MW00397195

CLIMATE CHANGE
LAW AND POLICY

ASPEN ELECTIVE SERIES

CLIMATE CHANGE LAW AND POLICY

Hari M. Osofsky
Associate Professor of Law
Affiliated Faculty with Geography
and Conservation Biology
Associate Director of Law, Geography &
Environment, Consortium on Law and Values in
Health, Environment & the Life Sciences
and
Fellow, Institute on the Environment
University of Minnesota

Lesley K. McAllister
Professor of Law
Stanley Legro Professor in Environmental Law
University of San Diego
and
Adjunct Associate Professor, School of International
Relations and Pacific Studies University of California
San Diego

 Wolters Kluwer
Law & Business

ISBN 978-0-7355-7716-9

Library of Congress Cataloging-in-Publication Data

Osofsky, Hari M., 1972-
    Climate change law and policy / Hari M. Osofsky, Lesley K. McAllister.
        p. cm.
    Includes bibliographical references and index.
    ISBN 978-0-7355-7716-9 (perfectbound : alk. paper)
    1. Climatic changes — Law and legislation. 2. Global warming — Law and legislation. I. McAllister, Lesley K. (Lesley Krista), 1970- II. Title.

K3585.5.O86 2012
344.04′633 — dc23   2012027492

About Wolters Kluwer Law & Business

Wolters Kluwer Law & Business is a leading global provider of intelligent information and digital solutions for legal and business professionals in key specialty areas, and respected educational resources for professors and law students. Wolters Kluwer Law & Business connects legal and business professionals as well as those in the education market with timely, specialized authoritative content and information-enabled solutions to support success through productivity, accuracy and mobility.

Serving customers worldwide, Wolters Kluwer Law & Business products include those under the Aspen Publishers, CCH, Kluwer Law International, Loislaw, Best Case, ftwilliam.com and MediRegs family of products.

CCH products have been a trusted resource since 1913, and are highly regarded resources for legal, securities, antitrust and trade regulation, government contracting, banking, pension, payroll, employment and labor, and healthcare reimbursement and compliance professionals.

Aspen Publishers products provide essential information to attorneys, business professionals and law students. Written by preeminent authorities, the product line offers analytical and practical information in a range of specialty practice areas from securities law and intellectual property to mergers and acquisitions and pension/benefits. Aspen's trusted legal education resources provide professors and students with high-quality, up-to-date and effective resources for successful instruction and study in all areas of the law.

Kluwer Law International products provide the global business community with reliable international legal information in English. Legal practitioners, corporate counsel and business executives around the world rely on Kluwer Law journals, looseleafs, books, and electronic products for comprehensive information in many areas of international legal practice.

Loislaw is a comprehensive online legal research product providing legal content to law firm practitioners of various specializations. Loislaw provides attorneys with the ability to quickly and efficiently find the necessary legal information they need, when and where they need it, by facilitating access to primary law as well as state-specific law, records, forms and treatises.

Best Case Solutions is the leading bankruptcy software product to the bankruptcy industry. It provides software and workflow tools to flawlessly streamline petition preparation and the electronic filing process, while timely incorporating ever-changing court requirements.

ftwilliam.com offers employee benefits professionals the highest quality plan documents (retirement, welfare and non-qualified) and government forms (5500/PBGC, 1099 and IRS) software at highly competitive prices.

MediRegs products provide integrated health care compliance content and software solutions for professionals in healthcare, higher education and life sciences, including professionals in accounting, law and consulting.

Wolters Kluwer Law & Business, a division of Wolters Kluwer, is headquartered in New York. Wolters Kluwer is a market-leading global information services company focused on professionals.

To our children — Erin, Nathan, Oz, and Scarlet — and our students.
We write this book in the hope that the next generation finds creative ways
to make progress in addressing climate change.

SUMMARY OF CONTENTS

TABLE OF CONTENTS

PREFACE

Climate change law and policy is currently taught in a variety of ways. Many law schools have two- or three-credit seminars on the subject, but climate change also is taught as a topic within international, comparative, and environmental law courses. In addition, other graduate and undergraduate programs such as environmental studies and political science offer courses on the subject.

In recognition of both the ever-changing legal landscape addressing climate change and the diversity of courses addressing the topic, *Climate Change Law and Policy* provides a succinct, modular text paired with a continuously updated Web site. The book and its accompanying Web site (http://aspenlawschool.com/books/osofsky_climate) create a flexible platform for exploring the issue of climate change and the role of law in addressing it, enabling instructors to expand where desired and have access to the most up-to-date information.

Because of its modular quality, the book can be used either as a primary text or as a supplemental text. Instructors can choose to purchase the whole book or particular chapters of interest. Each chapter provides a self-contained treatment of a key topic that can be taught on its own or in conjunction with other topics. The accompanying teacher's manual provides teaching suggestions and exercises to accompany each chapter.

The book intentionally pares down the material to its core, but the accompanying Web site provides links to additional primary documents and scholarship to allow for more in-depth exploration. Together, the book and Web site provide the timely material on a wide variety of issues to allow the instructor to focus on areas of particular interest without the bulk and expense of a traditional casebook. In our view, this approach to providing course materials fits the problem of climate change more effectively than a traditional casebook.

We would like to acknowledge and thank several people who have made invaluable contributions to this project. This book has had a long evolution to its present form, and five people have been particularly critical to its development. Hiram Chodosh helped to inspire this book, and served as a generous mentor to emerging international law scholars in so doing. Wil Burns, who originally planned to serve as a third co-author, helped frame the book and provided important insights into the subject and material. Carol McGeehan, the publisher at Aspen Publishers, nurtured this project from the beginning and became a wonderful mentor and friend over the course of the project. John Devins, our editor at Aspen Publishers who has also become a good friend, has done an excellent job of patiently working with us to improve the book; we have greatly appreciated his input and responsiveness. Finally, the book benefitted significantly from Lisa Connery's assistance in overseeing its production; she worked hard to perfect the book while keeping true to our vision.

Both of us have greatly appreciated the support of our law schools as we have worked on this project. In particular, Meghan Schwartz of the University of Minnesota and Arlene Penticoff of the University of San Diego spent many valuable hours working to shepherd the book through the copyright clearance process. Drew McNeill and Lynn Parins provided very good bluebooking assistance and helped develop the index. Early-adopters Jeffrey Atik of Loyola Law School and Maxine Burkett of University of Hawai'i School of Law, students in courses at our law schools, and anonymous reviewers contributed insightful feedback that improved the book greatly.

Last, but certainly not least, our families have provided endless love, support, and patience. We thank our spouses and children—Joshua, Oz, and Scarlet Gitelson; and Andrew, Erin, and Nathan McAllister—for reminding us of the future generations whose welfare depends upon our success in dealing with the problem of climate change.

Hari Osofsky
Lesley McAllister
August 2012

ACKNOWLEDGMENTS

Excerpts from the following copyrighted materials are reprinted with permission. Except where noted, the publication date is also the copyright date.

Randall S. Abate & Andrew B. Greenlee, *Sowing Seeds Uncertain: Ocean Iron Fertilization, Climate Change, and the International Environmental Law Framework*, 27 Pace Envtl. L. Rev. 555 (2010). Reprinted with permission of Pace Environmental Law Review.

Harro van Asselt & Joyeeta Gupta, *Stretching Too Far? Developing Countries and the Role of Flexibility Mechanisms Beyond Kyoto*, 28 Stan. Envtl. L.J. 311 (2009). Reprinted with permission of Stanford Environmental Law Journal.

Michele Betsill, Environmental NGOs and the Kyoto Protocol Negotiations: 1995 to 1997, in *NGO Diplomacy: The Influence of Nongovernmental Organizations in International Environmental Negotiations* 46–64 (Michele M. Betsill & Elisabeth Corell eds., 2008). Reprinted with permission of the MIT Press.

Statement of Richard Blumenthal, Attorney General of Connecticut, *The Role of State Attorneys General in National Environmental Policy: Welcome & Global Warming Panel, Part I*, 30 Colum. J. Envtl. L. 335 (2005). Reprinted with permission of Columbia Journal of Environmental Law.

Daniel Bodansky, *The Copenhagen Climate Change Conference: A Post-Mortem*, 104 Am. J. Int'l L. 230 (2010). Reprinted with permission of American Journal of International Law.

Daniel Bodansky, *The United Nations Framework Convention on Climate Change: A Commentary*, 18 Yale J. Int'l L. 451 (1993). Reprinted with permission of Yale Journal of International Law.

Cinnamon Carlarne, *Notes from a Climate Change Pressure-Cooker: Sub-Federal Attempts at Transformation Meet National Resistance in the USA*, 40 Conn. L. Rev. 1351 (2008). Reprinted with permission of Connecticut Law Review.

Center for Climate Change and Energy Solutions, *Climate Change 101: Understanding and Responding to Global Climate Change* (2011). Reprinted with permission of Center for Climate Change and Energy Solutions.

Center for Climate Change and Energy Solutions, *Sixteenth Session of the Conference of the Parties to the United Nations Framework Convention on Climate*

Change and Sixth Session of the Meeting of the Parties to the Kyoto Protocol (2010). Reprinted with permission of Center for Climate Change and Energy Solutions.

Committee on Strategic Advice on the U.S. Climate Change Science Program, National Research Council, *Evaluating Progress of the U.S. Climate Change Science Program: Methods and Preliminary Results* (2007). Reprinted with permission of National Research Council.

Robin Kundis Craig, *"Stationary is Dead"— Long Live Transformation: Five Principles for Climate Change Adaptation Law*, 34 Harv. Envtl. L. Rev. 9 (2010). Reprinted with permission of Harvard Environmental Law Review.

Lincoln L. Davies, *Alternative Energy and the Energy-Environment Disconnect*, 46 Idaho L. Rev. 473 (2010). Reprinted with permission of Idaho Law Review.

Bonnie Docherty & Tyler Giannini, *Confronting a Rising Tide: A Proposal for a Convention on Climate Change Refugees*, 33 Harv. Envtl. L. Rev. 349 (2009). Reprinted with permission of Harvard Environmental Law Review.

David Duff, *Carbon Taxation in British Columbia*, 10 Vt. J. Envtl. L. 87 (2008). Reprinted with permission of Vermont Journal of Environmental Law.

A. Denny Ellerman, Frank J. Convery & Christian de Perthius, *Pricing Carbon: The European Union Emissions Trading Scheme* (2010). Reprinted with permission of Cambridge University Press.

Endangerment and Cause or Contribute Findings for Greenhouse Gases Under Section 202(a) of the Clean Air Act, 74 Fed. Reg. 66,494, 66,516, 66,523–66,524, 66,536–66,537 (Dec. 15, 2009) (to be codified at 40 C.F.R. ch. 1). Reprinted with permission of United States Environmental Protection Agency.

Kirsten H. Engel, *Whither Subnational Climate Change Initiatives in the Wake of Federal Climate Legislation?*, 39 Publius: J. Federalism 432 (2009). Reprinted with permission of Oxford University Press on behalf of the American Political Science Association.

Victor B. Flatt, *Taking the Legislative Temperature: Which Federal Climate Change Legislative Proposal is "Best"?*, 102 Nw. U. L. Rev. Colloquy 123 (2007). Reprinted by special permission of Northwestern University School of Law, Northwestern University Law Review.

Frederic Forge & Tim Williams, Parliamentary Research and Information Service, Library of Parliament, Canada, *Policy Options to Reduce Greenhouse Gas Emissions* (Oct. 7, 2008). Reproduced with permission of the Library of Parliament, 2012.

Robert L. Glicksman, *Climate Change Adaptation: A Collective Action Perspective on Federalism Considerations*, 40 Envtl. L. 1159 (2010). Reprinted with permission of author and Environmental Law.

Ivan Gold & Nidhi Thakar, *A Survey of State Renewable Portfolio Standards: Square Pegs for Round Climate Change Holes?*, 35 Wm. & Mary Envtl. L. & Pol'y Rev. 183 (2010). Reprinted with permission of William & Mary Environmental Law & Policy Review.

Ruth Gordon, *Climate Change and the Poorest Nations: Further Reflections on Global Inequality*, 78 U. Colo. L. Rev. 1559 (2007). Reprinted with permission of author and University of Colorado Law Review.

Margaret Rosso Grossman, *Climate Change and the Law*, 58 Am. J. Comp. L. 223 (2010). Reprinted with permission of American Journal of Comparative Law.

Kathryn Harrison, *The Road Not Taken: Climate Change Policy in Canada and the United States*, 7 Global Envtl. Pol. 92–117 (Nov. 2007). Reprinted with permission of the Massachusetts Institute of Technology.

David Held & Angus Fane Hervey, *Democracy, Climate Change and Global Governance: Democratic Agency and the Policy Menu Ahead* (2009). Reprinted with permission of authors.

ICLEI, *Institutionalizing Climate Preparedness in Miami-Dade County, FL* (2010). Reprinted with permission of ICLEI.

The Independent Climate Change Emails Review (July 2010). Reprinted with permission of the Review.

Intergovernmental Panel on Climate Change, *Climate Change 2007: Synthesis Report. Contribution of Working Groups I, II and III to the Fourth Assessment Report of the Intergovernmental Panel on Climate Change, Summary for Policymakers*, pp. 1–22. Geneva, Switzerland. Reprinted with permission of the Intergovernmental Panel on Climate Change.

Intergovernmental Panel on Climate Change, *IPCC Statement on the Melting of Himalayan Glaciers* (Jan. 20, 2010). Reprinted with permission of the Intergovernmental Panel on Climate Change.

Intergovernmental Panel on Climate Change, *Statement of the IPCC Chairman on the Establishment of an Independent Committee to Review IPCC Procedures* (Feb. 27, 2010). Reprinted with permission of the Intergovernmental Panel on Climate Change.

Intergovernmental Panel on Climate Change, *The IPCC Fifth Assessment Report (AR5), Proposal for an IPCC Expert Meeting on Geoengineering*, 32d Sess., IPCC-XXXII/Doc. 5 (Oct. 11–14, 2010). Reprinted with permission of the Intergovernmental Panel on Climate Change.

Donald Kaniaru, Rajendra Shende & Durwood Zaelke, *Landmark Agreement to Strengthen Montreal Protocol Provides Powerful Climate Mitigation*, 8 Sustainable Dev. L. & Pol'y 46 (2008). Reprinted with permission of Sustainable Development Law & Policy.

Eli Kintisch, *Scientists Say Continued Warning Warrants Closer Look at Drastic Fixes*, 318 Science 1054 (2007). Reprinted with permission of Science.

Alexandra B. Klass, *Property Rights on the New Frontier: Climate Change, Natural Resource Development, and Renewable Energy*, 38 Ecology L.Q. 63 (2011). Reprinted with permission of Ecology Law Quarterly.

Katrina Fischer Kuh, *Capturing Individual Harms*, 35 Harv. Envtl. L. Rev. 155 (2011). Reprinted with permission of Harvard Environmental Law Review.

Kyoto Protocol to the United Nations Framework Convention on Climate Change (1992). Reprinted with permission of International Legal Materials.

Richard J. Lazarus, *Super Wicked Problems and Climate Change: Restraining the Present to Liberate the Future*, 94 Cornell L. Rev. 1153 (2009). Reprinted with permission of Cornell Law Review.

Peter Lehner, *Environment, Law, and Nonprofits: How NGOs Shape Our Laws, Health, and Communities*, 26 Pace Envtl. L. Rev. 19 (2009). Reprinted with permission of Pace Environmental Law Review.

Marcelo Leite, *The Brazilian Dilemma: A Nation Struggles Not to Exploit Its Own Greatest Resource*, Wash. Monthly (July/Aug. 2009). Reprinted with permission of Washington Monthly.

Joanna Lewis, *Energy and Climate Goals for China's 12th Five-Year Plan*, Ctr. for Climate & Energy Solutions (2011). Reprinted with permission of the Center for Climate and Energy Solutions.

Light-Duty Vehicle Greenhouse Gas Emission Standards and Corporate Average Fuel Economy Standards, Final Rule, 75 Fed. Reg. 25,323, 25,326–25,329 (May 7, 2010) (to be codified at 40 C.F.R. pts. 85, 86, and 600; 40 C.F.R. pts. 531, 533, 536, 537, and 538). Reprinted with permission of United States Environmental Protection Agency.

Albert C. Lin, *Geoengineering Governance*, Issues in Legal Scholarship 1 (Apr. 2009). Reprinted with permission of De Gruyter.

Jingjing Liu, *Overview of the Chinese Legal System*, 41 Envtl. L. Rep. News & Analysis 10885 (2011). Copyright © 2011 Environmental Law Institute®, Washington, DC. Reprinted with permission from ELR®.

David Markell & J.B. Ruhl, *An Empirical Survey of Climate Change Litigation in the United States*, 40 Envtl. L. Rep. News & Analysis 10644 (2010). Copyright © 2010 Environmental Law Institute®, Washington, DC. Reprinted with permission from ELR®.

Lesley K. McAllister, *Sustainable Consumption Governances in the Amazon*, 38 Envtl. L. Rep. News & Analysis 10873 (2008). Copyright © 2008 Environmental Law Institute®, Washington, DC. Reprinted with permission from ELR®.

Jeffrey McGee & Ros Taplin, *The Asia-Pacific Partnership and the United States' International Climate Policy*, 19 Colo. J. Int'l Envtl. L. & Pol'y 179 (2008). Originally published in the Colorado Journal of International Environmental Law and Policy, Volume 18, Issue 3 (2008). All rights reserved. Reprinted with permission of Colorado Journal of International Environmental Law & Policy.

Jay Michaelson, *Geoengineering: A Climate Change Manhattan Project*, 17 Stan. Envtl. L.J. 73 (1998). Reprinted with permission of Stanford Environmental Law Journal.

Jennifer Morgan & Edward Cameron, *WRI Insight: Reflections on COP 17 in Durban* (Dec. 16, 2011). Reprinted with permission of World Resources Institute.

Brian Moskal & Michael McDonough, *The Impact of 2010 Midterm Elections on Climate Change Legislation*, Climate Change L. & Pol'y Rep. (Dec. 2010). Excerpted with consent from the Climate Change Law & Policy Reporter, Copyright © 2010, 2012, Argent Communications Group, all rights reserved. E-mail: reporters@argentco.com.

Sean O'Hara, *The Importance of the United States Staying the Course While Implementing Environmental Policy in Accordance with the American Recovery and Reinvestment Act of 2009*, 17 U. Balt. J. Envtl. L. 85 (2009). Reprinted with permission of University of Baltimore Journal of Land & Development (successor to University of Baltimore Journal of Environmental Law).

Hari M. Osofsky, *Is Climate Change "International"?: Litigation's Diagonal Regulatory Role*, 49 Va. J. Int'l L. 585 (2009). Reprinted with permission of Virginia Journal of International Law.

Elinor Ostrom, *Polycentric Systems for Coping with Collective Action and Global Environmental Change*, 20 Global Envtl. Change 550 (2010). Reprinted with permission of Elsevier.

Uma Outka, *The Renewable Energy Footprint*, 30 Stan. Envtl. L.J. 241 (2011). Reprinted with permission of Stanford Environmental Law Journal.

Stephen Pacala & Robert Socolow, *Stabilization Wedges: Solving the Climate Problem for the Next 50 Years with Current Technologies*, 305 Science 968 (2004). Reprinted with permission of Science.

Holly L. Pearson & Kevin Poloncarz, *With Legislation Stalled, EPA Presses Forward with Greenhouse Gas Regulatory Program Under the Clean Air Act as Jan. 2, 2011, Trigger Date Approaches*, 587 PLI/Real 105 (2011). Excerpted with consent from the Climate Change Law & Policy Reporter, Copyright © 2010, 2012, Argent Communications Group, all rights reserved. E-mail: reporters@argentco.com.

Simone Pulver, *An Environmental Contestation Approach to Analyzing the Causes and Consequences of the Climate Policy Split in the Oil Industry*, 20 Org. & Env't 52 (2007). Reprinted by permission of SAGE Publications.

Kal Raustiala, Nonstate Actors in the Global Climate Regime, in *International Relations and Global Climate Change* 95–117 (Urs Luterbacher & Detlef F. Sprinz eds., 2001). Reprinted by permission of the MIT Press.

Johan Rockstrom et al., *A Safe Operating Space for Humanity*, 461 Nature 472 (2009). Reprinted with permission of Nature.

Miranda A. Schreurs & Yves Tiberghien, *Multi-Level Reinforcement: Explaining European Union Leadership in Climate Change Mitigation*, 7 Global Envtl. Pol. 19 (2007). Reprinted with permission of the Massachusetts Institute of Technology.

Nicholas Stern, *The Economics of Climate Change: The Stern Review, Summary of Conclusions* (2006). Reprinted with permission of the United Kingdom Government National Archives.

John W. Suthers, *The State Attorney General's Role in Global Climate Change*, 85 Denv. U. L. Rev. 757 (2007–2008). Reprinted with permission of Denver University Law Review.

Katherine A. Trisolini, *All Hands on Deck: Local Governments and the Potential for Bidirectional Climate Change Regulations*, 62 Stan. L. Rev. 669 (2010). Reprinted with permission of Stanford Law Review.

United Nations Framework Convention on Climate Change (1992). Reprinted with permission of United Nations Treaty Series.

Michael P. Vandenbergh & Anne C. Steinemann, *The Carbon-Neutral Individual*, 82 N.Y.U. L. Rev. 1687 (2007). Reprinted with permission of New York University Law Review.

David Vogel, *The Hare and the Tortoise Revisited: The New Politics of Consumer and Environmental Regulation in Europe*, 33 Brit. J. Pol. Sci. 557 (2003). Reprinted with permission of Cambridge University Press.

Mary Christina Wood, *"You Can't Negotiate With a Beetle": Environmental Law for a New Ecological Age*, 50 Nat. Resources J. 167 (2010). Reprinted with permission of Natural Resources Journal.

Tseming Yang, *The Problem of Maintaining Emission "Caps" in Carbon Trading Programs Without Federal Government Involvement: A Brief Examination of the Chicago Climate Exchange and the Northeast Regional Greenhouse Gas Initiative*, 17

Fordham Envtl. L. Rev. 271 (2006). Reprinted with permission of Fordham Environmental Law Review.

Dongsheng Zang, *From Environment to Energy: China's Reconceptualization of Climate Change*, 27 Wis. Int'l L.J. 543 (2009). Reprinted with permission of Wisconsin International Law Journal.

CHAPTER 1

THE CHALLENGE OF CLIMATE CHANGE: SCIENTIFIC, LEGAL, AND POLITICAL ELEMENTS

In the longer-term, we face what I term the "50-50-50 challenge." By 2050, the world's population will grow by 50 percent, reaching 9 billion people. By that time, by 2050, the world must reduce at least by 50 per cent global greenhouse gas emissions. That is the "50-50-50 challenge."

U.N. Secretary-General, *Better Global Governance Needed to Help Most Vulnerable, Stave Off Climate Change, Meet 'New Generation' Challenges, Says Secretary-General in Marrakesh*, U.N. Doc. SG/SM/13188 (Oct. 18, 2010), *available at* http://www.un.org/News/Press/docs/2010/sgsm13188.doc.htm.

The remarks by U.N. Secretary-General Ban Ki-moon capture well the core dilemmas facing the United States and the world in responding appropriately to climate change. Consensus science suggests that a wide range of human activities that emit greenhouse gases are causing changes in the climate that pose increasing dangers over time. Atmospheric concentrations of carbon dioxide exceeded 390 parts per million in 2011, well above both the 280 parts per million that existed prior to the industrial revolution in the nineteenth century and the 350 parts per million that scientists have recommended staying below to minimize risks of major climate change.

Policymakers in governments around the world have attempted to address these emissions and are beginning to respond to and plan for their effects. But, to date, these efforts — even with the legal progress made through international climate change negotiations — remain woefully inadequate to address the problem. Emissions are still far too high to prevent the worst effects, with no sign that many of the most significant emitters have the political will to bring them down adequately. Adaptation planning is still in its early stages in most places. Moreover, for each of these issues, widespread debate exists about appropriate law and policy.

Deep inequalities also permeate these debates. The countries that are the biggest greenhouse gas emitters have historically been rich, developed countries while many of the countries with low emission levels are physically vulnerable and poor, with limited capacity to adapt. Although rapidly developing countries like China, India, and Brazil represent an increasing share of global emissions—China has passed the United States as the world's largest emitter—their per capita emissions remain much lower. These countries also have the desire to continue raising their citizens' standard of living to that of developed countries.

This book explores these dilemmas. It analyzes the problem of climate change and efforts to address it through law. This first chapter provides a guide to the book and introduces climate change science, law, and policy options, and their accompanying daunting regulatory challenges, to frame the chapters that follow.

A. GUIDE TO THE BOOK

Throughout its discussion of climate change law and policy, this book is grounded in three key concepts. First, climate change is a tremendously complex problem at the interface of science, law, politics, culture, and economics. Any effective legal strategy to address climate change must take that complexity into account.

Second, and related to the first, the law relevant to climate change is not just environmental. Greenhouse gas emissions stem from behaviors at the core of economies around the world, and the effects of climate change will fundamentally alter life in many places. A legal treatment of climate change must think comprehensively and creatively about what types of law help to frame the problem and must be involved in solutions.

Finally, climate change cannot be fully addressed through international negotiations under the 1992 United Nations Framework Convention on Climate Change (UNFCCC). Those negotiations are a tremendously important piece of the legal solution, but a full treatment of climate change requires consideration of legal activity at multiple levels of government and by a wide range of actors.

The book builds from these concepts to explore climate change as a legal problem that cuts across levels of government, disciplines, and substantive areas of law. This book differs from others in its effort to give fairly equal emphasis to each level of governance and to the diversity of strategies being used to address climate change. This structure is intended to map the web of human interactions comprising this problem and its potential solutions.

The book identifies seven topics as critical to understanding climate change law and policy, and treats each of these topics in a chapter. This first chapter frames the rest of the book by introducing the complex nature of climate change science and of the laws attempting to address emissions and impacts. The chapter explores the ways in which human action interacts with efforts to understand climate change science, the areas of greater and lesser

certainty in current science, and contemporary controversies and their implications for the future of scientific inquiry and presentation in this area. It then
considers the options and challenges facing legal efforts to address this
problem, with a focus on mitigation, adaptation, and the complexities of
cross-cutting governance.

Chapter Two examines international legal efforts to approach climate
change. It begins by discussing the international treaty regime focused on climate change. The chapter explains the framework provided by the UNFCCC, its
implementation through the 1997 Kyoto Protocol, and the state of current
negotiations. The chapter then explores four other ways in which international
law has and continues to interact with climate change, including the Montreal
Protocol's climate change impacts, agreements among major economies, the
Asia-Pacific Partnership on Clean Development and Climate, and human rights
and world heritage petitions to international bodies.

Chapter Three provides an overview of the current state of climate change
law in the United States. It begins with the legislative branch, considering the
primary existing statutes focused on climate change and the difficulties of
passing more comprehensive climate change legislation. It then turns to the
judicial branch and explores the ways in which litigation, especially the
Supreme Court's decisions in *Massachusetts v. EPA* and *AEP v. Connecticut*,
has helped to shape regulatory action under the Clean Air Act and other environmental statutes. It concludes by considering the executive branch, with
a focus on how its implementation of the Supreme Court's decision in
Massachusetts and other regulatory action has led to steps to mitigate and
adapt to climate change in the United States.

Chapter Four moves beyond the United States to examine and compare
other national and regional action on climate change. The chapter begins by
introducing the comparative law approach and the complexities of making
legal comparisons among nations. It then turns to four key places that vary
significantly in how they have engaged with the problem of climate change:
the European Union, a model of energetic regulatory action; Canada, which
initially followed Europe's lead but then did not follow through; China, a
rapidly industrializing country that has become the world's largest greenhouse
gas emitter; and Brazil, an emerging economic power that is home to
threatened forests critical to climate stability. The chapter concludes by exploring the possibilities for global harmonization of climate change law.

Chapter Five looks within the nation-state to analyze the local, state,
provincial, and regional efforts to address climate change. The chapter first
observes that subnational greenhouse gas regulation presents a puzzle: Why
would a locality or state unilaterally incur the costs of encouraging or mandating greenhouse gas emission reductions? What benefits would it receive in
return? The chapter then surveys the large and diverse landscape of subnational mitigation and adaptation policies. The chapter concludes with a
close look at the phenomenon of transnational collaborations, in which localities in different national jurisdictions cooperate in nontraditional ways.

Chapter Six moves beyond governments to examine the role of nongovernmental organizations, corporations, and individuals in climate change law and
policy. It first examines the ways in which nongovernmental organizations

work collaboratively to influence U.S. law and engage in the international treaty-making process. It then turns to the role of major corporate emitters, both in blocking climate change regulation and in working voluntarily and cooperatively to reduce their emissions. The chapter concludes by considering the importance of individual efforts to reduce climate change, and possibilities for changes in the behavior of many individuals to add up to significant emissions reductions.

The final chapter looks to the future of climate change law and policy. Chapter Seven begins by positing two risky future scenarios and the role that law might play in each of them. In the first scenario, perhaps the most realistic, legal efforts to mitigate climate change have failed to prevent major impacts and the nations of the world have decided to attempt to intervene in the climate system to try to reverse climate change. In the second scenario, major climate change has transformed the globe, and leaders are contemplating major relocation and reconstitution of law and society in response. The book then concludes by considering how future lawyers and policymakers interested in this problem can work more effectively towards less risky pathways forward.

Collectively, these chapters aim both to provide a comprehensive introduction to climate change law and policy and to challenge those who will determine our future to think creatively. We hope that by examining the complexity of law's interaction with this problem, the book can be part of a constructive step forward.

B. CLIMATE CHANGE SCIENCE: CERTAINTIES AND UNCERTAINTIES

Effectively assessing the problem of climate change and potential solutions from a scientific perspective is extremely complex. Not only are the interactions of greenhouse gas emissions with the atmosphere and ocean extremely complicated, but the problem of climate change also involves the interactions between human beings and their environment. Human beings are causing the increased emissions of greenhouse gases, suffering the impacts, and trying to adapt.

Moreover, while a high level of certainty exists about the big picture of climate change, significant uncertainty exists over some of the particular effects in specific places. It is difficult to have a nuanced public conversation about the details of climate change science and the appropriate legal approaches to risk. The polarized nature of the current discourse, especially in the United States, has made such discussions even harder. These challenges have been exacerbated by public controversy over errors and inappropriate behavior by a handful of climate scientists. While independent assessments have found their mistakes to have minimal impact on the overall reliability of consensus climate change science and key institutions have changed procedures to address these lapses, these scandals have further shaken public confidence in the science.

This section explores these issues. It begins by examining the current state of climate change science, and then considers the barriers to scientific understanding and the ways in which controversies over science interact with public perceptions of risk.

1. THE CURRENT STATE OF CLIMATE CHANGE SCIENCE

Climate change science not only involves complicated interactions among the ocean, atmosphere, land masses, and people, but it is also developed and communicated in a complex political, legal, economic, and cultural context. This section provides an overview of the current state of climate change science by providing an excerpt from the *Climate Change 2007: Synthesis Report* by the Intergovernmental Panel on Climate Change (IPCC), the leading organization in the world assessing climate change science.

Since its establishment in 1988, the IPCC has examined the state of climate change science through a comprehensive assessment of peer-reviewed work of scientists around the world. That year, the World Meteorological Organization (WMO) and the United Nations Environment Program (UNEP) created the IPCC and the United Nations General Assembly passed a resolution providing it with responsibility for producing a comprehensive review and recommendations. From the start, the IPCC was charged with not only assessing the physical science, but also analyzing its interaction with people and proposing strategies for addressing both causes and impacts.

The IPCC has produced four comprehensive assessment reports and numerous specialized reports since its creation. It has three primary working groups: one that focuses on the state of the science; another that examines impacts, adaptation, and vulnerability; and a third that analyzes mitigation. The IPCC's assessment reports, which have come out every few years beginning in 1990, contain a volume on each of these three areas and a synthesis volume that considers the ways in which these three aspects of climate change interact. The fourth IPCC assessment report came out in 2007 and the fifth one is due out in 2013–2014. Recent IPCC specialized reports include 2011 reports on *Renewable Energy and Climate Change Mitigation* and *Managing the Risks of Extreme Events and Disasters to Advance Climate Change Adaptation.*

The following excerpt from the IPCC's 2007 *Synthesis Report* describes the complex interactions that constitute the problem of climate change. It provides background on the IPCC, explores human interactions with the climate system, and considers options for the future.

INTERGOVERNMENTAL PANEL ON CLIMATE CHANGE [IPCC], CLIMATE CHANGE 2007: SYNTHESIS REPORT. CONTRIBUTION OF WORKING GROUPS I, II AND III TO THE FOURTH ASSESSMENT REPORT OF THE INTERGOVERNMENTAL PANEL ON CLIMATE CHANGE: SUMMARY FOR POLICYMAKERS, AT 1–22 (BY CORE WRITING TEAM, R.K. PACHAURI & A. REISINGER EDS.)

http://www.ipcc.ch/publications_and_data/ar4/syr/en/contents.html

Foreword

The Intergovernmental Panel on Climate Change (IPCC) was jointly established in 1988, by the World Meteorological Organization (WMO) and the

United Nations Environment Programme (UNEP), with the mandate to assess scientific information related to climate change, to evaluate the environmental and socio-economic consequences of climate change, and to formulate realistic response strategies. The IPCC multivolume assessments have since then played a major role in assisting governments to adopt and implement policies in response to climate change, and in particular have responded to the need for authoritative advice of the Conference of the Parties (COP) to the United Nations Framework Convention on Climate Change (UNFCCC), which was established in 1992, and its 1997 Kyoto Protocol.

Since its establishment, the IPCC has produced a series of Assessment Reports (1990, 1995, 2001 and this one in 2007), Special Reports, Technical Papers and Methodology Reports, which have become standard works of reference, widely used by policymakers, scientists, other experts and students. The most recent publications include a Special Report on "Carbon Dioxide Capture and Storage" and one on "Safeguarding the Ozone Layer and the Global Climate System", published in 2005, and the "Guidelines for National Greenhouse Gas Inventories" re-edited in 2006. A Technical Paper on "Climate Change and Water" is under preparation.

This Synthesis Report (SYR), adopted in Valencia, Spain, on 17 November 2007, completes the four-volume Fourth Assessment Report (AR4), which was released in various steps throughout the year under the title "Climate Change 2007". It summarises the findings of the three Working Group reports and provides a synthesis that specifically addresses the issues of concern to policymakers in the domain of climate change: it confirms that climate change is occurring now, mostly as a result of human activities; it illustrates the impacts of global warming already underway and to be expected in future, and describes the potential for adaptation of society to reduce its vulnerability; finally it presents an analysis of costs, policies and technologies intended to limit the extent of future changes in the climate system.

The AR4 is a remarkable achievement involving more than 500 Lead Authors and 2000 Expert Reviewers, building on the work of a wide scientific community and submitted to the scrutiny of delegates from more than one hundred participating nations.

. . . .

Summary for Policymakers

1. Observed Changes in Climate and Their Effects

Warming of the climate system is unequivocal, as is now evident from observations of increases in global average air and ocean temperatures, widespread melting of snow and ice and rising global average sea level.

. . . .

2. Causes of Change

Changes in atmospheric concentrations of greenhouse gases (GHGs) and aerosols, land cover and solar radiation alter the energy balance of the climate system.

Global GHG emissions due to human activities have grown since pre-industrial times, with an increase of 70% between 1970 and 2004.

Carbon dioxide (CO_2) is the most important anthropogenic GHG. Its annual emissions grew by about 80% between 1970 and 2004. The long-term trend of declining CO_2 emissions per unit of energy supplied reversed after 2000.

Global atmospheric concentrations of CO_2, methane (CH_4) and nitrous oxide (N_2O) have increased markedly as a result of human activities since 1750 and now far exceed pre-industrial values determined from ice cores spanning many thousands of years.

Atmospheric concentrations of CO_2 (379ppm) and CH_4 (1774ppb) in 2005 exceed by far the natural range over the last 650,000 years. Global increases in CO_2 concentrations are due primarily to fossil fuel use, with land-use change providing another significant but smaller contribution. It is *very likely* that the observed increase in CH_4 concentration is predominantly due to agriculture and fossil fuel use. CH_4 growth rates have declined since the early 1990s, consistent with total emissions (sum of anthropogenic and natural sources) being nearly constant during this period. The increase in N_2O concentration is primarily due to agriculture.

There is *very high* confidence that the net effect of human activities since 1750 has been one of warming.

Most of the observed increase in global average temperatures since the mid-20th century is very likely due to the observed increase in anthropogenic GHG concentrations. It is *likely* that there has been significant anthropogenic warming over the past 50 years averaged over each continent (except Antarctica)

During the past 50 years, the sum of solar and volcanic forcings would *likely* have produced cooling. Observed patterns of warming and their changes are simulated only by models that include anthropogenic forcings. Difficulties remain in simulating and attributing observed temperature changes at smaller than continental scales.

Advances since the TAR show that discernible human influences extend beyond average temperature to other aspects of climate.

Human influences have:

- *very likely* contributed to sea level rise during the latter half of the 20th century
- *likely* contributed to changes in wind patterns, affecting extra-tropical storm tracks and temperature patterns
- *likely* increased temperatures of extreme hot nights, cold nights and cold days
- *more likely* than not increased risk of heat waves, area affected by drought since the 1970s and frequency of heavy precipitation events.

Anthropogenic warming over the last three decades has *likely* had a discernible influence at the global scale on observed changes in many physical and biological systems.

. . . .

3. Projected Climate Change and Its Impacts

There is *high agreement* and *much evidence* that with current climate change mitigation policies and related sustainable development practices, global GHG emissions will continue to grow over the next few decades.

The IPCC Special Report on Emissions Scenarios (SRES, 2000) projects an increase of global GHG emissions by 25 to 90% (CO_2-eq) between 2000 and 2030, with fossil fuels maintaining their dominant position in the global energy mix to 2030 and beyond. More recent scenarios without additional emissions mitigation are comparable in range.

Continued GHG emissions at or above current rates would cause further warming and induce many changes in the global climate system during the 21st century that would *very likely* be larger than those observed during the 20th century.

. . . .

There is now higher confidence than in the TAR in projected patterns of warming and other regional-scale features, including changes in wind patterns, precipitation and some aspects of extremes and sea ice.

Regional-scale changes include:

- warming greatest over land and at most high northern latitudes and least over Southern Ocean and parts of the North Atlantic Ocean, continuing recent observed trends
- contraction of snow cover area, increases in thaw depth over most permafrost regions and decrease in sea ice extent; in some projections using SRES scenarios, Arctic late-summer sea ice disappears almost entirely by the latter part of the 21st century
- *very likely* increase in frequency of hot extremes, heat waves and heavy precipitation
- *likely* increase in tropical cyclone intensity; less confidence in global decrease of tropical cyclone numbers
- poleward shift of extra-tropical storm tracks with consequent changes in wind, precipitation and temperature patterns
- *very likely* precipitation increases in high latitudes and *likely* decreases in most subtropical land regions, continuing observed recent trends.

. . . .

Some systems, sectors and regions are likely to be especially affected by climate change.

Systems and sectors:

- particular ecosystems:
  - terrestrial: tundra, boreal forest and mountain regions because of sensitivity to warming; mediterranean-type ecosystems because of reduction in rainfall; and tropical rainforests where precipitation declines
  - coastal: mangroves and salt marshes, due to multiple stresses
  - marine: coral reefs due to multiple stresses; the sea ice biome because of sensitivity to warming
- water resources in some dry regions at mid-latitudes and in the dry tropics, due to changes in rainfall and evapotranspiration, and in areas dependent on snow and ice melt

- agriculture in low latitudes, due to reduced water availability
- low-lying coastal systems, due to threat of sea level rise and increased risk from extreme weather events
- human health in populations with low adaptive capacity.

Regions:

- the Arctic, because of the impacts of high rates of projected warming on natural systems and human communities
- Africa, because of low adaptive capacity and projected climate change impacts
- small islands, where there is high exposure of population and infrastructure to projected climate change impacts
- Asian and African megadeltas, due to large populations and high exposure to sea level rise, storm surges and river flooding.
- Within other areas, even those with high incomes, some people (such as the poor, young children and the elderly) can be particularly at risk, and also some areas and some activities.

. . . .

4. Adaptation and Mitigation Options

A wide array of adaptation options is available, but more extensive adaptation than is currently occurring is required to reduce vulnerability to climate change. There are barriers, limits and costs, which are not fully understood.

Societies have a long record of managing the impacts of weather- and climate-related events. Nevertheless, additional adaptation measures will be required to reduce the adverse impacts of projected climate change and variability, regardless of the scale of mitigation undertaken over the next two to three decades. Moreover, vulnerability to climate change can be exacerbated by other stresses. These arise from, for example, current climate hazards, poverty and unequal access to resources, food insecurity, trends in economic globalisation, conflict and incidence of diseases such as HIV/AIDS.

Some planned adaptation to climate change is already occurring on a limited basis. Adaptation can reduce vulnerability, especially when it is embedded within broader sectoral initiatives. There is high confidence that there are viable adaptation options that can be implemented in some sectors at low cost, and/or with high benefit-cost ratios. However, comprehensive estimates of global costs and benefits of adaptation are limited.

. . . .

Adaptive capacity is intimately connected to social and economic development but is unevenly distributed across and within societies.

A range of barriers limits both the implementation and effectiveness of adaptation measures. The capacity to adapt is dynamic and is influenced by a society's productive base, including natural and man-made capital assets, social networks and entitlements, human capital and institutions, governance, national income, health and technology. Even societies with high adaptive capacity remain vulnerable to climate change, variability and extremes.

. . . .

5. The Long-Term Perspective

Determining what constitutes "dangerous anthropogenic interference with the climate system" in relation to Article 2 of the UNFCCC involves value judgements. Science can support informed decisions on this issue, including by providing criteria for judging which vulnerabilities might be labelled 'key'.

Key vulnerabilities may be associated with many climate-sensitive systems, including food supply, infrastructure, health, water resources, coastal systems, ecosystems, global biogeochemical cycles, ice sheets and modes of oceanic and atmospheric circulation.

. . . .

There is high confidence that neither adaptation nor mitigation alone can avoid all climate change impacts; however, they can complement each other and together can significantly reduce the risks of climate change.

Adaptation is necessary in the short and longer term to address impacts resulting from the warming that would occur even for the lowest stabilisation scenarios assessed. There are barriers, limits and costs, but these are not fully understood. Unmitigated climate change would, in the long term, be likely to exceed the capacity of natural, managed and human systems to adapt. The time at which such limits could be reached will vary between sectors and regions. Early mitigation actions would avoid further locking in carbon intensive infrastructure and reduce climate change and associated adaptation needs.

Many impacts can be reduced, delayed or avoided by mitigation. Mitigation efforts and investments over the next two to three decades will have a large impact on opportunities to achieve lower stabilisation levels. Delayed emission reductions significantly constrain the opportunities to achieve lower stabilisation levels and increase the risk of more severe climate change impacts.

In order to stabilise the concentration of GHGs in the atmosphere, emissions would need to peak and decline thereafter. The lower the stabilisation level, the more quickly this peak and decline would need to occur.

There is high agreement and much evidence that all stabilisation levels assessed can be achieved by deployment of a portfolio of technologies that are either currently available or expected to be commercialised in coming decades, assuming appropriate and effective incentives are in place for their development, acquisition, deployment and diffusion and addressing related barriers.

All assessed stabilisation scenarios indicate that 60 to 80% of the reductions would come from energy supply and use and industrial processes, with energy efficiency playing a key role in many scenarios. Including non-CO_2 and CO_2 land-use and forestry mitigation options provides greater flexibility and cost-effectiveness. Low stabilisation levels require early investments and substantially more rapid diffusion and commercialisation of advanced low-emissions technologies.

Without substantial investment flows and effective technology transfer, it may be difficult to achieve emission reduction at a significant scale. Mobilising financing of incremental costs of low-carbon technologies is important.

The macro-economic costs of mitigation generally rise with the stringency of the stabilisation target. For specific countries and sectors, costs vary considerably from the global average.

In 2050, global average macro-economic costs for mitigation towards stabilisation between 710 and 445ppm CO_2-eq are between a 1% gain and 5.5% decrease of global GDP. This corresponds to slowing average annual global GDP growth by less than 0.12 percentage points.

Responding to climate change involves an iterative risk management process that includes both adaptation and mitigation and takes into account climate change damages, co-benefits, sustainability, equity and attitudes to risk.

Impacts of climate change are very likely to impose net annual costs, which will increase over time as global temperatures increase. Peer-reviewed estimates of the social cost of carbon in 2005 average US$12 per tonne of CO_2, but the range from 100 estimates is large (-$3 to $95/t$CO_2$). This is due in large part to differences in assumptions regarding climate sensitivity, response lags, the treatment of risk and equity, economic and non-economic impacts, the inclusion of potentially catastrophic losses and discount rates. Aggregate estimates of costs mask significant differences in impacts across sectors, regions and populations and very likely underestimate damage costs because they cannot include many non-quantifiable impacts.

Limited and early analytical results from integrated analyses of the costs and benefits of mitigation indicate that they are broadly comparable in magnitude, but do not as yet permit an unambiguous determination of an emissions pathway or stabilisation level where benefits exceed costs.

Climate sensitivity is a key uncertainty for mitigation scenarios for specific temperature levels.

Choices about the scale and timing of GHG mitigation involve balancing the economic costs of more rapid emission reductions now against the corresponding medium-term and long-term climate risks of delay.

NOTES AND QUESTIONS

1. The synthesis report delineates areas of greater and lesser certainty. What are these areas and how does the language of the report differentiate among different levels of certainty? In your view, which certainties and uncertainties are most critical for law and policy?
2. The synthesis report captures an overwhelming mix of environmental and human interactions that both cause the problem of climate change and help to determine appropriate responses. How should policymakers respond to this overwhelming mix? More broadly, what is the role of law in addressing complex problems like climate change?
3. Issues of inequality emerge throughout the synthesis report. Beyond the economic differences between countries that affect their emissions levels and ability to adapt, the report highlights the systems, sectors, and regions

most vulnerable to climate change. How do these inequalities impact the ways in which law should be used as a tool in addressing climate change? Chapter Seven explores these problems of inequality in more depth.

4. The synthesis report makes clear that there are economic costs both to mitigating climate change and to failing to mitigate effectively. Which costs are more certain? When would these costs occur? How should these issues of competing costs and their different levels of certainty and timing affect climate change law and policy?

2. BARRIERS TO SCIENTIFIC UNDERSTANDING

The public discussion over climate change science often focuses on polarized battles between those who believe in climate change science and those who are skeptical. This discussion is important in framing the policy debates, and the next section will focus on controversies over climate change science. However, before focusing on those controversies, this section examines the certainties and uncertainties of climate change science in a more nuanced way than those debates often allow.

Climate change science analyzes a very complex system with interactions in many places and at many physical (local, state, national, international) and temporal (past, present, future) scales. The level of scientific certainty is not uniform across this system. Rather it depends upon what aspect of the system is being discussed; some aspects have been studied more than others and some are easier to understand and predict than others.

Although a high level of certainty exists about the global-level processes of climate change, more uncertainty exists about some of the impacts occurring locally and regionally at specific points in time. This uncertainty, however, varies depending on the type of impact. For example, while climate change increases the risk of severe storms, it is difficult to say that it caused a particular hurricane or blizzard. On the other hand, strong scientific consensus exists about climate change causing the sea level to rise and heat waves, even at smaller scales.

At both international and national levels, there are efforts to address knowledge gaps where possible. The U.S. National Research Council's 2007 assessment of the U.S. Climate Change Science Program helped to frame some of the most recent efforts in the United States through highlighting areas where progress was needed for more effective scientific understanding and policymaking. The following is an excerpt of that advice.

COMMITTEE ON STRATEGIC ADVICE ON THE U.S. CLIMATE CHANGE SCIENCE PROGRAM, NATIONAL RESEARCH COUNCIL, EVALUATING PROGRESS OF THE U.S. CLIMATE CHANGE SCIENCE PROGRAM: METHODS AND PRELIMINARY RESULTS 1, 41–46 (2007)

http://www.nap.edu/catalog/11934.html

The U.S. Climate Change Science Program (CCSP) was created in February 2002 under a new cabinet-level management structure designed to improve government-wide management of climate and related environmental science.

The CCSP integrated the then-existing U.S. Global Change Research Program (USGCRP) with the administration's Climate Change Research Initiative. The CCSP was formed with an ambitious, but practical, guiding vision: *a nation and the global community empowered with the science based knowledge to manage the risks and opportunities of change in the climate and related environmental systems.*

Although the U.S. government has sponsored research on climate and related environmental change through the CCSP or USGCRP for more than 15 years, the progress of either program has never been evaluated. Such evaluations are important for identifying strengths and weaknesses and determining what adjustments should be made to achieve program goals. At the request of Dr. James Mahoney, then director of the CCSP, the National Research Council (NRC) established the Committee on Strategic Advice on the U.S. Climate Science Program to carry out three tasks over a three-year period. The first task — an evaluation of program progress — is the subject of this report:
. . . .

Overarching Conclusions

Discovery science and understanding of the climate system are proceeding well, but use of that knowledge to support decision making and to manage risks and opportunities of climate change is proceeding slowly.

Good progress has been made in documenting climate changes and their anthropogenic influences and in understanding many aspects of how the Earth system works (e.g., aerosol direct forcing, glacier melting). Coupled ocean-atmosphere-land climate models have also improved, although models that enable exploration of feedbacks, assessment of human driving forces, or trade-offs of different resource management and mitigation options are still relatively immature. The program has made a significant contribution to international climate research, particularly to Working Group 1 of the Intergovernmental Panel on Climate Change (IPCC). CCSP research and the temperature trends report have also played a role in the findings of the recently released IPCC (2007) report.

In contrast, inadequate progress has been made in synthesizing research results, assessing impacts on human systems, or providing knowledge to support decision making and risk analysis. Reports on temperature trends and scenarios of greenhouse gas emissions were the only CCSP synthesis and assessment products completed in the last four years; most synthesis activities have been small, focused, community efforts. A previous review of the CCSP strategic plan found that decision support activities were underdeveloped. The committee's preliminary assessment of progress (Chapters 4 and 5) shows that decision support has been incorporated into some aspects of the ecosystems research element (i.e., management strategies that consider the effect of climate variability on fisheries) and the human contributions and responses research element (e.g., Decision Making Under Uncertainty [DMUU] centers). However, these programs are small, and decision support is treated primarily as a service activity, rather than a topic that requires fundamental research. As a result, decisions about climate and associated environmental change have had to be made without the benefit of a strong scientific underpinning.

Progress in understanding and predicting climate change has improved more at global, continental, and ocean basin scales than at regional and local scales.

The disparity in progress is partly a result of the site-specific nature of impacts and vulnerabilities and the much greater natural variability on smaller scales. For example, the interannual variability of surface temperature is an order of magnitude greater on the scale of an individual town than the global average. It is these smaller spatial scales that are most relevant for state and local resource managers, policy makers, and the general public. Future projected land cover changes and changes in the distribution of continental water due to dams and irrigation, for example, are just beginning to be included in climate models. However, improving understanding of regional-scale climate processes and their impacts in North America would require improved integrated modeling, regional-scale observations, and the development of scenarios of climate change and impacts. Improved predictions of climate change at local levels should help the CCSP bridge the gap between science and decision making.

Our understanding of the impact of climate changes on human well-being and vulnerabilities is much less developed than our understanding of the natural climate system.

The greatest progress in the CCSP has been made on basic climate science associated with overarching goals 1, 2, and 3 (although human driving forces have lagged) and the least has been made on the interaction of climate change with human systems (overarching goals 4 and 5). Improved progress toward overarching goals 4 and 5 will require stronger connections with the social science community and a more comprehensive and balanced research program. Indeed, a review of the draft CCSP strategic plan recommended accelerating efforts in human dimensions, economics, adaptation, and mitigation by strengthening science plans and institutional support. Yet only a small percentage of the CCSP research and observations budget is devoted to the human contributions and responses research element, making it difficult to carry out even the limited research agenda outlined in the CCSP strategic plan. The bundling of human dimensions research and decision support tools further deemphasizes the importance of social science research and is detrimental to both parts of the program.

Another reason for inadequate progress is that no agency has a program focused on the human dimensions of climate. A consequence is that expertise in the human dimensions of climate change is in short supply in the participating agencies, which in turn makes it difficult for the CCSP to exert leadership and forge the necessary links between these agencies and the academic social science community. The connections that the National Science Foundation established for its DMUU centers may provide a model for other CCSP social science research.

Finally, the human dimensions research community is small and unorganized and thus may be unable to advocate effectively for changing program priorities. However, the good quality of work achieved with the low level of investment to date suggests that the community is capable of supporting a more substantial program.

Science quality observation systems have fueled advances in climate change science and applications, but many existing and planned observing systems have been cancelled, delayed, or degraded, which threatens future progress.

Much of the progress in understanding the climate system has been fueled by the availability of a wide range of data. A rich resource of satellite and in situ observations has been collected, disseminated, and archived by agencies participating in the CCSP. However, the number and diversity of satellite observations are expected to diminish significantly with the cancellation or delay of several planned National Aeronautics and Space Administration (NASA) and National Oceanic and Atmospheric Administration (NOAA) satellite missions (e.g., Hydros, Global Precipitation Measurement mission, Landsat Data Continuity Mission, Geostationary Operational Environmental Satellite Series-R) and the elimination of climate instruments from NPOESS. By the end of the decade the number of operating sensors and instruments on board NASA platforms is expected to decrease by approximately 40 percent. In addition, a number of long-standing in situ networks (e.g., U.S. Geological Survey stream gauge network, U.S. Department of Agriculture Snowpack Telemetry snow observation system) are deteriorating, and planned carbon cycle field campaigns may be cancelled because of funding shortfalls. The anticipated decline in U.S. capability to monitor global- or regional-scale environmental changes and the degradation of climate data climate change research. Indeed, the reduction in remote sensing capability is perhaps the single greatest threat to the future progress of the CCSP. Yet the CCSP has no strategy for implementing, sustaining, and evolving an observing system to address crucial questions on climate and related environmental changes. It is also not clear what role the CCSP might play in cooperating with other countries to obtain necessary data. This is particularly worrisome, given the IPCC prediction that the large warming trend of the last two decades will continue for at least the next few decades.

Progress in communicating CCSP results and engaging stakeholders is inadequate.

One of the most important differences between the CCSP and the U.S. Global Change Research Program (USGCRP) is the increased emphasis on communicating research results to stakeholders and encouraging the use of science-based products to support decision makers. Indeed, using CCSP knowledge to manage risks and opportunities related to climate variability and change is an overarching goal of the program. However, a coherent communications strategy, informed by basic social science research, has not yet been developed. Most efforts to carry out the two-way dialogue envisioned in the CCSP strategic plan appear to be ad hoc and to rely more on communicating research results — especially to federal agencies and, to a lesser extent, the scientific community — than on hearing what others need from the program. NOAA's Regional Integrated Sciences and Assessments program has been effective in communicating research results to stakeholders in particular sectors (e.g., impact of seasonal-to-interannual climate variability on water resources) or regions, but this program is small and has limited reach. Other efforts to identify and engage state and local officials, nongovernmental organizations, and the climate change technology community are still in the early stages.

Building and maintaining relationships with stakeholders is not easy and requires more resources in the CCSP Office and participating agencies than are currently available. Yet a well-developed list of stakeholders, target audiences, and their needs is essential for educating the public and informing decision making with scientifically based CCSP products.

The separation of leadership and budget authority presents a serious obstacle to progress in the CCSP.

A principle in *Thinking Strategically* is that a leader with authority to direct resources and/or research effort is essential if the program is to succeed. However, the CCSP is an interagency program in which responsibility for program management and budget allocation is shared among the participating agencies. As a result, effective coordination mechanisms are essential. Strong coordination at all levels of the program — within research questions, among closely related research elements and cross-cutting issues, and across the program as a whole — can create new avenues of investigation and should enable the CCSP to achieve more than its participating agencies could accomplish alone. Advances in characterizing the carbon budget, for example, have been attributed in part to an active IWG and scientific steering committee, community-established implementation plans, and a long history of interagency cooperation on carbon cycle research projects. . . . Established coordination mechanisms exist at both the component level (IWGs for research elements and cross-cutting issues . . .) and the program level (CCSP principals and program office).

However, coordination of budgets has been less effective. In the early years of the USGCRP, the Office of Management and Budget worked closely with the program leadership to identify priorities and to communicate those priorities to the relevant agency heads. CCSP budget allocations are coordinated to a much lesser extent today. Budgets are reported for major components of the CCSP (e.g., overarching goals, research elements), although this is primary a post factum accounting exercise, not a true allocation of funds to carry out the program. The CCSP director and agency principals have only a small budget over which they have discretionary control, and they must rely on persuasion rather than authority to allocate or prioritize funding across the agencies. For example, the CCSP appears to have had little influence either on the decisions taken to cancel or delay satellite missions or on what resources should be allocated to expand or upgrade in situ networks, despite the importance of observing systems to achieving CCSP objectives. Instead, these decisions are made by the respective agencies. Similarly, the interagency working groups have few discretionary funds and little authority to implement the objectives that they define, unless these objectives coincide with their agency objectives. Even funding for the Climate Change Research Initiative is disbursed among agency programs. Such fragmented authority can only weaken coherent leadership and priority setting and slow progress in achieving the overall goals of the program.

NOTES AND QUESTIONS

1. Although greater focus on local and regional issues will increase scientific certainty, it still will be hard to know whether any particular weather event occurring at a specific place and time is caused by climate change. What is the appropriate way to deal with that uncertainty? Is it enough to know that climate change increases the risk of more frequent and severe weather events?

   One well-established approach to scientific uncertainty under international environmental law, known as the precautionary principle, is to act with caution in the face of risk. This principle has many different formulations, one of the most well-accepted of which is articulated in the 1992 Rio Declaration: "In order to protect the environment, the precautionary approach shall be widely applied by States according to their capabilities. Where there are threats of serious or irreversible damage, lack of full scientific certainty shall not be used as a reason for postponing cost-effective measures to prevent environmental degradation." United Nations Conference on Environment and Development, Rio de Janiero, Braz., June 3–14, 1992, *Rio Declaration on Environment and Development*, princ. 15, U.N. GAOR, 46th Sess., U.N. Doc. A/CONF. 151/26/Rev.1 (Vol. I), Annex I (Aug. 12, 1992), June 13, 1992, *available at* http://www.unep.org/Documents .Multilingual/Default.asp?documentid=78&articleid=1163.

   Do you agree with taking a precautionary approach to the scientific uncertainties in climate change science? How would you translate such an approach into law and policy?

2. The Rio Declaration, like the IPCC synthesis report above, highlights the complexity of the science–law interface. While many issues might be able to be addressed by involving government officials more effectively, a key gap will likely remain. Namely, the scientists understand science better than law and the lawmakers understand law better than science. What is the best way of addressing this gap? How should the proposed "two-way communication" be implemented?

3. This report also highlights the complexity of the human-science interface. Why is research at that interface critical to addressing the problem of climate change? Which types of human-science research seem most important to you based on what you know the problem thus far?

3. CONTROVERSIES AND PUBLIC PERCEPTIONS OF RISK

Climate change science and scientists have been challenged over the past few years based on the release of information that showed procedural and substantive problems with both the IPCC and its underlying science. These controversies have helped to effect a shift in public opinion in the United

States, where polls show that people have become less certain about climate change science. This section discusses two of the most serious incidents to give clearer context for the current debates over climate change science.

The first problem made public was an inaccurate paragraph of the 2007 IPCC synthesis report on the melting of Himalayan glaciers. Although it was a relatively limited error, the fact that it made it into the report undermined the IPCC's credibility and raised questions about its process. The IPCC responded both directly and proactively to the problematic paragraph in the IPCC synthesis report and the following two excerpts describe that response.

The following excerpt is the IPCC's direct response to the error and assessment of its effect on the document as a whole.

IPCC, IPCC STATEMENT ON THE MELTING OF HIMALAYAN GLACIERS (JAN. 20, 2010)

http://www.ipcc.ch/pdf/presentations/himalaya-statement-20january2010.pdf

The Synthesis Report, the concluding document of the Fourth Assessment Report of the Intergovernmental Panel on Climate Change (page 49) stated: "Climate change is expected to exacerbate current stresses on water resources from population growth and economic and land-use change, including urbanisation. On a regional scale, mountain snow pack, glaciers and small ice caps play a crucial role in freshwater availability. Widespread mass losses from glaciers and reductions in snow cover over recent decades are projected to accelerate throughout the 21st century, reducing water availability, hydropower potential, and changing seasonality of flows in regions supplied by meltwater from major mountain ranges (e.g. Hindu-Kush, Himalaya, Andes), where more than one-sixth of the world population currently lives."

This conclusion is robust, appropriate, and entirely consistent with the underlying science and the broader IPCC assessment.

It has, however, recently come to our attention that a paragraph in the 938-page Working Group II contribution to the underlying assessment refers to poorly substantiated estimates of rate of recession and date for the disappearance of Himalayan glaciers. In drafting the paragraph in question, the clear and well-established standards of evidence, required by the IPCC procedures, were not applied properly.

The Chair, Vice-Chairs, and Co-chairs of the IPCC regret the poor application of well-established IPCC procedures in this instance. This episode demonstrates that the quality of the assessment depends on absolute adherence to the IPCC standards, including thorough review of "the quality and validity of each source before incorporating results from the source into an IPCC Report." We reaffirm our strong commitment to ensuring this level of performance.

In addition to addressing the problematic paragraph, the IPCC established an independent committee to review its procedures and prevent a recurrence of these types of problems. The following IPCC statement describes that decision.

IPCC, Statement of the IPCC Chairman on the Establishment of an Independent Committee to Review IPCC Procedures (Feb. 27, 2010)

http://www.ipcc.ch/pdf/press/PA_IPCC_Chairman_Statement_27Feb2010.pdf

The IPCC strives to ensure that its procedures for use of published material in the preparation of its assessment reports are followed in all respects. But we recognize the criticism that has been leveled at us and the need to respond. While embarking on the preparation of its Fifth Assessment Report it was the intention of the IPCC that an independent committee of distinguished experts evaluate means by which IPCC procedures must be implemented fully and that they should also examine any changes in procedure that may be required. The proposal to set up such an independent committee was conveyed to governments by the IPCC Secretariat in a communication dated Tuesday 16 February.

Further, during the 11th Session of the Governing Council/Global Ministerial Environment Forum convened by the United Nations Environment Programme in Bali during February 24–26, IPCC pursued interaction with governments and the UN to establish an independent review of the IPCC procedures as proposed. The mechanism by which such an independent review will take place is under active consideration.

Meanwhile, we stand firmly behind the rigour and robustness of the 4th Assessment Report's conclusions, and are encouraged by the support demonstrated recently by scientists and governments around the world.

The 4th Assessment Report's key conclusions are based on an overwhelming body of evidence from thousands of peer-reviewed and independent scientific studies. Most significantly, they rest on multiple lines of analysis and datasets.

The second controversy resulted after the e-mail accounts of climate change scientists at the University of East Anglia in the United Kingdom were hacked and their e-mails were released on the Internet. The released e-mails allegedly showed inappropriate behavior by the scientists regarding the ways in which they handled their data, approached peer review, and reported their results to the public. Although an independent investigation found that these e-mails did not undermine the accuracy of the scientific work, the tone and content of these e-mails damaged the scientists' credibility.

The following excerpt summarizes the conclusions of the independent investigation. The report not only addresses the impact of the scientists' e-mails, but also the broader implications for how climate change science should be conducted.

The Independent Climate Change Emails Review 10–16 (July 2010)

http://www.cce-review.org/pdf/FINAL%20REPORT.pdf

1.1 Introduction

2. In November 2009, approximately 1000 e-mails from the Climatic Research Unit (CRU) of the University of East Anglia (UEA) were made public without authorisation.

3. CRU is a small research unit which over the last 30 years has played an important role in the development of climate science, in particular in their work on developing global temperature trends.
4. The e-mails fuelled challenges to the work of CRU, to the reliability of climate science generally, and to the conclusions of the Intergovernmental Panel on Climate Change (IPCC). All this happened shortly before the Copenhagen Summit, and was extensively referred to there.
5. In response, the UEA commissioned two inquiries. The first led by Lord Oxburgh, into the science being undertaken at CRU, has already reported. This document is the report of the second inquiry—The Independent Climate Change E-mails Review—which examines the conduct of the scientists involved and makes recommendations to the University of East Anglia. Our inquiry addresses a number of important allegations that were made following the e-mail release.
6. The allegations relate to aspects of the **behaviour** of the CRU scientists, such as their handling and release of data, their approach to peer review, and their role in the public presentation of results.
7. The allegations also include the assertion that actions were taken to promote a particular view of climate change by improperly influencing the process of advising policy makers. Therefore we have sought to understand the significance of the roles played by those involved from CRU and of the influence they had on the relevant outcomes.
8. The Review examines **the honesty, rigour and openness** with which the CRU scientists have acted. It is important to note that we offer no opinion on the validity of their scientific work. Such an outcome could only come through the normal processes of scientific debate and not from the examination of e-mails or from a series of interviews about conduct.
     . . . .

1.3 Findings

13. Climate science is a matter of such global importance, that the highest standards of honesty, rigour and openness are needed in its conduct. On the specific allegations made against the behaviour of CRU scientists, **we find that their rigour and honesty as scientists are not in doubt.**
14. In addition, we do not find that their behaviour has prejudiced the balance of advice given to policy makers. In particular, **we did not find any evidence of behaviour that might undermine the conclusions of the IPCC assessments.**
15. **But we do find that there has been a consistent pattern of failing to display the proper degree of openness,** both on the part of the CRU scientists and on the part of the UEA, who failed to recognise not only the significance of statutory requirements but also the risk to the reputation of the University and, indeed, to the credibility of UK climate science.

1.3.1 Land Station Temperatures

16. **On the allegation of withholding temperature data, we find that CRU was not in a position to withhold access to such data or tamper**

with it. We demonstrated that any independent researcher can download station data directly from primary sources and undertake their own temperature trend analysis.

17. **On the allegation of biased station selection and analysis, we find no evidence of bias.** Our work indicates that analysis of global land temperature trends is robust to a range of station selections and to the use of adjusted or unadjusted data. The level of agreement between independent analyses is such that it is highly unlikely that CRU could have acted improperly to reach a predetermined outcome. Such action would have required collusion with multiple scientists in various independent organisations which we consider highly improbable.

18. **On the allegation of withholding station identifiers we find that CRU should have made available an unambiguous list of the stations used in each of the versions of the Climatic Research Unit Land Temperature Record (CRUTEM) at the time of publication. We find that CRU's responses to reasonable requests for information were unhelpful and defensive.**

19. **The overall implication of the allegations was to cast doubt on the extent to which CRU's work in this area could be trusted and should be relied upon and we find no evidence to support that implication.**

1.3.2 Temperature Reconstructions from Tree Ring Analysis

20. The central implication of the allegations here is that in carrying out their work, both in the choices they made of data and the ways in which it was handled, CRU scientists intended to bias the scientific conclusions towards a specific result and to set aside inconvenient evidence. More specifically, it was implied in the allegations that this should reduce the confidence ascribed to the conclusions in Chapter 6 of the IPCC 4th Report, Working Group 1 (WG1).

21. **We do not find that the way that data derived from tree rings is described and presented in IPCC AR4 and shown in its Figure 6.10 is misleading.** In particular, on the question of the composition of temperature reconstructions, we found no evidence of exclusion of other published temperature reconstructions that would show a very different picture. The general discussion of sources of uncertainty in the text is extensive, including reference to divergence. In this respect it represented a significant advance on the IPCC Third Assessment Report (TAR).

22. **On the allegation that the phenomenon of "divergence" may not have been properly taken into account when expressing the uncertainty associated with reconstructions, we are satisfied that it is not hidden and that the subject is openly and extensively discussed in the literature, including CRU papers.**

23. **On the allegation that the references in a specific e-mail to a "trick" and to "hide the decline" in respect of a 1999 WMO report figure show evidence of intent to paint a misleading picture, we find that, given its subsequent iconic significance (not least the use of a similar figure in the IPCC Third Assessment Report), the figure supplied for the**

WMO Report was misleading. We do not find that it is misleading to curtail reconstructions at some point *per se*, or to splice data, but we believe that both of these procedures should have been made plain — ideally in the figure but certainly clearly described in either the caption or the text.

24. **On the allegations in relation to withholding data, in particular concerning the small sample size of the tree ring data from the Yamal peninsula, CRU did not withhold the underlying raw data (having correctly directed the single request to the owners).** But it is evidently true that access to the raw data was not simple until it was archived in 2009 and that this delay can rightly be criticized on general principles. In the interests of transparency, we believe that CRU should have ensured that the data they did not own, but on which their publications relied, was archived in a more timely way.

1.3.3 Peer Review and Editorial Policy

25. **On the allegations that there was subversion of the peer review or editorial process we find no evidence to substantiate this in the three instances examined in detail.** On the basis of the independent work we commissioned . . . on the nature of peer review, we conclude that it is not uncommon for strongly opposed and robustly expressed positions to be taken up in heavily contested areas of science. We take the view that such behaviour does not in general threaten the integrity of peer review or publication.

1.3.4 Misuse of IPCC Process

26. **On the allegations that in two specific cases there had been a misuse by CRU scientists of the IPCC process, in presenting AR4 to the public and policy makers, we find that the allegations cannot be upheld.** In addition to taking evidence from them and checking the relevant records of the IPCC process, we have consulted the relevant IPCC review Editors. Both the CRU scientists were part of large groups of scientists taking joint responsibility for the relevant IPCC Working Group texts, and were not in a position to determine individually the final wording and content.

1.3.5 Compliance with the Freedom of Information Act (FoIA) and the Environmental Information Regulations (EIR)

27. **On the allegation that CRU does not appear to have acted in a way consistent with the spirit and intent of the FoIA or EIR, we find that there was unhelpfulness in responding to requests and evidence that e-mails might have been deleted in order to make them unavailable should a subsequent request be made for them.** University senior management should have accepted more responsibility for implementing the required processes for FoIA and EIR compliance.

1.3.6 Other Findings on Governance

28. **Given the significance of the work of CRU, UEA management failed to recognise in their risk management the potential for damage to the University's reputation fuelled by the controversy over data access.**

1.4 Recommendations

29. Our main recommendations for UEA are as follows:
Risk management processes should be directed to ensuring top management engagement in areas which have the potential to impact the reputation of the university. Compliance with FoIA/EIR is the responsibility of UEA faculty leadership and ultimately the Vice-Chancellor. Where there is an organisation and documented system in place to handle information requests, this needs to be owned, supported and reinforced by University leadership. CRU should make available sufficient information, concurrent with any publications, to enable others to replicate their results.

1.5 Broader Issues

30. Our work in conducting the Review has led us to identify a number of issues relevant not only to the climate science debate but also possibly more widely, on which we wish to comment briefly.
31. **The nature of scientific challenge.** We note that much of the challenge to CRU's work has not always followed the conventional scientific method of checking and seeking to falsify conclusions or offering alternative hypotheses for peer review and publication. We believe this is necessary if science is to move on, and we hope that all those involved on all sides of the climate science debate will adopt this approach.
32. **Handling Uncertainty — where policy meets science.** Climate science is an area that exemplifies the importance of ensuring that policy makers — particularly Governments and their advisers, Non-Governmental Organisations and other lobbyists — understand the limits on what scientists can say and with what degree of confidence. Statistical and other techniques for explaining uncertainty have developed greatly in recent years, and it is essential that they are properly deployed. But equally important is the need for alternative viewpoints to be recognized in policy presentations, with a robust assessment of their validity, and for the challenges to be rooted in science rather than rhetoric.
33. **Peer review — what it can/cannot deliver.** We believe that peer review is an essential part of the process of judging scientific work, but it should not be overrated as a guarantee of the validity of individual pieces of research, and the significance of challenge to individual publication decisions should be not exaggerated.
34. **Openness and FoIA.** We support the spirit of openness enshrined in the FoIA and the EIR. It is unfortunate that this was not embraced by UEA, and we make recommendations about that. A well thought through publication scheme would remove much potential for disruption by the

submission of multiple requests for information. But at the level of public policy there is need for further thinking about the competing arguments for the timing of full disclosure of research data and associated computer codes etc, as against considerations of confidentiality during the conduct of research. There is much scope for unintended consequences that could hamper research: US experience is instructive. We recommend that the ICO should initiate a debate on these wider issues.

35. **Handling the blogosphere and non traditional scientific dialogue.** One of the most obvious features of the climate change debate is the influence of the blogosphere. This provides an opportunity for unmoderated comment to stand alongside peer reviewed publications; for presentations or lectures at learned conferences to be challenged without inhibition; and for highly personalized critiques of individuals and their work to be promulgated without hindrance. This is a fact of life, and it would be foolish to challenge its existence. The Review team would simply urge all scientists to learn to communicate their work in ways that the public can access and understand. That said, a key issue is how scientists should be supported to explain their position, and how a public space can be created where these debates can be conducted on appropriate terms, where what is and is not uncertain can be recognised.

36. **Openness and Reputation.** An important feature of the blogosphere is the extent to which it demands openness and access to data. A failure to recognize this and to act appropriately, can lead to immense reputational damage by feeding allegations of cover up. Being part of a like minded group may provide no defence. Like it or not, this indicates a transformation in the way science has to be conducted in this century.

37. **Role of Research Sponsors.** One of the issues facing the Review was the release of data. At various points in the report we have commented on the formal requirements for this. We consider that it would make for clarity for researchers if funders were to be completely clear upfront in their requirements for the release of data (as well as its archiving, curation etc).

38. **The IPCC.** We welcome the IPCC's decision to review its processes, and can only stress the importance of capturing the range of viewpoints and reflecting appropriately the statistical uncertainties surrounding the data it assesses. Our conclusions do not make a judgement on the work of IPCC, though we acknowledge the importance of its advice to policy makers.

NOTES AND QUESTIONS

1. How serious are problems with the IPCC report and e-mails by climate scientists? Do you see these independent assessments as an appropriate response to the incidents? What are the benefits and limitations of such assessments?

In addition to these independent assessments, a 2011 study led by a physicist who had previously expressed skepticism of climate science reaffirmed the underlying validity of the scientific research showing an increase in average world land temperature over the past 50 years. *See* Press Release, Berkeley Earth Surface Temperature, Cooling the Warming Debate: Berkeley Earth Releases Global Land Warming Analysis (Oct. 20, 2011), http://berkeleyearth.org/pdf/berkeley-earth-summary-20-october-2011.pdf. Moreover, this study was funded in part by a foundation affiliated with the oil corporation Koch Industries, which reportedly contributed $24.9 million to climate change denial groups between 2005 and 2008. *See* GREENPEACE, KOCH INDUSTRIES SECRETLY FUNDING THE CLIMATE DENIAL MACHINE: EXECUTIVE SUMMARY 6 (2010), *available at* http://www.greenpeace.org/usa/Global/usa/report/2010/3/executive-summary-koch-indus.pdf. How does this study complement the independent assessments?

2. Both the e-mails and the conclusions of the independent report on the e-mails were widely reported in the press and the media continues to be actively involved in discussing controversies over climate change science, often in ways that reflect the political polarization over climate change. For example, in October 2011, Jon Stewart on his late night show criticized Fox News for failing to cover the results of the study described in the previous note after its extensive coverage of "ClimateGate." *See The Daily Show with Jon Stewart: Weathering Fights* (Comedy Central television broadcast Oct. 26, 2011), *available at* http://www.thedailyshow.com/watch/wed-october-26-2011/weathering-fights. Similarly, in early 2012, the media role in the public discourse over climate change science was highlighted by a pair of dueling editorials in the *Wall Street Journal*, the first by 16 scientists expressing skepticism about climate change science and the second by an even larger group of scientists questioning the expertise of many of the 16 signatories and claiming that "[r]esearch shows that more than 97% of scientists actively publishing in the field agree that climate change is real and human caused." *Compare No Need to Panic About Global Warming*, WALL ST. J., Jan. 26, 2012, http://online.wsj.com/article/SB10001424052970204301404577171531838421366.html, *with Check with Climate Scientists for Views on Climate*, WALL ST. J., Feb. 1, 2012, http://online.wsj.com/article/SB100014240529702047409045777193270727472662.html. What should be the role of the media in addressing these sorts of controversies? How effectively can the media communicate the technical issues involved in assessing climate change science and how should it report on the politics surrounding the science?

3. These controversies and the media coverage of them not only highlight specific problems, but the broader political context in which climate science takes place. Scientists make choices aware that their work might be used by those who support or oppose lawmaking efforts to address climate change. Moreover, the growth of the Internet has intensified public scrutiny. Do you agree with the conclusions of the independent report on the e-mails about how scientists should operate in this environment?

C. ADDRESSING CLIMATE CHANGE THROUGH LAW: CORE OPTIONS AND CRITICAL DILEMMAS

The previous section makes clear that climate change science issues are tremendously complex because they intersect with human beings and their cultural, political, economic, and legal institutions and norms. This section connects these issues more directly to law, the focus of this book, in order to set the stage for the chapters that follow.

Although the initial focus of those concerned about human-caused climate change was *prevention*, the level of past emissions is already great enough to make some climate change certain. The focus has therefore shifted to *mitigation*, reducing greenhouse gas emissions to limit the extent of the change, and *adaptation*, preparing for the effects and responding to them to minimize their harm. To compensate for inadequate mitigation, there also has been an increasing focus on geoengineering, using technology to reverse climate change or its effects, which will be discussed in depth in Chapter Seven.

This section introduces the primary strategies being discussed and debated regarding both mitigation and adaptation and the dilemmas of regulating a fundamentally cross-cutting problem. The discussion in this section highlights three core challenges facing ongoing efforts to address the problem of climate change: (1) the need for law to evolve to engage scientific complexity; (2) the insufficiency of the current international climate change legal regime to address the problem; and (3) the multidimensional nature of the legal solutions needed.

1. MITIGATION

Much of the public discourse over climate change focuses on mitigation. Policymakers, business executives, nongovernmental organizations, and individuals have diverse views about what type of action is appropriate to reduce greenhouse gas emissions. This section explores two categories of core questions that animate debates over appropriate mitigation strategies: technological ones and law and policy ones.

The first type of issue that arises regarding mitigation is technological. The underlying problem of climate change involves complex and evolving science, but reducing emissions also raises disputes at the interface of law and technology. Legal measures that effectively reduce greenhouse gas emissions should focus on using existing technology effectively and on fostering the development of needed new technology. However, crafting such measures requires answering difficult questions: What technology is needed to reduce greenhouse gas emissions? Is it possible to reach reduction targets with existing technology and, if so, what would that look like? What types of technological breakthroughs would be most helpful in bringing emissions down without major economic impacts?

In 2004, Professors Stephen Pacala and Robert Socolow attempted to answer these questions. In an article that continued to inspire debate and discussion in the lead up to the Durban climate change negotiations in 2011, they argued that we have the technology necessary to address climate change and proposed a set of options that could be combined to do so. Specifically, they suggested that humanity should choose to employ seven wedges — where each wedge represents a technological approach that would reduce emissions by a particular amount — in order to put itself on a 50-year path through which stabilizing climate change is possible. The following excerpt from their article introduces their theory of wedges and the 15 wedge options they set forth.

STEPHEN PACALA & ROBERT SOCOLOW, STABILIZATION WEDGES: SOLVING THE CLIMATE PROBLEM FOR THE NEXT 50 YEARS WITH CURRENT TECHNOLOGIES

305 Science 968 (2004)

The debate in the current literature about stabilizing atmospheric CO_2 at less than a doubling of the preindustrial concentration has led to needless confusion about current options for mitigation. On one side, the Intergovernmental Panel on Climate Change (IPCC) has claimed that "technologies that exist in operation or pilot stage today" are sufficient to follow a less-than doubling trajectory "over the next hundred years or more." On the other side, a recent review in *Science* asserts that the IPCC claim demonstrates "misperceptions of technological readiness" and calls for "revolutionary changes" in mitigation technology, such as fusion, space-based solar electricity, and artificial photosynthesis. We agree that fundamental research is vital to develop the revolutionary mitigation strategies needed in the second half of this century and beyond. But it is important not to become beguiled by the possibility of revolutionary technology. Humanity can solve the carbon and climate problem in the first half of this century simply by scaling up what we already know how to do.

What Do We Mean by "Solving the Carbon and Climate Problem for the Next Half-Century"?

Proposals to limit atmospheric CO_2 to a concentration that would prevent most damaging climate change have focused on a goal of 500 +/− 50 parts per million (ppm), or less than double the preindustrial concentration of 280 ppm. The current concentration is 375 ppm. The CO_2 emissions reductions necessary to achieve any such target depend on the emissions judged likely to occur in the absence of a focus on carbon [called a business-as-usual (BAU) trajectory], the quantitative details of the stabilization target, and the future behavior of natural sinks for atmospheric CO_2 (i.e., the oceans and terrestrial biosphere). We focus exclusively on CO_2, because it is the dominant anthropogenic greenhouse gas; industrial-scale mitigation options also exist for subordinate gases, such as methane and N_2O.

Very roughly, stabilization at 500 ppm requires that emissions be held near the present level of 7 billion tons of carbon per year (GtC/year) for the next 50 years, even though they are currently on course to more than double. . . . The next 50 years is a sensible horizon from several perspectives. It is the length of a career, the lifetime of a power plant, and an interval for which the technology is close enough to envision. . . .

The Stabilization Triangle

We idealize the 50-year emissions reductions as a perfect triangle. . . . Stabilization is represented by a "flat" trajectory of fossil fuel emissions at 7 GtC/year, and BAU is represented by a straight-line "ramp" trajectory rising to 14 GtC/year in 2054. The "stabilization triangle," located between the flat trajectory and BAU, removes exactly one third of BAU emissions.

To keep the focus on technologies that have the potential to produce a material difference by 2054, we divide the stabilization triangle into seven equal "wedges." A wedge represents an activity that reduces emissions to the atmosphere that starts at zero today and increases linearly until it accounts for 1 GtC/year of reduced carbon emissions in 50 years. It thus represents a cumulative total of 25 GtC of reduced emissions over 50 years. In this paper, to "solve the carbon and climate problem over the next half-century" means to deploy the technologies and/or lifestyle changes necessary to fill all seven wedges of the stabilization triangle.

Stabilization at any level requires that net emissions do not simply remain constant, but eventually drop to zero. For example, in one simple model that begins with the stabilization triangle but looks beyond 2054, 500-ppm stabilization is achieved by 50 years of flat emissions, followed by a linear decline of about two-thirds in the following 50 years, and a very slow decline thereafter that matches the declining ocean sink. To develop the revolutionary technologies required for such large emissions reductions in the second half of the century, enhanced research and development would have to begin immediately.

Policies designed to stabilize at 500 ppm would inevitably be renegotiated periodically to take into account the results of research and development, experience with specific wedges, and revised estimates of the size of the stabilization triangle. But not filling the stabilization triangle will put 500-ppm stabilization out of reach. In that same simple model, 50 years of BAU emissions followed by 50 years of a flat trajectory at 14 GtC/year leads to more than a tripling of the preindustrial concentration.

It is important to understand that each of the seven wedges represents an effort beyond what would occur under BAU. Our BAU simply continues the 1.5% annual carbon emissions growth of the past 30 years. This historic trend in emissions has been accompanied by 2% growth in primary energy consumption and 3% growth in gross world product (GWP). If carbon emissions were to grow 2% per year, then 10 wedges would be needed instead of 7, and if carbon emissions were to grow at 3% per year, then 18 wedges would be required. Thus, a continuation of the historical rate of decarbonization of the fuel mix prevents the need for three additional wedges, and ongoing improvements in energy efficiency prevent the need for eight additional wedges. Most readers will reject at least one of the wedges listed here, believing that the corresponding deployment is certain to occur in BAU, but readers will disagree about which to reject on such grounds. On the other hand, our list of mitigation options is not exhaustive.

What Current Options Could Be Scaled Up to Produce at Least One Wedge?

Wedges can be achieved from energy efficiency, from the decarbonization of the supply of electricity and fuels (by means of fuel shifting, carbon capture and storage, nuclear energy, and renewable energy), and from biological storage in forests and agricultural soils. . . . Although several options could be scaled up to two or more wedges, we doubt that any could fill the stabilization triangle, or even half of it, alone. Because the same BAU carbon emissions cannot be displaced twice, achieving one wedge often interacts with achieving another. The more the electricity system becomes decarbonized, for example, the less the available savings from greater efficiency of electricity use, and vice versa. . . .

Category I: Efficiency and Conservation

Improvements in efficiency and conservation probably offer the greatest potential to provide wedges. For example, in 2002, the United States announced the goal of decreasing its carbon intensity (carbon emissions per unit GDP) by 18% over the next decade, a decrease of 1.96% per year. An entire wedge would be created if the United States were to reset its carbon intensity goal to a decrease of 2.11% per year and extend it to 50 years, and if every country were to follow suit by adding the same 0.15% per year increment to its own carbon intensity goal. However, efficiency and conservation options are less tangible than those from the other categories. Improvements in energy efficiency will come from literally hundreds of innovations that range from new catalysts and chemical processes, to more efficient lighting and insulation for buildings, to the growth of the service economy and telecommuting. Here, we provide four of many possible comparisons of greater and less efficiency in 2054.

Option 1: Improved fuel economy. Suppose that in 2054, 2 billion cars (roughly four times as many as today) average 10,000 miles per year (as they do today). One wedge would be achieved if, instead of averaging 30 miles per gallon (mpg) on conventional fuel, cars in 2054 averaged 60 mpg, with fuel type and distance traveled unchanged.

Option 2: Reduced reliance on cars. A wedge would also be achieved if the average fuel economy of the 2 billion 2054 cars were 30 mpg, but the annual distance traveled were 5000 miles instead of 10,000 miles.

Option 3: More efficient buildings. According to a 1996 study by the IPCC, a wedge is the difference between pursuing and not pursuing "known and established approaches" to energy efficient space heating and cooling, water heating, lighting, and refrigeration in residential and commercial buildings. These approaches reduce midcentury emissions from buildings by about one-fourth. About half of potential savings are in the buildings in developing countries.

Option 4: Improved power plant efficiency. In 2000, coal power plants, operating on average at 32% efficiency, produced about one fourth of all carbon emissions: 1.7 GtC/year out of 6.2 GtC/year. A wedge would be created if twice today's quantity of coal-based electricity in 2054 were produced at 60% instead of 40% efficiency.

Category II: Decarbonization of Electricity and Fuels

Option 5: Substituting natural gas for coal. Carbon emissions per unit of electricity are about half as large from natural gas power plants as from coal plants. Assume that the capacity factor of the average baseload coal plant in 2054 has increased to 90% and that its efficiency has improved to 50%. Because 700 GW of such plants emit carbon at a rate of 1 GtC/year, a wedge would be achieved by displacing 1400 GW of baseload coal with baseload gas by 2054. The power shifted to gas for this wedge is four times as large as the total current gas-based power.

Option 6: Storage of carbon captured in power plants. Carbon capture and storage (CCS) technology prevents about 90% of the fossil carbon from reaching the atmosphere, so a wedge would be provided by the installation of CCS at 800 GW of baseload coal plants by 2054 or 1600 GW of baseload natural gas plants. The most likely approach has two steps: (i) precombustion capture of CO_2, in which hydrogen and CO_2 are produced and the hydrogen is then burned to produce electricity, followed by (ii) geologic storage, in which the waste CO_2 is injected into subsurface geologic reservoirs. Hydrogen production from fossil fuels is already a very large business. Globally, hydrogen plants consume about 2% of primary energy and emit 0.1 GtC/year of CO_2. The capture part of a wedge of CCS electricity would thus require only a tenfold expansion of plants resembling today's large hydrogen plants over the next 50 years. . . . A worldwide effort is under way to assess the capacity available for multicentury storage and to assess risks of leaks large enough to endanger human or environmental health.

Option 7: Storage of carbon captured in hydrogen plants. The hydrogen resulting from precombustion capture of CO_2 can be sent offsite to displace the consumption of conventional fuels rather than being consumed onsite to produce electricity. The capture part of a wedge would require the installation of CCS, by 2054, at coal plants producing 250 MtH_2/year, or at natural gas plants producing 500 MtH_2/year. The former is six times the current rate of hydrogen production. The storage part of this option is the same as in Option 6.

Option 8: Storage of carbon captured in synfuels plants. Looming over carbon management in 2054 is the possibility of large-scale production of synthetic fuel (synfuel) from coal. Carbon emissions, however, need not exceed those associated with fuel refined from crude oil if synfuels production is accompanied by CCS. Assuming that half of the carbon entering a 2054 synfuels plant leaves as fuel but the other half can be captured as CO_2, the capture part of a wedge in 2054 would be the difference between capturing and venting the CO_2 from coal synfuels plants producing 30 million barrels of synfuels per day. . . . Currently, the Sasol plants in South Africa, the world's largest synfuels facility, produce 165,000 barrels per day from coal. Thus, a wedge requires 200 Sasol-scale coal-to-synfuels facilities with CCS in 2054. The storage part of this option is again the same as in Option 6.

Option 9: Nuclear fission. On the basis of the Option 5 estimates, a wedge of nuclear electricity would displace 700 GW of efficient baseload coal capacity in 2054. This would require 700 GW of nuclear power with the same 90% capacity factor assumed for the coal plants, or about twice the nuclear capacity currently deployed. The global pace of nuclear power plant construction from 1975 to 1990 would yield a wedge, if it continued for 50 years. Substantial expansion in nuclear power requires restoration of public confidence in safety and waste disposal, and international security agreements governing uranium enrichment and plutonium recycling.

Option 10: Wind electricity. We account for the intermittent output of windmills by equating 3 GW of nominal peak capacity (3 GW_p) with 1 GW of base-load capacity. Thus, a wedge of wind electricity would require the deployment of 2000 GW_p that displaces coal electricity in 2054 (or 2 million 1-MW_p wind turbines). Installed wind capacity has been growing at about 30% per year for more than 10 years and is currently about 40 GW_p. A wedge of wind electricity would thus require 50 times today's deployment. The wind turbines would "occupy" about 30 million hectares (about 3% of the area of the United States), some on land and some offshore. Because windmills are widely spaced, land with windmills can have multiple uses.

Option 11: Photovoltaic electricity. Similar to a wedge of wind electricity, a wedge from photovoltaic (PV) electricity would require 2000 GW_p of installed capacity that displaces coal electricity in 2054. Although only 3 GW_p of PV are currently installed, PV electricity has been growing at a rate of 30% per year. A wedge of PV electricity would require 700 times today's deployment, and about 2 million hectares of land in 2054, or 2 to 3 m_2 per person.

Option 12: Renewable hydrogen. Renewable electricity can produce carbon-free hydrogen for vehicle fuel by the electrolysis of water. The hydrogen produced by 4 million 1-MW_p windmills in 2054, if used in high-efficiency fuel-cell cars, would achieve a wedge of displaced gasoline or diesel fuel. Compared with Option 10, this is twice as many 1-MW_p windmills as would be required to produce the electricity that achieves a wedge by displacing high-efficiency baseload coal. This interesting factor-of-two carbon-saving advantage of wind-electricity over wind-hydrogen is still larger if the coal plant is less efficient or the fuel-cell vehicle is less spectacular.

Option 13: Biofuels. Fossil-carbon fuels can also be replaced by biofuels such as ethanol. A wedge of biofuel would be achieved by the production of about 34 million barrels per day of ethanol in 2054 that could displace gasoline, provided the ethanol itself were fossil-carbon free. This ethanol production rate would be about 50 times larger than today's global production rate, almost all of which can be attributed to Brazilian sugarcane and United States corn. An ethanol wedge would require 250 million hectares committed to high-yield (15 dry tons/hectare) plantations by 2054, an area equal to about one-sixth of the world's cropland. An even larger area would be required to the extent that the biofuels require fossil-carbon inputs. Because land suitable for annually harvested biofuels crops is also often suitable for conventional agriculture, biofuels production could compromise agricultural productivity.

Category III: Natural Sinks

Although the literature on biological sequestration includes a diverse array of options and some very large estimates of the global potential, here we restrict our attention to the pair of options that are already implemented at large scale and that could be scaled up to a wedge or more without a lot of new research.

Option 14: Forest management. Conservative assumptions lead to the conclusion that at least one wedge would be available from reduced tropical deforestation and the management of temperate and tropical forests. At least one half-wedge would be created if the current rate of clear-cutting of primary tropical forest were reduced to zero over 50 years instead of being halved. A second half-wedge would be created by reforesting or afforesting approximately 250 million hectares in the tropics or 400 million hectares in the temperate zone (current areas of tropical and temperate forests are 1500 and 700 million hectares, respectively). A third half-wedge would be created by establishing approximately 300 million hectares of plantations on nonforested land.

Option 15: Agricultural soils management. When forest or natural grassland is converted to cropland, up to one-half of the soil carbon is lost, primarily because annual tilling increases the rate of decomposition by aerating undecomposed organic matter. About 55 GtC, or two wedges' worth, has been lost historically in this way. Practices such as conservation tillage (e.g., seeds are drilled into the soil without plowing), the use of cover crops, and erosion control can reverse the losses. By 1995, conservation tillage practices had been adopted on 110 million hectares of the world's 1600 million hectares of cropland. If conservation tillage could be extended to all cropland, accompanied by a verification program that enforces the adoption of soil conservation practices that actually work as advertised, a good case could be made for the IPCC's estimate that an additional half to one wedge could be stored in this way.

Conclusions

In confronting the problem of greenhouse warming, the choice today is between action and delay. Here, we presented a part of the case for action by identifying a set of options that have the capacity to provide the seven stabilization wedges and solve the climate problem for the next half-century. None of the options is a pipe dream or an unproven idea. Today, one can buy electricity from a wind turbine, PV array, gas turbine, or nuclear power plant. One can buy hydrogen produced with the chemistry of carbon capture, biofuel to power one's car, and hundreds of devices that improve energy efficiency. One can visit tropical forests where clear-cutting has ceased, farms practicing conservation tillage, and facilities that inject carbon into geologic reservoirs. Every one of these options is already implemented at an industrial scale and could be scaled up further over 50 years to provide at least one wedge.

Even if people could agree on technological options, difficult legal issues would remain. A range of different legal mechanisms could be used to reach these mitigation goals. As with technology, deep disagreements exist over these legal options, and countries, states, and localities have proceeded along divergent paths. The mechanisms currently in use and the alternatives to them lead to this section's second set of questions: What types of legal mechanisms could incentivize individuals and companies to reduce their emissions? Which ones would be most effective and which ones would be most politically acceptable? What combination of mandatory and voluntary commitments at international, national, state, local, and individual levels would create the reductions that scientists say are needed to minimize impacts?

In 2008, the Canadian Library of Parliament published a document outlining three major policy options that governments have for mitigating greenhouse gas emissions: cap-and-trade systems, carbon taxes, and direct regulations. It explains that all of these options aim to set a price on carbon in a way that reduces its use in the market, but that each of them use different mechanisms for doing so. It considers both the political viability and potential effectiveness of each approach, and how the approaches might be used together. Because this document predates the 2010 failure of cap-and-trade legislation in the United States and Canada's 2011 decision not to recommit to the Kyoto Protocol, it particularly focuses on cap-and-trade. However, even in the current North American political environment, this document provides a helpful summary of policy options.

FRÉDÉRIC FORGE & TIM WILLIAMS, PARLIAMENTARY RESEARCH AND INFORMATION SERVICE, LIBRARY OF PARLIAMENT, CANADA, POLICY OPTIONS TO REDUCE GREENHOUSE GAS EMISSIONS 1–6 (OCT. 7, 2008)

http://www.parl.gc.ca/Content/LOP/researchpublications/prb0819-e.pdf

There are many policy tools available to the government to help induce greenhouse gas (GHG) emissions reductions, including voluntary actions and agreements, financial incentives and subsidies and information instruments. However, there is a growing consensus among economists, environmentalists, many politicians and business leaders that putting a price on (GHGs) is essential to reduce emissions.

Market-based approaches are thought to be most effective because they signal that GHG emissions have a monetary value, stimulating actions that will lead emitters to reduce their emissions. In effect, putting a price on GHG emissions would acknowledge that the atmosphere cannot be used as a free waste disposal site for these pollutants. Such a price would therefore take into account costs that are not reflected in the price of energy production and use, termed "external" costs. This would level the playing field with other, currently more expensive, lower carbon energy sources, making these sources more economically viable.

There are different ways of pricing carbon which can be used in combination with other mechanisms, such as regulation. While it is acknowledged that putting a price on carbon is an effective way to reduce emissions, the best market mechanism or combination of mechanisms for pricing carbon is much more difficult to establish. The following document gives a brief overview of market mechanisms and regulatory options for reducing GHG emissions.

Cap-and-Trade Systems

A cap-and-trade system is a regulatory program under which government sets a cap on the quantity of GHG emissions, distributes permits for allowable emissions that add up to the cap, and enables firms to buy and sell the permits after the initial distribution. Regulated sources must pay allowances at the end of a given period equal to their emissions. The price for emission allowances (the carbon price) is determined by supply and demand for allowances in an emissions trading market.

A. Upstream and Downstream Systems

Cap-and-trade systems can be focussed either on "upstream" or on "downstream" facilities. An upstream cap-and-trade (UCT) system applies to fuel suppliers and requires them to surrender allowances equivalent to the carbon content of fossil fuels they distribute. A UCT system would cover almost all energy-related emissions. This option has the advantage of being relatively simple, and it covers the entire economy. Analyses have shown that it would be environmentally efficient, minimize economic costs to the economy, be manageable administratively, and link easily to domestic and international offset programs. . . . On the other hand, a UCT system would likely drive up the cost of gasoline and home heating fuels, and it is a system that has yet to be implemented in any country.

A downstream cap-and-trade (DCT) program applies to sources of GHG emissions and requires them to pay allowances equal to their emissions. An all-source-DCT system would imply the regulation of millions of individual GHG sources, including cars and homes. Because of the difficulty in monitoring emissions from small sources, as well as the potential transaction costs involved with emissions trading from small sources, a DCT system could most effectively apply to a subset of sources consisting of large emitters.

. . . .

B. Carbon Offsets and Credits from the Kyoto Protocol

If a company does not have sufficient allowances to cover its emissions or if reducing actual emissions or purchasing credits within the cap-and-trade system is relatively expensive, the company may be permitted to supplement its allowances by purchasing emission reductions outside of the cap-and-trade system. This may include "carbon offsets" or credits associated with other emission reduction systems like those provided through the Kyoto Protocol.

Carbon offsets are certified emission reductions produced by individuals and businesses not regulated under the cap-and-trade system that regulated facilities can purchase. Carbon offsets can include such projects as those that produce renewable energy, energy efficiency, reforestation and GHG emission reductions resulting from changes in agricultural practices.

Though only certified offsets would be allowable under any trading system, the NRTEE [National Round Table on the Environment and the Economy] concluded that an offsets system would likely be ineffective because it would provide incentives to technology and behaviour that would likely have occurred in the absence of the program.

The Kyoto Protocol includes systems that allow the purchase of credits internationally. This will be done through the *emissions trading mechanism,* one of the three Kyoto mechanisms. The other two mechanisms are designed to create credits that then can be traded, if a country or industry so chooses:

- the *clean development mechanism* (CDM) allows developed countries to gain credit for projects with verifiable emission reductions in developing countries; and
- the *joint implementation* (JI) *mechanism* allows developed countries to gain credit through projects in another developed country, or in a country in transition to a market economy.

These credits may also be allowed to apply to a facility's target within a domestic cap-and-trade system. The price of international credits and carbon offsets, as well as the quantity of them that would be allowed for use against targets, will influence the price of credits within the cap-and-trade system. The credibility of the credits would influence the effectiveness of the scheme.

Emission (Carbon) Tax

A "carbon tax" or a tax on GHG emissions imposes a direct fee (the carbon price) on emission sources based on the amount of GHG they emit, but does not set a limit on GHG emissions. In a manner similar to cap-and-trade options, the tax could be imposed upstream or downstream. It could require importers, producers and distributors of fossil fuels to pay a fixed fee on the carbon dioxide contained in fuel sold and/or it could require emitters to pay based on their actual emissions.

In order to make a tax more politically acceptable, revenues generated by carbon taxes are typically recycled back to emitters and the general public, who may be paying higher prices for goods and services affected by the taxes. Revenue recycling could take many forms, including compensating adversely impacted firms and segments of society, proportionally returning revenue based on tax paid, reducing other labour or capital taxes, or investing in technology and innovation.

An emission tax program, unlike a cap-and-trade scheme, does not guarantee that a given emissions reduction target will be met, because emitters may choose either to pay the tax or to reduce emissions. As a result, the level of the tax will likely have to be adjusted over time to meet a given emission target. This system does, however, provide price certainty, because the tax level is set before the policy is implemented.

Analyses have shown that an emission tax is more likely to allow for adoption of the cheapest mitigation strategies, as well as easier administration, than a cap-and-trade scheme. How policy-makers distributed revenues from the tax would determine the economic impact and effectiveness of the tax. However, political acceptability is likely to be a major obstacle, since new taxes and fuel price increases would garner negative reaction. An emission tax may be more politically attractive as part of a larger tax reform program.

While the NRTEE analysis showed that an economy-wide carbon tax would result in significant GHG emission reductions, experience in various countries shows that the implementation of such a broad and effective tax is exceedingly difficult.

Generally speaking, existing carbon taxes are primarily aimed at fossil fuel use and related emissions, and have been mostly applied to the household sector and services sector. Industry typically benefits from various exemptions because of concerns about international competition. . . .

Although some correlations have been found between carbon taxes and greenhouse gas reductions, it is difficult to specifically attribute emission reductions to a carbon tax for a number of reasons, including:

- the countries that have implemented forms of carbon taxation have done so as one part of a suite of other programs aimed at reducing emissions, many of which could have cross-sectoral impacts on emissions;
- no country has put in place a true economy-wide carbon tax, choosing rather to target some areas while exempting others, often exempting the sectors where the most impact is required for emission reductions; and
- carbon tax regimes that do exist have generally been weak as a result of worries about competitiveness, given that other countries have not put such taxes in place.

Direct Regulations

Economy-wide regulatory mechanisms to force GHG emission reductions have never been seriously considered without a trading mechanism (cap-and-trade). They could, however, be used for parts of the economy that may not respond well to a price signal. There may be no response because:

- market failures and other barriers may reduce the responsiveness of certain sectors to changes in emission costs — particularly in the transportation and building sectors and some consumer markets, such as those for vehicles, houses and appliances; and
- emissions from some sectors of the economy, including agriculture, forestry, and waste management, may not be covered by the broad price signal.

Examples of this type of regulation might include energy efficiency standards and building codes or requirements to use alternative energy sources in buildings, equipment and transportation. Such actions would be relatively easy to take since they would simply involve modifying existing regulations. They would also avoid the politically difficult step of attaching a carbon cost to the price of gasoline and home heating. . . . Improving product efficiency standards yields limited results, [however,] because the incentive to reduce the use of inefficient products and to replace such products with more efficient ones is weak; indeed, the incentives may lead to greater use of energy-consuming products, since energy savings may allow consumers to buy more of these products, including some with elevated consumption levels. Energy use reduction through efficiency also effectively increases supply relative to demand, which could decrease energy prices, spurring greater demand.

There is a consensus that direct regulatory instruments would not lead to large reductions in GHG emissions but could be used as complementary policy tools to a market-based approach like an emission tax or a cap-and-trade scheme. For example, only by putting a significant price on carbon emissions would carbon capture and storage become economically attractive.

Conclusion

There is general agreement that putting a price on carbon through an emissions tax and/or a cap-and-trade approach is the most effective way to achieve GHG emission reductions. Taxes are generally seen as the most cost effective method, but they are not easy to couple with reduction targets and are politically very difficult to implement. Cap-and-trade systems are more complex to implement, must be very carefully planned (the compliance mechanisms and the volume and distribution of permits, in particular, must be well-thought-out) and do not provide cost assurance. In addition, companies may pass on to consumers the costs incurred by a cap-and-trade system in a way that is less transparent than a tax. Experience with these policies has delivered mixed results that are difficult to analyze.

Scandinavian countries pioneered the use of carbon taxes in the early 1990s. While a few other jurisdictions, most recently British Columbia, have since followed suit, carbon taxes have not been widely adopted. Rather, the cap-and-trade system has emerged as the internationally preferred market mechanism for mitigating GHG emissions. The European Union (EU) has operated a cap-and-trade system since January 2005. Despite some initial problems, the system is growing both in scope and in importance. Various legislative initiatives in the United States Congress also indicate that a cap-and-trade scheme is likely to become the dominant market mechanism for mitigating GHG emissions in the United States, particularly given the political difficulties involved with introducing a new tax.

NOTES AND QUESTIONS

1. In a September 2011 essay, *Wedges Reaffirmed*, Professor Socolow reflects on how he and Professor Pacala could have been more effective in motivating change and what updating their 2004 paper would entail:

   > Today, *nine* wedges are required to fill the stabilization triangle, instead of seven. A two-segment global carbon-dioxide emissions trajectory that starts now instead of seven years ago — flat for 50 years, then falling nearly to zero over the following 50 years — adds another 50 parts per million to the equilibrium concentration. The delayed trajectory produces nearly half a degree Celsius (three-quarters of a degree Fahrenheit) of extra rise in the average surface temperature of the earth. . . .
   >
   > Worldwide, policymakers are scuttling away from commitments to regulations and market mechanisms that are tough enough to produce the necessary streams of investments. Given that delay brings the potential for much additional damage, what is standing in the way of action?
   >
   > Familiar answers include the recent recession, the political influence of the fossil fuel industries, and economic development imperatives in countries undergoing industrialization. But, I submit, advocates for prompt

action, of whom I am one, also bear responsibility for the poor quality of the discussion and the lack of momentum. Over the past seven years, I wish we had been more forthcoming with three messages: We should have conceded, prominently, that the news about climate change is unwelcome, that today's climate science is incomplete, and that every "solution" carries risk. I don't know for sure that such candor would have produced a less polarized public discourse. But I bet it would have. Our audiences would have been reassured that we and they are on the same team—that we are not holding anything back and have the same hopes and fears.

It is not too late to bring these messages forward.

. . . .

I believe the messages of the wedges paper are as important as ever. The global greenhouse-gas emissions rate in 2061 is a better focus of attention than targets a century or more in the future. Achieving an emissions rate in 2061 no higher than today's is a goal that can be achieved by scaling up already deployed technologies. Given present knowledge, that goal is probably ambitious enough; pursuing tougher goals could lead us to opt for cures that are worse than the disease. And an iterative process for resetting goals is essential, in order to take into account both new science and newly revealed shortcomings of "solutions."

To motivate prompt action today, seven years later, our wedges paper needs supplements: insights from psychology and history about how unwelcome news is received, probing reports about the limitations of current climate science, and sober assessments of unsafe braking.

Robert Socolow, *Wedges Reaffirmed*, Bull. Atomic Scientists, Sept. 27, 2011, http://www.thebulletin.org/web-edition/features/wedges-reaffirmed.

Ten leading commentators, advocates, and policymakers provided solicited comments in response to *Wedges Reaffirmed*, which also can be found at http://www.thebulletin.org/web-edition/features/wedges-reaffirmed, for those interested in further exploration. These comments are largely complementary of the wedges approach, but provide a diversity of views on how to move climate change policy forward in the aftermath of cap-and-trade's failure in the United States and the limited progress since the original 2004 article.

As you reflect upon the original paper, Socolow's recent essay, and the commentaries, consider the following questions: What are the benefits and limitations of thinking about climate change mitigation in terms of wedges? Do you agree with Socolow's assessment that a different approach to the public discourse about climate change science by advocates is likely to result in more progress? If so, how might such a conversation be begun most effectively?

2. As noted above, the focus on cap-and-trade in the Canadian Library of Parliament report predates developments in 2010 and 2011 that make a fuller adoption of this approach in North America less likely. However, Australia, as part of meeting its obligations under the Kyoto Protocol's first commitment period, passed legislation establishing a carbon price in 2011, which relies on cap-and-trade mechanisms. For updates from the Australian government on its progress on implementing its climate change and clean energy plans, see Australian Government, *Clean Energy Future*, http://

www.cleanenergyfuture.gov.au/(last visited Apr. 10, 2012). At the 2011 Durban climate change negotiations, Australia remained open to a second Kyoto Protocol commitment period, which would rely on these national-level developments, even as Canada, Japan, and Russia refused to commit to additional targets and timetables. *See* Conference of the Parties serving as the meeting of the Parties to the Kyoto Protocol, Seventh Session, Durban, S. Africa, Nov. 28-Dec. 9, 2011, *Outcome of the work of the Ad Hoc Working Group on Further Commitments for Annex I Parties under the Kyoto Protocol at Its Sixteenth Session,* U.N. Doc. FCCC/KP/CMP/2011/10/Add.1 Decision 1/CMP.7 (Mar. 15, 2012) (advance version), *available at* http://unfccc.int/resource/docs/2011/cmp7/eng/10a01.pdf. Given these developments, how do you view the three policy options presented in the Canadian report? In the absence of effective national-level commitments in North America to climate change mitigation, how might those concerned about climate change proceed toward implementing strategies like those proposed by Pacala and Socolow?

2. ADAPTATION

As it has become clear that climate change will happen regardless of our mitigation strategies, policymakers and academics have increasingly examined adaptation strategies. Like mitigation, adaptation has a complex relationship with law because it involves so many different aspects of people's choices. But in many ways, adaptation is even more difficult than mitigation to regulate because it involves evolving ecosystems and the uncertainties of how climate change will affect them. This section explores both the big picture of what adaptation would entail and the nuances of addressing this complicated interface between people and the natural environment through often-too-rigid law.

The following excerpt is from the brief *Adaptation*, which is part of a series that the Center for Climate and Energy Solutions has prepared, called *Climate Change 101: Understanding and Responding to Global Climate Change*. It provides an introduction to adaptation issues, makes the case for why adaptation planning is needed, and proposes some strategies for effective policymaking.

CENTER FOR CLIMATE AND ENERGY SOLUTIONS,
CLIMATE CHANGE 101: ADAPTATION (2011)

http://www.c2es.org/docUploads/climate101-adaptation.pdf

The Case for Adaptation Planning

Limits on emissions will not be enough, or happen soon enough, to avoid all impacts of climate change. Reducing emissions will decrease the magnitude of global warming and its related impacts. But carbon dioxide and other greenhouse gases can remain in the atmosphere for decades or centuries after they are produced. This means that today's emissions will affect the climate for years to come, just as the warming we are experiencing now is the result of emissions produced in the past. Because of this time lag, the Earth is committed to some additional warming no matter what happens now to reduce emissions. As a result, there are unavoidable impacts already built into the climate system. With worldwide emissions continuing to rise, adaptation efforts are necessary to reduce both the cost and severity of both mitigation and climate change impacts for decades to come.

Model projections have underestimated actual rates of climatic changes and impacts. Recent scientific research demonstrates that many aspects of climate change are happening earlier or more rapidly than climate models and experts projected. The rate of change projected for global surface temperatures, and related impacts such as ice melt and sea-level rise, is unprecedented in modern human history. We now have nearly two decades of observations that overlap with model projections. Comparing the model projections to the observations shows the models underestimated the amount of change that has actually occurred. For instance, sea-level rise has occurred 50 percent faster than the projected rate, and the area of summer Arctic sea ice has decreased at three times the projected rate, while several other aspects of climate change have also been underestimated. Adapting to climate change will become that much harder, and that much more expensive, to the extent that the changes happen faster, or on a larger scale, than we expect going forward.

Acting now to limit the potential damage from climate change is often smarter—and costs less in the long run—than acting later. There is a human tendency to address current or near-term climate impacts in a just-in-time fashion (for example, water conservation measures to prevent droughts in some southeastern U.S. cities were started only after a severe shortage was evident). This approach may work when: the impacts are predictable or slow in developing; solutions are available and can be implemented in time to save lives, property, or natural resources; and there is low risk of irreparable harm. Even under these conditions, however, people often overlook or delay solutions that reduce the ultimate risk of harm. "Proactive adaptation" requires assessing the vulnerability of natural and man-made systems, as well as the costs and benefits of action versus inaction, and planning alternatives accordingly. This approach recognizes the need to factor climate change into decisions that affect the long-term susceptibility of systems to the impacts of climate change. From the methods for building or repairing bridges, dams, and other infrastructure, to the rules and regulations governing coastal development and wetland protection, the decision whether to consider climate change now will have implications down the line.

Some systems and societies are more vulnerable to the impacts of climate change than others. Climate change will affect a wide array of systems including coastal settlements, agriculture, wetlands, crops, forests, water supply and treatment systems, and roads and bridges. The vulnerability of different systems varies widely. For example, the ability of natural systems to adapt to increasing rates of climate change is generally more limited than built systems. Similarly, some countries or regions, such as the United States, may be better able to adapt to climate change, or have a greater "adaptive capacity," than others. By contrast, the adaptive capacity of many developing countries is often limited by a number of vital factors, such as economic or technological resources. Even within developed countries such as the United States, some areas have lower adaptive capacity than others. Smart planning ensures that governments and communities are paying attention to those systems that are most vulnerable, while laying the groundwork for actions to reduce the risk to human life, ecosystems, infrastructure, and the economy.

Successful Approaches to Adaptation

Adaptation services are emerging as governments, businesses, and communities worldwide are recognizing the need to address current and potential climate change impacts. Discussed below are several common elements in terms of methodology for adapting to climate change impacts.

Recognize that adaptation must happen at local and regional levels. Climate changes and their associated impacts vary greatly from location to location. Although national and international action is essential, many important decisions about how best to manage systems affected by climate change are made at local and regional levels. For example, states and localities have authority over land use planning decisions, including zoning and building codes, as well as transportation infrastructure. In some cases, state authority is extending to provide insurance coverage where the private market is retreating, exposing these states to larger financial risks. In exercising these authorities, managers, planners, and policy makers need to account for the potential outcomes of climate change. Yet systems such as water resources and species span city, county, and state lines. As a result, adaptation also requires planners from government, the private sector, and others to coordinate their activities across jurisdictions. Those engaged in planning need to share information, plan together, and collaboratively modify existing policies and procedures to ensure efficient and effective solutions. The exchange of information, resources, best practices, and lessons learned across jurisdictional lines and among different groups of stakeholders is a key element of successful adaptation planning.

Identify key vulnerabilities. Adaptation planning requires an understanding of those systems that are most at risk—and why. That means finding answers to questions in three key areas:

- **Exposure:** What types of climate changes and impacts can we expect, and which systems will be exposed? What is the plausible range of severity of exposure, including the duration, frequency, and magnitude of changes in average climate and extremes?
- **Sensitivity:** To what extent is the system (or systems) likely to be affected as a result of projected climate changes? For instance, will the impacts be irreversible (such as death, species extinction or ecosystem loss)? What other substantial impacts can be expected (such as extensive property damage or food or water shortages)?
- **Adaptive Capacity:** To what extent can the system adapt to plausible scenarios of climate change and/or cope with projected impacts? What is feasible in terms of repair, relocation, or restoration of the system? Can the system be made less vulnerable or more resilient?

Involve all key stakeholders. Successful adaptation planning relies on input from, and the alignment of, all key stakeholders. This means broadening the participants involved in identifying problems and solutions. Because the impacts of climate change span entire regions, adaptation planning should involve representatives from federal, state, and local government; science and academia; the private sector; and local communities. Successful planning will require creativity, compromise, and collaboration across agencies, sectors, and traditional geographic and jurisdictional boundaries. It also requires the involvement of experts who can help participants understand historical and current climate and other trends affecting various sectors, and who can provide completed impact assessments for other locations with similar sectors and/or projected impacts.

Set priorities for action based on projected and observed impacts. For vulnerable systems, prioritizing adaptive measures based on the nature of the projected or observed impacts is vital. The Intergovernmental Panel on Climate Change published a list of criteria to aid in identifying key vulnerabilities. Some of these criteria include:

- **Magnitude:** Impacts are of large scale (high number of people or species affected) and/or high-intensity (catastrophic degree of damage caused such as loss of life, loss of biodiversity).
- **Timing:** Impacts are expected in the short term and/or are unavoidable in the long term if not addressed. Consider also those impacts with variable and unpredictable timing.
- **Persistence/Reversibility:** Impacts result in persistent damage (e.g., near permanent water shortage) or irreversible damage (e.g., disintegration of major ice sheets, species extinction).
- **Likelihood/Certainty:** Projected impacts or outcomes are likely, with a high degree of confidence (e.g., damage or harm that is clearly caused by rising temperatures or sealevel). The higher the likelihood, the more urgent the need for adaptation.
- **Importance:** Systems at risk are of great importance or value to society, such as a city or a major cultural or natural resource.
- **Equity:** The poor and vulnerable will likely be hurt the most by climate change, and are the least likely to be able to adapt. Pay special attention to those systems that lack the capacity and resources to adapt.

Choose adaptation options based on a careful assessment of efficacy, risks, and costs. Due to uncertainties in projected climate changes and in how systems will respond to those changes, adaptation options carry varying degrees of uncertainty, or risk, as well. Timing, priority setting, economic and political costs, availability of resources and skills, and the efficacy of various solutions all should be a part of the discussion. The range of options includes but is not limited to:

- **No-regret:** Actions that make sense or are worthwhile regardless of additional or exacerbated impacts from climate change. Example: protecting/restoring systems that are already vulnerable or of urgent concern for other reasons.
- **Profit/opportunity:** Actions that capitalize on observed or projected climatic changes. Example: a farmer is able to shift to different crops that are better suited to changing climatic conditions.
- **"Win-win":** Actions that provide adaptation benefits while meeting other social, environmental, or economic objectives, including climate change mitigation. Example: improving the cooling capacity of buildings through improved shading or other low-energy cooling solutions.
- **Low-regret:** Measures with relatively low costs for which benefits under climate change scenarios are high. Example: incorporating climate change into forestry, water, and other public land management practices and policies, or long-term capital investment planning.
- **Avoiding unsustainable investments:** Policies or other measures that prevent new investment in areas already at high risk from current climatic events, where climate change is projected to exacerbate the impacts. Example: prohibiting new development in flood-prone areas where sea-level rise is increasing and protective measures are not cost effective.
- **Averting catastrophic risk:** Policies or measures intended to avert potential or eventual catastrophic events — i.e., events so severe or intolerable that they require action in advance based on available risk assessment information. Example: relocating Alaskan villages in areas at or near sea-level with projected sea-level rise and increasing severe weather events.

Effectively addressing climate change, both in the context of mitigation and adaptation, requires legal institutions and rules that have the flexibility to respond to and drive the changes that are needed. Unfortunately, our law and legal institutions often lack such flexibility because of the ways in which they are constituted to create stability. The following excerpt from an article by Professor Robin Craig argues that adapting to climate change impacts requires a fundamental rethinking of legal approaches to environmental and natural resources problems.

ROBIN KUNDIS CRAIG, "STATIONARITY IS DEAD" — LONG LIVE TRANSFORMATION: FIVE PRINCIPLES FOR CLIMATE CHANGE ADAPTATION LAW

34 Harv. Envtl. L. Rev. 9, 10–18 (2010)

On Halloween, 2008, PBS's nightly news program *The NewsHour* reported the plight of Montana's $300 million recreational fishing industry and $2.4 billion agricultural industry, both of which depend on Montana's rivers and streams. Trout fishing makes up a substantial component of the fishing industry, but the trout begin to die when water temperatures reach 78°F or higher.

Unfortunately for the trout, average spring air temperatures have been rising since the 1950s, at a pace consistent with projected climate change impacts, and will continue to increase. Higher temperatures mean earlier snowmelt and hence less and slower-moving water in the summer, which in turn allows instream temperatures to rise above the trout's tolerance — and temperatures are expected only to keep increasing. As for agriculture, the decrease in the total volume of water available during the summer makes irrigation increasingly difficult. Thus, climate change appears to be simultaneously putting at risk Montana's trout, fishing industry, agriculture industry, and the human communities dependent on all three.

As Montana's trout streams demonstrate, climate change is already altering the base conditions of ecosystems in the United States and hence is beginning to impact the human economies that depend on those ecosystems' services. To list three additional recent examples:

- Climate change is altering hydrological regimes, creating new and exacerbating existing conflicts between species' and humans' needs for water. In May 2007, the U.S. District Court for the Eastern District of California noted that the Delta smelt, "a small, slender bodied fish endemic to" the Sacramento-San Joaquin Delta and already at risk from the joint operations of the federally managed Central Valley Project and California's State Water Project ("CVP/SWP"), would likely be put further at risk by climate change-driven decreases in water volume and increases in water temperature in the Delta. Because the U.S. Fish and Wildlife Service ("FWS") failed to consider the effects of these changing hydrological conditions on the smelt, its Biological Opinion issued pursuant to the federal Endangered Species Act ("ESA") was arbitrary and capricious. The resulting injunction threatened to shut down water delivery to millions of southern Californians — indeed, delivery of water to southern California in summer 2009 (the start of the dry season) was only forty percent of users' expectations, a result of both continued drought and species considerations. To complicate the water delivery problem still further, in June 2009 the National Marine Fisheries Service ("NMFS") concluded that CVP/SWP operations are likely to jeopardize five other species protected under the ESA — the endangered Sacramento River winter-run Chinook salmon, the threatened Central Valley spring-run Chinook salmon, the threatened Central Valley steelhead, the threatened southern distinct population segment of North American green sturgeon, and Southern Resident killer whales — especially considering shifting ecological baselines for these species as a result of climate change.

- Climate change is already allowing destructive pest species to invade new territory, threatening both ecosystems and commercial interests. As is true of most insects, "[e]very aspect of [the mountain pine beetle's] life-cycle is dependent upon temperature." This pest invades pines, particularly lodgepole pines, and kills them. The beetle's territory is normally limited by cold winters, but since the 1970s, warming temperatures have expanded the beetle's potential range by more than seventy-five percent.

Mountain pine beetles have been taking advantage of this new habitat in British Columbia, Canada, and the northern Rockies in the United States (especially Colorado and Wyoming), and the expansion of the species can only be explained by changes in climate. By the end of 2006, the beetle had infested 130,000 square kilometers of British Columbia and western Canada, an invasion that is an order of magnitude larger than any previous invasion. Moreover, between 1997 and 2007, the beetle destroyed thirteen million hectares of pine in this part of Canada, many areas of which are considered critical timber supply areas. To deal with the economic disruption that the infestation and its effects on the Canadian logging industry have caused, the Canadian government "invest[ed] over $33 million in projects that support economic growth, job creation and future sustainability of communities adversely affected by the widespread beetle infestation."

- Climate change is creating positive feedback loops that may irreversibly push ecosystems over ecological thresholds, destroying coupled socio-ecological systems. In January 2009, the U.S. Climate Change Science Program ("USCCSP") reported that the Arctic tundra represents a "clear example" of climate change pushing an ecosystem beyond an ecological threshold. Warmer temperatures in the Arctic reduces the duration of snow cover, which in turn reduces the tundra's ability to reflect the sun's energy, leading to an "amplified, positive feedback effect." The result has been "a relatively sudden, domino-like chain of events that result in conversion of the arctic tundra to shrubland, triggered by a relatively slight increase in temperature," and the consequences for people living in these areas have been severe. For example, the Inupiat Eskimo village of Kivalina, Alaska, is suing for the costs of moving elsewhere, in response to the steady erosion of the village itself. Similarly, most Canadian Inuit live near the coast, on lands that exist only because of permafrost. Warming Arctic conditions threaten to deprive them of their homelands.

Thus, a variety of natural systems and the humans who depend on them — what are termed socio-ecological systems — are vulnerable to climate change impacts.

While developing and implementing successful mitigation strategies clearly remains critical in the quest to avoid worst-case climate change scenarios, we have passed the point where mitigation efforts alone can deal with the problems that climate change is creating. Because of "committed" warming — climate change that will occur regardless of the world's success in implementing mitigation measures, a result of the already accumulated greenhouse gases ("GHGs") in the atmosphere — what happens to socio-ecological systems over the next decades, and most likely over the next few centuries, will largely be beyond human control. The time to start preparing for these changes is now, by making adaptation part of a national climate change policy.

Nevertheless, American environmental law and policy are not keeping up with climate change impacts and the need for adaptation. To be sure, adjustments to existing analysis requirements are relatively easy, as when the Eastern

District of California ordered the FWS to consider the impacts of climate change in its Biological Opinion under the ESA. Agencies and courts have also already incorporated similar climate change analyses into the National Environmental Policy Act's ("NEPA") Environmental Impact Statement ("EIS") requirement and similar requirements in other statutes.

Even so, adapting law to a world of continuing climate change impacts will be a far more complicated task than addressing mitigation. When the law moves beyond analysis requirements to actual environmental regulation and natural resource management, it will find itself in the increasingly uncomfortable world of changing complex systems and complex adaptive management—a world of unpredictability, poorly understood and changing feedback mechanisms, nonlinear changes, and ecological thresholds. As noted, climate change alters baseline ecosystem conditions in ways that are currently beyond immediate human control, regardless of mitigation efforts. These baseline conditions include air, water, and land temperatures; hydrological conditions, including the form, timing, quality, and amount of precipitation, runoff, and groundwater flow; soil conditions; and air quality. Alterations in these basic ecological elements, in turn, are prompting shifts and rearrangements of species, food webs, ecosystem functions, and ecosystem services. Climate change thus complicates and even obliterates familiar ecologies, with regulatory and management consequences.

Nor are these regulatory and management consequences an as-yet-still-hypothetical problem. In February 2008, a group of researchers noted in *Science* that current water resource management in the developed world is grounded in the concept of stationarity — "the idea that natural systems fluctuate within an unchanging envelope of variability." However, because of climate change, "stationarity is dead." These researchers emphasized that impacts to water supplies from climate change are now projected to occur "during the multi-decade lifetime of major water infrastructure projects" and are likely to be wide-ranging and pervasive, affecting every aspect of water supply. As a result, the researchers concluded that stationarity "should no longer serve as a central, default assumption in water-resource risk assessment and planning. Finding a suitable successor is crucial for human adaptation to changing climate."

Further, these authors realized the critical question is what a successor regime to stationarity should look like. With the onset of climate change impacts, humans have decisively lost the capability—to the extent that we ever had it—to dictate the status of ecosystems and their services. As a result, and perhaps heretically, this Article argues that, for adaptation purposes, we are better off treating climate change impacts as a long-term natural disaster rather than as anthropogenic disturbances, with a consequent shift in regulatory focus: we cannot prevent all of climate change's impacts, but we can certainly improve the efficiency and effectiveness of our responses to them. As this slow-moving tsunami bears down on us, some loss is inevitable—but loss of everything is not. Climate change is creating a world of triage, best guesses, and shifting sands, and the sooner we start adapting legal regimes to these new regulatory and management realities, the sooner we can marshal energy and resources into actions that will help humans, species, and ecosystems cope with the changes that are coming.

The problem is, in this brave new world of climate change adaptation, there will be no panaceas—"one size fits all" solutions to environmental problems—particularly in the realm of natural resource management. We need new ways of thinking about law, and a new legal framework that will allow a multiplicity of techniques to be brought to bear in crafting adaptation responses to particular local impacts while still promoting actions consistent with overall ecological and social goals.

Specifically, in formulating the law that will govern adaptation to ecological and socio-ecological impacts ("climate change adaptation law"), two issues are of most immediate consequence. First, existing environmental and natural resources laws are preservationist, grounded in the old stationarity framework that no longer reflects ecological realities. In contrast, the new climate change adaptation law needs to incorporate a far more flexible view of the natural world, because both the identity of the regulatory objects—the things such as rivers that such statutes are trying to protect—and the regulatory objectives will themselves be continually transforming, especially at the ecosystem level.

Second, legal flexibility in the past has occasionally operated as the means for avoiding tough decisions and needed actions, as the Environmental Protection Agency's ("EPA") attempted ducking of carbon dioxide regulation under the Clean Air Act ("CAA") demonstrates. Given the societal importance of climate change adaptation, however, increased legal flexibility should not become a mechanism for avoiding effective environmental regulation and natural resource management. To deal effectively with adaptation and climate change impacts, the law will need to differentiate aspects of flexibility and discretion. Specifically, the law will have to embrace flexibility and adaptive management in the implementation of specific adaptation measures. However, it will simultaneously need to limit actors' discretion to do nothing or to deviate materially from general regulatory and management precepts and goals. That is, the specific means of adaptation can reflect local circumstances and needs, but the fact of adaptation and the general goals and policies climate change adaptation law seeks to effectuate should not be subject to local veto or avoidance.

In other words, climate change adaptation law should be based on principled flexibility. As used in this Article, principled flexibility means that both the law and regulators (1) distinguish in legally significant ways uncontrollable climate change impacts from controllable anthropogenic impacts on species, resources, and ecosystems that can and should be actively managed and regulated, and (2) implement consistent principles for an overall climate change adaptation strategy, even though the application of those principles in particular locations in response to specific climate change impacts will necessarily encompass a broad and creative range of adaptation decisions and actions.

This Article takes a first step toward a new climate change adaptation regime for environmental regulation and natural resource management in the United States by suggesting an across-the-board shift in legal objectives, from preservation and restoration to the improvement of resilience and adaptive capacity.

NOTES AND QUESTIONS

1. Although mitigation and adaptation strategies are being treated in separate sections, they interact with one another in many ways. Roger N. Jones, Paul Dettmann, Geoff Park, Maureen Rogers, and Terry White have explored the complexity of this relationship in their scholarship. They argue:

> The complementarity between adaptation and mitigation is critical. Exercising adaptive capacity (adapting) allows an activity to cope with successively larger changes produced by successively higher levels of global warming. Exercising mitigative capacity (mitigating) reduces the risk of climate hazards from the upper end of the projected range of change.
>
> . . . .
>
> However, there is a discontinuity between the local and global scale that can be expressed as the difference between mitigative capacity and the demand for mitigation for a particular activity at a given time and place. The capacity to mitigate is not related to the mitigative demand for each activity, instead being related to its adaptive capacity and whether exercising this capacity is sufficient to cope with serious impacts likely to be encountered at a given level of change. Where adaptive capacity can be exercised locally, the benefits are also felt locally. Demand for mitigation will be highest when and where adaptive capacity is exceeded. The supply of mitigative capacity is local, as is the demand, but that demand is for a global good. This is the largest hurdle facing the institutions of north central Victoria. While it makes good sense to exercise both adaptive and mitigative capacity . . . mitigation needs to be integrated within a global market to meet a host of demands at the local scale.
>
> Roger N. Jones, Paul Dettmann, Geoff Park, Maureen Rogers & Terry White, *The Relationship between Adaptation and Mitigation in Managing Climate Change Risks: A Regional Response from North Central Victoria, Australia*, 12 MITIGATION & ADAPTION STRATEGIES GLOBAL FOR CHANGE 685 (2007).

   Given these dynamics, how should policymakers approach mitigation and adaptation efforts?
2. To what extent are you persuaded by the *Adaptation* brief's arguments for acting now? Can you think of additional arguments for turning to adaptation? Which of the proposed strategies seem easiest to implement and which seem most likely to face political and legal barriers?
3. What are the benefits and limitations of introducing greater regulatory flexibility to address the problem of climate change? How could that flexibility be used as a tool to implement adaptive management techniques, and how could it be used as a tool to prevent needed action? What are the downsides of legal flexibility?

These questions over legal flexibility are made more complex by the interaction between law and science. If solutions need to be situation-specific but also take place in an environment of some level of scientific uncertainty, how should lawmakers and regulators craft appropriate responses? To what extent are flexibility and evaluating risk in the face of uncertainty compatible, and when might tensions arise?

4. The need for lawyers to engage science with respect to climate change and other problems raises questions about our current approach to legal education in the United States. To what extent should the legal curriculum mandate exposure to other disciplines? What are the benefits and limitations of having a more interdisciplinary curriculum? How, if at all, would you alter the law school curriculum to incorporate this interdisciplinary education?

3. COMPLEXITIES OF CROSS-CUTTING REGULATORY STRATEGIES

The previous sections have explored numerous complexities regarding climate change science and using law as an effective tool in both mitigation and adaptation. However, what makes climate change difficult to address through law is that each of these challenges is only one piece of the regulatory puzzle. This section considers the big picture, focusing on what the problem looks like when these pieces are put together and the difficulties of interacting with multiple levels of government and numerous substantive areas of law.

The following excerpt of an article by Professor Richard Lazarus provides such a big picture view. It explains why climate change is even more difficult to regulate than the types of public policy problems that scholars have termed "wicked," making it "super wicked."

RICHARD J. LAZARUS, SUPER WICKED PROBLEMS AND CLIMATE CHANGE: RESTRAINING THE PRESENT TO LIBERATE THE FUTURE

94 Cornell L. Rev. 1153, 1159–61 (2009)

Even once one accepts the current scientific consensus that significant global climate change is happening, human activities are a significant contributing cause of that change, and the associated public health and welfare impacts are sufficiently serious to warrant climate change legislation, crafting that legislation is extraordinarily difficult. Scholars long ago characterized a public-policy problem with the kinds of features presented by climate change as a "wicked problem" that defies resolution because of the enormous interdependencies, uncertainties, circularities, and conflicting stakeholders implicated by any effort to develop a solution. Sometimes described as "social messes," classic wicked problems include AIDS, healthcare, and terrorism.

Climate change, however, has been fairly described as a "super wicked problem" because of its even further exacerbating features. These features include the fact that time is not costless, so the longer it takes to address the problem, the harder it will be to do so. As greenhouse gas emissions continue to increase, exponentially larger, and potentially more economically disruptive, emissions reductions will be necessary in the future to bring atmospheric concentrations down to desired levels. Future technological advances, therefore, would likewise have to be able to achieve those exponentially greater reductions to make up for lost time. The climate change that happens in the interim may itself cause sufficient economic disruption, for instance, by slowing growth rates, so as to make it much harder to accomplish the necessary technological innovation.

Another problematic characteristic of climate change is that those who are in the best position to address the problem are not only those who caused it, but also those with the least immediate incentive to act within that necessary shorter timeframe. The major sources of greenhouse gas emissions include many of the world's most powerful nations, such as the United States, which are not only reluctant to embrace restrictions on their own economies but are least susceptible to demands by other nations that they do so. In addition, by a perverse irony, they are also the nations least likely to suffer the most from climate change that will unavoidably happen in the nearer term.

A third feature is the absence of an existing institutional framework of government with the ability to develop, implement, and maintain the laws necessary to address a problem of climate change's tremendous spatial and temporal scope. Climate change is ultimately a global problem. But there is an absence of any global lawmaking institution with a jurisdictional reach and legal authority that match the scope of the problem.

As Professor Lazarus explains, climate change has global dimensions but is not being addressed effectively at a global scale; these failures have to do with the limits of international institutions, vagaries of international negotiations, and political will. However, even with more functional international regulatory mechanisms, climate change arguably would still be challenging to regulate because both mitigation and adaptation interact with multiple levels of government in ways that would pose challenges for a top-down approach driven by treaties. The following excerpt from an article by Professor Osofsky explores this dilemma by analyzing the ways in which climate change poses a multi-level regulatory problem.

HARI M. OSOFSKY, IS CLIMATE CHANGE "INTERNATIONAL"?: LITIGATION'S DIAGONAL REGULATORY ROLE

49 Va. J. Int'l L. 585, 591–602 (2009)

I. The Need for Multiscalar Climate Regulation

The structure of law poses a fundamental difficulty for effective regulation of multiscalar [involving multiple levels of government] problems like climate change. Namely, law's scales are sticky despite the fluid scalar nature of greenhouse gas emissions and impacts. In other words, we have subdivided law into levels of governance—a sensible idea for creating order and administrability—and formal regulation tends to happen within the fixed frames of those structures. As a result, we generally approach regulation as choosing or coordinating among those levels.

The current dilemmas over climate regulation reflect those constraints. This Part analyzes climate change as an example of a multiscalar problem that law struggles to address effectively. It begins by examining the multiscalar nature of emissions and impacts, and then turns to the barriers to an effective regulatory regime.

A. The Nature of the Problem

Much has been written about the problem of anthropogenic climate change. The purpose of this Section is not to summarize that literature, but rather to look at it through a scalar lens. This Section argues that the scientific consensus over climate change reveals not only near certainty that anthropogenic contributions matter, but also that emissions and impacts intersect with decision making from the smallest to the largest levels. Using the United States and its states and localities as examples, the Section explores this interaction.

1. Emissions

Greenhouse gas emissions result from individual, local, state, national, regional, and international decisions. At an individual level, each person, within parameters, makes choices about what his or her carbon footprint will be. Regarding transportation, for example, people decide whether to walk or to rely upon a bike or motor vehicle; if a motor vehicle, whether to use public, carpool, or individual options; and, if individual options, whether to use high or low emissions cars. Although each individual's choices have a minor impact on total greenhouse gas emissions, trends in personal decisions add up, even at the global scale.

Those individual choices occur not simply in a sociocultural context — the past couple of years, for instance, have seen a significant shift in public opinion about climate change—but also in a multiscalar legal one. As explored in recently settled litigation between California and San Bernardino County, urban growth plans significantly impact emissions trajectories. Many studies have shown, for example, the ways in which suburban zoning and planning — with large individual lots, separation between residential and commercial uses, and limited public transportation — increase vehicle miles traveled and, as a result, overall emissions from that locality. Moreover, although little of this research has been disaggregated for gender, it appears from the few studies that have taken place that this variable may matter for what types of urban planning will be most effective; for example, women in developed countries tend to make different transportation choices than men.

State-level decision making further impacts those individual transportation choices. Following California's lead, a number of states have attempted to exceed federal limitations on motor vehicle emissions by enacting more stringent regulations. As cases challenging and supporting these efforts wind their way through state and federal courts and interact with the Bush administration Environmental Protection Agency's (EPA) decision to deny California's waiver request and the Obama administration EPA's reconsideration of it, the future of these regulations remains uncertain. It appears likely, however, that the Obama administration EPA, upon completing its reconsideration, will take steps to allow California and other states to move forward. Whether and when these state regulations go into effect will have a significant impact on which cars consumers will be allowed to drive in those states — the reason for the auto industry's concern — and, as a result, on individual transportation choices.

As the disputes over these state laws make clear, the federal government also regulates individual transportation decisions through each of its three branches. Congress has passed several statutes impacting vehicle emissions — which the executive branch then implements — and is considering additional legislation targeted at climate change. The judicial branch evaluates agency choices about whether and how those statutes should be used to regulate vehicle emissions. These standards drive what options consumers have and how expensive they will be.

In the globalized economy and its web of legal interconnections, these interactions do not stop at U.S. borders. Regional and international trade agreements determine which vehicles we import and export and how expensive they will be, again impacting what options are available to consumers. U.S. participation in international negotiations — as well as formal and informal agreements — regarding climate change puts pressure on our national policies, which influence the price and availability of high and low emissions vehicles.

This type of analysis does not simply apply to vehicles, of course, but to the broad panoply of emissions decisions that individuals and governmental and nongovernmental entities make. From the multiscalar energy industry to the emergence of complex transnational coalitions on climate change, current and future emissions are shaped through multiscalar regulatory dynamics.

The Fourth IPCC Report's volume on mitigation reinforces this point; it relies on a mix of what it calls bottom-up and top-down economic studies to assess emissions reduction scenarios. The bottom-up studies consider specific options, generally with an unchanged macroeconomy, whereas the top-down studies engage economy-wide options. The IPCC summary for policymakers reports:

> Bottom-up and top-down models have become more similar since the TAR [Third Assessment Report] as top-down models have incorporated more technological mitigation options and bottom-up models have incorporated more macroeconomic and market feedbacks as well as adopting barrier analysis into their model structures. Bottom-up studies in particular are useful for the assessment of specific policy options at [the] sectoral level, e.g. options for improving energy efficiency, while top-down studies are useful for assessing cross-sectoral and economy-wide climate change policies, such as carbon taxes and stabilization policies. However, current bottom-up and top-down studies of economic potential have limitations in considering life-style choices, and in including all externalities such as local air pollution. They have limited representation of some regions, countries, sectors, gases, and barriers. The projected mitigation costs do not take into account potential benefits of avoided climate change.

This consensus analysis suggests that in order to regulate emissions most efficiently, we must consider strategies at multiple levels, as well as find ways of incorporating cultural questions into economic models.

In addition, the mitigation volume makes clear how difficult the multiple geographic and time scales make this project. For example, the chapter entitled "Transport and Its Infrastructure" covers transportation issues in mostly sweeping terms and does not have the space to delve into the nuances of how its approach can be applied within specific contexts. More generally, the introduction to the volume explains that inertia in both climate and socio-economic systems, combined with the multiple time scales involved regarding the problem and responses to it, pose serious challenges. Not only will many measures need to be taken in the short term in order to prevent medium and long term issues, but policymakers also will have to navigate the fact that the same radiative forcing may cause the atmosphere to respond in decades as the ocean changes over centuries. Effective legal regulation somehow must bridge these complexities of how emissions and their interaction with the physical environment are scaled and of the greater scientific uncertainty that currently exists at smaller scales.

2. Impacts and Adaptation

These complexities of scale are not limited to emissions, but also span issues of mitigation and adaptation. The Fourth IPCC Report makes clear that we have passed the point at which prevention of impacts is possible. Rather, a host of impacts already have been felt, and scientific consensus suggests that they will only get worse as time passes. The explosion of climate change litigation over the past few years, and its increasing viability in courts around the world, reflects this reality.

Just as the extent of emissions interacts with multiscalar regulatory behavior, mitigation and adaptation present quandaries at every level of governance. As a physical matter, climate change manifests uniquely in each specific place, and the likelihood of severe impacts are not distributed equally. Unfortunately, current predictions suggest that the places with the least economic and political resources often will bear the brunt of these physical changes.

At an individual level, people must make hard choices in response to the changes in their physical environment. As glacial lakes loom above them or risks from coastal storms grow more severe, should individuals leave their communities? Are they able to do so? What steps are realistic options to limit the damages that they will suffer from the changing climate where they live? These are not just decisions facing the very poor; European ski resorts have begun wrapping their glaciers, and wine growers try to take climate change into account when planting new grapes. But the choices are often more fundamental for those who have few resources and live in close connection with the land.

As with emissions, these individual choices occur within a multiscalar regulatory framework. Localities, states, and national governments decide what their plans will be in response to these changes and the extent to which they want to and are able to support the individuals making those hard decisions. From the details of land use planning to the availability of federal disaster relief, governmental decision makers help to structure how palatable life will be in particular places as climates change.

Moreover, these policy decisions have impacts at multiple time scales. As time passes, impacts evolve and, in many places, according to consistent scientific data, likely will worsen. In addition, as we load the atmosphere with more and more greenhouse gases, the risks of a sudden catastrophic event — such as ice sheet collapse — increase. Decision making on impacts thus has to grapple with current and predicted future issues.

Together, the multiscalar dimensions of both emissions and impacts suggest that climate change will be very difficult to regulate effectively at any one scale. Local action must be tied to larger-scale decision making, whereas international action must make room for the nuances of smaller-scale variation. Moreover, because the substances being regulated are so deeply embedded in economies and cultures, political complexities abound that likely will manifest differently at each level of governance.

B. Current Regulatory Failures

This need to cross cut levels of governance is, of course, not lost on those attempting to address climate change at any particular level. The major treaties on climate change build in flexibility mechanisms to allow for the nation-state parties to address emissions in ways that work for their particular contexts. Local efforts often use international standards as a benchmark, such as in cities' pledges to comply with the Kyoto Protocol's emissions reductions. Moreover, a wide range of actors at different levels of governance — including governmental entities, nongovernmental and quasigovernmental organizations, corporations, and individuals — are working collaboratively on crafting better regulatory strategies.

But even with this recognition, multiscalar efforts on climate change at this point are falling short. The international legal regime suffers from both a lack of political will and the complexities of national implementation. Although the United States agreed under great pressure to rejoin negotiations over the post-2012 regime at the December 2007 climate meetings in Bali and President Obama has pledged to "re-engage with the U.N. Framework Convention on Climate Change," there are few signals that international consensus can be reached on the major reductions that scientists say are needed to avoid the most serious dangers. Moreover, many parties to the Kyoto Protocol are likely to miss its not very ambitious targets. In some countries, such as Canada, the implementation problem has stemmed in part from the fact that important subnational governmental entities are not prepared to make the needed reductions and the national government cannot force that change.

Once one gets below the international level, however, policy efforts on climate change become more piecemeal, which is a persistent issue in discussions of the appropriate role of smaller-scale regulation and the difficulties of leakage at the subnational level. The national and international coalitions of cities, for example, continue to grow — and at this point these cities represent fifteen percent of global emissions — but they do not yet come close to including all cities around the world. Those that join these coalitions also tend to be more amenable to taking needed regulatory steps than those that do not join. Moreover, many cities still face major internal political battles as they try to navigate the practical effect of meeting those obligations on their other goals.

Furthermore, as a formal matter, multiscalar regulatory approaches not only have to deal with specific barriers at each level of governance, but also have to bridge the way in which we categorize and cabin law. For example, treaties and customary international law — the bulwarks of international legal regulation — are based on the nation-state as the key decision maker. Under current legal models, international law can only be created through the consent of sovereign and equal nation-states. With such an approach, the ability of subnational governments to interact with international law is limited; even if their participatory role increases, the structure of how formal international law is created prevents entities other than nation-states from being treated as full subjects and objects of international law.

Formal barriers occur at the other end of the scale spectrum as well. Localities are constituted through a combination of state and local law and entities. When localities choose to make Kyoto Protocol commitments, they are not binding themselves to the treaty but rather incorporating its terms into local law. In fact, if they tried to do more, national and state governments might attempt to intervene on the basis that the localities are overstepping their boundaries. Similarly, their freedom to revise their greenhouse gas policies and commitments over time stems from the fact that international entities have no binding authority over them. . . . [S]ome of the primary efforts to push localities on emissions policies that have showed some teeth are those undertaken by states in the context of direct litigation, such as the suit by the State of California against San Bernardino County, which resulted in a settlement agreement.

The combination of regulatory barriers at each level of governance and structural constraints on meaningful multiscalar regulation poses a formidable obstacle to addressing climate change. Despite determined advocacy by numerous committed entities, the world is still far from adequately addressing emissions and their looming impacts at any level of governance. Although particular localities certainly have shown leadership, even those at the forefront of emissions control are not reducing them at the rate scientists say are needed, and regulatory failures elsewhere are dwarfing their efforts.

The complexities of cross-cutting governance do not end with the challenge of bringing together different levels of government. Climate change also implicates many different areas of law, most fundamentally energy and environmental law. Many legal systems, including that of the United States, treat each substantive area of law under a separate statutory regime with its own regulatory apparatus. The result is that climate change governance must overcome simultaneous overlap and fragmentation, where more than one area of law with distinct mechanisms applies to mitigation and adaptation initiatives.

The following excerpt by Professor Lincoln Davies explores this dilemma in the context of the United States. It explains why the disconnect between energy and environmental law makes effective approaches to alternative energy difficult and proposes ways to overcome this divide.

LINCOLN L. DAVIES, ALTERNATIVE ENERGY
AND THE ENERGY-ENVIRONMENT DISCONNECT

46 Idaho L. Rev. 473, 474-77, 499-506 (2010)

It is one of the most important—and unspoken—paradoxes of the modern American regulatory state: Energy law and environmental law rarely, if ever, merge. The fact that energy and environmental law do not work together has massive implications for the nation's future, particularly if we aim to curb our addiction to oil. Suggestions for how to change our energy trajectory are not in short supply. We need a smarter grid, and more of it. We need new transmission rules, and better ways of resolving siting conflicts. We need different transportation technologies, and better incentives for transitioning to them. We need to halt climate change, and move to electricity production that helps us do so. We need to reduce energy demand, and change our behavior to shift that curve. We need more efficiency, and fast.

All of these suggestions have merit. Taken together, they undoubtedly would propel us to a much different—and superior—future than the place to which our present energy policies have delivered us. Yet such specific policy reforms, as necessary as they are, do not take into account an overarching problem, a problem that may be their undoing if left unaddressed. Until the disjunction between energy and environmental law is repaired, one of the most fundamental barriers to a new and different energy future remains. Changing our course requires admitting our problem: Separating discussions of energy and environment works only to help us live the lie, to enable our addiction.

. . . .

II. The Historical Divorce of Energy and Environmental Law

That energy law and environmental law have been so historically disconnected may not grab newspaper headlines, but the reasons for this odd result are hardly secret. The fields trace to disparate traditions. Energy law was born largely from public utility and antitrust law, which emphasize economic analysis, monopolistic presumptions, and market preferences. Environmental law, on the other hand, arose not from the world of economics but from a melding of risk assessment and policy, a search for regulatory tools to prevent mass tort-like harms, the erosion of ecosystems and deterioration of public health, the "tragedy of the commons," and overexploitation of natural resources. Moreover, while the fields crystallized at roughly the same time—in the 1970s—environmental law has captured the public conscious far more readily than its energy law counterpart. "Even though energy policy had a prime role during [the 1970s and 1980s], environmental policy was the new star."

The irony is that while energy and environmental law derive from different places, they increasingly look more and more alike. Where energy law once placed faith in the judgment of expert agency regulators, it now has found religion in the verdicts of markets. Likewise for environmental law, the dominance of the 1970s technocratic command-and-control directives continue to give way to market- and information-based policy mechanisms. Where energy law once drew bright lines between federal and state jurisdiction, it progressively blurs those distinctions by relying on federal-state cooperation for, among other things, market restructuring, transmission siting, and reliability governance. The same is true for environmental law. The field's primacy once lay in the states; the 1970s "statutory big bang" shifted that center toward the federal government; and the emerging sense now is that cooperative, or "dynamic," federalism may have the best chance at regulatory success.

. . . .

III. Manifestations of the Divorce

. . . .

That energy and environmental law generally seek to achieve different goals — for energy law, economic development; for environmental law, conservation of resources and protection of public health — should already be clear. This is perhaps the most important distinction between energy law and environmental law. The fields' core thrusts differ because their ultimate aims differ.

. . . .

IV. Implications of the Divorce

Although there certainly are exceptions, the general trajectory of energy and environmental law should thus be clear. The fields work in separate spheres. They promote different objectives and, even where they share commonalities, such as the trend toward market-based regulation, fail to regulate in a coordinated, holistic manner.

On its face, this disconnect would seem problematic. Laws that address problems completely, rather than piecemeal, make for better regulation. Still, the question of whether connecting energy and environmental law would lead to better governance remains. That is, once the fields' disjunction is clear, are its implications really that problematic? Given that both fields have helped promote social welfare, the question is a fair one. Abundant energy is the lifeblood of our modern economy, and environmental protection helps guarantee the very basis of life.

This Part takes up the question by briefly assessing what deficiencies the disconnect between energy and environmental law might create for energy governance in general. It then applies those factors to the question of alternative energy development. Finally, on this foundation, it asks whether combining energy and environmental law may help forge a path to a new energy future.

A. For Energy Governance

Despite energy and environmental regulation's substantial accomplishments, a new approach could garner important improvements. Sufficient governance is not optimal governance, and there is a strong argument that the way we have been regulating energy questions is not sufficient: climate change looms, peak oil is either already here or just around the corner, and yet the profile of our national energy supply looks strikingly like it did when John F. Kennedy took office. All law is evolutionary. To account for the deficiencies that the disconnect between energy and environmental law creates, it may be time for these fields to evolve again — toward each other.

There are at least four deficiencies that disconnecting energy law and environmental law may produce. They are the risks of (1) inefficaciousness, (2) inefficiency, (3) foregone synergies, and (4) incompleteness. . . .

. . . .

B. For Alternative Energy Development

Certainly the problems created by the energy-environmental law disconnect arise in many areas, but they may be most acute for alternative energy development. The disconnect exerts a subtle, if inexorable, force pushing against a transition from traditional fuels to a more sustainable energy future.

The problem is clearest from an efficacy perspective. To the extent that alternative energy is seen as promoting environmental objectives — less pollution, more conservation — the fact that energy law and environmental law promote different goals clearly has restrained the adoption of more renewables. Both energy law's focus on reliability and its emphasis on cost temper any incentive that environmental law might create for alternative energy production. Clean Air Act limits on pollution emissions, for instance, should at least indirectly promote use of fewer traditional coal plants and more emission-free facilities such as wind and solar farms, but energy law pushes the other way. Generation resources such as solar and wind are intermittent (not always available) and have comparably high capital costs, even if their operating costs are low. As Warren Kotzmann has observed, "[a]t some point, if a significant percentage of resource need is based on wind, then back up power plants must be built to supplement when the wind resources are not available. Obviously, this would result in a cost prohibitive duplication of facilities." Thus, the environmental benefits achievable by switching to such power sources have been slow to come, at least in part, because energy and environmental law stand at cross purposes.

The flipside is also true. The United States would be full of more dams, more nuclear power plants, and the lower electrical bills that come with them were it not for environmental regulation. True, were these two fields more closely coordinated, one could argue that where we stand today is actually a careful legislative balance of competing, yet equally valid, economic and environmental considerations. Given how separately the two fields operate, however, that case is a hard one to make. Instead, it looks much more like inefficaciousness.

The other problems created by the energy-environmental law disconnect also manifest in alternative energy development. Consider inefficiency. If promoting alternative energy were a goal of both fields, the most efficient solution for carrying it out would be a coordinated effort between their administrators. The least expensive and most reliable energy sources could be sought based on economic and scientific criteria nationwide: a synthesized, consistent national energy plan. Instead, the picture today is much different. Some states have adopted laws requiring renewable electricity development—the aforementioned renewable portfolio standards—while many have not. The result is a crazy-quilt patchwork of laws and regulations that frustrate efficiency instead of promoting it. Over two dozen national RPS proposals have been introduced in Congress, but none have gained enough traction to pass—in no small part because energy and environmental law remain at war.

The story is just as troublesome for alternative transportation fuels. In that context, "agribusiness and their political allies have foisted [a] snake oil [biofuels program that mandates the use of ethanol and biodiesel] on the American consumer in a successful effort to transfer billions of dollars from the public to corn farmers, and ethanol and biodiesel producers." The result is not a transition to sustainability but a short-sighted, inefficient energy strategy based on special interests. In short, at least partially because energy and environmental laws remain separate, whatever incremental moves the nation has made away from archetype fuels have been fractured and inefficient, not coordinated and economical.

Likewise, the fields' divorce frustrates regulatory synergies. Take again alternative energy in electricity generation. One set of agencies—state public service commissions and FERC—exercises authority over the energy side of this sector, while an entirely different group of agencies—EPA and state environmental quality divisions—regulates the industry's environmental effects. This is the "heart of the problem" with energy-environmental regulation: "[T]he division of authority among several separate agencies, each of which is almost wholly oblivious to the technological alternatives that lie outside its own particular area of expertise . . . [means that] systematic intertechnology comparisons are impossible."

Were regulatory authority structured differently, such that pollution control technologies and clean energy technologies could be compared side by side, for instance, energy and environmental regulation might look much different. By bringing agencies together, a more deliberate alternative energy strategy could be crafted. Regulation might not only be more successful and less costly, it could be better too. This is not just because coordination would promote cooperation on alternative energy. It is also because agencies could learn from each other how to best achieve it.

Finally, the example of alternative energy development shows just how incomplete energy and environmental law are. If a sustainable energy future were a shared goal of both energy and environmental law, then the fields' targets would likely change in two ways. First, they both would likely focus more on transitioning to a more renewable-heavy electricity and transportation profile. Second, they would target areas for sustainable energy they now largely ignore. They might, for instance, aggressively chase efficiency gains in electricity, transportation, the built environment, and consumption generally. They would seek to fundamentally change the way energy is priced and used. They would target everyday consumers and the vast portion of energy use they comprise. They would target culture, and the "ossified" path of fossil fuel dependence we are now on. They would, in other words, extend their grasp to precisely the areas that energy and environmental law do not now reach.

C. Marrying Energy and Environmental Law —
Toward a New Energy Future?

How do we move energy and environmental law closer together? Assessing with detailed precision what a merged body of energy-environmental law would look like is beyond this article's scope. Nevertheless, it should be clear that the marriage must happen. The disconnect between energy and environmental law hardly is alone as a roadblock to a more sustainable energy future, but the reality of this barrier is plain. Whether it is the need for new transmission capacity, or the lack of a comprehensive climate change regulatory scheme, or the on-again, off-again nature of alternative energy production tax credits that stands immediately in the way of moving to renewable energy, a key reason these barriers exist at all is because energy and environmental law continue to work in different worlds, promoting conflicting objectives. Changing that even incrementally would be a step in the right direction — a step toward removing barriers to alternative energy development. While finding the specific contours for merging energy and environmental law thus calls for further reflection, some initial outlines of the merger's architecture are apparent.

To begin, any marriage of environmental law must be more holistic than the fields are today. The combined field must "look at the essential characteristics of the energy system as a whole, to think how they are intertwined, and to use that knowledge as a basis for deriving a more effective environmental policy." As Gary Bryner has explained, "[a] cautious, conservative, ethically defensible, and balanced energy policy" must be centered "in the idea of ecological sustainability." The idea is that for regulation to be effective, it must not separate root causes from core effects. The idea is that to better promote alternative energy, all issues must be considered. The idea is that environmental and energy law must be remade to work together as a unified whole.

One way to begin making energy-environmental regulation more holistic is to find areas where the two fields' objectives can be reconciled. To a degree, this has already started. Renewable portfolio standards, federal fuel efficiency standards for cars, and even climate change legislation, can all be seen as simultaneously promoting both energy and environmental aims: cleaner energy use, but reliable and abundant energy supplies nevertheless. Still, much work remains. From an economic perspective, it is true that any environmental law which makes energy markets more accurately reflect social costs does not conflict with the goals of energy regulation. But law is not evaluated under economic theory alone, and any increase in energy costs is often seen as anathema.

Part of how energy and environmental law must move together, then, is by crafting a common metric that melds both fields' goals. There is much promise on this front in the concept of sustainability, because sustainability values both economic development and environmental protection. It also measures these values over a long-term frame, so that short-term losses lose some of their current overemphasis. Sustainability as a legal concept, however, is still largely nascent. Getting it off the ground unquestionably will take much time and effort, and merging energy and environmental law may be part of that broader campaign. Clearly, though, regulation centered in the notion that economics and environmental protection must be balanced, rather than left at war, would do much for a transition to alternative energy development.

The good news is that at least some groundwork for merging energy and environmental law already has been laid. Because both fields increasingly rely on the same regulatory tools, finding a way to coordinate them should be less difficult than it once might have been. They already speak much of the same language, or at least close dialects. Certainly this is not to say that the task will be easy. Environmental regulators use markets for much different purposes than energy administrators, but from this common ground, both might be able to find areas where the fields can most easily become symbiotic. In the alternative energy context, this is precisely what it means to make inter-technology comparisons. The merging of energy and environmental law will allow regulators to evaluate a much broader array of possible solutions, because the merger should help break down regulatory silos.

Moreover, because energy and environmental law both excise large, and similar, swaths of activity from their regulatory grasps, the promise of merging the fields should be significant. That is, fertile ground for blending the two fields rests in the areas where neither currently regulates at all: for instance, small individual actions that have large cumulative effects, such as household electricity use or personal motor vehicle gasoline consumption — in short, realms ripe for work in alternative energy. In these areas, because regulation is currently light or non-existent, there may be room for a new approach altogether. Writing on a blank slate should be simpler than revamping an entire book, especially a tome as complex as energy and environmental law.

Law, of course, has limits. Apart from its symbolic and moral-setting properties, law can only really control behavior on the margins. That may well be why energy and environmental law currently do not regulate many of the areas they leave unrestrained. Nevertheless, to the extent that a merged energy-environmental field begins to extend into areas such as nonpoint source pollution or household energy consumption, a prime opportunity for coordinating energy and environmental law may be available. One way of thinking of the challenge of sustainability is that we must transform both our infrastructure and our culture. Present moves to alternative energy address primarily the former. For the latter, room for a newly wedded field of energy and environmental law to experiment should be vast indeed.

. . . .

NOTES AND QUESTIONS

1. How can law most effectively address the challenges described by Lazarus? What kinds of legal structures are likely to be most able to engage the "wicked" aspects of climate change and the additional "super wicked" challenges that it poses?

As discussed in more depth in Chapter Five's discussion of state and local government efforts, Nobel Prize winner Elinor Ostrom has argued for the important role that a multilevel, polycentric approach (one based on many key stakeholders taking action at different levels simultaneously) could play in addressing the collective action problem posed by climate change. Does thinking about climate change as a multiscalar and/or polycentric regulatory problem require a legal paradigm shift in the ways in which international negotiations are treated? How might multiscalar solutions vary in the context of mitigation and of adaption?

Could an effective multiscalar approach be crafted through viewing the smaller-scale activity as simply part of a nation's compliance with an international regime as a legal matter, or would this be inadequately polycentric in its focus? If one considers legal approaches within a nation-state in addition to international ones, how might solutions look different within a country and at an international level?

As discussed in more depth in Chapters Two and Five, state, provincial, and local governments have increasingly become involved in climate change. Beyond their individual efforts and the use of local land use planning law to address climate change, these smaller-scale governments have been collaborating transnationally. How should these efforts fit into a multiscalar approach to climate change governance?

2. To the extent that Davies is correct that energy and environmental law need to be brought together, how should that be done in the short-term and long-term? Piecemeal efforts focused on a particular issue can sometimes move forward, but comprehensive reform of the statutory regime will likely be politically difficult to accomplish. Chapter Three considers an example of the Obama Administration bringing energy and environmental law together to address motor vehicle emissions' contribution to climate change; its "National Program" merges "energy law" fuel efficiency standards and "environmental law" tailpipe emissions standards through collaborative agency rulemaking.

3. What other areas of law besides those addressing energy and environment interact with the problem of climate change? How might all these different areas of law be integrated or harmonized?

CHAPTER 2

INTERNATIONAL LEGAL APPROACHES: TREATIES AND NON-BINDING AGREEMENTS

Because of the global dimensions of climate change, policymakers have attempted to address it at an international level through treaty law. The United Nations Framework Convention on Climate Change (UNFCCC) and the agreements under it form the core international legal response to climate change. Opened for signature in 1992, the UNFCCC has 195 Parties (194 nation-states and 1 regional economic integration organization, the European Union), and thus includes nearly every country in the world.

However, the Parties to the UNFCCC have failed to reach an agreement that would achieve the reductions scientists say are needed, both because of lack of political will in key countries and because of political differences among countries. In the context of these difficulties, other international approaches pursued simultaneously serve as an important complement to negotiations under the UNFCCC.

This chapter provides an overview of the efforts to use international law to solve climate change. It begins with a brief introduction to international law, and then explores the core climate change treaty framework and other important international legal developments.

A. THE COMPLEXITIES OF INTERNATIONAL LAW

The problem of climate change cannot be solved by any single country. As Chapter One explores in depth, the physical and human dynamics of climate change involve action by governments, corporations, nongovernmental organizations, and individuals around the world. These global and transnational dynamics require international-level agreements as part of legal efforts to address the issue.

However, international law functions differently than domestic law; no overarching government exists to enforce the law. Instead, the core of international law consists of agreements among nation-states, which are presumed to be sovereign and equal. Countries participating in these agreements enforce the law collectively and through international institutions that they create. This structure has led to long-standing debates over the extent to which international law is truly law, debates which at times have become quite politicized. The discussion in this section does not attempt to enter such debates, but rather presents the primary forms of international law and the way in which these forms are being used to address climate change.

The Statute of the International Court of Justice, the principal judicial organ of the United Nations, provides a list of the primary sources of international law that has been accepted by most commentators as definitive:

a.   international conventions, whether general or particular, establishing rules expressly recognized by the contesting states;
b.   international custom, as evidence of a general practice accepted as law [customary international law];
c.   the general principles of law recognized by civilized nations;
d.   subject to the provisions of Article 59, judicial decisions and the teachings of the most highly qualified publicists of the various nations, as subsidiary means for the determination of rules of law.

Statute of the International Court of Justice art. 38(1), June 26, 1945, 59 Stat. 1055, 33 U.N.T.S. 993, *available at* http://www.icj-cij.org/documents/index.php?p1=4&p2=2&p3=0.

This chapter will focus on the first category in the list of primary sources, "international conventions," which are also referred to as treaties. The Vienna Convention on the Law of Treaties (VCLT) defines a treaty as "an international agreement concluded between States in written form and governed by international law, whether embodied in a single instrument or in two or more related instruments and whatever its particular designation." Vienna Convention on the Law of Treaties art. 2, May 23, 1969, 1155 U.N.T.S. 331, 333, *available at* http://untreaty.un.org/ilc/texts/instruments/english/conventions/1_1_1969.pdf. The UNFCCC and the Kyoto Protocol, as well as a number of the agreements discussed in Section C, below, are all treaties so defined. The countries that agree to a treaty are referred to as "parties" to it. Although the United States is not party to the Vienna Convention on the Law of Treaties, it considers many provisions of that convention to be customary international law. United States Dep't of State, *Vienna Convention on the Law of Treaties*, DIPLOMACY IN ACTION, http://www.state.gov/s/l/treaty/faqs/70139.htm (last visited Apr. 12, 2012).

An understanding of international law would be incomplete without also including the other three sources of international law; in various contexts they have relevance to international legal dialogues regarding climate change. "International custom," also referred to as "customary international law," and, in older documents, "the law of nations," has two primary dimensions: many nations agree to it, and they believe that they are bound by it. Disputes occur about how broad that agreement must be and what can be used as evidence of binding consent. "General principles of law" fill the gaps in treaties and customary international law. These widely accepted principles of the legal systems of nations supplement the often-limited language of international agreements. Finally, the "judicial decisions" and "teachings" are used in order to help resolve disagreements about treaties or customary international law. Commentators have a wide range of perspectives regarding what should fall into this category and how decisions and teachings should be used, particularly because international legal scholarship has evolved over time from treatises summarizing existing law to more normatively focused work. For further exploration of these sources and an overview of public international law, see IAN BROWNLIE, PRINCIPLES OF PUBLIC INTERNATIONAL LAW (Oxford University Press, 7th ed. 2008).

Even a brief overview of international law is useful for understanding the nation-state-led efforts to address climate change occurring primarily under the auspices of the UNFCCC and treaties like the Montreal Protocol. But the cross-cutting nature of climate change discussed in Chapter One also highlights the limitations of addressing it solely through such a top-down regime. International legal theorists continually grapple with how to capture dynamics outside of agreements among nation-states. For example, New Haven School scholars describe law as "a process of authoritative decision by which the members of a community clarify and secure their common interests," and include a wide range of interactions in different arenas as relevant to international lawmaking. HAROLD D. LASSWELL & MYRES S. MCDOUGAL, JURISPRUDENCE FOR A FREE SOCIETY: STUDIES IN LAW, SCIENCE AND POLICY vol. 1, at xxi (New Haven Press/Kluwer Law, 1992). Global legal pluralists and those arguing for polycentric approaches to climate change similarly favor an analysis that treats international law among nation-states as only one component of addressing climate change. In addition, some international legal scholars, such as those from the Third World Approaches to International Law (TWAIL) school, question the presumption of legitimacy at the core of the international legal system and explore the roles that colonialism, post-colonial legacy, and inequality play in the international order. This chapter's exploration of international legal efforts to address climate change approaches these issues by including the treaties among countries and other international-level interactions that help to shape multilevel governance of climate change and by highlighting issues of inequality. Chapter Seven provides a deeper examination of the injustices associated with major climate change.

NOTES AND QUESTIONS

1. Although the Vienna Convention on the Law of Treaties provides a widely accepted definition of a treaty, distinguishing between a binding international treaty and a non-binding international agreement is often difficult. Many treaties, including the ones discussed below, include broad or ambiguous language, or both, in order to allow for the agreement of as many countries as possible. The UNFCCC is an example of a treaty that contains quite a bit of such wording, because its goal was to establish a

framework on which as many of the countries of the world as possible, especially the major emitters, could agree. As you examine the language of the treaties in the sections that follow, consider what are the advantages and disadvantages of broad and ambiguous treaties with many parties versus narrower and clearer treaties with fewer parties. When treaties contain such broad or vague provisions, how are they different from non-binding declarations?

2. How might your view of climate change treaty negotiations be affected by your view of the international legal system? For example, if you view the UNFCCC structure as the primary way to address climate change instead of as one piece of a complex puzzle, how would your assessment of the status and importance of the treaty negotiations vary? If you reject the legitimacy of the international legal system on the basis that there are governments that do not democratically represent their people and that countries have unequal places at the negotiating table, how would you view current efforts to address climate change and how would you like to see future ones structured?

For those wanting to explore international legal theory further, many resources exist. This brief note cannot do justice to all of them, but a few possibilities for further inquiry follow. Oona Hathaway and Harold Koh provide a helpful compilation of different perspectives at the law-political science intersection. Oona Anne Hathaway & Harold Hongju Koh, Foundations of International Law and Politics (Foundation Press, 2005). Paul Berman's *Global Legal Pluralism*, 80 S. Cal. L. Rev. 1155 (2007), introduces global legal pluralism and explains how pluralism might assist with understanding and approaching the global legal environment. James Gathii creates a history of TWAIL and extensive bibliography of its scholarship. James Thuo Gathii, *TWAIL: A Brief History of Its Origins, Its Decentralized Network, and a Tentative Bibliography* 3 Trade L. & Dev. 26 (2011). For those wanting to delve further into the controversies over customary international law and its status in the U.S. legal system, Carlos Vázquez summarizes the various positions and advocates his own in Carlos M. Vázquez, *Customary International Law as U.S. Law: A Critique of the Revisionist and Intermediate Positions and a Defense of the Modern Position*, 86 Notre Dame L. Rev. 1495 (2011).

B. THE CLIMATE CHANGE TREATY REGIME

The primary treaty regime on climate change follows a "framework-protocol" model. The UNFCCC establishes a broad framework for making international progress on climate change, with an understanding that subsequent protocols negotiated under its auspices will provide more specific commitments. Under the auspices of this treaty, all of the Parties agree to the broad principles of the framework and to developed country major emitters having more significant obligations than developing countries, in accordance with the international law principle of common but differentiated responsibility. This principle recognizes that climate change and its impacts are a common concern of humankind, but that obligations to address the problem should be differentiated based on notions of equity.

Each year Parties to the UNFCCC gather at a Conference of the Parties (COP) to negotiate their additional commitments. However, negotiations on the protocols and the long-term approach to climate change — often under the auspices of the Ad Hoc Working Group on Long-term Cooperative Action (AWG-LCA) — have been stymied by disagreement over what form detailed mitigation commitments should take. Most importantly, some developed country major emitters have been willing to make commitments even if developing country major emitters do not. Others — most prominently, the United States — have insisted on a universal agreement that includes commitments from developing countries. As a result, negotiations regarding mitigation have split along two different tracks, reflecting these divergent visions.

The Kyoto Protocol, which was adopted in 1997 and entered into force in 2005, reflects the first instance of developed country major emitters making specific commitments to targets and timetables for emissions reductions that do not include developing countries; these commitments are the most significant to date under the UNFCCC. Since 2005, Parties to the Kyoto Protocol have met annually at a Meeting of the Parties of the Kyoto Protocol (MOP), in conjunction with the COP. The first commitment period of the Kyoto Protocol expires in 2012, and, at the 2011 Durban COP, many of its Parties committed to a period that begins in 2013. However, the impact of the Kyoto Protocol has been limited by several obstacles. First, the United States, the largest developed country emitter, is not a party to it. Second, many Parties are struggling to make their first-period commitments. Finally, and most troubling for the future, some key developed country emitters like Canada, Japan, and Russia — all of which were crucial to the treaty being able to enter into force without U.S. participation — have not agreed to specific commitments for the second period.

In parallel with some major emitters making ongoing Kyoto Protocol commitments, UNFCCC Parties have worked toward developing a universal agreement. The 2011 Durban COP made some progress on an agreement to reach a universal binding agreement by 2015, and established an Ad Hoc Working Group on the Durban Platform to develop a new protocol or other legal approach. However, until Parties reach such an agreement, rather than just agreeing on a procedure for trying to reach an agreement, only the Kyoto Protocol Parties have specific, binding commitments to mitigate climate change. The other UNFCCC Parties track and report their emissions (a requirement for developed countries) and make voluntary commitments and actions.

While these disagreements over mitigation commitments have persisted, UNFCCC Parties have reached agreement on initiatives to help developing countries obtain needed technology and to support adaptation efforts, especially in poor countries that will be particularly impacted but have limited capacity to adapt. The last several COPs have resulted in progress on both fronts.

The following sections provide an overview of these issues. They analyze the framework-protocol approach of the climate change treaty regime, core provisions of the UNFCCC and the Kyoto Protocol, and the current state of negotiations.

1. THE FRAMEWORK-PROTOCOL APPROACH TO CLIMATE CHANGE TREATIES

Before looking at the specifics of the UNFCCC, Kyoto Protocol, and ongoing negotiations, it is important to understand the overall structure of the climate change treaty regime and why negotiators decided to follow a framework-protocol approach. This approach with respect to climate change has had a significant impact on how the regime has developed since. It has ensured a broad commitment to principles and a structure for negotiations, but the details continue to be difficult to negotiate.

The following excerpt, written by Professor Bodansky soon after the UNFCCC was negotiated, introduces the climate change treaty regime and describes the decision to take a framework-protocol approach.

DANIEL BODANSKY, THE UNITED NATIONS FRAMEWORK CONVENTION ON CLIMATE CHANGE: A COMMENTARY

18 Yale J. Int'l L. 451, 453–54, 493–96 (1993)

In response to this threat [of climate change], the U.N. General Assembly established the Intergovernmental Negotiating Committee for a Framework Convention on Climate Change (INC) in December 1990, with the mandate to negotiate a convention containing "appropriate commitments" in time for signature at the U.N. Conference on Environment and Development (UNCED) in June 1992. The INC met six times between February 1991 and May 1992, and adopted the U.N. Framework Convention on Climate Change (Climate Change Convention, or Convention) on May 9, 1992. The Convention was opened for signature at UNCED, where it was signed by 154 states and the European Community. It requires fifty ratifications for entry into force.

To many, the Convention was a disappointment. Despite early hopes that it would seek to stabilize or even reduce emissions of greenhouse gases by developed countries, the Convention contains only the vaguest of commitments regarding stabilization and no commitment at all on reductions. It fails to include innovative proposals to establish a financial and technology clearinghouse or an insurance fund, or to use market mechanisms such as tradeable emissions rights. Furthermore, it not only contains significant qualifications on the obligations of developing countries, but gives special consideration to the situation of fossil-fuel producing states.

Nevertheless, given the complexity both of the negotiations, which involved more than 140 states with very different interests and ideologies, and of the causes, effects, and policy implications of global warming, reaching agreement at all in such a limited period of time was a considerable achievement. In fact, the final text is significantly more substantive than either the bare-bones convention advocated by some delegations or previous framework conventions dealing with transboundary air pollution and depletion of the ozone layer. While the Convention does not commit states to specific limitations on greenhouse gas emissions, it recognizes climate change as a serious threat and establishes a basis for future action. First, it defines as a common long-term objective the stabilization of atmospheric concentrations of greenhouse gases "at a level that would prevent dangerous anthropogenic interference with the climate system." Second, to guide future work, it sets forth principles relating to inter- and intra-generational equity, the needs of developing countries, precaution, cost-effectiveness, sustainable development, and the international economy. More importantly, it establishes a process designed to improve our information base and reduce uncertainties, to encourage national planning, and to produce more substantive international standards should scientific evidence continue to mount that human activities are changing the Earth's climate.

   . . . .

A. Framework vs. Substantive Approach

In establishing the INC, the U.N. General Assembly charged it with drafting "an effective framework convention on climate change, containing appropriate commitments." This mandate left open a fundamental question that ran throughout the negotiations: was the INC's task to draft a framework convention — that is, a largely procedural convention, establishing a basis for future action — or a substantive convention committing states to specific measures and policies?

Early proposals for the climate change negotiations focused on the framework convention/protocol approach, which had been used with considerable success to deal with the problems of acid rain and depletion of the ozone layer. Under this model, states first negotiate a framework convention, establishing general obligations concerning such matters as scientific research and exchange of information, as well as a skeletal legal and institutional framework for future action. States later develop specific pollution control measures (including emissions limitations targets) and more detailed implementation mechanisms in protocols.

The framework convention/protocol model serves two basic functions. First, it allows work to proceed in an incremental manner. States can begin to address a problem without waiting for a consensus to emerge on appropriate response measures, or even before there is agreement that a problem exists. Lawmaking can thus proceed "amidst great uncertainty." For example, when both the ECE Long-Range Transboundary Air Pollution Convention (LRTAP) and the Vienna Convention for the Protection of the Ozone Layer (Vienna Ozone Convention) were adopted, some states remained unconvinced of the need for action. Nevertheless, even skeptical states acquiesced in the adoption of these conventions, since the conventions did not commit them to any specific measures. Later, when the scientific evidence became stronger, protocols could be adopted more quickly, since the framework conventions had cleared away many of the preliminary procedural and institutional issues.

Second, the framework convention approach can produce positive feedback loops, making the adoption of specific substantive commitments more likely. Scientific research and assessments carried out under the convention help reduce uncertainties and lay a basis for action. The institutions established by the framework convention play a catalytic role by collecting data, providing technical assistance, and issuing reports. The meetings held under the convention provide a forum for discussions among the technical elites in different countries, and serve to focus international public scrutiny on countries that lag behind an emerging international consensus. In effect, once a framework convention is adopted, the international lawmaking process takes on a momentum of its own. States that were initially reluctant to undertake substantive commitments, but that acquiesce in the seemingly innocuous process set in motion by the framework convention, feel increasing pressure not to fall out of step as that process gains momentum.

Despite the advantages and historical successes of the framework convention/protocol model, many countries wanted the INC to produce more than a framework convention. Given the perceived urgency of the problem as well as the extensive preparatory work of the IPCC, they viewed the two-step, framework convention/protocol process as unnecessarily slow. . . .

States did not necessarily fall on the same side of the framework/substantive convention split for commitments and for mechanisms. At one extreme, some oil-exporting states favored at most a barebones convention that set general principles rather than specific commitments and that did not establish subsidiary bodies to the COP or binding dispute settlement procedures. In contrast, the United States supported what it characterized as a "process-oriented convention," which, although limited on the commitments side, established quite ambitious implementation mechanisms, including advisory committees on science and implementation; detailed provisions on scientific research, information exchange, and education; and flexible noncompliance procedures. Many developing countries expressed support for specific commitments, as long as those commitments were differentiated so as to apply primarily to developed countries. However, they questioned many of the more detailed procedural proposals, including those for the creation of subsidiary institutions to the COP. Finally, the European Community, generally joined by Austria, Sweden, Switzerland, AOSIS [Alliance of Small Island States], and the CANZ group (Canada, Australia, and New Zealand), supported detailed provisions on both substantive commitments and procedural mechanisms, including a specific commitment by developed countries to stabilize emissions of carbon dioxide at 1990 levels by the year 2000, a scientific advisory committee, an implementation and/or executive committee, and binding dispute-settlement procedures.

The debate between the framework and substantive approaches persisted right up to the end of the INC, when the INC considered whether the title of the Convention should be, the "U.N. Convention on Climate Change," or, as was ultimately agreed, the "U.N. *Framework* Convention on Climate Change." In the end, the Convention lies somewhere between a framework and a substantive convention. It establishes more extensive commitments than those contained in LRTAP or the Vienna Ozone Convention, but falls short of the type of specific emissions control measures contained in the Sulfur Dioxide or Montreal Protocols. While there are few procedural or institutional innovations in the Convention, it does establish scientific and implementation committees and provides for scientific assessment, reporting and review of greenhouse gas levels, financial and technical support to aid implementation, and a financial mechanism.

NOTES AND QUESTIONS

1. Professor Jutta Brunnée analyzes the ways in which the predominant framework-protocol approach to multilateral environmental agreement design may have contributed to the diminished leadership of the United States on international environmental law treaties. Professor Brunnée explains:

> The primary approach to global MEA [multilateral environmental agreement] design today is the 'framework-protocol' model, first employed at the global level by the 1985 Vienna Convention for the Protection of the Ozone Layer and its 1987 Montreal Protocol. Typically, the initial framework treaty contains only general commitments and establishes information-gathering and decision-making structures. Subsequent protocols to the framework treaty provide binding emission reduction or other environmental protection commitments.
>
> The framework-protocol approach is designed to promote consensus building around the need for and parameters of collective action, to focus binding commitments on priority concerns, and to adapt or expand the regime over time. This regime development is accomplished through regular meetings of the treaty's Conference of the Parties (COP) and its various scientific and political subsidiary bodies. With an institutional core and ongoing regulatory agenda, modern MEAs therefore resemble international organizations in many respects. Treaty parties become participants in rolling information gathering, negotiation and consensus-building processes, and COPs have emerged as forums for much of the international environmental law-making activity. In these ongoing multilateral processes, it is more difficult for individual parties to determine agendas, to resist regime development, and to extricate themselves from regime dynamics. In addition, a range of techniques have evolved that facilitate treaty development by COP decision, reducing reliance on formal amendments and softening consent requirements in various ways.
>
> Even this brief overview of MEA growth suggests a number of reasons why the early pattern of US leadership on treaty development and quick ratification may have abated. First, and most importantly, the ongoing interactions and negotiations among parties to an MEA tend to generate patterns of expectations and normative understandings that guide and constrain subsequent policy choices and legal development within the regime. In addition, these multilateral negotiations provide opportunities for coalition building that enhance the ability of smaller states to influence outcomes and help dilute the influence of more powerful states. Second, the sheer number and the growing complexity of MEAs make multilateral engagement increasingly resource-intensive. Significant human and financial resources are required in the development of MEAs, as well as in the various ongoing

multilateral engagements once agreements are adopted. Increasingly, agreements are also tackling complex global issues in which environmental concerns are intertwined with development issues. The environment-development dimension to most global MEAs not only entails protracted negotiation processes. Typically, global environmental governance also requires significant financial and technological transfers from North to South. Finally, the easier agreements have likely been reached already, so that the remaining treaties tend to impose more onerous obligations. Thus, rather than target relatively discrete issues of international concern, MEAs now tackle matters that implicate the domestic spheres of parties to a growing extent, and often require significant adjustments of domestic regulatory standards or approaches.

Jutta Brunnée, *The United States and International Environmental Law: Living with an Elephant*, 15 EUR. J. INT'L L. 617, 636–38 (2004).

Based on the analyses of Bodansky and Brunnée, what are the advantages and disadvantages of beginning with a broad framework that many countries can agree to and that establishes the framework for binding negotiations? In the context of climate change in particular, what are arguments for and against establishing a broad agreement among many nations with limited direct obligations that could serve as the basis for future commitments?

2. How does climate change compare to other problems, such as transboundary air pollution and ozone depletion, for which a framework-protocol approach has been used? In which context does such an approach seem most likely to succeed?

3. If you were to design an alternative to the framework-protocol approach to address climate change, what would it be? Are there other approaches that seem more likely to be successful, or do all approaches seem likely to encounter similar political obstacles?

2. CORE PROVISIONS OF THE UNITED NATIONS FRAMEWORK CONVENTION ON CLIMATE CHANGE

The provisions of the UNFCCC establish general goals for reducing climate change and divide countries into three groups, which are listed through annexes to the convention, based on their level of development. Annex I includes both developed countries that were members of the Organization for Economic Cooperation and Development (OECD) in 1992 and countries with economies in transition, which includes the Russian Federation and a number of other former Soviet republics. Annex II list is a subset of the Annex I list; it includes only the OECD members from that first group. The Annex II Parties have the greatest obligations to limit emissions and assist developing countries with technology and adaptation. All other Parties form a third group, referred to as "Non-Annex I." These countries are mostly poorer, developing nations. A subset of 49 of the Non-Annex I Parties have been classified by the United Nations as least developed countries (LDCs), and the UNFCCC and negotiations under it focus on their particular technological and adaptation needs.

The following excerpt from the UNFCCC delineates the treaty's core goals and principles, as well as some of the key commitments of Parties.

UNITED NATIONS FRAMEWORK CONVENTION ON CLIMATE CHANGE, MAY 9, 1992, S. TREATY DOC. NO. 102-38, 1771 U.N.T.S. 164, 166, 170

http://unfccc.int/resource/docs/convkp/conveng.pdf

Article 2

Objective

The ultimate objective of this Convention and any related legal instruments that the Conference of the Parties may adopt is to achieve, in accordance with the relevant provisions of the Convention, stabilization of greenhouse gas concentrations in the atmosphere at a level that would prevent dangerous anthropogenic interference with the climate system. Such a level should be achieved within a time frame sufficient to allow ecosystems to adapt naturally to climate change, to ensure that food production is not threatened and to enable economic development to proceed in a sustainable manner.

Article 3

Principles

In their actions to achieve the objective of the Convention and to implement its provisions, the Parties shall be guided, inter alia, by the following:

1. The Parties should protect the climate system for the benefit of present and future generations of humankind, on the basis of equity and in accordance with their common but differentiated responsibilities and respective capabilities. Accordingly, the developed country Parties should take the lead in combating climate change and the adverse effects thereof.

2. The specific needs and special circumstances of developing country Parties, especially those that are particularly vulnerable to the adverse effects of climate change, and of those Parties, especially developing country Parties, that would have to bear a disproportionate or abnormal burden under the Convention, should be given full consideration.

3. The Parties should take precautionary measures to anticipate, prevent or minimize the causes of climate change and mitigate its adverse effects. Where there are threats of serious or irreversible damage, lack of full scientific certainty should not be used as a reason for postponing such measures, taking into account that policies and measures to deal with climate change should be cost-effective so as to ensure global benefits at the lowest possible cost. To achieve this, such policies and measures should take into account different socio-economic contexts, be comprehensive, cover all relevant sources, sinks and reservoirs of greenhouse gases and adaptation, and comprise all economic sectors. Efforts to address climate change may be carried out cooperatively by interested Parties.

4. The Parties have a right to, and should, promote sustainable development. Policies and measures to protect the climate system against human-induced change should be appropriate for the specific conditions of each

Party and should be integrated with national development programmes, taking into account that economic development is essential for adopting measures to address climate change.

5. The Parties should cooperate to promote a supportive and open international economic system that would lead to sustainable economic growth and development in all Parties, particularly developing country Parties, thus enabling them better to address the problems of climate change. Measures taken to combat climate change, including unilateral ones, should not constitute a means of arbitrary or unjustifiable discrimination or a disguised restriction on international trade.

Article 4

Commitments

1. All Parties, taking into account their common but differentiated responsibilities and their specific national and regional development priorities, objectives and circumstances, shall:

(a) Develop, periodically update, publish and make available to the Conference of the Parties, in accordance with Article 12, national inventories of anthropogenic emissions by sources and removals by sinks of all greenhouse gases not controlled by the Montreal Protocol, using comparable methodologies to be agreed upon by the Conference of the Parties;

(b) Formulate, implement, publish and regularly update national and, where appropriate, regional programmes containing measures to mitigate climate change by addressing anthropogenic emissions by sources and removals by sinks of all greenhouse gases not controlled by the Montreal Protocol, and measures to facilitate adequate adaptation to climate change;

(c) Promote and cooperate in the development, application and diffusion, including transfer, of technologies, practices and processes that control, reduce or prevent anthropogenic emissions of greenhouse gases not controlled by the Montreal Protocol in all relevant sectors, including the energy, transport, industry, agriculture, forestry and waste management sectors;

(d) Promote sustainable management, and promote and cooperate in the conservation and enhancement, as appropriate, of sinks and reservoirs of all greenhouse gases not controlled by the Montreal Protocol, including biomass, forests and oceans as well as other terrestrial, coastal and marine ecosystems;

(e) Cooperate in preparing for adaptation to the impacts of climate change; develop and elaborate appropriate and integrated plans for coastal zone management, water resources and agriculture, and for the protection and rehabilitation of areas, particularly in Africa, affected by drought and desertification, as well as floods;

(f) Take climate change considerations into account, to the extent feasible, in their relevant social, economic and environmental policies and actions, and employ appropriate methods, for example impact assessments, formulated and determined nationally, with a view to minimizing adverse effects on the economy, on public health and on the quality of the environment, of projects or measures undertaken by them to mitigate or adapt to climate change;

(g) Promote and cooperate in scientific, technological, technical, socio-economic and other research, systematic observation and development of data archives related to the climate system and intended to further the understanding and to reduce or eliminate the remaining uncertainties regarding the causes, effects, magnitude and timing of climate change and the economic and social consequences of various response strategies;

(h) Promote and cooperate in the full, open and prompt exchange of relevant scientific, technological, technical, socio-economic and legal information related to the climate system and climate change, and to the economic and social consequences of various response strategies;

(i) Promote and cooperate in education, training and public awareness related to climate change and encourage the widest participation in this process, including that of non-governmental organizations; and

(j) Communicate to the Conference of the Parties information related to implementation, in accordance with Article 12.

2. The developed country Parties and other Parties included in Annex I commit themselves specifically as provided for in the following:

(a) Each of these Parties shall adopt national policies and take corresponding measures on the mitigation of climate change, by limiting its anthropogenic emissions of greenhouse gases and protecting and enhancing its greenhouse gas sinks and reservoirs. These policies and measures will demonstrate that developed countries are taking the lead in modifying longer-term trends in anthropogenic emissions consistent with the objective of the Convention, recognizing that the return by the end of the present decade to earlier levels of anthropogenic emissions of carbon dioxide and other greenhouse gases not controlled by the Montreal Protocol would contribute to such modification, and taking into account the differences in these Parties' starting points and approaches, economic structures and resource bases, the need to maintain strong and sustainable economic growth, available technologies and other individual circumstances, as well as the need for equitable and appropriate contributions by each of these Parties to the global effort regarding that objective. These Parties may implement such policies and measures jointly with other Parties and may assist other Parties in contributing to the achievement of the objective of the Convention and, in particular, that of this subparagraph;

(b) In order to promote progress to this end, each of these Parties shall communicate, within six months of the entry into force of the Convention for it and periodically thereafter, and in accordance with Article 12, detailed information on its policies and measures referred to in subparagraph (a) above, as well as on its resulting projected anthropogenic emissions by sources and removals by sinks of greenhouse gases not controlled by the Montreal Protocol for the period referred to in subparagraph (a), with the aim of returning individually or jointly to their 1990 levels these anthropogenic emissions of carbon dioxide and other greenhouse gases not controlled by the Montreal Protocol. This information will be reviewed by the Conference of the Parties, at its first session and periodically thereafter, in accordance with Article 7;

(c) Calculations of emissions by sources and removals by sinks of greenhouse gases for the purposes of subparagraph (b) above should take into account the best available scientific knowledge, including of the effective capacity of sinks and the respective contributions of such gases to climate change. The Conference of the Parties shall consider and agree on methodologies for these calculations at its first session and review them regularly thereafter;

(d) The Conference of the Parties shall, at its first session, review the adequacy of subparagraphs (a) and (b) above. Such review shall be carried out in the light of the best available scientific information and assessment on climate change and its impacts, as well as relevant technical, social and economic information. Based on this review, the Conference of the Parties shall take appropriate action, which may include the adoption of amendments to the commitments in subparagraphs (a) and (b) above. The Conference of the Parties, at its first session, shall also take decisions regarding criteria for joint implementation as indicated in subparagraph (a) above. A second review of subparagraphs (a) and (b) shall take place not later than 31 December 1998, and thereafter at regular intervals determined by the Conference of the Parties, until the objective of the Convention is met;

(e) Each of these Parties shall:

(i) coordinate as appropriate with other such Parties, relevant economic and administrative instruments developed to achieve the objective of the Convention; and

(ii) identify and periodically review its own policies and practices which encourage activities that lead to greater levels of anthropogenic emissions of greenhouse gases not controlled by the Montreal Protocol than would otherwise occur;

(f) The Conference of the Parties shall review, not later than 31 December 1998, available information with a view to taking decisions regarding such amendments to the lists in Annexes I and II as may be appropriate, with the approval of the Party concerned;

(g) Any Party not included in Annex I may, in its instrument of ratification, acceptance, approval or accession, or at any time thereafter, notify the Depositary that it intends to be bound by subparagraphs (a) and (b) above. The Depositary shall inform the other signatories and Parties of any such notification.

3. The developed country Parties and other developed Parties included in Annex II shall provide new and additional financial resources to meet the agreed full costs incurred by developing country Parties in complying with their obligations under Article 12, paragraph 1. They shall also provide such financial resources, including for the transfer of technology, needed by the developing country Parties to meet the agreed full incremental costs of implementing measures that are covered by paragraph 1 of this Article and that are agreed between a developing country Party and the international entity or entities referred to in Article 11 [which defines and describes the Financial Mechanism by which developed countries assist developing countries], in accordance with that Article. The implementation of these commitments shall take into account the need for adequacy and predictability in the flow of funds and the importance of appropriate burden sharing among the developed country Parties.

4. The developed country Parties and other developed Parties included in Annex II shall also assist the developing country Parties that are particularly vulnerable to the adverse effects of climate change in meeting costs of adaptation to those adverse effects.

5. The developed country Parties and other developed Parties included in Annex II shall take all practicable steps to promote, facilitate and finance, as appropriate, the transfer of, or access to, environmentally sound technologies and know-how to other Parties, particularly developing country Parties, to enable them to implement the provisions of the Convention. In this process, the developed country Parties shall support the development and enhancement of endogenous capacities and technologies of developing country Parties. Other Parties and organizations in a position to do so may also assist in facilitating the transfer of such technologies.

6. In the implementation of their commitments under paragraph 2 above, a certain degree of flexibility shall be allowed by the Conference of the Parties to the Parties included in Annex I undergoing the process of transition to a market economy, in order to enhance the ability of these Parties to address climate change, including with regard to the historical level of anthropogenic emissions of greenhouse gases not controlled by the Montreal Protocol chosen as a reference.

7. The extent to which developing country Parties will effectively implement their commitments under the Convention will depend on the effective implementation by developed country Parties of their commitments under the Convention related to financial resources and transfer of technology and will take fully into account that economic and social development and poverty eradication are the first and overriding priorities of the developing country Parties.

8. In the implementation of the commitments in this Article, the Parties shall give full consideration to what actions are necessary under the Convention, including actions related to funding, insurance and the transfer of technology, to meet the specific needs and concerns of developing country Parties arising from the adverse effects of climate change and/or the impact of the implementation of response measures, especially on:

(a) Small island countries;

(b) Countries with low-lying coastal areas;

(c) Countries with arid and semi-arid areas, forested areas and areas liable to forest decay;

(d) Countries with areas prone to natural disasters;

(e) Countries with areas liable to drought and desertification;

(f) Countries with areas of high urban atmospheric pollution;

(g) Countries with areas with fragile ecosystems, including mountainous ecosystems;

(h) Countries whose economies are highly dependent on income generated from the production, processing and export, and/or on consumption of fossil fuels and associated energy-intensive products; and

(i) Landlocked and transit countries.

Further, the Conference of the Parties may take actions, as appropriate, with respect to this paragraph.

9. The Parties shall take full account of the specific needs and special situations of the least developed countries in their actions with regard to funding and transfer of technology.

10. The Parties shall, in accordance with Article 10, take into consideration in the implementation of the commitments of the Convention the situation of Parties, particularly developing country Parties, with economies that are vulnerable to the adverse effects of the implementation of measures to respond to climate change. This applies notably to Parties with economies that are highly dependent on income generated from the production, processing and export, and/or consumption of fossil fuels and associated energy-intensive products and/or the use of fossil fuels for which such Parties have serious difficulties in switching to alternatives.

. . . .

Article 12

Communication of Information Related to Implementation

1. In accordance with Article 4, paragraph 1, each Party shall communicate to the Conference of the Parties, through the secretariat, the following elements of information:

(a) A national inventory of anthropogenic emissions by sources and removals by sinks of all greenhouse gases not controlled by the Montreal Protocol, to the extent its capacities permit, using comparable methodologies to be promoted and agreed upon by the Conference of the Parties;

(b) A general description of steps taken or envisaged by the Party to implement the Convention; and

(c) Any other information that the Party considers relevant to the achievement of the objective of the Convention and suitable for inclusion in its communication, including, if feasible, material relevant for calculations of global emission trends.

2. Each developed country Party and each other Party included in Annex I shall incorporate in its communication the following elements of information:

(a) A detailed description of the policies and measures that it has adopted to implement its commitment under Article 4, paragraphs 2(a) and 2(b); and

(b) A specific estimate of the effects that the policies and measures referred to in subparagraph (a) immediately above will have on anthropogenic emissions by its sources and removals by its sinks of greenhouse gases during the period referred to in Article 4, paragraph 2(a).

3. In addition, each developed country Party and each other developed Party included in Annex II shall incorporate details of measures taken in accordance with Article 4, paragraphs 3, 4 and 5.

4. Developing country Parties may, on a voluntary basis, propose projects for financing, including specific technologies, materials, equipment, techniques or practices that would be needed to implement such projects, along with, if possible, an estimate of all incremental costs, of the reductions of emissions and increments of removals of greenhouse gases, as well as an estimate of the consequent benefits.

5. Each developed country Party and each other Party included in Annex I shall make its initial communication within six months of the entry into force of the Convention for that Party. Each Party not so listed shall make its initial communication within three years of the entry into force of the Convention for that Party, or of the availability of financial resources in accordance with Article 4, paragraph 3. Parties that are least developed countries may make their initial communication at their discretion. The frequency of subsequent communications by all Parties shall be determined by the Conference of the Parties, taking into account the differentiated timetable set by this paragraph.

6. Information communicated by Parties under this Article shall be transmitted by the secretariat as soon as possible to the Conference of the Parties and to any subsidiary bodies concerned. If necessary, the procedures for the communication of information may be further considered by the Conference of the Parties.

7. From its first session, the Conference of the Parties shall arrange for the provision to developing country Parties of technical and financial support, on request, in compiling and communicating information under this Article, as well as in identifying the technical and financial needs associated with proposed projects and response measures under Article 4. Such support may be provided by other Parties, by competent international organizations and by the secretariat, as appropriate.

8. Any group of Parties may, subject to guidelines adopted by the Conference of the Parties, and to prior notification to the Conference of the Parties, make a joint communication in fulfilment of their obligations under this Article, provided that such a communication includes information on the fulfilment by each of these Parties of its individual obligations under the Convention.

9. Information received by the secretariat that is designated by a Party as confidential, in accordance with criteria to be established by the Conference of the Parties, shall be aggregated by the secretariat to protect its confidentiality before being made available to any of the bodies involved in the communication and review of information.

10. Subject to paragraph 9 above, and without prejudice to the ability of any Party to make public its communication at any time, the secretariat shall make communications by Parties under this Article publicly available at the time they are submitted to the Conference of the Parties.

NOTES AND QUESTIONS

1. What have the Parties actually committed to in the provisions of Articles 3, 4, and 12? To what extent would acting in accordance with these commitments be adequate to address the problem of climate change?
2. Notions of equity, grounded in the principle of common but differentiated responsibility, are expressed throughout these core provisions. Does the

way in which obligations have been divided in the UNFCCC seem appropriate? As discussed in more depth in Chapter Four, total emissions of leading developing country emitters have increased greatly since these UNFCCC provisions were crafted in the early 1990s, but their per capita emissions are still well below that of major developed countries. How if at all should the application of common but differentiated responsibility evolve to address their growing emissions?

3. Article 26 of the Vienna Convention on the Law of Treaties states: "Every treaty in force is binding upon the parties to it and must be performed by them in good faith." Vienna Convention on the Law of Treaties art. 26, May 23, 1969, 1155 U.N.T.S. 331, *available at* http://untreaty.un.org/ilc/texts/instruments/english/conventions/1_1_1969.pdf. If parties to the UNFCCC have an obligation to act in "good faith" with the treaty, which actions should be viewed as required and which actions should be viewed as prohibited?

4. The UNFCCC puts a strong emphasis on emissions cataloging and reporting, as detailed in Article 12. What are the benefits and limitations of countries tracking their own emissions and sharing them?

3. KYOTO PROTOCOL

The Kyoto Protocol was adopted in 1997 and entered into force in 2005. As the only agreement on climate change to set binding targets and timetables for its Parties, it represents the most significant, specific commitments that major emitters have taken on climate change.

The Kyoto Protocol ultimately included the European Union and all of the major developed countries except the United States during the first commitment period of 2008–2012. Australia did not ratify the Kyoto Protocol by the time it came into force in 2005, but did by 2007, with the treaty entering into force there in 2008. The United States participated actively in the negotiations, but President Clinton did not even bring the treaty to the Senate for ratification because key senators had made it clear that ratification would fail. His successor, President George W. Bush, then indicated in 2001 that the United States would no longer participate in the treaty.

As discussed in more depth in Chapter Four, the Kyoto Protocol Parties vary significantly in the extent to which they have been meeting their obligations during the first commitment period. For example, the European Union is on target to meet its emission reduction goals, whereas Canada will clearly fail to do so. Moreover, as considered in Chapter Four with respect to Canada, the Protocol's limited enforcement mechanisms make it difficult to force noncompliant countries to change their behavior.

The 2011 Durban COP resulted in a second commitment period beginning in 2013 of a length not fully determined, but many of the key developed country emitters seem unlikely to commit to additional targets and timetables during it. While European Union Annex I countries have made commitments, and Australia and New Zealand have indicated their potential willingness to do so, Canada, Japan, and Russia — three key developed countries — have indicated that they will not make specific commitments during the second period.

Article 3 of the Kyoto Protocol, excerpted below, describes the agreement's core obligations for the first commitment period. The Durban COP's outcomes included proposed amendments providing commitments and a timetable for the second period, which the Ad Hoc Working Group on Further Commitments for Annex I Parties under the Kyoto Protocol will continue to work on at its seventeenth session.

KYOTO PROTOCOL TO THE UNITED NATIONS FRAMEWORK CONVENTION
ON CLIMATE CHANGE ART. 3, DEC. 10, 1997, 37 I.L.M. 22, 33 (1997)

---

http://unfccc.int/resource/docs/convkp/kpeng.pdf

Article 3

1. The Parties included in Annex I shall, individually or jointly, ensure that their aggregate anthropogenic carbon dioxide equivalent emissions of the greenhouse gases listed in Annex A do not exceed their assigned amounts, calculated pursuant to their quantified emission limitation and reduction commitments inscribed in Annex B and in accordance with the provisions of this Article, with a view to reducing their overall emissions of such gases by at least 5 percent below 1990 levels in the commitment period 2008 to 2012.

2. Each Party included in Annex I shall, by 2005, have made demonstrable progress in achieving its commitments under this Protocol.

3. The net changes in greenhouse gas emissions by sources and removals by sinks resulting from direct human-induced land-use change and forestry activities, limited to afforestation, reforestation and deforestation since 1990, measured as verifiable changes in carbon stocks in each commitment period, shall be used to meet the commitments under this Article of each Party included in Annex I. The greenhouse gas emissions by sources and removals by sinks associated with those activities shall be reported in a transparent and verifiable manner and reviewed in accordance with Articles 7 and 8.

4. Prior to the first session of the Conference of the Parties serving as the meeting of the Parties to this Protocol, each Party included in Annex I shall provide, for consideration by the Subsidiary Body for Scientific and Technological Advice, data to establish its level of carbon stocks in 1990 and to enable an estimate to be made of its changes in carbon stocks in subsequent years. The Conference of the Parties serving as the meeting of the Parties to this Protocol shall, at its first session or as soon as practicable thereafter, decide upon modalities, rules and guidelines as to how, and which, additional human-induced activities related to changes in greenhouse gas emissions by sources and removals by sinks in the agricultural soils and the land-use change and forestry categories shall be added to, or subtracted from, the assigned amounts for Parties included in Annex I, taking into account uncertainties, transparency in reporting, verifiability, the methodological work of the Intergovernmental Panel on Climate Change, the advice provided by the Subsidiary Body for Scientific and Technological Advice in accordance with Article 5 and the decisions of the Conference of the Parties. Such a decision shall apply in the second and subsequent commitment periods. A Party may choose to apply such a

decision on these additional human-induced activities for its first commitment period, provided that these activities have taken place since 1990.

5. The Parties included in Annex I undergoing the process of transition to a market economy whose base year or period was established pursuant to decision 9/CP.2 of the Conference of the Parties at its second session shall use that base year or period for the implementation of their commitments under this Article. Any other Party included in Annex I undergoing the process of transition to a market economy which has not yet submitted its first national communication under Article 12 of the Convention may also notify the Conference of the Parties serving as the meeting of the Parties to this Protocol that it intends to use an historical base year or period other than 1990 for the implementation of its commitments under this Article. The Conference of the Parties serving as the meeting of the Parties to this Protocol shall decide on the acceptance of such notification.

6. Taking into account Article 4, paragraph 6, of the Convention, in the implementation of their commitments under this Protocol other than those under this Article, a certain degree of flexibility shall be allowed by the Conference of the Parties serving as the meeting of the Parties to this Protocol to the Parties included in Annex I undergoing the process of transition to a market economy.

7. In the first quantified emission limitation and reduction commitment period, from 2008 to 2012, the assigned amount for each Party included in Annex I shall be equal to the percentage inscribed for it in Annex B of its aggregate anthropogenic carbon dioxide equivalent emissions of the greenhouse gases listed in Annex A in 1990, or the base year or period determined in accordance with paragraph 5 above, multiplied by five. Those Parties included in Annex I for whom land-use change and forestry constituted a net source of greenhouse gas emissions in 1990 shall include in their 1990 emissions base year or period the aggregate anthropogenic carbon dioxide equivalent emissions by sources minus removals by sinks in 1990 from land-use change for the purposes of calculating their assigned amount.

8. Any Party included in Annex I may use 1995 as its base year for hydrofluorocarbons, perfluorocarbons and sulphur hexafluoride, for the purposes of the calculation referred to in paragraph 7 above.

9. Commitments for subsequent periods for Parties included in Annex I shall be established in amendments to Annex B to this Protocol, which shall be adopted in accordance with the provisions of Article 21, paragraph 7. The Conference of the Parties serving as the meeting of the Parties to this Protocol shall initiate the consideration of such commitments at least seven years before the end of the first commitment period referred to in paragraph 1 above.

10. Any emission reduction units, or any part of an assigned amount, which a Party acquires from another Party in accordance with the provisions of Article 6 or of Article 17 shall be added to the assigned amount for the acquiring Party.

11. Any emission reduction units, or any part of an assigned amount, which a Party transfers to another Party in accordance with the provisions of Article 6 or of Article 17 shall be subtracted from the assigned amount for the transferring Party.

12. Any certified emission reductions which a Party acquires from another Party in accordance with the provisions of Article 12 shall be added to the assigned amount for the acquiring Party.

13. If the emissions of a Party included in Annex I in a commitment period are less than its assigned amount under this Article, this difference shall, on request of that Party, be added to the assigned amount for that Party for subsequent commitment periods.

14. Each Party included in Annex I shall strive to implement the commitments mentioned in paragraph 1 above in such a way as to minimize adverse social, environmental and economic impacts on developing country Parties, particularly those identified in Article 4, paragraphs 8 and 9, of the Convention. In line with relevant decisions of the Conference of the Parties on the implementation of those paragraphs, the Conference of the Parties serving as the meeting of the Parties to this Protocol shall, at its first session, consider what actions are necessary to minimize the adverse effects of climate change and/or the impacts of response measures on Parties referred to in those paragraphs. Among the issues to be considered shall be the establishment of funding, insurance and transfer of technology.

The Kyoto Protocol emphasizes flexibility and equity in the way in which it structures its commitments. Differential obligations are established based on countries' levels of development. Parties are allowed to trade emissions, so that a country that does not need its full allotment can sell that excess to Parties struggling to meet their commitments. Joint implementation (JI) allows a country to count as part of its reductions ones that it makes in territories of another Kyoto Protocol country that has emissions reduction obligations. Finally, the Clean Development Mechanism (CDM) allows countries with Kyoto Protocol emissions reduction obligations to receive reduction credit for projects in developing countries.

This approach has been controversial. While some commentators praise these flexibility mechanisms as allowing for economically efficient and politically feasible emissions reductions, others view them as limiting developed country obligations and perpetuating inequality. The following excerpt by Harro van Asselt and Professor Joyeeta Gupta provides an overview of the three flexibility mechanisms and some of the concerns that have been raised about them.

HARRO VAN ASSELT & JOYEETA GUPTA, STRETCHING TOO FAR?
DEVELOPING COUNTRIES AND THE ROLE OF FLEXIBILITY MECHANISMS BEYOND KYOTO

28 Stan. Envtl. L.J. 311, 331–42 (2009)

II. Developing Countries and Flexibility Mechanisms in the Climate Regime

A. Flexibility Mechanisms in the Climate Regime: Background and History

[T]he Kyoto Protocol introduced three new market-based flexibility instruments: International emissions trading, JI, and the CDM. The main rationale behind these flexibility mechanisms is cost effectiveness — ensuring that greenhouse gas emission reductions take place where they are cheapest.

International emissions trading can be classified as a "cap-and-trade" system, where a certain emission cap is set, and a fixed number of emission allowances are distributed. Article 17 of the Kyoto Protocol, in conjunction with Annex B — indicating the list of countries with binding targets — provides developed countries with an opportunity to realize the necessary emission reductions under the cap through emissions trading. If a country has low marginal abatement costs, it can sell its surplus allowances on the international market. Likewise, those countries with high marginal abatement costs can buy allowances at the market price. By putting a price on emissions, emissions trading can provide economic incentives for technological innovation, since new technologies can lead to greater reductions.

In implementing emissions trading, two broad methods for the initial allocation of allowances are commonly distinguished: allowances can be sold to the highest bidder ("auctioning"), or they can be allocated for free on the basis of historical or current emissions ("grandfathering"). Allocation of emission allowances could also take place based on other factors (e.g. on a per capita basis or based on geographical circumstances) or through hybrid methods, whereby allowances are partly granted and partly sold. If allowances were allocated per capita, a large majority of allowances would flow to the developing world (mainly China and India). The Kyoto Protocol adopted the grandfathering approach: allowances are distributed on the basis of past emissions, with arbitrary adjustments for national conditions, such as wealth, growth projections, and domestic emission reduction potential. However, there was no standard formula underlying the division of allowances — rather, they were allocated mainly through "horse-trading" between the industrialized countries at the negotiating table.

In contrast with international emissions trading, both the CDM and JI can be classified as "baseline-and-credit" systems, through which credits can be earned by reducing greenhouse gas emissions against a constructed baseline. It is important to note that the mechanisms do not reduce greenhouse gas emissions; instead, they allow developed country investors to increase their emissions when they purchase credits.

Under the CDM, developed (Annex B) countries may form voluntary partnerships with non-Annex B countries to undertake greenhouse gas emission reduction projects. The dual purpose of the CDM as outlined in the Kyoto Protocol is to assist non-Annex B countries in achieving sustainable development through new technologies and efficiency techniques, while allowing Annex B countries to achieve their Kyoto targets at lower cost through certified emissions reductions (CERs), which may be counted against their national emission reduction targets. Whereas the CDM establishes the possibility for developed countries to cooperate with developing countries on greenhouse gas emission reduction projects, JI enables cooperation between two Parties to the Kyoto Protocol that both have binding quantitative commitments. Given that JI does not involve developing countries, the instrument will not be examined in depth in this Article.

. . . .

Although the Kyoto Protocol was unique in that it introduced partial emissions trading at the global level, some countries had previously used the policy instrument for domestic pollution reduction programs. The United States, for example, launched a domestic trading scheme for sulfur dioxide in 1990. Hence, it is logical that the United States pushed for the inclusion of emissions trading in the Kyoto Protocol. With the rejection of the Kyoto Protocol by the Bush Administration in 2001, it is rather ironic that the European Union — initially opposed to the idea of emissions trading — has now ended up as the main proponent of the instrument. Possibly a key consideration for putting so much effort in developing emissions trading was the hope that the United States would ultimately ratify the Protocol, but self interest probably also played a role, as emissions trading reduced the costs of emission reductions within the European Union. The European Union started the first regional scheme for trading carbon dioxide emission allowances in January 2005.

B. Flexibility Mechanisms and Developing Countries: Structural Concerns

. . . .

In this Part, we discuss some of the main concerns that have been voiced about the use of these mechanisms.

1. Diffusing Western Structures and Values

The first general objection to flexibility mechanisms is an ideological one that opposes imposition of one policy instrument on all countries. Through international emissions trading, Richman argues, Western structures and values are being diffused to developing countries. Some have deemed this to be a form of "carbon colonialism." The concept of emissions trading, and other market-based mechanisms to control environmental pollution, is compatible with Western, neo-liberal conceptions of achieving cost effectiveness through markets and the establishment of property rights. . . .

2. Historical Responsibility and Shunning Leadership

For the second concern, the basic contention is that because developed countries have emitted greenhouse gases without regulatory constraints since preindustrial times, they are responsible for the observed and projected climate change impacts. Through emissions trading, however, developed countries can, to some extent, buy themselves out of their commitment to reduce emissions domestically, and receive credit for carbon reductions that result from their assistance to other countries. Even though the Kyoto Protocol demands that the use of flexibility mechanisms should be supplemental to domestic emission reductions, this "supplementarity" is not defined. Thus, it is possible for developed countries to evade their responsibility and leadership obligation, as there would be "'virtual' compliance without physical compliance." By permitting credits from emissions trading, the incentives for domestic action are reduced, which could result in less — rather than more — technological innovation in the countries buying the credits.

Moreover, acceptance of the idea of grandfathering brings with it a rejection of the idea of allocations based on other rights. Under grandfathering, the polluter gets paid as countries are allocated emission rights more or less in accordance with their current emission levels, and the largest polluters can get compensated for reducing their emissions beyond their commitment levels. If this principle is accepted as legitimate, then allocating on the basis of other principles, such as the per capita principle, inevitably gets labeled as "hot air." "Hot air" in this context refers to providing allocations to countries in excess of their current pollution levels. The issue of hot air has also provoked other responses, not only in developing countries. It has been defined as the "degree to which a country's assigned amount exceeds what its emissions would be in the absence of any abatement measures." Effectively, it allows developed countries to increase their emissions by purchasing emission allowances from countries with economies in transition — mainly the countries that were part of the Former Soviet Union and its satellite states. Many of these latter countries are emitting far below their allocated levels as their economies have undergone extensive restructuring in the transition phase, and it will take some time before their economies recover. These countries could thus benefit from selling their surplus emissions. Buying emission allowances from these countries through international emissions trading would endanger the environmental integrity of the Kyoto Protocol, as the countries with economies in transition do not have to take any particular steps, at least in the short term, to reduce emissions. Although hot air would not technically lead Annex I countries to exceed their emission targets, the practical and ethical argument against it is that it can lead to higher emissions than would occur without emissions trading.

. . . .

3. Differences in Negotiating Power

After the adoption of the Kyoto Protocol, an extensive rulebook has developed on international emissions trading and the CDM. It is a daunting task for anyone to understand the detailed, and often complicated, rules and procedures. However, whereas developed countries often send large delegations to climate change negotiations, developing countries' delegations usually consist of one to four persons. For any delegate, it is a formidable challenge to master all the ins and outs of, for example, requirements related to monitoring, reporting and verifying emissions, modalities and procedures of the CDM, technology transfer, adaptation funding, and so on. Developed countries, however, have at least some domestic experience with emissions trading schemes (for example, the member states of the European Union have established a supranational cap-and-trade system for greenhouse gases, and the United States gained experience through its sulfur dioxide trading scheme), with either staff devoted to flexibility mechanism negotiation, or easy access to independent experts. As a result, it is likely that the details of emissions trading at the global level will be based on experiences and proposals stemming from developed countries. The establishment of a Trust Fund for Participation in the UNFCCC Process, which is aimed at facilitating developing countries' participation in climate change negotiations, has mitigated this concern to some extent. However, any contributions to this fund are made on a voluntary basis, and the fund only sponsors a limited number of delegates per country. While nongovernmental organizations provide negotiator training, capacity building exercises, and ad hoc legal assistance for some small developing countries, these efforts are more focused on medium-term issues than short-term negotiations. Furthermore, where they are focused on short-term negotiation, they are generally only available for, and utilized by, small developing island states, rather than all developing countries.

4. High Administrative Burdens

The design and implementation of emissions trading schemes pose new challenges to developed nations, as is illustrated by the European Union's struggle with the European emissions trading scheme. For developing countries, where institutional structures take different forms, this undertaking would be even more challenging. For any emissions trading scheme to function properly, countries need to fulfill certain basic conditions, which could imply high administrative costs. This includes establishing a reliable emissions monitoring, reporting and verification system, as well as putting in place a national registry for emission allowances. As Baumert et al. point out, "developing countries will need to weigh the potential benefits of financial inflows through international emissions trading against the costs of adhering to their eligibility requirements. It is net benefits that matter." Without sufficient resources, developing countries would thus not be able to participate on equal footing in an international emissions trading scheme or reap the benefits from the CDM. Developing countries could be further at a disadvantage, because they lack the "infrastructure and managerial capabilities necessary to evaluate and negotiate potential bargains." Although the Kyoto Protocol does not yet extend international emissions trading to developing countries, it is important to keep this concern in mind in the light of calls to create a global carbon market.

NOTES AND QUESTIONS

1. Article 3 of the Kyoto Protocol differentiates between Annex I countries with developed economies and those in transition. However, the inclusion of transitional economies in Annex I raises fairness questions. Why should transitional economies be included in Annex I and subject to Kyoto Protocol reduction commitments when rapidly developing countries like China, India, Brazil, and Mexico are not? These developing countries, moreover, have opposed any changes to the current categorization. Is the climate change treaty regime dealing with difference among countries appropriately?

2. Although the flexibility mechanisms play an important role in making it possible for Parties to meet their commitments, commentators have raised difficult questions about whether they allow Parties to avoid meaningful reductions, as the Asselt and Gupta excerpt indicates. The Clean Development Mechanism, in particular, through which Kyoto Protocol parties meet commitments by creating emissions reductions in developing countries, has come under scrutiny on both equity and effectiveness grounds. For example, a study by Professor Michael Wara found that a significant

percentage of CDM projects did not focus on core areas of sustainable energy technology development. Michael Wara, *Measuring the Clean Development Mechanism's Performance and Potential*, 55 UCLA L. Rev. 1759, 1803 (2008). What is the appropriate role of flexibility mechanisms, particularly ones that allow developed countries to meet their obligations through actions in developing countries?

3. What is the significance of the Kyoto Protocol moving forward without the United States for the future of international climate change treaties? Does it signal a more powerful role for other major emitters, or the limits of forward motion without the participation of all major emitters?

4. The Kyoto Protocol targets for the first commitment period fall well below the level of reductions scientists say are needed to avoid the most serious impacts of climate change. However, many Parties are having trouble meeting even those obligations, which is part of why several key countries are unwilling to commit to a second period. How should the difficulties of meeting even these limited obligations impact future international efforts on climate change?

5. Which vision, the Kyoto Protocol approach or a universal agreement, seems more likely to be effective in addressing climate change? Professor John Dernbach argues that "The Kyoto Protocol essentially provides for only one type of commitment—absolute nation-wide emission reduction targets. A multi-track framework—a framework that provides for several different types of commitments or agreements—would provide a legal structure more capable of delivering substantial early emission reductions than a one-track framework." John C. Dernbach, *Achieving Early and Substantial Greenhouse Gas Reductions Under a Post-Kyoto Agreement*, 20 Geo. Int'l Envtl. L. Rev. 573, 599–600 (2008). What are the benefits and limitations of the two approaches, and how would each need to be structured to reduce emissions fast enough?

4. ONGOING NEGOTIATIONS

The question of what to do when the Kyoto Protocol's first reporting period ends in 2012 has dominated negotiations under the UNFCCC in recent years. As noted in the introduction to this section, although many important issues are being discussed, the most crucial one has been what form commitments will take after 2012. Deep divisions exist over whether to continue the two-track system of the Kyoto Protocol, in which major developed country emitters have specific, binding obligations and developing countries lack such obligations, or to move to a one-track system in which developed and developing country major emitters have obligations.

The 2011 Durban negotiations made progress (though experts dispute how much) in resolving this dispute by providing procedural mechanisms and some level of agreement on both tracks. However, in order to understand these steps, it is helpful to consider the context in which the Durban COP took place.

The following excerpt by Professor Bodansky describes the history of COP negotiations and the results of the 2009 Copenhagen COP. The Copenhagen negotiations were particularly significant because many major heads of states participated, including President Obama, and many hoped that major progress would result. Instead, the very limited Copenhagen Accord, which the Parties could not reach a full consensus to adopt and so merely took note of, represented the challenges facing efforts to craft a coherent regime to replace the Kyoto Protocol.

DANIEL BODANSKY, THE COPENHAGEN CLIMATE CHANGE CONFERENCE: A POST-MORTEM

104 Am. J. Int'l L. 230, 230–38 (2010)

I. The Evolution of the International Climate Change Regime

Since the international climate change negotiations began in 1991, the climate change regime has developed in three phases. The first phase involved the establishment of the basic framework of governance, set forth in the Framework Convention, which was adopted in 1992 and entered into force two years later. The second phase, running from 1995 to 2001, involved the negotiation and elaboration of the Kyoto Protocol, which sets forth quantitative emission reduction targets for developed (Annex I) countries through 2012, and establishes market-based mechanisms (including emissions trading) for achieving those targets. The current phase—which the Copenhagen conference had been intended to conclude—addresses the post-2012 period, after the conclusion of the first commitment period of the Kyoto Protocol.

. . . .

The focus on developing country emissions in the Copenhagen process—and, in particular, the emissions of China and the other major developing country economies—represents a significant reorientation of the climate change negotiations. During the first decade of the regime, from the initiation of negotiations in 1991 through the adoption of the Marrakesh Accords in 2001, the negotiating process focused almost exclusively on emissions reductions by developed countries. Although the United States fitfully pushed the parties to address the issue of "developing country participation," the 1995 Berlin Mandate, which launched the negotiations of the Kyoto Protocol, effectively took this issue off the table by excluding any new commitments for non-Annex I countries. Even after the Protocol was adopted in 1997, the same pattern continued for an additional four years, through 2001, when the Marrakesh conference adopted a detailed rule book for implementing the Kyoto targets. Although developing countries participated actively, the primary axis of the negotiations was the split of the developed countries between the European Union and the United States—the EU member states pushing for strong emission reduction targets, implemented primarily through domestic measures, and the United States (together with "Umbrella Group" allies such as Australia and Japan) pushing for the unrestricted use of market-based mechanisms, including emissions trading.

The more recent phase in the climate negotiations, which began after Marrakesh, shifted the primary axis of the negotiations from EU-U.S. to developed-developing (and, in particular, U.S.-China). The new negotiating dynamic was initially obscured by the rejection of the Kyoto Protocol by the Bush administration and its unwillingness to discuss any alternative architecture, which put the negotiations in a holding pattern for several years. But when the negotiating process began to emerge from its deep freeze, the shift in dynamics became apparent, and the developed-developing country divide moved to center stage at the Bali conference in 2007.

Although the U.S.-EU negotiations were always difficult — even during the Clinton administration when one might have thought the policy differences would be less significant — the split between the United States and the European Union pales in comparison to the gulf between developed and developing countries. On one side, developed countries insist that the post-2012 regime address the emissions of all of the major economies, developing as well as developed. On the other side, developing countries continue to argue, as they have done since the negotiations began back in 1991, that they are not historically responsible for the climate change problem, have less capacity to respond to it, and should therefore not be expected to undertake specific international commitments to reduce emissions.

. . . .

II. The Copenhagen Accord

The Copenhagen Accord is a political rather than a legal document. It is very brief — only about two-and-a-half pages long — and leaves many details to be filled in later.

Elements of the Accord

Shared vision. The Framework Convention defines the climate regime's objective as the prevention of "dangerous anthropogenic interference with the climate system" but does not further identify what level of emissions or concentrations such interference entails.

. . . .

In Copenhagen, developing countries strongly objected to setting a date for the peaking of their emissions, and also resisted adopting a global emissions goal or a greenhouse gas concentration target because of the implications these would have for their own emissions. (Although developed countries have pledged to reduce their emissions by 80 percent by 2050, the 50-by-50 goal would still require developing country emissions to peak and begin to decline prior to 2050.) In the end, states could agree only that "deep cuts" in emissions are necessary, with a view to keeping the increase in global temperature below 2°C. In deference to the Maldives and other small island states, which had pushed for a 1.5° limit on global temperature change, the Copenhagen Accord provides for consideration of a stronger long-term goal as part of the assessment of the Accord's implementation that will be completed by 2015.

Developed country mitigation.

. . . .

The Copenhagen Accord establishes a bottom-up process that allows each Annex I party to define its own target level, base year, and accounting rules, and to submit its target in a defined format, for compilation by the UNFCCC Secretariat. Under the terms of the Accord, Annex I countries "commit to implement" their targets, individually or jointly, subject to international MRV [monitoring, reporting, and verification].

Developing country mitigation. There has been widespread agreement that developing country NAMAs (nationally appropriate mitigation actions) that receive international support should be subject to some type of international review, and that a "matching mechanism" should be established to link developing countries' proposals with financing by developed countries. This consensus is reflected in the Copenhagen Accord, which establishes a registry for listing NAMAs for which support is sought, and provides that supported NAMAs "will be subject to international measurement, reporting and verification in accordance with guidelines adopted by the Conference of the Parties."

The principal issues relating to developing country mitigation have concerned "autonomous" mitigation actions—that is, emission reduction measures that do not receive any financial support from developed countries. Should these be purely a matter of national discretion, subject only to national reporting and verification? Or should they be internationalized in some fashion—for example, through inclusion in a schedule that is subject to international review? And, more generally, should developing country mitigation actions (both supported and autonomous) be expected to add up to a particular quantitative reduction below business as usual?

In Copenhagen, these issues became the principal bone of contention between the United States and China, as the United States and many other developed countries insisted on measurement, reporting, and some form of international review, while China rejected any international review. The Copenhagen Accord represents a tortuous compromise in its paragraph 5:

— As with developed country emissions targets, it establishes a bottom-up process by which developing countries will submit their mitigation actions in a defined format, for compilation by the UNFCCC Secretariat (including both autonomous and supported mitigation actions).
— It provides that non-Annex I parties "will implement" these actions.
— It provides that developing country mitigation actions will be subject to domestic MRV and that developing countries will report on the results of this MRV in biennial national communications, "with provisions for international consultations and analysis under clearly defined guidelines that will ensure that national sovereignty is respected."

Financial assistance. Although states generally agree on the need for substantial new funding to help developing countries mitigate and adapt to climate change, they conceptualize this funding differently. The United States and other developed countries see financial assistance, in essence, as part of an implicit quid pro quo linked to developing country mitigation commitments. Developing countries, in contrast, see it as payment of the "carbon debt" that they believe developed countries owe for their historical emissions.

In Copenhagen, the discussions about financial support revolved around the typical issues: how much money, from what sources, and with what governance arrangements? The Copenhagen Accord addresses only the first of these issues, leaving the other two for future resolution. It creates a "collective commitment" for developed countries to provide "new and additional resources . . . approaching USD 30 billion" in so-called fast start money for the 2010-2012 period, balanced between adaptation and mitigation, and sets a longer-term collective "goal" of mobilizing $100 billion per year by 2020 from all sources (public and private, bilateral and multilateral), but links this money to "meaningful mitigation actions and transparency on implementation." It calls for governance of adaptation funding through equal representation by developing and developed country parties, but does not establish a governance arrangement for finance more generally. Finally, it calls for the establishment of a Copenhagen Green Climate Fund as an operating entity of the Convention's financial mechanism, as well as a high-level panel to consider potential sources of revenue to meet the $100 billion per year goal, and provides that a "significant portion" of international funding should flow through the Green Climate Fund.

Forestry. In the run-up to the Copenhagen conference, the potential to reduce emissions from deforestation and forest degradation (known as "REDD-plus") received considerable attention. The principal question has been whether to finance REDD-plus from public funds or by providing carbon credits. The Copenhagen Accord calls for the "immediate establishment" of a mechanism to help mobilize resources for REDD-plus from developed countries and acknowledges the "need to provide positive incentives," but does not resolve the issue of public versus private support.

Adaptation. The Copenhagen Accord recognizes the "urgent" need for "enhanced action and international cooperation on adaptation," and agrees that "developed countries shall provide adequate, predictable and sustainable financial resources, technology and capacity-building" to help implement adaptation actions in developing countries.

Monitoring, reporting, and verification. As with the mitigation issue, the discussions on MRV have concerned its level, as well as the parallelism/differentiation between developed and developing country MRV. The Copenhagen Accord calls for "rigorous, robust and transparent" MRV of Annex I emissions reductions and financing, "in accordance with existing and any further guidelines adopted by the Conference of the Parties." As noted above, supported NAMAs by developing countries will be subject to international MRV under guidelines adopted by the COP, while autonomous mitigation actions will be verified nationally and reported in national communications every two years, and will be subject to "international consultations and analysis" under international guidelines that ensure that national sovereignty is respected.

Legal form. The Copenhagen Accord sidesteps the issues about the legal form of the post-2012 climate regime. Although the penultimate draft of the COP decision accompanying the Copenhagen Accord called for the completion of negotiations on a new "legally binding instrument" at next year's conference in Cancún, Mexico, this reference was deleted from the final version. As a result, the questions of one versus two outcomes and legal versus nonlegal form remain unresolved.

The Future of the Copenhagen Accord

Following agreement on the Copenhagen Accord by heads of state and government, the remaining question on the final night was how the Accord would be reflected in the official decisions of the conference. The Danes proposed that the Copenhagen Accord be adopted as a COP decision, which requires consensus (usually defined as the absence of formal objection). But a small group of countries that had played a spoiler role throughout the conference (led by Bolivia, Sudan, and Venezuela) objected, arguing that the negotiation of the Accord represented a "coup d'état" against the United Nations because it bypassed the formal meetings. After an all-night session, the impasse was ultimately broken by a decision to "take note of" the Copenhagen Accord, which gives it some status in the UNFCCC process but not as much as endorsement by the COP. Those countries that wish to "associate" themselves with the Copenhagen Accord are to notify the UNFCCC Secretariat, for inclusion in the list of countries in the chapeau.

As of March 30, 2010, the UNFCCC Secretariat had received submissions from more than one hundred countries regarding their plans to reduce their GHG emissions and/or their wish to be associated with the Copenhagen Accord. In many cases, countries providing information on their mitigation actions have explicitly "associated" themselves with the Copenhagen Accord (including Brazil, China, the European Union and its member states, India, Japan, South Africa, and the United States), but, as of this writing, a few countries — most notably Russia — have not done so expressly.

After the difficult negotiations at Copenhagen, Parties set more modest goals for the 2010 Cancún meetings. As described by this excerpt from a report by the Pew Center on Climate Change, the Cancún negotiations made progress, but still left major questions open for the post-2012 landscape and future negotiations.

PEW CENTER ON CLIMATE CHANGE, SIXTEENTH SESSION OF THE CONFERENCE OF THE PARTIES TO THE UNITED NATIONS FRAMEWORK CONVENTION ON CLIMATE CHANGE AND SIXTH SESSION OF THE MEETING OF THE PARTIES TO THE KYOTO PROTOCOL (2010)

http://www.pewclimate.org/docUploads/cancun-climate-conference-cop16-summary.pdf

Agreeing to put aside for now issues that have stalemated international climate talks for years, governments meeting at the U.N. Climate Change Conference in Cancún, Mexico, approved a set of decisions anchoring national mitigation pledges and taking initial steps to strengthen finance, transparency and other elements of the multilateral climate framework.

In large measure, the Cancún Agreements import the essential elements of the Copenhagen Accord into the U.N. Framework Convention on Climate Change (UNFCCC). They include the mitigation targets and actions pledged under the Accord — marking the first time all major economies have pledged explicit actions under the UNFCCC since its launch nearly two decades ago. The Agreements also take initial steps to implement the operational elements of the Accord, including a new Green Climate Fund for developing countries and a system of "international consultations and analysis" to help verify countries' actions.

Agreement in Cancún hinged on finding a way to finesse for now the more difficult questions of if, when, and in what form countries will take binding commitments. In particular, the deal had to strike a balance between developing country demands for a new round of developed country targets under the Kyoto Protocol and the refusal of Japan and others to be boxed in. The final outcome leaves all options on the table and sets no clear path toward a binding agreement.

The meeting — known formally as the Sixteenth Session of the Conference of the Parties to the UNFCCC (COP 16) and the Sixth Session of the Meeting of the Parties to the Kyoto Protocol (CMP 6) — was a stark contrast to the drama, chaos and bitter disappointment of a year earlier in Copenhagen.

With the Mexican government working hard to keep the negotiating process open and inclusive, there were no pitched procedural battles or dramatic walkouts. The United States and China avoided any open sparring, and India emerged as a key broker between the two. Parties generally, fearing that another "failure" could cripple the U.N. process, were quicker to accept incremental outcomes falling well short of their initial demands. In the final hours, only Bolivia fought to keep the package from being adopted, while country after country heaped praise on the Mexican presidency for delivering success.

Apart from its specific substantive outcomes [described above], the major accomplishment of Cancún was demonstrating that the U.N. negotiations can still produce tangible results — the most tangible since the Marrakesh Accords nearly a decade ago.

The 2011 Durban COP took place in the shadow of the limited progress in 2009 and 2010 on the key question of form, and of the looming expiration of the Kyoto Protocol's first commitment period. The conference, to the surprise of many, made progress on both of these issues — the Durban Platform for Enhanced Action committed the Parties to reaching a universal agreement by 2015 and provided a procedure for working towards that agreement while the Kyoto Protocol Parties negotiated a second commitment period. The Durban negotiations also built on the often less controversial steps made at the previous two COPs regarding technology transfer, adaptation, financing, transparency, and reducing emissions from deforestation and forest degradation (REDD).

The following excerpt from a World Resources Institute Insight, written just after the negotiations ended two days later than originally scheduled, discusses the implications of the steps made at the Durban COP and the complexities of evaluating them.

JENNIFER MORGAN & EDWARD CAMERON, WRI INSIGHTS:
REFLECTIONS ON COP 17 IN DURBAN (DEC. 16, 2011)

http://insights.wri.org/news/2011/12/reflections-cop-17-durban

As weary negotiators return home from the marathon United Nations Framework Convention on Climate Change (UNFCCC) talks in Durban, South Africa, opinion is divided on the deal that was struck.

Some believe the package — consisting of a new "Durban Platform" to nego-tiate the long-term future of the regime, a second commitment period for the Kyoto Protocol, and an array of decisions designed to implement the Cancun agreements — represents a significant step forward and cause for hope. Others are more cautious, viewing these outputs as insufficient in ambition, content, and timing to tackle the far-reaching threat of climate change.

Are the outcomes from Durban sufficient to solve the climate crisis? No. Tackling climate change will be a multi-generational effort requiring sus-tained political engagement and a complete transition to a low-carbon economy. It is clear that our collective action remains inadequate and requires an urgent injection of ambition.

Perhaps a more suitable question to assess the Durban deal would be: Are the outcomes a step in the right direction? In principle yes, but in practice we will have to wait and see. The Durban Platform holds promise, signifying a departure on many important levels from past COP agreements. It reinforces some key building blocks for a sustained and comprehensive attempt to tackle the climate crisis. It further removes a series of contentious issues that have previously been used to block progress. Meanwhile, the Kyoto Protocol will continue into a second commitment period and thus retains the important political value of rules-based emissions reductions from a group of industrialized countries, while preserving important mechanisms such as emissions trading, the Clean Devel-opment Mechanism (CDM), and Joint Implementation. However, in the more detailed discussions concerning the Long-term Cooperative Action (LCA) track, many observers were disappointed with the lack of progress in some areas.

. . . .

I. Assessing the Durban Platform

While opinion is divided on the Durban Platform for Enhanced Action, overall it holds a great deal of merit. The Platform seeks to establish the future direction of the climate regime by initiating a new round of negotiations to be concluded by 2015 and operationalized by 2020. We have a text that ulti-mately brings all Parties — from both the developed and developing world — onto one track, recognizes the emissions gap, and tries to resolve the difficult conflict between equity and environmental integrity.

When assessing the merits of the Durban Platform it is important to note the alternatives going into the final weekend. At the last moments of the negotiations the situation looked bleak. The first proposal under consideration by Parties seemed devoid of ambition, doing little to break the fundamental political problems in this process. A second option would have brought post-ponement of a decision or even collapse. In that context, the Durban Platform emerged as a significantly more ambitious alternative.

The Platform also has value in its own right:

- The text calls for "the widest possible cooperation by all countries and their participation in an effective and appropriate international response". This begins to break down the traditional divide between developed and developing countries and points to an inclusive collective action approach.

- It also provides for reintegration under the same agreement of the developed countries that have remained outside Kyoto or withdrawn.
- The text recognizes the need to strengthen the multilateral, rules-based regime and anticipates this through development of a "protocol, another legal instrument or an agreed outcome with legal force under the Convention applicable to all Parties" by 2015.
- Importantly, the text notes and expresses concern at the significant emissions gap and reconfirms the long-term global goal of limiting warming to 2°C. It further provides an option for strengthening the goal to 1.5°C, which is both an important concession to the most vulnerable countries, and a vital link to forthcoming scientific assessments.
- The tacit criticism of existing pledges, coupled with the commitment to an inclusive rules-based approach, seems to suggest that the voluntary "pledge and review" system in vogue since Copenhagen is now time-bound. This is a significant concession by many major emitters. . . .

II. The Second Commitment Period of the Kyoto Protocol

The agreement in Durban extended the Kyoto Protocol, providing a transition period for the European Union and other countries to maintain a common legal framework as they head toward a new future agreement.

Parties who sign up to the Second Commitment Period are committing to reduce emissions by at least 25%-40% below 1990 levels by 2020. It is still unclear which additional countries will join the EU in this effort. The second commitment period under the Kyoto Protocol is set to begin on January 1, 2013 and end either on December 31, 2017 or December 31, 2020.

Looking at it from a high level, with this decision the EU gained a major diplomatic victory and the developing countries ensured that the cherished instruments and rules-based principles of the Kyoto Protocol survived in the short-term. WRI will look further into the details of the Kyoto Protocol decision and publish a separate blog in the coming weeks.

III. Evaluating Progress on Implementation of the LCA Track

While the Durban Platform and the Kyoto Protocol have received most of the COP-related press coverage, it is important to recognize that negotiators tackled more than fifty related issues as part of the Durban Package.

Many of these sought to operationalize decisions taken in Cancun in December 2010 and covered vital interests including work on climate finance, transparency and reporting (MRV), the Periodic Review, adaptation, technology, ambition, and REDD.

NOTES AND QUESTIONS

1. Although the vast majority of the UNFCCC Parties supported the Copenhagen Accord, the consensus rules meant that a small group of nation-states

could block it from being adopted. What are the advantages and disadvantages of this consensus approach?

2. How much progress did the Durban COP make in resolving the two competing visions? To what extent did it address underlying concerns about each approach, such as: Is a single track approach capable of addressing developing country concerns about maintaining the Kyoto Protocol's focus on targets and timetables and distinction between Annex I and other countries? Is a dual approach capable of satisfying the developed countries that think the U.S. commitments need to be integrated with those of the Kyoto Protocol Parties?

3. Given the outcomes of the recent COPs, how optimistic are you that the UNFCCC negotiations will result in a binding treaty that could help avoid risking the worst impacts of climate change? If you think this outcome is unlikely, how should the international legal community proceed?

Professor William Boyd argues, in a piece written just after the Copenhagen COP, that these failures to achieve such a binding agreement suggest the need for a more pluralist approach to conceptualizing climate change law and policy:

> [T]he difficulties facing international climate policy stem from an unrealistic embrace of top-down, global approaches to the problem and a corresponding lack of attention to the realities of a plural, fragmented international legal and political order. This posture of "globalism," which derives in part from a distinctive set of knowledge practices that has sought to make the Earth system into a unitary, governable domain, has pushed international climate policy into what appears to be an intractable political impasse regarding the prospects of fashioning a binding legal instrument capable of coordinating an effective global response to the problem.
>
> To be sure, an alternative approach to climate governance that is more sensitive to the facts of globalization, pluralism, and fragmentation at multiple levels of authority cannot simply devolve into a naïve celebration of localism or, even worse, a fatalism that acknowledges the enormous complexity of it all, recognizes that the clock has run in terms of any possibility of achieving prudent stabilization targets, and urges that all remaining resources and attention be shifted to adaptation or, in more extreme cases, geoengineering. The "solutions" to climate change, if they can even [be] called that, will be as varied and complicated as the problem itself, assembled through many new connections across and within levels of governance, implicating a vast array of actors, institutions, laws, and values. Understanding how these varied and partial solutions are emerging thus becomes a critical component of the larger effort to learn from experience and expand the conditions of possibility for effective forms of climate governance.
>
> Viewed from this perspective, post-Copenhagen climate governance looks much more like the messy, multi-layered forms of governance emerging in response to other global threats such as terrorism, financial crisis, or infectious disease—forms of governance marked not by a single, overarching regulatory system but a complex, nested set of institutions and actors. Wrapped up in all of this is a recognition that conventional regulatory structures associated with traditional notions of government cannot combat these problems effectively without tapping into a much broader and more fluid set of practices that spans multiple geographies and publics. Confronted by a set

of problems arising out of the exceedingly complex interplay of social, economic, and ecological systems and faced with an increasingly tenuous sphere of competence, the contemporary state appears as only one element (albeit a critical one) in a broader emerging assemblage of actors, institutions, and knowledge practices. By taking these emerging assemblages on their own terms, by viewing them as partial, contingent forms of governance, and by seeking to understand how they hold together (or not) we can gain insight into the possibilities and the challenges of building enabling environments that can harness ongoing efforts and direct them toward realistic forms of climate governance.

William Boyd, *Climate Change, Fragmentation, and the Challenges of Global Environmental Law: Elements of a Post-Copenhagen Assemblage*, 32 U. Pa. J. Int'l L. 457, 548–49 (2010).

Do you agree with Professor Boyd? What would be the advantages and disadvantages of the approach to climate change governance that he suggests? How does this approach compare to the one presented by Osofsky in the final section of Chapter One?

C. OTHER INTERNATIONAL LEGAL ACTION WITH RELEVANCE TO CLIMATE CHANGE

The slow pace of UNFCCC negotiations, as described in the section above, has led many policymakers and scholars to consider alternative, parallel approaches. This section explores four of those approaches: other environmental treaties, agreements among sub-groups of UNFCCC Parties, voluntary public–private partnerships, and petitions regarding impacts upon human rights and world heritage.

In addition, as Chapter Five discusses in more depth, subnational governments, despite their limited status under international law as subunits of the nation-states making decisions, have established transnational agreements on climate change. Leaders of cities, states, and provinces around the world are meeting, making commitments to each other that cross national borders, and pushing for national action. These activities raise important questions about models of international lawmaking and strategies for multilevel climate change governance, which Chapter Five addresses.

1. THE MONTREAL PROTOCOL

Climate change is not the focus of the Montreal Protocol on Substances That Deplete the Ozone Layer. Rather, this treaty, which entered into force in 1989 and has been ratified by 196 Parties (including all U.N. member states and the European Union), was created to phase out substances leading to ozone depletion. The Montreal Protocol Parties have accomplished its goals very effectively, in part because there was an easy technological fix: The companies producing the substances impacting the ozone layer were able to find economical substitutes for them.

However, some of the substances that deplete ozone are also greenhouse gases. The Montreal Protocol's elimination of chlorofluorocarbons (CFCs), which are potent greenhouse gases, has resulted in more effective binding climate change mitigation thus far than the UNFCCC process. A further agreement in 2007 to accelerate the phase-out of hydrochlorofluorocarbons (HCFCs), the transitional substitute for CFCs, which also have an important climate impact, will make the treaty an even more important tool in climate change mitigation.

The following excerpt describes the impact of the 2007 amendments to the Montreal Protocol and of the original agreement on greenhouse gas emissions.

DONALD KANIARU, RAJENDRA SHENDE & DURWOOD ZAELKE,
LANDMARK AGREEMENT TO STRENGTHEN MONTREAL PROTOCOL
PROVIDES POWERFUL CLIMATE MITIGATION

8 Sustainable Dev. L. & Pol'y 46, 46–49 (2008)

Introduction

September [2007]'s historic agreement under the Montreal Protocol to accelerate the phase-out of hydrochlorofluorocarbons ("HCFCs") marked the first time both developed and developing countries explicitly agreed to accept binding and enforceable commitments to address climate change. This is particularly significant because the decision was taken by consensus by the 191 Parties to the Protocol — all but five countries recognized by the United Nations. Accelerating the HCFC phase-out could reduce emissions by sixteen billion tons of carbon dioxide-equivalent ("CO_2e") through 2040. In terms of radiative forcing, this will delay climate change by up to 1.5 years. This is because, in addition to depleting the ozone layer, HCFCs also are potent greenhouse gases ("GHGs") with some thousands of times more powerful than carbon dioxide ("CO_2") at warming the planet. Thus, from September 2007 both Montreal and Kyoto can be considered climate protection treaties.

The HCFC agreement and its climate benefits were possible largely because of the Montreal Protocol's unique history of continuous adjustment to keep pace with scientific understanding and technological capability. The Parties to the Protocol generally regard the treaty as fair, due to its objective technical assessment bodies and its effective financial mechanism, the Multilateral Fund. These features and others have made the Protocol the world's most successful multilateral environmental agreement, phasing out ninety-five percent of global production of ozone-depleting substances in just twenty years and placing the ozone layer on a path to recovery.

. . . .

Rapid Increase in HCFC Use Threatens Climate as Well as Ozone

At their nineteenth meeting on September 22, 2007, the Parties agreed to adjust the Montreal Protocol to accelerate the phase-out of HCFCs. Fittingly, the meeting celebrated the twentieth anniversary of the Montreal Protocol.

HCFCs are ozone-depleting substances regulated under the Montreal Protocol as "transitional" substitutes for the more damaging CFCs. Like CFCs, they were used in a variety of applications, including refrigerators and air conditioners, as foam blowing agents, and as chemical solvents. By 2006, it was clear that the use of HCFCs in developing countries was growing rapidly and threatening the recovery of the ozone layer and potentially undermining efforts to mitigate climate change.

Estimates reported by the Montreal Protocol's Technology and Economic Assessment Panel ("TEAP") showed that HCFC use could exceed 700,000 tonnes by 2015 — roughly five times more than the TEAP's 1998 projection of just 163,000 tonnes. The Protocol's Scientific Assessment Panel reported in 2006 that the recovery of the ozone layer to pre-1980 levels would likely be delayed by fifteen years over Antarctica, to 2065, and by five years at mid-latitudes, to 2049, with the delay at mid-latitudes partly due to the high estimates of future production of HCFCs. In addition, the Environmental Investigation Agency reported in 2006 that HCFC emissions by 2015 could cancel out the reductions achieved by the Kyoto Protocol during its first commitment period of 2008-2012.

The increased HCFC use was driven partly by economic growth in developing countries and by a "perverse incentive" under the Kyoto Protocol's Clean Development Mechanism ("CDM"). The most commonly used HCFC is HCFC-22, which produces by-product emissions of HFC-23 when it is manufactured. Under the CDM, eligible HCFC-22 producers in developing countries could generate Certified Emissions Reductions ("CERs") by capturing and destroying HFC-23 by-product emissions. HFC-23 is a super-GHG with a global warming potential ("GWP") of 11,700. HFC-23 CERs could earn up to ten times the cost of capturing and destroying HFC-23 emissions and are exceeding the sales revenue of HCFC-22, effectively subsidizing the cost of producing HCFC-22 and driving its expanded use, including in applications where it has not been widely used or had already been replaced.

The original HCFC control measures were not negotiated with these higher than expected levels in mind. Originally, the Montreal Protocol required developing countries to freeze HCFC consumption by 2016 at 2015 levels and phase-out one hundred percent of HCFC production by 2040. It required developed countries to phase out 99.5 percent of HCFCs by 2020, with 0.5 percent allowed for servicing existing equipment until 2030. By early 2007, there was concern that without urgent action, developing countries would have difficulty in complying with the 2016 freeze and the 2040 phase-out.

Montreal Protocol's Success Made It the World's Best Climate Treaty

As it approached its twentieth anniversary, the Montreal Protocol already was widely considered the world's most successful multilateral environmental agreement. But what many did not know is that its success in phasing out ozone-depleting substances also made it the world's best climate treaty — so far.

The publication of a groundbreaking paper in the Proceedings of the National Academy of Sciences ("PNAS") calculated the climate benefits of the Montreal Protocol, and the results helped spur the international community to action. Because CFCs are such potent GHGs, the Montreal Protocol is reducing emissions by 135 $GtCO_2e$ between 1990 and 2010 and delaying climate forcing by seven to twelve years. When pre-Montreal Protocol efforts to protect the ozone layer are included, such as voluntary reductions in CFCs and domestic regulations in the 1970s, the delay in climate forcing is thirty-five to forty-one years.

The PNAS article drew greater attention to both the ozone and the climate impacts of the increased HCFC use. It became the foundation for key Parties and non-governmental organizations to make the case for strengthening the Montreal Protocol by accelerating the HCFC phase-out to maximize its climate benefits — as well as to ensure the continued success of the treaty in protecting the ozone layer. In particular, the article received considerable attention at meetings of the Stockholm Group, an informal gathering of ozone and climate experts that played a critical role in reviewing the technical and economic data supporting an accelerated HCFC phase-out and building consensus among developed and developing country governments.

. . . .

HCFC Agreement Provides for Climate-Friendly Substitutes and Financing

After a week of intense negotiations in Montreal, the Parties reached an agreement to accelerate the HCFC phase-out. For developing countries, the new control measures shift the base year from 2015 to an average of 2009 and 2010 and the freeze date from 2016 to 2013. Developing countries must then phase-out ten percent of production by 2015, thirty-five percent by 2020, 67.5 percent by 2025, and 97.5 percent by 2030, with 2.5 percent allowed for servicing existing equipment until 2040. Developed countries, many of which have already completed a transition out of HCFCs, must now phase-out seventy-five percent of production by 2010, instead of sixty-five percent, with a 99.5 percent phase-out by 2020, and 0.5 percent allowed for servicing existing equipment until 2030.

Accelerating the HCFC phase-out will reduce emissions an estimated sixteen $GtCO_2e$ or more through 2040, with the actual climate benefits depending on the success replacing HCFCs with zero and low GWP substitutes, and/or preventing future emissions of these substitutes by providing for a robust system to recover and recycle or destroy used chemicals at equipment end-of-life.

In an effort to maximize these potential climate benefits, the adjustment decision calls on the Parties to "promote the selection of alternatives to HCFCs that minimize environmental impacts, in particular impacts on climate" and to give priority to "substitutes and alternatives that minimize other impacts on the environment, including on the climate, taking into account global-warming potential, energy use, and other relevant factors."

By explicitly referencing the climate impacts of HCFC substitutes and alternatives, the adjustment marks the first time that both developed and developing countries have agreed to accept binding commitments to mitigate climate change.

The adjustment decision also includes provisions to ensure that developing countries receive financial assistance through the Multilateral Fund to make the transition out of HCFCs, although the details of implementation will continue to be negotiated at the Fund's Executive Committee meetings.

The agreement was hailed worldwide. Achim Steiner, the Executive Director of the United Nations Environment Programme, called it "the most important breakthrough in an environmental negotiation process for at least five or six years because it sets a very specific target with an ambitious timetable." Romina Picolotti, Argentina's Minister of Environment and an early and vocal proponent of the accelerated HCFC phase-out, described it as "important for the ozone layer, and even more important for the climate. It shows us what we can do when we have the spirit to cooperate."

NOTES AND QUESTIONS

1. The diminishing ozone layer has been an easier problem to address than climate change because of the relative simplicity and cost-effectiveness of addressing the ozone problem. Companies quickly found substitutes for ozone-depleting substances, and supported the international treaty. Greenhouse gas emissions stem from economy-wide activities that have no simple substitute. Do these differences help to explain why the Montreal Protocol's elimination of specific substances has reduced these emissions more effectively than the more comprehensive process of the UNFCCC?

2. Scholars and policymakers have debated the reasons for the Montreal Protocol achieving greater policy success than the Kyoto Protocol. Professor Cass Sunstein, for example, has argued that "both the success of the Montreal Protocol and the mixed picture for the Kyoto Protocol were largely driven by the decisions of the United States, and those decisions were driven in turn by a form of purely domestic cost-benefit analysis." Cass R. Sunstein, *Of Montreal and Kyoto: A Tale of Two Protocols*, 31 HARV. ENVTL. L. REV. 1, 5 (2008). Professor Sunstein concludes that,

   > The position of the United States will not shift unless the domestic benefits of emissions reductions are perceived to increase or unless the perceived domestic costs drop, perhaps as a result of technological innovation. It follows that for the future, the task remains to devise an international agreement that resembles the Montreal Protocol in one critical respect: its signatories, including the United States, have reason to believe that they will gain more than they will lose.
   > *Id.* at 65.

   Do you agree with his conclusion? If so, what should its implications be for international climate change negotiations?

3. If a wide range of treaty regimes all have climate change impacts, how should the UNFCCC deal with those regimes? Can the UNFCCC craft comprehensive solutions in such a scenario?

2. AGREEMENTS AMONG MAJOR ECONOMIES

Given the difficulties of reaching agreement among all the UNFCCC Parties, the most significant greenhouse gas emitters have attempted to make progress in smaller, alternative fora. In 2009, in conjunction with the G8 meetings — in which the heads of France, Germany, Italy, the United Kingdom, Japan, the United States, Canada, and Russia convened to discuss economic and political matters — leaders from 16 countries and the European Union formed a new group to work on climate change, the Major Economies Forum on Energy and Climate. The countries participating in this forum, all of which emit significant quantities of greenhouse gases, are members of the UNFCCC; their efforts in this forum take place in parallel to their efforts at the UNFCCC conferences of the Parties.

The following joint declaration, which includes a commitment to keep temperature rise attributable to climate change at under two degrees Celsius, describes this undertaking.

MAJOR ECONOMIES FORUM, L'AQUILA, ITALY, JULY 9, 2009, DECLARATION OF THE LEADERS: THE MAJOR ECONOMIES FORUM ON ENERGY AND CLIMATE

http://www.majoreconomiesforum.org/past-meetings/
the-first-leaders-meeting.html

We, the leaders of Australia, Brazil, Canada, China, the European Union, France, Germany, India, Indonesia, Italy, Japan, the Republic of Korea, Mexico, Russia, South Africa, the United Kingdom, and the United States met as the Major Economies Forum on Energy and Climate in L'Aquila, Italy, on July 9, 2009, and declare as follows:

Climate change is one of the greatest challenges of our time. As leaders of the world's major economies, both developed and developing, we intend to respond vigorously to this challenge, being convinced that climate change poses a clear danger requiring an extraordinary global response, that the response should respect the priority of economic and social development of developing countries, that moving to a low-carbon economy is an opportunity to promote continued economic growth and sustainable development, that the need for and deployment of transformational clean energy technologies at lowest possible cost are urgent, and that the response must involve balanced attention to mitigation and adaptation.

We reaffirm the objective, provisions and principles of the UN Framework Convention on Climate Change. Recalling the Major Economies Declaration adopted in Toyako, Japan, in July 2008, and taking full account of decisions taken in Bali, Indonesia, in December 2007, we resolve to spare no effort to reach agreement in Copenhagen, with each other and with the other Parties, to further implementation of the Convention.

Our vision for future cooperation on climate change, consistent with equity and our common but differentiated responsibilities and respective capabilities, includes the following:

1. Consistent with the Convention's objective and science:

Our countries will undertake transparent nationally appropriate mitigation actions, subject to applicable measurement, reporting, and verification, and prepare low-carbon growth plans. Developed countries among us will take the lead by promptly undertaking robust aggregate and individual reductions in the midterm consistent with our respective ambitious long-term objectives and will work together before Copenhagen to achieve a strong result in this regard. Developing countries among us will promptly undertake actions whose projected effects on emissions represent a meaningful deviation from business as usual in the midterm, in the context of sustainable development, supported by financing, technology, and capacity-building. The peaking of global and national emissions should take place as soon as possible, recognizing that the timeframe for peaking will be longer in developing countries, bearing in mind that social and economic development and poverty eradication are the first and overriding priorities in developing countries and that low-carbon development is [indispensable] to sustainable development. We recognize the scientific view that the increase in global average temperature above pre-industrial levels ought not to exceed 2 degrees C. In this regard and in the context of the ultimate objective of the Convention and the Bali Action Plan, we will work between now and Copenhagen, with each other and under the Convention, to identify a global goal for substantially reducing global emissions by 2050. Progress toward the global goal would be regularly reviewed, noting the importance of frequent, comprehensive, and accurate inventories.

We will take steps nationally and internationally, including under the Convention, to reduce emissions from deforestation and forest degradation and to enhance removals of greenhouse gas emissions by forests, including providing enhanced support to developing countries for such purposes.

2. Adaptation to the adverse effects of climate change is essential. Such effects are already taking place. Further, while increased mitigation efforts will reduce climate impacts, even the most aggressive mitigation efforts will not eliminate the need for substantial adaptation, particularly in developing countries which will be disproportionately affected. There is a particular and immediate need to assist the poorest and most vulnerable to adapt to such effects. Not only are they most affected but they have contributed the least to the build up of greenhouse gases in the atmosphere. Further support will need to be mobilized, should be based on need, and will include resources additional to existing financial assistance. We will work together to develop, disseminate, and transfer, as appropriate, technologies that advance adaptation efforts.

3. We are establishing a Global Partnership to drive transformational low-carbon, climate-friendly technologies. We will dramatically increase and coordinate public sector investments in research, development, and demonstration of these technologies, with a view to doubling such investments by 2015, while recognizing the importance of private investment, public-private partnerships and international cooperation, including regional innovation centers. Drawing on global best practice policies, we undertake to remove barriers, establish incentives, enhance capacity-building, and implement appropriate measures to aggressively accelerate deployment and transfer of key existing and new low-carbon technologies, in accordance with national circumstances. We welcome the leadership of individual countries to spearhead efforts among interested countries to advance actions on technologies such as energy efficiency; solar energy; smart grids; carbon capture, use, and storage; advanced vehicles; high-efficiency and lower-emissions coal technologies; bio-energy; and other clean technologies. Lead countries will report

by November 15, 2009, on action plans and roadmaps, and make recommendations for further progress. We will consider ideas for appropriate approaches and arrangements to promote technology development, deployment, and transfer.

4. Financial resources for mitigation and adaptation will need to be scaled up urgently and substantially and should involve mobilizing resources to support developing countries. Financing to address climate change will derive from multiple sources, including both public and private funds and carbon markets. Additional investment in developing countries should be mobilized, including by creating incentives for and removing barriers to funding flows. Greater predictability of international support should be promoted. Financing of supported actions should be measurable, reportable, and verifiable. The expertise of existing institutions should be drawn upon, and such institutions should work in an inclusive way and should be made more responsive to developing country needs. Climate financing should complement efforts to promote development in accordance with national priorities and may include both program-based and project-based approaches. The governance of mechanisms disbursing funds should be transparent, fair, effective, efficient, and reflect balanced representation. Accountability in the use of resources should be ensured. An arrangement to match diverse funding needs and resources should be created, and utilize where appropriate, public and private expertise. We agreed to further consider proposals for the establishment of international funding arrangements, including the proposal by Mexico for a Green Fund.

5. Our countries will continue to work together constructively to strengthen the world's ability to combat climate change, including through the Major Economies Forum on Energy and Climate. In particular, our countries will continue meeting throughout the balance of this year in order to facilitate agreement in Copenhagen.

At the 2010 G8 summit, the meeting's declaration reiterated those countries' commitments on climate change, with several paragraphs on climate change and energy issues.

G8, Muskoka, Canada, June 25–26, 2010, Muskoka Declaration: Recovery and New Beginnings

http://www.whitehouse.gov/sites/default/files/g8_muskoka_declaration.pdf

Environmental Sustainability and Green Recovery

21. Among environmental issues, **climate change** remains top of mind. As we agreed in L'Aquila, we recognize the scientific view that the increase in global temperature should not exceed 2 degrees Celsius compared to pre-industrial levels. Achieving this goal requires deep cuts in global emissions. Because this global challenge can only be met by a global response, we reiterate our willingness to share with all countries the goal of achieving at least a 50% reduction of global emissions by 2050, recognizing that this implies that global emissions need to peak as soon as possible and decline thereafter. We will

cooperate to that end. As part of this effort, we also support a goal of developed countries reducing emissions of greenhouse gases in aggregate by 80% or more by 2050, compared to 1990 or more recent years. Consistent with this ambitious long-term objective, we will undertake robust aggregate and individual mid-term reductions, taking into account that baselines may vary and that efforts need to be comparable. Similarly, major emerging economies need to undertake quantifiable actions to reduce emissions significantly below business-as-usual by a specified year.

22. We strongly support the negotiations underway within the UN Framework Convention on Climate Change (UNFCCC). We reiterate our support for the Copenhagen Accord and the important contribution it makes to the UNFCCC negotiations. We urge those countries that have not already done so to associate themselves with the Accord and list their mitigation commitments and actions. Recognizing the scientific view that the increase in global temperature should not exceed 2 degrees Celsius, we also call for the full and effective implementation of all the provisions of the Accord, including those related to measurement, reporting and verification thereby promoting transparency and trust. In this context, we are putting in place our respective fast-start finance contributions to help address the most urgent and immediate needs of the most vulnerable developing countries and to help developing countries lay the ground work for long-term, low-emission development. We express our commitment to cooperate actively and constructively with Mexico as the President of the sixteenth meeting of the UNFCCC Conference of the Parties on November 29–December 10, 2010. We support related initiatives, including the UN Secretary-General's High-Level Advisory Group on identifying long-term public and private financing, and the Paris-Oslo Process on REDD+. We want a comprehensive, ambitious, fair, effective, binding, post-2012 agreement involving all countries, and including the respective responsibilities of all major economies to reduce greenhouse gas emissions.

23. While remaining committed to fighting climate change, we discussed the importance of ensuring that economies are climate resilient. We agreed that more research was needed to identify impacts at the global, regional, national and sub-national levels, and the options for adaptation, including through infrastructural and technological innovation. We particularly recognize the situation of the poorest and most vulnerable countries. We will share our national experiences and plans for adaptation, including through a conference on climate change adaptation in Russia in 2011.

24. To address climate change and increase energy security, we are committed to building low carbon and climate resilient economies, characterized by green growth and improved resource efficiency. We recognize the opportunities provided by a transition to low carbon and renewable energies, in particular for job creation. We encourage the IEA [International Energy Agency] to develop work on an International Platform for low-carbon technologies, in order to accelerate their development and deployment. The elimination or reduction of tariff and non-tariff barriers to trade in environmental goods and services is essential to promote the dissemination of cleaner low-carbon energy technologies and associated services worldwide. Carbon capture and storage (CCS) can play an important role in transitioning to a low-carbon

emitting economy. We welcome the progress already made on our Toyako commitments to launch the 20 large-scale CCS demonstration projects globally by 2010 and to achieve the broad deployment of CCS by 2020, in cooperation with developing countries. Several of us commit to accelerate the CCS demonstration projects and set a goal to achieve their full implementation by 2015. We also recognize the role nuclear energy can play in addressing climate change and energy security concerns, acknowledging the international commitment to safety, security and safeguards for non-proliferation as prerequisites for its peaceful use. We also [recognize] the potential of bioenergy for sustainable development, climate change mitigation and energy security. We welcome the work of the Global Bioenergy Partnership (GBEP) and commit to facilitating swift adoption of voluntary sustainability criteria and indicators, as well as on capacity building activities.

NOTES AND QUESTIONS

1. How meaningful are these commitments, especially in light of the Copenhagen, Cancún, and Durban COPs? To what extent does a non-binding commitment among these countries to keep temperature rise below two degrees Celsius advance efforts to address global climate change?
2. What are the advantages and disadvantages of major emitters making commitments outside of the UNFCCC process? How should such agreements interact with the UNFCCC process? How do such agreements affect the inequities of emissions, impacts, and the UNFCCC negotiation process?

    Jacob Werksman and Kirk Herbertson have argued that statements by the Major Economies Forum on Climate Change and Energy in the lead up to the Copenhagen negotiations played a role in reducing expectations for what could be accomplished there:

    The MEF [Major Economies Forum] Declaration raised expectations that a Copenhagen agreement could demonstrate how all major economies will take actions to reduce global emissions by more than fifty percent by 2020 and by more than eighty percent by 2050. If so, for the first time, both developed and developing countries would need to design, declare, and be held accountable for either NAMAs [Nationally Appropriate Mitigation Actions] or commitments that put humanity on track towards a low-carbon future. However, as Copenhagen approached, the MEF statements also began to reveal emerging views on legal form and review procedures that would represent a significant retreat from a UNFCCC process that had been premised on the importance of a legally binding instrument. By the time they met in London in October 2009, MEF leaders had begun to describe their goal as merely to "internationalize" domestic climate policies in the form of "listings" subject only to a party-led peer-review process. As COP-15 approached, both the UN Secretary General and the Danish government, which would play host for and preside over the Copenhagen COP, picked up on the MEF signals and began to lower expectations as to the legal character of any COP-15 outcome.

> Jacob Werksman & Kirk Herbertson, *The Aftermath of Copenhagen: Does International Law Have a Role to Play in the Global Response to Climate Change?*, 25 Md. J. Int'l L. 109, 114 (2010).

What does this assessment by Werksman and Herbertson suggest about the potential for parallel forums to render climate change agreements more or less effective, depending on their approach?

3. Are these the most critical countries for mitigating climate change? How might you add to or subtract from the Major Economies and G8 lists? How might such changes impact the ability of the group to reach such an agreement, or one that goes further?

3. ASIA-PACIFIC PARTNERSHIP ON CLEAN DEVELOPMENT AND CLIMATE

After President Bush announced in 2001 that the United States would not ratify the Kyoto Protocol, his administration pursued alternative approaches to addressing climate change. The Asia-Pacific Partnership on Clean Development and Climate represents the most significant of these alternative approaches. This Partnership, which concluded in April 2011, included Australia, Canada, China, India, Japan, Korea, the United States, and a number of private sector partners. Its work on climate change, energy security, and reduction of air pollution aimed to augment clean energy investment and trade. The partners formed eight public-private task forces focusing on aluminum, buildings and appliances, cement, cleaner fossil fuel energy, coal mining, power generation and transmission, renewable energy and distributed generation, and steel.

The following excerpt, from an article written near the end of the Bush administration, describes this partnership and the ways in which it embodied the administration's focus on voluntarism and greenhouse gas intensity targets.

JEFFREY McGEE & ROS TAPLIN, THE ASIA-PACIFIC PARTNERSHIP AND THE UNITED STATES' INTERNATIONAL CLIMATE POLICY

19 Colo. J. Int'l Envtl. L. & Pol'y 179, 207 (2008)

Japan, China, South Korea, India, Australia and the United States announced the Asia Pacific Partnership on Clean Development and Climate (AP6) in July 2005. The AP6 is an international agreement on technology cooperation and information exchange broadly focused on energy, environment and development issues. The AP6 specifically focuses on air pollution, poverty eradication, climate change, development, and energy security. Its Charter explicitly states that it is voluntary and non-binding. The Charter is clearly not in treaty form or intended to be binding, so it is best characterized as a soft-law memorandum of understanding between the six partner nations. The AP6 therefore continues the voluntarist policy direction of the Bush Administration climate change partnerships and multilateral technology development partnerships discussed above. The AP6 emphasizes the continued U.S. retreat from hard law international commitments on climate change during the Bush Administration.

Under the AP6 Charter, the partner nations form a Policy and Implementation Committee ("PIC") to "govern the overall framework, policies, and procedures of the Partnership, periodically review progress of collaboration, and provide direction to the Administrative Support Group." The PIC will implement AP6 activities by engaging the private sector, development banks, research institutions, and other governmental, intergovernmental, and non-governmental organizations. The United States is the first chair of the PIC of the AP6. The Administrative Support Group ("ASG") will organize meetings and serve as an information clearinghouse. The United States has also taken on the ASG role for at least the first two years of the AP6.

During the January 2006 AP6 meeting in Sydney, Australia, the members devised a Work Plan that created eight sector-based "Task Forces" to address cleaner fossil energy, renewable energy and distributed generation, power generation and transmission, steel, aluminum, cement, coal mining, and buildings and appliances. Representatives of the partner nations will act as a chair and co-chair of each task force, although non-state actors may also be invited to join. After the Sydney meeting the new PIC met with private sector and research institutions in Berkeley, California to devise Action Plans for each of the eight task forces. The PIC again formally convened in Jeju, South Korea six months later and agreed on an initial set of projects and activities for each Action Plan.

Business leaders participated in both the Sydney and Berkeley meetings. However, representatives from environmental non-governmental organizations, academics, and members of the public were not offered similar access. While the AP6 Charter indicates that only representatives of member governments may sit on the PIC, it is clear that non-state actors, particularly business interests, have a formal leading role in the Task Forces. Indeed, the AP6 Action Plans show that non-state actors have a leading management and participatory role in a number of projects. There is a widespread delegation to non-state actors in the Action Plans, particularly to business and public research bodies. The AP6 is pluralist in that non-state interests are key in formulating and implementing the activities of the Task Forces.

The AP6 internationalizes the United States' climate change policy of using greenhouse gas intensity targets rather than absolute reduction targets. The Vision Statement of the AP6, released at its launch in July 2005, clearly raises nationally-determined greenhouse gas intensity targets as the preferred approach to international climate change policy:

The partnership will share experiences in developing and implementing our national sustainable development and energy strategies, and explore opportunities to reduce the greenhouse gas intensities of our economies.

The Charter of the AP6 also references reducing greenhouse gas intensity. The AP6 therefore internationalizes the goal of greenhouse intensity reduction contained in the Bush Administration GCCPB.

This partnership among a number of critical developed and developing countries in collaboration with industry did not end with the Bush administration, but the tone of U.S. participation changed under President Obama in the period prior to Partnership's dissolution. The Obama administration framed its participation in the Asia-Pacific Partnership as a complement to its efforts at the UNFCCC and in the Major Economies Forum, rather than as an alternative approach. Consider, for example, the following excerpt from the U.S. Statement at the Third Ministerial Meeting, which took place in the lead-up to the Copenhagen negotiations.

U.S. COUNTRY STATEMENT, ASIA-PACIFIC PARTNERSHIP MINISTERIAL MEETING (OCTOBER 26–27, 2009)

http://www.asiapacificpartnership.org/pdf/shanghai/statements/US-cs.pdf

- I am very pleased to join you in this partnership, which we see as one vehicle to help us realize this transformation more quickly and more effectively. As has been said often, this is an important group of countries — our leaders oversee fully half of the world's economic activity and we have a unique capacity, individually and collectively, to shape our children's future.

     . . . .
- This is the first ministerial we have held in 2 years, and much has changed since we last met in Delhi.
- Overall, we have achieved solid results. The Partnership has approved more than 150 projects in its time. The United States has committed some $65 million to promote the objectives of the [Asia-Pacific Partnership], and we have funded over 40 projects across all eight task forces.
- These projects have achieved measurable results — not only through direct benefits such as reduced greenhouse gas emissions, increased capacity to reduce energy use, improved access to renewable energy technologies, and improved access to financing for clean energy — but also through the extensive leveraging of market forces to engage the private sector in promoting clean energy technology transfer.

     . . . .
- Looking forward — we are all now deeply involved in an effort to establish a framework that substantially ramps up our cooperative efforts to promote technology development, dissemination and transfer. This effort is occurring through many channels — global, regional and bilateral.
- We expect Copenhagen to be a signal meeting in our efforts to define measurable, reportable and verifiable national actions, as well as the international framework to support such efforts through finance, technology transfer and capacity building.
- We expect a significant outcome in technology to emerge from Copenhagen, where we have advocated for the creation of a new "hub and spokes" technology assistance vehicle to assist countries [to] identify and secure the technologies they need to develop more cleanly.

- All of us are also working to establish a Global Partnership through the Major Economies Forum process, and we have been deeply involved in the development of action plans that will soon be provided to our leaders.
- These action plans will help us deepen cooperation among the countries at this table, and broaden our cooperation to include partners from other regions of the world.
- It is also clear that in the future, the carbon market will play a substantially larger role in the effort to mobilize private capital, and that efforts to assist in carbon market readiness will be a key part of our effort going forward.
- And we see a trend toward low carbon growth plans that will inform our decisions to transform our economies.
- All of us are planning new and more ambitious actions at the domestic level to address climate change and develop more cleanly — from India's recently announced clean energy missions, the efforts underway . . . in China to meet a carbon intensity goal, and the efforts in several of our countries, including my own, to establish broad-based cap-and-trade legislation.
- We will have a continuing need to evaluate the [Asia-Pacific Partnership's] niche as our approaches and the broader framework for technology cooperation develops, both over the coming year and beyond.
- We appreciate the Australian initiative to review our flagship projects, which will inform our view of how the work of the public and private members of the task forces should go forward.
- It notes the importance of linking technology with capacity building for finance, and suggests that the international system can do more to match finance with needs.
- We would like to reaffirm that we see this Partnership as playing a useful, and we hope, important role in our future efforts, and we look forward to continuing the dialogue over coming months about the concrete and tangible ways that [Asia-Pacific Partnership] can contribute.
- I'd like to thank Japan for offering to host the next meeting of the Policy and Implementation Committee, and I'd like to suggest that it would be useful for the PIC to explicitly consider how the [Asia-Pacific Partnership] can best contribute to implementation of the outcomes we achieve in Copenhagen and through the Global Partnership, building on the collaborative, practical model that has worked for us thus far.

NOTES AND QUESTIONS

1. How does viewing the Asia-Pacific partnership as a UNFCCC alternative versus a UNFCCC complement affect its role in transnational climate change governance?
2. What are the comparative strengths and weaknesses of the approaches to international climate change agreements under the UNFCCC, Major Economies Declaration, and Asia-Pacific Partnership?

3. The regional governance structures in the Asia-Pacific region are relatively weak compared to those in other regions with major greenhouse gas emitters, such as Europe and North America. Professor Mercurio, for example, has argued that these agreements have played a limited role in the expansion of trade in Asia:

> As a result of the focus on trade in goods and corresponding low level of ambition, the business community in Asia has essentially ignored the intra-regional RTAs [Regional Trade Agreements]. The utilization rates of intra-Asian RTAs, that is, the percentage of businesses which actually make use of the RTAs, are appallingly low when compared to other regions. Thus, while it is true that intra-Asian trade has increased throughout the last three decades, and particularly in the last decade, the low utilization rates demonstrate that the increased regional trade has not directly occurred as a result of the trade agreements.
>
> Brian Mercurio, *Trade Liberalisation in Asia: Why Intra-Asian Free Trade Agreements Are Not Utilised by the Business Community*, 6 ASIAN J. WTO & INT'L HEALTH L. & POL'Y 109, 111 (2011).

How might the less well-developed regional governance in this region have affected the role of the Asia-Pacific partnership?

4. HUMAN RIGHTS AND WORLD HERITAGE PETITIONS

The impacts of climate change and the complexities of adapting to them raise international legal issues with a far broader scope than just international environmental law. The petitions to the Inter-American Commission on Human Rights and the World Heritage Commission reflect that breadth. In both sets of actions, the petitioners claimed that the climate change harms implicate areas of international law that would not traditionally be associated with climate change. The Inuit's petition to the Inter-American Commission claimed that failure of the United States to adopt effective climate change policies violated their rights. The World Heritage Commission petitions argued that protected world heritage sites were being harmed by climate change and should be placed on the list of world heritage in danger as a result.

The following excerpt from an article written by Professor Carlarne describes these petitions in the broader context of efforts to affect U.S. climate change policy.

CINNAMON CARLARNE, COMMENTARY, NOTES FROM A CLIMATE CHANGE PRESSURE-COOKER: SUB-FEDERAL ATTEMPTS AT TRANSFORMATION MEET NATIONAL RESISTANCE IN THE USA

40 Conn. L. Rev. 1351, 1400–04 (2008)

Measures to influence the course of U.S. climate change policy extend beyond internal players and institutions. Domestic and foreign citizens alike look to international institutions, such as the Inter-American Commission on Human Rights and the World Heritage Convention, as mechanisms for holding the U.S. government accountable for alleged international responsibilities and liabilities for climate change.

In the first instance, on December 7, 2005, the Center for International Environmental Law (CIEL) filed petitions with the Inter-American Commission on Human Rights (IACHR) against the United States on behalf of sixty-three Inuit petitioners, representing both American and Canadian citizens. The petitions concerned the "impact of global warming on the Inuit and other vulnerable communities in the Americas and the implication of these impacts for human rights."

The Inuit petitions were based on the United States' alleged contribution to and its failure to address global warming. The petitions emphasized that the U.S., with only five percent of the world's population, is responsible for twenty-five percent of the world's emissions, and that the U.S. government is not only refusing to participate in the international climate change regime but is "actively impeding the ability of the global community to take collective action."

The IACHR rejected CIEL's petition on November 16, 2006, without prejudice. Although the petition was dismissed, in February 2007, the IACHR invited the petitioners to return to the Commission to provide testimony on the links between climate change and human rights. On March 5, 2007, Sheila Watt-Cloutier, an Inuit petitioner and Former Chair of the Inuit Circumpolar Conference (as well as Nobel Prize nominee), CIEL Senior Attorney Donald Goldberg, and Earthjustice Managing Attorney Martin Wagner gave testimony before the Commission. Together, the three witnesses used their testimony to create a full picture of the physical, cultural and legal links between climate change and human rights in the hopes of creating enforceable links between international human rights law and global climate change.

While the IACHR is one of the first international institutions to confront the links between climate change and international law, it will not be the last. The Inuit petitions signal a trend whereby sovereign states and members of civil society seek redress for the harms posed by climate change through international mechanisms. This trend is evidenced by statements made by the government of the island nation of Tuvalu that it plans to lodge similar complaints against either the United States and/or Australia to the International Court of Justice (ICJ).

The Inuit petitions to the IACHR and Tuvalu's threat to bring a dispute before the ICJ have attracted considerable public attention. However, the Inuit petitions were dismissed and the Tuvalu case has yet to materialize. Nevertheless, the IACHR request for testimony from CIEL and from Sheila Watt-Cloutier and the decision by affected groups to challenge the United States' climate change strategy in international tribunals suggests that, both within the United States and extra-jurisdictionally, states, citizens, and international institutions are increasingly willing and able to contest the United States' current legal and political stance on climate change.

. . . .

Another international venue that is confronting the connections between climate change and international law is the UNESCO Convention Concerning the Protection of the World Cultural and Natural Heritage (World Heritage Convention).

The underlying goal of the World Heritage Convention is to highlight that certain sites of "cultural or natural heritage are of outstanding interest and therefore need to be preserved as part of the world heritage of mankind as a whole." The World Heritage Convention reflects increasing acceptance of the concept of "cultural internationalism," which "views cultural property as belonging to the world's peoples and not limited to the citizens of the state where the property is located."

On February 16, 2006 — the first anniversary of the Kyoto Protocol coming into force — twelve conservation groups from the U.S. and Canada lodged a petition with the World Heritage Committee to list Waterton-Glacier International Peace Park, located across the U.S. and Canadian borders, on the List of World Heritage Sites in Danger as a consequence of the threats that climate change pose to the natural environment at the site. The petition alleged that "less than one fifth of the park's glaciers still exist — and those precious few that remain are melting rapidly due to human-induced climate change." Based on the risk posed to the site by climate change, the petitioners requested that the World Heritage Committee list the site as in danger and adopt a management plan with a set of corrective measures that should "focus on reductions in U.S. greenhouse gas emissions because the glaciers, which are so rapidly melting, are within the United States' territory, implicating the obligation of the World Heritage Convention to conserve and protect natural and cultural heritage within a Party's boundaries." The petition has the two-fold goal of protecting the site from further degradation and finding a legal foothold for forcing the United States to regulate greenhouse gas emissions.

Four other petitions have been filed by conservation organizations worldwide to add Mount Everest, the Peruvian Andes, the Great Barrier Reef and the Belize Barrier Reef to the list of sites in danger due to climate change. In 2005, in response to mounting concern, the World Heritage Committee commissioned an expert report on the effects of climate change on heritage. The report found that the effects of climate change may jeopardize World Heritage natural and cultural sites and the "fact that Climate Change poses a threat to the outstanding universal values (OUV) of some World Heritage sites" requires the Committee to, among other things, "design appropriate measures for monitoring the impacts of Climate Change and adapting to the adverse consequences." After recognizing that climate change is a threat to heritage, the report analyzes the key issues for the World Heritage Committee to consider when deciding how to respond to climate change.

At its annual meeting in July 2006, the World Heritage Committee took the issue into consideration. After consultation, the Committee issued a Decision on the question of climate change and heritage. The Decision acknowledges the links between climate change and heritage and the importance of creating an institutional strategy for responding to this new challenge. The Decision, however, fell short of the expectations of many people. With the Decision, the Committee created an institutional framework for beginning to respond to the impacts of climate change. It did not, however, create any mechanisms for addressing the causes of global climate change. The Committee rejected a call by campaigners to cut greenhouse gas emissions and took no direct action on the pending petitions to place properties on the "in danger" list. In addition, the final Decision reflected concessions to State Parties, including the United States, to delete references to the Kyoto Protocol and IPCC scientific findings.

———————

NOTES AND QUESTIONS

1. Climate change differs from the type of problems typically addressed through environmental rights claims or the danger listing problems because of its geographic scope and complexity. Typically, those bodies remedy the issues brought before them by having a particular country or countries take particular steps. If a commission found a human rights violation or endangered world heritage, what would be the appropriate remedy? Would it be fair to focus on the countries that have the highest per capita or total emissions? How might such a remedy interact with the UNFCCC process?
2. The then-Chair of the Inuit Circumpolar Conference Sheila Watt-Cloutier, in a presentation during the 2005 UNFCCC Conference of the Parties, described the petition as an important way of initiating a dialogue about climate change and human rights with the United States regardless of its changes of formal success:

   > A declaration from the commission may not enforceable, but it has great moral value. We intend the petition to educate and encourage the United States to join the community of nations in a global effort to combat climate change. . . .
   >
   >   . . .
   >   This petition is our means of inviting the United States to talk with us and to put this global issue into a broader human and human rights context. Our intent is to encourage and to inform.
   >   Sheila Watt-Cloutier, Chair, Inuit Circumpolar Conference, Address before the Eleventh Conference of Parties to the U.N. Framework Convention on Climate Change (Dec. 7, 2005).

   Do you agree that there is value in framing climate change as a human rights issue regardless of the likelihood of a petition succeeding or a declaration being formally enforceable? To what extent, if at all, do such petitioners form part of climate change governance?
3. Because climate change potentially implicates so many areas of international law, commentators have explored the possibility of claims before other international bodies such as the International Court of Justice, the World Trade Organization, and international financial institutions. How might those claims compare to the ones that have been brought before the Inter-American Commission and World Heritage Commission? Do they seem more or less appropriate as mechanisms to address climate change?

CHAPTER 3

U.S. LEGAL DEVELOPMENTS: LEGISLATIVE, EXECUTIVE, AND JUDICIAL ACTION

The United States has produced new federal climate change regulations over the past several years. However, its path to regulation, unlike that of many other countries, has been shaped significantly by litigation. Rather than greenhouse gas emissions regulation taking place under a new statute focused on climate change, the U.S. federal government is developing regulation under the Clean Air Act, a law broadly focused on air pollution that was initially passed in 1963 and amended significantly into its modern formulation in 1970.

The U.S. approach to federal climate change regulation emerged out of a 2007 Supreme Court decision. The Court's holding in *Massachusetts v. EPA* (*Massachusetts*) that the Environmental Protection Agency (EPA) had abused its discretion by the way in which it decided not to regulate greenhouse gas emissions under the Clean Air Act has provided the basis for significant new climate change regulation. In the period since the *Massachusetts* decision, Congress has neither eliminated this Clean Air Act regulatory authority nor added substantially to the very limited legislation directly addressing climate change, other than through investing in clean energy through the American Recovery and Reinvestment Act of 2009 (ARRA).

This combination of limited new legislation with a major Supreme Court ruling has resulted in a U.S. regulatory regime largely constructed under the Clean Air Act and through litigation, a state of affairs that has led to disagreement and uncertainty. Those who desire climate change regulation generally would prefer comprehensive climate change legislation, and they often view greenhouse gas emissions regulation under the Clean Air Act as a second-best path forward. Those who oppose climate change regulation think that the new regulations under the Clean Air Act are problematic.

The Supreme Court's 2011 decision in *American Electric Power v. Connecticut* (*AEP*) reinforced the current U.S. regulatory approach under the Clean Air Act. While largely foreclosing a parallel path of federal common law nuisance suits over climate change, the Court indicated that regulatory suits under the Clean Air Act were an appropriate way of influencing the current federal approach to climate change. The Court's decision in *AEP* left open the door to federal common law nuisance suits in a scenario in which Congress eliminates the EPA's regulatory authority over greenhouse gas emissions under the Clean Air Act.

This chapter reviews the evolution of U.S. federal regulatory policy on climate change. It begins by detailing the existing legislation directly addressing climate change in the United States and the political battles over more comprehensive climate change legislation. It then examines the ways in which the Clean Air Act, through a mix of judicial and executive action, has come to serve as the primary statute regulating greenhouse gas emissions in the United States. It concludes by surveying some of the other key federal developments, with a particular focus on the ARRA funding of and President Obama's emphasis on "clean energy," the complexities of renewable energy siting and climate change adaptation, and the continuing development of climate change litigation under other environmental statutes and tort law.

A. EXISTING AND PROSPECTIVE CLIMATE CHANGE LEGISLATION

Although the U.S. Congress looks unlikely to pass any sort of comprehensive climate change legislation in the short term, the United States does have some statutory law directly related to climate change. This section explores that law, as well as the failed efforts to produce a more comprehensive legislative approach to this problem. In so doing, the section grounds the rest of the chapter, as it clarifies why those wanting to address climate change more comprehensively at a national level have turned to more general environmental and energy law.

1. LIMITED DIRECT STATUTORY REGIME

The United States lacks comprehensive climate change legislation, but it does have statutes directly focused on climate change that address research, monitoring, and reporting. None of these statutes requires specific greenhouse gas emissions reductions or adaptation measures, but they have resulted in the United States assessing the state of its emissions, which is a crucial first step in making effective reductions.

The following excerpt, which predates the failure of comprehensive climate change legislation, provides an overview of how the United States helps to cause and is affected by climate change, and the current statutes directly addressing the problem. It supplements Chapter One's broader discussion of science, law, and policy by examining the U.S. interaction with the problem.

MARGARET ROSSO GROSSMAN, CLIMATE CHANGE AND THE LAW

58 Am. J. Comp. L. 223, 223, 226–28, 241–43 (2010)

Human activities, in the United States and elsewhere, contribute to the emission of greenhouse gases, which persist in the global atmosphere and lead to climate change, including global warming and other climate variability. The United States has begun to cooperate more fully with international measures to mitigate climate change, but has not yet enacted comprehensive climate legislation. Nonetheless, federal statutes and regulations in the areas of environmental, energy, and climate law help to reduce greenhouse gas emissions and to mitigate climate change. States have also adopted measures to mitigate climate change, and several regional programs exist. Although fewer regulatory efforts in the United States have focused on adaptation to climate change, both the federal government and the states will require programs to adapt to the effects of unavoidable climate change.

   . . . .

B. Climate Change in the United States

Global warming is significant for the United States. In the last fifty years, U.S. average air temperature increased more than 2°F, and precipitation increased 5%, with more rain falling in heavier downpours. Other changes include more frequent and intense extreme weather events (heat waves, droughts), more destructive hurricanes, higher water temperatures, rising sea levels, and stronger winter storms. Impacts of climate change are likely to become more severe, affecting water resources, altering ecosystems, and challenging crop and livestock production. Higher sea levels and storm surges will threaten coastal areas. Climate change may exacerbate other social and environmental stresses and threaten human health. Moreover, "[f]uture climate change and its impacts depend on choices made today," both to reduce emissions and to adapt to unavoidable changes.

In the United States, as in other nations, carbon dioxide is the GHG emitted in the largest quantities. Other GHGs, however, have more global warming potential (GWP). For example, methane has a GWP of 25 (25 times more potent, for equal weights, than CO_2); nitrous oxide, 298. High GWP gases are sulfur hexafluoride (SF_6, GWP of 22,800), hydrofluorocarbons (HFCs, 12-14,800), and perfluorocarbons (PFCs, 7390-12,200). Emissions data are often expressed as CO_2 equivalents, a unit of measurement that expresses the GWP of other gases in terms of the warming potential of CO_2.

Total anthropogenic GHG emissions for 2008 in the United States were 6,956.8 teragrams of CO_2 equivalent (Tg CO_2e), 14% more than in 1990. Net emissions in 2008, however, were 6,016.4 Tg CO_2e, after reduction of 940.3 Tg CO_2e for carbon "sinks" (carbon sequestration from land use, land-use change, and forestry activities). Total U.S. emissions of GHGs in 2008 were 2.9% lower than in 2007, a decrease attributed to higher fuel costs that resulted in less demand for transportation fuels and for electricity; a drop in CO_2 emissions offset small increases in emissions of other GHGs.

Between 2007 and 2008, GHG intensity (metric tons CO_2e per million dollars of gross domestic product) fell by 2.6%, while between 2006 and 2007, emissions intensity had fallen by only 0.6%, a relatively slow rate of improvement.

The majority of 2008 GHG emissions in the United States were CO_2 (85.1%), most of which is energy-related. Other significant emissions were methane (8.2%), nitrous oxide (4.6%), and high-GWP gases (2.2%). Most

CO_2 emissions resulted from fossil fuel combustion, primarily in five major sectors: electricity generation, transportation, industry, residential, and commercial. Methane emissions were from enteric fermentation from livestock, manure management, decomposition of landfill wastes, and natural gas systems. Agricultural soil management and fuel combustion from mobile sources emitted N_2O; high GWP emissions (HGCs, PFCs and SF_6) resulted from various industrial processes.

. . . .

III. U.S. Law and Climate Change

As of April 2010, the United States had not enacted a comprehensive climate law. Indeed, until recently, the federal government's attitude toward climate change ranged from "simple inaction to outright obstructionism," with little meaningful federal regulation and documented efforts to play down the extent and serious effects of climate change. Even so, however, environmental and energy laws and regulations help to reduce emissions and mitigate climate change. These measures, which affect climate change directly and indirectly, govern areas like fuel conservation, energy efficiency, and reporting of GHG and other emissions. The legal environment continues to change, as the Environmental Protection Agency (EPA) and other agencies promulgate regulations and Congress debates climate change proposals.

. . . .

C. Climate Law

Since the late 1970s, U.S. laws have focused to some extent on climate specifically. The first U.S. climate laws recognized the threat of global warming and authorized research to help the government understand the problem and draft effective solutions. Later measures developed goals and policies in response to climate change, including monitoring and reporting of GHGs and carbon capture and sequestration. Proposals pending in Congress are comprehensive and include an emissions cap-and-trade program.

1. Research

The 1978 National Climate Program Act established a National Climate Program and a National Climate Program Office with requirements for research and planning. Similarly, the 1987 Global Climate Protection Act called for a policy response based on scientific information generated by the 1978 law. It required a national policy on global climate change, with goals of understanding the greenhouse effect, fostering international cooperation, and mitigating GHG emissions. The 1990 Global Change Research Act established the interagency U.S. Global Change Research Program, which demanded comprehensive research to assist the United States and the world to "understand, assess, predict, and respond to human-induced and natural processes of global change."

2. Monitoring and Reporting

Research led to more direct focus on causes of climate change. Thus, the Energy Policy Act of 1992, which implemented U.S. obligations under the Framework Convention, required an annual inventory of aggregate GHG emissions. Voluntary reporting helped the United States to track GHG emissions, but the law did not require reduction of emissions.

More recently, Congress, moving from research toward response, asked for mandatory reporting of GHG emissions. The Consolidated Appropriations Act, 2008 called for a "comprehensive and effective national program of mandatory, market-based limits and incentives . . . that slow, stop, and reverse the growth of [GHG] emissions . . ." and identified funds for EPA development of a rule to require mandatory reporting of GHG emissions. The Omnibus Appropriations Act, 2009 required EPA to promulgate a GHG reporting rule, and the resulting regulation requires reporting by facilities that produce about 85% of all U.S. GHG emissions. Although EPA's rule does not require mitigation of GHG emissions, it lays the foundation for future limitations and reductions.

In late 2009, Congress debated legislation to impose the "mandatory, market-based limits and incentives" mentioned above. Proposed legislation would include a GHG registry, a cap-and-trade program, scheduled reduction of emissions, and other measures. Debates have continued, but by April 2010, Congress had enacted no comprehensive climate change legislation.

3. Sequestration

Both the Energy Policy Act [EPA Act] and EISA [2007 Energy Independence and Security Act] encourage carbon capture, sequestration, and storage. Under the 2005 law, the Secretary of Energy must implement a "10-year carbon capture research and development program to develop carbon dioxide capture technologies on combustion-based systems." EISA authorizes research and testing of carbon capture, storage, and sequestration. Proposed legislation would encourage sequestration and authorize regulations for minimizing risks of storage and a program to ensure compensation for damages and limit long-term liability for sequestration facilities.

NOTES AND QUESTIONS

1. What do the existing laws focused on climate change accomplish? How do research, monitoring, and reporting provide the basis for further efforts on climate change? What are their limitations?

2. Does it matter if the United States never passes comprehensive climate change legislation? Could the problem be addressed adequately through environmental and energy law in conjunction with the limited existing climate change legislation?

3. Perhaps in part as a result of the dearth of direct legislation on climate change, many of the governmental programs in the United States relevant to climate change, such as ones encouraging energy conservation and efficiency practices, involve voluntary measures by corporations. An extensive debate has taken place over how much value voluntary environmental programs have. A recent empirical study by Professors Robert Innes and Abdoul Sam concludes that such programs can be a helpful component of an overall regulatory scheme.

Overall, this work lends support to the view that [Voluntary Pollution Reduction] VPR programs, carefully combined with regulatory and enforcement rewards for program participation, can be useful and effective tools to reduce pollution and save government costs of overseeing firms' environmental performance. Voluntary programs may also offer firms the opportunity to convey their environmental commitment to potential political adversaries and thereby deter costly boycotts and political conflicts. As a result, even when consumer free riding prevents firms from obtaining any "green premia" in the marketplace — a failure that would otherwise doom VPR efforts — voluntary environmental programs can succeed.

Robert Innes & Abdoul G. Sam, *Voluntary Pollution Reductions and the Enforcement of Environmental Law: An Empirical Study of the 33/50 Program*, 51 J.L. & Econ. 271, 293 (2008).

What role do you think voluntary pollution reduction programs should play in climate change regulation, particularly given the relatively weak direct legislative regime?

2. FAILED EFFORTS AT COMPREHENSIVE CLIMATE CHANGE LEGISLATION

The 2010 defeat of proposed cap-and-trade legislation in Congress was not the first such failure. The U.S. Congress has considered comprehensive climate change legislation numerous times in the past decade. Most bills never even made it out of congressional committees. This pattern of repeated failure, paired with current political realities, makes comprehensive climate change legislation a dim prospect in the United States.

The following excerpt details the most recent failures during the Obama administration.

BRIAN MOSKAL & MICHAEL McDONOUGH, THE IMPACT OF THE 2010 MIDTERM ELECTIONS ON CLIMATE CHANGE LEGISLATION

Climate Change L. & Pol'y Rep. (Dec. 2010)

Enacting climate change legislation was one of the pillars of President Obama's presidential campaign in 2007 and 2008, and as early as November 2008, the President-elect called for Congress to craft and pass a comprehensive climate bill in its upcoming 2009 term. Following the President's call for a bill, Congress spent a significant amount of time and effort addressing various bills related to GHG emissions. The American Clean Energy and Security Act of 2009 (ACES), often informally called the Waxman-Markey bill, was passed by the House in 2009. ACES would have established a nationwide cap-and-trade system within the existing CAA for GHG emissions, requiring a reduction in GHG emissions to 83% of 2005 levels by 2020, and to 17% of those levels by 2050. ACES also would have prevented GHGs from being categorized as criteria pollutants or hazardous air pollutants under the CAA, and would have exempted major GHG-emitting facilities from the New Source Review and Title V provisions of the CAA.

Shortly after ACES' passage, the Senate considered various pieces of companion climate legislation. In September 2009, Sens. John Kerry (D - Mass.) and

Barbara Boxer (D - Calif.) introduced a climate bill entitled the Clean Energy Jobs and American Power Act. This bill would have required GHG reductions to 80% of 2005 levels by 2020 by instituting caps on GHG emissions and a nationwide allowance system similar to the cap-and-trade provisions of ACES. The bill would have prohibited EPA from creating national ambient air quality standards for GHG emissions or regulating them as hazardous air pollutants, but would have allowed New Source Review and Title V permitting for sources emitting at least 25,000 metric tons per year CO_2 equivalent. The bill passed the Senate Committee on Environment and Public Works, chaired by Sen. Boxer, in November 2009. But due to the shifting political landscape and worsening economy in the summer of 2010, the bill lost momentum in the Senate, with many observers believing it had little chance of garnering enough bipartisan support to survive a filibuster.

In May 2010, Sens. Kerry and Joe Lieberman (I - Conn.) released a modified climate bill simply entitled the American Power Act. Sen. Lindsey Graham (R - S.C.), once another co-sponsor of the bill, withdrew from the sponsor team the month before. The American Power Act would not have included a comprehensive cap-and-trade system like ACES and the predecessor Clean Energy Jobs and American Power Act. Rather, it would have employed a cap-and-trade system for some industries, delayed implementation of that system for others, and possibly imposed a carbon tax on still others, while also focusing more heavily on creating jobs in the energy sector and providing incentives for nuclear power, offshore exploration and production, clean coal, and carbon sequestration. This bill would have excluded GHGs from triggering New Source Review for any facility that is initially permitted or modified after January 1, 2009, and would have prohibited EPA from setting performance standards for certain GHG sources covered by the cap. The bill also would have prevented EPA from regulating GHGs as hazardous air pollutants, setting national ambient air quality standards for GHGs, or using GHGs as a trigger for Title V simply based on climate effects alone. Provisions designed to attract bipartisan backing included support for nuclear energy development and expansion of offshore drilling.

In the summer of 2010, with the passage of climate change legislation becoming more unlikely in the Senate and the political winds continuing to favor Republicans, attention turned to direct efforts to rein in EPA's regulation of GHGs. In June 2010, the Senate considered but ultimately defeated a resolution introduced by Sen. Lisa Murkowski (R - Alaska) that would have eliminated EPA's authority to regula[te] GHG emissions. Senate attention then turned to measures to delay implementation of GHG regulations, led by a call for a two-year moratorium on stationary source regulation by Sen. Rockefeller (D. - W. Va.) and other Democrats from states with significant coal production. Supporters cited the deteriorating economic climate and pointed out that further job losses would result from adoption of aggressive GHG regulations.

One of the key questions throughout debates over what form, if any, comprehensive climate change legislation should take has been whether cap-and-trade or carbon taxation is a preferable way to price carbon. As discussed in more depth in Chapter One, a cap-and-trade approach establishes a market for carbon with a limit on the total amount of carbon. Those with carbon dioxide emissions allocations, whether purchased or given to them, trade; those who do not need all their allocations sell them to those who need more, a process that creates a price for those allocations. In contrast, a taxation approach directly sets the price for carbon by making people and companies pay an additional amount for each unit of carbon dioxide they emit. Many economists prefer a carbon tax approach, but cap-and-trade had been seen prior to the 2010 failure of comprehensive climate change legislation to be more politically viable given the aversion to new taxation in the U.S. political system.

The following excerpt from Professor Victor Flatt, written toward the end of the Bush administration when climate change legislation looked likely, compares the then-pending round of legislative proposals, all of which died by mid-2010. It builds upon Chapter One's broader introduction to cap-and-trade and tax-based approaches by looking at their benefits and limitations in a U.S. context.

Victor B. Flatt, Taking the Legislative Temperature: Which Federal Climate Change Legislative Proposal Is "Best"?

102 Nw. U. L. Rev. Colloquy 123, 135–39 (2007)

Interestingly all of the climate change legislative proposals would be considered market-based control regimes, with Bingaman-Specter, Udall-Petri, Lieberman-McCain, Kerry-Snowe, Waxman, Feinstein-Carper, and Alexander-Lieberman, all envisioning a cap-and-trade scheme for CO_2, and Stark and Larson proposing an economy wide tax.

A tax system can control pollution by setting a tax on emissions (such as for CO_2) at a high enough level to discourage such emissions. For instance, one could presumably set a tax on CO_2 emissions (or energy production associated with CO_2 emissions) that would discourage emissions enough to reach a CO_2 reduction target. Cap-and-trade systems adopt the target first and then allocate the overall amount allowed by the target to parties in the market to use, sell, or buy (trade) as they please. Cap-and-trade can be an efficient pollution reduction mechanism because the trading allows the private sector to control emissions at the lowest possible cost (to the private sector) and also encourages innovation.

Currently, none of our environmental laws attempt to control pollution through a tax and we have only one cap and trade system, the one for sulfur dioxide ("SO_2") to control acid rain that was passed in 1990. That all of the climate change legislative proposals embrace a tax or cap-and-trade system shows just how much these systems have gained in respectability in the last seventeen years. But there are disadvantages to such a system that indicate the issue must be examined more closely.

There are several good critiques of market-based systems to control pollution and comparisons of market based regimes, command and control regimes, and other regimes. The primary critiques of market-based systems are that they may create hot-spots of pollution which hurt specific groups, usually the poor or politically powerless; that they are not fair because they do not necessarily penalize a polluter with the money to purchase pollution rights; that they send the wrong moral signals; and that they are difficult to enforce.

Of these criticisms, three do not appear to be of much concern when addressing the regulation of CO_2 specifically. Because CO_2's harm is worldwide and dispersed, there are no "hotspots" for concern. Moreover, concerns over moral signals seem lessened with CO_2 as compared to almost any other pollutant because CO_2 historically has not been seen as a "bad" thing, so producers are not said to have historically engaged in a bad behavior. Fairness is not as large a concern since all high-energy sector use usually has direct benefit to the general public.

The enforcement issue, however, could be more important than the others for the regulation of CO_2. One of the unique features of the cap-and-trade market in SO_2, is that only large coal-fired power plants are involved in the market. These are relatively limited in number, and already regulated. Therefore, the enforcement and administration costs as well as the possibility of costs from regulatory failure are relatively low for the benefit that can be derived from the system. CO_2 regulation would be a different animal altogether. First, CO_2 and other greenhouse gases are not limited to coal-fired power plants, though they are a major source. Mobile sources play a large role, and if a system were to include offsets (see discussion, *infra*), the entities that must be monitored and regulated mushroom exponentially.

None of the legislative cap-and-trade proposals would subject every CO_2 source to the market mechanism, but in such cases, significant sources that are left out of the system must still be regulated. For instance Corporate Average Fuel Efficiency (or CAFE) standards for automobiles, which require an automotive seller's fleet to have a certain fuel efficiency (which in turn reduces CO_2 emissions) is an effective way of controlling CO_2 from automobiles. These have been debated in the related energy bill and should be part of the climate change solution. Consideration of CAFE standards (or other method to control CO_2 from cars, such as a tax) needs to occur at the same time as a consideration of any cap and trade proposal to see how much the relative reductions would cost and how the cost would be allocated.

Even if CO_2 met all of the criteria necessary for the efficient use of cap and trade, some kinds of command and control, particularly those that mandate the adoption of some market standard in certain sectors, can overcome commons problems and "split actor" problems and bring reductions at lower cost because of the ease of enforcement. For instance, the EU consideration on the ban of incandescent light bulb sales seems a very cost-effective way to increase energy efficiency and thereby reduce the production of CO_2. Thus, efficient reduction of climate-changing emissions might be accompanied by command and control systems, at least in some arenas, such as automobile design.

In addition, a major nationwide survey demonstrated that a majority of the American public would actually prefer a command and control system rather than a market system to control climate change. The fact that this has not had a major impact on the legislative proposals to date suggests either that the parties proposing the laws have a better sense of what regulation will be effective, or those who propose the laws realize that market systems may not be as fair and effective but may benefit a particular favored industry or constituency — or some combination of the two.

The difficulty with cap-and-trade enforcement may be why two of the proposals (Feinstein-Carper and Alexander-Lieberman) only apply to the electricity sector. It has already been demonstrated that this sector can be efficiently regulated in a cap-and-trade system. However, limiting the law to this one sector means that overall emissions reductions cannot be as large. Moreover, it raises fairness concerns. While most Americans use electricity and would presumably share the cost of increases, the public at large will not see equitable distribution of costs to the extent that power plants have their rates set by inconsistent state regulation.

Feinstein-Carper and Alexander-Lieberman could be seen as compromise proposals that anticipate further legislation in other sectors, but propose the electricity generation sector first because of the ease of regulation. Nevertheless, the very concept of proceeding in sectors raises concern. First, there is no guarantee that future legislation will occur after one sector passes. Moreover, as discussed above, experience with cap-and-trade in the electricity generating sector may not be applicable to all industries, requiring individual sector systems in any future legislation. Sector-by-sector regulation might reduce cheating because trading within sectors will likely be easier to monitor, but the lack of inter-sector trading or offsets would defeat many of the benefits of a market system in the first place. Economy-wide proposals may be considered the most efficient and the most fair, but this consideration must be balanced against the enforceability of economy-wide limits.

The enforcement problems inherent to a cap-and-trade system should spur a closer look at the legislative proposals that embrace taxation of CO_2 content. Such taxes are easier to enforce than cap and trade because they are picked up at product and service origination and added to final prices. Economists generally favor a tax because it internalizes any efficiencies of a trading system (if the price of producing carbon is not recouped in one sector, it will cease production) without having to monitor a complicated trading system.

The main objection to a tax system seems to be the belief that the American public abhors any "tax" and will punish any legislator who proposes or votes for one, even if the tax is incorporated into final prices. Representative Dingell has recently challenged this assumption, and I leave it to political scientists to further analyze this question and educate the public. There is also some concern that the appropriate level of "tax" will not be selected to reach the intended reduction target, a problem that one need not worry about in cap-and-trade. This is considered an economic science problem, but a general aversion to taxes may mean that this "target" gets set by other considerations than the most efficient production of CO_2.

Nevertheless, because of ease of administration, a tax system is probably superior with respect to enforcement and fairness and could be tweaked to provide relief for the poor or others whom we feel deserve relief from regulatory impacts.

NOTES AND QUESTIONS

1. Why did comprehensive climate change legislation fail? Are there forms it could take in the foreseeable future that would avoid these difficulties?
2. Do you agree with Professor Flatt that a tax approach would likely be superior but is not as politically viable? If so, why are taxes less popular? Do you think that there are strategies that might address those concerns?
3. Professor Richard Epstein argues that cap-and-trade and tax are actually not that different, but rather have the same benefits and limitations:

   > In principle, it should always be possible to design a first-best tax that operates exactly like a first-best regulation. Put otherwise, the perfect tax and the perfect regulation system will have the same level of overall pollution, and the same production and outcomes by all firms within the system. All superficial differences will disappear.
   >
   > . . . .
   >
   > The problems, however, are a mirror image of one another. If we cannot set the tax in a carbon tax system, then for the same reasons we cannot set the cap in a cap and trade system. The same problems remain: too much leakage to small emitters, including farm animals, no real knowledge of the magnitude of the harm that one is trying to avert, and no confidence that we can decide who gets the trading rights for free and who has to purchase them at some auction.
   >
   > Richard A. Epstein, *Carbon Dioxide: Our Newest Pollutant*, 43 Suffolk U. L. Rev. 797, 823, 824 (2010).

   Do you agree with Professor Epstein? Do you think that there are comparative advantages and disadvantages of cap-and-trade versus carbon tax approaches to comprehensive climate change regulation? Why have efforts focused so heavily on cap-and-trade approaches?
4. Professors Holly Doremus and Michael Hanemann have argued that a cap-and-trade regime would be insufficient to control climate change on its own and that the federal government should also adopt a climate law modeled on the Clean Air Act's cooperative federalism approach. *See* Holly Doremus & W. Michael Hanemann, *Of Babies and Bathwater: Why the Clean Air Act's Cooperative Federalism Framework Is Useful for Addressing Global Warming*, 50 ARIZ. L. REV. 799, 811–12, 834 (2008). Professor Alice Kaswan similarly proposes a cooperative federalism approach to climate change legislation that includes federal minimum standards which states can exceed and delegation of program implementation. Alice Kaswan, *A Cooperative Federalism Proposal for Climate Legislation: The Value of State Autonomy in the Federalism System*, 85 DENV. U. L. REV. 791, 814–23 (2008). If you were designing climate change legislation, what would its key elements be? Would you create some sort of a cap-and-trade approach, a carbon tax approach, or some other alternative? What mechanisms would you put in to make it maximally effective?

B. SUPREME COURT AND EXECUTIVE ACTION UNDER THE CLEAN AIR ACT

The Clean Air Act is the primary federal environmental statute under which U.S. greenhouse gas regulation is occurring. A limited 1963 version of the Clean Air Act was passed in response to growing concern about the public health impacts of severe air pollution, especially smog. Through major amendments and the creation of the Environmental Protection Agency (EPA) in 1970, the Clean Air Act became a more comprehensive federal response to air pollution. Since then, the EPA has played an important role in implementing the statute through the creation of regulations and programs. Amendments to the Clean Air Act in 1990 further expanded the EPA's authority to promulgate and enforce regulations to reduce air pollutant emissions.

As U.S. legislative efforts on climate change repeatedly floundered, the EPA, under multiple presidential administrations, grappled with whether greenhouse gas emissions should be viewed as air pollutants under the Clean Air Act. Although these emissions are quite different from the smog that motivated the creation of the Clean Air Act, the statute defines the term *air pollution* broadly. After years of unsuccessful internal and external efforts to have the EPA regulate greenhouse gas emissions as air pollutants, a diverse group of governmental and nongovernmental entities petitioned the agency to do so. This petition ultimately resulted in the 2007 U.S. Supreme Court decision in *Massachusetts v. EPA*, which has provided the basis for greenhouse gas regulation to move forward.

This section discusses that landmark case, the motor vehicle and stationary sources regulations that have followed, challenges to these regulatory efforts, and the impact of the Supreme Court's 2011 opinion in *AEP v. Connecticut*. It explores how a combination of judicial and executive decision making, grounded in environmental law, has moved greenhouse gas regulation forward in the absence of comprehensive climate change legislation.

1. *MASSACHUSETTS v. EPA*

The U.S. Supreme Court decision in *Massachusetts v. EPA*, 549 U.S. 497 (2007), underlies the federal efforts to regulate greenhouse gas emissions. It also represents the deep divisions within the United States over climate change regulation. The 26 petitioners before the Supreme Court included 12 states, a U.S. territory, 3 cities, and 13 nongovernmental organizations. The respondents included not only the EPA, but also 10 other states and 19 industry and utility groups.

This case, the first in which the Supreme Court engaged the problem of climate change, involved important threshold and substantive issues. Before the Supreme Court could reach the substantive issues, it had to decide the threshold question of whether petitioners had standing to bring the case. This determination required the Supreme Court to analyze the nature of the problem of climate change in order to decide if petitioners could satisfactorily demonstrate the required elements of standing: injury, causation, and remedy.

As a substantive matter, the Supreme Court had to determine whether the Clean Air Act's broad definition of air pollutant applied to greenhouse gas emissions even though their relevant atmospheric interactions are quite different than many of the substances previously regulated under the statute.

The following excerpts from the majority opinion and dissents reveal the controversies in the case with respect to both standing and the merits of interpreting the statute.

MASSACHUSETTS v. EPA

549 U.S. 497, 504–06, 516–29, 532–37, 539–51, 553, 555–58, 560 (2007)

JUSTICE STEVENS delivered the opinion of the Court.

A well-documented rise in global temperatures has coincided with a significant increase in the concentration of carbon dioxide in the atmosphere. Respected scientists believe the two trends are related. For when carbon dioxide is released into the atmosphere, it acts like the ceiling of a greenhouse, trapping solar energy and retarding the escape of reflected heat. It is therefore a species—the most important species—of a "greenhouse gas."

Calling global warming "the most pressing environmental challenge of our time," a group of States, local governments, and private organizations alleged in a petition for certiorari that the Environmental Protection Agency (EPA) has abdicated its responsibility under the Clean Air Act to regulate the emissions of four greenhouse gases, including carbon dioxide. Specifically, petitioners asked us to answer two questions concerning the meaning of §202(a)(1) of the Act: whether EPA has the statutory authority to regulate greenhouse gas emissions from new motor vehicles; and if so, whether its stated reasons for refusing to do so are consistent with the statute.

In response, EPA, supported by 10 intervening States and six trade associations, correctly argued that we may not address those two questions unless at least one petitioner has standing to invoke our jurisdiction under Article III of the Constitution. Notwithstanding the serious character of that jurisdictional argument and the absence of any conflicting decisions construing §202(a)(1), the unusual importance of the underlying issue persuaded us to grant the writ. 548 U.S. 903, 126 S. Ct. 2960, 165 L. Ed. 2d 949 (2006).

I

Section 202(a)(1) of the Clean Air Act, as added by Pub. L. 89-272, §101(8), 79 Stat. 992, and as amended by, *inter alia,* 84 Stat. 1690 and 91 Stat. 791, 42 U.S.C. §7521(a)(1), provides:

> "The [EPA] Administrator shall by regulation prescribe (and from time to time revise) in accordance with the provisions of this section, standards applicable to the emission of any air pollutant from any class or classes of new motor vehicles or new motor vehicle engines, which in his judgment cause, or contribute to, air pollution which may reasonably be anticipated to endanger public health or welfare. . . ."

The Act defines "air pollutant" to include "any air pollution agent or combination of such agents, including any physical, chemical, biological, radioactive . . . substance or matter which is emitted into or otherwise enters the ambient air." §7602(g). "Welfare" is also defined broadly: among other things, it includes "effects on . . . weather . . . and climate." §7602(h).

. . . .

IV

Article III of the Constitution limits federal-court jurisdiction to "Cases" and "Controversies." Those two words confine "the business of federal courts to questions presented in an adversary context and in a form historically viewed as capable of resolution through the judicial process." Flast v. Cohen, 392 U.S. 83, 95, 88 S. Ct. 1942, 20 L.Ed.2d 947 (1968). It is therefore familiar learning that no justiciable "controversy" exists when parties seek adjudication of a political question, Luther v. Borden, 7 How. 1, 12 L.Ed. 581 (1849), when they ask for an advisory opinion, Hayburn's Case, 2 Dall. 409, 1 L.Ed. 436 (1792), see also Clinton v. Jones, 520 U.S. 681, 700, n. 33, 117 S. Ct. 1636, 137 L.Ed.2d 945 (1997), or when the question sought to be adjudicated has been mooted by subsequent developments, California v. San Pablo & Tulare R. Co., 149 U.S. 308, 13 S. Ct. 876, 37 L.Ed. 747 (1893). This case suffers from none of these defects.

The parties' dispute turns on the proper construction of a congressional statute, a question eminently suitable to resolution in federal court. Congress has moreover authorized this type of challenge to EPA action. See 42 U.S.C. §7607(b)(1). That authorization is of critical importance to the standing inquiry. . . .

EPA maintains that because greenhouse gas emissions inflict widespread harm, the doctrine of standing presents an insuperable jurisdictional obstacle. We do not agree. At bottom, "the gist of the question of standing" is whether petitioners have "such a personal stake in the outcome of the controversy as to assure that concrete adverseness which sharpens the presentation of issues upon which the court so largely depends for illumination." Baker v. Carr, 369 U.S. 186, 204, 82 S. Ct. 691, 7 L.Ed.2d 663 (1962).

. . . .

Only one of the petitioners needs to have standing to permit us to consider the petition for review. See Rumsfeld v. Forum for Academic and Institutional Rights, Inc., 547 U.S. 47, 52, n. 2, 126 S. Ct. 1297, 164 L.Ed.2d 156 (2006). We stress here, as did Judge Tatel below, the special position and interest of Massachusetts. It is of considerable relevance that the party seeking review here is a sovereign State and not, as it was in Lujan, a private individual.

Well before the creation of the modern administrative state, we recognized that States are not normal litigants for the purposes of invoking federal jurisdiction.

. . . .

Just as Georgia's independent interest "in all the earth and air within its domain" supported federal jurisdiction a century ago, so too does Massachusetts' well-founded desire to preserve its sovereign territory today. . . . That Massachusetts does in fact own a great deal of the "territory alleged to be affected" only reinforces the conclusion that its stake in the outcome of this case is sufficiently concrete to warrant the exercise of federal judicial power.

When a State enters the Union, it surrenders certain sovereign prerogatives. . . .

These sovereign prerogatives are now lodged in the Federal Government, and Congress has ordered EPA to protect Massachusetts (among others) by prescribing standards applicable to the "emission of any air pollutant from any class or classes of new motor vehicle engines, which in [the Administrator's] judgment cause, or contribute to, air pollution which may reasonably be anticipated to endanger public health or welfare." 42 U.S.C. §7521(a)(1). Congress has moreover recognized a concomitant procedural right to challenge the rejection of its rulemaking petition as arbitrary and capricious. §7607(b)(1). Given that procedural right and Massachusetts' stake in protecting its quasi-sovereign interests, the Commonwealth is entitled to special solicitude in our standing analysis.

With that in mind, it is clear that petitioners' submissions as they pertain to Massachusetts have satisfied the most demanding standards of the adversarial process. EPA's steadfast refusal to regulate greenhouse gas emissions presents a risk of harm to Massachusetts that is both "actual" and "imminent." Lujan, 504 U.S., at 560, 112 S. Ct. 2130 (internal quotation marks omitted). There is, moreover, a "substantial likelihood that the judicial relief requested" will prompt EPA to take steps to reduce that risk. Duke Power Co. v. Carolina Environmental Study Group, Inc., 438 U.S. 59, 79, 98 S. Ct. 2620, 57 L.Ed.2d 595 (1978).

The Injury

The harms associated with climate change are serious and well recognized. Indeed, the NRC Report itself—which EPA regards as an "objective and independent assessment of the relevant science," 68 Fed. Reg. 52930—identifies a number of environmental changes that have already inflicted significant harms, including "the global retreat of mountain glaciers, reduction in snow-cover extent, the earlier spring melting of ice on rivers and lakes, [and] the accelerated rate of rise of sea levels during the 20th century relative to the past few thousand years. . . ." NRC Report 16.

Petitioners allege that this only hints at the environmental damage yet to come. According to the climate scientist Michael MacCracken, "qualified scientific experts involved in climate change research" have reached a "strong consensus" that global warming threatens (among other things) a precipitate rise in sea levels by the end of the century, MacCracken Decl. ¶ 5, Stdg.App. 207, "severe and irreversible changes to natural ecosystems," id., ¶ 5(d), at 209, a "significant reduction in water storage in winter snowpack in mountainous regions with direct and important economic consequences," ibid., and an increase in the spread of disease, id., ¶ 28, at 218-219. He also observes that rising ocean temperatures may contribute to the ferocity of hurricanes. Id., ¶¶ 23-25, at 216-217.

That these climate-change risks are "widely shared" does not minimize Massachusetts' interest in the outcome of this litigation. See Federal Election Comm'n v. Akins, 524 U.S. 11, 24, 118 S. Ct. 1777, 141 L.Ed.2d 10 (1998) ("[W]here a harm is concrete, though widely shared, the Court has found 'injury in fact'"). According to petitioners' unchallenged affidavits, global sea levels rose somewhere between 10 and 20 centimeters over the 20th century as a result of global warming. MacCracken Decl. ¶ 5(c), Stdg.App. 208. These rising seas have already begun to swallow Massachusetts' coastal land. *Id.,* at 196 (declaration of Paul H. Kirshen ¶ 5), 216 (MacCracken Decl. ¶ 23). Because the Commonwealth "owns a substantial portion of the state's coastal property," *id.,* at 171 (declaration of Karst R. Hoogeboom ¶ 4), it has alleged a particularized injury in its capacity as a landowner. The severity of that injury will only increase over the course of the next century: If sea levels continue to rise as predicted, one Massachusetts official believes that a significant fraction of coastal property will be "either permanently lost through inundation or temporarily lost through periodic storm surge and flooding events." *Id.,* ¶ 6, at 172. Remediation costs alone, petitioners allege, could run well into the hundreds of millions of dollars. . . .

Causation

EPA does not dispute the existence of a causal connection between man-made greenhouse gas emissions and global warming. At a minimum, therefore, EPA's refusal to regulate such emissions "contributes" to Massachusetts' injuries.

EPA nevertheless maintains that its decision not to regulate greenhouse gas emissions from new motor vehicles contributes so insignificantly to petitioners' injuries that the Agency cannot be hauled into federal court to answer for them. . . .

But EPA overstates its case. Its argument rests on the erroneous assumption that a small incremental step, because it is incremental, can never be attacked in a federal judicial forum. Yet accepting that premise would doom most challenges to regulatory action.

. . . .

And reducing domestic automobile emissions is hardly a tentative step. Even leaving aside the other greenhouse gases, the United States transportation sector emits an enormous quantity of carbon dioxide into the atmosphere — according to the MacCracken affidavit, more than 1.7 billion metric tons in 1999 alone. ¶ 30, Stdg.App. 219. That accounts for more than 6% of worldwide carbon dioxide emissions. *Id.,* at 232 (Oppenheimer Decl. ¶ 3); see also MacCracken Decl. ¶ 31, at 220. To put this in perspective: Considering just emissions from the transportation sector, which represent less than one-third of this country's total carbon dioxide emissions, the United States would still rank as the third-largest emitter of carbon dioxide in the world, outpaced only by the European Union and China. Judged by any standard, U.S. motor-vehicle emissions make a meaningful contribution to greenhouse gas concentrations and hence, according to petitioners, to global warming.

The Remedy

While it may be true that regulating motor-vehicle emissions will not by itself *reverse* global warming, it by no means follows that we lack jurisdiction to decide whether EPA has a duty to take steps to *slow* or *reduce* it. . . .

We moreover attach considerable significance to EPA's "agree[ment] with the President that 'we must address the issue of global climate change,'" 68 Fed.

Reg. 52929 (quoting remarks announcing Clear Skies and Global Climate Initiatives, 2002 Public Papers of George W. Bush, Vol. 1, Feb. 14, p. 227 (2004)), and to EPA's ardent support for various voluntary emission-reduction programs, 68 Fed. Reg. 52932. As Judge Tatel observed in dissent below, "EPA would presumably not bother with such efforts if it thought emissions reductions would have no discernable impact on future global warming." 415 F.3d, at 66.

In sum — at least according to petitioners' uncontested affidavits — the rise in sea levels associated with global warming has already harmed and will continue to harm Massachusetts. The risk of catastrophic harm, though remote, is nevertheless real. That risk would be reduced to some extent if petitioners received the relief they seek. We therefore hold that petitioners have standing to challenge EPA's denial of their rulemaking petition.

V

The scope of our review of the merits of the statutory issues is narrow. As we have repeated time and again, an agency has broad discretion to choose how best to marshal its limited resources and personnel to carry out its delegated responsibilities. See Chevron U.S.A. Inc. v. Natural Resources Defense Council, Inc., 467 U.S. 837, 842-845, 104 S. Ct. 2778, 81 L.Ed.2d 694 (1984). That discretion is at its height when the agency decides not to bring an enforcement action. Therefore, in Heckler v. Chaney, 470 U.S. 821, 105 S. Ct. 1649, 84 L.Ed.2d 714 (1985), we held that an agency's refusal to initiate enforcement proceedings is not ordinarily subject to judicial review. Some debate remains, however, as to the rigor with which we review an agency's denial of a petition for rulemaking.

There are key differences between a denial of a petition for rulemaking and an agency's decision not to initiate an enforcement action. See American Horse Protection Assn., Inc. v. Lyng, 812 F.2d 1, 3-4 (C.A.D.C.1987). In contrast to nonenforcement decisions, agency refusals to initiate rulemaking "are less frequent, more apt to involve legal as opposed to factual analysis, and subject to special formalities, including a public explanation." Id., at 4; see also 5 U.S.C. §555(e). They moreover arise out of denials of petitions for rulemaking which (at least in the circumstances here) the affected party had an undoubted procedural right to file in the first instance. Refusals to promulgate rules are thus susceptible to judicial review, though such review is "extremely limited" and "highly deferential." National Customs Brokers & Forwarders Assn. of America, Inc. v. United States, 883 F.2d 93, 96 (C.A.D.C.1989).

EPA concluded in its denial of the petition for rulemaking that it lacked authority under 42 U.S.C. §7521(a)(1) to regulate new vehicle emissions because carbon dioxide is not an "air pollutant" as that term is defined in §7602. In the alternative, it concluded that even if it possessed authority, it would decline to do so because regulation would conflict with other administration priorities. As discussed earlier, the Clean Air Act expressly permits review of such an action. §7607(b)(1). We therefore "may reverse any such action found to be . . . arbitrary, capricious, an abuse of discretion, or otherwise not in accordance with law." §7607(d)(9).

VI

On the merits, the first question is whether §202(a)(1) of the Clean Air Act authorizes EPA to regulate greenhouse gas emissions from new motor vehicles in the event that it forms a "judgment" that such emissions contribute to climate change. We have little trouble concluding that it does. In relevant part, §202(a)(1) provides that EPA "shall by regulation prescribe . . . standards applicable to the emission of any air pollutant from any class or classes of new motor vehicles or new motor vehicle engines, which in [the Administrator's] judgment cause, or contribute to, air pollution which may reasonably be anticipated to endanger public health or welfare." 42 U.S.C. §7521(a)(1). Because EPA believes that Congress did not intend it to regulate substances that contribute to climate change, the agency maintains that carbon dioxide is not an "air pollutant" within the meaning of the provision.

The statutory text forecloses EPA's reading. The Clean Air Act's sweeping definition of "air pollutant" includes "*any* air pollution agent or combination of such agents, including *any* physical, chemical . . . substance or matter which is emitted into or otherwise enters the ambient air. . . ." §7602(g) (emphasis added). On its face, the definition embraces all airborne compounds of whatever stripe, and underscores that intent through the repeated use of the word "any." Carbon dioxide, methane, nitrous oxide, and hydrofluorocarbons are without a doubt "physical [and] chemical . . . substance[s] which [are] emitted into . . . the ambient air." The statute is unambiguous.

. . . .

While the Congresses that drafted §202(a)(1) might not have appreciated the possibility that burning fossil fuels could lead to global warming, they did understand that without regulatory flexibility, changing circumstances and scientific developments would soon render the Clean Air Act obsolete. The broad language of §202(a)(1) reflects an intentional effort to confer the flexibility necessary to forestall such obsolescence. . . . Because greenhouse gases fit well within the Clean Air Act's capacious definition of "air pollutant," we hold that EPA has the statutory authority to regulate the emission of such gases from new motor vehicles.

VII

The alternative basis for EPA's decision — that even if it does have statutory authority to regulate greenhouse gases, it would be unwise to do so at this time — rests on reasoning divorced from the statutory text. While the statute does condition the exercise of EPA's authority on its formation of a "judgment," 42 U.S.C. §7521(a)(1), that judgment must relate to whether an air pollutant "cause[s], or contribute[s] to, air pollution which may reasonably be anticipated to endanger public health or welfare," *ibid*. Put another way, the use of the word "judgment" is not a roving license to ignore the statutory text. It is but a direction to exercise discretion within defined statutory limits.

. . . .

In short, EPA has offered no reasoned explanation for its refusal to decide whether greenhouse gases cause or contribute to climate change. Its action was therefore "arbitrary, capricious, . . . or otherwise not in accordance with law."

42 U.S.C. §7607(d)(9)(A). We need not and do not reach the question whether on remand EPA must make an endangerment finding, or whether policy concerns can inform EPA's actions in the event that it makes such a finding. Cf. Chevron U.S.A. Inc. v. Natural Resources Defense Council, Inc., 467 U.S. 843-844, 104 S. Ct. 2778, 81 L.Ed.2d 694, at 1. We hold only that EPA must ground its reasons for action or inaction in the statute.

VIII

The judgment of the Court of Appeals is reversed, and the case is remanded for further proceedings consistent with this opinion.

It is so ordered.

CHIEF JUSTICE ROBERTS, with whom JUSTICE SCALIA, JUSTICE THOMAS, and JUSTICE ALITO join, dissenting.

Global warming may be a "crisis," even "the most pressing environmental problem of our time." Pet. for Cert. 26, 22. Indeed, it may ultimately affect nearly everyone on the planet in some potentially adverse way, and it may be that governments have done too little to address it. It is not a problem, however, that has escaped the attention of policymakers in the Executive and Legislative Branches of our Government, who continue to consider regulatory, legislative, and treaty-based means of addressing global climate change.

Apparently dissatisfied with the pace of progress on this issue in the elected branches, petitioners have come to the courts claiming broad-ranging injury, and attempting to tie that injury to the Government's alleged failure to comply with a rather narrow statutory provision. I would reject these challenges as nonjusticiable. Such a conclusion involves no judgment on whether global warming exists, what causes it, or the extent of the problem. Nor does it render petitioners without recourse. This Court's standing jurisprudence simply recognizes that redress of grievances of the sort at issue here "is the function of Congress and the Chief Executive," not the federal courts. Lujan v. Defenders of Wildlife, 504 U.S. 555, 576, 112 S. Ct. 2130, 119 L.Ed.2d 351 (1992). I would vacate the judgment below and remand for dismissal of the petitions for review.

I

. . . .

Our modern framework for addressing standing is familiar: "A plaintiff must allege personal injury fairly traceable to the defendant's allegedly unlawful conduct and likely to be redressed by the requested relief." DaimlerChrysler, supra, at 342, 126 S. Ct., at 1861 (quoting Allen v. Wright, 468 U.S. 737, 751, 104 S. Ct. 3315, 82 L.Ed.2d 556 (1984); (internal quotation marks omitted)). Applying that standard here, petitioners bear the burden of alleging an injury that is fairly traceable to the Environmental Protection Agency's failure to promulgate new motor vehicle greenhouse gas emission standards, and that is likely to be redressed by the prospective issuance of such standards.

Before determining whether petitioners can meet this familiar test, however, the Court changes the rules. It asserts that "States are not normal litigants for the purposes of invoking federal jurisdiction," and that given

"Massachusetts' stake in protecting its quasi-sovereign interests, the Commonwealth is entitled to *special solicitude* in our standing analysis." *Ante,* at 1454,
1455 (emphasis added).

Relaxing Article III standing requirements because asserted injuries are
pressed by a State, however, has no basis in our jurisprudence, and support
for any such "special solicitude" is conspicuously absent from the Court's
opinion.

. . . .

What is more, the Court's reasoning falters on its own terms. The Court
asserts that Massachusetts is entitled to "special solicitude" due to its "quasi-
sovereign interests," *ante,* at 1455, but then applies our Article III standing test
to the asserted injury of the Commonwealth's loss of coastal property. . . .

On top of everything else, the Court overlooks the fact that our cases cast
significant doubt on a State's standing to assert a quasi-sovereign interest — as
opposed to a direct injury — against the Federal Government. . . .

II

It is not at all clear how the Court's "special solicitude" for Massachusetts
plays out in the standing analysis, except as an implicit concession that petitioners cannot establish standing on traditional terms. But the status of Massachusetts as a State cannot compensate for petitioners' failure to demonstrate
injury in fact, causation, and redressability.

When the Court actually applies the three-part test, it focuses, as did the
dissent below, see 415 F.3d 50, 64 (C.A.D.C.2005) (opinion of Tatel, J.), on the
Commonwealth's asserted loss of coastal land as the injury in fact. If petitioners rely on loss of land as the Article III injury, however, they must ground
the rest of the standing analysis in that specific injury. That alleged injury must
be "concrete and particularized," Defenders of Wildlife, 504 U.S., at 560, 112
S. Ct. 2130, and "distinct and palpable," Allen, 468 U.S., at 751, 104 S. Ct. 3315
(internal quotation marks omitted). Central to this concept of "particularized"
injury is the requirement that a plaintiff be affected in a "personal and
individual way," Defenders of Wildlife, 504 U.S., at 560, n. 1, 112 S. Ct.
2130, and seek relief that "directly and tangibly benefits him" in a manner
distinct from its impact on "the public at large," id., at 573-574, 112 S. Ct.
2130. . . .

The very concept of global warming seems inconsistent with this particu-
larization requirement. Global warming is a phenomenon "harmful to humanity at large," 415 F.3d, at 60 (Sentelle, J., dissenting in part and concurring in
judgment), and the redress petitioners seek is focused no more on them than
on the public generally — it is literally to change the atmosphere around the
world.

If petitioners' particularized injury is loss of coastal land, it is also that
injury that must be "actual or imminent, not conjectural or hypothetical,"
Defenders of Wildlife, supra, at 560, 112 S. Ct. 2130 (internal quotation
marks omitted), "real and immediate," Los Angeles v. Lyons, 461 U.S. 95,
102, 103 S. Ct. 1660, 75 L.Ed.2d 675 (1983) (internal quotation marks omitted),
and "certainly impending," Whitmore v. Arkansas, 495 U.S. 149, 158, 110
S. Ct. 1717, 109 L.Ed.2d 135 (1990) (internal quotation marks omitted).

As to "actual" injury, the Court observes that "global sea levels rose somewhere between 10 and 20 centimeters over the 20th century as a result of global warming" and that "[t]hese rising seas have already begun to swallow Massachusetts' coastal land." *Ante,* at 1456. But none of petitioners' declarations supports that connection. . . . Thus, aside from a single conclusory statement, there is nothing in petitioners' 43 standing declarations and accompanying exhibits to support an inference of actual loss of Massachusetts coastal land from 20th-century global sea level increases. It is pure conjecture.

The Court's attempts to identify "imminent" or "certainly impending" loss of Massachusetts coastal land fares no better. . . . "Allegations of possible future injury do not satisfy the requirements of Art. III. A threatened injury must be *certainly impending* to constitute injury in fact." Whitmore, supra, at 158, 110 S. Ct. 1717 (internal quotation marks omitted; emphasis added).

III

Petitioners' reliance on Massachusetts's loss of coastal land as their injury in fact for standing purposes creates insurmountable problems for them with respect to causation and redressability. . . .

Petitioners view the relationship between their injuries and EPA's failure to promulgate new motor vehicle greenhouse gas emission standards as simple and direct: Domestic motor vehicles emit carbon dioxide and other greenhouse gases. Worldwide emissions of greenhouse gases contribute to global warming and therefore also to petitioners' alleged injuries. Without the new vehicle standards, greenhouse gas emissions — and therefore global warming and its attendant harms — have been higher than they otherwise would have been; once EPA changes course, the trend will be reversed.

The Court ignores the complexities of global warming, and does so by now disregarding the "particularized" injury it relied on in step one, and using the dire nature of global warming itself as a bootstrap for finding causation and redressability. First, it is important to recognize the extent of the emissions at issue here. . . . According to one of petitioners' declarations, domestic motor vehicles contribute about 6 percent of global carbon dioxide emissions and 4 percent of global greenhouse gas emissions. Stdg.App. 232. The amount of global emissions at issue here is smaller still; §202(a)(1) of the Clean Air Act covers only *new* motor vehicles and *new* motor vehicle engines, so petitioners' desired emission standards might reduce only a fraction of 4 percent of global emissions.

This gets us only to the relevant greenhouse gas emissions; linking them to global warming and ultimately to petitioners' alleged injuries next requires consideration of further complexities.

. . . .

Petitioners are never able to trace their alleged injuries back through this complex web to the fractional amount of global emissions that might have been limited with EPA standards. In light of the bit-part domestic new motor vehicle greenhouse gas emissions have played in what petitioners describe as a 150-year global phenomenon, and the myriad additional factors bearing on petitioners' alleged injury — the loss of Massachusetts coastal land — the connection is far too speculative to establish causation.

IV

Redressability is even more problematic. To the tenuous link between petitioners' alleged injury and the indeterminate fractional domestic emissions at issue here, add the fact that petitioners cannot meaningfully predict what will come of the 80 percent of global greenhouse gas emissions that originate outside the United States . . . .

. . . .

No matter, the Court reasons, because *any* decrease in domestic emissions will "slow the pace of global emissions increases, no matter what happens elsewhere." *Ante,* at 1458. Every little bit helps, so Massachusetts can sue over any little bit.

The Court's sleight of hand is in failing to link up the different elements of the three-part standing test. What must be *likely* to be redressed is the particular injury in fact. The injury the Court looks to is the asserted loss of land. The Court contends that regulating domestic motor vehicle emissions will reduce carbon dioxide in the atmosphere, *and therefore* redress Massachusetts's injury. But even if regulation *does* reduce emissions—to some indeterminate degree, given events elsewhere in the world—the Court never explains why that makes it *likely* that the injury in fact—the loss of land—will be redressed. Schoolchildren know that a kingdom might be lost "all for the want of a horseshoe nail," but "likely" redressability is a different matter. The realities make it pure conjecture to suppose that EPA regulation of new automobile emissions will *likely* prevent the loss of Massachusetts coastal land.

V

Petitioners' difficulty in demonstrating causation and redressability is not surprising given the evident mismatch between the source of their alleged injury—catastrophic global warming—and the narrow subject matter of the Clean Air Act provision at issue in this suit. The mismatch suggests that petitioners' true goal for this litigation may be more symbolic than anything else. The constitutional role of the courts, however, is to decide concrete cases—not to serve as a convenient forum for policy debates. . . .

When dealing with legal doctrine phrased in terms of what is "fairly" traceable or "likely" to be redressed, it is perhaps not surprising that the matter is subject to some debate. But in considering how loosely or rigorously to define those adverbs, it is vital to keep in mind the purpose of the inquiry. The limitation of the judicial power to cases and controversies "is crucial in maintaining the tripartite allocation of power set forth in the Constitution." DaimlerChrysler, 547 U.S., at 341, 126 S. Ct., at 1860-1861 (internal quotation marks omitted). In my view, the Court today—addressing Article III's "core component of standing," Defenders of Wildlife, supra, at 560, 112 S. Ct. 2130, fails to take this limitation seriously.

. . . .

Perhaps the Court recognizes as much. How else to explain its need to devise a new doctrine of state standing to support its result? The good news is that the Court's "special solicitude" for Massachusetts limits the future applicability of the diluted standing requirements applied in this case. The bad news is that the Court's self-professed relaxation of those Article III requirements has caused us to transgress "the proper — and properly limited — role of the courts in a democratic society." Allen, 468 U.S., at 750, 104 S. Ct. 3315 (internal quotation marks omitted).

I respectfully dissent.

JUSTICE SCALIA, with whom THE CHIEF JUSTICE, JUSTICE THOMAS, and JUSTICE ALITO join, dissenting.

I join THE CHIEF JUSTICE's opinion in full, and would hold that this Court has no jurisdiction to decide this case because petitioners lack standing. The Court having decided otherwise, it is appropriate for me to note my dissent on the merits.

I

A

The provision of law at the heart of this case is §202(a)(1) of the Clean Air Act (CAA or Act), which provides that the Administrator of the Environmental Protection Agency (EPA) "shall by regulation prescribe . . . standards applicable to the emission of any air pollutant from any class or classes of new motor vehicles or new motor vehicle engines, which *in his judgment* cause, or contribute to, air pollution which may reasonably be anticipated to endanger public health or welfare." 42 U.S.C. §7521(a)(1) (emphasis added). . . . There is no dispute that the Administrator has made no such judgment in this case. . . .

The question thus arises: Does anything *require* the Administrator to make a "judgment" whenever a petition for rulemaking is filed? Without citation of the statute or any other authority, the Court says yes. Why is that so? . . . Where does the CAA say that the EPA Administrator is required to come to a decision on this question whenever a rulemaking petition is filed? The Court points to no such provision because none exists.

Instead, the Court invents a multiple-choice question that the EPA Administrator must answer when a petition for rulemaking is filed. The Administrator must exercise his judgment in one of three ways: (a) by concluding that the pollutant *does* cause, or contribute to, air pollution that endangers public welfare (in which case EPA is required to regulate); (b) by concluding that the pollutant *does not* cause, or contribute to, air pollution that endangers public welfare (in which case EPA is *not* required to regulate); or (c) by "provid[ing] some reasonable explanation as to why it cannot or will not exercise its discretion to determine whether" greenhouse gases endanger public welfare, *ante,* at 1462, (in which case EPA is *not* required to regulate).

I am willing to assume, for the sake of argument, that the Administrator's discretion in this regard is not entirely unbounded — that if he has no reasonable basis for deferring judgment he must grasp the nettle at once. The Court, however, with no basis in text or precedent, rejects all of EPA's stated "policy judgments" as not "amount[ing] to a reasoned justification," *ante,* at 1463, effectively narrowing the universe of potential reasonable bases to a single one: Judgment can be delayed *only* if the Administrator concludes that "the scientific uncertainty is [too] profound." *Ibid.* The Administrator is precluded from concluding *for other reasons* "that it would . . . be better not to regulate at this time." *Ibid.* Such other reasons — perfectly valid reasons — were set forth in the Agency's statement.

. . . .

EPA's interpretation of the discretion conferred by the statutory reference to "its judgment" is not only reasonable, it is the most natural reading of the text. The Court nowhere explains why this interpretation is incorrect, let alone why it is not entitled to deference under Chevron U.S.A. Inc. v. Natural Resources Defense Council, Inc., 467 U.S. 837, 104 S. Ct. 2778, 81 L.Ed.2d 694 (1984). As the Administrator acted within the law in declining to make a "judgment" for the policy reasons above set forth, I would uphold the decision to deny the rulemaking petition on that ground alone.

B

Even on the Court's own terms, however, the same conclusion follows. As mentioned above, the Court gives EPA the option of determining that the science is too uncertain to allow it to form a "judgment" as to whether greenhouse gases endanger public welfare. . . . EPA *has* said precisely that — and at great length, based on information contained in a 2001 report by the National Research Council (NRC) entitled Climate Change Science: An Analysis of Some Key Questions. . . .

I simply cannot conceive of what else the Court would like EPA to say.

II

A

Even before reaching its discussion of the word "judgment," the Court makes another significant error when it concludes that "§202(a)(1) of the Clean Air Act *authorizes* EPA to regulate greenhouse gas emissions from new motor vehicles in the event that it forms a 'judgment' that such emissions contribute to climate change." *Ante,* at 1459 (emphasis added). For such authorization, the Court relies on what it calls "the Clean Air Act's capacious definition of 'air pollutant.'" *Ante,* at 1460.

. . . The Court is correct that "[c]arbon dioxide, methane, nitrous oxide, and hydrofluorocarbons," *ante,* at 1462, fit within the second half of that definition: They are "physical, chemical, . . . substance[s] or matter which [are] emitted into or otherwise ente[r] the ambient air." But the Court mistakenly believes this to be the end of the analysis. In order to be an "air pollutant" under the Act's definition, the "substance or matter [being] emitted into . . . the ambient air" must also meet the *first* half of the definition — namely, it must be an "air pollution agent or combination of such agents." The Court simply pretends this half of the definition does not exist.

The Court's analysis faithfully follows the argument advanced by petitioners, which focuses on the word "including" in the statutory definition of "air pollutant." See Brief for Petitioners 13-14. As that argument goes, anything that *follows* the word "including" must necessarily be a subset of whatever *precedes* it. Thus, if greenhouse gases qualify under the phrase following the word "including," they must qualify under the phrase preceding it. Since greenhouse gases come within the capacious phrase "any physical, chemical, . . . substance or matter which is emitted into or otherwise enters the ambient air," they must also be "air pollution agent[s] or combination[s] of such agents," and therefore meet the definition of "air pollutant[s]."

That is certainly one possible interpretation of the statutory definition. The word "including" can indeed indicate that what follows will be an "illustrative" sampling of the general category that precedes the word. Federal Land Bank of St. Paul v. Bismarck Lumber Co., 314 U.S. 95, 100, 62 S. Ct. 1, 86 L.Ed. 65 1941). Often, however, the examples standing alone are broader than the general category, and must be viewed as limited in light of that category. . . .

In short, the word "including" does not require the Court's (or the petitioners') result. It is perfectly reasonable to view the definition of "air pollutant" in its entirety. . . . This is precisely the conclusion EPA reached. . . . Once again, in the face of textual ambiguity, the Court's application of Chevron deference to EPA's interpretation of the word "including" is nowhere to be found. Evidently, the Court defers only to those reasonable interpretations that it favors.

. . . .

In the end, EPA concluded that since "CAA authorization to regulate is generally based on a finding that an air pollutant causes or contributes to air pollution," 68 Fed. Reg. 52928, the concentrations of CO_2 and other greenhouse gases allegedly affecting the global climate are beyond the scope of CAA's authorization to regulate. "[T]he term 'air pollution' as used in the regulatory provisions cannot be interpreted to encompass global climate change." *Ibid.* Once again, the Court utterly fails to explain why this interpretation is incorrect, let alone so unreasonable as to be unworthy of Chevron deference.

* * *

The Court's alarm over global warming may or may not be justified, but it ought not distort the outcome of this litigation. This is a straightforward administrative-law case, in which Congress has passed a malleable statute giving broad discretion, not to us but to an executive agency. No matter how important the underlying policy issues at stake, this Court has no business substituting its own desired outcome for the reasoned judgment of the responsible agency.

NOTES AND QUESTIONS

1. What are the key arguments that the majority and dissenting opinions make on standing and the substantive law? Which arguments do you find most persuasive and least persuasive?
2. What is the EPA required to do after *Massachusetts v. EPA*? Is there a scenario in which the EPA could have continued not to engage in greenhouse gas regulation after this opinion?
3. Why does the Supreme Court focus on the special nature of states in its standing analysis? Does the Court's reasoning on this issue make it more or less likely that private parties could have standing in climate change cases?

4. Consider the following interchange during the oral argument of *Massachusetts v. EPA*:

> Justice Scalia: But I always thought an air pollutant was something different from a stratospheric pollutant, and your claim here is not that the pollution of what we normally call "air" is endangering health. . . . [Y]our assertion is that after the pollution leaves the air and goes up into the stratosphere it is contributing to global warming.
>
> Mr. Milkey: Respectfully, Your Honor, it is not the stratosphere. It's the troposphere.
>
> Justice Scalia: Troposphere, whatever. I told you before I'm not a scientist. (Laughter.)
>
> Justice Scalia: That's why I don't want to deal with global warming, to tell you the truth.
>
> Transcript of Oral Argument at 22–23, *Massachusetts v. EPA*, 127 S. Ct. 1438 (2007) (No. 05-1120), 2006 WL 3431932 at 22–23.

Although Justice Scalia was likely being humorous, his remarks raise questions about how courts should engage complex climate change science. What do you think is the most appropriate way for judges to approach the scientific issues that these cases raise?

Professor Holly Doremus has raised broader concerns over the scientizing of politics, that is, both sides using science as an argumentative device. She notes that, "The combination of actual uncertainty and public expectations of certainty makes the rhetoric of science equally available to the regulatory offense and defense." *See* Holly Doremus, *Science Plays Defense: Natural Resource Management in the Bush Administration*, 32 Ecology L.Q. 249, 255 (2005). How did these issues play out in *Massachusetts v. EPA*?

5. How do debates over the appropriate roles of different levels of government in climate change regulation play out in this case? Professor Hari Osofsky has explored this question in some depth, arguing that those wanting less regulation claimed that climate change was too big for regulatory action at state and national levels, and that those wanting more regulation argued for the smaller-scale nature of emissions and impacts. *See* Hari M. Osofsky, *The Intersection of Scale, Science, and Law in* Massachusetts v. EPA, 9 Or. R. Int'l L. 233 (2007). Professor Alice Kaswan has argued that these suits play an important role in addressing jurisdictional overlap. Alice Kaswan, *The Domestic Approach to Global Climate Change: What Role for Federal, State, and Litigation Initiatives?*, 42 U.S.F. L. Rev. 39, 79–80 (2008). What role do you think the federal and state governments should play in addressing problems like climate change that also have international dimensions, and when it is appropriate for courts to help resolve these conflicts over regulatory scale?

2. ENDANGERMENT FINDING AND SUBSEQUENT REGULATION

Although the Bush administration did not take significant action in the aftermath of *Massachusetts v. EPA*, the Obama administration began implementing the decision upon taking office. The first step in the implementation was to decide whether or not greenhouse gas emissions cause or contribute to the endangerment of public health and welfare. In order for the EPA to issue regulations limiting the emissions of greenhouse gases under the Clean Air Act, it had to make such an endangerment finding. Over the course of 2009, the EPA issued a draft and then final finding under Clean Air Act Section 202(a), a decision that provides the basis for further regulatory action.

The following is an excerpt from that finding. It contains two primary parts: a general finding that greenhouse gases endanger health and public welfare and a more specific finding that the greenhouse gas emissions covered by Clean Air Act Section 202(a) cause or contribute to that endangerment.

ENDANGERMENT AND CAUSE OR CONTRIBUTE FINDINGS FOR GREENHOUSE GASES UNDER SECTION 202(A) OF THE CLEAN AIR ACT; FINAL RULE, 74 FED. REG. 66,494, 66,516, 66,523–24, 66,536–37 (DEC. 15, 2009) (TO BE CODIFIED AT 40 C.F.R. CH. 1)

http://www.epa.gov/climatechange/endangerment/downloads/
Federal_Register-EPA-HQ-OAR-2009-0171-Dec.15-09.pdf

IV. Greenhouse Gases Endanger Public Health and Welfare

The Administrator finds that elevated concentrations of greenhouse gases in the atmosphere may reasonably be anticipated to endanger the public health and to endanger the public welfare of current and future generations. The Administrator is making this finding specifically with regard to six key directly-emitted, long-lived and well-mixed greenhouse gases: Carbon dioxide, methane, nitrous oxide, hydrofluorocarbons, perfluorocarbons, and sulfur hexafluoride. The Administrator is making this judgment based on both current observations and projected risks and impacts into the future. Furthermore, the Administrator is basing this finding on impacts of climate change within the United States. However, the Administrator finds that when she considers the impacts on the U.S. population of risks and impacts occurring in other world regions, the case for endangerment to public health and welfare is only strengthened.

. . . .

B. The Air Pollution Is Reasonably Anticipated to Endanger Both Public Health and Welfare

The Administrator finds that the elevated atmospheric concentrations of the well-mixed greenhouse gases may reasonably be anticipated to endanger the public health and welfare of current and future generations. This section describes the major pieces of scientific evidence supporting the Administrator's endangerment finding, discusses both the public health and welfare nature of the endangerment finding, and addresses a number of key issues the Administrator considered when evaluating the state of the science as well as key public comments on the Proposed Findings. . . .

As described in Section II of these Findings, the endangerment test under CAA section 202(a) does not require the Administrator to identify a bright line, quantitative threshold above which a positive endangerment finding can be made. The statutory language explicitly calls upon the Administrator to use her judgment. This section describes the general approach used by the Administrator in reaching the judgment that a positive endangerment finding should be made, as well as the specific rationale for finding that the greenhouse gas air pollution may reasonably be anticipated to endanger both public health and welfare. First, the Administrator finds the scientific evidence linking human emissions and resulting elevated atmospheric concentrations of the six well-mixed greenhouse gases to observed global and regional temperature increases and other climate changes to be sufficiently robust and compelling. This evidence is briefly explained in more detail in Section V of these Findings. The Administrator recognizes that the climate change associated with elevated atmospheric concentrations of carbon dioxide and the other well-mixed greenhouse gases have the potential to affect essentially every aspect of human health, society and the natural environment. The Administrator is therefore not limiting her consideration of potential risks and impacts associated with human emissions of greenhouse gases to any one particular element of human health, sector of the economy, region of the country, or to any one particular aspect of the natural environment. Rather, the Administrator is basing her finding on the total weight of scientific evidence, and what the science has to say regarding the nature and potential magnitude of the risks and impacts across all climate-sensitive elements of public health and welfare, now and projected out into the foreseeable future. The Administrator has considered the state of the science on how human emissions and the resulting elevated atmospheric concentrations of well-mixed greenhouse gases may affect each of the major risk categories, *i.e.,* those that are described in the TSD [Technical Support Document], which include human health, air quality, food production and agriculture, forestry, water resources, sea level rise and coastal areas, the energy sector, infrastructure and settlements, and ecosystems and wildlife. The Administrator understands that the nature and potential severity of impacts can vary across these different elements of public health and welfare, and that they can vary by region, as well as over time.

The Administrator is therefore aware that, because human-induced climate change has the potential to be far-reaching and multi-dimensional, not all risks and potential impacts can be characterized with a uniform level of quantification or understanding, nor can they be characterized with uniform metrics. Given this variety in not only the nature and potential magnitude of risks and impacts, but also in our ability to characterize, quantify and project into the future such impacts, the Administrator must use her judgment to weigh the threat in each of the risk categories, weigh the potential benefits where relevant, and ultimately judge whether these risks and benefits, when viewed in total, are judged to be endangerment to public health and/or welfare.

This has a number of implications for the Administrator's approach in assessing the nature and magnitude of risk and impacts across each of the risk categories. First, the Administrator has not established a specific threshold metric for each category of risk and impacts. Also, the Administrator is not necessarily placing the greatest weight on those risks and impacts which have been the subject of the most study or quantification.

Part of the variation in risks and impacts is the fact that climbing atmospheric concentrations of greenhouse gases and associated temperature increases can bring about some potential benefits to public health and welfare in addition to adverse risks. The current understanding of any potential benefits associated with human-induced climate change is described in the TSD and is taken into consideration here. The potential for both adverse and beneficial effects are considered, as well as the relative magnitude of such effects, to the extent that the relative magnitudes can be quantified or characterized. Furthermore, given the multiple ways in which the buildup of atmospheric greenhouse gases can cause effects (*e.g.,* via elevated carbon dioxide concentrations, via temperature increases, via precipitation increases, via sea level rise, and via changes in extreme events), these multiple pathways are considered. For example, elevated carbon dioxide concentrations may be beneficial to crop yields, but changes in temperature and precipitation may be adverse and must also be considered. Likewise, modest temperature increases may have some public health benefits as well as harms, and other pathways such as changes in air quality and extreme events must also be considered.

The Administrator has balanced and weighed the varying risks and effects for each sector. She has judged whether there is a pattern across the sector that supports or does not support an endangerment finding, and if so whether the support is of more or less weight. In cases where there is both a potential for benefits and risks of harm, the Administrator has balanced these factors by determining whether there appears to be any directional trend in the overall evidence that would support placing more weight on one than the other, taking into consideration all that is known about the likelihood of the various risks and effects and their seriousness. In all of these cases, the judgment is largely qualitative in nature, and is not reducible to precise metrics or quantification. Regarding the timeframe for the endangerment test, it is the Administrator's view that both current and future conditions must be considered. The Administrator is thus taking the view that the endangerment period of analysis extend from the current time to the next several decades, and in some cases to the end of this century. This consideration is also consistent with the timeframes used in the underlying scientific assessments. The future timeframe under consideration is consistent with the atmospheric lifetime and climate effects of the six well-mixed greenhouse gases, and also with our ability to make reasonable and plausible projections of future conditions.

The Administrator acknowledges that some aspects of climate change science and the projected impacts are more certain than others. Our state of knowledge is strongest for recently observed, large-scale changes. Uncertainty tends to increase in characterizing changes at smaller (regional) scales relative to large (global) scales. Uncertainty also increases as the temporal scales move away from present, either backward, but more importantly forward in time. Nonetheless, the current state of knowledge of observed and past climate changes and their causes enables projections of plausible future changes under different scenarios of anthropogenic forcing for a range of spatial and temporal scales. In some cases, where the level of sensitivity to climate of a particular sector has been extensively studied, future impacts can be quantified whereas in other instances only a qualitative description of a directional change, if that, may be possible. The inherent uncertainty in the direction, magnitude, and/or rate of certain future climate change impacts opens up the possibility that some changes could be more or less severe than expected, and the possibility of unanticipated outcomes. In some cases, low probability, high impact outcomes (*i.e.*, known unknowns) are possibilities but cannot be explicitly assessed.

. . . .

V. The Administrator's Finding That Emissions of Greenhouse Gases from CAA Section 202(a) Sources Cause or Contribute to the Endangerment of Public Health and Welfare

As discussed in Section IV.A of these Findings, the Administrator is defining the air pollution for purposes of the endangerment finding to be the elevated concentration of well-mixed greenhouse gases in the atmosphere. The second step of the two-part endangerment test is for the Administrator to determine whether the emission of any air pollutant emitted from new motor vehicles cause or contribute to this air pollution. This is referred to as the cause or contribute finding, and is the second finding by the Administrator in this action.

. . . .

B. The Administrator's Finding Regarding Whether Emissions of the Air Pollutant from Section 202(a) Source Categories Cause or Contribute to the Air Pollution That May Be Reasonably Anticipated to Endanger Public Health and Welfare

The Administrator finds that emissions of the well-mixed greenhouse gases from new motor vehicles contribute to the air pollution that may reasonably be anticipated to endanger public health and welfare. This contribution finding is for all of the CAA section 202(a) source categories and the Administrator considered emissions from all of these source categories. The relevant mobile sources under CAA section 202(a)(1) are "any class or classes of new motor vehicles or new motor vehicle engines, * * *." CAA section 202(a)(1) (emphasis added). The new motor vehicles and new motor vehicle engines (hereinafter "CAA section 202(a) source categories") addressed are: Passenger cars, light-duty trucks, motorcycles, buses, and medium and heavy-duty trucks. . . .

The Administrator reached her decision after reviewing emissions data on the contribution of CAA section 202(a) source categories relative to both global greenhouse gas emissions and U.S. greenhouse gas emissions. Given that CAA section 202(a) source categories are responsible for about 4 percent of total global greenhouse gas emissions, and for just over 23 percent of total U.S. greenhouse gas emissions, the Administrator finds that both of these comparisons, independently and together, support a finding that CAA section 202(a) source categories contribute to the air pollution that may be reasonably anticipated to endanger public health and welfare. The Administrator is not placing primary weight on either approach; rather she finds that both approaches clearly establish that emissions of the well-mixed greenhouse gases from section 202(a) source categories contribute to air pollution with may reasonably be anticipated to endanger public health and welfare. As the Supreme Court noted, "[j]udged by any standard, U.S. motor-vehicle emissions make a meaningful contribution to greenhouse gas concentrations and hence, * * * to global warming." *Massachusetts v. EPA,* 549 U.S. at 525–38.

———————

The EPA used its endangerment finding as the basis for rulemaking that regulates motor vehicle greenhouse gas emissions. It began in 2010 by promulgating—jointly with the National Highway Traffic Safety Administration (NHTSA)—the "National Program," which for the first time intertwined fuel efficiency and vehicle tailpipe emissions for 2012–2016 model year cars and light trucks. Before this new program, regulation regarding fuel efficiency and vehicle tailpipe emissions took place separately. The EPA and NHSTA are also establishing rules for model years 2017–2025. In addition, the EPA and NHTSA adopted a Heavy-Duty National Program in 2011, which regulates greenhouse gas emissions and establishes fuel efficiency standards for medium- and heavy-duty vehicles.

The National Program has significance beyond its groundbreaking regulation of motor vehicle greenhouse gas emissions and collaboration between EPA and NHTSA. It also represents an important moment of compromise among the federal government, the State of California, and automakers. The Clean Air Act allows California to set its own tailpipe emissions standards that exceed federal standards if it receives a waiver to do so. States then choose between following the federal and California standards. After a Bush administration denial of California's petition for a waiver to regulate tailpipe greenhouse gas emissions, which resulted in lawsuits, the Obama administration granted that waiver. However, the National Program creates a convergence between the higher California standards allowed by the waiver and federal standards, a uniformity which automakers prefer. In January 2010, the EPA, Department of Transportation, and the State of California continued their collaboration on cars and light trucks by announcing a unified timeframe for proposing greenhouse gas emissions and fuel economy standards for 2017–2025. The EPA and NHSTA provided notice of proposed rulemaking regarding those standards in November 2011.

The following is an excerpt from the joint rulemaking establishing the initial National Program. It provides an overview of the program and a description of the core elements of the rule.

Light-Duty Vehicle Greenhouse Gas Emission Standards and Corporate Average Fuel Economy Standards; Final Rule, 75 Fed. Reg. 25,323, 25,326–29 (May 7, 2010) (to be codified at 40 C.F.R. pts. 85, 86, and 600; 40 C.F.R. pts. 531, 533, 536, 537, and 538)

http://www.gpo.gov/fdsys/pkg/FR-2010-05-07/pdf/2010-8159.pdf

I. Overview of Joint EPA/NHTSA National Program

A. Introduction

The National Highway Traffic Safety Administration (NHTSA) and the Environmental Protection Agency (EPA) are each announcing final rules whose benefits will address the urgent and closely intertwined challenges of energy independence and security and global warming.

These rules will implement a strong and coordinated Federal greenhouse gas (GHG) and fuel economy program for passenger cars, light-duty-trucks, and medium-duty passenger vehicles (hereafter light-duty vehicles), referred to as the National Program. The rules will achieve substantial reductions of GHG emissions and improvements in fuel economy from the light-duty vehicle part of the transportation sector, based on technology that is already being commercially applied in most cases and that can be incorporated at a reasonable cost. NHTSA's final rule also constitutes the agency's Record of Decision for purposes of its NEPA analysis.

This joint rulemaking is consistent with the President's announcement on May 19, 2009 of a National Fuel Efficiency Policy of establishing consistent, harmonized, and streamlined requirements that would reduce GHG emissions and improve fuel economy for all new cars and light-duty trucks sold in the United States. The National Program will deliver additional environmental and energy benefits, cost savings, and administrative efficiencies on a nationwide basis that would likely not be available under a less coordinated approach. The National Program also represents regulatory convergence by making it possible for the standards of two different Federal agencies and the standards of California and other states to act in a unified fashion in providing these benefits. The National Program will allow automakers to produce and sell a single fleet nationally, mitigating the additional costs that manufacturers would otherwise face in having to comply with multiple sets of Federal and State standards. This joint notice is also consistent with the Notice of Upcoming Joint Rulemaking issued by DOT and EPA on May 19, 2009 and responds to the President's January 26, 2009 memorandum on CAFE standards for model years 2011 and beyond, the details of which can be found in Section IV of this joint notice.

Climate change is widely viewed as a significant long-term threat to the global environment. As summarized in the Technical Support Document for EPA's Endangerment and Cause or Contribute Findings under Section 202(a) of the Clear Air Act, anthropogenic emissions of GHGs are very likely (90 to 99 percent probability) the cause of most of the observed global warming over the last 50 years. The primary GHGs of concern are carbon dioxide (CO_2), methane, nitrous oxide, hydrofluorocarbons, perfluorocarbons, and sulfur hexafluoride. Mobile sources emitted 31 percent of all U.S. GHGs in 2007 (transportation sources, which do not include certain off-highway sources, account for 28 percent) and have been the fastest-growing source of U.S. GHGs since 1990. Mobile sources addressed in the recent endangerment and contribution findings under CAA section 202(a) — light-duty vehicles, heavy-duty trucks, buses, and motorcycles — accounted for 23 percent of all U.S. GHG in 2007. Light-duty vehicles emit CO_2, methane, nitrous oxide, and hydrofluorocarbons and are responsible for nearly 60 percent of all mobile source GHGs and over 70 percent of Section 202(a) mobile source GHGs. For light-duty vehicles in 2007, CO_2 emissions represent about 94 percent of all greenhouse emissions (including HFCs), and the CO_2 emissions measured over the EPA tests used for fuel economy compliance represent about 90 percent of total light-duty vehicle GHG emissions.

Improving energy security by reducing our dependence on foreign oil has been a national objective since the first oil price shocks in the 1970s. Net petroleum imports now account for approximately 60 percent of U.S. petroleum consumption. World crude oil production is highly concentrated, exacerbating the risks of supply disruptions and price shocks. Tight global oil markets led to prices over $100 per barrel in 2008, with gasoline reaching as high as $4 per gallon in many parts of the U.S., causing financial hardship for many families. The export of U.S. assets for oil imports continues to be an important component of the historically unprecedented U.S. trade deficits. Transportation accounts for about two-thirds of U.S. petroleum consumption. Light-duty vehicles account for about 60 percent of transportation oil use, which means that they alone account for about 40 percent of all U.S. oil consumption.

1. Building Blocks of the National Program

The National Program is both needed and possible because the relationship between improving fuel economy and reducing CO_2 tailpipe emissions is a very direct and close one. The amount of those CO_2 emissions is essentially constant per gallon combusted of a given type of fuel. Thus, the more fuel efficient a vehicle is, the less fuel it burns to travel a given distance. The less fuel it burns, the less CO_2 it emits in traveling that distance. While there are emission control technologies that reduce the pollutants (e.g., carbon monoxide) produced by imperfect combustion of fuel by capturing or converting them to other compounds, there is no such technology for CO_2. Further, while some of those pollutants can also be reduced by achieving a more complete combustion of fuel, doing so only increases the tailpipe emissions of CO_2. Thus, there is a single pool of technologies for addressing these twin problems, i.e., those that reduce fuel consumption and thereby reduce CO_2 emissions as well.

. . . .

B. Summary of the Joint Final Rule and Differences from the Proposal

In this joint rulemaking, EPA is establishing GHG emissions standards under the Clean Air Act (CAA), and NHTSA is establishing Corporate Average Fuel Economy (CAFE) standards under the Energy Policy and Conservation Action of 1975 (EPCA), as amended by the Energy Independence and Security Act of 2007 (EISA). The intention of this joint rulemaking is to set forth a carefully coordinated and harmonized approach to implementing these two statutes, in accordance with all substantive and procedural requirements imposed by law.

NHTSA and EPA have coordinated closely and worked jointly in developing their respective final rules. This is reflected in many aspects of this joint rule. For example, the agencies have developed a comprehensive Joint Technical Support Document (TSD) that provides a solid technical underpinning for each agency's modeling and analysis used to support their standards. Also, to the extent allowed by law, the agencies have harmonized many elements of program design, such as the form of the standard (the footprint-based attribute curves), and the definitions used for cars and trucks. They have developed the same or similar compliance flexibilities, to the extent allowed and appropriate under their respective statutes, such as averaging, banking, and trading of credits, and have harmonized the compliance testing and test protocols used for purposes of the fleet average standards each agency is finalizing. Finally, under their respective statutes, each agency is called upon to exercise its judgment and determine standards that are an appropriate balance of various relevant statutory factors. Given the common technical issues before each agency, the similarity of the factors each agency is to consider and balance, and the authority of each agency to take into consideration the standards of the other agency, both EPA and NHTSA are establishing standards that result in a harmonized National Program.

This joint final rule covers passenger cars, light-duty trucks, and medium-duty passenger vehicles built in model years 2012 through 2016. These vehicle categories are responsible for almost 60 percent of all U.S. transportation-related GHG emissions. EPA and NHTSA expect that automobile manufacturers will meet these standards by utilizing technologies that will reduce vehicle GHG emissions and improve fuel economy. Although many of these technologies are available today, the emissions reductions and fuel economy improvements finalized in this notice will involve more widespread use of these technologies across the light-duty vehicle fleet. These include improvements to engines, transmissions, and tires, increased use of start-stop technology, improvements in air conditioning systems, increased use of hybrid and other advanced technologies, and the initial commercialization of electric vehicles and plug-in hybrids. NHTSA's and EPA's assessments of likely vehicle technologies that manufacturers will employ to meet the standards are discussed in detail below and in the Joint TSD.

The National Program is estimated to result in approximately 960 million metric tons of total carbon dioxide equivalent emissions reductions and approximately 1.8 billion barrels of oil savings over the lifetime of vehicles sold in model years (MYs) 2012 through 2016. In total, the combined EPA and NHTSA 2012-2016 standards will reduce GHG emissions from the U.S. light-duty fleet by approximately 21 percent by 2030 over the level that would occur in the absence of the National Program. These actions also will provide important energy security benefits, as light-duty vehicles are about 95 percent dependent on oil-based fuels. The agencies project that the total benefits of the National Program will be more than $240 billion at a 3% discount rate, or more than $190 billion at a 7% discount rate. In the discussion that follows in Sections III and IV, each agency explains the related benefits for their individual standards.

Together, EPA and NHTSA estimate that the average cost increase for a model year 2016 vehicle due to the National Program will be less than $1,000. The average U.S. consumer who purchases a vehicle outright is estimated to save enough in lower fuel costs over the first three years to offset these higher vehicle costs. However, most U.S. consumers purchase a new vehicle using credit rather than paying cash and the typical car loan today is a five year, 60 month loan. These consumers will see immediate savings due to their vehicle's lower fuel consumption in the form of a net reduction in annual costs of $130-$180 throughout the duration of the loan (that is, the fuel savings will outweigh the increase in loan payments by $130-$180 per year). Whether a consumer takes out a loan or purchases a new vehicle outright, over the lifetime of a model year 2016 vehicle, the consumer's net savings could be more than $3,000. The average 2016 MY vehicle will emit 16 fewer metric tons of CO_2-equivalent emissions (that is, CO_2 emissions plus HFC air conditioning leakage emissions) during its lifetime. Assumptions that underlie these conclusions are discussed in greater detail in the agencies' respective regulatory impact analyses and in Section III.H.5 and Section IV.

This joint rule also results in important regulatory convergence and certainty to automobile companies. Absent this rule, there would be three separate Federal and State regimes independently regulating light-duty vehicles to reduce fuel consumption and GHG emissions: NHTSA's CAFE standards, EPA's GHG standards, and the GHG standards applicable in California and other States adopting the California standards. This joint rule will allow automakers to meet both the NHTSA and EPA requirements with a single national fleet, greatly simplifying the industry's technology, investment and compliance strategies. In addition, to promote the National Program, California announced its commitment to take several actions, including revising its program for MYs 2012-2016 such that compliance with the Federal GHG standards will be deemed to be compliance with California's GHG standards. This will allow the single national fleet used by automakers to meet the two Federal requirements and to meet California requirements as well. California is proceeding with a rulemaking intended to revise its 2004 regulations to meet its commitments. EPA and NHTSA are confident that these GHG and CAFE standards will successfully harmonize both the Federal and State programs for MYs 2012-2016 and will allow our country to achieve the increased benefits of a single, nationwide program to reduce light-duty vehicle GHG emissions and reduce the country's dependence on fossil fuels by improving these vehicles' fuel economy.

A successful and sustainable automotive industry depends upon, among other things, continuous technology innovation in general, and low GHG emissions and high fuel economy vehicles in particular. In this respect, this action will help spark the investment in technology innovation necessary for automakers to successfully compete in both domestic and export markets, and thereby continue to support a strong economy.

While this action covers MYs 2012-2016, many stakeholders encouraged EPA and NHTSA to also begin working toward standards for MY 2017 and beyond that would maintain a single nationwide program. The agencies recognize the importance of and are committed to a strong, coordinated national program for light-duty vehicles for model years beyond 2016.

NOTES AND QUESTIONS

1. Why was it important for the EPA to find not only that greenhouse gases endanger public health and welfare, but also that the specific emissions regulated in the Clean Air Act's Section 202(a) do so? On what basis does

the EPA make both findings? What are the strengths and weaknesses of its analysis?

2. How did the endangerment finding provide the basis for the motor vehicles regulations that followed? To what extent is the finding framed in a way that it might have implications beyond motor vehicles?

3. What are the advantages and disadvantages of the EPA and NHSTA jointly regulating? Why do you think that such joint regulation has not taken place in the past?

4. What are the benefits and limitations of the State of California being able to petition for a waiver from federal standards, and states being able to choose between those standards? What might have motivated the federal government and California to work to harmonize their standards in the coming years? Why might the federal government have decided to include the automobile industry in those negotiations?

3. EXTENSION TO STATIONARY SOURCES AND JUDICIAL AND LEGISLATIVE CHALLENGES

In May 2010, the EPA took the first major step in extending its greenhouse gas regulatory efforts to stationary sources such as power plants, refineries, and other major industrial emitters. It issued a final rule establishing the threshold greenhouse gas permit requirements for new and existing facilities under the New Source Review Prevention of Significant Deterioration (PSD) and Title V.

These two permitting programs cover air pollution arising from stationary sources (as opposed to motor vehicles). They provide permits when constructing new facilities, modifying existing facilities, and operating these facilities will lead to emissions of substances defined as pollutants under the Clean Air Act. The PSD permitting process was created in 1977 through Clean Air Act amendments, and requires review of new facilities or facility modifications that would significantly increase a pollutant regulated under the Act. Title V focuses on pollution arising from operations. These permits provide limits on the types and quantities of emissions and requirements regarding pollution control devices, pollution prevention activities, and monitoring.

The May 2010 rule addresses concerns over which emitters will have obligations under the initial greenhouse gas regulations of stationary sources. It tailors the permitting programs so that they only cover the most significant greenhouse gas facilities (which produce 70 percent of greenhouse gas emissions from stationary sources) in order to avoid overburdening state regulators or smaller emitters. In December 2010, the EPA promulgated additional rules that further refine these requirements and address the varying regulatory conditions in different states. The EPA also proposed a schedule for establishing greenhouse gas National Source Performance Standards for power plants and petroleum refineries as part of its settlement of two additional lawsuits.

EPA's regulation of greenhouse gases has been challenged in both Congress and the courts, but has not yet been significantly undermined. The following excerpt provides an overview of the EPA's initial efforts to regulate stationary sources and these challenges.

HOLLY L. PEARSON & KEVIN POLONCARZ, WITH LEGISLATION STALLED, EPA PRESSES FORWARD WITH GREENHOUSE GAS REGULATORY PROGRAM UNDER THE CLEAN AIR ACT AS JANUARY 2, 2011 TRIGGER DATE APPROACHES

587 PLI/Real 105, 107–11 (2011)

Ever since the U.S. Supreme Court's decision in *Massachusetts v. U.S. EPA*, 549 U.S. 497 (2007), when the Court held that GHGs fall within the definition of "air pollutant" for purposes of CAA section 202(a)(1), EPA has been figuring out how it is going to regulate GHGs under the CAA. In the past year, after issuing a number of proposals and receiving thousands of comments, EPA began to finalize its approach. In particular, EPA finalized four actions that the Agency believes, taken together, trigger PSD applicability for certain GHG sources.

Endangerment and Cause or Contribute Findings

First, EPA finalized two distinct findings regarding GHGs under section 202(a) of the CAA (74 Fed. Reg. 66,496 (Dec. 15, 2009)). In the "Endangerment Finding," EPA found that the current and projected concentrations of six key GHGs in the atmosphere—namely, carbon dioxide (CO_2), methane (CH4), nitrous oxide (N2O), hydrofluorocarbons (HFCs), perfluorocarbons (PFCs), and sulfur hexafluoride (SF6)—may reasonably be anticipated to endanger public health and welfare of current and future generations. In the "Cause or Contribute Finding," EPA found that the combined emissions of these GHGs from new motor vehicles and new motor vehicle engines contribute to the GHG air pollution that endangers public health and welfare. These findings were a prerequisite for finalizing the light-duty vehicle GHG standards.

Johnson Memo Reconsideration

Second, EPA issued its final reconsideration of the Bush Administration's "Johnson Memo," a December 18, 2008 memorandum by former EPA Administrator Stephen L. Johnson that set forth a policy on when a pollutant is "subject to regulation" under the CAA (75 Fed. Reg. 17004 (Apr. 2, 2010)). EPA's reconsideration of the Johnson Memo affirmed the interpretation that "subject to regulation" for PSD permitting requirements includes only those pollutants subject to regulations that require actual control of emissions. In addition, EPA clarified that the date that a pollutant becomes "subject to regulation" is the date that a regulation "takes effect." Based on EPA's interpretations and the then-anticipated promulgation of the light-duty vehicle standards, PSD permitting requirements would be triggered on January 2, 2011, the earliest date that model year 2012 vehicles meeting the GHG light-duty vehicle standards could be sold in the U.S.

Light-Duty Vehicle Rule

Third, in a joint final rulemaking with the National Highway Traffic Safety Administration (NHTSA), EPA issued the first national rule limiting GHG emissions from cars and light trucks (75 Fed. Reg. 25,324 (May 7, 2010)). Applicable to passenger cars, light-duty trucks, and medium-duty passenger vehicles, the standards will go into effect with model year 2012 and push NHTSA's corporate average fuel economy (CAFE) standards to a fleetwide average of 30.1 miles per gallon in 2012 to 35.5 miles per gallon in 2016, with corresponding CO_2 emissions limits (in grams per mile).

The Final PSD Tailoring Rule

Finally, early . . . summer [2010], EPA finalized the "Tailoring Rule" to "tailor" the requirements of the CAA—namely, the statutory PSD and Title V thresholds—and phase in GHG permitting of stationary sources (75 Fed. Reg. 31,514 (June 3, 2010)). (*See*, "EPA Issues Final 'Tailoring Rule' Establishing Permitting Requirements for Greenhouse Gas Emissions," 3 *Climate Change Law & Pol'y Rptr* 86 (July 2010).) According to EPA, the Tailoring Rule is necessary because, without it, PSD and Title V requirements would apply at the statutory 100 and 250 tons per year (tpy) levels as of January 2, 2011, triggering a need for agencies to issue tens of thousands of PSD permits and millions of Title V permits. The Tailoring Rule established the first two steps of EPA's phase-in approach and outlined a third.

Under Step 1, from January 2, 2011 to June 30, 2011, PSD or Title V requirements will apply to a source's GHG emissions only if the source is subject to PSD or Title V anyway due to its non-GHG pollutants. For these so-called "anyway" sources, the applicable requirements of PSD, most notably, the BACT [Best Available Control Technology] requirement, will apply to projects that increase net GHG emissions by at least 75,000 tpy total GHGs (on a CO_2e basis), but only if the PSD requirement is triggered by a non-GHG pollutant. For Title V, only existing sources with, or new sources obtaining, Title V permits for non-GHG pollutants will be required to address GHGs.

Under Step 2, from July 1, 2011 to June 30, 2013, PSD permitting requirements will apply for the first time to new construction projects that emit GHGs of at least 100,000 tpy even if a project's emissions do not exceed the permitting thresholds for any other pollutant. In addition, sources that emit or have the potential to emit at least 100,000 tpy CO_2e and that undertake a modification that increases net GHG emissions by at least 75,000 tpy CO_2e will be subject to PSD requirements. For Title V, new sources and existing sources not already subject to Title V that emit at least 100,000 tpy CO_2e will become subject to Title V requirements. According to EPA estimates, approximately 900 additional PSD permitting actions and 550 Title V permitting actions will be required.

In addition, EPA outlined a third step, consisting of another rulemaking to begin in 2011 and conclude by July 1, 2012 that may subject smaller sources to permitting requirements beginning July 1, 2013. EPA also committed (i) to explore streamlining techniques, (ii) to not include sources with emissions below 50,000 tpy CO_2e and modifications with net GHG increases of 50,000 tpy CO_2e before April 30, 2016, (iii) to complete a study by April 30, 2015 to evaluate the status of PSD and Title V permitting for GHG-emitting sources, and (iv) to complete further rulemaking based on the study by April 30, 2016 to address smaller sources.

Legal Challenges

Given the stakes involved, it is not surprising that each of EPA's four actions has been challenged. All told, more than 75 petitions for review filed by, among others, industry groups, businesses, states and governors, U.S. representatives, and environmental groups, are pending with the U.S. Court of Appeals for the D.C. Circuit.

After issuing its Endangerment and Cause or Contribute Findings, EPA received ten petitions for reconsideration that challenged the validity of the climate science used as a basis for EPA's findings. On July 29, 2010, EPA denied all ten petitions. Legal battles continue, however, through petitions for review filed with the D.C. Circuit Court of Appeals; a lawsuit filed by the U.S. Chamber of Commerce challenging the legality of EPA's rejection of its petition for reconsideration; and a petition to EPA under the Data Quality Act filed by Peabody Energy challenging the temperature data supporting EPA's findings.

Multiple pending petitions for review challenge EPA's other three actions. For the Johnson Memo Reconsideration and the Tailoring Rule, procedural motions were due by September 15, 2010, and dispositive motions and EPA's certified index of the administrative record were due by September 30, 2010. For the Light-Duty Vehicle Rule, procedural motions were due by September 10, 2010, and dispositive motions and EPA's certified index of the administrative record were due by September 24, 2010.

In addition, a group of industry associations filed a petition for reconsideration of the Tailoring Rule on grounds that only those pollutants for which EPA has established a national ambient air quality standard (NAAQS), *i.e.*, criteria pollutants, and for which the area is designated attainment or unclassifiable are able to trigger PSD permitting requirements. In other words, the approach that EPA is taking under Step 1 of the Tailoring Rule in regulating only "anyway" sources is the correct one under the CAA. EPA has not yet issued a decision on the petition for reconsideration.

NOTES AND QUESTIONS

1. Why did the Obama administration decide to confine its initial permitting efforts on greenhouse gases to the most significant emitters? What are the benefits and limitations of such a decision?
2. What makes greenhouse gas regulation so controversial? Are there any ways to frame regulations to make them less controversial, or is such contestation inherent to regulating these emissions?
3. States play a major role in the implementation of standards for stationary sources through their state implementation plans. Robert McKinstry, Jr., Thomas Peterson, Adam Rose, and Dan Wei have argued that state

implementation plans under the Clean Air Act play a constructive role in cost-effective greenhouse gas emissions:

> States and regional organizations have been in the forefront of programs to address climate change in the United States. The Supreme Court's decision in *Massachusetts v. Environmental Protection Agency* means that a strong federal response is now also inevitable. Expeditious implementation of a federal program requires that existing state and regional programs be coordinated and incorporated into a federal program. The federal Clean Air Act provides a medium for accomplishing this. Scale up of the climate mitigation planning efforts of twenty states suggests that an effective federal response can be achieved expeditiously at economy-wide net cost savings, provided all socio-economic sectors are addressed and vertical and horizontal linkages are considered through a mixture of policy tools. Analysis of the portfolios of policy tools identified in state climate plans indicates that many essential policy tools fall exclusively within state jurisdiction. Planning and implementation at the state level is critical for identifying the mix of technical and policy approaches that will be most effective and coordinating mechanisms across sectors. The state implementation planning mechanism creates by the Clean Air Act can be adapted to allow federal coordination and oversight of the full range of state, local and federal policy mechanisms necessary for cost-effective reductions of greenhouse gas emissions.
>
> Robert B. McKinstry, Jr., Thomas D. Peterson, Adam Rose & Dan Wei, *The New Climate World: Achieving Economic Efficiency in a Federal System for GHG Regulation through State Planning* (Mar. 5, 2009) (unpublished manuscript), *available at* http://ssrn.com/abstract=1354146.

Do you agree with them? How does this state role impact the appropriate strategies for federal efforts to regulate power plants, refineries, and other major industrial emitters?

4. *AMERICAN ELECTRIC POWER V. CONNECTICUT*

In June 2010, the U.S. Supreme Court issued its second decision involving climate change, *AEP v. Connecticut*. In this case, the petitioners directly challenged major corporate emitters rather than the decisions of governmental regulators. Unlike *Massachusetts*, the opinion was largely unanimous other than on the "threshold issues"; these issues included standing (where there is a 4–4 plurality following the *Massachusetts* approach) and the political question doctrine, a major issue in the lower courts and oral argument, but only referenced briefly in a footnote in the opinion.

Justice Ginsburg wrote an opinion that Justices Roberts, Scalia, Kennedy, Breyer, and Kagan joined. Justice Alito, joined by Justice Thomas, concurred in part and concurred in judgment. Justice Sotomayor, who was part of a lower court panel hearing the case, recused herself. The justices agreed that, assuming the EPA remained authorized to regulate greenhouse gas emissions under the Clean Air Act, litigation should take place under that statute rather than under federal common law.

The following excerpts from the majority and concurring opinions include a description of the case, the justices' views on threshold issues, its core analysis regarding why EPA's Clean Air Act regulatory authority displaces common law federal public nuisance, and the issues that it chooses not to reach. Together, the holding and dicta reinforce the current U.S. regulatory path based on the *Massachusetts* opinion and define that path's parameters further.

AMERICAN ELECTRIC POWER CO. v. CONNECTICUT

131 S. Ct. 2527, 2532–41 (2011)

JUSTICE GINSBURG delivered the opinion of the Court.

We address in this opinion the question whether the plaintiffs (several States, the city of New York, and three private land trusts) can maintain federal common law public nuisance claims against carbon-dioxide emitters (four private power companies and the federal Tennessee Valley Authority). As relief, the plaintiffs ask for a decree setting carbon-dioxide emissions for each defendant at an initial cap, to be further reduced annually. The Clean Air Act and the Environmental Protection Agency action the Act authorizes, we hold, displace the claims the plaintiffs seek to pursue.

I

In Massachusetts v. EPA, 549 U.S. 497, 127 S. Ct. 1438, 167 L.Ed.2d 248 (2007), this Court held that the Clean Air Act, 42 U.S.C. §7401 et seq., authorizes federal regulation of emissions of carbon dioxide and other greenhouse gases. "[N]aturally present in the atmosphere and . . . also emitted by human activities," greenhouse gases are so named because they "trap . . . heat that would otherwise escape from the [Earth's] atmosphere, and thus form the greenhouse effect that helps keep the Earth warm enough for life." 74 Fed. Reg. 66499 (2009). Massachusetts held that the Environmental Protection Agency (EPA) had misread the Clean Air Act when it denied a rulemaking petition seeking controls on greenhouse gas emissions from new motor vehicles. 549 U.S., at 510–511, 127 S. Ct. 1438. Greenhouse gases, we determined, qualify as "air pollutant[s]" within the meaning of the governing Clean Air Act provision, id., at 528–529, 127 S. Ct. 1438 (quoting §7602(g)); they are therefore within EPA's regulatory ken. Because EPA had authority to set greenhouse gas emission standards and had offered no "reasoned explanation" for failing to do so, we concluded that the agency had not acted "in accordance with law" when it denied the requested rulemaking. Id., at 534–535, 127 S. Ct. 1438 (quoting §7607(d)(9)(A)).

Responding to our decision in Massachusetts, EPA undertook greenhouse gas regulation. In December 2009, the agency concluded that greenhouse gas emissions from motor vehicles "cause, or contribute to, air pollution which may reasonably be anticipated to endanger public health or welfare," the Act's regulatory trigger. §7521(a)(1); 74 Fed. Reg. 66496. The agency observed that "atmospheric greenhouse gas concentrations are now at elevated and essentially unprecedented levels," almost entirely "due to anthropogenic emissions," id., at 66517; mean global temperatures, the agency continued, demonstrate an "unambiguous warming trend over the last 100 years," and particularly "over the past 30 years," *ibid*. Acknowledging that not all scientists agreed on the causes and consequences of the rise in global temperatures, id., at 66506, 66518, 66523–66524, EPA concluded that "compelling" evidence supported the "attribution of observed climate change to anthropogenic" emissions of greenhouse gases, id., at 66518. Consequent dangers of greenhouse gas emissions, EPA determined, included increases in heat-related deaths; coastal inundation and erosion caused by melting icecaps and rising sea levels; more frequent and intense hurricanes, floods, and other "extreme weather events" that cause death and destroy infrastructure; drought due to reductions in mountain snowpack and shifting precipitation patterns; destruction of ecosystems supporting animals and plants; and potentially "significant disruptions" of food production. Id., at 66524–66535.

EPA and the Department of Transportation subsequently issued a joint final rule regulating emissions from light-duty vehicles, see 75 Fed. Reg. 25324 (2010), and initiated a joint rulemaking covering medium- and heavy-duty vehicles, see *id.*, at 74152. EPA also began phasing in requirements that new or modified "[m]ajor [greenhouse gas] emitting facilities" use the "best available control technology." §7475(a)(4); 75 Fed. Reg. 31520–31521. Finally, EPA commenced a rulemaking under §111 of the Act, 42 U.S.C. §7411, to set limits on greenhouse gas emissions from new, modified, and existing fossil-fuel fired power plants. Pursuant to a settlement finalized in March 2011, EPA has committed to issuing a proposed rule by July 2011, and a final rule by May 2012. See 75 Fed. Reg. 82392; Reply Brief for Tennessee Valley Authority 18.

II

The lawsuits we consider here began well before EPA initiated the efforts to regulate greenhouse gases just described. In July 2004, two groups of plaintiffs filed separate complaints in the Southern District of New York against the same five major electric power companies. The first group of plaintiffs included eight States and New York City, the second joined three nonprofit land trusts; both groups are respondents here. The defendants, now petitioners, are four private companies and the Tennessee Valley Authority, a federally owned corporation that operates fossil-fuel fired power plants in several States. According to the complaints, the defendants "are the five largest emitters of carbon dioxide in the United States." App. 57, 118. Their collective annual emissions of 650 million tons constitute 25 percent of emissions from the domestic electric power sector, 10 percent of emissions from all domestic human activities, *ibid.*, and 2.5 percent of all anthropogenic emissions worldwide, App. to Pet. for Cert. 72a.

By contributing to global warming, the plaintiffs asserted, the defendants' carbon-dioxide emissions created a "substantial and unreasonable interference with public rights," in violation of the federal common law of interstate nuisance, or, in the alternative, of state tort law. App. 103–105, 145–147. The States and New York City alleged that public lands, infrastructure, and health were at risk from climate change. App. 88–93. The trusts urged that climate change would destroy habitats for animals and rare species of trees and plants on land the trusts owned and conserved. App. 139–145. All plaintiffs sought injunctive relief requiring each defendant "to cap its carbon dioxide emissions and then reduce them by a specified percentage each year for at least a decade." App. 110, 153.

The District Court dismissed both suits as presenting non-justiciable political questions, citing Baker v. Carr, 369 U.S. 186, 82 S. Ct. 691, 7 L.Ed.2d 663 (1962), but the Second Circuit reversed, 582 F.3d 309 (2009). On the threshold questions, the Court of Appeals held that the suits were not barred by the political question doctrine, id., at 332, and that the plaintiffs had adequately alleged Article III standing, id., at 349.

Turning to the merits, the Second Circuit held that all plaintiffs had stated a claim under the "federal common law of nuisance." Id., at 358, 371. . . .

The Court of Appeals further determined that the Clean Air Act did not "displace" federal common law. . . .

We granted certiorari. 562 U.S. ___, 131 S. Ct. 2527, ___ L.Ed.2d ___, 2011 WL 2437011 (2010).

III

The petitioners contend that the federal courts lack authority to adjudicate this case. Four members of the Court would hold that at least some plaintiffs have Article III standing under Massachusetts, which permitted a State to challenge EPA's refusal to regulate greenhouse gas emissions, 549 U.S., at 520–526, 127 S. Ct. 1438; and, further, that no other threshold obstacle bars review. Four members of the Court, adhering to a dissenting opinion in Massachusetts, 549 U.S., at 535, 127 S. Ct. 1438, or regarding that decision as distinguishable, would hold that none of the plaintiffs have Article III standing. We therefore affirm, by an equally divided Court, the Second Circuit's exercise of jurisdiction and proceed to the merits. See Nye v. United States, 313 U.S. 33, 44, 61 S. Ct. 810, 85 L.Ed. 1172 (1941).

IV

A

"There is no federal general common law," Erie R. Co. v. Tompkins, 304 U.S. 64, 78, 58 S. Ct. 817, 82 L.Ed. 1188 (1938), famously recognized. In the wake of Erie, however, a keener understanding developed. See generally Friendly, In Praise of Erie—And of the New Federal Common Law, 39 N.Y.U.L.Rev. 383 (1964). Erie "le[ft] to the states what ought be left to them," id., at 405, and thus required "federal courts [to] follow state decisions on matters of substantive law appropriately cognizable by the states," id., at 422. Erie also sparked "the emergence of a federal decisional law in areas of national concern." Id., at 405. The "new" federal common law addresses "subjects within national legislative power where Congress has so directed" or where the basic scheme of the Constitution so demands. Id., at 408, n. 119, 421–422. Environmental protection is undoubtedly an area "within national legislative power," one in which federal courts may fill in "statutory interstices," and, if necessary, even "fashion federal law." Id., at 421–422.

. . . .

Recognition that a subject is meet for federal law governance, however, does not necessarily mean that federal courts should create the controlling law. Absent a demonstrated need for a federal rule of decision, the Court has taken "the prudent course" of "adopt[ing] the readymade body of state law as the federal rule of decision until Congress strikes a different accommodation."

. . . .

We need not address the parties' dispute in this regard. For it is an academic question whether, in the absence of the Clean Air Act and the EPA actions the Act authorizes, the plaintiffs could state a federal common law claim for curtailment of greenhouse gas emissions because of their contribution to global warming. Any such claim would be displaced by the federal legislation authorizing EPA to regulate carbon-dioxide emissions.

B

. . . .

We hold that the Clean Air Act and the EPA actions it authorizes displace any federal common law right to seek abatement of carbon-dioxide emissions from fossil-fuel fired power plants. Massachusetts made plain that emissions of carbon dioxide qualify as air pollution subject to regulation under the Act. 549 U.S., at 528–529, 127 S. Ct. 1438. And we think it equally plain that the Act "speaks directly" to emissions of carbon dioxide from the defendants' plants.

. . . .

If EPA does not *set* emissions limits for a particular pollutant or source of pollution, States and private parties may petition for a rulemaking on the matter, and EPA's response will be reviewable in federal court. See §7607(b)(1); Massachusetts, 549 U.S., at 516–517, 529, 127 S. Ct. 1438. As earlier noted, see *supra,* at 2530–2531, EPA is currently engaged in a §7411 rulemaking to set standards for greenhouse gas emissions from fossil-fuel fired power plants. To settle litigation brought under §7607(b) by a group that included the majority of the plaintiffs in this very case, the agency agreed to complete that rulemaking by May 2012. 75 Fed. Reg. 82392. The Act itself thus provides a means to seek limits on emissions of carbon dioxide from domestic power plants — the same relief the plaintiffs seek by invoking federal common law. We see no room for a parallel track.

C

The plaintiffs argue, as the Second Circuit held, that federal common law is not displaced until EPA actually exercises its regulatory authority, *i.e.,* until it sets standards governing emissions from the defendants' plants. We disagree.

. . . .

The critical point is that Congress delegated to EPA the decision whether and how to regulate carbon-dioxide emissions from power plants; the delegation is what displaces federal common law. Indeed, were EPA to decline to regulate carbon-dioxide emissions altogether at the conclusion of its ongoing §7411 rulemaking, the federal courts would have no warrant to employ the federal common law of nuisance to upset the agency's expert determination.

EPA's judgment, we hasten to add, would not escape judicial review. Federal courts, we earlier observed, see *supra,* at 2537–2538, can review agency action (or a final rule declining to take action) to ensure compliance with the statute Congress enacted. As we have noted, see *supra,* at 2537, the Clean Air Act directs EPA to establish emissions standards for categories of stationary sources that, "in [the Administrator's] judgment," "caus[e], or contribut[e] significantly to, air pollution which may reasonably be anticipated to endanger public health or welfare." §7411(b)(1)(A). "[T]he use of the word 'judgment,'" we explained in Massachusetts, "is not a roving license to ignore the statutory text." 549 U.S., at 533, 127 S. Ct. 1438. "It is but a direction to exercise discretion within defined statutory limits." Ibid. EPA may not decline to regulate carbon-dioxide emissions from power plants if refusal to act would be "arbitrary, capricious, an abuse of discretion, or otherwise not in accordance with law." §7607(d)(9)(A). If the plaintiffs in this case are dissatisfied with the outcome of EPA's forthcoming rulemaking, their recourse under federal law is to seek Court of Appeals review, and, ultimately, to petition for certiorari in this Court.

Indeed, this prescribed order of decision making — the first decider under the Act is the expert administrative agency, the second, federal judges — is yet another reason to resist setting emissions standards by judicial decree under federal tort law. The appropriate amount of regulation in any particular greenhouse gas-producing sector cannot be prescribed in a vacuum: as with other questions of national or international policy, informed assessment of competing interests is required. Along with the environmental benefit potentially achievable, our Nation's energy needs and the possibility of economic disruption must weigh in the balance.

. . . .

It is altogether fitting that Congress designated an expert agency, here, EPA, as best suited to serve as primary regulator of greenhouse gas emissions. The expert agency is surely better equipped to do the job than individual district judges issuing ad hoc, case-by-case injunctions. Federal judges lack the scientific, economic, and technological resources an agency can utilize in coping with issues of this order. See generally Chevron U.S.A. Inc. v. Natural Resources Defense Council, Inc., 467 U.S. 837, 865–866, 104 S. Ct. 2778, 81 L.Ed.2d 694 (1984). Judges may not commission scientific studies or convene groups of experts for advice, or issue rules under notice-and-comment procedures inviting input by any interested person, or seek the counsel of regulators in the States where the defendants are located. Rather, judges are confined by a record comprising the evidence the parties present. Moreover, federal district judges, sitting as sole adjudicators, lack authority to render precedential decisions binding other judges, even members of the same court.

Notwithstanding these disabilities, the plaintiffs propose that individual federal judges determine, in the first instance, what amount of carbon-dioxide emissions is "unreasonable," App. 103, 145, and then decide what level of reduction is "practical, feasible and economically viable," App. 58, 119. These determinations would be made for the defendants named in the two lawsuits launched by the plaintiffs. Similar suits could be mounted, counsel for the States and New York City estimated, against "thousands or hundreds or tens" of other defendants fitting the description "large contributors" to carbon-dioxide emissions. Tr. of Oral Arg. 57.

The judgments the plaintiffs would commit to federal judges, in suits that could be filed in any federal district, cannot be reconciled with the decision-making scheme Congress enacted. The Second Circuit erred, we hold, in ruling that federal judges may set limits on greenhouse gas emissions in face of a law empowering EPA to set the same limits, subject to judicial review only to ensure against action "arbitrary, capricious, . . . or otherwise not in accordance with law." §7607(d)(9).

V

The plaintiffs also sought relief under state law, in particular, the law of each State where the defendants operate power plants. See App. 105, 147. The Second Circuit did not reach the state law claims because it held that federal common law governed. . . . None of the parties have briefed preemption or otherwise addressed the availability of a claim under state nuisance law. We therefore leave the matter open for consideration on remand.

* * *

For the reasons stated, we reverse the judgment of the Second Circuit and remand the case for further proceedings consistent with this opinion.
It is so ordered.

JUSTICE SOTOMAYOR took no part in the consideration or decision of this case.

JUSTICE ALITO, with whom JUSTICE THOMAS joins, concurring in part and concurring in the judgment.

I concur in the judgment, and I agree with the Court's displacement analysis on the assumption (which I make for the sake of argument because no party contends otherwise) that the interpretation of the Clean Air Act, 42 U.S.C. §7401 et seq., adopted by the majority in Massachusetts v. EPA, 549 U.S. 497, 127 S. Ct. 1438, 167 L.Ed.2d 248 (2007), is correct.

NOTES AND QUESTIONS

1. The Supreme Court chose to take a broad view of displacement rather than make it depend on the EPA actually regulating under its authority. What are the advantages and disadvantages of taking such a broad approach?
2. In an article that pre-dates the Supreme Court decision in *AEP*, Attorney James Shelson argues that public nuisance should not be applied to climate change because its standards are too hard to define and these claims are subject to abuse:

> The decisions that have not dismissed public nuisance claims in climate change cases sustain these claims on the naïve and incorrect assumption that common law provides sufficient standards to resolve climate change issues. The Fifth Circuit found that "common law tort rules provide long-established rules for adjudicating the nuisance, trespass and negligence claims at issue." The Second Circuit found that federal courts have successfully adjudicated complex public nuisance cases "for over a century." The decisions, however, fail to say what those standards are. Indeed, "[o]ne searches in vain . . . for anything resembling a principle in the common

law of nuisance." "There is perhaps no more impenetrable jungle in the entire law than that which surrounds the word 'nuisance.' It has meant all things to all people, and has been applied indiscriminately to everything from an alarming advertisement to a cockroach baked in a pie." Nuisance law "straddles the legal universe, virtually defies synthesis, and generates case law to suit every taste." The Fourth Circuit correctly got to the heart of the matter when it concluded that if we are to regulate greenhouse gas emissions "by the same principles we use to regulate prostitution, obstacles in highways, and bullfights, we will be hard pressed to derive any manageable criteria." Moreover, public nuisance claims in climate change cases are potentially subject to abuse. In other words, they "scapegoat the regulated community by extracting piecemeal relief from those entities for a regulatory failure that rests primarily with the federal government."

James W. Shelson, *The Misuse of Public Nuisance Law to Address Climate Change*, 78 Def. Couns. J. 195, 218–19 (2011).

Do you agree with Shelson? Does climate change as a problem have qualities that are different than other issues like tobacco about which public nuisance suits have been brought to influence public policy? If so, what are those differences? If not, what is your view of the value and limitations of public nuisance as a tool in social and environmental policy?

3. Professor Maxine Burkett has argued that the *AEP* decision poses serious climate justice concerns because it eliminates an avenue through which those injured by climate change can achieve corrective justice, in which the perpetrator compensates them for their harm. In that context, she explains the way in which public nuisance can serve as an important justice mechanism:

Corrective justice is one of the most important goals of tort law because of its focus on the relationship between the tortfeasor and victim. While there are myriad interpretations of corrective justice theory and its application, this approach at its core counsels simply that individuals who are responsible for the wrongful losses of others have a duty to repair those losses. Further, rectification of harms suffered can help restore the moral balance upset by the externalized costs that climate change inflicts on individuals and communities. The corollary, therefore, is that tort law should provide a venue and possible damages remedy for [climate justice] CJ plaintiffs whose claims — namely, injuries to life and property — demand compensation from the worst offenders.

. . . .

Public nuisance theory, with its emphasis on the unreasonableness of a plaintiff's *injury*, provides an appropriate focus for understanding climate impact claims. Instead of assessing the worth of defendant's actions — often riddled with the politics of wealth and power — nuisance law shines a spotlight on the unprecedented events climate change introduces. Public nuisance claims, as Professor Randall Abate explains, may succeed where disparate impact litigation failed in the environmental justice context. They can provide the specific relief — funding for physical relocation in this case — that these particular CJ plaintiffs deserve. Even with a comprehensive regulatory scheme for emissions reduction in place, public nuisance law should remain a means by which climate impacted communities can seek compensation from major-emitters.

Maxine Burkett, *Climate Justice and the Elusive Climate Tort*, 121 Yale L.J. Online 115 (2011), *available at* http://yalelawjournal.org/2011/09/13/burkett.html.

What is the appropriate role for corrective justice in the context of climate change? To what extent should these justice concerns have entered into the Court's determination in *AEP*? In the aftermath of *AEP*, what are the best strategies for helping climate change victims achieve corrective justice?

Burkett's essay is part of a symposium published by *Yale Law Journal Online* that explores different aspects of the *AEP* opinion. The symposium contains analysis of implications for climate change litigation (Professor Hari Osofsky), standing (Professor Daniel Farber), political question doctrine (Professor Jim May), displacement (Professor Jonathan Adler), nuisance suits to address climate change (Professor Michael Gerrard), and climate justice (Professor Maxine Burkett). All of these essays can be accessed through the introductory essay of the symposium, Hari M. Osofsky, AEP v. Connecticut*'s Implications for the Future of Climate Change Litigation*, 121 Yale L.J. Online 101 (2011), *available at* http://yalelawjournal.org/2011/09/13/osofsky.html.

4. The Supreme Court left open the possibility that state law nuisance suits could proceed. In an article written prior to the *AEP* decision, Jonathan Zasloff argues that public nuisance climate change suits function as a form of judicial carbon tax. Jonathan Zasloff, *The Judicial Carbon Tax: Reconstructing Public Nuisance and Climate Change*, 55 UCLA L. Rev. 1827 (2008). Assuming he is correct, could these suits — if they are allowed to move forward in state courts when the preemption question is fully litigated — serve as a way of getting the efficiencies of taxation without a formal tax? Or, for those who oppose carbon taxation, is Zasloff's argument yet another reason to find these lawsuits problematic?

C. OTHER RELEVANT FEDERAL DEVELOPMENTS

Although the Clean Air Act currently serves as the primary federal regulatory vehicle for mitigating climate change in the United States, other important developments are shaping federal efforts to address climate change. First, the American Recovery and Reinvestment Act of 2009, passed in response to the U.S. financial crisis, has provided considerable funding for clean energy initiatives that help to mitigate climate change. Second, the federal government plays a role, through separate energy and environmental law regimes, in land use planning relevant to clean energy. Third, policymakers and commentators have begun to explore the role of the federal government in climate change adaptation. Finally, climate change litigation has continued its explosive growth in the years since *Massachusetts v. EPA*, and continues to have a significant regulatory influence. The following section details each of these developments.

1. LEGISLATIVE AND EXECUTIVE FUNDING OF CLEAN ENERGY

Even as it failed to pass comprehensive climate change legislation, the U.S. Congress took a significant step in 2009 to address the financial crisis. The

American Recovery and Reinvestment Act (ARRA) attempted to jumpstart the economy in a range of ways, including through major new funding for clean energy. The Act focused on transforming the electric power grid, supporting research into cleaner ways of using fossil fuel, energy efficiency, and renewable energy.

The following excerpt details the primary relevant provisions of this statute. It considers the goals of the Act and the components of its clean energy initiatives.

SEAN O'HARA, THE IMPORTANCE OF THE UNITED STATES STAYING THE COURSE WHILE IMPLEMENTING ENVIRONMENTAL POLICY IN ACCORDANCE WITH THE AMERICAN RECOVERY AND REINVESTMENT ACT OF 2009

17 U. Balt. J. Envtl. L. 85, 85–92 (2009)

I. Introduction

The 111th United States Congress enacted the American Recovery and Reinvestment Act of 2009 (ARRA), which President Barack Obama signed into law on February 17, 2009. Congress enacted the ARRA in response to the economic recession currently felt by many Americans. The ARRA has many objectives, including preserving and creating jobs, providing assistance to those most impacted by the recession and investing in environmental protection that will provide long term economic benefits. The measures proposed by Congress amount to approximately 787 billion dollars and over the next ten years and will include 501 billion dollars in increased spending as well as 286 billion dollars in tax cuts. From these funds, approximately 60 billion dollars in loans are expected to be guaranteed to support renewable energy and electric transmission technologies.

II. ARRA Objectives

One of the main objectives of the ARRA is to lessen the United States dependence on foreign sources of energy by investing in the domestic renewable energy industry. Specifically, the ARRA seeks to provide long term economic benefits in four main areas: the national electric grid, fossil energy, renewable fuels and energy efficiency.

III. National Electric Grid

Approximately 11 billion dollars of the funding from ARRA will go towards improving the national transmission system. This money will be spent on updating the power transmission system to what is referred to as a "Smart Grid" and building new high-voltage power lines. A "Smart Grid" is a modernized electricity network that is less centralized than a producer controlled network and more consumer-interactive. The transformation to a "Smart Grid" therefore "enables the industry's best ideas for grid modernization to reach their full potential." Of the 11 billion dollars allocated, approximately 4.5 billion dollars will go toward the development of the "Smart Grid" system. This initiative includes placing more "Smart Meters" in consumers' homes and businesses. "Smart Meters" are advanced meter systems that identify energy consumption in more detail than a conventional meter. This allows consumers to more easily manage their energy consumption and hopefully reduce consumer demand and energy bills.

The rest of the money allocated for improving the national electric grid, about 6.5 billion dollars, will go toward constructing new power lines. Most of the new power lines will transport energy output from renewable energy sources such as solar power collection devices and wind turbines. The focus of this construction will be in areas constrained by transmission access.

. . . .

IV. Fossil Energies

The ARRA dedicates approximately 3.4 billion dollars to the development of cleaner fossil energies. Coal makes up more than half of the United States energy portfolio and is a cheap power source. The funds allocated for fossil energies will be used to research and develop new ways for businesses to use coal technologies. These funds will go toward carbon capture and sequestration projects, also known as "clean coal." This policy will help to reduce the sulfur, nitrogen and mercury pollutants emitted from power plants.

The ARRA allocates 1.5 billion dollars for large-scale geological carbon capture projects. Carbon capturing and storage is a way to mitigate the effects of fossil fuel emissions on global warming. This is done by capturing carbon dioxide at large point sources, such as fossil fuel power plants, before they are released into the atmosphere.

In addition, about 1 billion dollars will go to research and development programs. Approximately 800 million dollars will be spent to enhance the United States Clean Coal Power Initiative and the government-funded FutureGen project. This project's goal is to construct a coal-fueled power plant, emitting almost no emissions, that produces electricity while utilizing carbon capture and storage.

. . . .

V. Renewable Energy

ARRA will provide an additional 13 billion dollars in loans and bonds and 18 billion dollars in estimated tax credits for the purpose of renewable energy. Providing money towards developing domestic renewable energy is important because renewable fuels and energy sources have recently experienced "unprecedented growth as an industry." From this funding, about 6 billion dollars will be allocated to support renewable energy projects under the Innovative Technology Loan Guarantees Program, and each project is limited to 500 million dollars. As part of the Energy Policy Act of 2005, and as required by the ARRA, the DOE [Department of Energy] must implement a Loan Guarantee Program, which will only provide loans to construction projects starting before September 30, 2011 that promote renewable energy systems, electric power transmission systems and leading-edge biofuel projects. This Energy Policy Act "provides broad authority for the DOE to guarantee loans that support early commercial use of advanced technologies."

Approximately 2 billion dollars has been allocated for new manufacturing and capacity testing of advanced battery technologies and another 1.25 billion dollars will be put toward biomass and geothermal projects. Additionally, through the creation of an Alternative Fueled Vehicles Pilot Grant Program, the government is providing 300 million dollars to buy hybrid vehicles for the federal fleet. Lastly, approximately 3 billion dollars will be allocated for pass-through grants that support the State Energy Program. This Program provides grants and directs funding to state energy offices from the DOE's Office of Energy Efficiency and Renewable Energy technology programs. States will use these grants "to address their energy priorities and program funding to adopt emerging renewable energy and energy efficiency technologies" locally.

The ARRA also estimates that approximately 18 billion dollars will be received in tax credits for individuals and companies utilizing renewable energy. One way the government plans to implement this policy is to extend the Federal Renewable Energy Production Tax Credit (PTC) for three years. PTC is a "per-kilowatt, per-hour tax credit for electricity generated by qualified energy sources." This should "mainly help spur wind projects" because a company will receive the largest credit for using this type of resource (2.1 cents per kilowatt-hour for wind). It is also estimated that approximately 2.3 billion dollars in various competitive tax credits and bonds will be awarded for up to 30 percent of costs associated with alternative energy equipment manufacturing facilities. Finally, about 2 billion dollars will be applied towards "qualified hybrid vehicle purchases by individual taxpayers."

VI. Energy Efficiency

ARRA's funding in relation to energy efficiency is likely to reduce the amount of energy that the nation's buildings consume. Since offices and homes are two of the "biggest sources of domestic power demand," owners of these buildings should receive the bulk of the funds and tax credits awarded. The remaining funds allocated from the ARRA to promote environmental protection towards the development of domestic energy efficiency are about 16 billion dollars, and an additional 2 billion dollars are estimated in tax credits.

The ARRA specifies that 4.5 billion dollars will be allotted towards the Federal Buildings Fund to make federal buildings greener. Approximately 3 billion dollars from the Energy Efficiency and Conservation Block Grants are for state and local governments to partake in energy efficiency investments and reductions in energy use and fossil fuels emissions. Additionally, about 5 billion dollars is going towards the Low Income Home Energy Assistance Program, which assists low income households that pay a high proportion of household income for home energy. Individual homeowners have the potential to receive a tax credit for up to 30 percent of costs incurred if they utilize certain energy efficient home improvements through 2010.

NOTES AND QUESTIONS

1. How do the clean energy incentives address the problem of climate change? More broadly, can the problem of climate change mitigation be addressed

through a focus on clean energy, or are there aspects of needed change that would be missing?

2. Although climate change has become increasingly politically controversial in the years since President Obama took office, a broader consensus exists about the need to transition energy production and use in the United States in ways that promote conservation, efficiency, and cleaner sources. President Obama's 2012 State of the Union Address reflected the divergent political discourse regarding climate change and clean energy:

> The differences in this chamber may be too deep right now to pass a comprehensive plan to fight climate change. But there's no reason why Congress shouldn't at least set a clean energy standard that creates a market for innovation. So far, you haven't acted. Well, tonight, I will. I'm directing my administration to allow the development of clean energy on enough public land to power 3 million homes. And I'm proud to announce that the Department of Defense, working with us, the world's largest consumer of energy, will make one of the largest commitments to clean energy in history — with the Navy purchasing enough capacity to power a quarter of a million homes a year.
>
> President Barack Obama, Remarks by the President in State of the Union Address (Jan. 24, 2012), *available at* http://www.whitehouse.gov/the-press -office/2012/01/24/remarks-president-state-union-address.

Do you agree that a clean energy standard is more politically viable than comprehensive climate change legislation? Why or why not? Do you think that tying clean energy to innovation will make it more politically viable?

3. What role are the deep cuts to energy and environmental spending that emerged out of the debt crisis and compromise likely to play in the future of such incentive programs? What are the benefits and limitations of this fiscal austerity in the context of climate change?

2. FEDERAL INTERACTIONS WITH ENERGY SITING AND LAND USE PLANNING

Transitioning to cleaner energy involves more than just funding innovative initiatives. Although much of energy regulation in the United States occurs at state and local levels, the regulatory initiatives of the Federal Energy Regulatory Commission (FERC) also play an important role in transmission siting, more effective pricing of renewables in the energy market, and smart grid development. These regulatory steps by FERC, as a legal matter, occur separately from the EPA's efforts under the Clean Air Act and other environmental laws. However, because both regulatory regimes guide the behavior of utilities producing energy and the regional-level transmission organizations coordinating their interaction with each other and the grid, they together shape possibilities for energy transition.

These interactions among energy and environmental law and the agencies that implement them are further complicated by their relationship with land use planning, which is traditionally controlled by state and local governments. The following excerpt from an article by Professor Uma Outka describes this intersection of substantive areas of law and levels of government.

UMA OUTKA, THE RENEWABLE ENERGY FOOTPRINT
30 Stan. Envtl. L.J. 241, 254–69 (2011)

Land use regulation is primarily a state and local function in the U.S. Although Congress may regulate land use to the extent permissible under the Commerce Clause, the authority to govern land use—"to define and limit property rights, including the right to use the land and its natural resources"—rests squarely within the states' police power. States have delegated much of this land use control to local governments. With over 39,000 local governments across the 50 states, it should come as no surprise that land use law is highly decentralized and variable. As Professor Tony Arnold aptly describes it, "the land use regulatory system is a system of 'regulatory patches' that are located in the United States primarily at the local level of governance and decision making, but operate in the shadows of: a) the super-dominance of private control of land, and b) overlays of federal and state land use regulations." Federal influence over land use is exerted, for example, through the National Environmental Policy Act (NEPA), which requires environmental analysis of federal actions including land development, and the Coastal Zone Management Act (CZMA), arguably "the first major federal land use model." In the context of electricity generation, federal agencies exert exclusive permitting authority over hydroelectric facilities, but this is the exception, not the rule. And even in that atypical setting, states traditional role is honored by the right to influence terms in the permits.

In recognition of the statewide and often regional importance of power plants and transmission lines, many states have taken a more active role in guiding energy siting than is typical for other, even industrial, land uses. Nonetheless, the regulatory context for siting energy infrastructure can vary significantly jurisdiction to jurisdiction. New law tailored to large-scale renewable projects necessarily modifies, supplements, or supplants a pre-existing and often long-standing regulatory context for energy siting.

1. Power Plant Siting

Nearly all of the electricity consumed in the U.S. is generated at large-scale power plants, transmitted across high-voltage power lines, and delivered via substations for residential, commercial, and industrial end use. This model of "centralized" power production is decidedly dominant across the U.S. The alternative model, "distributed" generation of electricity, involves power produced onsite or in small-scale facilities close to end users. The model has potential, but its penetration of the energy market to date remains small. The siting frameworks discussed here are and have been an integral part of supplying nearly all of the nation's electricity.

Prior to the 1970s, siting power plants was an almost entirely local process. Many of the same complaints we hear today about local and environmental opposition to energy facilities are the same sentiments that forty years ago provided impetus for a shift toward siting at the state-level. In 1970, the National Association of Regulatory Utility Commissioners developed a model siting statute to promote "the provision of a reliable, abundant and economical energy supply with due regard for the preservation and enhancement of the environment." Legislation emerged across many states to assign ultimate siting decisions to a state agency and to coordinate and expedite permitting, licensing, and streamline challenges to site approvals. State siting for large power plants is law, for example, in Arkansas, California, Connecticut, Florida, Iowa, Kentucky, Maine, Maryland, Massachusetts, Minnesota, Montana, Nevada, New Jersey, New York, Ohio, Oregon, Rhode Island, Vermont, Washington, Wisconsin. Despite significant variation state to state, these statutes taken together marked a departure from the traditional state-to-local delegation of land use authority, a move to prevent parochial preference from blocking new power plants.

Local influence remains strong, however, even under state siting law. Virtually all of the statutes provide a mechanism for local involvement in the siting process and strive for consistency with local regulation, though some allow the state to act against local objection when the "necessity" or the "public interest" justifies it. Still, roughly half the states did not alter the local land use process for energy siting, which can mean "a virtually unregulated siting process" in "rural areas where zoning, noise and land-use ordinances are not in place." These states are likely to limit their role in siting to the determination of "need" for a new facility. A need determination, when required, functions as generic state approval to build a large power plant, but not at a particular site—that is, the project is deemed necessary to meet demand as a prerequisite for construction, wherever that may occur.

2. Transmission Line Siting

FERC has traditionally regulated interstate transmission and wholesale cost of electricity, but much as they have with non-hydroelectric power plants, "states have traditionally assumed all jurisdiction to approve or deny permits for the siting and construction of electric transmission facilities." Centralized state authority as described for the siting of power plants is more common still for siting transmission lines. Over half the states have adopted a "one stop shopping" regime for transmission siting—consolidated state powers in a centralized siting agency, exercised in a single forum in which the public can participate, applying "a single set of statewide policies for making siting decisions" that either preempts or allows for overruling local authorities. In the remaining states, siting is subject to local land use regulation.

Though generally regarded as sufficient for siting in-state, state frameworks are often blamed for inhibiting grid expansion across state lines. Since the 1970s, "chronic underinvestment" in transmission has led to "bottlenecks in the electric grid and congestion is worsening in many places." The difficulty of interstate siting has focused attention on two aspects of transmission siting law primed for reform. The first is the extent to which state law supports or hinders interstate coordination. A recent study by the National Council on Electricity Policy found that state statutes vary in the degree to which they address interstate transmission siting or encourage and provide guidance for planning with other states. At least twelve states were silent on these issues, and those that do have law structuring interstate relations are hardly uniform in their approach. To overcome these differences, many states participate in regional planning via a Regional Transmission Organization (RTO) as "an entry-point for addressing interstate siting complications," but a range of other models exist, from the formal end of the spectrum, such as interstate compacts, to informal models, such as advisory committees. Still, regulators can only act within the confines of state law.

The second aspect is the outdated conception of "need" that states use to determine if a transmission line should be built. Just as it is for power plants, the "need" determination is typically the prerequisite to siting new transmission. Yet as Ashley Brown and Jim Rossi have argued, state definitions of "need" have not kept pace with changes in the electricity industry such as the shift away from vertically integrated monopolies to competitive energy markets, the disaggregation of generation, distribution, and transmission into separate enterprises. As they explain, state siting statutes have typically "envisioned a determination of need based on benefits to in-state customers" and limit state siting authorities' "ability to even consider, let alone rely on, export and import opportunities in the interstate wholesale markets as a basis for siting transmission lines." These impediments to interstate siting have been seen for some time as hindering grid expansion needed to remedy congestion as well as hobbling wholesale power markets.

The Energy Policy Act of 2005 altered the tradition of exclusive state authority by creating limited federal siting authority "for the first time in U.S. history." In response to concern over black-outs and grid congestion in highly populated areas, the Act authorized the U.S. Department of Energy (DOE) to designate "National Interest Electric Transmission Corridors" and granted the Federal Energy Regulatory Commission (FERC) limited jurisdiction to site power lines with those corridors if states "withheld approval [of a permit application] for more than 1 year." This shift of authority to federal agencies has been noted extensively in the legal literature and elsewhere, but so far it has done little to reduce state primacy. The DOE designated only two limited corridors, one in the mid-Atlantic and one in the Southwest. FERC initially interpreted its new authority as a broad grant of jurisdiction that allowed the agency to approve permits that a state affirmatively denied within one year. However, a closely watched case in the Fourth Circuit, Piedmont Environmental Council v. FERC, rejected FERC's position, holding that "the continuous act of withholding approval does not include the final administrative act of denying a permit." The Court reasoned that "[i]f Congress had intended to take the monumental step of preempting state jurisdiction every time a state commission denies a permit in a national interest corridor, it would surely have said so directly" (emphasis in original). Thus, it is a remedy for inaction only. States retain siting jurisdiction so long as they minimally keep state review processes on track to approve or disapprove a site within one year. Piedmont clarified that FERC has no authority at present to approve new "national interest" transmission lines that state regulators oppose.

3. NEPA and Cumulative Impacts

NEPA dominates among the federal statutes that may affect siting decisions. Under NEPA, federal agencies have long been required to assess the environmental impacts of major federal actions and their alternatives.

Where environmental effects of a proposed action will be significant, an environmental impact statement (EIS) must be prepared. Permitting energy projects on federal land is an obvious federal action that may require NEPA review by multiple agencies with an interest in a selected site. A less obvious NEPA trigger can be Department of Energy loan guarantees for renewable projects, whether on public or private land. When NEPA applies, a project will receive a much more thorough and comprehensive environmental review than it would under most state and local regimes. Indeed, considering "cumulative impacts" is explicitly required. What the NEPA review reveals, however, does not dictate a particular outcome — it is an "essentially procedural" overlay designed to inform, not direct, decisionmaking.

The "cumulative impacts" analysis under NEPA fundamentally recognizes that environmental review of a federal action in isolation leaves important questions unanswered. NEPA regulations define "cumulative impacts" as "the impact on the environment which results from the incremental impact of the action when added to other past, present, and reasonably foreseeable future actions." This definition, read literally, is almost limitless in scope; in practice, the predecisional posture of the analysis inevitably binds it to the particular project proposed. Yet where to draw the line between relevant impacts and those that are too remote has been the source of confusion for agency analysts, NEPA practitioners, and courts reviewing the adequacy of NEPA documents. As one analyst put it, "the problem arises when an agency must decide how to address the cumulative impacts of a proposal in conjunction with 'reasonably foreseeable future actions.'" Nonetheless, case law and agency interpretation have leaned toward discerning this boundary in favor of reining in the geographic and forward-looking aspects of "cumulative impacts" under NEPA. The Supreme Court in Kleppe v. Sierra Club seemed to impose a temporal limitation on the concept by declaring that "when several proposals . . . will have cumulative or synergistic environmental impact upon a region are pending concurrently before an agency, their environmental consequences must be considered together." In 1997, the Council on Environmental Quality (CEQ), which is responsible for NEPA regulations, issued guidance to analysts focused on "the cause and effect relationships between the multiple actions and the resources, ecosystems, and human communities of concern." The guidance bounds the analysis by differentiating "project specific analyses," which are usually "conducted on the scale of counties, forest management units, or installation boundaries," with cumulative effects analyses, for which the geographic boundary is conceived of as a "project impact zone" and may include "human communities, landscapes, watersheds, or airsheds." Consistent with but preceding the CEQ guidance, the Fifth Circuit in Fritiofson v. Alexander identified at least the following factors as part of the EIS analysis of cumulative effects: "(1) the area in which the effects of the proposed project will be felt; (2) the impacts that are expected in that area from the proposed project; (3) other actions past, proposed, and reasonably foreseeable that have had or are expected to have impacts in the same area; (4) the impacts or expected impacts from these or other actions, and (5) the overall impact that can be expected if the individual impacts are allowed to accumulate."

A recent survey of NEPA "cumulative impacts" cases in the Ninth Circuit confirms adherence to the Fifth Circuit's emphasis on the immediate geographical surroundings of the project proposal. It is probably safe to assume that environmental plaintiffs challenging "cumulative impacts" analysis under NEPA must base their case on "the potential effects of several actions on one particular resource" — a narrower but more manageable conception of "cumulative impacts" than the CEQ definition might suggest.

4. Renewable Energy and Existing Frameworks

Renewable energy is poorly matched with existing siting frameworks for at least four reasons. First, many of the states with centralized authorities afford one-stop permitting for very large facilities only. North Dakota and Massachusetts, for example, certify energy facilities greater than 100 MW, while New York's threshold is 80 MW, Florida's is 75 MW, Ohio's is 50 MW, and the list goes on. Although there are large-scale renewable energy facilities being constructed, many are often much smaller, 25 MW or less. Thus, even in states with centralized siting agencies, many projects are likely to fall below the MW threshold and require a long list of separate state and local permit applications with no single point of contact.

Second, the longstanding challenge of interstate transmission siting looms larger still in the renewable context because resource availability often determines where a renewable project can be viable. The richest terrestrial wind resources, for example, are found in mid-western states, while large-scale geothermal energy is considered most viable in the west and southwest. Solar energy is ubiquitous but areas with the greatest intensity, such as the southwest, are considered the best locations for large-scale concentrated solar power plants. For this reason, the variability in state approaches to interstate relations may especially constrain transmission projects supporting renewables. The option to choose a site that avoids the need for interstate transmission is not always available as it might be for non-renewable projects. Likewise, given that most states make the "need" determination a siting prerequisite, statutes restricting the analysis to in-state need may exact the heaviest burden on remote renewable projects. As Jim Rossi has observed, these laws adhere to dated assumptions based on "indifference to the sources of energy, and primarily local environmental impacts" — they remain largely oblivious to the broader climate agenda to reduce greenhouse gas emissions that renewable energy serves.

Third, in states that rely on local governance for some or all energy siting, the local approval process can be lengthy, costly, and unpredictable. Much as state-by-state need determinations can neglect regional and national benefits of interstate transmission, local review typically fails to credit the extra-local benefits renewable projects offer. These benefits exceed the electricity made available to the immediate surrounding geographic area to include incremental reduction in GHG emissions from energy production. Renewable energy projects offer more than their non-renewable counterparts in the sense that the benefits are global rather than just local; however, their benefits are also long-term and abstract. These features play to the tendency to discount policies designed to address "delayed harm," as Professor Eric Biber puts it, of which renewable energy as a component of climate policy is a prime example.

Finally, the existing frameworks do not directly respond with sufficient urgency to site renewable projects quickly that is unique to this political moment. This urgency stems in some states from renewable portfolio standards and their timetables. For example, Colorado passed a bill in 2010 requiring 30 percent of the state's electricity to come from renewables by 2020. California's goal is 33 percent by 2020, New York's is 29 percent by 2015, while Nevada and Ohio are both aiming for 25 percent by 2025, and the list goes on. The urgency is also incentive-driven as federal loan guarantees under the Recovery Act, for example, are only available to projects that break ground by 2011. Similar pressure exists to site new power lines to support renewable energy development. The Edison Electric Institute (EEI) claims that nearly $37 billion has been invested in transmission infrastructure to support renewable energy development. Still, one of the most cited barriers to new transmission is insufficient investment, which the complexity of siting regulation only exacerbates. This is not a new concern, but frustration with current law is intensifying, as a "chicken-and-egg dilemma hinders the development" of remote renewable energy resources. The dilemma presents a critical planning problem: "transmission developers are hesitant to build transmission to a region without certainty that a power plant will be built to use the line, just as wind and solar developers are hesitant to build a power plant without certainty that a transmission line will be built."

The urgency to site new infrastructure has focused significant attention on these and other regulatory "barriers." In the face of pressure to break ground, existing frameworks can seem cumbersome and inadequate, hindering rather than facilitating the shift to renewable energy. The Solar Energy Industries Association (SEIA) cites "protracted permitting processes for generation projects" as a threat to "the momentum of utility-scale solar power." Under the existing regulatory structure, SEIA and the American Wind Energy Association (AWEA), assert that "it is almost impossible to build an interstate transmission network."

NOTES AND QUESTIONS

1. In light of the issues discussed by Professor Outka, what is the most effective way of addressing the problem of siting transmission lines? A forthcoming article by Professors Alexandra Klass and Elizabeth Wilson explores possibilities for addressing this problem. It concludes that some federal preemption of state siting authority over interstate transmission lines would be a good solution, but presents political feasibility concerns. In light of that, the article proposes: "(1) a "process preemption approach" using the current federal model for siting cell phone towers; or (2) movement toward regional collaborations with an ultimate transfer of at least some state siting authority to regional organizations through interstate compacts or other legal mechanisms." Alexandra B. Klass & Elizabeth Wilson, *Renewable Energy*

and Transmission Challenges, 65 VAND. L. REV. (forthcoming 2012) (on file with authors), *available at* http://papers.ssrn.com/sol3/papers.cfm?abstract _id=2012075.

2. Regional transmission organizations, which direct the production and distribution of power among participating utilities, are not only playing a role in addressing transmission problems. They also are innovating to bring renewable energy into their market structures. For example, the Midwestern regional transmission organization, MISO, introduced a new FERC-approved product designed to integrate wind more effectively into the market despite its intermittency. For a discussion of this new standard, see MISO, *Wind Integration*, https://www.midwestiso.org/WhatWeDo/Strategic Initiatives/Pages/WindIntegration.aspx (last visited Apr. 16, 2012); NAT'L RENEWABLE ENERGY LAB., *MISO Furthers Wind Integration into Market*, http://www.nrel.gov/wind/news/2011/1561.html (last visited Apr. 16, 2012).

3. THE ROLE OF THE FEDERAL GOVERNMENT IN ADAPTATION

Climate change impacts are already happening in the United States. According to the latest IPCC assessments, even if mitigation efforts are successful, these impacts will only worsen in the coming years due to past and present emissions. As a result, efforts to adapt to climate change have become more important.

In October 2009, President Obama created through executive order the Interagency Climate Change Adaptation Task Force, which is co-chaired by three crucial entities for federal adaptation planning: the Council on Environmental Quality, the National Oceanic and Atmospheric Administration, and the Office of Science and Technology Policy. The task force has begun meeting but is still in the beginning stages of its work.

While the focus in this chapter is on the federal government, addressing adaptation requires action by federal, state, and local governments, which raises difficult questions of how the federal government should invoke its authority in relation to these other levels of government. The following excerpt from an article by Professor Robert Glicksman explores the contours of these federalism dilemmas.

ROBERT L. GLICKSMAN, CLIMATE CHANGE ADAPTATION: A COLLECTIVE ACTION PERSPECTIVE ON FEDERALISM CONSIDERATIONS

40 Envtl. L. 1159 (2010)

The longer Congress dithers and stumbles in its efforts to pass climate change legislation aimed at reducing greenhouse gas emissions, the greater will be the need for the adoption and implementation of climate change adaptation measures. As the Congressional Budget Office has recognized, "[t]he world is committed to some degree of warming from emissions that have already occurred, and even very aggressive emissions restrictions are unlikely to halt the growth of concentrations for many years to come." Most climate change scientists seem to agree. Although the exact nature, extent, and distribution of the adverse effects of climate change is unknowable, the climate change to which the world is already committed threatens to transform natural ecosystems and disrupt human social and economic systems that rely on them, perhaps to an unprecedented degree and within a relatively short time period. According to the Intergovernmental Panel on Climate Change (IPCC), the expected impacts of climate change include melting of glaciers, intensifying droughts and runoff, rising sea levels, and changes in the morphology, physiology, phenology, reproduction, species distribution, community structure, ecosystem processes, and species evolutionary processes among marine, freshwater, and terrestrial biological systems.

. . . .

Despite the critical need for the development of adaptive responses to climate change, the federal government has done little to stake out its turf on adaptation policy or to coordinate the responses of lower levels of government. This Article takes the need for the development of an effective adaptation policy as a given and focuses on the proper allocation of decision making authority within our federal system of government. While much has been written about the federalism implications of climate change mitigation policy, relatively less has been written about the federalism issues arising from climate change adaptation policy. This disproportionate emphasis on mitigation is not because the problems facing adaptation policymakers are any simpler than those relating to adaptation, or because the government is further along in devising solutions. President Obama's Interagency Climate Change Task Force has posited that that "[a]daptation and resilience will require action from all segments of society — the public sector . . . the nonprofit sector and individuals. This challenge provides Federal, Tribal, State, and local governments with significant opportunities for innovation." The Task Force also stated that significant gaps in the United States government's approach to climate change adaptation and building resilience exist, including the absence of a unified strategic vision and approach, an understanding of the challenges at all levels of government, and an organized and coordinated effort among federal, state, local, and tribal actors.

One argument for devolving considerable control over the formulation and implementation of adaptation policy to the state and local levels is that the effects of climate change will vary by location, requiring different strategies. If a "one size fits all" approach was ill-suited to pollution control regimes, it is likely to be that much more problematic when addressing climate change adaptation issues. Accordingly, some have advocated placing the power and responsibility of dealing with adaptation issues principally in the hands of local governments. The German federal government has accepted this view, postulating that "[p]eople on the spot often know best what is good for their specific case. . . . The Federal Government is therefore relying on strengthening individual capacity and adaptive capacity at the local level."

On the other hand, federal participation and leadership is likely to be necessary for several reasons: state and local authorities may lack the resources to lead the adaptation effort, they are likely to have incentives to put their citizens at an advantage vis-à-vis those of other jurisdictions fighting for scarce resources such as water, the actions of one jurisdiction may have adverse spill-over effects in other places, and coordination of the policies of multiple jurisdictions may be needed to ensure effectiveness. These have long been the justifications offered for affording a prominent role to the federal government in many environmental regulatory programs. As one observer noted, "federal systems always seem to face substantial pressure to devolve implementing policy choices to the local level. On the other hand, joint action is the raison d'être for federalism, and hence, the lines of authority must facilitate unity."

. . . .

II. The Design of Federal Climate Change Adaptation Policy

The options for the design of a federal policy for climate change adaptation range from affording state and local governments broad discretion to determine the nature of their responses, to divesting state and local power in favor of exclusive federal control. The appropriate option may differ depending on the strength of federal, state, and local interests in the traditional allocation of decision making authority over, and the nature of, the collective action problem implicated by the various resources and activities affected by climate change. The institutional considerations and federalism concerns are not necessarily the same for climate change adaptation as for mitigation policy. In particular, they may tilt more heavily in favor of an expansive role for state and localities in the adaptation context.

A. Models of Adaptation Federalism

The allocation of power among the federal government, states, and localities to determine the nature of governmental responses to the anticipated or actual effects of climate change can follow one of three models. First, the federal role could be confined to developing and providing information, or providing financial support for actions designed and implemented by state and local governments. The federal government could retain greater control while still leaving implementation authority primarily in state or local hands by conditioning the receipt of federal funds on adherence to federal standards or policies. Second, Congress could choose to follow the traditional cooperative federalism model in fashioning a climate change adaptation regime by setting goals, but delegating to the states the primary authority to achieve them through means selected by the states. Third, federal authority could displace state or local power, at least over certain aspects of the adaptation effort.

The first model is the one Congress used in the initial stages of the modern environmental area. Congress, during the 1960s, enacted legislation into the causes and effects of pollution, for example, but depended on the states to use that information to control the sources of pollution that created health and environmental risks. It also provided financial support for state regulatory efforts. Under the Clean Water Act, for example, the United States Environmental Protection Agency (EPA) has administered a program of grants and loans to state and local governments for the construction of sewage treatment plants. To this day, the federal environmental laws identify these kinds of information and resource-sharing efforts as critical statutory purposes.

The Clean Air Act, for example, includes among its purposes the "initiat[ion] and accelerat[ion of] a national research and development program . . . [to] prevent[] and control air pollution," and the "provi[sion of] technical and financial assistance to State and local governments . . . [to] develop[] and execut[e] . . . their air pollution prevention and control programs." Other environmental statutes reflect similar goals. Although the federal role in controlling air and water pollution has moved well beyond providing federal technical and financial support to state and local programs, federal statutes specifically directed at climate change to date focus on information gathering and distribution, not regulatory action. Other nations with federal systems have concluded that an appropriate role for the federal government is supplying information on climate change adaptation to lower level units of government.

One way to increase the federal government's role in the development of climate change adaptation strategies without displacing state and local authorities as the primary policymaking bodies would be to use Congress's authority under the Spending Clause to condition the provision of federal funds for adaptation planning on compliance with federal standards or criteria. In particular, federal funding could be conditioned on compliance with adaptation strategies that do not interfere with federal purposes or damage the national interest. This approach would leave state and local governments with the option of choosing not to follow the federal lead if they are willing to forego federal financial assistance. Some of the major climate change bills considered by Congress in 2009 and 2010 would have conditioned federal funds for adaptation planning in this way. The federal government could condition the receipt of federal flood insurance, funding for infrastructure projects, and agricultural subsidies, among other things, on the willingness of states and localities to comply with federal adaptation planning procedures and criteria. The imposition of conditions on the receipt of federal funds obviously results in a greater coercive impact than the distribution of unconditional federal grants for activities such as adaptation planning by the states. Depending on the nature and scope of the conditions, conditional funding may nevertheless impose a measure of federal oversight while retaining considerable state discretion.

A second model, which would increase the extent to which the federal government controls the design and implementation of climate adaptation policy without ousting state or local exercises of power, is the cooperative federalism model reflected in the major federal pollution control statutes such as the Clean Air and Clean Water Acts. In those contexts, cooperative federalism involves shared governmental responsibility for achieving federally prescribed environmental protection goals. Under the Clean Air Act, for example, the federal government retains the authority to set national ambient air quality standards, delegates to the states the authority to achieve those standards through the preparation of implementation plans which must be approved by EPA, allows states to administer the permit program through which emission controls are applied to individual sources, requires sources to comply with federal technology-based standards such as those that apply to new stationary sources or sources of hazardous air pollutants but allows states to adopt more stringent standards, and shares enforcement authority with the states. Some European nations, including the Netherlands, have created climate change adaptation strategies that build on the cooperative federalism model.

A third model involves displacement of state and local authority to devise and implement climate change adaptation policy. Such preemption of state and local authority is rare in the federal environment laws. Most statutes explicitly preserve state authority to adopt standards that are more stringent than the federal floor. In rare instances, however, Congress has barred the states from adopting standards or other regulatory approaches that differ from federal standards in any way. The most important example is the Clean Air Act's prohibition on adoption by the states of motor vehicle emission standards that differ from EPA's standard. Congress carved out an exception from that prohibition for California because of the severity of its air pollution problems and the fact that it began regulating motor vehicle emissions before Congress adopted the Clean Air Act. If EPA waives the prohibition on state standards for California, other states may adopt standards equivalent to California's. In similar fashion, Congress could decide that the federal government should retain exclusive, or near-exclusive, control over certain aspects of climate change adaptation policy.

B. Mitigation and Adaptation Compared

It is unlikely that the same model is appropriate for all aspects of federal climate change adaptation policy. A federal information-sharing role may be best suited to some aspects, while others would accommodate conditional funding or traditional cooperative federalism arrangements. Even displacement of state and local authority may be appropriate in some areas. Some participants in the debate over climate change mitigation legislation have advocated displacement of state cap-and-trade programs for reducing GHG emissions. A federal trading program with a larger market than state schemes may enhance market liquidity, for example. In addition, leakage and race-to-the-bottom concerns may deter sufficient state level mitigation. Regardless of whether Congress decides to preempt state cap-and-trade programs, the considerations that bear on whether to preempt state and local measures relating to climate change mitigation policy are not necessarily the same as those relevant to the role of the states and localities in adapting to climate change.

Some of the analysis of whether the federal government should preempt state and local efforts to abate GHG emissions is likely to be applicable to analysis of adaptation federalism questions, too. As Professor Robin Craig has noted, for example, pollution control laws bear on adaptation as well as mitigation because a reduction in some forms of pollution will reduce ecological stressors and thus enhance ecosystem resilience to climate change. As a result, a legislative decision that federal mitigation policy demands a minimal level of controls on GHG emissions (and preemption of less stringent state measures) might also support federal displacement of state control over adaptation policies that seek to foster ecosystem resilience. Two aspects of climate change adaptation policy, however, suggest that preservation of a strong state and local role is even more important than it is in the mitigation context.

First, climate change adaptation policy will need to address a broader and more diffuse set of problems than the ones targeted by mitigation policy. As Professor J.B. Ruhl has noted, "Mitigation policy is . . . all about the same goal — cutting down greenhouse gas concentrations in the atmosphere. Adaptation, by contrast, is about many different effects, varied across the nation, operating at many different and sometimes competing scales." As a result, while the federal government will have an important role in formulating the broad goals of adaptation policy, effective adaptation strategies are likely to be site-specific. The problems will differ by location — drought may be the problem in one place, while another is prone to flooding — and, even when the problems are similar, what is effective in preparing for and accommodating to the effects of climate change in one place, such as preparing for flooding resulting from rising sea levels along the coast, may be ineffective or even counterproductive in another, where flooding may be due to increased snow-melt in the spring due to rising temperatures. In short, effective adaptation policy may depend on knowledge of and the ability to respond to diverse local conditions. State and local policymakers may be able to make the necessary adjustments more effectively than the federal government can.

Second, climate change adaptation policy will involve areas in which law and policy have traditionally been set at the state and local level, and in which the federal government has been loath to intervene. Two obvious examples are land use control and water allocation law. Land use controls such as zoning are likely to be important parts of climate change adaptation strategies. It may be necessary to restrict development in areas vulnerable to flooding or to preserve open space to provide connective corridors for migrating wildlife species unable to survive in existing habitat. Congress has almost always steered clear of establishing anything that remotely resembles a federal land use regulatory program — other than for lands and resources owned by the federal government — and has remained committed to protecting the sovereignty of state and local governments to control land use. This commitment, or the fear of the political backlash that the adoption of federal land use controls might cause, is a principal explanation, for example, of the Clean Water Act's failure to regulate nonpoint source pollution. It also at least partially explains why Congress has chosen not to regulate the construction of or access to structures that are magnets for automobiles — called indirect sources — under the Clean Air Act, even in areas of the country in which automotive pollution has contributed to persistent failures to attain the health-based primary national ambient air quality standards.

Climate change also will affect the distribution of water resources, providing too much water in some places and not enough in others. Adaptation policy can play a useful role in preventing waste in areas in which water is plentiful and assuring that water is diverted to areas in which shortages exist. Congress has been just as skittish about infringing on state authority to control water allocation as it has been to jump into the land use regulation business. As Robert Adler has explained, "since at least the middle of the nineteenth century, state water law has reigned supreme as the primary authority governing the allocation and use of water resources, as proclaimed by Congress, the executive branch, and the courts." Congress went to great lengths in the Clean Water Act to steer clear of any such infringement. Somewhat less absolutely, the Endangered Species Act declares a federal policy "that Federal agencies shall cooperate with State and local agencies to resolve water resources issues in concert with conservation of endangered species." These precedents suggest that Congress will, if possible, tread lightly on state and local authority to decide on climate change adaptation measures that entail decisions about land use and water allocation.

C. Resolving the Tension Between Historic Tradition and Current Need

The fact that states and localities have traditionally played a dominant role in controlling land use and water allocation does not mean they will or should continue to do so in addressing the risks posed by climate change. Changes are likely to occur. These traditions do mean, however, that efforts to enhance the federal government's authority to dictate land use and water [allocation] policy, or even to adopt minimal federal standards under a cooperative federalism-like regime, are likely to generate at least as much political opposition as the efforts to adopt mandatory controls on GHG emissions or to price carbon have generated. A tension between leaving sacrosanct state and local prerogatives in areas such as land and water use and recognizing the need for a larger federal role is therefore apt to shape the institutional design of federal climate change adaptation policy, whenever the federal government is prepared to tackle climate change adaptation. In striking the appropriate balance, collective action analysis may provide environmental policymakers with important insights on when it is appropriate for the federal government to establish a presence even in areas in which it has thus far been reluctant to stake out a significant role and on related institutional design questions.

. . . .

IV. Conclusion

The uncertainty about the magnitude and distribution of the effects of climate change makes it impossible to predict exactly what kinds of adaptive measures will be needed in different parts of the country and when they will be needed. There seems to be a consensus among those who have focused on climate change adaptation policy that the effort will necessarily involve federal, state, and local government participation. In an optimal world, policymakers at different levels would coordinate their responses so that adaptation proceeds as efficiently and effectively as possible, the burdens resulting from climate change are minimized, and the unavoidable burdens are distributed as equitably as possible, even though climate change is likely to affect some areas of the country, such as coastal areas vulnerable to flooding and severe storm activity, more than others.

It is inevitable, however, that clashes of interest will develop between jurisdictions when desired goods, such as potable water, are scarce or efforts by one state or locality to avoid the undesirable aspects of climate change shift the burden of those changes to other jurisdictions. Collective action analysis can help avoid or resolve such conflicts by assigning the authority to control the development of climate change adaptation policy to the level of government best situated to address a problem without exacerbating the adverse consequences of climate change for others. The conflicts are likely to arise both when states and localities fail to do enough to anticipate and react to climate change and when they do "too much." As the analysis above indicates, collective action analysis supports the exercise of federal power to create minimal protections against the ravages of climate change in the face of state or local reluctance to react to its consequences. The federal role, which would exist concurrently with the exercise of state and local power to respond to climate change, could involve providing technical and financial assistance to state and local governments or the creation of the kinds of cooperative federalism regulatory programs that have become entrenched in U.S. environmental law over the last forty years. In limited contexts, collective action analysis also supports displacement of the aggressive exercise of state and local authority to adapt to climate change in favor of exclusive federal control. These situations are most likely to involve state and local efforts that result in interstate externalities.

NOTES AND QUESTIONS

1. How do the regulatory challenges of adaptation compare to those of mitigation? What are the key similarities and differences?
2. Why does the federal government have a role to play in climate change adaptation? Do you agree with Professor Glicksman's conclusions about how the balance among federal, state, and local government should be struck in this context?
3. In addition to the taskforce, one role that the federal government has taken on is funding state and local adaptation efforts. For an overview of current initiatives by smaller scale governments, and of federal funding for state and local adaptation planning under President Clinton, see PEW CTR. ON GLOBAL CLIMATE CHANGE, ADAPTATION PLANNING — WHAT U.S. STATES AND LOCALITIES ARE DOING (2008), *available at* http://www.pewclimate.org/docUploads/ State_Adapation_Planning_02_11_08.pdf.

4. ONGOING INFLUENCE OF LITIGATION

The U.S. Supreme Court has thus far decided two climate change cases, *Massachusetts v. EPA* and *AEP v. Connecticut*, which are discussed in depth above. However, these two cases represent only a small sample of the many ways in which courts have been used to debate the problem of climate change. Over the past several years, climate change litigation has evolved from a few cases to a major emerging field. The following excerpt from an article by Professors David Markell and J.B. Ruhl provides a comprehensive empirical assessment of the cases that have been brought in U.S. federal and state courts.

DAVID MARKELL & J.B. RUHL, AN EMPIRICAL SURVEY OF CLIMATE
CHANGE LITIGATION IN THE UNITED STATES

40 Envtl. L. Rep. News & Analysis 10644, 10646–50 (2010)

The foundational gap we seek to begin to fill in this Article is a chronicling of developments in the judicial arena. In performing this chronicling function, we hope to contribute in two important respects to understanding of the climate change action in the courts to date. First, we compile and present basic information about the cases brought to date, e.g., the types of cases, where they have been brought, the types of plaintiffs and defendants involved, and the outcomes. In addition, we provide a further layer of analysis through our synthesis of this basic information and our identification of trends that have emerged thus far.

Some commentators have suggested that the courts are already significant drivers of climate change policy, and their role is likely to increase. Carol Browner, Director of the White House Office of Energy and Climate Change Policy, for example, has suggested that "the courts are starting to take control" of climate change. A December 2009 *Wall Street Journal* op-ed contends that, because of the lack of progress internationally and in domestic legislation, the "climate-change lobby is already shifting to Plan B . . . Meet the carbon tort." A recent *New York Times* article similarly concludes that we are likely to see increasing numbers of common-law nuisance cases in the climate change arena:

> In a report issued last year, Swiss Re, an insurance giant, compared the [common-law nuisance] suits to those that led dozens of companies in asbestos industries to file for bankruptcy, and predicted that "climate change-related liability will develop more quickly than asbestos-related claims." The pressure from such suits, the report stated, "could become a significant issue within the next couple of years."

Echoing this theme, Prof. Hari Osofsky suggests in a forthcoming article that courts have "become a critical forum in which the future of greenhouse gas emissions regulation and responsibility are debated."

Judicial action is not important solely because of the direction courts provide through their decisions, though that direction itself is of substantial significance. Scholars, policymakers, and others have begun to think about the implications of judicial decisions on the work of other branches. Prof. Richard Lazarus, for example, following the U.S. Court of Appeals for the Second Circuit's recent decision in *Connecticut v. American Electric Power*, a significant victory for activists because of its favorable holdings on standing and justiciability grounds, notes that a major challenge for "environmentalists" is "how best to use this win to help promote meaningful climate change legislation in Congress and regulatory action by EPA, where the issues will best be addressed." White House Director Browner similarly suggests that recent court decisions have "increased the pressure on Congress to pass legislation to curb heat-trapping gases."

This Article unpacks the realities of what one *New York Times* headline describes as courts serving as "battlefields" in "climate fights." We have read and coded every climate change case that has been resolved to date; and, if a case has been filed but no resolution has yet been reached, we have reviewed (and coded) the complaint and other documents in the court docket.

Some of what we have found is in line with our expectations, while other findings frankly took us by surprise. Briefly, with more detail and description following in later sections, eight of our findings include:

- Most of the cases brought to date are suits that environmental nongovernmental organizations (NGOs) have brought against the federal and/or state government, with a handful of "professional" environmental NGOs serving as plaintiffs in many of the cases;
- Most of the cases have been brought in federal court;
- Most of the cases are based on statutory causes of action (rather than constitutional or common-law claims);
- Many of the cases are based on National Environmental Policy Act (NEPA) or state "Little NEPA" claims and are focused on stopping coal-fired power plants;
- Adaptation is not on the litigation radar screen;
- Common-law nuisance cases are a very small component of the case mix, despite the significant attention they have received;
- Of the relatively small number of cases that have been resolved, the success rate for plaintiffs is roughly 50%; and
- The use of the courts to raise climate change issues really gained steam in 2006; before that year, climate change litigation was quite rare.

In the following section, we explain the methodology we used in this initial effort to provide a comprehensive picture of the role of the courts to date in the development of the law on climate change.

II. Study Method

The goal of this study is to evaluate what is happening on the ground in the world of climate change litigation. As we indicate in the introductory section of this Article, there are a number of articles about different facets of climate change litigation, but we believe that ours is the first to attempt a comprehensive empirical description of all of the climate change litigation initiated to date. In this section, we explain how we defined climate change litigation, identified cases that met the criteria, and coded each case for relevant attributes.

A. Defining Climate Change Litigation

. . . .

We decided, therefore, to define climate change litigation as any piece of federal, state, tribal, or local administrative or judicial litigation in which the party filings or tribunal decisions directly and expressly raise an issue of fact or law regarding the substance or policy of climate change causes and impacts. So, in the power plant example, if the claim were that the environmental impact analysis failed to take into account GHG emissions, or that the permit hearing was defective because the tribunal refused to allow evidence of GHG emissions, that would qualify the case as climate change litigation.

. . . .

To help add details to our general definition of climate change, we also developed a typology of different claims that might be expected to arise in the climate change litigation world (see Table 1). The typology includes claims that are actively being litigated in numerous cases, such as claims that a species should be listed under the ESA [Endangered Species Act] because of threats stemming from climate change, as well as claims not yet likely to arise in litigation but which could arise as policy develops, such as disputes over offset contracts and claims that a property owner failed to take adequate adaptation measures to respond to sea-level rise. This typology proved robust, accounting for all but a few of the cases we ultimately deemed to qualify as climate change litigation (see Table 1, Case Type 18, "Other").

. . . .

III. Findings

Based on sheer number of cases, the prototype of climate change litigation in the United States involves an environmental NGO suing a federal agency in federal court to prevent the agency from taking an action by alleging that the agency violated NEPA. Yet, this configuration by no means defines the breadth and depth of the cases in our study. Indeed, the rich diversity of attributes in the cases suggests the future holds a broadening of litigation themes over time. In this section, we delve into some of those attributes by examining the full scope of: (1) parties and forums; (2) types of claims and litigation objectives; and (3) the outcomes, status, and trends of the cases.

A. Parties and Forums

One clear finding of our study is that NGOs are driving climate change litigation as plaintiffs, and their primary targets are the federal government and states . . . [E]nvironmental NGOs were plaintiffs in almost two thirds of the cases, and industry NGOs were involved in over 10%, meaning NGOs were involved as plaintiffs in almost three-quarters of the cases. Companies and state and local governments were also frequently involved as plaintiffs. On the defendant side, . . . the federal government was a named defendant in over one-third of the cases, and states were defendants in over one-quarter of the cases. Companies and local governments were also frequently named as defendants.

. . . .

Intergovernmental litigation was not a common occurrence. The federal government was not a plaintiff in any case. States were named plaintiffs in 11 suits against the federal government, and local governments were named plaintiffs in eight such cases. Also, in one case, a state government sued a local government. There were no other examples of intergovernmental litigation. Of course, as *Massachusetts v. EPA* demonstrates, small numbers in this sense do not necessarily mean small impact.

As Figure 3 shows, over one-half of climate change cases have been filed in federal court, and over one-quarter in state court. Litigation in federal and state agencies accounted for just over 10% of the cases, while we found no examples of local court or agency litigation.

. . . .

Table 1. Case Typology

Category	Case Type	Cases # (%)
Substantive Mitigation Regulation	1. Action to prevent or limit a legislative or agency decision to carry out, fund, or authorize a direct or indirect source of GHG emissions, e.g., building, funding, or permitting a coal power plant.	25 (18%)
	2. Action challenging a legislative or agency decision to refuse or place limits on proposals to carry out, fund, or authorize a direct or indirect source of GHG emissions, e.g., to overturn denial of a power plant permit.	5 (3.5%)
	3. Action to require a legislature or agency to promulgate a statute, rule, or policy establishing new or more stringent limits on GHG emissions by regulating direct or indirect sources, e.g., to force EPA to regulate GHG emissions; to force local government to impose green building requirements.	10 (6.5%)
	4. Action challenging legislative or agency promulgation of statute, rule, or policy establishing new or more stringent limits on [GHG] emissions that regulate direct or indirect sources, e.g., to prevent EPA from regulating GHG emissions; to challenge local decisions to require green building.	13 (9.5%)
	5. Government enforcement action against direct or indirect GHG emissions source alleging violation of regulatory or permit limits.	0
	6. Citizen enforcement action against direct or indirect GHG emissions source alleging violation of regulatory or permit limits.	4 (3%)
Substantive Adaptation Measures	7. Action to require legislative or agency action on statute, rule, policy, or permit to require new or more extensive climate change adaptation actions, e.g., to require a coastal development permittee to retain wetlands as sea level buffer.	0
	8. Action to prevent legislative or agency action on statute, rule, policy, or permit that proposes to require new or more extensive climate change adaptation actions, e.g., to challenge proposed sea wall.	0
	9. Government enforcement action against public or private entity alleging violation of regulatory or permit condition related to climate change adaptation.	0
	10. Citizen enforcement action against public or private entity alleging violation of regulatory or permit condition related to climate change adaptation.	0

Category	Description	Count
Procedural Monitoring, Impact Assessment, and Information Reporting	11. Action to impose on public or private entities a new or more extensive monitoring, impact assessment, or information disclosure requirement focused on GHG emissions, impacts of climate change, or means and success of climate change adaptation, e.g., to require NEPA documentation for coastal development to account for sea-level rise in EIS; to require public companies to disclose GHG emissions.	57 (41%)
	12. Action to prevent imposition on public or private entities a new or more extensive monitoring, impact assessment, or information disclosure requirement focused on GHG emissions, impacts of climate change, or means and success of climate change adaptation, e.g., to challenge proposed GHG emissions monitoring requirement.	0
Rights & Liabilities	13. Action to extend scope of human rights, property rights, or civil rights to provide protection of individual or public against effects of or responses to climate change, e.g., claim that GHG source violates civil rights; claim that immigration policy for climate refuges violates human rights.	0
	14. Action to impose statutory, tort, nuisance, or other property damage or personal injury liability on source of GHG emissions or for inadequate climate change mitigation or adaptation measures, e.g., public-nuisance action against GHG emission sources; public-nuisance claim for destruction of coastal dunes.	6 (4.5%)
	15. Action to impose contract, insurance, securities, fraud, failure to disclose, or other business or economic injury liability on source of GHG emissions or for inadequate climate change mitigation or adaptation measures, e.g., insurance recovery claim for effects of sea-level rise; dispute over carbon credit market transaction.	2 (1.5%)
Identification of Climate-Threatened Resources	16. Action to force agency to identify species or other resource as climate-threatened and list under federal or state ESA or other statute.	7 (5%)
	17. Action to reverse decision by agency to identify species or other resource as climate-threatened and list under federal or state ESA or other statute.	2 (1.5%)
Other	18. Other — not defined by other categories.	8 (6%)

B. Types of Cases and Litigation Objectives

Table 1 shows our typology of cases and the number of cases in our study fitting each category. As noted above, we developed the typology based on our review of literature about the status and future of climate change litigation. Thus, some of the litigation types had no matching cases. This is a significant finding, in that it shows that some forms of climate change litigation remain anticipated. For example, no case involved a claim regarding substantive climate change adaptation measures, whereas over 40% of the cases focused on substantive mitigation measures. The other major category, also accounting for over 40% of the cases, involved claims that causes or effects of climate change had not adequately been incorporated into impact assessment or information disclosure procedures, such as NEPA. The rest of the cases involved a range including ESA listing litigation and tort and contract liability litigation.

Table 2 digs a little deeper into the attributes of cases in the two major litigation thrusts — substantive mitigation and procedural defects. The patterns are quite similar in both categories, but a few noteworthy differences are apparent. For example, most industry NGO and company-initiated litigation is focused on substantive mitigation issues, whereas most environmental NGO litigation is focused on procedural claims. Also, state governments are the most frequent defendant in substantive mitigation cases, whereas the federal government is the most frequent defendant in the procedural cases.

We designed the typology also to allow us to differentiate between what we refer to as "pro" and "anti" cases, with "pro" cases having the objective of increasing regulation or liability associated with climate change, and "anti" cases being aimed in the opposite direction . . . [W]ith 85% of the cases, "pro" litigation is the dominant thrust. Not surprisingly, our data show that "pro" litigation is most associated with environmental NGO plaintiffs, and "anti" litigation is most associated with industry NGO and company-initiated litigation.

. . . .

Clearly, cases designed to prevent government action predominate, with NEPA and similar state statutes accounting for over one-third of the claims. Litigation to prevent issuance of permits to coal-fired power plants is also a significant component of this category, as are cases to prevent issuance of permits to other industrial facilities. In the much smaller category of cases to force government action, ESA listing cases accounted for the largest number, though other statutes were not far behind.

. . . .

C. Outcomes, Status, and Trends

[C]limate change litigation is a relatively recent phenomenon, with only 18 cases having been filed prior to 2006. Not surprisingly, therefore, most of the federal cases are pending or reached final resolution in district courts, . . . with a small percentage reaching appellate stages.

. . . .

[H]owever, . . . many cases have attained some degree of success on the merits. Almost one-third of all "pro" cases and a little over 10% of all "anti"

Table 2. Attributes of Substantive Mitigation and Procedural Cases

Category	Attribute	Substantive Cases (#)	Procedural Cases (#)
Plaintiff	Federal	0	0
	State	5	4
	Local	3	5
	Tribal	0	3
	Env. NGO	40	52
	Ind. NGO	11	2
	Company	11	1
	Individual	0	2
Defendant	Federal	17	38
	State	28	14
	Local	7	11
	Tribal	0	0
	Company	20	11
	Individual	2	0
Forum	Federal Court	27	36
	State Court	16	19
	Local Court	0	0
	U.S. EPA	8	1
	Other Federal Agency	0	0
	State Agency	6	1
	Local Agency	0	0
Source of Law	Constitutional	7	3
	Statutory	50	55
	Common Law	1	0

cases have achieved partial or total success on the climate change-related claims. More cases in both categories, however, have been unsuccessful, either due to procedural defects or on the substantive merits—the climate change claims in over one-third of the "pro" cases and just under one-quarter of the "anti" cases have failed for one or the other reason.

Overall, the distribution of types of cases, their outcomes, and the relative recency of the filings suggests that the profile of climate change litigation is likely to be dynamic over the next decade. Over one-half of the cases in our study were filed in 2007 or later. Only 5% of cases have reached the appeals stage. No claims involving adaptation have been filed, and very few cases have involved tort, contract, human rights, or property rights claims. Moreover, one has to bear in mind that there is no comprehensive federal climate change legislation to begin with, thus accounting for the complete lack of federal enforcement litigation. Hence, climate change litigation has the potential to broaden in scope on many fronts and intensify across the board, including in areas where it is already quite active. In all likelihood, therefore, the findings of our study of cases filed through 2009 will be much different in many respects from our updated study in, say, 2015.

NOTES AND QUESTIONS

1. What are primary forms that climate change litigation takes? What is the appropriate role of courts in resolving these different types of controversies?
2. Cases focused on increased consideration of climate change in procedural decision-making, especially in the context of coal power plants, are by far the most common type of climate change litigation. Why do you think these cases are the most common and what influence do you think they will have?
3. What is the likely future of climate change litigation? Do you think the significance of these cases rests primarily in their direct regulatory influence, or in the indirect ways in which they change the discourse and put pressure on regulators and major emitters? For more discussion of this issue, see Hari M. Osofsky, *The Continuing Importance of Climate Change Litigation*, 1 CLIMATE L. 3 (2010).

CHAPTER 4

FOREIGN LEGAL DEVELOPMENTS: COMPARATIVE LAW AND POLICY

Countries around the world have varied widely in their response to the threat of climate change. The policies and actions of the United States federal government — considered in detail in Chapter Three — have been weak in comparison to many other industrialized countries. In the United States, as described at greater length in Chapter Five, subnational entities such as states and cities have emerged as leaders in devising laws and policies to address climate change. In contrast, the countries of the European Union (EU) have responded strongly and directly to the issue of climate change, most notably by establishing an EU-wide regulatory program to reduce greenhouse gas emissions. Other industrialized countries such as Canada fall somewhere between the U.S. and the EU countries in terms of their national commitment. Canada, for example, joined the Kyoto Protocol, but has struggled to meet its commitments and decided not to recommit to a second Kyoto Protocol period. Large developing countries such as China and Brazil are emerging as climate change policy leaders, but they face many challenges.

With the failure thus far of United Nations Framework Convention on Climate Change (UNFCCC) negotiations to produce a binding agreement that would reduce emissions adequately to avoid risks of major climate change impacts, the question emerges: To what extent can voluntary national policies, such as the ones countries commit to as Nationally Appropriate Mitigation Actions (NAMAs) under the UNFCCC, substitute for a coordinated international approach? Considering that 60 percent of greenhouse gas emissions come from just 10 countries (*see* Table 4.1), significant progress could be made on greenhouse gas reductions through agreements among small groups of countries. The Major Economies Forum approach described in Chapter Two reflects that understanding, but has yet to result in significant, specific commitments. While the world waits for more successful UNFCCC negotiations, great importance lies in the actions that each major emitter takes.

Table 4.1: Greenhouse Gas Emissions and Other Climate Change–Related Indicators for 2005 Top 10 Emitting Countries

2005 Rank	Country	2005 GHG Emissions (MMTCE)	2005 GHG Emissions (% of World)	1990 GHG Emissions (MMTCE)	1990-2005 Emissions Difference (MMTCE)	1990-2005 Increase or Decrease (%)	2005 Per Capita GHG Emissions (tons C/person)
1	China	1,974	19.1%	981	993	101.2%	1.5
2	United States	1,892	18.3%	1,634	258	15.8%	6.4
[3][a]	European Union-27	1,378	13.4%	1,467	-89	-6.1%	2.8
3	Russian Federation	532	5.2%	800	-268	-33.5%	3.7
4	India	509	4.9%	302	207	68.5%	0.5
5	Japan	370	3.6%	326	44	13.5%	2.9
6	Brazil	276	2.7%	188	88	46.8%	1.5
7	Germany	266	2.6%	326	-60	-18.4%	3.2
8	Canada	202	2.0%	159	43	27.0%	6.2
9	United Kingdom	176	1.7%	194	-18	-9.3%	2.9
10	Mexico	176	1.7%	125	51	40.8%	1.7
Total[b] (Top 10)		6,373	61.8%	5,035	1,338	26.6%	
WORLD		10,320	100.0%	8,380	2,189	26.1%	1.6

Source: Adapted from LARRY PARKER & JOHN BLODGETT, CONG. RESEARCH SERV., RL32721, GREENHOUSE GAS EMISSIONS: PERSPECTIVE ON THE TOP 20 EMITTERS AND DEVELOPED VERSUS DEVELOPING NATIONS app. B, tbl.B-1 (2010). Notes: (a) If the EU-27 were ranked in terms of its 2005 GHG emissions, it would place 3rd; (b) Totals are of the 10 individual nations; they do not include the European Union.

Studying the different approaches of countries to climate law and policy is important for additional reasons. In many cases, principles and strategies that are ultimately adopted at the international level are first developed or used in one or more countries. Countries also can learn from the successes and failures of policies in other countries. Finally, studying other countries allows us to evaluate the strength and appropriateness of our own national policies more honestly and thoroughly. To provide this comparative perspective, this chapter analyzes the climate change policies of several of the world's largest emitters outside the United States—the EU, Canada, China, and Brazil.

A. COMPARATIVE LAW APPROACHES

Significant legal and policy development will be required in most, if not all, countries in order to address climate change adequately. Even countries that are not large emitters are likely to need policies to adapt to climate change and prevent growth of emissions. Comparative law provides an approach or framework to understand how and why legal development differs in different places.

Traditionally, comparative law consisted primarily of rule-comparison, wherein experts focused on the text of legal rules, especially those embodied in legislative acts, as their principal object of study. Based on this approach, comparative lawyers would often advocate that countries "borrow" or "transplant" laws from other countries, particularly those viewed as more advanced in their legal development. *See* ALAN WATSON, LEGAL TRANSPLANTS: AN APPROACH TO COMPARATIVE LAW (1974). For example, the American and French Revolutionary legal reforms were widely emulated in other nations. John Henry Merryman, *Comparative Law Scholarship*, 21 HASTINGS INT'L & COMP. L. REV. 771, 773–74 (1998). In the environmental field, laws requiring the preparation of environmental impact studies originated in the United States and have been widely adopted elsewhere.

Comparative law scholars have often categorized the legal systems of countries as part of either the civil law tradition or the common law tradition. The legal systems of most European and Latin American countries are derived more directly from Roman law and are referred to as civil law legal systems, while England and the United States have common law legal systems. JOHN HENRY MERRYMAN, THE CIVIL LAW TRADITION: AN INTRODUCTION TO THE LEGAL SYSTEMS OF WESTERN EUROPE AND LATIN AMERICA (1969). In civil law countries, there is a stricter separation of powers among the branches of government that precludes considering judicial opinions as a source of law. Rather, the legislature makes law and the judges' role is to apply it to the case at hand. For these reasons, judges and courts in civil law countries are less likely to be influential actors in resolving cutting-edge legal and policy issues.

More recently, comparativists have emphasized the importance of a contextual approach, in which the law's social and cultural context is more fully taken into account. Professor John Henry Merryman suggests that comparative law scholars should consider a wide variety of differences in legal culture, legal institutions, legal actors, and legal processes. John Henry Merryman, *Comparative Law Scholarship*, 21 HASTINGS INT'L & COMP. L. REV. 771, 771 (1998). Comparative law scholars have also questioned the viability of legal transplants, doubting whether a law that emerged in one country's legal system can be inserted into another legal system with similar effect. Professor Pierre Legrand has argued that legal transplants are "impossible" because when a legal rule is moved to a new legal system, the meaning of the rule will inevitably change, given its new social and cultural context. *See* Pierre Legrand, *The Impossibility of 'Legal Transplants,'* 4 MAASTRICHT J. EUR. & COMP. L. 111 (1997).

In addition to the field's theoretical and methodological complexities, there are also practical barriers to effectively comparing the laws of different countries. Although differences in language can be overcome, difficulties of translation are real and important. Moreover, the cultural and historical nuances that affect legal processes and outcomes in different places often require that the legal comparativist use the research tools of social science. As Professor Legrand has written, "what is anthropology if not the study of foreign cultures? And, what does comparative legal studies address if not the study of foreign legal cultures?" Pierre Legrand, *How to Compare Now*, 16 LEGAL STUDIES 232, 238 (1996). As a practical matter, it may be difficult for one—or even of group of scholars—to amass the expertise necessary to fully understand the meaning and significance of legal change in different countries.

NOTES AND QUESTIONS

1. Assuming you can read French, how much do you think you would learn about French climate change policy by reading a French climate change law? What limits or barriers would you face? How useful of an exercise do you think it would be to compare the text of the French law with the text of California's Global Warming Solutions Act? If you were to propose to conduct research comparing climate change law in France and California, what research activities would you include in the proposal?
2. What elements of climate change law do you think might be good candidates for legal transplantation? Could rules setting forth a carbon tax or a cap-and-trade system be transplanted from one country to another? What about rules regarding coastal development or energy efficiency standards?
3. A large body of comparative scholarship exists about how environmental law is written, implemented, and enforced in different countries. Most often focusing on industrialized countries, such scholarship has found different "national styles of regulation." The United States for example has been found to rely more on adversarial processes and adjudication to enforce environmental laws. ROBERT A. KAGAN, ADVERSARIAL LEGALISM: THE AMERICAN WAY OF LAW (2001). The environmental agencies of countries such as Germany and Great Britain tend to deal with polluters in a more collaborative and conciliatory way. *Id.*; DAVID A. VOGEL, NATIONAL STYLES OF REGULATION: ENVIRONMENTAL POLICY IN GREAT BRITAIN AND THE UNITED STATES (1986). How might

differences in regulatory style influence how different countries undertake climate change law and regulation?

B. THE EUROPEAN UNION: ENERGETIC REGULATORY ACTION

The European Union (EU), which is the third largest greenhouse gas emitter when considered as a whole, has led in establishing a regulatory regime to reduce greenhouse gases. In 2005, the EU started an ambitious emissions trading program that covered about half of its carbon dioxide emissions. The EU took this action at the same time that the U.S. federal government was largely stagnant in developing a legal and policy response to climate change. How were European lawmakers able to move forward when U.S. policymakers were apparently bedeviled by arguments that climate change science was uncertain, and that climate change regulation would hurt the country's economy?

In order to understand the EU's climate change policy, some background on the EU's political and legal structure is helpful. The EU is composed of 27 member states, including Austria, Belgium, Bulgaria, Cyprus, the Czech Republic, Denmark, Estonia, Finland, France, Germany, Greece, Hungary, Ireland, Italy, Latvia, Lithuania, Luxembourg, Malta, the Netherlands, Poland, Portugal, Romania, Slovakia, Slovenia, Spain, Sweden, and the United Kingdom. Its origins date from the 1957 Treaty of Rome, in which six states (Belgium, France, Germany, Italy, Luxembourg, and the Netherlands) formed the European Economic Community to pursue common economic objectives. In 1993, the Treaty on European Union, or Maastricht Treaty, formally constituted the EU with the membership of 12 states. Additional countries joined in 1995, 2004, and 2007.

Three institutions are primarily responsible for making law and policy in the EU. The European Council, composed of the heads of state, is the primary policy-setting and decision-making body. The European Parliament, the members of which are directly elected, is responsible for passing legislation in coordination with the European Council. The European Commission acts as the EU's executive arm; it is responsible for initiating legislation and the day-to-day running of the EU.

The first and second sections below focus on how the EU became a world leader in climate change policy. The third section details the workings and outcomes of the EU's emissions trading program. The final section analyzes European progress towards meeting the emissions reductions target that it committed to in the Kyoto Protocol.

1. THE PRECAUTIONARY TURN

The European Union's aggressive action on climate change is consistent with a broader trend since the 1990s: environmental law in Europe has become more proactive and precautionary than environmental law in the United States. The following excerpt by Professor David Vogel explores this divergence.

DAVID VOGEL, THE HARE AND THE TORTOISE REVISITED: THE NEW POLITICS
OF CONSUMER AND ENVIRONMENTAL REGULATION IN EUROPE

33 Brit. J. Pol. Sci. 557, 557–68, 571–74 (2003)

This article describes and explains an important shift in the pattern of divergence between consumer and environmental protection policies in Europe and the United States. From the 1960s through the mid 1980s American regulatory standards tended to be more stringent, comprehensive and innovative than in either individual European countries or in the European Union (EU). The period between the mid 1980s and 1990 was a transitional period: some important regulations were more stringent and innovative in the EU, while others were more stringent and innovative in the United States. The pattern since 1990 is the obverse of the quarter-century between 1960 and the mid 1980s: recent EU consumer and environmental regulations have typically been more stringent, comprehensive and innovative than those of the United States.

To borrow Lennart Lundqvist's formulation, which he used to contrast American and Swedish air pollution control standards during the 1970s, since around 1990 the American 'hare' has been moving forward at a tortoise pace, while since the mid 1980s the pace of the European 'tortoise' resembles that of a hare. To employ a different metaphor, in a number of significant respects European and American regulatory politics have 'traded places'. Regulatory issues were formerly more politically salient and civic interests more influential in the United States than in most individual European countries or the EU. More recently, this pattern has been reversed. Consequently, over the last fifteen years, the locus of policy innovation with respect to many areas of consumer and environmental regulation has passed from the United States to Europe.

This historical shift in the pattern of divergence of European and American consumer and environmental regulations poses two questions. First, why has consumer and environmental regulation become more stringent, comprehensive and innovative in Europe since the mid 1980s? Secondly, why did it become less stringent, comprehensive and innovative in the United States after 1990? This article addresses both these questions, but it focuses primarily on describing and explaining the shift in European regulatory politics and policies. . . .

The EU has . . . replaced the leadership role of the United States in addressing global environmental problems. Through the 1980s most major international environmental agreements — most notably the London Convention on Dumping at Sea (1972), the Conventional on International Trade in Endangered Fauna and Flora (1973) and the Montreal Protocol (1987), which phased out the use of CFCs [chlorofluorocarbons] to protect the ozone layer — were both initiated and strongly supported by the United States, and subsequently ratified by either individual European countries or the EU. 'Since the early 1990s, however, effective US international environmental policy leadership has lapsed.' By contrast, by 1994 the Basel Convention on Hazardous Wastes (1989) had been ratified by every EU Member State but has yet to be ratified by the United States. Both the

Convention on Biological Diversity (1992) and the Biosafety Protocol (2000) were signed by the EU, but not by the United States.

The EU, as well as each of the member states, has ratified the Kyoto Protocol, an international treaty to reduce emissions of greenhouse gases, and a number of European nations have established policies to reduce carbon emissions. The United States refused to ratify the 1997 Kyoto Protocol, was not a party to the 2001 Bonn Agreement, and there are no federal controls on carbon emissions, only a set of voluntary guidelines. . . .

Another important indicator of the extent to which the United States and Europe have 'traded places' has to do with the transatlantic direction of regulatory emulation. During the 1970s and 1980s, the European environmental agenda was strongly influenced by the United States. Thus throughout the debates in Europe during this period over automotive emission standards, American standards often served as a benchmark, with environmentalists and their supporters pressuring the national governments and the EU to adopt them. Indeed, for both Sweden and the EU, the existence of more stringent American standards actually facilitated the strengthening of European standards; since global automobile manufacturers were now producing less polluting cars for the American market, it made both economic and environmental sense to require these firms to market similar vehicles in Europe. As a Swedish panel noted: 'the only realistic solution to the problem of strengthening the Swedish exhaust gas regulations seems, for the moment, to be an adaptation to the United States regulations.' . . .

More recently the transatlantic flow of influence has been in the opposite direction. American restrictions on leg-traps and its ban on animal feed for cattle have been influenced by developments in Europe.

Changes in European Regulatory Policies and Institutions

The emergence of the precautionary principle as a guide to regulatory decision making represents an important dimension of the new European approach to risk regulation. This principle legitimates regulation when 'potentially dangerous effects deriving from a phenomenon, product or process have been identified, and . . . scientific evaluation does not allow the risk to be determined with sufficient certainty [because] of the insufficiency of the data or their inconclusive or imprecise nature.' Originally developed in Germany during the 1970s and 1980s, it was incorporated in the 1993 Treaty of the European Union. Since 1994, it has been referenced in more than thirty reports and resolutions of the European Parliament.

While the precautionary principle cannot be divorced from science, since 'a scientific view of the risk is an essential component of the evaluation of risk that the principle anticipates', its growing popularity in Europe reflects the perception that scientific knowledge is an insufficient guide to regulatory policy. It requires the extension of scientific knowledge while simultaneously acknowledging 'the possible intrinsic limitations of scientific knowledge in providing the appropriate information in good time'. The principle thus both increases public expectations of science and reflects the public's skepticism of scientific knowledge. In effect, it reduces the scientific threshold for regulatory policy making. By mandating or precluding regulatory action, in advance of scientifically confirmed cause–effect relationships, the principle, 'curtails the ability of politicians to invoke scientific uncertainty as a justification for avoiding or delaying the imposition of more stringent protection measures'. While its legal significance at both the EU and national level remains unclear, the practical effect of the precautionary principle has frequently been to permit, or even require, the adoption of more risk-averse policies. It explicitly acknowledges the inherently political nature of regulatory decision making by enabling policy makers to take into account a wide variety of non-scientific factors, including public opinion and social values. . . .

Explaining the New European Regulatory Regime

What accounts for these changes in European regulatory policies and institutions? Explaining a complex set of developments over a period of nearly two decades presents a difficult analytical challenge. However, three sets of inter-related factors appear to have contributed to these institutional and policy shifts. They are: a series of regulatory failures and crises; broader citizen support for more risk-averse regulatory policies within Europe; and the growth of the regulatory competence of the EU. The former two factors have affected policies at both the national and EU levels; the latter has affected regulatory policies at the European level.

Regulatory Failures and Crises

The most important factor contributing to the increased stringency of health, safety and environmental regulation in Europe has been a series of regulatory failures and crises that placed new regulatory issues on the political agenda and pressured policy makers to adopt more risk averse or precautionary policies. In 1986 both the nuclear accident at Chernobyl and the Sandoz chemical fire on the Rhine, had significant trans-border impacts as well as important health and environmental consequences. The *Washington Post* observed in December 1988: 'Dead seals in the North Sea, a chemical fire on the Loire, killer algae off the coast of Sweden, contaminated drinking water in Cornwall. A drumbeat of emergencies has intensified the environmental debate this year in Europe, where public concern about pollution has never been higher.' According to Elizabeth Bomberg,

> These disasters made an impact. In 1992, the protection of the environment and the fight against pollution had become an 'immediate and urgent problem' in the view of 85% of EU citizens. . . . Eurobarometer surveys in 1989 and the early 1990s registered up to 91% of EU citizens expressing support for a common European policy for protecting the environment. . . . Questions on the environment evoked stronger and more positive support for unified EU action than did questions concerning any other area of policy.
>
> . . .

Regulatory failures or crises do not automatically lead to shifts in public attitudes or public policy. After all, Europe had experienced regulatory failures prior to the mid 1980s. But the policy impact of the regulatory failures and crises during the second half of the 1980s and the 1990s has been broader and deeper. Their cumulative impact has been to increase the public's sense of vulnerability to and anxiety about the risks associated with modern society and this in turn has affected the political context in which regulatory policies have been made. . . .

Political Developments

A second, related, explanation for the change in European regulatory policies and institutions has to do with political developments within individual European countries. During much of the 1980s, support for strict environmental, health and safety regulations in Europe was geographically polarized. Often, Germany, the Netherlands and Denmark favoured stricter and more risk-averse regulations, while Britain, France and Italy opposed them. Much of EU environmental policy making thus represented a struggle between the EUs three 'green' member states, where constituencies representing civic interests enjoyed considerable public support and influence (the Green party has played an important role in Germany since 1983), and Britain, France and Italy, where they did not. But while Germany, the Netherlands and Denmark continue to play a role as environmental 'pioneers', in the EU (subsequently joined in 1995 by Sweden, Austria and Finland), strong public interest and support for stricter health and environmental standards has spread south and west within Europe. This change has been particularly significant in Britain and France, which are no longer regulatory 'laggards' within Europe.

During the 1990s, British public opinion became 'greener' and Britain's green lobbies become more influential. This in turn has affected a number of British policies. In 1990, as part of a broader re-examination of its environmental policies, Britain formally adopted the precautionary principle as one of the 'basic aims and principles supporting sustainable development'. The application of this principle has affected a number of British regulatory policies, including the dumping of sewer sludge in the North Sea and domestic water pollution standards. It has also strained Britain's consultative regulatory style, challenging the ability of regulators to justify lax controls or regulatory delays on the grounds that they have inadequate knowledge of harm and forcing them to take preventive action in advance of conclusive scientific opinion. . . .

The European Union

In addition to a series of regulatory failures, and related broadening and deepening of public support for more stringent regulatory polices within Europe, the emergence of the EU as a more important source of regulatory policy making has also affected the stringency and scope of European regulatory policies. It is significant that the changes in European regulatory policies and politics described in this article began around the time of the enactment of the Single European Act (SEA) in 1987. This amendment to the Treaty of Rome, by enabling directives to be enacted by a system of qualified majority voting instead of unanimity, significantly accelerated the EU's regulatory competence. The EU has played a critical role in changing the dynamics of European regulatory policies: each subsequent revision of the Treaty of Rome has accorded civic interests greater weight in the policy process. Combined with growing public support for risk-averse policies, these revisions have had important policy impacts.

The SEA gave environmental policy a treaty basis for the first time, specifying that preventive action should be taken whenever possible and requiring that harmonized standards take as a base 'a high level of protection'. The Treaty on the European Union (1993) made precaution a guiding principle of EU environmental policy: 'Community policy shall aim at a high level of protection taking into account the diversity of situations in the various regions of the Community. It shall be based on the precautionary principle and on the principles that preventive action should be taken'. The Treaty of Amsterdam (1997) called upon the Council and the Parliament to achieve high levels of health, safety, environmental and consumer protection in promulgating single market legislation and Article 153 explicitly defined consumer policy and health protection as 'rights'. It also extended the precautionary principle to consumer protection.

As Majone has noted, the EU is primarily a regulatory state: issuing rules is its most important vehicle for shaping public policy in Europe. Notwithstanding frequent criticisms of the EU's 'democratic deficit', its institutions have played an important role in strengthening the representation of civic or diffused interests. The influence of consumer and environmental pressure groups on the Commission remains limited and they typically enjoy less access than representatives of business. There are, however, exceptions: the European Consumers Union did lead a successful campaign calling for the EU to ban beef hormones, while Greenpeace worked with Green parties to mobilize public and political opposition against the approval of GMOs in Europe. In addition, the 'European Court of Justice has often played a crucial role in promoting civic interests' and has been repeatedly willing 'to be influenced by consumer and civic concerns in reaching its judgments'.

EU treaties have also steadily expanded the role of the European Parliament, a body in which consumer and environmental interests have been relatively influential, in shaping European legislation. The SEA granted Parliament legislative power under 'cooperation' procedures, and these were expanded by the Maastricht Treaty which established 'co-decision' procedures, thus giving the Parliament and the Council of Ministers co-responsibility for writing legislation. The Parliament's purview over environmental legislation was expanded by the Amsterdam Treaty. 'Despite the limitations of co-decision, its use as the legislative procedure for environmental measures considerably strengthens the Parliament's role in the adoption of new environmental legislation.' The Green party has been an important political presence in the European Parliament since 1989, when it captured thirty-seven seats; following the June 1999 election it again had thirty-seven members. The Parliament has often been an effective source of pressure on the Council for the adoption of more stringent regulations. . . .

NOTES AND QUESTIONS

1. Since its first articulation in international law in 1987, the precautionary principle has become a common element in international environmental agreements. More than 90 international agreements include the precautionary principle in one form or another, including the UNFCCC. Perhaps the most authoritative statement of the principle is in the Rio Declaration of 1992: "Where there are threats of serious or irreversible damage, lack of full scientific certainty shall not be used as a reason for postponing cost-effective measures to prevent environmental degradation." United Nations Conference on Environment and Development, Rio de Janiero, Braz., June 3–14, 1992, *Rio Declaration on Environment and Development*, princ. 15, U.N. GAOR, 46th Sess., U.N. Doc. A/CONF. 151/26/Rev.1 (Vol. I), Annex I (Aug. 12, 1992), June 13, 1992, *available at* http://www.unep.org/Documents.Multilingual/Default.asp?documentid=78&articleid=1163.

What aspects of climate change make it a good candidate for the application of the precautionary principle? What other environmental threats or problems do you think might be well-suited for the application of the precautionary principle?

2. The United States and Europe differ greatly in their reception of the precautionary principle. The 1992 Treaty on European Union, which created the EU and instituted the euro currency, states that policy "shall be based on the precautionary principle and on the principles that preventative action should be taken, that environmental damage should as a priority be rectified at source and that the polluter should pay." In 2000, the European Commission, which acts as the EU's executive arm, adopted a communication that endorsed and explained the role of the precautionary principle in the management of risk. *See Communication from the Commission on the Precautionary Principle*, COM (2000) 1 final (Feb. 2, 2000). How does Europe's action on climate change accord with the precautionary principle? Do you think that Europe's formal adoption of the precautionary principle helps explains its leadership in climate change policy? Would full implementation of the precautionary principle require going even further than Europe has?

3. In the United States, in contrast, some academics and policymakers have criticized the precautionary principle as being antiscientific and unworkable as a regulatory decision-making tool, while others have supported greater incorporation of this principle into policy. For an example of such a critique, see Cass R. Sunstein, Laws of Fear: Beyond the Precautionary Principle (2005). While the principle has not been formally recognized in national or state law in the United States, a couple of cities have incorporated it into their municipal codes. In 2003, San Francisco adopted the precautionary principle as the first chapter of the city's environment code. San Francisco, Cal., Ordinance 171-03 (2003). Also, the City of Berkeley amended its municipal code to add a chapter on the precautionary principle in 2006. Berkeley, Cal., Ordinance 6,911-N.S. (2006). How can this great difference in the level of acceptance of the precautionary principle be explained? Why do you think the precautionary principle has had most success at the local level?

2. INSTITUTIONS AND LEADERSHIP

In addition to the role of ideas, the role of institutions must be considered in explaining the EU's commitment to action on climate change. The

following account by Professors Miranda Schreurs and Yves Tiberghien analyzes the role that different EU institutions have played in shaping its policy in
the wake of the United States choosing not to move forward with Kyoto
Protocol commitments.

MIRANDA A. SCHREURS & YVES TIBERGHIEN, MULTI-LEVEL REINFORCEMENT:
EXPLAINING EUROPEAN UNION LEADERSHIP IN CLIMATE CHANGE MITIGATION

7 Global Envtl. Pol., no. 4, 2007 at 19, 20–21, 40–41

The most significant instance of EU leadership is arguably its decision to
move forward with ratification of the Kyoto Protocol after President George W.
Bush made clear on March 28, 2001, that his intention was to withdraw the US
from the agreement. The US pull-out left Europe in a conundrum. The US
accounted for 36.1 percent of the 1990 CO_2 emissions of industrialized
countries. The EU as a whole was responsible for a somewhat smaller 24.2
percent. If the protocol was to survive, the EU would have to convince states
representing another 30.8 percent of 1990 industrialized country CO_2 emissions to join it in ratifying the agreement in order to meet the Kyoto Protocol's
somewhat arbitrary requirement that 55 percent of industrialized states' 1990
CO_2 emissions be represented by ratifying states in order for the agreement to
go into effect. This meant that the EU, at a minimum, would have to convince
Japan (responsible for 8.5 percent of 1990 industrialized states' emissions) and
Russia (responsible for 17.4 percent) to ratify.

Despite these obstacles, the European Council formally agreed to the
Kyoto Protocol on 25 April 2002. . . .

Why did the European Union feel so strongly about preserving Kyoto? What
were the factors motivating the Europeans to be so disapproving of the Bush
administration's actions? The US pull out could have provided Europe with an
easy way out of a treaty that few states in Europe would find easy to fulfill. As of
2000, many states were already far off their Kyoto targets. Why then was European
reaction so strongly opposed to Bush's abandonment of the agreement?

EU leadership has been driven by a combination of factors. While public
opinion and the presence of green parties were certainly important to creating
a milieu supportive of action, EU leadership resulted from a process of mutual
leadership reinforcement by different actors involved in the EU's process of
multi-level governance. The leadership roles played by several Member States
(especially Germany, the UK, the Netherlands, and Denmark but also Austria,
Finland, Luxembourg, and Sweden) were important. This leadership often
played out in particularly strong ways at times when Member States held
the presidency of the European Council. Perhaps recognizing the importance
of this responsibility, Member States at times also showed a willingness to
strategically pass the leadership baton off to the next player. As UK Foreign
Secretary Margaret Beckett said during a speech in Berlin just prior to Germany
assuming the dual responsibility of the presidency of the European Union and
of the G8: "We are willing to work with you on a concrete proposal [for climate
change] to come out of your twin presidencies. . . . [W]e will support you. But
you must lead. . . . The baton has passed to Germany. Please don't drop it."

The [European] Commission has also played a central role. In many ways, for the Commission, climate change is seen as one of the European Union's most important and defining issues, and the Kyoto Protocol a crucial show case of the EU's willingness and ability to lead on foreign policy matters. . . . The Commission is well aware that a failure to fulfill Kyoto Protocol obligations could hurt European credibility in any future global environmental negotiations and raise legitimate questions regarding Europe's ability to lead. To remedy the emerging gap between the Kyoto target and reality, a first batch of implementation measures was introduced by the Commission under the European Climate Change Program adopted in June 2001. Since then, the Commission has pushed several new directives dealing with the promotion of renewables, higher efficiency in heat and power generation, the energy performance of buildings, and emissions trading, among others.

The [European Parliament] has also been a frequent champion of EU leadership, supported by green parties and environmental NGOs. In many ways, its role has been reinforcing of the leadership exhibited by key member states and the Commission.

EU leadership on climate change may also have been partly self-serving. It became a wedge issue for the EU, a way for the EU to build coalitional strength with other nations and in the process enhance its strength vis-à-vis the United States. It can also be argued that not only has the EU successfully promoted Member State and international cooperation in the obtainment of a collective good, despite at times high individual costs, but also enhanced its own institution building goals in the process.

NOTES AND QUESTIONS

1. Professors Schreurs and Tiberghien explain how the European Council, Commission, and Parliament have all acted in support of climate change policies. In the same period of time, the roughly parallel institutions of the United States, namely the executive and legislative branches, have been gridlocked on the issue. How can this difference be explained? Are U.S. political institutions ossified in a way that prevents them from being able to respond to new environmental threats? It is perhaps worthy of note that almost all significant environmental laws in the United States date from the 1970s and 1980s. The 1990s and 2000s have, in contrast, been a period of "regulatory recoil and reinvention," during which U.S. environmental law has been on the defensive against claims that it is inefficient and bad for the economy. ROBERT V. PERCIVAL ET AL., ENVIRONMENTAL REGULATION: LAW, SCIENCE AND POLICY 88 (2006).

2. At COP 15 in Copenhagen in 2009, the European Union pushed for a binding agreement to succeed the Kyoto Protocol. The European Union was effectively sidelined toward the end of the negotiations, when the United States, China, India, Brazil, and South Africa brokered the nonbinding Copenhagen Accord. At COP 16 in Cancún in 2010, the European Union favored legally binding emissions reduction targets, but the Cancún

agreements instead endorsed the voluntary commitments of the Copenhagen Accord. At COP 17 in Durban in 2011, the Kyoto Protocol parties decided to establish a second commitment period, but only the European Union has made clear commitments thus far, and other parties such as Canada, Japan, and Russia have indicated that they will not commit to further targets and timetables under that agreement. What do the outcomes of these COPs imply about the EU's future role in international climate change negotiations? Can the EU regain the leadership role that it once had, or will the United States and China play the leading roles?

3. THE EUROPEAN UNION EMISSIONS TRADING SCHEME

The largest regulatory system ever established to address climate change has been operating in the EU since 2005. The EU Emissions Trading Scheme (ETS) is a cap-and-trade program that regulates about 11,500 stationary sources in the 27 European member states. As Chapter One discusses in more depth, a cap-and-trade program establishes an overall limit (or cap) on the emissions of covered sources, creates a corresponding number of emissions allowances, and allows sources to trade allowances in markets. The EU ETS covers about 40 percent of all greenhouse gas emissions in the EU.

A cap-and-trade program was first suggested as an important component of the European Climate Change Programme in a Green Paper issued by the European Commission in March 2000. *See* A. DENNY ELLERMAN & PAUL L. JOSKOW, PEW CTR. ON GLOBAL CLIMATE CHANGE, THE EUROPEAN UNION'S EMISSIONS TRADING SYSTEM IN PERSPECTIVE (2008), *available at* http://www.pewclimate.org/docUploads/EU-ETS-In-Perspective-Report.pdf. The European Parliament and Council issued the final Emissions Trading Directive in October 2003, just over a year before the program was slated to begin. *See* Directive 2003/87/EC, of the European Parliament and of the Council of 13 October 2003 Establishing a Scheme for Greenhouse Gas Emission Allowance Trading Within the Community and Amending Council Directive 96/61/EC, *available at* http://eur-lex.europa.eu/LexUriServ/LexUriServ.do?uri=OJ:L:2003:275:0032:0046:en:PDF.

An EU Directive is a framework that has to be given legal force and implementation through a process called *transposition*, which requires each member state government to issue legislative and regulatory measures to implement the directive. In late 2003 and 2004, European member states developed the national laws and policies necessary to implement the program, including the National Allocation Plans that set forth how greenhouse gas emission allowances would be allocated to affected industry sectors. Despite the tight timetable, the program began in 2005 as scheduled.

An interesting aspect of Europe's pioneering adoption of the EU ETS is that Europe had initially been against the use of emissions trading to reduce the emissions of greenhouse gases. In the Kyoto Protocol negotiations, the United States advocated for using this new market-based instrument to achieve reductions more efficiently, while Europe argued that traditional command-and-control-type regulatory mandates would be more effective and reliable. The excerpt below explores why the EU ultimately embraced emissions trading.

A. Denny Ellerman, Frank J. Convery & Christian De Perthius, Pricing Carbon: The European Union Emissions Trading Scheme

29–31 (2010)

As a result of the adoption of the EU Emissions Trading Directive, a somewhat paradoxical situation has emerged in the international climate change arena. In a very short period of time, emissions trading has evolved from being a non-option for the European Union to the cornerstone of European climate policy. Meanwhile, the United States, so long the proponent of emissions trading, turned largely to voluntary measures as part of its climate strategy and refusal to ratify the Kyoto Protocol. Considering that it was only in 1997 that trading began moving from being a mainly academic interest to taking centre stage in Europe, progress with adopting this instrument has been remarkable. The European Environment Agency describes this situation as one in which Europe has gone 'from follower to leader' in terms of both understanding and applying this economic instrument to environmental policy.

The Union has a population of almost 500 million people, living in twenty-seven countries, embracing twenty-three languages, with per capita GDP in 2005 on a purchasing power parity basis ranging from €32,197 (Ireland) to €7,913 (Bulgaria). It is not always a harmonious club. Sometimes it seems that Edward Mortimer's view captures the Union's essence: 'A nation . . . is a group of people united by a common dislike of their neighbors, and a shared misconception about their ethnic origins.'

Why was agreement reached? Several factors contributed to the successful establishment of the EU ETS.

First, the idea of the European common market and the Single European Act of 1986 that made it a reality were fundamental to the creation of the emissions trading scheme. By enabling the free movement of goods, people and capital across borders, the act linked the economies of member states and made the idea of a common emissions reduction objective — as expressed in the burden-sharing agreement of 1998 — a real possibility. It also helped member states overcome industry's objections to the implementation of a pan-European trading system.

Second, both the content and the political fallout of the Kyoto Protocol were key to the introduction of emissions trading within the European Union. European negotiators failed to prevent the inclusion of emissions trading in the Kyoto Protocol. It was precisely this failure, however, that led the Union to reconsider its GHG management strategy and to turn from a tax-centred [sic] approach to the creation of a carbon market. Then the US refusal to ratify the Kyoto Protocol prompted Europe to take the lead in moving the treaty forward. The Union's ability to make trade-offs on the world stage — and in particular to secure Russian agreement to ratify the Kyoto Protocol in exchange for EU support for WTO [World Trade Organization] membership — allowed the protocol to come into effect, which in turn re-emphasized the role of the EU ETS.

Third, early actions by individual European member states gave further impetus to the swift creation of a pan-European trading scheme following the Kyoto negotiations. States such as the United Kingdom, Denmark and the Netherlands were choosing to pursue their own environmental taxation and trading schemes in the absence of European action. Fears about the further expansion of this regulatory patchwork—and the implications it could have for the proper functioning of the common market—enabled the tripartite EU government to come to agreement on the EU ETS in a relatively short period of time. This agreement was facilitated by supportive information on trading from the United States, which, based on its experience with the Acid Rain Program, relayed the message that business can co-exist and prosper with emissions trading.

Finally, the design features of the EU ETS itself facilitated consensus between the EU government, industry and NGOs. A firm limit on emissions and the prospective availability of transparent data from installations assuaged environmental advocates; free allowances and allocation at the member state level helped diminish industry opposition; and the inclusion of an obligatory three-year pilot period temporarily indulged some member state preoccupations, including opt-out and pooling, and served as a way of identifying weaknesses to be corrected after 2007. These provisions, combined with a willingness on all sides to compromise and a high degree of skill and commitment at the levels of the European Commission, European Parliament, member states and some businesses and NGOs, enabled the EU ETS to go forward.

NOTES AND QUESTIONS

1. The first compliance period of the EU ETS, sometimes called the "pilot phase," covered the years 2005 through 2007. At the end of the period, each facility included in the program would have to demonstrate that it was in compliance by holding enough emissions allowances to cover its emissions. For example, if a facility emitted 500,000 tons of carbon dioxide in the years 2005 through 2007, it would have to show that it held 500,000 EUAs (European Union Allowances) at the end of 2007. By 2006, however, it became clear that there was an oversupply of EUAs in the allowance market, and allowance prices collapsed. Studies showed that the EU had overallocated allowances by distributing more allowances than would be required to cover "business as usual" emissions. *See* Lesley K. McAllister, *The Overallocation Problem in Cap-and-Trade: Moving Toward Stringency*, 34 Colum. J. Envtl. L. 395 (2009); A. Denny Ellerman & Barbara Buchner, *Over-Allocation or Abatement? A Preliminary Analysis of the EU Emissions Trading Scheme based on the 2005–06 Emissions Data*, 41 Envtl. & Resource Econ., no. 2, Oct. 2008, at 267.

2. While the pilot phase of the EU ETS was ineffective in establishing an allowance price that could lead to sustained emissions reductions, it can be considered a success in setting the stage for the second compliance period of the EU ETS, which spanned 2008 to 2012. This second phase of the program is called the "Kyoto Phase" because it was designed to ensure that Europe met its Kyoto Protocol emissions reduction commitment that applies in these years. A third phase of the EU ETS program is anticipated to

cover the years from 2013 to 2020, with even more stringent emissions caps. As the Kyoto phase began, commentators observed that "the trading infrastructure of markets, registries and monitoring, reporting and verification is in place, and a significant segment of European industry is incorporating the price of CO_2 emissions into their daily production decisions." A. Denny Ellerman & Paul L. Joskow, Pew Ctr. on Global Climate Change, The European Union's Emissions Trading System in Perspective 45 (2008), *available at* http://www.pewclimate.org/docUploads/EU-ETS-In-Perspective-Report.pdf.

3. The implantation of the EU ETS has, of course, not been without legal conflict. Indeed, the scheme has spurred more litigation than other major environmental regulations instituted by the European Union. *See* Navraj Singh Ghaleigh, *Emissions Trading Before the European Court of Justice: Market Making in Luxembourg, in* LEGAL ASPECTS OF CARBON TRADING 374–83 (2009). Most of the lawsuits have either contested the legal validity of the directive that established the EU ETS or Commission decisions on the national allocation plans. The European Court of Justice has generally upheld the scheme and the Commission's decisions.

4. The EU ETS is one facet of Europe's larger climate change policy. In 2007, then-president of the European Union Angela Merkel laid out what would become known as the EU's 20-20-20 plan: to cut CO_2 emissions by 20 percent, increase energy efficiency by 20 percent, and expand renewable use to 20 percent of energy by 2020. The plan was officially agreed to by the European Parliament and Council in 2008 and became law in 2009. *See What is the EU Doing on Climate Change?*, EUROPEAN COMMISSION (Oct. 18, 2010), http://ec.europa.eu/environment/climat/climate_action.htm. The plan was adopted with the hope that international climate treaty negotiations would be successful in yielding a successor agreement to the Kyoto Protocol. The EU leaders offered to increase the EU emissions reduction goal to 30 percent, on the condition that other major emitting countries committed to doing their fair share in a binding treaty.

    The international meetings that followed failed to produce such a treaty, but debate ensued in Europe about whether it should commit to the 30 percent emissions reductions anyhow. What arguments can be raised for and against making such a strong unilateral commitment? For the European Commission's thoughts, see *Communication from the Commission to the European Parliament, the Council, the European Economic and Social Committee and the Committee of the Regions: Analysis of Options to Move Beyond 20% Greenhouse Gas Emission Reductions and Assessing the Risk of Carbon Leakage,* COM (2010) 265/3 (May 26, 2010).

4. EUROPEAN COMPLIANCE WITH THE KYOTO PROTOCOL

    The European Environmental Agency (EEA) reported in 2009 that the EU was on track to meet its Kyoto target. European Environmental Agency, *Greenhouse Gas Emission Trends and Projections in Europe 2009*, Report No. 9/2009 (2009), *available at* http://www.eea.europa.eu/publications/eea_report_2009_9. The EEA further stated that the EU-15, which comprises the 15 countries that were part of the EU at the time that the Kyoto Protocol was negotiated (Austria, Belgium, Denmark, Finland, France, Germany, Greece, Ireland, Italy, Luxembourg, the Netherlands, Portugal, Spain, Sweden, and the United Kingdom), may significantly beat its target of 8 percent below 1990 levels:

> The EU-15 could over-achieve its Kyoto target by an average 217 MT [mega-tons] CO2-equivalent per year over the Kyoto period if all existing and planned additional measures are fully implemented in a timely manner and if Member States use Kyoto mechanisms and enhance carbon sinks as planned. This represents a 5.1% overachievement beyond the 8% Kyoto target.
> *Id.*

The following excerpt further explains the EU's emissions targets and compliance projections.

EUROPEAN ENVIRONMENT AGENCY, TRACKING PROGRESS TOWARDS KYOTO AND 2020 TARGETS IN EUROPE, AT 12, 17, No. 7/2010 (2010)

http://www.eea.europa.eu/publications/progress-towards-kyoto

2. Emission targets and Kyoto compliance

2.1 Emission Targets under the Kyoto Protocol and the Burden-Sharing Agreement

Under the Kyoto Protocol, the EU-15 has taken on a common commitment to reduce emissions between 2008 and 2012 by 8% on average, compared to base-year emissions. Within this overall target, differentiated emission limitation or reduction targets have been agreed for each of the 15 pre-2004 Member States under an EU accord known as the 'burden-sharing agreement'. . . .

The EU-27 does not have a Kyoto target, since the Protocol was ratified before 2004 when 12 countries became EU Member States. Therefore 10 of these EU-12 Member States have individual targets under the Kyoto Protocol, while Cyprus and Malta do not have targets. Of the other EEA member countries, Iceland, Liechtenstein, Norway and Switzerland have individual targets under the Kyoto Protocol while Turkey, which acceded to the Kyoto Protocol in February 2009 has no quantified emission reduction commitment, like Cyprus and Malta. Croatia has an individual target under the Kyoto Protocol.

2.2 Achieving 2008–2012 Objectives: The 'Kyoto Compliance Equation'

To comply with its objective under the Kyoto Protocol, a Party must keep its total GHG emissions during the five years of the Kyoto Protocol's first commitment period (2008–2012) within a specific emission budget. In other words, total GHG emissions during that period must remain equal or below the Party's assigned amount, which is the total quantity of valid Kyoto units it holds (within its registry). One Kyoto unit corresponds to 1 tonne of CO_2-equivalent emissions.

Each Party's assigned amount is equal to:

- an initial assigned amount, determined according to the Party's base-year emissions and its Kyoto target. This initial assigned amount is measured in assigned amount units (AAUs);

- *plus/minus* any additional Kyoto units that the Party has acquired from or transferred to other Parties through the Kyoto mechanisms (CERs [Certified Emission Reductions] from clean development mechanism projects, ERUs [Emission Reduction Units] from joint implementation projects or AAUs [Assigned Amount Units] from international emission trading between governments);
- *plus/minus* any additional Kyoto units that the Party has issued/cancelled for net removals/emissions from a [land use change or forestry] activity (RMUs [Removal Units]).

To comply with its Kyoto obligations, a Party needs to satisfy a 'Kyoto compliance equation', which can be summarised as follows:

$$\text{`2008–2012 total GHG emissions'} \leqslant \text{`total Kyoto units'}$$

With: 'total Kyoto units' = 'initial assigned amount (AAUs)' + 'use of flexible mechanisms (AAUs + CERs + ERUs)' + 'carbon sink removals (RMUs)'

Therefore to achieve its target, a Party can act on two sides of the 'compliance equation':

- *emissions side*: limiting or reducing its own emissions by acting at national level,
- *assigned amount side*: increasing its assigned amount, by acquiring additional Kyoto units at international level and by further enhancing CO_2 removals from carbon sink activities.

Compliance of EU-15 Member States under the internal EU burden-sharing agreement relies on the same principles, with each Member State's initial assigned amount being determined according to its individual burden-sharing target, instead of the –8% reduction target of the whole EU-15 under the Kyoto Protocol.

After final emissions have been reported and reviewed for the entire commitment period, Parties to the Kyoto Protocol will have 100 days to undertake final transactions necessary to achieve compliance with their commitment (the 'true-up period'). A final Kyoto compliance assessment will therefore not be possible before end 2014 or 2015.

. . .

3. Current Progress Towards Kyoto Targets

- In 2008, the first year of the commitment period, GHG emissions in eight EU-15 Member States (Belgium, Germany, Greece, Finland, France, the Netherlands, Sweden and the United Kingdom), nine EU-12 Member States (Bulgaria, Czech Republic, Estonia, Hungary, Lithuania, Latvia, Poland, Romania and Slovakia) and one other EEA member country (Norway) were lower than their respective Kyoto targets, taking into account the effect of domestic emission trading schemes. These countries were therefore on track towards achieving their Kyoto commitments in 2008.
- Taking into account the intended use of flexible mechanisms and emission reductions from LULUCF [land use, land-use change and forestry] activities

over the full commitment period, five additional Member States (Ireland, Luxembourg, Portugal, Slovenia and Spain) and one other EEA member country (Iceland) are also on track towards their targets in 2008.

• Three EU Member States (Austria, Denmark and Italy), two other EEA member countries (Liechtenstein and Switzerland) as well as one EU candidate country (Croatia) need to further reduce emissions by 2012 or plan to increase their quantity of Kyoto units further than they currently do in order to achieve their respective Kyoto targets.

. . . .

• The EU-15 is well on track towards achieving its commitment under the Kyoto Protocol of reducing its emissions by 8% compared to base-year levels, with a current total overachievement of 253 Mt CO_2-equivalent per year (5.9% of base year emissions) for the two years 2008 and 2009, when the intended use of flexible mechanisms and carbon sinks removals are taken into account. This assumes that the overachievement of their target by certain Member States could cover for any shortfall existing in other Member States. . . .

NOTES AND QUESTIONS

1. The EU-15's 2008 emissions were approximately 6.2 percent below 1990 emissions. European Environmental Agency, *Greenhouse Gas Emission Trends and Projections in Europe 2009,* Report No. 9/2009 (2009), *available at* http://www.eea.europa.eu/publications/eea_report_2009_9. In considerable contrast, 2008 emissions in the United States were 13.5 percent higher than its 1990 emissions. E.P.A, OFFICE OF ATMOSPHERIC PROGRAMS, INVENTORY OF U.S. GREENHOUSE GAS EMISSIONS AND SINKS: 1990–2008 (2010), *available at* www.epa.gov/climatechange/emissions/downloads11/US-GHG-Inventory -2011-Complete_Report.pdf. One important question is how much of this difference can be attributed to the EU ETS and other regulatory measures. Notably, most of the difference is accounted for by varying emissions trajectories in the 1990s, before the EU ETS came into effect. In the 1990s, the EU-15's emissions remained relatively stable at 1990 levels while U.S. emissions grew by about 15 percent. *U.S. Inventory* at ES-6.

2. Do the EU's emissions reductions since 1990 really represent a success story in the decarbonization of major industrial economies? A report by the English NGO, Policy Exchange, asserts that the answer depends on how you allocate responsibility for carbon emissions among countries. *See* ANDREW BRINKLEY & DR. SIMON LESS, POLICY EXCHANGE, CARBON OMISSIONS: CONSUMPTION-BASED ACCOUNTING FOR INTERNATIONAL CARBON EMISSIONS, (2010), *available at* http://www.policyexchange.org.uk/publications/publication .cgi?id=215. The report shows that Europe's "consumed carbon," the amount of carbon emitted to produce all the products and services consumed in Europe, actually rose 47 percent since 1990. In other words, Europe "off-shored" many of its emissions, consuming more imported

products that emitted greenhouse gases in the countries where they were produced. Should countries be responsible for the carbon emissions embedded in the products they consume, or just for the carbon emissions produced within their national borders?

C. CANADA: COMMITMENT WITHOUT COMPLIANCE

Canada and the United States share many political and economic interests, as well as a similar cultural and legal heritage. Both of these North American countries are predominantly common law jurisdictions with colonial histories involving the United Kingdom and France. Both have federal systems with complex dynamics between the national government and subnational units — the 50 U.S. states and the 10 Canadian provinces, as well as territories, counties, and cities. Both also have complex cultural and legal relationships with their original indigenous inhabitants.

Unlike the United States, however, Canada is simultaneously a parliamentary democracy and a constitutional monarchy. The Prime Minister is appointed by the Governor General, acting in the name of the Queen, but generally is the leader of the political party that a plurality of the popularly-elected members of the House of Commons supports. The Prime Minister acts as head of government, initiating most legislation and appointing cabinet members, senior diplomats, Supreme Court judges, and a variety of other key public officials. The most powerful opposition party's leader becomes the Leader of Her Majesty's Loyal Opposition, which creates dynamics somewhat like the two-party system in the United States.

Because of these similarities and differences, especially interesting lessons can be learned through comparing the development of Canada's climate change policies with those of the United States. As the following sections discuss, Canada committed to emissions reductions through the Kyoto Protocol, but its decisions and actions since then have made it clear that it will fail to meet its targets and timetables for the first commitment period. Moreover, Canada announced at the 2011 Durban COP that, like the United States, it would not participate in a second Kyoto Protocol commitment period.

1. PARTICIPATION IN THE KYOTO PROTOCOL

In the course of international climate change negotiations, Canada and the United States often have taken similar positions. Both countries handily ratified the United National Framework Convention on Climate Change in the early 1990s. Yet, as the 1990s progressed, concerns arose in each country about the potential economic impacts of internationally committing to emissions reductions. In the United States, businesses warned that energy prices could rise significantly, and the Senate passed a resolution in 1997 against the ratification of any treaty that required emissions limits for developed countries but not for developing countries. In Canada, energy-intensive manufacturing industries also became more vocal, and the provinces that relied most heavily on these industries voiced their opposition. Ultimately in 1997, federal and provincial energy and environment ministers agreed to support the idea of reducing 2010 emissions to 1990 levels but no further.

Despite internal politics, the federal governments of both countries were also responding to international pressures to commit to more significant reductions. In the Kyoto negotiations, Canada explicitly based its willingness to commit on that of its neighbor: Canada was willing to commit to a reduction target that was one percentage point less stringent than the reduction target agreed to by the United States. Indeed, as adopted in December 1997, the Kyoto protocol set forth a U.S. target of a 7 percent reduction of greenhouse gases below 1990 levels in the years 2008 to 2012, and a Canadian target of 6 percent.

In light of their similar trajectory, the next turn of events would have been very hard to predict: Canada ratified the Kyoto Protocol even after the U.S. announced that it would not. The following excerpt by Professor Kathryn Harrison explains this surprising outcome.

KATHRYN HARRISON, THE ROAD NOT TAKEN: CLIMATE CHANGE POLICY
IN CANADA AND THE UNITED STATES

7 Global Envtl. Pol., no. 4, 2007 at 92, 105–08

Canada's commitment to a 6% reduction below 1990 emissions also met with strong opposition at home. If the Prime Minister's unilateral announcement of a –3% target had not done enough damage to federal-provincial relations, provincial officials and Ministers were outraged by Canada's acceptance of a final target of –6%. Fortuitously, a First Ministers Conference was scheduled to begin in Ottawa just as the meeting in Kyoto concluded. The Premiers emerged from the meeting placated by three reassurances from the Prime Minister. First, the Prime Minister committed that "no region [would be] asked to bear an unreasonable burden," a phrase that would become something of a mantra for the provinces in the years to follow. Second, the leaders agreed to undertake a study of the costs and benefits of implementation before proceeding to ratification. Third, the First Ministers agreed that development of an implementation plan would be done in partnership with provincial and territorial governments, a concession Alberta Premier, Ralph Klein, enthusiastically declared equivalent to a "provincial veto" over implementation.

In early 1998, the federal and provincial energy and environment Ministers established the National Climate Change Process, co-chaired by Alberta and the federal government. A massive public consultation exercise ensued involving some 450 experts and 225 stakeholders in 16 "issue tables." For four years after the Kyoto meeting there with few outward signs of federal-provincial discord, largely reflecting that, although there was much discussion, little progress was being made toward a realistic plan to meet Canada's Kyoto Protocol commitment.

The nature of the challenge Canada faced changed dramatically in the spring of 2001 when President George W. Bush confirmed that the US would not ratify the Kyoto Protocol. As discussed above, Canada's commitment in Kyoto was predicated on the US accepting a comparable target. The US withdrawal thus had implications for the competitiveness of Canadian industry. The US' withdrawal from the Protocol also meant that the international community needed both Japan and Russia to ratify in order to reach the 55% hurdle for the treaty to take effect. In that context, the European Union adopted a more generous stance toward the remaining members of the umbrella group at COP-6bis in July 2001. Riding on Japan's coat tails, Canada received credit for 30 MT [megatons] for business-as-usual forestry practices, which was *more* than it asked for going into the negotiations, as well as authorization for unlimited reliance on carbon sinks and international mechanisms. However, the gains made at COP-6 satisfied neither critics within the federal government nor among the provinces. Thus, after the Bonn deal was finalized at COP-7 in Marrakesh, Canada renewed an argument, already many times rebuffed by the international community, that it should receive credits for exporting natural gas to the United States, on the grounds that Americans would otherwise be burning more greenhouse gas-intensive oil or coal.

To understand the events that followed, it is critical to situate the Kyoto issue within the context of a leadership struggle ongoing in the federal Liberal party in the summer of 2002. Tensions between the Prime Minister and his long-time rival, Finance Minister Paul Martin, came to a head in June 2002, when Mr. Martin either resigned or was fired from Cabinet, depending on whose account one accepts. There was increasing pressure on the Prime Minister from the Liberal caucus, a majority of whom supported Mr. Martin's leadership bid. In response, Mr. Chrétien promised both a bold policy agenda in the months to come, and that after completing that agenda he would retire in early 2004.

In the lead up to the "Rio +10" Conference on Environment and Development in Johannesburg in late 2002, there was speculation that the government would use the occasion to ratify Kyoto, spurring an increase in lobbying from both sides. The business community released estimates that ratification of the Kyoto Protocol would cost Canada 450,000 jobs. In response, over half (96 out of 172) of Liberal members of Parliament and 23 Liberal Senators signed a letter to the Prime Minister calling on the government to ratify the Kyoto Protocol, with or without "clean energy export credits." Ultimately, Prime Minister Chrétien announced in his plenary speech in Johannesburg that a resolution to ratify Kyoto would be placed before Canada's Parliament by the end of the year. Although the Prime Minister's speech was widely reported as a commitment that Canada would ratify, that was not in fact what Mr. Chrétien promised. In Canada, the decision to ratify international treaties rests with Cabinet, not Parliament. At the time of the Prime Minister's speech, no decision on the Kyoto Protocol had been made by Cabinet, which senior officials interviewed recalled was "evenly divided" on the issue. However, with the receipt of the backbenchers' letter, and the knowledge that ratification would be guaranteed support from both the Bloc Quebecois and New Democratic Party, the Prime Minister was confident that a resolution would pass, in turn forcing Cabinet's hand. The plan to place a resolution before Parliament thus was not an announcement of a decision on ratification so much as a strategy to circumvent dissent within Mr. Chrétien's own Cabinet.

In the fall of 2002, the business community formed the Coalition for Responsible Energy Solutions, which, among other activities, placed a series of full-page newspaper ads across Canada, arguing that ratification of Kyoto would "place Canadian business at a severe disadvantage relative to the United States" and require Canada "to make payments to countries with no targets." Federal provincial relations concerning ratification also remained contentious. Only two of ten provinces, Quebec and Manitoba, supported ratification. In contrast, the Premier of Ontario, representing almost 40% of Canadians, stated that his province would not support Kyoto if it killed "even one job." When the federal government released its much anticipated "Climate Change Plan for Canada" in late November, *all* provincial premiers signed a statement declaring the federal implementation plan "inadequate" and calling instead for a jointly devised national plan. Negotiations between the provinces and the federal government ground to a halt, effectively terminating the joint National Climate Change Process.

What is most striking about the federal implementation plan is its lack of specifics. There was a call to negotiate covenants with industrial sectors but no details as to which facilities would be asked to reduce their emissions by how much. There were promises of public spending but no budgetary commitments for particular projects. There were proposals for measures such as revisions to building codes that could only be undertaken by provincial governments, but no commitment to do so by the provinces. Almost five years to the day after Canada agreed to the Kyoto Protocol, and after a massive national consultation exercise, the federal government released what was essentially a plan to develop a plan.

In the lead-up to the House resolution, even federal Cabinet Ministers were remarkably open in their reservations concerning ratification. Fearful of risking support for his leadership campaign in Western Canada, Prime Minister-in-waiting Paul Martin maintained a position of "studied ambiguity" on the question of ratification. With the position on Kyoto not only of many back-benchers but of several of his key Cabinet Ministers uncertain, the Prime Minister declared the Kyoto resolution to be a matter of confidence, an unusual measure given that non-binding resolutions are normally free votes. The Liberal caucus duly fell into line, and on December 10, 2002, the House of Commons passed a resolution calling "upon the government to ratify the Kyoto Protocol on climate change" by a vote of 195 to 77, with all Liberal members present voting in favour. The motion was passed by the Senate two days later, and the day after that the decision to ratify the Kyoto Protocol was made by Cabinet without debate, all Ministers having already publicly supported the resolution in the House. The Environment Minister personally delivered Canada's ratification papers to the United Nations on December 17, 2002.

NOTES AND QUESTIONS

1. Canada ratified the Kyoto Protocol, but it became clear over the course of the 2000s that Canada would not meet its 6 percent emissions reduction target. Emissions continued increasing due in large part to a booming oil

and gas sector. In 2006, a new Conservative government came into power that cut funding for climate change policies and declared the Kyoto target impossible to meet. *See* Doug Struck, *Canada Alters Course on Kyoto: Budget Slashes Funding Devoted to Goals of Emissions Pact*, WASH. POST, May 3, 2006, http://www.washingtonpost.com/wp-dyn/content/article/2006/05/02/AR2006050201774.html. In 2010, the government projected that Canada's total emissions between 2008 and 2012 would be 29 percent over its Kyoto target. *See* ENVIRONMENT CANADA, NATIONAL INVENTORY REPORT 1990-2008: GREENHOUSE GAS SOURCES AND SINKS IN CANADA (2010), *available at* http://www.ec.gc.ca/Publications/default.asp?lang=En&xml=492D914C-2EAB-47AB-A045-C62B2CDACC29. Canada's ratification seems to have had little effect on its behavior. Does that mean that Canada's ratification was not worthwhile? What value might Canada's ratification have had even in light of its later lack of compliance?

2. Environmental NGOs in Canada sought to force the federal government to comply with its Kyoto target through litigation in the Canadian courts. Specifically, Friends of the Earth (FOE) Canada filed suit in 2007 alleging that the government violated the Kyoto Protocol Implementation Act (KPIA) of 2007. Passed by the Canadian Parliament without the support of the sitting government, the KPIA required the government to prepare annual climate change plans based on meeting Kyoto targets and to draft and enact legally binding regulations to combat climate change. In 2008, the lower federal court held that the government's obligations under the KPIA were not justiciable and that the controversy should be resolved by Parliament rather than by the courts. *See Friends of the Earth v. Canada*, 2008 F.C. 1183 (2008), *available at* http://reports.fja.gc.ca/eng/2008/2008fc1183/2008fc1183.pdf. The decision was affirmed by the appeals court in 2009 and denied review by the Canadian Supreme Court in 2010. Do you think that the Canadian courts were correct in finding the case nonjusticiable? Does this ruling place the Canadian government above the law in a way that jeopardizes the rule of law? For an argument that it does, see Dianne Saxe, *Climate Change, KPIA and The Rule of Law*, ENVIROLAW.COM (Mar. 17, 2010), *available at* http://envirolaw.com/climate-change-kpia-rule-law/.

3. What should the ramifications be of Canada's disregard for its Kyoto commitments? Although the Kyoto Protocol is considered to have the strongest compliance mechanism in international environmental law, it does not provide for financial penalties. Rather, countries that are not in compliance with their emissions targets will be required to make up for the deficiency in the next commitment period (post-2012) plus an additional 30 percent emissions allowance deduction. However, Canada has decided not to participate in the next commitment period, limiting the impact of that mechanism. Do you think Canada's Kyoto breach will harm its reputation as a law-abiding country? Should it?

4. In 2010, Canada signed the Copenhagen Accord with a stated target of 17 percent below 2005 emissions levels by 2020. This is the same Copenhagen Accord target inscribed by the United States. With respect to the 1990 baseline, Canada's target actually represents an increase of 2.5 percent. How should the nations complying with the Kyoto Protocol react to Canada's setting voluntary targets that indicate non-compliance with the Protocol?

2. ALBERTA'S OIL SANDS

Part of the explanation for Canada's inability or unwillingness to comply with its Kyoto commitments relates to its growing status as a fossil-fuel exporting nation. The Canadian province of Alberta is home to a huge reserve of unconventional oil in the form of bituminous sands, generally referred to as oil sands or tar sands. As the price of oil rose in the 2000s, investment in oil sands production grew quickly. The report, excerpted below, was commissioned by the Royal Society of Canada, Canada's national academy of scientists.

THE ROYAL SOCIETY OF CANADA EXPERT PANEL, EXECUTIVE SUMMARY:
ENVIRONMENTAL AND HEALTH IMPACTS OF CANADA'S OIL SANDS INDUSTRY 1–2
(2010)

http://www.rsc.ca/documents/expert/RSC_ExP_ExecutiveSummary_
ENG_Dec14_10_FINAL_v5.pdf

Development of the oils sands of northern Alberta has become an issue of growing public interest in recent years, with highly polarized views being presented by different stakeholders, including First Nations, environmentalists, industries and governments, about the merits of oil sands development in relation to its environmental and health impacts. Regardless of what any individual chooses to believe about these divergent views, the scale of investment and development in the oil sands is a major factor in Canada's economy, making the issues involved of vital importance to Canadians. . . .

Context for the Project

The oil sands (or tar sands) have become a focus of intense development in recent years, and production from the oil sands has raised the prospect of Canada being a substantial net exporter of petroleum products. The oil sands have become increasingly controversial because of environmental and health issues, including: overall greenhouse gas emissions (the oil sands contribute about 5% of Canada's total emissions, but are Canada's fastest growing source); major landscape disruption from surface mining; massive tailings ponds holding wastes toxic to fish and waterfowl; and major consumptive water use.

These features have drawn the attention of international environmental groups, some of which have labeled the product from this source as "dirty oil." The deaths of more than 1,600 ducks on a tailings pond in April 2008, and ongoing claims of a cancer cluster being caused by oil sands contamination in the downstream (primarily aboriginal) community of Fort Chipewyan, have drawn media attention.

On the economic side, the oil sands have been a major source of investment in Canada, supporting not only Alberta, but the federal government (through increased taxes), the Ontario Manufacturing sector, and skilled tradespeople from across Canada who have migrated to Fort McMurray [Alberta] for employment.

The major findings in the report addressing health and environmental issues include, in brief:

Feasibility of reclamation and adequacy of financial security: Reclamation is not keeping pace with the land disturbance but research indicates that sustainable uplands reclamation is achievable and ultimately should be able to support traditional land uses. Current practices for obtaining financial security for reclamation liability leave Albertans vulnerable to major financial risks.

Impacts of oil sands contaminants on downstream residents: There is currently no credible evidence of environmental contaminant exposures from oil sands reaching Fort Chipweyan at levels expected to cause elevated human cancer rates. More monitoring focused on human contaminant exposures is needed to address First Nation and community concerns.

Impacts on population health in Wood Buffalo: There is population level evidence that residents of the regional Municipality of Wood Buffalo (RMWB) experience a range of health indicators, consistent with "boom town" impacts and community infrastructure deficits, which are poorer than those of a comparable Alberta region and provincial averages.

Impacts on regional water supply: Current industrial water use demands do not threaten the viability of the Athabasca River system if the water Management framework developed to protect in-stream, ecosystem flow needs is fully implemented and enforced.

Impacts on regional water quality and groundwater quantity: Current evidence on water quality impacts on the Athabasca River system suggests that oil sands development activities are not a current threat to aquatic system viability. However, there are valid concerns about the current Regional Aquatics Monitoring Program (RAMP) that must be addressed. The regional cumulative impact on groundwater quantity and quality has not been assessed.

Tailings pond operation and reclamation: Technologies for improved tailings management are emerging but the rate of improvement has not prevented a growing inventory of tailings ponds. Reclamation and management options for wet landscapes derived from tailings ponds have been researched but are not adequately demonstrated.

Impacts on ambient air quality: The current ambient air quality monitoring data for the region show minimal impacts from oil sands development on regional air quality except for noxious odour emission problems over the past two years. Control of NOx [nitrogen oxide] emissions and regional acidification potential remain valid concerns.

Impacts on greenhouse gas emissions (GHG): Progress has been made by the oil sands industry in reducing its GHG emission per barrel of bitumen produced. Nonetheless, increasing GHG emissions from growing bitumen production creates a major challenge for Canada to meet our international commitments for overall GHG emission reduction that current technology options do not resolve.

Environmental regulatory performance: the environmental regulatory capacity of the Alberta and Canadian Governments does not appear to have kept pace with the rapid expansion of the oil sands industry over the past decade. The EIA [Environmental Impact Assessment] process relied upon by decision-makers to determine whether proposed projects are in the public interest has serious deficiencies in relation to international best practices. Environmental data access for cumulative impact assessment needs to improve.

———————

NOTES AND QUESTIONS

1. The mining of oil from oil sands is associated with a wide range of local air, water, and land pollution issues. Local communities, including Canadian aboriginal communities referred to as "First Nations," bear the brunt of these impacts, while benefits flow to others. How should the environmental justice concerns inherent in this situation be addressed?

2. Alberta's oil sands are second to only Saudi Arabia in their potential to supply the world's oil demand. Moreover, because of higher energy requirements, producing a barrel of oil from oil sands generates several times as many greenhouse gases as producing a conventional barrel of oil. Emissions from mining oil sands are Canada's fastest growing source of greenhouse gas emissions, and are expected to remain so. *See* Alastair R. Lucas, *Mythology, Fantasy and Federalism: Canadian Climate Change Policy and Law*, 20 Pac. McGeorge Global Bus. & Dev. L.J. 41, 52–56 (2007).

3. How strong of an influence would you expect Albertan and Canadian oil interests generally to have on Canadian climate politics? Might their influence be so strong that Canada would lobby against laws in other countries that could restrict markets for its oil? *See* Climate Action Network Canada, The Tar Sands' Long Shadow: Canada's Campaign to Kill Climate Policies Outside Our Borders (2010), *available at* http://www.climateactionnetwork .ca/e/news/2010/release/index.php?WEBYEP_DI=66 (alleging that Alberta's government and the Canadian federal government have lobbied against California's low carbon fuel standard and the EU's Fuel Quality Directive, two provisions that aim to encourage cleaner transportation fuels).

4. The United States consumes nearly all exports from the Canadian oil sands. Indeed, the United States imports more oil from Canada than from any other country, and those imports amount to about 20% of the total U.S. oil supply. *See* Shawn McCarthy, *Oil Sands on Track to Be Biggest Source of U.S. Oil Imports*, The Globe and Mail, May 19, 2010, http://www.theglobeandmail.com/report -on-business/industry-news/energy-and-resources/oil-sands-on-track-to-be -biggest-source-of-us-oil-imports/article1574854/. For the United States, Canada's reserves seem to represent a safe, secure, long-term supply of oil. Should the United States increase its reliance on oil from Alberta's oil sands? The proposed Keystone XL pipeline would run from Alberta through the mid-western United States to Texas, allowing for an increase in oil sands production and an expansion of its markets. Faced with opposition from environmentalists and affected landowners in Nebraska, the Obama administration delayed approval in 2011 pending further study.

5. Like Canada and the United States, Australia is very rich in fossil fuel resources. According to the U.S. Energy Information Administration,

Australia was the world's largest coal exporter and fourth-largest liquefied natural gas exporter in 2010. For many years, Australia and the United States were the only two signatories that refused to ratify the Kyoto Protocol. In 2007, however, after a change of government, Australia ratified it and in 2011, Australia passed major climate change legislation. Its Clean Energy Legislative Package introduced a fixed carbon price of AU$23/tonne effective July 1, 2012, which moves to a flexible price after three years.

3. BRITISH COLUMBIA'S CARBON TAX

Like some states of the United States, some provinces of Canada became leaders in climate change policy in the face of inaction at the federal level. In 2008, Canada's western province, British Columbia, became the first jurisdiction in North America to enact a carbon tax. The following excerpt from Professor David Duff describes this development.

DAVID DUFF, CARBON TAXATION IN BRITISH COLUMBIA

10 Vt. J. Envtl. L. 87, 90–95 (2008)

On February 19, 2008, the Government of British Columbia announced that it would introduce a consumption-based carbon tax of $10 per ton of CO_2e, rising to $30 per ton by 2012 — making the Province the most aggressive jurisdiction in Canada (and perhaps North America) when it comes to addressing climate change.

For several reasons, it is perhaps not surprising that British Columbia would be a leader in the development of public policies to reduce GHG emissions. With almost half the Province's population concentrated in a metropolitan area (Vancouver) that enjoys a more moderate climate than the rest of Canada and almost 93% of its electricity currently generated from hydroelectric power, carbon emissions in British Columbia are among the lowest in Canada on a per capita basis at 15.5 tons in 2005 compared to 23.1 tons in the country as a whole. Despite low emissions per capita, however, total emissions increased by 30% between 1990 and 2005, with the greatest growth resulting from fossil fuel production and fugitive emissions from oil and natural gas, which almost doubled during this period. At the same time, British Columbia is particularly vulnerable to the effects of global climate change, having already lost half of its lodgepole pines to the ravages of the mountain pine beetle, experiencing summer droughts and severe winter storms, and facing a major risk of flooding from sea level increases.

. . . .

As its name suggests, the British Columbia carbon tax does not apply to all GHG emissions, but only to emissions from the combustion of fossil fuels and other specified combustibles in the Province, with rates based on CO_2e emissions associated with the various fuels and combustibles that are subject to the tax. As a result, while the tax applies to emissions of CO_2 and other GHGs from the combustion of fossil fuels, it does not apply to CO_2 emissions from industrial processes such as the production of oil, gas, aluminum, or cement;

or to the emission of other GHGs such as methane and nitrous oxide from the disposal of solid waste and the agricultural sector. Nor does the tax apply to the combustion of biofuels such as firewood, woodwaste, ethanol, biodiesel, and bio-heating oil, which are arguably carbon-neutral. Instead, the Provincial Budget explains:

> The tax base includes fossil fuels used for transportation by individuals and in all industries, including the combustion of natural gas to operate pipelines, as well as road, rail, marine and air transportation. As well, the tax base includes fuel used to create heat for households and industrial processes, such as producing cement and drying coal.

Additionally, since the tax applies only to the combustion of fossil fuels within the Province, it also excludes or specifically exempts fuels exported from British Columbia and fuels used for inter-jurisdictional commercial marine and aviation purposes. As a result, the budget explains, "neither the emissions released elsewhere to produce fuel imported to BC or the emissions released elsewhere from burning fuel exported from BC are included in the tax base."

Although the British Columbia carbon tax does not apply to all GHG emissions, the substantial share of CO_2 in total GHG emissions and the equally substantial role of fossil fuel combustion as a cause of CO_2 emissions means that the tax base is quite broad, reaching approximately 70% of aggregate GHG emissions within the Province. While the exclusion of GHG emissions from industrial processes has been sharply criticized by the Opposition New Democratic Party (NDP), administrative challenges to the measurement of these emissions — which depend on production processes and can vary from facility to facility — suggest that their initial exclusion from the carbon tax is reasonable. Additionally, it seems reasonable to exclude CO_2 emissions from industrial processes and other GHG emissions from waste disposal and agriculture from the carbon tax because, as the budget explains, "many of these emissions will be subject to the cap-and-trade system or other GHG reduction measures under development." The exclusion of fuels for export and fuels used for interjurisdictional commercial, marine, and aviation purposes may also be justified on the basis that the tax is intended to apply only to emissions from the combustion of fossil fuels within the Province.

NOTES AND QUESTIONS

1. Although many economists and others believe that a carbon tax is a more efficient and effective way to reduce greenhouse gas emissions than a cap-and-trade program, carbon tax proposals have not appeared politically viable in the United States. In British Columbia, the carbon tax was popular at its introduction, but opposition grew in the economic downturn of 2008. A provincial election in May 2009 effectively served as a referendum on the governing party's adoption of the carbon tax. Notably, the party won

reelection as voters stood by the tax. *See id.; see also* John Lorinc, *British Colum-bia's Carbon Tax Survives*, N.Y. Times, May 14, 2009, http://green.blogs.nytimes .com/2009/05/14/british-columbias-carbon-tax-survives/. Why might a carbon tax be viable in British Columbia, but not in a U.S. state such as California?

2. British Columbia, as well as Manitoba, Ontario, and Quebec, are all partners in the Western Climate Initiative (WCI), described in Chapter Five. As part of the WCI, British Columbia also developed a cap-and-trade program for greenhouse gases. British Columbia's Greenhouse Gas Reduction (Cap and Trade) Act, which provides the statutory basis to establish the cap-and-trade program, was passed into law in May 2008. When implemented, British Columbia's approach may provide an important example of how a cap-and-trade program and a carbon tax can work together.

D. CHINA: INDUSTRIALIZATION IN THE ERA OF CLIMATE CHANGE

China has undergone an incredible surge of development in the past two dec-ades, making it not just a major player in economic terms, but also a major player in global climate change policy. As Professor Edward Ziegler explains, "The largest construction boom in world history is currently underway in China. . . . As China rapidly develops a modern industrial and technological economy, it joins the United States and other industrialized nations as a major consumer of resources and energy, as well as a major polluter of local and global ecosystems." Edward H. Ziegler, *China's Cities, Globalization, and Sustain-able Development: Comparative Thoughts on Urban Planning, Energy, and Environ-mental Policy*, 5 Wash. U. Global Stud. L. Rev. 295 (2006). In the first decade of the 2000s, China became the world's largest greenhouse gas emitter on an annual basis and the world's largest energy consumer. Spencer Swartz & Shai Oster, *China Tops U.S. in Energy Use*, Wall St. J., July 18, 2010, http:// online.wsj.com/article/SB10001424052748703720504575376712353150310 .html. With over 1.3 billion citizens, China is the world's most populous country and accounts for almost 20 percent of the world's population. Increases in its per capita emissions will therefore substantially influence global mitigation efforts.

China's economic transformation has been intertwined with a rapidly developing legal system. Although China has a long legal tradition, its legal system was effectively dismantled during the Cultural Revolution as lawyers were persecuted and law schools were closed. The number of lawyers in China has expanded from approximately 5,500 in 1981 to approximately 190,000 in 2009, mostly concentrated in major cities, with people in rural areas often having limited access to them. The training and standards for lawyers evolved significantly over this period. In 1985, less than 8 percent of judicial employees held university degrees. A unified bar exam for new judges and lawyers, paired with a university education requirement, was only instituted in 2002; 360,000 people took that first unified bar exam, which had a 7 percent pass rate.

Because the bar exam and education requirements do not apply retroactively, many older members of the Chinese judiciary have only received some on-the-job training. The Chinese legal system still struggles with corruption, bureaucracy, instability, and political interference. For an in-depth discussion of these developments and issues, see Stanley B. Lubman, Bird in a Cage: Legal Reform in China After Mao (1999); Yuanyuan Shen, *Conceptions and Receptions of Legality: Understanding the Complexity of Law Reform in Modern China*, in The Limits of the Rule of Law in China 20–44 (Karen G. Turner, James V. Feinerman & R. Kent Guy, eds. 2000); William P. Alford & Fang Liufang, Legal Training and Education in the 1990s: An Overview and Assessment of China's Needs 21 (1994); Mo Zhang, *The Socialist Legal System with Chinese Characteristics: China's Discourse for the Rule of Law and a Bitter Experience*, 24 Temp. Int'l & Comp. L.J. 1 (2010); Hari M. Osofsky, *Social Change Through Active, Reflective Learning? Clinical Legal Education in China and the United States* (draft manuscript on file with author).

China's current legal and economic context helps to shape its approach to climate change. This section explores that approach by providing a brief introduction to the Chinese legal system, an overview of how China's approach to climate change has evolved over time, and a discussion of its current approach.

1. INTRODUCTION TO THE CHINESE LEGAL SYSTEM

Since Deng Xiaoping began pursuing reform in 1978, China has been on a path he described as "socialism with Chinese characteristics," a hard-to-define term that attempts to capture a mix of traditions and philosophies. Structurally, China is a centrally-controlled, single-party state with 33 provincial-level divisions. Its subnational units — and its citizens generally — answer to the national government with more limited degrees of freedom than those in the other major emitters described in this book, though economic development has loosened that control somewhat.

The following excerpt by Professor Jingjing Liu provides an overview of the Chinese legal system and its evolution that will help to contextualize the Chinese approach to climate change.

Jingjing Liu, Overview of the Chinese Legal System

41 Envtl. L. Rep. News & Analysis 10885, 10885–887 (2011)

The People's Republic of China (PRC) was founded in 1949 by the Chinese Communist Party (CCP). For almost three decades after the PRC's establishment, there was a perception that a formal legal system for many areas of national life was unnecessary since the economy was centrally controlled and conflicts could thus be resolved through mediation or administrative means without reference to legal rights and obligations. However, the "Reform and Open Door" policy in the late 1970s, which began China's current rapid economic development and initiated the ongoing transition to a market economy, has had enormous implications for the country's legal development. The 1980s and 1990s saw massive and rapid enactment of laws, including many environmental laws, regulations, and rules.

The rebuilding of China's legal system over the past few decades has generally abandoned ideological requirements and embarked on a massive effort of law transplantation from western legal systems and internationally recognized practices, especially matters related to economic management, as a tool for attracting foreign investment. Modern Chinese law in its forms, structure, and methodologies thus exhibits many western characteristics, though it is generally modeled on the European continental civil law tradition in its legislative techniques. There has also been development in the public law areas and significant implications for protecting human rights (written into the 2004 Constitutional Amendment) since China's entry into the World Trade Organization (WTO), which imposes requirements on transparency and accessibility of law, reasonable administration of law, and impartiality, independence, and effectiveness of judicial review.

I. The Political Structure

Modern China is in form a unitary state, as compared to the federal system of the United States. All power flows from the central government in Beijing. However, economic reform has brought significant decentralization of economic administration, and in many cases, Beijing has been unable to supervise effectively the exercise of local government power, leading to substantial de facto autonomy for local governments in many areas of activities.

. . . .

According to the Constitution, all power in the PRC belongs to the people and is to be exercised through the National People's Congress (NPC) and local people's congresses at lower governmental levels. Thus, the NPC in appearance sits on top of China's political power structure as the supreme organ of the state. As a matter of practical reality, however, most governmental power is exercised by the Standing Committee of the Politburo of the CCP. Because the CCP has party organizations attached to government institutions at all levels and because the great majority of government officials are CCP members, the party plays an important but nontransparent role in and has enormous influence over the operation of China's government at all levels. The result is that even if the law specifies particular requirements, the policies of the Communist Party organization, through the party's influence over the government officials who are also CCP members, may greatly influence how the government implements or otherwise follows the law. The result has been significant transparency issues regarding governmental decisionmaking, including decisionmaking related to projects that have major impacts on the environment.

The NPC, as the supreme organ of state power, has the authority to issue laws binding across China, appoints the president of the nation (currently President Hu Jintao), the premier (the head of the State Council, China's cabinet, currently Premier Wen Jiabao), and the presidents of the Supreme People's Court and the Supreme People's Procuratorate (the national prosecutorial agency). NPC delegates are not elected by a popular vote; they are chosen by the people's congresses at the provincial level. Similarly, provincial people's congress delegates are chosen by people's congresses immediately below them. Direct popular elections are only held at the township and county levels. The

NPC has no more than 3,000 delegates, and representation of women and ethnic minorities is required. The delegates are selected for a term of five years and can be reappointed for further terms. The NPC convenes once a year, usually in March, for several weeks to discuss important matters of the state.

The large number of delegates in the NPC and the infrequency of its meetings prevent the NPC from exercising its stipulated supreme power. To facilitate the functioning of the government, the Constitution also establishes the Standing Committee of the NPC (SCNPC) as a permanent body of the NPC. The 175 members of the SCNPC are elected by the NPC. The SCNPC is vested by the Constitution with extensive powers, including the power to interpret the Constitution, make and revise laws, certain powers to appoint top government and judicial officials, and otherwise act when the NPC as a whole is not in session. Within the environmental arena, the SCNPC and the Environment and Natural Resources Protection Committee of the NPC play an important role in making, revising, and interpreting environmental statutes, inspecting the implementation of environmental laws, as well as supervising the work of environmental protection agencies and courts.

The State Council in the central government is responsible for the day-to-day work of operating the government as the highest organ of state administration. The premier is the head of the State Council, which is divided into various ministries and commissions. This structure of a people's congress on the one hand and a day-to-day government on the other hand is replicated at the local levels as well.

The Supreme People's Court is the highest judicial organ, and the Supreme People's Procuratorate is the highest state organ for legal supervision, which includes functions of both bringing criminal prosecutions and ensuring that government agencies act in accordance with the law. The State Council, the Supreme People's Court and the Supreme People's Procuratorate are all responsible to the NPC and the SCNPC. A similar structure exists at the provincial, municipal/prefectural, and district/county level with the local governments, people's courts and people's procuratorates being responsible to the local people's congresses. An important ministry within the State Council is the Ministry of Justice, which administers prisons, oversees the People's Mediation Committees, the lawyer system and the notary system, manages legal education, and otherwise disseminates legal knowledge.

. . . .

Though the NPC and the SCNPC are the main legislative bodies, the State Council is de facto the most powerful lawmaking institution, given its extensive inherent and delegated powers of lawmaking. It issues administrative regulations that touch upon almost every aspect of political, social, and economic life in China, and over 70% of the laws considered by the NPC and the SCNPC are initiated and drafted by the State Council.

II. History and Legal Context

China's modern legal system combines a number of legal traditions, including features of the continental European civil law tradition, substantial elements borrowed from the socialist law system of the former Soviet Union, and principles inherited from imperial Chinese law. In recent years, especially in the environmental area, American legal principles are also increasingly reflected in China's legal system. Unlike the western legal systems of continental Europe, however, which have been shaped by their roots in the private-law system of Rome or their early religious basis, traditional Chinese law instead centered on state concerns and dealt with private matters only incidentally. There was no special, differentiated institution, such as a "court," before which disputing parties could advance their legal claims. Instead, law was considered to be primarily an instrument for the sovereign to protect and advance the interests of the state and the rulers. As a result, traditional Chinese law was largely penal in nature; civil matters, those dealing with the interests of private parties, were largely left in the hands of customary law.

While ancient China had a highly developed and sophisticated administrative law system, its primary purpose was to ensure that officials followed the law and to increase government efficiency, not to protect individual rights from abuse by public power. The development and operation of the legal profession was strongly discouraged, and lawyers were seen primarily as "litigation tricksters." The emphasis was on substantive justice, with significant attention paid to fact-finding. Notions of procedural justice and due process were virtually nonexistent. In criminal trials, confessions were generally required for conviction, and torture was common. The heavy influence of Confucian values on traditional Chinese legal philosophy is particularly reflected in the general antipathy toward litigation and preference for extra-judicial mechanisms such as mediation as the primary means for dispute resolution. Some of these features in traditional Chinese law, to a certain degree, still influence the development of many aspects of the modern legal regime.

One of the most visible set of characteristics of China's modern legal system arises from the principles adopted from the civil-law tradition: statutory laws are of key importance; court judgments have formally no precedential effect, though they may serve as guidance. . . .

The hierarchy of China's laws and regulations is as follows:

- *Constitution*
- *Laws* by the NPC and the SCNPC
- *Administrative Regulations* by the State Council
- *Local People's Congress Regulations* by local people's congresses and their standing committees at the provincial level
- *Rules*, including *Government Rules* by local governments of provinces, and *Ministry Rules* by central-level ministries, commissions, and agencies directly under the State Council

International treaties ratified by China are directly applicable and prevail if they conflict with domestic law.

NOTES AND QUESTIONS

1. How does China's legal system compare to that of the other countries studied in this book? What are the primary similarities and differences?
2. In what ways does China's political and legal system influence its capacity to address climate change? Does China's centralized approach make it more likely that its policies will be implemented because there will be less opportunity for democratic contestation? Or does implementation benefit from robust public participation?

   Professor Wang Mingyuan has found inadequacies in the implementation of China's energy conservation and renewable energy laws due to weaknesses in governmental administration, law enforcement, and budget resources. *See* Wang Mingyuan, *Issues Related to the Implementation of China's Energy Law: Analysis of the Energy Conservation Law and the Renewable Energy Law as Examples*, 8 VT. J. ENVTL. L. 225 (2006–2007); *see also* Dr. Xuehua Zhang, *China's Environmental Administrative Enforcement System*, 41 ENVTL. L. REP. NEWS & ANALYSIS 10890 (2011).

2. THE EVOLUTION OF THE CHINESE APPROACH TO CLIMATE CHANGE

The Chinese approach to climate change has evolved substantially from its initial stance during the UNFCCC negotiations. The following excerpt by Professor Dongsheng Zang describes that transition and how it results from China increasingly treating climate change as an energy rather than environmental problem.

DONGSHENG ZANG, FROM ENVIRONMENT TO ENERGY: CHINA'S
RECONCEPTUALIZATION OF CLIMATE CHANGE

27 Wis. Int'l L.J. 543, 548–72 (2009)

II. Negotiating the UN Climate Change Convention

China's environment suffers long lasting deficits in two areas: investment and governance. Investment refers to the financial, technological input, while governance means the institutional channel through which environment issues are identified and managed. Environmental pollution was largely ignored in Mao's China during the 1950s-1970s. In the 1980s, when China was on its "four modernization" path there were some efforts to control pollution but with little success. On the eve of the 1989 crisis, Baruch Boxer, an ecologist who closely followed China's environmental situation during this period, observed: "China's potential for finding a workable balance between conservation and growth remains problematic." This was the domestic context of China's participation of climate negotiations that eventually led to the Climate Change Convention and the Kyoto Protocol.

This Part of the essay presents a brief history of the climate negotiations, largely from 1989, when the Climate Change Convention negotiations started, to late 1997, when the Kyoto Protocol was concluded. It pays particular attention to how the Chinese government understood the issue of climate change. Framing an issue like climate change is, of course, a complex process in which many actors and elements are involved. In this essay, discussion is limited to the official actors and their views, because the focus is on how the government in China conceptualized climate change. This Part considers the following elements to reflect this complex process: (a) who is in charge of the negotiations, (b) whose perspectives are influential in the internal deliberation, and (c) who is making decisions in response to the issues identified.

A. Before Climate Negotiations Began

In the 1980s, the basic bureaucratic structure for the negotiations was already in place. The State Council—China's cabinet—set up an Environment Protection Committee (SC-EPC) in 1984. Its stated mission was to formulate policies on the environment and to lead and coordinate the nation's environmental protection work. From 1984 to 1998, the SC-EPC was the top policymaker on the environment in the Chinese government. In 1984, the National Environmental Protection Bureau (NEPB), headed by Qu Geping, was set up under the Ministry of Urban and Rural Construction. NEPB was the executive arm of the SC-EPC. From 1984 to 1988, the SC-EPC was chaired by Li Peng, then the Vice-Premier. After he became Premier in 1987, Li Peng was succeeded by Song Jian, then Commissioner of the State Science and Technology Commission and a State Counselor of Vice-Premier level in the Chinese bureaucratic hierarchy.

In 1988, when the United Nations' Intergovernmental Panel on Climate Change (IPCC) was formed, China Meteorological Administration (CMA) became the contact agency in China. The year 1988 also saw the formation of the National Environmental Protection Agency (NEPA), an expanded and more independent governmental agency to succeed NEPB. In the meantime, the NEPA was working on national environmental legislation, the Environmental Protection Act, which was passed by the national legislature—the National People's Congress—in December 1989. However, work with the U.N. was temporarily disrupted in June 1989 when the Tiananmen Massacre occurred on June 4th. The incident, which resulted in widespread condemnation and economic sanctions from the West, pushed Beijing into diplomatic isolation. Despite all the uncertainty at the time, the scientific community in China was strongly in favor of continuing the work with the UN and keeping communications with the international environment movements open. Environmental engineers looked to the West, especially the United States, for inspiration and, increasingly, research funding. In 1991, the U.S. National Science Foundation established a "Panel on Global Climate Change Sciences in China," which organized a couple of visits to China in 1991 and interviewed members of the Chinese scientific community. The American experts observed, there "has been ever increasing pressure on Chinese institutions to seek international cooperation to carry out research projects, to gain access to expertise, training opportunities and equipment." On the other hand, for the hardliners who have now been in control, the environment became one of the few diplomatic channels still open to the outside world. Thus, they also needed the work with the UN to continue so as to "break the ice" of isolation. The decision to continue the climate talks eventually led to China's signing of the Climate Change Convention on June 1, 1992 and ratification on January 5, 1993. The Kyoto Protocol was signed on May 29, 1998 and ratified on August 30, 2002.

B. China's 1990 Position on Climate Change

Even though the hardliners in Beijing decided to continue climate talks, attempts were made to control the processes. This is most clearly demonstrated in China's first policy statement on climate change, "China's Principles and Position on Global Environmental Issues," announced in July 1990 at SC-EPC's 18th meeting. The statement set fundamental principles in a variety of global environmental issues covering climate, ozone, and biodiversity. These principles and positions were to be restated over and over again in subsequent years. The principles included: (a) environmental protection and economic development must be promoted hand in hand; (b) developed countries are mainly responsible for the environment problems, thus must bear the costs accordingly; (c) sovereignty is inalienable and any interference in domestic issues is not allowed; (d) developing countries should be given a stronger voice in global environmental issues, and developed countries should assist developing countries in finance and technology transfer; and (e) as a responsible nation, China will actively take part in global environmental issues. On climate change, the 1990 policy statement laid out the following positions: that China would actively participate in the negotiations; that developed countries are mainly responsible for climate change, including their duty to provide assistance to developing countries; and that China will take efforts to improve energy efficiency, but not to promise any specific cap on carbon dioxide emission.

It is important to note that most of these viewpoints laid out in the principles were not new. China's developing-country perspective, its insistence on sovereignty, and emphasis on developed countries' taking responsibility were all present in ozone layer and hazardous waste negotiations before the 1989 Tiananmen tragedy. What was new was the last point, that China would not make any commitment on carbon dioxide. This is perhaps where the top leadership decided to take a hard line approach in response to the sanctions from the West. This was a political decision because at the time the top leadership in China did not have scientific data on climate change and could not have possibly comprehended the implications of that stance. IPCC did not adopt their first scientific report until August 1990.

Bureaucratic control soon followed the position statement. As international environmental negotiations intensified, the State Planning Commission, the Ministry of Energy, and the Ministry of Foreign Affairs dominated the subsequent climate negotiations that eventually led to the Rio de Janeiro Conference in 1992. These departments' interests differed from those of environmental engineers at NEPA and climate scientists from the CMA. The Ministry of Foreign Affairs (MFA) was, of course, tightly controlled by the top leadership, particularly in the aftermath of the Tiananmen incident when China was facing a hostile diplomatic environment. The State Council formally decided early in 1991 that MFA would lead the climate negotiations. The State Planning Commission and the Ministry of Energy were the prototype central planning bureaucracy in the command economy. They were exclusively focused on production and largely regarded the environment as irrelevant or an obstacle to their goals.

C. The Climate Group I

Despite the attempts for political control, international climate talks helped the environmentalists and climatic scientists in China. This was in part because governments in the West largely defined and understood climate change as an environmental issue. This helped those environmental engineers and climate scientists in the Chinese delegations since they could better understand the substances than the political appointees. This became a crucial advantage giving the environmentalists some control in identifying and framing issues in their memos and proposals when they came back home. These memos and proposals addressed to the State Council became part of the framing process because they were written either in response to the strong opposition from the powerful industry ministries or with their opposition in mind.

One such memo was by the Chinese delegation to a London international conference on ozone layer in March 1989. The delegation was impressed that China's experience in warm winters was quite consistent with the global phenomenon. In its report to the State Council in China, the delegation concluded that climate change needed leadership from the State Council and the involvement of multiple departments, since the meteorological and environmental bureaus were not enough. Thus, the delegation proposed that a planning group should be established. Another delegation, which attended the UNEP's Fifteenth Meeting from May 15 to 26, 1989 in Nairobi, Kenya, made two proposals in China. First, they proposed that because environmental issues had become major political issues in the world the SC-EPC should set up a coordinating group on international environmental issues. Second, in order to change its "awkward position" (beidong diwei) in the international arena, the delegation suggested, China should improve air quality and make necessary changes to energy policy so that CO_2 would be reduced effectively. These proposals led to the creation of the Coordinating Group on Climate Change (Climate Group I) under the SC-EPC in January 1990. Climate Group I was chaired by Song Jian.

From October 29 to November 7, 1990, another Chinese delegation was dispatched to attend the Second World Climate Conference in Geneva. In public, the delegation, led by Song Jian, expressed some skepticism on whether global warming was caused by human activities (most likely, under political instruction). In its report to the State Council, however, the delegation made four proposals, all arguing that China should play a more active role on climate change issues. First, the delegation reiterated that climate change was a serious issue and thus must be handled seriously. The memo stated that, "since we are the third largest country in terms of energy consumption and our emission is high, and both energy consumption and emission are growing rapidly, . . . we are getting a lot of attention." Second, the delegation noted that China still lacked the scientific data on climate change issues and suggested that State Planning Commission and the State Science and Technology Commission allocate more funds to support research and monitoring equipment. Third, it called for more efforts dedicated to the preparation for the climate change negotiations at Rio de Janeiro. Fourth, the delegation proposed policy changes to promote more efficient use of energy and clean energy, so as to reduce emissions. It reiterated that "since our per capita energy consumption and emission are still low, the international community cannot blame us. But once we have signed the climate change treaty, the general trend would still be to reduce emission, sooner or later."

In January 1991, the SC-EPC convened a meeting on climate change. The meeting was to hear reports of the Geneva Second World Climate Conference, a report by the CMA on warmer winters in China, and to begin planning for the upcoming UNFCCC negotiations. CMA's report confirmed that between 1980 and 1989, winter in northern China was "clearly" getting warmer, average temperatures in northern China during the 1980s was 0.3-1.0°C higher than it was in the 1950s. In his address, Song Jian highlighted this finding and suggested that more funds should be allocated to climate research. He said, "We feel awkward when attending international conferences with no data in hand." Song Jian also instructed the Ministry of Agriculture to do research on the impacts of climate change on agriculture and the State Bureau of Oceans to estimate the impacts of higher sea levels. Taking this opportunity, Song Jian suggested that, "when we run into significant questions on science in negotiations, we should invite our scientists to speak their opinions. They will make a great contribution." In this process, the SC-EPC and NEPA gradually reinforced themselves by bringing in more members of the scientific community. When preparatory work for the Rio de Janeiro Conference started in September 1990, the Climate Group I invited a large number of scientists and engineers to act as advisors on technical issues. One year later, Song Jian made two suggestions at a SC-EPC meeting to further strengthen the influence of the scientific community. One was to set up a Scientific Advisory Group under the SC-EPC, making the channel between the Climate Group I and the scientific community official. The Scientific Advisory Group was officially formed in August 1991. The second proposal was to set up a high-level advisory group on broader policy issues, the China Council for International Co-operation on Environment and Development (CCICED, or the International Council), in order to facilitate communication between China and international organizations, foreign foundations, businesses, and experts. With support from the Canadian International Development Agency (CIDA), the International Council officially started on April 22, 1992 in Beijing.

D. The International Council

Initially, the International Council was composed of forty-three experts and publicists from China and abroad. Song Jian was elected the Chairman, and Qu Geping and Dr. Marcel Massé, President of CIDA, were elected as Vice-Chairmen. NEPA was designated as the host institution for the International Council. It maintains a Council Secretariat, also at NEPA, for administrative functions. The first Secretary General was Mr. Xie Zhenhau, then Deputy Administrator of NEPA. There were twenty-four Chinese members; four were from the scientific community, the rest were all vice-ministerial level officials representing a variety of government agencies, including SPC, SSTC, CMA, and

NEPA. The nineteen international members were from a mixture of international institutions such as UNESCO, the World Bank, nonprofit organizations, such as the Rockefeller Foundation, businesses such as Royal Dutch/ Shell Group, current or former government officials, and international environmental NGOs such as the World Wide Fund for Nature. The mandate of the International Council was to "provide advice and assistance to the Chinese Government in the development of an integrated, coherent approach across the areas of environmental protection, economic and social development, science and technology and related areas."

As a high-level advisory group, the International Council had access to decision-makers that any think tank would envy. In 1992, when it was formed, the members held a two-hour meeting with Premier Li Peng, who discussed in great detail China's policy on a variety of issues, from the environment to energy. The initial plan was for the International Council to be in place for five years. Apparently the Chinese government developed a viable working relationship with it so that the parties all agreed that the Council would continue. The first five years became known as Phase I (1992-97), but it has now been extended three times: Phase II (1997-2002), Phase III (2002-07) and Phase IV (2008-13). The International Council's regular channel of communication with the policymakers is its annual general meeting (AGM) where it adopts formal written recommendations. Recommendations are deliberated during its AGMs based on information from its Task Forces and Expert Working Groups covering a wide variety of issues including pollution control, environmental economics, energy strategy, scientific research, trade and sustainable development, and biodiversity.

From the configuration of its membership, the International Council seems as much an environmental advisory body as an energy advisory group. Nevertheless, it was probably behind some of the vital decisions that tend to contribute to the framing of climate change as an environmental issue. First, immediately after the Rio Conference, China was among the first to develop the Agenda 21 action plan to implement the principles of the Earth Summit. Second, the International Council pushed for China to embrace the climate change negotiations which eventually led to the Kyoto Protocol. In 1993, the Council already recommended that, "China should play an active role in international efforts to cope with global environmental problems. For example, China should make efforts to reduce atmospheric carbon emissions which are related to international efforts." In 1996, it again called for the development of a national plan for coping with such global problems as climate change. Prior to the Kyoto Conference, the Council recommended "full Chinese participation in the negotiation of a package." Third, the International Council supported strengthening the government agency in charge of environmental protection. In 1995, it recommended that "NEPA must be given sufficient power to be able to enforce its legislation, and of course it must have corresponding resources." It linked this to the international UNFCCC, "This is all the more important if China is to observe its obligations under international treaties such as the Convention on Climate Change."

E. Climate Change as Environment: The Limits

However, despite the efforts from the elite environmentalists during the period from 1989 to 1998, success was very limited. The greatest achievement was conceptual, introducing the notion of total emission control in the Climate Change Convention and the Kyoto Protocol and translating it into domestic environmental law. Previously, China's pollution control had been based on concentration of pollutants, not total emission control, like the cap in the FCCC and the Kyoto Protocol. However, total emission control was introduced into the newly amended Water Pollution Prevention and Control Act of 1996, which allowed provincial governments to control the total discharge of major pollutants. In June 1996, the State Council's Information Office published a white paper on environmental protection, where it was declared, as a "strategic move," that pollution control be changed from focusing on concentration control of specific pollutants to a combination of concentration and "total quantity control." In August, the State Council issued a "Decision on Several Issues in Environment Protection," where the term "total emission control" was put at the center of the overall rethinking of pollution control in China. Total emission control was also written into the Air Pollution Prevention and Control Act (APPCA) of 2000.

In terms of governance, the environmentalists in NEPA and the national legislature, the National People's Congress, consciously pushed for a series of legislation on the environment. In the process, there were some signs of progress. For example, the amendment processes of APPCA in 1995 and 2000 showed the more active and independent role that the national legislature played. Western observers were initially excited by the rise of the National People's Congress, but that rise turned out to be very limited. There was also expectation of the rise of the judiciary, but the judiciary remained weak and marginal in the 1990s. More fundamentally, there was still a great mismatch between law as inspirational statement of norms and the complex economic and social structure that law had little power to shape. NEPA as the national environment agency was in no better shape. With its meager budget, SEPA was overwhelmed by its work on other more pressing issues such as acid rain (caused by sulfur dioxide) and water pollution in major lakes and river basins. Things got worse in 1998 when Premier Zhu Rongji reorganized the government. NEPA was elevated to ministry level to become the State Environmental Protection Administration (SEPA), but its staff was not expanded accordingly.

III. The "Energy Turn"

After 2003, however, climate change was conceptualized as an energy policy issue. Some Chinese officials divide China's participation in international climate diplomacy into three stages: (a) negotiation of the Climate Change Convention, from 1990 to 1992; (b) negotiation of the Kyoto Protocol, from 1992 to 1997; and (c) the post-Kyoto period, from late 1997 to the present. This periodization closely follows the development of international negotiations. The Kyoto Protocol negotiations concluded in December 1997, but China did not ratify it until September 2002. This period would obscure two events in the development of climate policy in China that occurred during this period of time: one is bureaucratic change—the lead agency in charge of climate was shifted to NDRC (which was also responsible for energy policy) in 1998, when Premier Zhu Rongji reorganized the government. The other occurred early in 2003. Development Research Center of the State Council—the top think tank within the establishment—started working on a new energy strategy that proved to set the theoretical foundation for the subsequent years. These two events suggest the beginning of China's reconceptualization of climate change.

A. NDRC in Control

In 1998, Song Jian left the Climate Group I. Premier Zhu Rongji's decided to dismantle Climate Group I and establish a new group called State Coordinate Group on Responses to Climate Change ("Climate Group II"). The new entity was led by Zeng Peiyan, then Vice Premier and Chief Commissioner of the State Development and Planning Commission (SDPC, successor to the State Planning Commission). Climate Group II's office was relocated from the China Meteorological Administration to the newly formed SDPC. This is significant as the office functioned as the secretariat, in practice the office carries a lot of responsibility for climate work in China. In October 2003, when the Hu Jintao-Wen Jiabao administration took power, Climate Group II was chaired by Ma Kai, the newly appointed head of the National Development and Reform Commission (NDRC, successor to the SDPC). In 2007, the State Small Leadership Group on Climate Change, Energy Conservation and Emission Reduction (Climate Group III) was formed to replace Climate Group II, and its office was set in NDRC. Climate Group III is a high-level policy deliberation and decision-making body chaired by Premier Wen Jiabao, composed of mostly ministers from different departments. Ma Kai, the head of NDRC, was appointed as Office Director. In terms of bureaucratic structure, 1998 saw a significant change in China's conceptualization of climate change. Since 1998, the Climate Groups II and III were both heavily influenced by NDRC.

As noted earlier, during the U.N. Climate Change Convention negotiations, the State Planning Commission was not enthusiastic about climate change. The reformed NDRC is now in charge of energy policy (through its National Energy Administration), and it still closely works with the Ministry of Foreign Affairs. But the energy situation was changing dramatically for China after 1998. China has a long standing concern for dependence on foreign oil, given its experiences in the 1960s. Internal debates on energy security started as soon as China became a net oil importer in 1993. Concerns about energy were lessened temporarily by the Asian Financial Crisis in 1997-98, when the main policy focus was stimulating the economy. The debate on energy security intensified again in 2003 when China became the world's second largest consumer of oil, the United States being the first. In the volatile market of the 2000s, dependence on imported oil means vulnerability in national security and domestic stability. Power outages in 2004 in major cities across China also added to the sense of crisis. Politically, it was also the right time to think about the long term. In November 2002, Hu Jintao succeeded Jiang Zemin to become the Party's Secretary-General, and in March 2003, Hu was to become China's

President at the National People's Congress. As Hu Jintao and Wen Jiabao prepared for the leadership transition, it was natural to rethink the energy policy for the nation.

. . . .

B. Rethinking China's Energy Strategy

Early in 2003, the Development Research Center of the State Council, a top establishment think tank, along with the NDRC, Chinese Academy of Science, etc., led a large-scale study on China's energy policy. The study covered a wide range of topics from energy demand and supply, oil security, conservation, environment, climate change, clean coal technology, renewable energy, to research and development (R&D) in the energy sector. The final product of the study, "Strategy and Policy for China's Energy" (Strategy) was the keynote speech and center of discussion at a high-level international workshop in November 2003 in Beijing. The Strategy set the intellectual foundation of China's subsequent energy policies of the 2000s.

The Strategy first reviewed energy during the 1980-2000 period. It noted that China's GDP grew at an annual rate of 9.7 percent, while energy only grew at 4.6 percent, less than half of the economic growth. Energy intensity — measured by the energy consumption for each unit of GDP—went down by 64 percent. This is an enormous achievement considering the world average went down by only 19 percent, and that of the Organization for Economic Co-operation and Development (OECD) countries went down 20 percent during the same period. The Strategy attributed the success to three elements. First, the change in industrial structure—the proportion of metallurgy industries decreased while that of light industries such as electronics and communication increased. Second, as result of the reform, the market forces started playing an important role in allocating resources and eliminating some of the energy- and raw material-consuming firms.

However, this trend of energy intensity going down would not continue, the Strategy projected. This is because the industrial structure would change again in the next twenty years. As living standards go up and consumption patterns change over time, demand for energy would change, especially in the areas of transportation and construction, which would grow faster than the overall economy. China is facing a tension here, asserted the Strategy. On the one hand, it is heavily dependent on fossil fuel (coal and oil), and on the other, its energy efficiency remained considerably lower than that of the world average. This creates two major concerns. One is carbon dioxide emission. China's emission of carbon dioxide increased from 394 million tons in 1980 to 832 million tons in 2001. By 2020, emissions will be even higher, "thus China would be facing increasingly more international pressure to reduce greenhouse gas emission." The other concern, the Strategy noted, is energy security. By 2020, almost 60 percent of oil would have to be imported from abroad, which would leave China in an extremely vulnerable position. There-fore, the Strategy reasoned, it is crucial that China adopt a long-term energy strategy aiming at a transformation in terms of development direction and development pattern.

At the core of a sustainable energy strategy are three elements: priority on conservation and efficiency, multiple sources, and environment-friendliness. On conservation and efficiency, the Strategy set the goal that by the year 2020 China's total energy consumption goes down by 15 to 27 percent. The Strategy reiterated that as the top priority in the new energy strategy, conservation and efficiency should be given higher priority than increasing energy supply. On multiple sources, the Strategy recommended that China should increase the use of natural gas and actively develop renewable energy such as hydraulic power and nuclear power. The Strategy recommended the target capacity for nuclear to be 40 gigawatts (GWs), small-scale hydraulic power to be 70 GWs, wind power to be 20 GWs, and biomass to be 10 GWs. On the environment, the Strategy recommended that, "environment should be considered as an inherent element in decision-making on energy strategy." In other words, the Strategy conveyed the message that the environment is not an externality and should not be treated as one. It projected that by 2020 China's emission of carbon dioxide would be between 1.3 to 2 billion tons, reaching a per capita emission between 0.9 to 1.3 tons. Given the amount of emission, the Strategy speculated that there would be no doubt that "China would be forced to commit a cap as soon as the United States accedes into the Kyoto Protocol." At the end of the day, "it would be really hard for China to avoid any cap on greenhouse gases after 2020."

C. The National Program on Climate Change

The ideas laid out in the Strategy gradually found their way into official policy. In December 2004, the Communist Party took up the energy conservation and efficiency principle in its landmark Central Economic Work Conference. Then the energy strategy was further formulated and became part of the "Eleventh Five-Year Plan" approved by the National People's Congress in March 2006. The new energy strategy eventually became the foundation of the "National Climate Change Program," (the Program) announced by NDRC in June 2007. As the nation's second general official statement on climate change, the Program embodies the way NDRC defined climate change as an energy policy, an enormous change from the first period 1989-1998, discussed earlier.

The Program covered a broad range of issues. It described endeavors China had taken (Chapter I), the challenges China is still facing (Chapter II), its policy principles and objectives (Chapter III), measures and policies China is prepared to apply (Chapter IV), and its basic positions on climate change in the international arena (Chapter V). Though it covers industrial processes, agriculture, forestry, urban waste, etc. as key areas for emission mitigation, the Program largely defined China's climate policy through the lens of energy — energy efficiency, conservation, technology, and renewable status. The main targets the Program sets are energy targets that: (a) China will reduce energy consumption per unit of output value in GDP by 20%, and (b) China will raise the proportion of renewable energy to 10 percent of its primary energy supply by 2010. This is in part because China does not want to set a cap for its carbon emissions, even in this purely domestic context. More fundamentally, the central theme of the Program, based on the new energy strategy, is not just to cut emissions, but to change China's economic growth pattern by improving energy conservation and efficiency. In other words, the Program saw a strategic value in energy conservation and efficiency as a means to fuel economic growth by upgrading the whole economic structure.

D. Climate Change as Energy: Challenges

The differences between climate change understood as energy policy and climate change understood as environmental policy lie in the specific context of the Chinese policymaking process. There are differences in both governance and investment. In terms of governance, NDRC preferred certain policy instruments to others based on its own experience, tradition, and jurisdiction. The National Program on Climate Change is more in favor of a "command and control" approach — it sets standards, rules, targets, and timetables, but remains ambiguous on market incentive-based measures. SEPA, or its successor, the Ministry of Environment Protection (MEP), was interested in "cap-and-trade" and has conducted pilot projects on sulfur dioxide and chemical oxygen demand (COD), but "cap-and-trade" was not even mentioned in the Program. SEPA was also interested in a carbon tax. The Program is silent on carbon tax as well. NDRC, however, has recently made it clear that it opposes the idea. Climate change as environment would prefer a measure that can be applied across a broad range of industries and economic sectors, as a carbon tax or cap-and-trade suggest, but climate change as energy would not tolerate that because they may hurt NDRC itself. Thus climate change as energy's biggest problem is conflict of interests.

However, there are some positive elements in China's new policy. In recent years, NDRC has been aggressively investing in cleaner technology to reduce emissions. In the power generation sector, as a result, bigger (typically with capacity of 600 MW) and more efficient power generators employing super-critical (SC) or ultra-supercritical (USC) technology are replacing the smaller and old power generators. A report published in April 2009 by the International Energy Agency suggests that about ninety-five SC or USC units with a capacity of 600 MW or more had been put into operation by mid-2007, with another seventy units under construction, scheduled to be operational before 2010. Another area is renewable energy. A recent example is that a 10 GW wind farm in Jiuquan, Gansu province, northwest China, has just started construction. The Global Wind Energy Council, a Brussels-based institution, reported that in 2008, China again doubled its installed capacity by adding about 6.3 GW, to reach a total of 12.2 GW, making China the fourth in the world in terms of installed capacity. The United States added the biggest capacity in the same year, surpassing Germany to become the number one market in wind power. For China, this is the fourth consecutive year when its total capacity doubled every year. As a result of these investments 12.8 billion kilowatt-hour (kWh) of electricity came from wind power in 2008.

These areas show some signs of what Giddens calls "economic convergence," meaning that environmentally sound policy often coincides with what is good for the economy and wider political goals. China is contributing to the global move towards renewable energy. In the United States, wind power investment also has the benefit of "economic convergence." The wind industry added 35,000 jobs in 2008 resulting in a total of about 85,000 people employed in the wind industry today, up from 50,000 a year ago. In 2008, combined with new large hydropower stations, renewable energy represented 41 percent of total new global capacity, making 2008 the first year that investment in new power generation capacity sourced from renewable energy technologies (approximately $140 billion including large hydro) was more than the investment in fossil-fueled technologies (approximately $110 billion).

. . . .

___

NOTES AND QUESTIONS

1. How does Zang's analysis of the evolution of Chinese climate change law and policy fit within the rest of this book's exploration of the complex intersection of environment and energy? What are the advantages and disadvantages of each framing? Is there any way to get a greater convergence of environmental and energy issues, both legally and conceptually, with respect to climate change?
2. There are a variety of ways to measure China's contribution to climate change. When China is described as the largest emitter in the world, its responsibility to reduce its emissions seems clear. Yet other measures cast China's emissions in a different light. China's per capita emissions remain less than a quarter of the per capita emissions of the United States and Canada, and about half those of the European Union. Also, between 1850 and 2002, of all the carbon dioxide emitted into the atmosphere, the United States and the EU nations were each responsible for about 30 percent, and China was responsible for only about 8 percent. KEVIN A. BAUMERT, TIMOTHY HERZOG, & JONATHAN PERSHING, WORLD RES. INST., NAVIGATING THE NUMBERS: GREENHOUSE GAS DATA AND INTERNATIONAL CLIMATE POLICY 32, fig. 6.1 (2005).

   Which of these measures matters most in deciding which countries should reduce emissions and by how much? China and other developing countries do not bear the historical responsibility for climate change, and their people do not on average enjoy the highly energy-consumptive lifestyles of North-Americans and Europeans. Yet, if left unchecked, the emissions of major developing countries will overwhelm any emissions reductions achieved in developed countries.
3. Another important perspective is gained by making the link between China's emissions and developed country consumption. One-third of China's carbon emissions come from manufacturing electronics and other goods that are exported, often to the United States and Europe. *See* Elsa Wenzel, *One-Third of China's Carbon Emissions Tied to Exports*, CNET NEWS, July 29, 2008, http://news.cnet.com/8301-11128_3-10001150-54.html. Does this mean that the responsibility for a large part of China's emissions should lie with the final consumers in the United States, Europe, and other countries? Professor Michael Vandenbergh suggests that the government

or non-profit organizations in the United States should label consumer products to make clear their carbon footprint. This approach, he argues, would create consumer pressure that would induce importers of goods in the United States to impose carbon reduction requirements on Chinese suppliers. *See* Michael P. Vandenbergh, *Climate Change: The China Problem*, 81 S. Cal. L. Rev. 905 (2008). Do you agree that this approach could create strong incentives for emissions reductions in China? If not, why not?

3. CURRENT CHINESE CLIMATE CHANGE LAW AND POLICY

In line with Zang's analysis, China's 2011 Five-Year Plan interweaves energy and climate change goals. The targets China has set for itself have generally been phrased in terms of a reduction in carbon (or energy) intensity, which is defined as the amount of carbon emissions (or energy used) per unit of economic output. A carbon intensity reduction does not require an actual reduction in carbon emissions. When economic output (i.e., gross domestic product) is growing, carbon emissions may also grow, and carbon intensity will fall as long as economic output grows more quickly than emissions.

In the excerpt below, Professor Joanna Lewis analyzes the current Chinese approach.

JOANNA LEWIS, CENTER FOR CLIMATE AND ENERGY SOLUTIONS, ENERGY AND CLIMATE GOALS OF CHINA'S 12TH FIVE-YEAR PLAN (2011)

---

http://www.c2es.org/docUploads/energy-climate-goals-china-twelfth-five-year-plan.pdf

The 12th Five-Year Plan (FYP) adopted by the Chinese government in March 2011 devotes considerable attention to energy and climate change and establishes a new set of targets and policies for 2011-2015. While some of the targets are largely in line with the status quo, other aspects of the plan represent more dramatic moves to reduce fossil energy consumption, promote low-carbon energy sources, and restructure China's economy. Among the goals is to "gradually establish a carbon trade market." Key targets include:

- A 16 percent reduction in energy intensity (energy consumption per unit of GDP);
- Increasing non-fossil energy to 11.4 percent of total energy use; and
- A 17 percent reduction in carbon intensity (carbon emissions per unit of GDP).

Energy

The relationship between energy and economic growth matters greatly in China; without a reduction in energy intensity since the late 1970s, the country would need to consume three times the energy it does today to sustain its economic growth. At the center of China's 11th Five-Year Plan (2006-2010) was a target to decrease the overall energy intensity of the economy by 20 percent. This target was implemented in response to increases in energy intensity experienced between 2002 and 2005, the first increase experienced after several decades of rapidly decreasing energy intensity. To reverse the unexpected increases in energy intensity, the government mobilized a national campaign to promote energy efficiency, targeting in particular the largest and least efficient energy consuming enterprises. The Top 1,000 Program targeted approximately 1,000 companies (consuming about one-third of the country's energy) for efficiency improvements.

The 12th FYP builds directly on the 11th FYP energy intensity target and its associated programs, setting a new target to reduce energy intensity by an additional 16 percent by 2015. While this may seem less ambitious than the 20 percent reduction targeted in the 11th FYP, it likely represents a much more substantial challenge. It is likely the largest and least efficient enterprises have already undertaken efficiency improvements, leaving smaller, more efficient plants to be targeted in this second round. Under preparation is a new "Top 10,000" program, which is modeled after the Top 1,000 Program but adds an order of magnitude of companies to the mix. But as the number of plants grows, so do the challenges of collecting accurate data and enforcing targets.

The closure of inefficient power and industrial facilities also helped contribute to the decline in energy intensity during the 11th FYP period, with a reported 72.1 GW [gigawatts] of thermal capacity closed. Total plant closures are equivalent to 16 percent of the size of the capacity added over the period. An additional 8 GW of coal plants are reportedly to be shut down in 2011 alone with further closures no doubt on tap over the next five years.

While final data are not yet available, the country likely fell short of meeting its 11th FYP energy intensity target of 20 percent, instead achieving in the range of 19.1 percent. There is no doubt, however, that much was learned though efforts to improve efficiency nationwide. Many changes were made to how such national targets are enforced at the local level, including the incorporation of compliance with energy intensity targets into the evaluation for local officials.

The 12th FYP includes a target to increase non-fossil energy sources (including hydro, nuclear and renewable energy) to 11.4 percent of total energy use (up from 8.3 percent in 2010). While not formally enshrined in the 12th FYP, another recent notable announcement is a cap on total energy consumption of 4 billion tons of coal equivalent (tce) in 2015. To meet the cap on energy consumption, annual energy growth would need to slow to an average of 4.24 percent per year, from 5.9 percent between 2009 and 2010. The government is also trying to slow GDP growth rates, targeting 7 percent per year — far below recent growth rates. Lower GDP growth rates make it even more challenging for China to meet energy and carbon intensity targets, since energy and carbon need to grow more slowly than GDP for the country to achieve declining energy and carbon intensity.

Carbon

In the lead-up to the Copenhagen climate negotiations in the fall of 2009, the Chinese government pledged a 40-45 percent reduction in national carbon intensity from 2005 levels by 2020. To achieve this 2020 target, the 12th FYP sets an interim target of reducing carbon intensity 17 percent from 2010 levels by 2015. Whether this target will result in a deviation from China's expected carbon emissions over this time period depends on the corresponding GDP growth, but many studies have found that this target will be challenging for China to achieve without additional, aggressive policies to promote low carbon energy development.

Also promised in the 12th FYP is an improved system for monitoring greenhouse gas emissions, which will be needed to assess compliance with the carbon intensity target, and to prepare the national GHG inventories that, under the Cancún Agreements, are to be reported more frequently to the UNFCCC and undergo international assessment.

The 12th FYP establishes the goal of "gradually establish[ing] a carbon trade market," but does not elaborate. A handful of provinces have announced interest in piloting carbon trading schemes. The Tianjin Climate Exchange, partially owned by the founders of the Chicago Climate Exchange, is positioning itself to be the clearinghouse for any future carbon trading program. While some have suggested that Guangdong province may be targeted for a pilot program at the provincial level, other reports speculate that the program would begin within a single sector, such as the power sector, or begin by including only state-owned enterprises, which are often the target of early government policy experiments (as was the case with mandatory market shares for renewable energy placed on the large state-owned power companies). Other likely locations for pilots might include China's low-carbon cities and provinces.

Implementing a carbon trading scheme in China, even on a small-scale or pilot basis, will not be without significant challenges. Concerns have already been raised from both domestic and foreign-owned enterprises operating in China about how the regulation could affect their bottom lines. But the key challenge is likely technical, resulting from the minimal capacity currently in place to measure and monitor carbon emissions in China.

Industrial Policy

The 12th FYP also includes many new industrial policies to support clean energy industries and related technologies. Industries targeted include the nuclear, solar, wind and biomass energy technology industries, as well as hybrid and electric vehicles, and energy savings and environmental protection technology industries. These "strategic and emerging" industries are being promoted to replace the "old" strategic industries such as coal and telecom, (often referred to as China's pillar industries), which are heavily state-owned and have long benefited from government support. This move to rebrand China's strategic industries likely signals the start of a new wave of industrial policy support for the new strategic industries which may include access to dedicated state industrial funds, increased access to private capital, or industrial policy support through access to preferential loans or R&D funds.

Other targets encourage increased innovative activity, including a target for R&D expenditure to account for 2.2 percent of GDP, and for 3.3 patents per 10,000 people. During the 11th FYP period, an estimated 15.3 percent of government stimulus funding was directed towards innovation, energy conservation, ecological improvements and industrial restructuring.

Other Targets

The 12th FYP also includes targets to increase the rate of forest coverage by just over 21 percent and the total forest stock by 12.5 million hectares by 2015. Also mentioned are targets for the construction of 35,000 km of high-speed rail and improvements in subway and light rail coverage, as well as a goal to connect every city with a population greater than 500,000.

Outlook

The 12th FYP provides a glimpse into the minds of China's leadership as it lays out a methodological plan for moving the country forward. It includes a strong emphasis on new energy and climate programs and clearly illustrates China's commitment to increased environmental protection. The Plan itself provides a framework for progress, but leaves the details of implementation to policy makers, with many new policies and programs likely to follow in the coming weeks.

Some of the targets will no doubt prove challenging to implement. The national energy and carbon intensity targets will prove particularly difficult if economic growth rates slow in line with targets put forth in the plan. Implementation of energy conservation and efficiency programs at the facility level will prove increasingly demanding as more and more facilities are incorporated into current programs. The non-fossil energy target relies on extensive increases in nuclear energy capacity, but growth in nuclear plants may slow as efforts to improve safety and regulation will be implemented in the aftermath of the recent Japanese nuclear disaster. If nuclear targets are reduced, the share of renewable energy will need to increase even more than current targets propose.

Overall, China's Plan represents many ambitious climate and energy goals, and lays out a strategic roadmap for the county to endeavor to pursue over the next five years.

NOTES AND QUESTIONS

1. What is your assessment of this plan in the broader context of global emissions reductions efforts? To what extent does this combined focus on energy, carbon, and industry seem like an appropriate and effective approach to China addressing climate change? What are the benefits and limitations of having a five-year planning horizon?

2. In 2010, China joined the Copenhagen Accord with the following pledge:

> China will endeavor to lower its carbon dioxide emissions per unit of GDP by 40-45% by 2020 compared to the 2005 level, increase the share of non-fossil fuels in primary energy consumption to around 15% by 2020 and increase forest coverage by 40 million hectares and forest stock volume by 1.3 billion cubic meters by 2020 from the 2005 levels.

See United Nations Framework Convention on Climate Change, Information Provided by Parties to the Convention Relating to the Accord, Letter from China, Jan. 28, 2010, http://unfccc.int/files/meetings/cop_15/copenhagen_accord/application/pdf/chinacphaccord_app2.pdf.

Based on widely varying projections for China's GDP in 2020, China's pledge may represent anywhere from a 15 percent decrease to a 204 percent increase in emissions as compared to 1990 levels. *Who's On Board With The Copenhagen Accord?*, U.S. CLIMATE ACTION NETWORK, http://www.usclimatenetwork.org/policy/copenhagen-accord-commitments (last visited Apr. 7, 2012). Do you think this commitment should satisfy U.S. politicians and others who have argued that the United States should not commit to reducing its emissions unless China takes similar action?

3. In February 2010, Reuters reported that the Chinese city of Tianjin had launched a small-scale energy-intensity trading scheme, a possible first step toward a nationwide carbon cap-and-trade scheme. *See* Emma Graham-Harrison, *Chinese City Dips Toe in Carbon Cap and Trade*, REUTERS, Feb. 9, 2010, http://www.reuters.com/article/idUSTRE6182V620100209. Would establishing a nationwide cap-and-trade program be a good way for China to reach its carbon intensity goal? Ruth Greenspan Bell advises caution in the use of cap-and-trade and other market-based regulatory instruments in developing countries. Ruth Greenspan Bell, *Culture and History Count: Choosing Environmental Tools to Fit Available Institutions and Experience,* 38 IND. L. REV. 637 (2005). She argues that such regulatory instruments require legal and market infrastructure that is often not sufficiently present. In China, for example, she points out the extent to which governance has traditionally been based on personal relationships, and the lack of an independent judiciary.

E. BRAZIL: DEFORESTATION AND DEVELOPMENT

Like China, Brazil is a developing country that will play a key role in averting dangerous climate change. It is the world's fifth largest country, both by geographical area and by population. In terms of its economic and political development, Brazil successfully transitioned from dictatorship to democracy in the 1980s, and along with Russia, India, and China (the "BRIC" countries), is viewed as one of the world's largest emerging economies.

Brazil is a federal constitutional democracy, with 27 states and a federal district that comprises the capital city of Brasilia (*see* Figure 4.1, below). Its judiciary, both at the federal and state levels, has become an important actor in environmental law, as public prosecutors and environmental groups are constitutionally empowered to file environmental public interest lawsuits. *See* LESLEY K. MCALLISTER, MAKING LAW MATTER: ENVIRONMENTAL PROTECTION AND LEGAL INSTITUTIONS IN BRAZIL (2008). Southern Brazil, where São Paulo and Rio de Janeiro are located, has well developed industrial, agricultural, and urban economies. Northern Brazil is less economically developed, and it is home to the Amazon,

Figure 4.1: Map of the Brazilian States

Source: Map courtesy of www.theodora.com/maps, used with permission.

which contains the world's largest river by volume, a great deal of biodiversity, and over half of earth's remaining rainforests.

Tropical deforestation is a major source of greenhouse gas emissions, esti-mated to contribute about 20 percent of global emissions. Yet deforestation in tropical countries has proven difficult to control, in part because of the weak-ness of national legal and regulatory institutions for environmental protec-tion. In Brazil and several other countries, deforestation is closely linked to agricultural exports, which tend to be significant in the development of the national economy.

In the past five years, Brazil has emerged as a leader among develop-ing countries in climate change policy. As described below, Brazil has made significant strides in reducing deforestation in the Amazon forest and has committed to reducing it further. Brazil is also the first developing country to pass a national law that commits it to meeting a certain emissions reduc-tions target. These developments are explored in the sections below.

1. REDUCING EMISSIONS FROM DEFORESTATION

In Brazil, deforestation—primarily in the Amazon forest—is responsible for about 75 percent of the country's greenhouse gas emissions each year. However, because Brazil's energy sector relies on hydropower for electricity and biofuels for transportation more than most other major emitters, there are relatively few opportunities for emissions reductions.

The reading that follows by Brazilian journalist Marcelo Leite gives a sense of both the strides Brazil has made in reducing deforestation and the continuing threats that the Amazon faces.

MARCELO LEITE, THE BRAZILIAN DILEMMA: A NATION STRUGGLES NOT TO EXPLOIT ITS OWN GREATEST RESOURCE

Wash. Monthly, July/August 2009,
http://www.washingtonmonthly.com/features/2009/0907.leite.html

Seen from the height of 36,000 feet aboard a Brazilian Air Force jet, the Amazon rainforest looks tranquil as we approach our destination, the town of Tabatinga, a jungle outpost in the state of Amazonas where Brazil meets Colombia and Peru. A dark green velvet blankets the land as far as we can see through the fluffy clouds below us. The monotone is free of vehicle tracks, broken only by muddy threads of rivers flowing into the Upper Solimões, as the main branch of the mighty Amazon River is called where it enters the country on its 4,000-mile descent from the Peruvian Andes to the Atlantic.

But if this five-hour flight from São Paulo offers a glimpse of a vast and untouched Amazon, it also highlights the checkerboarding created by recent development. To reach the wilderness from the south, we first fly over countless towns, coffee and sugar cane plantations, and processing plants covering the state of São Paulo. Then the flight continues northward over immense cattle areas that lay siege to the unique, biologically diverse floodplain called the Pantanal, in the state of Mato Grosso do Sul. Passing over Rondônia state, an hour or so before we land, we see how soybean plantations—prominent newer stars in the country's growing array of exports—have replaced whole swaths of Amazon rainforest.

In sum, the flight gives the passenger a quick snapshot of a massive ecological dilemma. Of the original 1.5 million square miles of Brazilian Amazon forest, far and away the world's largest, some 82 percent remains intact. This entire area, roughly the size of India, is home to only twenty-four million people and is endowed with incredible biodiversity of global significance. But it continues to give way to logging, cattle, and soy plantations.

The big question is whether this southern giant will follow the development path favored by many Brazilians, once again plundering Amazonia's natural capital and suffering the severe consequences of deforestation. Or will it learn from unsustainable prior experience along its Atlantic coast, and resist dragging the Amazon rainforest into the same trap? The recent news has been good. According to satellite photos taken by Brazil's highly regarded National Institute for Space Research, deforestation rates have been dropping steadily since 2004. That was the year that President Luiz Inácio Lula da Silva, responding to increasing pressure from the international community and a growing contingent of ecologically minded Brazilian voters, revealed the Amazon Deforestation Action Plan. The plan involves tighter controls over loggers and ranchers, including fines and even imprisonment, and the refusal of credit by official banks to farmers who are not able to document that they abide by environmental regulations. Chief among these is the Forestry Code, which requires the preservation of at least 80 percent of forest cover on Amazonian properties.

Another piece of good news is Brazil's Amazon Fund, an innovative idea first announced by former Environment Minister Marina Silva at the United Nations climate conference in Bali in 2007. The fund, newly operational this year, collects voluntary contributions from other nations, companies, and even individuals: the government of Norway has pledged $1 billion to it, of which a first installment of $110 million was deposited at the end of March. Another $18 million is expected to come from Germany soon. Fund officials working at the National Economic and Social Development Bank, a federal agency, then channel these funds to conservation groups and projects — but only after a country-wide reduction in deforestation has been achieved and documented.

The emergence of this government-run fund, a spinoff from international discussions about Reduced Emissions from Deforestation and Forest Degradation (REDD), constitutes an advance in several important ways. First, by retaining Brazilian control over how the money is spent, the fund's structure counters nationalist objections to receiving foreign funds in exchange for forest conservation and the reduction of carbon dioxide emissions. Control over the national patrimony has been a strongly valued concept in Brazil ever since the bad old days of the mid-twentieth century, when foreign interests owned local electric power and oil companies. Dreams of Amazonian prosperity arouse similar feelings. Second, for the first time after decades of resistance, the fund commits Brazil to deforestation targets. The goal is to achieve an 80 percent reduction in Amazon deforestation by 2020. Third, the willingness of Norway and other countries to hand over substantial monies to Brazil, for projects chosen by Brazil only, reflects growing international confidence in the country's ability to measure deforestation rates and select anti-deforestation controls.

But even as Brazil pursues policies to slow deforestation, it advances others that could speed it up. In particular is the government's $328 billion Accelerated Development Plan, an ambitious long-term national effort to strengthen Brazilian infrastructure and ties with neighboring countries by means of new highways, bridges, airfields, and electric power installations. Support for such initiatives comes from powerful farming and mining interests. Each new mile of road in the Amazon creates new opportunities to exploit the forests. Meanwhile, agribusiness leaders and sympathetic members of Congress have launched an offensive against the Forestry Code and some of its more restrictive provisions. They are, for example, trying to restore the 80 percent reserve rule in the Amazon to the 50 percent level previously required.

The bottom line: the battle is far from over when it comes to balancing Amazonian economic growth and conservation, and in Brasilia the tug of war continues. The severe effects of Amazonian deforestation on regional weather and the global climate are becoming ever better understood. The forest's bio-diversity remains impressive, and there are still countless plant and animal species yet to be analyzed for their possible benefits to all of us. Still, the reality is that if Brazilians were forced to choose today between forest and develop-ment, many would favor the latter, matching the amount of forest that has already been lost and abandoning another 18 percent or more to development, exports, and short-term prosperity for some. Most would gladly retrace the path the nation followed along the coast while eradicating the no less diverse Atlantic forest — thus replicating the fate of most of the temperate forests in the developed world.

The factors that lead to deforestation in the Amazon are complex. While local actors, such as farmers and cattle ranchers, may be responsible for defor-estation on the ground, larger political and economic forces often influence their actions. As explained in the following excerpt by Professor Lesley McAll-ister, in the last couple decades, Amazonian deforestation has been driven by the expansion of agro-industry, which produces food and other products for national and international markets.

LESLEY K. McALLISTER, SUSTAINABLE CONSUMPTION GOVERNANCE
IN THE AMAZON

38 Envtl. L. Rep. News & Analysis 10873, 10873–877 (2008)

I. Amazonian Deforestation and Its Commodity Drivers

The deforestation of tropical forests is driven by complex social, political, and environmental factors that differ by region and country. Brazil, home to about 40% of the world's remaining tropical rainforests, has become one of the world's agroindustrial giants, and agroindustry has become an important driver of deforestation. This section describes historical deforestation rates in the Amazon, analyzes how expansion in the beef, soybeans and biofuel industries stimulates deforestation, and discusses the surge in Brazilian law enforcement to address deforestation in the 2000s.

A. Deforestation in the Amazon

The Amazon basin (or biome) extends through much of South America, with 60% of it within Brazil's boundaries. The Brazilian Amazon as used herein refers not just to the area of the Amazon basin with Brazil, but to a somewhat larger administrative region that in Brazil is referred to as the Legal Amazon (*Amazônia Legal*). The region is comprised of nine Brazilian states (Acre, Amapá, Amazonas, Pará, Rondônia, Roraima, Mato Grosso, Maranhão, and Tocantins) and covers more than half of Brazil's total land area [*see* Figure 4.1 above]. So defined, almost three-quarters of the Brazilian Amazon consists of forests of the Amazon biome. Large areas of the states of Mato Grosso, Tocantins, and Maranhão consist of the tropical shrub-savannas of the Cerrado biome.

Studies of the Amazon refer to an "arc of deforestation" that runs through the eastern and southern extents of the Amazon forests, primarily in the states of Pará, Mato Grosso, and Rondônia. This is the Brazilian frontier, where the socially and culturally complex drama (or tragedy) of deforestation unfolds. The cast of characters is large, with primary roles played (in rough order of appearance) by landgrabbers who claim land using fraud and violence; loggers who extract the most valuable species from the land; colonists and other subsistence farmers who buy or simply occupy land; and capitalized farmers and large cattle ranchers who often buy land from the landgrabbers, colonists and subsistence farmers. Supporting roles are played by goldminers and money launderers, as well as migrant laborers who sometimes become debt slaves to landgrabbers, farmers, and ranchers. The stage is a mosaic of often-contested land tenures, consisting roughly of untitled public lands (*terras devolutas*) (35%), private lands (24%), indigenous lands (21%), and publicly protected lands (20%).

Most deforestation in the Brazilian Amazon has occurred since the 1960s, when the Brazilian government began to subsidize the settlement and development of the region. In the 1970s and 1980s, the main drivers of Amazonian deforestation involved smallholder agriculture and cattle-grazing undertaken by colonists drawn to the Amazonian frontier by governmental road-building projects and other incentives. While logging has not been a direct cause of deforestation because only a few valuable species are selectively harvested, it has often been a precursor to deforestation as farmers and ranchers move into areas made accessible by illegal logging roads and logged forests become more susceptible to fire. Between 1960 and 2001, the human population of the Amazon grew from about 4 million to over 20 million.

According to official statistics, annual deforestation in the years from 1977 to 1988 averaged about 21,000 km^2, an area roughly the size of New Jersey. International concern about tropical deforestation and the loss of biological diversity in the 1980s culminated in the negotiation of the Convention on Biological Diversity at the 1992 "Earth Summit" in Rio de Janeiro. In the 1990s, annual deforestation in the Amazon tended to be lower, averaging about 16,000 km^2. By the turn of the twenty-first century, close to 15% of the original extent of Brazilian Amazon forests had been cleared.

Scientists have expressed concern that positive feedbacks between deforestation and climate change could devastate the Amazon, with grave consequences for the climate. With climate change, the Amazon could experience dieback as vegetation dies because of reduced precipitation and rising air temperatures, accompanied by increased risk of forest fire. A recent study suggests that without policy interventions, more than half of the Amazon forest will be destroyed or degraded by logging, agriculture, fires and drought by 2030.

B. Commodity Drivers

In the late 1990s, a new export-driven paradigm of commodity production involving primarily cattle ranching and soybean cultivation, emerged as the greatest threat to the Brazilian Amazon. The extent to which Amazonian deforestation has become responsive to international market conditions is evident in the recent fluctuations in annual deforestation rates. The years 2002 through 2004, when deforestation rates were increasing, were favorable for agroindustry expansion in Brazil because international market prices for many agricultural commodities including soy and beef were increasing and Brazil's currency devaluation lowered the price of Brazilian commodities in the international market. After 2004, the market prices of soy and beef declined and the Brazilian currency gained value against the dollar, curbing agroindustry expansion and contributing to the decline in deforestation rates from 2004 through 2007. In late 2007, when commodity prices began to rise precipitously, so too did deforestation. An analysis comparing annual deforestation rates with the annual average market prices of soy and beef in the years from 1994 through 2006 substantiated a strong correlation with beef prices and a weaker correlation with soy prices. This section describes the trajectory of the cattle and soybean industries in the Amazon, as well as the potential for world demand for biofuels to put further pressure on Amazonian forests.

1. Cattle

Cattle ranching has long been the largest driver of deforestation in the Amazon. Overall, about 70% of the area deforested in the Amazon is cattle pasture. In 1981, Norman Myers coined the term "hamburger connection" to describe how the growth in beef exports from Central America to the United States was contributing to deforestation. However, this term was not applicable to Brazil in the 1980s because almost all Brazilian beef was consumed domestically.

In the 2000s, however, a hamburger connection emerged as Brazil became the world's largest beef exporter. Between 1994 and 2005, Brazil expanded its beef exports over 450% in volume and 385% in value. Kaimowitz attributes the rapid expansion in the industry to dual causes: the favorable international market conditions for Brazilian exports and Brazil's progress towards the eradication of foot-and-mouth disease. Before 1998, the presence of foot-and-mouth disease in Brazil prevented most exports, but by 2003, 85% of the country's cattle herd was in areas that were certified as disease-free.

While the large majority of Brazil's beef exports come from southern Brazil, most of the expansion of the national herd has occurred in the Amazon. From 1990 to 2002, 80% of all growth in Brazil's livestock population occurred in the Amazon as the region's herd more than doubled from 26 million to 57 million. By 2005 the Amazon was home to about a third of the national cattle herd. The states with most growth in cattle ranching were Mato Grosso, Para and Rondônia, which were also the states with the most deforestation. In 2004, Brazil became the world's largest beef exporter, with 38% of its exports going to the European Union, 12% to the Middle East, and 10% to Russia.

2. Soybeans

Soybean cultivation in the Amazon began in the 1990s as varieties suitable to its climate were developed and worldwide demand for soybeans as animal feed protein grew. Significant private and governmental investment in infrastructure to facilitate the inflow of agricultural inputs and the outflow of harvests occurred including the construction of storage and processing facilities, the development of a barge system and associated deepwater ports, and the paving of interstate highways. International agroindustry firms such as Cargill,

Archer Daniels Midland, and Bunge have become important players in the Brazilian soybean industry. While pasture remains the dominant land use after deforestation, studies have identified "a new paradigm of forest loss" involving "larger clearing sizes and faster rates of forest conversion" for soybean cultivation.

Brazil is the world's second largest producer of soy, exceeded only by the United States. In the 2006-07 harvest, about 30% of Brazil's soy crop came from the state of Mato Grosso. While most of the crop is grown in the lowland savannah and transition areas in southern Mato Grosso, an increasing amount is being grown in the previously forested areas of northern Mato Grosso. In the forested areas of the Amazon generally, soybean cultivation grew by 15% annually from 1999 to 2004. The state of Mato Grosso has been at the center of that growth and of the related deforestation: in the years of 2001 to 2004, the state accounted for 40% of new deforestation in the Amazon. While a recent study in Mato Grosso showed that deforestation for large-scale cropland accounted for 17% of all deforestation between 2001 and 2004, most of the impact of soybean cultivation on deforestation is likely to be indirect. As prices for land risen because of the profitability of growing soy, cattle ranchers sell their lands to soybean farmers and move to more remote areas which they deforest for cattle ranching.

In 2006, Brazil replaced the United States as the world's largest exporter of soybeans. The European Union is the largest consumer of Brazilian soy, where it is used primarily as animal feed. The European Union has been especially interested in buying soy produced in the Amazon rather than in southern Brazil because the Amazonian crop is mostly free of genetically modified soy. China is also a major importer of Brazilian soy.

3. Biofuels

The quest to develop biofuels could exacerbate the conversion of forests to pasture and agriculture in the Brazilian Amazon. The United States, the European Union, Brazil, China, and India along with more than 20 other countries have enacted laws with mandatory targets for the use of biofuel in transportation fuels. Brazil is the largest producer and exporter of sugar cane ethanol to world markets, and it seeks to double its production by 2012. In addition, soybean oil can be used to make biodiesel. While biofuels were originally thought to emit fewer GHGs than petroleum fuel, studies that incorporate the deforestation and other land use changes associated with biofuels have found that they often lead to greater GHG emissions than petroleum.

The worldwide push toward biofuels could lead to increased Amazonian deforestation through several direct and indirect pathways. Most obviously, soybean cultivation for use in the production of biofuels may expand in the Amazon. It is also possible that palm plantations might be established for the production of palm oil, as is occurring in tropical Asia. Less directly, the production of biofuels elsewhere in the world may, in a variety of ways increases in the price of soybeans or cattle on the international market, thus stimulating further production of these commodities in the Amazon and the resultant deforestation. Brazilian sugar cane is cultivated primarily in southern Brazil, but increased cultivation there may displace soybean cultivation and cattle grazing, exerting pressure on the Amazon. Similarly, the cultivation of corn for ethanol may displace soy cultivation in the United States.

C. Brazilian Law Enforcement

Brazilian laws relating to deforestation in the Amazon are very strict, but have often not been enforced. In the 2000s, however, there have been signs of increasing governmental capacity at the federal and state levels in Brazil to enforce laws relating to Amazonian deforestation. The federal government has visibly cracked down on illegal logging in the Amazon and has stated its intention to establish a licensing system for rural properties in the Amazon that would enable documentation of illegal forest clearings. These initiatives are supported by the Brazilian government's sophisticated system of detecting and analyzing land clearing through satellite images.

Each year, an area of forest is selectively logged in the Amazon approximately equal to the area of forest loss. By law, a Sustainable Forest Management Plan must be prepared before a logging permit is issued by the environmental agency. However, it has been estimated that about 80% of logging in the Amazon is illegal, often because it comes from lands that are not legal owned or controlled by the loggers using logging permits based on fraudulent information. In 2004, the federal environmental agency IBAMA, in coordination with the federal police and federal prosecutors, began a campaign targeting illegal logging in the Amazon. By 2007, more than 15 sting operations had been conducted, resulting in the arrests of over 500 people for environmental crimes, including 116 IBAMA employees; the closure of 1,500 illegal sawmills; and the issuance of over 2.8 billion reais (almost US$ 1.2 billion) in fines. With the news of the spike in deforestation in late 2007, IBAMA initiated another round of sting operations. Moreover, the campaign sends an important signal regarding the government's ability and willingness to enforce environmental laws in the region.

A great deal of deforestation could be avoided if landowners complied with the Brazilian Forest Code (*Código Florestal*) that requires landowners in the Amazon to maintain a forest reserve (*reserva legal*) comprising 80% of their landholding. Landowners are also required to maintain forest cover in riparian zones, hilltops, and other "areas of permanent protection" (*áreas de preservação permanente*). Most landowners, however, do not meet these legal requirements. In 1999, the state of Mato Grosso's environmental agency initiated an ambitious licensing program for rural properties in which the agency identified land clearings through satellite data and mapped them to specific rural properties to find out whether they were licensed or not. The Rural Property Environmental Licensing System (SLAPR) revealed that 95% of large clearings in the state were illegal. The decline in the state's rate of deforestation in 2000 suggested that the program was effective in slowing forest loss. While the program was weakened after 2003 when Brazil's largest soybean entrepreneur was elected governor of Mato Grosso, the federal government and other Brazilian states have viewed it as a model for the licensing of rural properties throughout the Amazon.

Despite Brazil's growing capacity for enforcement of laws against deforestation, it should be noted that many national laws and policies stimulate infrastructural and economic development that lead to deforestation. Since the late 1990s, the federal government's development programs have consistently called for large infrastructure projects to facilitate industrial agriculture and other economic activities in the Amazon. Such projects, including new highways, railroads, river-channelizations, gas and power lines, and hydroelectric facilities, are often viewed as drivers of deforestation in their own right. A recent study also showed that between 2002 and 2007, the Brazilian government subsidized cattle ranching in the Amazon to the tune of almost 2 billion reais or approximately US$ 840 million.

NOTES AND QUESTIONS

1. Given that Amazon deforestation is driven by export-oriented agro-industry, are the consumers in other countries who buy Brazilian beef and soybeans also partly responsible? What can consumers of these products do to improve the situation? Professor Lesley McAllister describes the emergence of "sustainable consumption governance," which encompasses a "diverse array of private and public activities and institutions that seek to lead market participants toward more sustainable consumption." *Id.* at 10873. For example, in the Amazon, one soybean export company has required its local suppliers to certify that they are in compliance with Brazilian forest law or moving towards it. See Chapter Six for more discussion of the links between consumption and climate change.

2. As shown in Figure 4.2 below, in the latter 2000s, annual deforestation declined markedly. Some of this decline may be explained by economic factors such as lower agro-export commodity prices and the recession of the late 2000s. However, the Brazilian federal government's increasing attention to and vigilance against Amazonian deforestation also seems to be having a positive effect. As part of implementing the Amazon Deforestation Action Plan, the federal government initiated a series of sting operations targeting illegal deforestation in the Amazon and created over a hundred new protected areas that together are about the size of France. ENVTL. DEF. FUND, BRAZIL NATIONAL AND STATE REDD (2009), *available at* http://www.edf.org/sites/default/files/10438_Brazil_national_and_state_REDD_report.pdf.

    In 2009, the Brazilian government announced an ambitious deforestation reduction goal for the Amazon: by 2020, annual deforestation should be 80 percent below the 1996-2005 average of 19,500 sq. km/year (or about 4,000 sq. km). *See id.*; Mario Osava, *Brazil Deforestation Down 45 Percent*, IPSNEWS.NET, http://ipsnews.net/news.asp?idnews=49257. Aside from the climate change-related benefits, what other benefits could reducing Amazonian deforestation have for Brazil?

Figure 4.2: Area of the Brazilian Amazon Deforested by Year, 1995-2011 (August 1 to July 31), square kilometers per year

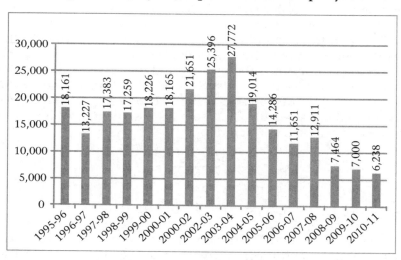

Source: Instituto Nacional de Pesquisas Espaciais (INPE), Ministry of Science and Technology, *available at* http://www.obt.inpe.br/prodes/prodes_1988_2011.htm.

3. To achieve its deforestation reduction goal, Brazil has made clear that it will need international help. Indeed, REDD (Reducing Emissions from Deforestation and Forest Degradation) has become an important aspect of international climate change treaty negotiations, as endorsed by the Copenhagen Accord and further specified in the Cancún Agreements. A REDD mechanism would enable developed countries to pay developing countries to preserve their tropical forests as a means of cutting global carbon emissions. In the past, REDD has been excluded from international climate change treaties because of concerns about monitoring, leakage, additionality, and permanence. *See* Randall S. Abate & Todd A. Wright, *A Green Solution to Climate Change: The Hybrid Approach to Crediting Reductions in Tropical Deforestation*, 20 Duke Envtl. L. & Pol'y F. 87 (2010).

Debates about REDD have centered on how it should be financed. Brazil has advocated for the establishment of a giant fund financed with donations from industrialized nation governments. Developing countries would receive the funds after they credibly demonstrate that they have reduced their emissions from deforestation. Brazil's Amazon Fund would serve as the model for this approach. Many other countries have favored a market-based approach, in which forest carbon credits generated from REDD projects could be used by companies and national governments to meet emission reduction targets in national cap-and-trade systems and international treaties like the Kyoto Protocol. For detailed information on the various REDD proposals, see Global Canopy Program, The Little Redd+ Book (2008), *available at* http://www.globalcanopy.org/sites/default/files/lrb_en.pdf.

Why do you think that Brazil has favored financing REDD through public funds rather than carbon credits? Why might the United States and other donor countries be concerned about a REDD mechanism that channels funds through developing country governments? In general, why do you think developing countries would be concerned about industrialized countries (and their companies) using forest carbon credits for compliance with their emissions reduction obligations?

4. Even in the absence of a REDD mechanism in international law, domestic laws of developed countries could allow for the purchase of credits generated by deforestation reduction projects in developing countries. The Waxman-Markey Bill, discussed in Chapter Three, was passed by the U.S. House of Representatives in 2009 but later abandoned. It would have allowed U.S. companies to offset six billion tons of carbon dioxide emissions before 2025 by investing in forest conservation projects before 2025. If the United States were to ever pass comprehensive climate change legislation, do you think U.S. companies should be able to fulfill emissions reduction obligations that they have under U.S. law by buying credits from deforestation reduction projects in Brazil? Why or why not?

In March 2010, Brazil and the United States signed a Memorandum of Understanding (MOU) pledging to "cooperate in areas related to capacity-building, research, development, deployment and dissemination of technologies to address climate change and its adverse effects." *U.S. and Brazil Sign Deforestation Agreement*, MONGABAY.COM, Mar. 7, 2010, http://news.mongabay.com/2010/0307-brazil_us_mou.html. Under the MOU, Brazil and the United States established a Climate Change Policy Dialogue, which will meet at least once a year to facilitate cooperation.

2. A NATIONAL CLIMATE CHANGE LAW

In 2008, Brazil released a National Policy on Climate Change, and in 2009, just days after the end of the Copenhagen COP, the president signed it into law. The following excerpt from the law highlights its key elements.

LAW NO. 12.187, OF DECEMBER 29, 2009

Diário Oficial da União [D.O.U.] de 12.30.2009 (Braz.)

Art. 1. This Law institutes the National Policy on Climate Change — PNMC (*Política Nacional sobre Mudança do Clima*) and establishes its principles, objectives, directives and instruments.

. . . .

Art. 3. The PNMC and resulting activities, performed under the responsibility of political entities and administrative bodies, shall observe the principles of precaution, prevention, citizen participation, sustainable development as well as the principle of common but differentiated responsibilities at international level, and, with regard to the measures adopted for their implementation, shall consider the following:

I - all have the duty to act, for the sake of the present and future generations, to reduce the impacts of anthropogenic interference with the climate system;

II - measures shall be taken to prevent, avoid or minimize identified causes of climate change with anthropogenic origin within the national territory, on which there is reasonable consensus among scientists and technicians engaged in the study of phenomena concerned;

III - adopted measures shall take into consideration the different socio-economic contexts of their application, distribute the resulting financial burden and charges across economic sectors and populations and communities concerned in an equitable and balanced way, and weigh individual responsibilities with regard to the origin of sources and occasioned effects on climate;

IV - sustainable development is the key to address climate change while conciliating it with serving the common and particular needs of the populations and communities that live in the national territory;

V - action at national level to address current, present and future climate change shall consider and integrate activities promoted at state and city level by public and private bodies.

Art. 4. The National Policy on Climate Change — PNMC shall aim at:

I - making social-economic development compatible with the protection of the climate system;

II - reducing anthropogenic greenhouse gas emissions with regard to their different sources;

. . . .

IV - strengthening anthropogenic removals by sinks of greenhouse gases in national territory;

V - implementing measures to promote adaptation to climate change, across the 3 (three) tiers of the Federation, with the participation and collaboration of economic and social agents concerned and of beneficiaries, particularly those especially vulnerable to the adverse effects of climate change;

VI - preservation, conservation, recovery and rehabilitation of environmental resources, with particular attention to the large natural biomes regarded as National Heritage;

VII - consolidation and expansion of legally protected areas and incentives to reforestation and recomposition of vegetation cover in degraded areas;

VIII - encouraging the development of the Brazilian Emissions Reduction Market — MBRE (*Mercado Brasileiro de Redução de Emissões*).

. . . .

Art. 11. Other public policy and governmental program principles, objectives, directives and instruments shall be made compatible with the principles, objectives, directives and instruments of this National Policy on Climate Change.

Sole Paragraph. A Decree from the Executive Power shall, in accordance with the National Policy on Climate Change, establish the Sectoral Plans of mitigation and adaptation to climate change, aiming at the consolidation of a low-carbon consuming economy, for the sectors of energy generation and distribution; urban public transport and modal interstate cargo and passenger transportation systems; manufacturing industry and durable consumer goods industry; fine chemicals industry and basic chemicals industry; paper and cellulose industry; mining; civil construction industry; healthcare services; and agriculture and ranching, with a view to meeting gradual quantifiable and verifiable anthropogenic emissions reduction targets, considering the specificities of each sector, including via the Clean Development Mechanism — CDM and via Nationally Appropriate Mitigation Actions — NAMAs.

Art. 12. To attain the PNMC objectives, the country shall adopt actions to mitigate greenhouse gas emissions with the purpose of reducing between 36.1% and 38.9% of projected emissions by 2020 as a national voluntary commitment.

Sole Paragraph. The projection of emissions for 2020 as well as the detailing of actions to attain the objective stated by the present article shall be stipulated by decree, based on the second Brazilian Inventory of Emissions . . . to be concluded in 2010.

NOTES AND QUESTIONS

1. Article 12 of Law No. 12.187 establishes a national greenhouse gas reduction target, and the law's passage made Brazil the first developing country to formalize such a target in national law. Brazil also pledged as one of its Nationally Appropriate Mitigation Actions (NAMA) under the Copenhagen Accord to undertake a series of voluntary domestic actions to achieve a reduction of 36.1 percent to 38.9 percent below projected "business-as-usual" emissions in 2020. For a listing of all of NAMAs that Brazil committed to under the Accord, see Letter from Embassy of the Federated Republic of Brazil, to United Nations Framework Convention on Climate Change (Jan. 29, 2010), *available at* http://unfccc.int/files/meetings/cop_15/copenhagen _accord/application/pdf/brazilcphaccord_app2.pdf. Why do you think that Brazil became a leader among developing countries in making a national commitment of this type?

2. In 1988, Brazilians wrote a new Federal Constitution after the country's transition from dictatorship to democracy. The constitution included an article dedicated to environmental protection. Article 225 declares that:

   > "[e]veryone has the right to an ecologically equilibrated environment, a good used in common by all citizens and essential to a healthy quality of life, imposing a duty on the government and the community to defend and preserve it for present and future generations."
   > Constituição da República Federativa do Brasil, art. 225 (Braz., 1988).

   Does the Brazilian constitution's articulation of an environmental right help explain Brazil's leadership in climate change policy?

3. To what extent are ambitious environmental laws in developing countries actually implemented and enforced? In Brazil, state and federal prosecutors

have emerged as some of the most vocal and active agents in environmental enforcement. *See* Lesley K. McAllister, Making Law Matter: Environmental Protection & Legal Institutions in Brazil (2008). Prosecutors have authority to bring legal actions against not just private citizens who violate environmental laws, but also governmental agencies that fail to implement them. Their role thus bears some resemblance to the role of citizen enforcers in U.S. environmental law. Why might these Brazilian prosecutors be better situated than governmental environmental agencies to enforce environmental laws?

F. TOWARD GLOBAL CLIMATE LAW

An important idea within comparative law has been that by comparing legal rules across jurisdictions, it may be possible to derive "general principles of law" that are valid and useful across many jurisdictions. Professors Tseming Yang and Robert Percival have embraced a similar view in their work on global environmental law. They suggest that by comparing the laws of various countries, we can identify basic environmental provisions and principles that have become globalized.

Tseming Yang & Robert V. Percival, The Emergence of Global Environmental Law

36 Ecology L.Q. 615, 616–17, 627–28, 631, 635–36, 652–53 (2009)

Worldwide growth of public concern for the natural environment has been one of the most important developments in recent decades. Globalization has helped connect societies and their environmental fates more closely than ever before. At the same time, environmental problems increasingly transcend national borders and pose serious challenges to the health of the planet. The development of more effective environmental laws and legal systems throughout the world has thus become critical to directing economic development and growth onto a path of environmental sustainability.

The responses have been surprisingly progressive. Countries are transplanting law and regulatory policy innovations of other nations, even when they have very different legal and cultural traditions. Short of deliberate copying, many national regulatory initiatives also exhibit design and functional similarities that reveal a growing convergence around a few principal approaches to environmental regulation. Increased cross-border collaboration between governments, non-governmental organizations (NGOs), multinational corporations, and the growth of transnational environmental networks have also significantly influenced the development of environmental law and regulation. Such growing international linkages are blurring the traditional divisions between private and public law and domestic and international law, promoting integration and harmonization. The result has been the emergence of "global environmental law"—a field of law that is international, national, and transnational in character all at once. . . .

1. Transplantation: Environmental Impact Assessment Requirements

The Kyoto Protocol's borrowing of the U.S. Clean Air Act's pollution trading principles is a highly visible instance of legal transplantation. Yet, it is not the most significant. That designation must be reserved for the international spread of environmental impact assessment requirements, arguably the most widely adopted environmental management tool across the world.

First adopted in the United States as part of the National Environmental Policy Act of 1969 (NEPA), the tool calls for the assessments of environmental impacts of proposed projects. Its purpose is to improve environmental decision making by requiring that information be gathered about the environmental effects and potential alternatives to the project or activity at issue. In the United States, at least at the federal level, this tool has largely remained a procedural requirement. There is no mandate for particular substantive action based on the information that is revealed. Nevertheless, the significance of this tool as a mechanism of environmental governance is clear based on how ingrained it has become in environmental decision making in the United States and worldwide. For example, from 1970 to 2007, American agencies filed 33,605 Environmental Assessments and resulting Environmental Impact Statements. Since then, the use of environmental impact assessments has spread to many nations and environmental treaties. . . .

2. Convergence: Regulatory Evolution and the Broadening of Civil Society Involvement in Environmental Governance

Apart from deliberate acts of borrowing, convergence through independent regulatory evolution has also contributed to the emergence of global environmental law. Common functional goals, governance considerations, and ecological and public health constraints have driven design, implementation, and operation of regulatory systems in similar directions. For example, the greater involvement of civil society in environmental concerns has been reflected in increased activism at the state and local levels when national governments fail to address critical environmental problems. In the United States, this heightened involvement has been especially visible in the increased activism of lower levels of governmental organizations on global environmental matters and the involvement of private actors in promoting global environmental governance.

The broadening of civil society involvement in environmental governance can serve as an important check on the economic and political influence of polluters, which can be strong at the local level. An engaged civil society and affected communities can provide important voices in regulatory decision making. Environmental behaviors by businesses and private individuals are shaped not only by laws and regulation but also by social norms, customs, and expectations.

Laws and regulations cannot be enforced by government officials all of the time. Indeed, voluntary compliance and social pressures must fill in more often than not. The role of civil society in shaping such informal influences has been especially visible in American efforts to curb climate change. . . .

3. Integration and Harmonization: Global Responses to Climate Change

One additional pathway contributing to the emergence of global environmental law is integration and harmonization. We define integration as the process of linking national legal systems and harmonization as the adjusting and conforming of their standards and requirements to an international system or to each other. Together, integration and harmonization are designed to coordinate and facilitate cooperation in order to achieve an environmental objective. The results are visible in emerging global environmental regulatory regimes. As Professor Richard Stewart explains, there has been:

> A vast increase in transnational regulation to address the consequences of global interdependency in such fields as . . . environmental protection. . . . These consequences can no longer be effectively managed by separate national regulatory and administrative measures. In response, many different systems of transnational regulation or regulatory cooperation have been established by states, international organizations, domestic administrative officials, and multinational businesses and NGOs, producing a wide variety of global regulatory regimes.

One of the most important regimes that has emerged is the climate change treaty system. It is made up of two primary treaties: the U.N. Framework Convention on Climate Change and the 1997 Kyoto Protocol. These treaties have given rise to a variety of implementing mechanisms, including the emission trading system, the CDM [Clean Development Mechanism], the Joint Implementation Mechanism, and the Non-compliance Mechanism. The emission trading system, designed to facilitate compliance with Annex B emission limitation obligations, and the CDM, which is intended to stimulate developing country participation in an effort to curb global greenhouse gas emissions, are among the most far-reaching institutions. Both have extended their influence beyond traditional governmental activities to private and business behaviors traditionally under the sole control of national regulatory authorities. . . .

The globalization of environmental law means that regulatory approaches, legal principles, and institution structures will be similar or have analogues across different national and international systems. As a result, knowledge gained by scholars and practioners [sic] in one system is more likely to transcend geographic and political boundaries and be relevant and meaningful to the operation and effectiveness of environmental regulatory systems elsewhere. Hence, the possibility for trans-jurisdictional practice and application of environmental legal doctrines, principles, and approaches seems to be increasing.

Environmental regulatory systems at an "earlier" stage of development can profitably use many of the lessons of more developed regulatory systems. As such, environmental lawyers and regulatory specialists can share knowledge and expertise outside of their own home jurisdictions, fueling the prospect for greatly increased opportunities for environmental lawyers to supply multi-jurisdictional legal services. Though many leading international law firms are already engaged in international, multi-jurisdictional practice, the emergence of global environmental law will accelerate and broaden such opportunities.

Global environmental law suggests an additional conclusion. Our shared interest in the global environmental commons makes the creation and development of environmental law a communal endeavor. Its collective nature necessitates that environmental regulation not remain the responsibility, or sovereign prerogative, of individual national legal systems or the specialized province of international lawyers and diplomats. Instead, it is an enterprise in which environmental law practitioners, scholars, activists, regulators, and legislators worldwide share an interest.

For environmentalists, the idea that the environment and pollution do not respect political boundaries may be self-evident. Comparative law scholars, however, have long maintained that law transplantation must be considered in the context of a system's specific legal history, culture, and social mores. In other words, even if law transplantation is a common phenomenon, and legal systems appear to share common elements, Watson has denied that "one can set up a theory of general legal development applicable to all or many unrelated societies." Contrary efforts are bound to be "superficial," simply "wrong," and "scarcely systematic." The endeavor of global environmental law hardly seeks to set out a "theory of general legal development." However, it does break with Watson's premise that legal systems and cultures cannot share fundamental similarities, at least in the field of law that regulates and addresses human interactions with parts of a common external world.

NOTES AND QUESTIONS

1. In another part of this article, Professors Tseming Yang and Robert Percival warn that American lawyers should not mistake the emergence of global environmental law for a mere extension of U.S. environmental law to the rest of the world. Rather, they explain, "American lawyers can profitably learn about environmental governance from the experiences and approaches developed elsewhere, especially in the areas of regulatory non-compliance and environmental human rights." *Id.* at 617. What can the United States learn from the climate change laws and policies of the European Union, Canada, China, and Brazil?
2. How is the concept of global law different from comparative law? How is it similar? Do you think that global environmental law provides a useful approach for synthesizing and coordinating the study of domestic, foreign, and international environmental law?
3. How do these ideas of global environmental law compare to the general principles of law discussed in Chapter Two as one of the four primary sources of international law recognized by the International Court of Justice? Are they filling the gaps left by treaty law or serving in some additional function?

5

STATE AND LOCAL ACTION: GOVERNMENTAL EFFORTS AND TRANSNATIONAL COLLABORATION

Subnational entities such as states and localities have been key actors in climate change law and policy. This is particularly true in countries such as the United States, where the national government has been slow to act. Some of the most noteworthy climate change governance to date has come from coordinated action by states and localities in different national jurisdictions. This chapter examines such subnational action and its transnational component.

A. THE PUZZLE OF SUBNATIONAL ACTION

State and local governments in the United States have adopted a wide variety of legal and policy measures to address climate change. As described below, many of these measures are oriented toward reducing greenhouse gas emissions, such as regulating greenhouse gas emitters, incentivizing renewable energy, and rewriting transportation plans. Because such measures may be costly, a question emerges: why would localities voluntarily incur these costs when the emissions reductions achieved are not likely to significantly reduce the impact of climate change on their communities? In other words, what are the benefits of these measures that justify the costs? And if the benefits are primarily other than emissions reductions, what are they? This section explores these questions by examining the reasons for subnational action and its importance.

1. DEFYING THE TRAGEDY OF THE COMMONS

As elaborated by Garrett Hardin in his classic work, some forms of environmental degradation result from what he terms a tragedy of the commons. Garrett Hardin, *The Tragedy of the Commons*, 162 SCIENCE 1243 (1968). Hardin asks his readers to imagine herdsmen with free access to grazing land. Each herdsman will have the incentive to maximize his own animals' use of the land because the herdsman reaps the full benefit of selling the animal. In contrast, the negative effects of overgrazing are shared by all herdsmen. The freedom of each herdsman to do the same on the commons leads to the tragedy. "Each man is locked in a system that compels him to increase his herd without limit — in a world that is limited. Ruin is the destination toward which all men rush, each pursuing his own best interest in a society that believes in the freedom of the commons. Freedom in a commons brings ruin to all. . . ." *Id.* at 1244. Hardin observes that the tragedy of the commons also appears in problems of pollution. Here, polluters reap the full benefit of manufacturing and selling a product, while the cost of the pollution is shared by all.

Climate change can easily be viewed as an example of a tragedy of the commons. As Professors J.R. Deshazo and Jody Freeman explain:

> Global warming is a classic public bad; it poses a global collective action problem. Neither a single state, nor a small handful of states, should be willing to invest in emissions regulation — both because a few jurisdictions acting alone cannot hope to make meaningful progress on the problem, and because the nature of global warming means that proactive states cannot fully internalize the benefits of their regulatory efforts, and must instead share those benefits. Thus, although state regulation in response to climate change may create negative externalities under some circumstances (e.g., if it burdens out-of-state interests), it necessarily creates positive externalities. States that generate these benefits for others (and for the world, really) may bear significant in-state costs. Generally, such conditions — significant costs and an inability to fully capture benefits — are the conditions under which we would expect to see either state inaction or a race to the bottom.
>
> J.R. DeShazo & Jody Freeman, *Timing and Form of Federal Regulation: The Case of Climate Change*, 155 U. Pa. L. Rev. 1499, 1518-19 (2007).

And therein lies the puzzle of subnational climate change action: instead of doing nothing, states and localities have become leaders in climate change policy. Why and how have they defied the logic of the tragedy of the commons?

One key to answering this question is recognizing that the benefits that states and localities may derive by acting on climate change are broad and varied. The tragedy of the commons paradigm focuses on one kind of benefit: reducing local environmental harm. In the case of climate change policy, however, there are many types of benefits that states and localities may derive from acting alone and together. Consider again the analysis of Professors DeShazo and Freeman:

> On closer examination, however, the emergence of state initiatives is not so puzzling. There are a variety of alternative explanations for why states are acting, the most plausible of which is that governors and state legislators are simply responding to the preferences of their electorates. This explains why some states are pushing forward even though they face strong industry opposition and the benefits of their efforts may be minimal — or, if not minimal, not able to be internalized. Bolstering this account are national and state-level

> polling data indicating strong public support for state action to address climate change. For example, data from California, New York, and the cluster of states that signed the Regional Greenhouse Gas Initiative (RGGI) — the "leader" states on climate regulation — show strong public support for state regulatory efforts.
>
> *Id.* at 1519–20.

As the authors suggest, state and local leaders may stand to gain by satisfying their electorate's concerns about climate change and showing political leadership. Mayors and governors of leader jurisdictions around the United States have garnered headlines and other favorable publicity for their proactive stances on climate change. *See* Kirsten H. Engel, *Whither Subnational Climate Change Initiatives in the Wake of Federal Climate Legislation?* 39 PUBLIUS: J. FEDERALISM 432 (2009).

Many other benefits may also motivate state and local governments. Some state and regional actions are taken with the intent to compel or induce emissions reduction at larger scales. State-led litigation such as *Massachusetts v. EPA* (*see supra* Chapter Three) and *American Electric Power Co. v. Connecticut* (*see supra* Chapter Three, and *infra* this chapter) seeks to compel national emissions reductions. Regional and state cap-and-trade programs may help induce national emissions reductions by designing and testing a model for *national* climate policy. Moreover, the businesses and industries of states that regulate first may gain a competitive advantage if similar federal regulations are later adopted. State and local climate policy may, for example, expand economic opportunities for new high-growth industries pertaining to energy efficiency and renewable energy. Finally, states and localities may be attracted by possible "co-benefits" of limiting greenhouse gas emissions, such as reducing energy costs, traffic congestion, air pollution, and solid wastes. *Id.* at 439–43; *see also* Kirsten H. Engel, *Mitigating Global Climate Change in the United States: A Regional Approach*, 14 N.Y.U. ENVTL. L.J. 54, 60–65 (2005).

NOTES AND QUESTIONS

1. Professors DeShazo and Freeman find that the most plausible of the alternative explanations for why states are acting is that state leaders are simply responding to the preferences of their electorates. Do you agree? Of the reasons suggested above, which do you find most convincing? In what situations would early-action states gain a competitive advantage, and in what situations might they instead be disadvantaged? For further exploration of these issues, Professors Katherine Trisolini and Jonathan Zasloff draw from international relations theory to try to understand this behavior. Katherine Trisolini & Jonathan Zasloff, *Cities, Land Use, and the Global Commons: Genesis and the Urban Politics of Climate Change*, in ADJUDICATING CLIMATE CHANGE: SUB-NATIONAL, NATIONAL, AND SUPRA-NATIONAL APPROACHES (William C.G. Burns & Hari M. Osofsky eds., Cambridge Univ. Press, 2009).
2. In many ways, state and local initiatives in the United States have been shaped by the absence of federal leadership in climate policy. Professor Jonathan Adler usefully identifies both "vices" and "virtues" of having states

and localities take action on climate change in the absence of federal action. Jonathan H. Adler, *Hothouse Flowers: The Vices and Virtues of Climate Federalism*, 17 TEMP. POL. & CIV. RTS. L. REV. 443 (2008). In his view, the main problem is that the scale of the action does not match the scale of the problem and is thus likely to be inefficient: "A local cap-and-trade system, for example, will cover a more limited set of sources, and fewer savings opportunities, than a national system with a broader base. Subjecting businesses to a variety of state standards may also be less efficient than a standardized federal regulatory regime." *Id.* at 449. However, he also points to virtues:

> Among other things, state initiatives may serve as useful experiments on the efficacy of various climate policy measures and do a better job addressing local preferences and information about sources of climate emissions and the relative costs and benefits of mitigation strategies. In addition, insofar as the threat of climate change calls for greater consideration of adaptation, state and local governments may be particularly well-situated to develop such measures.
> *Id.* at 450.

How has the absence of federal leadership enabled state and local initiatives? As the federal government becomes more active in climate policy, how do you expect states and localities to respond?

2. THE MULTISCALAR NATURE OF CLIMATE CHANGE

Based on the view that climate change is a global problem, there have been many calls for a global solution. But is climate change only a global problem? Is it not also a local, state, regional, and national problem? Climate change is inherently multiscalar: it is the result of actions taken by actors at all scales and it will have effects at all scales. Moreover, the opportunities and capacities to reduce their emissions that different localities in the world have vary widely, as will the impacts that climate change will have on local environments and livelihoods. As such, appropriate policies for mitigation and adaptation will likewise vary.

In the following excerpt, Professor Elinor Ostrom explains the need for a multiscalar approach to this multiscalar problem.

ELINOR OSTROM, POLYCENTRIC SYSTEMS FOR COPING WITH COLLECTIVE ACTION AND GLOBAL ENVIRONMENTAL CHANGE

20 Global Envtl. Change 550, 552–53, 555–56 (2010)

GHG emissions are the result of an extraordinarily large number of actions taken at multiple scales. Decisions within a family as to what forms of transportation to use, what car to purchase, and what investments to make regarding power consumption within their home affect not only the family budget but also the amount of GHGs released into the atmosphere. Similarly, decisions within business firms affect their budget as well as emissions.

Communities that have established power networks that enable households to invest in solar power to be used for household energy needs and, when not needed, contributed to a larger power network can reduce local energy costs and GHG emissions. Investments in better waste disposal facilities also generate local benefits as well as help decrease global emissions. Efforts to reduce pollution levels in large metropolitan areas focus on both total energy use and emissions of particulates and thus generate benefits at a metropolitan level as well as globally. Given that many of the actions generating GHG emissions are taken at multiple scales, activities that are organized at multiple scales generate benefits to those who act, ranging from households, farms, and cities at a local scale to regions within a state, states, regional units that cross state boundaries, and the globe.

A Polycentric Approach

. . . . Given that multiple benefits at diverse scales are generated from efforts taken to reduce GHG emissions as discussed above, polycentricity is a useful analytical approach for understanding and improving efforts to reduce the threat of climate change.

During the 1950s, massive criticism was leveled at the existing governance arrangements in metropolitan areas across the United States and Europe because of the large number of small-, medium-, and large-scale government units operating in the same metropolitan area. Many scholars thought that the high number of governments serving an area was evidence of a chaotic system. Ostrom et al. introduced the concept of polycentricity in their effort to understand whether the activities of a diverse array of public and private agencies engaged in providing public services in a metropolitan area were chaotic or potentially a productive arrangement:

> "Polycentric" connotes many centers of decision making that are formally independent of each other. . . . To the extent that they take each other into account in competitive relationships, enter into various contractual and cooperative undertakings or have recourse to central mechanisms to resolve conflicts, the various political jurisdictions in a metropolitan area may function in a coherent manner with consistent and predictable patterns of interacting behavior. To the extent that this is so, they may be said to function as a "system". . . .

Some readers will ask, What is the relevance of the polycentric approach for the analysis of global public goods? The initial relevance of the polycentric approach is the parallel between the earlier theoretical presumption that only the largest scale was relevant for the provision and production of public goods for metropolitan areas, and the contemporary presumption by some scholars that only the global scale is relevant for policies related to global public goods. Extensive empirical research found, however, that while large-scale units were part of effective governance of metropolitan areas, small- and medium-scale units were also necessary components. An important lesson is that simply recommending a single governance unit to solve global collective-action problems — because of global impacts — needs to be seriously rethought.

As discussed above, instead of the benefits derived from reducing GHGs existing only at the global level, multiple benefits are created by diverse actions at multiple scales. Potential benefits are even generated at a household level. Better health is enhanced by members of a household who bike to work rather than drive. Family expenditures allocated to heating and electricity may be reduced when investments have been made in better construction of a building, reconstruction of existing buildings, installation of solar panels, and many other investments that families as well as private firms can make that pay off in the long run. As more information is provided about these small-scale, but cumulatively additive, benefits, one can expect further efforts to be undertaken that cumulatively and significantly reduce GHG emissions.

. . . .

Given the complexity and changing nature of the problems involved in coping with climate change, "optimal" solutions for making substantial reductions in the level of GHGs emitted into the atmosphere are only a dream. A major reduction in emissions is, however, needed. The advantage of a polycentric approach is that it encourages experimentation by multiple actors, as well as the development of methods for assessing the benefits and costs of particular strategies adopted in one setting and comparing these with results obtained in other settings. A strong commitment to finding ways of reducing individual emissions is an important element for coping with climate change. Building such a commitment, and trusting that others are also taking responsibility, can be more effectively undertaken in small- to medium-scale units that are linked together through diverse information networks.

We need to recognize that doing nothing until a global treaty is negotiated maximizes the risk involved for everyone. Rather than only a global effort, it would be better to self-consciously adopt a polycentric approach to the problem of climate change in order to gain benefits at multiple scales as well as to encourage experimentation and learning from diverse policies adopted at multiple scales.

NOTES AND QUESTIONS

1. Professor Ostrom calls for a polycentric governance approach to climate change. In her view, international and national action on climate change will not be sufficient, and lower levels of governance at many scales will have key roles to play. Proceeding from this premise, difficult questions arise as to what actions should occur at each scale and how they should be coordinated. To what extent should the responsibilities of different jurisdictional scales be overlapping and to what extent should they be mutually exclusive? To what extent should they be firmly set and to what extent should they be flexible and dynamic? *See generally* Jonathan H. Adler, *Jurisdictional Mismatch in Environmental Federalism*, 14 N.Y.U. ENVTL. L.J. 130 (2005); Kirsten Engel, *Harnessing the Benefits of Dynamic Federalism in Environmental Law*, 56 EMORY L.J. 159 (2006).

2. At the COP 15 meeting in Copenhagen in 2009, local and regional leaders from many national jurisdictions met outside the formal negotiations and made agreements among themselves about how they would collaborate and coordinate. What importance could agreements such as these have to international lawmaking? Professor Hari Osofsky argues that while such

agreements have no formal status in international law, they have practical import for the capacity of the international community to meet its emissions reductions goals and they suggest the need for a rethinking of the narrow conception of international law that includes only agreements among national units. *See* Hari M. Osofsky, *Multiscalar Governance and Climate Change: Reflections on the Role of States and Cities at Copenhagen*, 25 MD. J. INT'L L. 64, 73 (2010).

B. STATES AND COALITIONS OF STATES

State governments in the United States have primary authority in several policy areas that are central to climate change mitigation and adaptation. Examples include land use, transportation policy, water policy, and economic development. Also, in the key area of energy policy, regional and state interests have historically predominated over national interests.

In the early 2000s, many states moved forward in the climate policy arena. California led with its passage of the Global Warming Solutions Act of 2006, which determined that the state's 2020 emissions shall be no greater than its 1990 emissions. California has also participated in the Western Climate Initiative, which, like the Regional Greenhouse Gas Initiative in the Northeast, aims to regulate greenhouse gas emissions in a significant region of the country. Moreover, according to the Center for Climate and Energy Solutions, about three-quarters of U.S. states have written state Climate Action Plans; about half have adopted Renewable Portfolio Standards requiring their electric utilities to generate energy from renewable sources; and about one-third have established "public benefit funds" to support energy efficiency and renewable energy projects. *See U.S. Climate Policy Maps*, CTR. FOR CLIMATE AND ENERGY SOLUTIONS, http://www.pewclimate.org/what_s_being_done/in_the_states/state_action _maps.cfm (last visited Apr. 20, 2012).

As discussed in Chapter Three, a primary question in the design of any potential future federal climate law in the Unites States will be how to balance and coordinate any newly created federal powers with these traditional state powers and innovative state programs. In the subnational context that is the focus of this chapter, questions arise as well: Why should states continue to have significant authority under future national climate legislation or regulation? In what situations should federal authority replace state authority? After discussing the most relevant state initiatives, this section concludes with an exploration of these federalism questions.

1. CALIFORNIA AND THE WESTERN CLIMATE INITIATIVE

Among U.S. states, California emits more greenhouse gases than any other state except for Texas. In fact, California's emissions place it among the top 20 emitters in the world, including all countries. Matching its importance as an emitter, California has been on the forefront of climate change policy in the United States, and indeed in the world. This section first discusses California's landmark climate change law, Assembly Bill 32 (AB 32). It then examines

California's collaboration with other U.S. states and Canadian provinces in the Western Climate Initiative.

ASSEMBLY BILL 32, 2005–2006 SESSION, GLOBAL WARMING SOLUTIONS ACT, CALIFORNIA 2006

http://www.arb.ca.gov/cc/ab32/ab32.htm

. . . .

The people of the State of California do enact as follows:

. . . .

38500. This division shall be known, and may be cited, as the California Global Warming Solutions Act of 2006.

. . . .

38501. The Legislature finds and declares all of the following:

(a) Global warming poses a serious threat to the economic well-being, public health, natural resources, and the environment of California. The potential adverse impacts of global warming include the exacerbation of air quality problems, a reduction in the quality and supply of water to the state from the Sierra snowpack, a rise in sea levels resulting in the displacement of thousands of coastal businesses and residences, damage to marine ecosystems and the natural environment, and an increase in the incidences of infectious diseases, asthma, and other human health-related problems.

(b) Global warming will have detrimental effects on some of California's largest industries, including agriculture, wine, tourism, skiing, recreational and commercial fishing, and forestry. It will also increase the strain on electricity supplies necessary to meet the demand for summer air-conditioning in the hottest parts of the state.

(c) California has long been a national and international leader on energy conservation and environmental stewardship efforts, including the areas of air quality protections, energy efficiency requirements, renewable energy standards, natural resource conservation, and greenhouse gas emission standards for passenger vehicles. The program established by this division will continue this tradition of environmental leadership by placing California at the forefront of national and international efforts to reduce emissions of greenhouse gases.

(d) National and international actions are necessary to fully address the issue of global warming. However, action taken by California to reduce emissions of greenhouse gases will have far-reaching effects by encouraging other states, the federal government, and other countries to act.

(e) By exercising a global leadership role, California will also position its economy, technology centers, financial institutions, and businesses to benefit from national and international efforts to reduce emissions of greenhouse gases. More importantly, investing in the development of innovative and pioneering technologies will assist California in achieving the 2020 statewide limit on emissions of greenhouse gases established by this division and will provide an opportunity for the state to take a global economic and technological leadership role in reducing emissions of greenhouse gases.

(f) It is the intent of the Legislature that the State Air Resources Board coordinate with state agencies, as well as consult with the environmental justice community, industry sectors, business groups, academic institutions, environmental organizations, and other stakeholders in implementing this division.

(g) It is the intent of the Legislature that the State Air Resources Board consult with the Public Utilities Commission in the development of emissions reduction measures, including limits on emissions of greenhouse gases applied to electricity and natural gas providers regulated by the Public Utilities Commission in order to ensure that electricity and natural gas providers are not required to meet duplicative or inconsistent regulatory requirements.

(h) It is the intent of the Legislature that the State Air Resources Board design emissions reduction measures to meet the statewide emissions limits for greenhouse gases established pursuant to this division in a manner that minimizes costs and maximizes benefits for California's economy, improves and modernizes California's energy infrastructure and maintains electric system reliability, maximizes additional environmental and economic co-benefits for California, and complements the state's efforts to improve air quality.

(i) It is the intent of the Legislature that the Climate Action Team established by the Governor to coordinate the efforts set forth under Executive Order S-3-05 continue its role in coordinating overall climate policy.

. . .

38599. (a) In the event of extraordinary circumstances, catastrophic events, or threat of significant economic harm, the Governor may adjust the applicable deadlines for individual regulations, or for the state in the aggregate, to the earliest feasible date after that deadline. (b) The adjustment period may not exceed one year unless the Governor makes an additional adjustment pursuant to subdivision (a).

———————

California also led the development of the Western Climate Initiative (WCI), a regional emissions reduction pact formed in 2007. Seven U.S. states (Arizona, California, Montana, New Mexico, Oregon, Utah, and Washington) and four Canadian provinces (British Columbia, Manitoba, Ontario, and Quebec) became partners in the WCI. In 2010, the WCI released a design document—excerpted below—that laid the groundwork for a regional cap-and-trade program and other strategies to meet a regional goal of reducing emissions to 15 percent below 2005 levels by 2020.

WESTERN CLIMATE INITIATIVE, DESIGN FOR THE WCI REGIONAL PROGRAM 1–6 (JULY 2010)

http://westernclimateinitiative.org/the-wci-cap-and-trade-program/
program-design

The WCI Partner jurisdictions have developed a comprehensive strategy to reduce regional GHG emissions to 15 percent below 2005 levels by 2020. This goal is based on the individual GHG emission reduction goals of the Partner jurisdictions. Our strategy will also spur investment in and development of clean-energy technologies, create green jobs, and protect public health. The WCI Partner jurisdictions' plan includes the following elements:

- **Using the power of the market.** A market-based approach that caps GHG emissions and uses tradable permits will provide incentives for companies and inventors to create new technologies that increase efficiency, promote greater use of renewable or lower-polluting fuels, and foster process improvements that reduce dependence on fossil fuels.
- **Encouraging reductions throughout the economy.** To reduce compliance costs and encourage emissions reductions, offset certificates will reward emissions reductions in sectors such as forestry and agriculture that are not covered by emissions caps.
- **Advancing core policies and programs to speed the transition to a clean energy economy** by targeting cost-effective emissions reductions, including:
  - Expanding energy efficiency programs that reduce customer utility bills;
  - Encouraging additional renewable energy sources that diversify supply resources and reduce air and water pollution;
  - Tackling transportation emissions through vehicle emissions standards, fuel standards, and incentives for improved community and transportation planning;
  - Establishing performance benchmarks and standards for high-emitting industries to spur innovation and improve competitiveness; and
  - Identifying best practices in workforce and community programs to help individuals transition to new jobs in the clean energy economy.

The WCI Partner jurisdictions' comprehensive strategy is good for the environment and good for the economy. It encourages the lowest cost reductions in GHG emissions and improved energy efficiency. Economic modeling conducted by the Partner jurisdictions indicates that the program will result in modest cost savings between 2012 and 2020. The strategy balances the principles adopted by the WCI Partner jurisdictions to maximize total benefits throughout the region, including reducing air pollutants, diversifying energy sources, and advancing economic, environmental, and public health objectives, while also avoiding localized or disproportionate environmental or economic impacts.

From the beginning, the Partner jurisdictions' strategy for addressing climate change has recognized the need for broad collaborative action to reduce GHG emissions. All of the WCI Partner jurisdictions have adopted climate action plans, and are taking steps to reduce emissions. We also are in discussions with other regional greenhouse gas initiatives—the Regional Greenhouse Gas Initiative (RGGI) and the Midwestern Greenhouse Gas Reduction Accord—to further broaden the collaboration on mitigation activities. In addition, WCI Partner jurisdictions are working closely with our federal governments to promote national and international action, and to ensure coordination among state, provincial, regional, and national programs.

The WCI Partner jurisdictions understand that even if it were possible to substantially reduce or even eliminate GHG emissions today, our jurisdictions would still feel the impacts of climate change due to emissions that have already occurred. Scientific research continues to confirm that our water resources, natural ecosystems, air quality, and environment-dependent industries like agriculture and tourism will be significantly impacted by changes in climate. Consequently, in addition to limiting GHG emissions, efforts are needed to address the impacts of climate change. The WCI Partner jurisdictions are therefore also committed to undertaking preparation and adaptation efforts.

Expanding Collaborative Action on Climate Change

GHG emissions are emitted from a broad range of activities worldwide. Unlike other air pollutants, GHG emissions contribute equally to climate change regardless of source or location. Efforts to mitigate climate change must ultimately address emissions from all major sources on a global basis.

As the WCI Partner jurisdictions move forward in the months and years ahead, the Partners will continue collaborating to develop a portfolio of core policies and programs to reduce GHG emissions. The governors and premiers of the Partner jurisdictions invite their colleagues across North America, including leaders of Native American tribes and Canada's First Nations, to join us to expand our effort to reduce GHG emissions and limit the impacts of a changing climate.

. . . .

2. The WCI Cap-and-Trade Program

As part of a comprehensive strategy to reduce GHG emissions, the WCI Partner jurisdictions have recommended a market-based program that provides an incentive to limit emissions and promotes technological innovation. Cap-and-trade has proven to be a successful means of reducing air pollution. It also is considered one of the most cost-effective and reliable strategies for pricing carbon emissions and providing emitters of GHG emissions with an incentive to limit pollution. With the trading component, cap-and-trade allows emitters to be flexible and creative in how to make needed reductions. . . .

The WCI program design includes a broad scope, encompassing nearly 90 percent of economy-wide emissions in the WCI Partner jurisdictions. The merits of pricing emissions broadly throughout the economy have been recognized in most of the recent federal proposals in the U.S. A forthcoming study by the National Research Council also recommends a broad scope, stating: "An economy-wide carbon pricing policy would provide the most cost-effective reduction opportunities, would lower the likelihood of significant emissions leakage, and could be designed with a capacity to adapt in response to new knowledge." Similarly, in 2009 the National Round Table on the Environment and the Economy published a report on carbon pricing in Canada, including: "To achieve stated reduction targets at the least possible cost, all emissions must be covered as fully as possible. This requires a unified pricing policy that consciously takes into account all emissions across all sectors and all jurisdictions."

The WCI Partner jurisdictions understand that in addition to covering most sectors of the economy, a broad geographic scope will also reduce overall compliance costs and can help mitigate leakage risks. A larger carbon market across a diverse set of emission sources provides a wider range of reduction opportunities. There are multiple paths for achieving the broad geographic and economy-wide coverage that is preferred for a cap-and-trade program. The WCI Partner jurisdictions also recognize alternative schedules for implementation can be accommodated and will continue to encourage additional jurisdictions to join the program after the expected start date of January 1, 2012.

NOTES AND QUESTIONS

1. AB 32 established explicit implementation deadlines for the California Air Resources Board (CARB). In 2007, CARB was required to adopt "early action" measures to reduce greenhouse gas emissions. Adopted measures included regulations to reduce emissions from fuels and mobile air-conditioning units and capture methane from landfills. By January 1, 2008, CARB was required to adopt mandatory emission reporting regulations for sources and a greenhouse gas emissions cap for 2020 based on 1990 emissions levels. By January 1, 2009, CARB was required to adopt a "scoping plan" detailing how CARB intended to meet the 2020 cap. By January 1, 2011, CARB was required to adopt the emissions reductions rules that would become effective on January 1, 2012, to meet the 2020 cap.

2. The scoping plan adopted in 2008 was challenged in state court for failing to comply with the California Environmental Quality Act (CEQA). Assoc. of Irritated Residents v. Cal. Air Res. Bd., No. CPF-09-509562 (Cal. App. Dep't Super. Ct. 2008), *available at* http://webaccess.sftc.org/Scripts/Magic94/mgrqispi94 .dll?APPNAME=IJS&PRGNAME=ROA22&ARGUMENTS=-ACPF09509562. Plaintiff environmental justice organizations argued that the scoping plan had selected a cap-and-trade approach without adequately analyzing alternatives that might be more environmentally effective. More specifically, plaintiffs expressed concern that a cap-and-trade approach would allow power plants and other large facilities to continue polluting disproportionately in poor communities as long as they purchase allowances or offsets. If you were the leader of an environmental organization that supported California's passage and implementation of AB32, what concerns might you have about the lawsuit? If you were the leader of an environmental justice organization, how would you respond to these concerns?

   The California court decided in favor of plaintiffs, and CARB completed additional studies to comply with CEQA. CARB then proposed and adopted a similar final regulation that included a cap-and-trade program beginning in 2013.

3. California has a long history of being a leader in environmental law, particularly in the area of air pollution regulation. Because California had already established emissions standards for motor vehicles before the Clean Air Act gave authority to the federal government to do so in 1970, Congress granted California an authority unique among states to retain its stricter standards and develop new vehicle standards in the future if it successfully petitions the federal government for a waiver. Other states may choose to adopt either the California standards or the default federal standards. In the early 2000s, California relied on this special authority to set greenhouse gas emissions standards for vehicles. As described in Chapter Three, the Bush Administration denied the waiver, which resulted in a lawsuit by California with 18 other states that wished to follow its standard intervening on its behalf, but then the Obama Administration granted the waiver in 2009. Do you think it was wise of Congress to give this special authority to California? Consider the arguments that would be made from the perspectives of both air quality advocates and the auto industry.

4. WCI sought to create a comprehensive cap-and-trade system in the region, encompassing nearly 90 percent of economy-wide emissions. Pollutants covered by the program would include carbon dioxide, methane, nitrous oxide, hydrofluorocarbons, perfluorocarbons, and sulfur hexafluoride. Covered facilities were in the electricity, industry, transportation, and commercial sectors. What are the advantages and disadvantages of such a broad regional cap-and-trade program? Consider not just environmental and economic aspects, but also political and administrative aspects.

   WCI is broad not only in its coverage, but also in its geographic scope, representing a view of "region" that cross-cuts national borders. What constitutional issues are raised by the fact that the WCI includes not just U.S. states but also Canadian provinces? Recent Supreme Court decisions have struck down individual states' transnational efforts as preempted by the federal prerogative in foreign affairs. In *Crosby v. National Foreign Trade Council*, 530 U.S. 363 (2000), the Court struck down a Massachusetts law that prohibited its state or local governments from contracting with companies doing business in Burma. In *American Insurance Association v. Garamendi*, 539 U.S. 396 (2003), the Court struck down a California law that mandated that insurers disclose information relating to whether they had compensated victims of the Holocaust under insurance policies sold before and during World War II. For more discussion, see generally Daniel A. Farber, *Climate Change, Federalism and the Constitution*, 50 ARIZ. L. REV. 879 (2008).

5. Because the WCI is a regional pact, states are free to withdraw. In 2011, six of the seven participating U.S. states withdrew from the WCI, leaving only California and four Canadian provinces as WCI partners. *See* Gordon Hamilton, *Six U.S. States Abandon Carbon-trade Partnership; B.C.'s Future in Ambitious Greenhouse-Gas Deal Unclear*, VANCOUVER SUN, Nov. 18, 2011, at A3. In several states, the governor who had agreed to the pact was no longer in office, and the new governor decided that remaining in the WCI was not in the state's interest. *See, e.g.*, Exec. Order No. 2010-06, 16 Ariz. Admin. Reg. 359 (Feb. 26, 2010), *available at* http://www.azgovernor.gov/dms/upload/EO_2010_06.pdf. How do you think the reality that states can withdraw anytime affected the work of the WCI and the design of its cap-and-trade program?

2. THE REGIONAL GREENHOUSE GAS INITIATIVE

The Regional Greenhouse Gas Initiative (RGGI) is a cap-and-trade program to regulate carbon dioxide emissions in ten Northeastern and Mid-Atlantic states. Seven states—Connecticut, Delaware, Maine, New Hampshire, New Jersey, New York, and Vermont—signed the original Memorandum of Understanding that established RGGI in 2005. The program became operational in 2009 with the participation of these states and three others, Maryland, Massachusetts, and Rhode Island.

RGGI caps the emission of carbon dioxide from power plants within these states at projected 2009 levels through 2014, and then the cap declines by 2.5 percent per year through 2018. The RGGI cap-and-trade program is thus substantially narrower than the cap-and-trade programs envisioned by California and the Western Climate Initiative. While the latter programs seek to include six major greenhouse gases from a wide variety of sectors, RGGI caps only the emissions of one greenhouse gas from one sector.

While more limited in scope, RGGI has been an early and valuable experiment in using cap-and-trade to regulate greenhouse gas emissions in the United States. To understand its importance, study the Memorandum of Understanding (MOU) below and consider the notes and questions that follow.

REGIONAL GREENHOUSE GAS INITIATIVE, MEMORANDUM OF UNDERSTANDING (DEC. 20, 2005)

---

http://www.rggi.org/docs/mou_12_20_05.pdf

WHEREAS, the States of Connecticut, Delaware, Maine, New Hampshire, New Jersey, New York, and Vermont (the "Signatory States") each individually have a policy to conserve, improve, and protect their natural resources and environment in order to enhance the health, safety, and welfare of their residents consistent with continued overall economic growth and to maintain a safe and reliable electric power supply system; and

WHEREAS, there is a growing scientific consensus that the increase in anthropogenic emissions of greenhouse gases is enhancing the natural greenhouse effect resulting in changes in the Earth's climate; and

WHEREAS, climate change poses serious potential risks to human health and terrestrial and aquatic ecosystems globally and in the Signatory States including: more severe droughts and floods; atmospheric warming resulting in increased concentrations of ground-level ozone (smog) and associated adverse health effects; changes in forest composition as dominant plant species change; increases in habitat for disease-carrying insects like mosquitos and other vectors; increases in algal blooms that damage shellfish nurseries and can be toxic to humans; sea level rise that threatens coastal communities and infrastructure, saltwater contamination of drinking water and the destruction of coastal wetlands; increased incidence of storm surges and flooding of low-lying coastal areas which would lead to the erosion of beaches; and

WHEREAS, a carbon constraint on fossil fuel-fired electricity generation and the development of a CO_2 allowance trading mechanism will create a strong incentive for the creation, development, and deployment of more efficient fuel burning technologies and processes, as well as renewable energy supplies, demand-side management practices and actions to increase energy efficiency, and will lead to less dependence on the import of fossil fuels; and

WHEREAS, reducing our dependence on imported fossil fuels will enhance the region's economy by augmenting the region's energy security and by retaining energy spending and investments in the region; and

WHEREAS, the Signatory States wish to establish themselves and their industries as world leaders in the creation, development, and deployment of carbon emission control technologies, renewable energy supplies, and energy-efficient technologies, demand-side management practices and increase the share of energy used within the Signatory States that is derived from secure and reliable supplies of energy; and

WHEREAS, climate change is occurring now, and continued delay in taking action to address the emissions that cause climate change will make any later necessary investments in mitigation and adaptive infrastructure much more difficult and costly; and

WHEREAS, to address global climate change and in order to do their fair share in addressing their contribution to this collective problem while preserving and enhancing the economic welfare of their residents, the Signatory States find it imperative to act together to control emissions of greenhouse gases, particularly carbon dioxide, into the Earth's atmosphere from within their region.

NOW THEREFORE, the Signatory States express their mutual understandings and commitments as follows:

1. OVERALL ENVIRONMENTAL GOAL

The Signatory States commit to propose for legislative and/or regulatory approval a CO_2 Budget Trading Program (the "Program") aimed at stabilizing and then reducing CO_2 emissions within the Signatory States, and implementing a regional CO_2 emissions budget and allowance trading program that will regulate CO_2 emissions from fossil fuel-fired electricity generating units having a rated capacity equal to or greater than 25 megawatts.

2. CO_2 BUDGET TRADING PROGRAM

A. Program Adoption. Each of the Signatory States commits to propose, for legislative and/or regulatory approval, the Program substantially as reflected in a Model Rule that will reflect the understandings and commitments of the states contained herein. The Program launch date will be January 1, 2009 as provided in 3.C. below.

B. Regional Emissions Cap. The regional base annual CO_2 emissions budget will be equal to 121,253,550 short tons.

C. State Emissions Caps. The regional base annual CO_2 emissions budget will be apportioned to the States so that each state's initial base annual CO_2 emissions budget is as follows:

Connecticut:	10,695,036 short tons
Delaware:	7,559,787 short tons
Maine:	5,948,902 short tons
New Hampshire:	8,620,460 short tons
New Jersey:	22,892,730 short tons

New York: 64,310,805 short tons
Vermont: 1,225,830 short tons

For the years 2009 through 2014, each state's base annual CO_2 emissions budget shall remain unchanged.

D. Scheduled Reductions. Beginning with the annual allocations for the year 2015, each state's base annual CO_2 emissions budget will decline by 2.5% per year so that each state's base annual emissions budget for 2018 will be 10% below its initial base annual CO_2 emissions budget.

E. Compliance Period and Safety Valve.

   (1) Compliance Period. The compliance period shall be a minimum of three (3) years, unless extended after a Safety Valve Trigger Event (described below). A subject facility must have a sufficient number of allowances at the end of each compliance period to cover its emissions during that period.

   (2) Safety Valve Trigger.

       (a) Safety Valve Trigger. If, after the Market Settling Period (as defined below), the average regional spot price for CO_2 allowances equals or exceeds the Safety Valve Threshold (defined below) for a period of twelve months on a rolling average (a "Safety Valve Trigger Event"), then the compliance period may be extended by up to 3 one-year periods.

       (b) Safety Valve Threshold. The Safety Valve Threshold shall be equal to $10.00 (2005$), as adjusted by the Consumer Price Index (CPI) plus 2% per year beginning January 1, 2006.

       (c) Market Settling Period. The Market Settling Period is the first 14 months of each compliance period.

. . .

G. Allocations of Allowances. Each Signatory State may allocate allowances from its CO_2 emissions budget as determined appropriate by each Signatory State, provided:

   (1) each Signatory State agrees that 25% of the allowances will be allocated for a consumer benefit or strategic energy purpose. Consumer benefit or strategic energy purposes include the use of the allowances to promote energy efficiency, to directly mitigate electricity ratepayer impacts, to promote renewable or non-carbon-emitting energy technologies, to stimulate or reward investment in the development of innovative carbon emissions abatement technologies with significant carbon reduction potential, and/or to fund administration of this Program; and

   (2) the Signatory States recognize that, in order to provide regulatory certainty to covered sources, state-specific rules for allocations should be completed as far in advance of the launch of the Program as practicable.

H. Early Reduction Credits. Each Signatory State may grant early reduction credits for projects undertaken after the date this Memorandum is signed and prior to the launch of the Program as defined in 3.C. at facilities subject to the Program, which projects have the effect of reducing emissions from the facility by (a) an absolute reduction of emissions through emission rate improvements; or (b) permanently reducing utilization of one or more units at the facility.

I. Banking. The banking of allowances, offset allowances and early reduction credits will be allowed without limitation.

3. MODEL RULE FOR ESTABLISHMENT OF THE CO_2 BUDGET TRADING PROGRAM

A. Model Rule. The Signatory States are collectively developing a draft Model Rule to serve as the framework for the creation of necessary statutory and/or regulatory authority to establish the Program. The Signatory States will use their best efforts to collectively release this draft Model Rule within 90 days after the execution of this MOU for a 60-day public review and comment period. Comments received during this comment period shall be reviewed by the Signatory States, and revisions to the draft Model Rule will be considered. A revised Model Rule will be developed and released within 45 days of the close of the public comment period after consultation among the Signatory States.

B. Legislation and/or Rulemaking. Each Signatory State commits to seek to establish in statute and/or regulation the Program and have that State's component of the regional Program effective as soon as practicable but no later than December 31, 2008.

C. Launch of Program. The Signatory States intend that the first compliance period of the Program will commence January 1, 2009.

. . . .

6. PROGRAM MONITORING AND REVIEW

The Signatory States agree to monitor the progress of the Program on an ongoing basis.

. . . .

D. Comprehensive 2012 Review. In 2012, the Signatory States will commence a comprehensive review of all components of the Program, including but not limited to:

(1) Program Success. The Signatory States will review whether the Program has been successful in meeting its goals.

(2) Program Impacts. The Signatory States will review the impacts of the Program as to price and system reliability.

(3) Additional Reductions. The Signatory States will consider whether additional reductions after 2018 should be implemented.

. . . .

8. AMENDMENT

This MOU may be amended in writing upon the collective agreement of the authorized representatives of the Signatory States.

NOTES AND QUESTIONS

1. The Model Rule referred to in Section 3 was published in 2006. *See* REG'L GREENHOUSE GAS INITIATIVE, MODEL RULE (2006), *available at* http://www.rggi .org/docs/Model%20Rule%20Corrected%208.15.06.pdf. The Model Rule set forth the basic administrative functioning of the program, including detailed provisions regarding allowance distribution, monitoring, and reporting, and other elements that are key to the establishment of a cap-and-trade program. The states then adopted their own versions of the Model Rule, legally enabling their participation in the program. In this way, the ultimate legal authority for the program comes from each state individually rather than from the states as a collective. This structure arguably helped RGGI avoid conflict with the Constitution's Compact Clause which prohibits any inter-state "agreement or compact" without congressional consent. U.S. CONST. art. I, §10, cl. 3. Why would the Framers have wanted to prohibit interstate agree-ments? Do you think they would have wanted to prohibit an agreement like RGGI? For further discussion, see Note, *The Compact Clause and the Regional Greenhouse Gas Initiative*, 120 HARV. L. REV. 1958 (2007).

2. Although RGGI is "not in any way supported or encouraged by federal law," Professor Ann Carlson argues that it would be a mistake "to view RGGI as regulatory action adopted independent of the federal government." Ann E. Carlson, *Iterative Federalism and Climate Change*, 103 NW. U. L. REV. 1097, 1142 (2009). She shows that RGGI was built using the ideas and organiza-tional architecture of prior cap-and-trade programs implemented under the federal Clean Air Act, including the Acid Rain Program (Title IV) and the NOx Budget Trading Program. What does the recognition that levels of government often share and borrow regulatory ideas suggest about the importance of initiatives such as AB32, WCI, and RGGI?

3. Overallocation of allowances is a problem that has plagued cap-and-trade programs, and it appears to be present in RGGI. A cap-and-trade program is overallocated if its emissions caps are higher than business-as-usual emis-sions. In an overallocated program, the price of emissions allowances is likely to be low, and regulated entities will need to make few, if any, emis-sions reductions to comply. *See* Lesley K. McAllister, *The Overallocation Problem in Cap-and-Trade: Moving Toward Stringency*, 34 COLUM. J. ENVTL. L. 395, 413–18 (2009). The RGGI cap was set at 188 million tons CO_2 for the years 2009 through 2014, followed by incremental annual reductions to reach about 169 million tons CO_2 by 2018. However, the region's emissions declined in the late 2000s due to energy supply and demand factors unre-lated to the program, and actual emissions in 2009 amounted to only 123 million tons CO_2, far below not just the 2009 cap but also the 2018 cap. *See* N.Y. STATE ENERGY RESEARCH & DEV. AUTH., RELATIVE EFFECTS OF VARIOUS FACTORS ON RGGI ELECTRICITY SECTOR CO_2 EMISSIONS: 2009 COMPARED TO 2005, at 3 (Nov. 2, 2010), *available at* http://www.rggi.org/docs/Retrospective_Analysis_Draft _White_Paper.pdf. RGGI did not incorporate a mechanism to adjust the cap downward, so such an adjustment would require additional legal action in each state. Why might the RGGI states be motivated to make such an adjust-ment? What barriers or problems could arise?

4. Another joint state effort, the Midwestern Greenhouse Gas Reduction Accord (MGGRA), was signed in November 2007. Founding members included the U.S. states of Illinois, Iowa, Kansas, Michigan, Minnesota, and Wisconsin, and the Canadian province of Manitoba. MIDWESTERN GOVERNORS ASSOC., MIDWESTERN GREENHOUSE GAS ACCORD 2007, at 4 (Nov. 15, 2007), *available at* http://www.iaenvironment.org/documents/MGAAccord.pdf. The members agreed to work jointly to establish greenhouse gas reduction targets and develop a multisector cap-and-trade program by November 2008, but the MGGRA Advisory Group's final recommendations and a model rule were not released until May 2010. In early 2011, the Web site of the MGGRA stated that "[t]he recommendations are from the advisory group only, and have not been endorsed or approved by any state." What do you think happened? Why didn't the MGGRA move forward to implementation? Is it possible that some states might have participated in the MGGRA not to advance the prospects for meaningful state or federal greenhouse gas regulation but to restrain them? How could participating in the pact serve anti-regulatory interests?

5. The phenomenon of states coordinating in this way to reduce greenhouse gas emissions regionally is surprising in many ways. Such collaboration runs contrary to prevalent theories of competition in state environmental policy, namely that states are likely to engage in a "race to the bottom" or a "race to the top." States engage in a "race to the bottom" when they compete to lower their environmental standards to attract new businesses or otherwise provide economic advantages. States engage in a "race to the top" when they compete to raise their environmental standards for such an advantage. Why have some states been motivated to collaborate instead of compete in the area of climate law? *See* Lesley K. McAllister, *Regional Climate Regulation: From State Competition to State Collaboration*, 1 SAN DIEGO J. CLIMATE & ENERGY L. 81, 86–88 (2009) (suggesting that they collaborate to facilitate policy diffusion, to achieve efficiencies in emissions trading, and to engage in a regional race to national influence).

3. STATE EFFORTS TO PROMOTE RENEWABLE ENERGY

Although California is the only U.S. state that has set a legally binding cap on its future greenhouse gas emissions, many states have adopted policies on renewable energy and energy efficiency that have the effect of reducing emissions. These policies often take the form of Renewable Portfolio Standards (RPS), Public Benefit Funds, and legislatively established property rights. A Renewable Portfolio Standard is a regulation that requires electricity supply companies such as electric utilities to produce or acquire a certain percentage of their electricity from renewable energy sources. A Public Benefit Fund generally involves the use of a surcharge on consumer electric bills to establish a fund dedicated to supporting energy efficiency and renewable energy development. Property rights approaches protect people's investment in renewable energy projects and provide an overall scheme to order them.

The following excerpt by attorneys Ivan Gold and Nidhi Thakar provides an overview of state renewable portfolio standards and their impact on climate change mitigation. It also explains the way in which states create regional tracking systems for renewable energy, which complement but are separate from the regional greenhouse gas emissions reduction accords described above.

Ivan Gold & Nidhi Thakar, A Survey of State Renewable Portfolio Standards: Square Pegs for Round Climate Change Holes?

35 Wm. & Mary Envtl. L. & Pol'y Rev. 183, 185, 189, 192–95, 205–06, 208–09, 212–16, 218–20, 222 (2010)

Since 1978, the federal and state governments have provided various incentives such as tax credits, loan guarantees, and favorable accounting treatments to subsidize electricity produced from renewable energy. Recently, these incentives have been augmented by statutory renewable portfolio standards or renewable energy standards (collectively, "RPS") that require utilities to include more renewable energy in their generation portfolios. Initially, RPS statutes were not a response to the threat of climate change. However, state RPS programs are now one of the most effective programs available domestically to minimize CO_2 emissions and address climate change.

    . . . .

I. Background

    . . . .

By 2002, twelve states had mandatory RPS programs. Two years later, an additional six states followed. By 2010, a total of thirty states had mandatory RPS programs. Before 2002, state RPS programs generally relied on legislative findings that RPS programs were needed to subsidize renewable energy resources, reduce utility reliance on fossil fuels, diversify energy supply, promote energy independence, create jobs, protect the environment, and achieve similar goals. Starting in 2002, control of climate change began to be cited as another express legislative purpose underlying state RPS statutes.

As of 2010, thirty state RPS programs are in effect. Many of these programs have compliance targets already in place or mandate compliance beginning in 2010, 2011, or 2012. These state programs constitute the major effort to control GHG emissions and climate change in the United States.

II. Survey of State RPS Programs

    . . . .

B. State RPS Programs and How They Work

State RPS programs vary widely in terms of their specific provisions. One review of differences in state RPS programs concluded that "[e]very state renewable portfolio standard . . . is unique because each state has its own policy objectives, political context and constituencies. As a result, RPS policies vary in many ways, including such elements as eligibility, compliance mechanisms, resource categories and program administration."

Although the specifics vary, most state RPS programs share a similar basic structure. Each defines which energy resources are "renewable" and lists which utilities must comply with RPS requirements. A utility subject to an RPS must meet its load during a specified period (the "compliance period") from sources (the "portfolio") that include a certain percentage of renewably generated electric power (the "minimum percentage"). After each compliance period, each utility must report the total amount of electric power supplied during the period and present evidence that at least the minimum percentage of that power came from RPS-eligible renewable sources.

. . . [A]ll state RPS programs include photovoltaic, biomass, hydro, landfill gas, and wind energy as renewable resources. Some of the thirty-six RPS programs include additional resources as renewable. These sources are often related to more traditional renewable technologies recognized in all states. For example, municipal waste is a subcategory of biomass, and solar thermal energy taps the same resource as photovoltaics.

. . . .

Each state sets it own compliance periods and minimum percentages. Some states also require that all or part of the renewable generation come from in-state generators. In some states, existing renewable capacity may qualify to meet RPS obligations. In other states, only new renewable generation qualifies to meet the first years of RPS obligations. Some also include energy saved by utility efficiency programs as renewable energy. Some permit utilities to "bank" excess renewable generation against future compliance obligations, while others permit utilities to defer current compliance to later years with increased future obligations to compensate for the deferral.

A utility typically has various ways to meet its obligation to add renewable generation. For example, it can:

- Generate electric power from a renewable resource it owns or controls;
- Purchase renewable electric power and its associated renewable energy credits ("REC") from another utility's renewable resource;
- Generate electric power using a non-renewable resource, such as coal, that does not produce RECs, but purchase an equivalent number of "unbundled" RECs from another utility's renewable resources;
- Apply excess "banked" renewable energy acquired or generated in previous compliance periods;
- "Borrow" (defer) compliance obligations to future compliance periods; and
- Make a monetary compliance payment to the state's RPS regulator in lieu of acquiring the minimum percentage of renewable generation.

Most utilities meet their RPS goals. If a utility fails to meet its RPS compliance obligations, most states provide penalties, frequently priced as a multiple of the then-current REC market price. However, in recent practice, penalties are often waived or deferred by regulators. To date, state RPS enforcement actions have been unusual, and some states simply have excused failures to comply.

RPS states also have different percentage requirements for renewable energy and impose different compliance deadlines. . . . Five states required mandatory compliance before 2010. Nine states will require first compliance in 2010. The rest require initial compliance to start in 2011, 2012, or later.

. . . .

Some differences in state RPS programs are noteworthy. As noted above, some states require renewable generation to be located in-state; however, most permit compliance using out-of-state resources. Some states require renewable energy to include some minimum percentage of specific technologies, usually wind or solar. Some states permit utilities to meet all or part of their RPS requirements with activities that increase efficient energy usage. Most RPS states have adapted their programs to permit regional RPS tracking systems to track and integrate their utilities' compliance.

The majority of states allow renewable generation to be purchased separate ("unbundled") from its associated RECs. Unbundled RECs provide utilities greater flexibility to meet requirements, as physical delivery of energy among utilities is often difficult for reasons such as transmission congestion, or the lack of a physical interconnection between the generator and the purchasing utility. Some utilities have fossil fuel generation sufficient to meet their total load and cannot accept additional renewable energy in their service territory without shutting down some fossil-fueled generation. Unbundled RECs "provide buyers flexibility: [i]n procuring green power across a diverse geographical area [and] [i]n applying the renewable attributes" to electric power produced at another source.

. . . .

Since their enactment, almost all state RPS programs have been revised, usually to increase minimum compliance levels. . . .

As a consequence of the 2007-09 recession, some states recently delayed or weakened their commitment to reduced GHG emissions. . . . However, despite the relaxation of some states' GHG programs, none of the states reduced or waived their RPS goals. The state RPS statutes remain intact and effective.

C. State RPS Programs and Climate Change

. . . .

RPS programs regulate renewable energy but do not directly regulate GHG emissions. However, such "limitations" are relatively unimportant. For example:

- Although RPS programs apply to only one emissions sector, electric generation, the electric power sector in the United States produced forty percent of 2007 national CO_2 emissions (thirty-two percent of total U.S. GHG emissions). On a global basis, the energy sector produces twenty-six percent of worldwide GHG emissions.
- Although RPS programs apply only in some states, RPS states currently cover forty-six percent of all U.S. electric generation. By 2025, the thirty-six states with voluntary and mandatory RPS programs will produce more than fifty-six percent of all electric power consumed in the United States and will emit more than sixty percent of electric power-related U.S. CO_2 (twenty percent of total U.S. CO_2 emissions).
- Although some RPS programs exempt selected utilities, or cover only a portion of a state's electric generation, this trend is reversing, and a number of states have amended their RPS programs to include utilities previously exempted. Today, sixteen of the thirty state RPS programs cover 90-100% of state generation and twenty-four of the thirty

mandatory programs cover more than seventy-five percent of their state utilities.

- Although RPS programs primarily affect CO_2 emissions, rather than all GHG emissions, CO_2 is the primary GHG released when fossil fuels make electricity. In 2007, CO_2 represented approximately eighty-two percent of all U.S. GHG emissions. . . .
- Although RPS programs only control GHGs indirectly, renewable electric generators generally emit far less CO_2 than coal, oil, or natural gas generators. Generators using coal can emit as much as 2000 lbs of CO_2 for each kWh generated, and natural gas generators emit approximately one-half that amount or less. Renewables like wind, hydro, and solar energy actually produce almost no GHGs. Renewable biomass generators can produce 1500 lbs of CO_2e (lbs/CO_2e) per megawatt hour of energy. The carbon content of natural gas is half that of coal, and natural gas-fired combined-cycle gas turbines, the most efficient fossil fueled generators, use fewer BTUs to produce a kWh of electricity than coal plants.
- Most RPS programs typically exclude zero-GHG resources such as nuclear power and hydroelectric dams, which are generally disfavored by the public. However, from 1999 to 2008, more than ninety percent of RPS-driven projects were zero-GHG wind projects, and the future for state RPS projects includes increasing amounts of other zero-GHG generation such as solar energy.
- Finally, some RPS permit technologies emit GHGs, such as biomass. However, these sources still emit significantly less GHGs than fossil-fueled generators because their fuel is recycled and are therefore still an attractive alternative to fossil fuels.

. . . .

D. Regional REC Tracking Systems and Regional GHG Accords

Regional tracking systems support individual state RPS programs. They track, record, and certify electric power produced from eligible renewable resources. Their primary and standard medium of exchange is an REC, which represents 1000 kWh of renewably produced electric power. In contrast, regional GHG accords are multi-state, multi-sector cap-and-trade programs that manage GHG emissions within each accord member state. Regional accords focus on GHG emissions rather than on renewable energy, although some make special provisions to favor renewable energy generation. Their medium of exchange is a GHG allowance or offset, which represents one ton of CO_2e emissions.

REC and GHG programs are both variants of cap-and-trade systems. An authority sets a maximum permitted level for GHG emissions or non-renewable energy during a compliance period, and this is the "cap." The cap is generally less than historic levels, and it reduces over time. Each regulated entity is required to meet its assigned share of the cap; to meet its cap, a regulated entity must report its actual GHG emissions, or the nonrenewable energy it used to meet its actual load. Typically, a GHG program requires the emitter to surrender one GHG offset for each ton of CO_2 emitted. The RPS program requires surrender of one REC to prove use of each MWh of renewable energy. Regulated entities with less than the required evidence of compliance must acquire the necessary certificates from regulated entities with excess certificates or pay a penalty. These exchanges and all their variations are the "trade" portion of "cap-and-trade."

Regional GHG programs and regional RPS tracking systems are creatures of state law, developed in the absence of federal controls on GHG and renewable generation. These programs are not explicitly or clearly integrated. Nor are RECs easily exchanged for tons of CO_2. Regional GHG accords and trading systems may overlap with state RPSs, but they do not replace them.

. . . .

E. Regional REC Tracking Systems

RPS programs require subject utilities to show that they acquired at least the minimum percentage amount of renewable energy during each compliance period. Regional REC tracking systems substantiate utility RPS compliance and facilitate regional RPS transactions between states. Individual RPS tracking systems usually cover the regional interconnected transmission operating or control systems to which their member states belong. RECs from each regional tracking system trade in the growing local, regional and national markets for renewable electricity.

. . . .

There are five major U.S. regional REC tracking systems: (i) Western Renewable Energy Generation Information System ("WREGIS"); (ii) Midwest Renewable Energy Tracking System ("MRETS"); (iii) Electric Reliability Council of Texas ("ERCOT"); (iv) PJM Generation Attribute Tracking System ("PJM GATS"); and (v) New England Power Pool Generation Information System ("NEPOOL GIS").

. . . .

———————

Although RPS programs create requirements for renewable energy and incentivize it, they generally do not address the property rights issues that renewable energy projects raise. Specifically, those investing in projects need to be able to protect their access to the renewable resource and prevent encroachment on it by neighbors. The following excerpt by Professor Alexandra Klass discusses the ways in which states have provided such protection for solar and wind access.

ALEXANDRA B. KLASS, PROPERTY RIGHTS ON THE NEW FRONTIER: CLIMATE CHANGE, NATURAL RESOURCE DEVELOPMENT, AND RENEWABLE ENERGY

38 Ecology L.Q. 63, 95–100, 102–06, 108–09 (2011)

III. Property Rights on the New Frontier

A. Property Rights in Solar and Wind Access and Related State Permitting Frameworks

This subpart explores the extent to which state and local governments have created, defined, and protected property rights in access to solar and wind as well as the extent to which they have removed local impediments to solar and wind development and created permitting, siting, and land use frameworks for such development. Regulatory activity in regards to solar and wind projects on private land has thus far occurred almost exclusively at the state and local levels, with the federal government limiting its involvement to financial assistance and permitting of solar and wind development on federal public lands. Many states have created similar property structures and regulatory frameworks for solar and wind. There is also significant diversity among the states, however, revealing that productive state experimentation is taking place, and that these initiatives can serve not only as potential models for other states but, ultimately, for the federal government.

1. Solar

Although the amount of solar energy generated in the United States currently represents less than one percent of annual U.S. electricity sales, many state and local governments are attempting to facilitate the development of solar energy. Thus far, both the federal government and state governments have created incentive programs, grants, and loans to promote its use. Many state and local governments, however, drawing on historical natural resources law, have also created property rights in solar access.

Solar energy is harnessed commercially primarily through the use of two main technologies: concentrating solar power (CSP) and photovoltaic (PV). As of 2009, the total CSP and PV electric power capacity installed in the United States was just over 2000 megawatts (MW). CSP converts solar power into thermal energy by using mirrors or lenses to concentrate radiation onto a receiver. Because the most cost-efficient CSP plants are large, they are typically associated with energy suppliers to utilities or with utilities themselves. By contrast, a PV system, the most common method of using solar power, converts sunlight into energy when solar radiation hits a semiconductor, releasing electrons. PV systems, which allow for solar energy production on a smaller level, are generally made up of ground mounted or roof mounted panels containing several individual solar cells or a single thin layer. Because PV solar systems are most closely associated with commercial and residential development on private lands (as opposed to the CSP plants more often located on public lands), the remainder of this section focuses primarily on the use of PV technology in the residential and commercial setting.

Some argue that a major barrier to the widespread use of PV systems in the United States is the failure of states to recognize "solar rights" or otherwise engage in land use planning in a manner that provides some assurance to installers of PV and other systems that neighboring property owners will not engage in development that will block access to the sun. At one time, American courts recognized the English doctrine of "ancient lights," which granted a property owner the right to prevent a neighbor from blocking light that reached the interior of a building and that had been enjoyed continuously for twenty years. This cause of action was eliminated in all U.S. jurisdictions by the late nineteenth century. As a result of the energy crisis of the 1970s, however, states began to focus on solar power and enacted some of the first laws to encourage solar energy. With the renewed focus on solar power today, some states are revising their statutes from this earlier period while others are enacting solar legislation for the first time.

State legislation to regulate and encourage solar development has taken many forms. For instance, some states have enacted laws that void any property conveyances, agreements, or deed transfers between parties that specifically prohibit the use of solar collectors. Other state laws invalidate covenants in common interest communities or local zoning ordinances that prohibit solar collectors, although those same laws allow for reasonable regulation of such collectors. Another form of state regulation is aimed at encouraging local governments to implement zoning or permitting ordinances to protect solar rights.

Some states have focused specifically on recognizing property rights in solar access. Many states now officially recognize "solar easements" as a type of property agreement that can be voluntarily entered into by two parties and will run with the land to subsequent property owners. In states that recognize such easements, the easement agreement serves to protect the landowner from a neighbor who may interfere with solar access once the system is installed. These easement statutes often outline the specific information that must be included in the creation of such an easement, and some go so far as to provide a sample easement agreement. The availability of solar easements may be limited, however, because they are voluntary in nature and servient owners may overcharge because of bilateral monopoly problems. To address this issue, Iowa has enacted a statute that allows local regulatory boards to create easements without the servient owner's consent; the statute requires that the servient landowners receive payment of just compensation based on the difference in the fair market value of the servient property before and after granting the solar access easement.

Other states and local governments have created permit systems and zoning ordinances to address solar access. New Mexico and Wyoming use a prior appropriation approach modeled after water law where the owner of a solar collector obtains rights to solar access if the owner used the collector before other uses that may block sunlight and if the use is considered to be beneficial. . . .

Wisconsin uses the reasonable use rule from private nuisance law by allowing municipal agencies to grant a permit to a solar user if doing so would not unreasonably interfere with development plans, and if the benefits of the solar system to the applicant and the public outweigh the burdens. . . .

Although it does not have a permit system, California has one of the most extensive statutory frameworks relating to solar energy rights, and it includes multiple elements of the different statutory schemes found nationwide. California provides protection for residents on the installation end of the process and protects their rights to continued solar access from neighboring properties. The statutory scheme includes the Solar Rights Act and the Solar Shade Control Act. The Solar Rights Act prohibits property conveyances and common interest community regulations that unreasonably limit the installation of solar systems, allows for the creation of solar easements, and limits the ability of local governments to restrict solar access. The Solar Rights Act also requires certain subdivisions to provide for future passive easements and authorizes local governments to enact regulations requiring solar easements in certain subdivisions.

The Solar Shade Control Act seeks to promote the use of vegetation for temperature control while limiting the effect of that vegetation on solar collection energy systems. . . .

At the local level, Boulder, Colorado has the most elaborate solar zoning ordinances through which it has created a system of "solar envelopes" and "solar fences" for different neighborhoods that creates space where no construction or vegetation can occur that interferes with the solar rights of neighbors. In this way, Boulder has integrated solar access issues into land use planning and zoning to provide expectations and certainty regarding solar access. Ashland, Oregon provides another example of a city that has implemented solar access laws at the local level. Its solar access ordinance includes formulas for lot classification that correspond to solar setback requirements, and provides protection from shade created by vegetation in the form of solar access permits. These solar access permits place limits on neighbors by requiring vegetation not to exceed a certain height. Additionally, Ashland has established a hearing process to resolve disputes when informal discussions fail, and the City also requires the Staff Advisor to file the solar access permit with the County Clerk so that it is registered. Similar to the Boulder ordinance, Ashland is attempting to provide its residents with some certainty regarding solar energy rights, with the stated purpose of the ordinance being "to provide protection of a reasonable amount of sunlight from shade from structures and vegetation whenever feasible to all parcels in the City to preserve the economic value of solar radiation falling on structures, investments in solar energy systems, and the options for future uses of solar energy."

. . . .

2. Wind

Unlike the situation with solar energy, where numerous states have statutes recognizing solar easements, only a few states have recognized wind easements or otherwise attempted to address property rights in wind specifically. Instead, most states are still at the stage of creating a range of incentives for wind development. . . . The creation of property rights in wind is becoming increasingly important as quality wind resources and the land on which to install turbines becomes scarcer. Wind turbines placed too close together can have significant negative impacts on energy production. Indeed, some state setback requirements are insufficient to avoid wind access conflicts between neighboring turbines under separate ownership. Thus, this section discusses in more detail how states with significant wind capacity have used a variety of incentives, sometimes coupled with explicit provisions relating to property rights in wind access, to increase wind energy capacity and avoid conflicts between wind energy systems and between wind energy systems and neighbors.

. . . .

As with solar property rights, the wind easement is the most commonly recognized wind energy property right, but whereas thirty states have recognized some form of solar easement, only six states have enacted similar laws for wind. Further, many statutes that have explicit descriptions of what must be contained in a solar easement have no such description for wind easements.

North Dakota, South Dakota, and Nebraska have addressed other property rights considerations by enacting laws that prevent the severing of wind rights from the surface estate. The stated reason for the severance ban is to prevent large companies wishing to install turbines from taking advantage of land owners.

Beyond recognizing individual easements and other property rights agreements, some states have embraced a statewide permitting and planning system for wind energy. As noted, some of the states with the highest wind capacity, such as Minnesota and Oregon, along with other states, like Washington, have replaced or supplemented local approvals with a statewide permitting process for some wind projects. Michigan has avoided a traditional property rights approach to wind development and instead has adopted a broader land-use approach at the state level. The Clean, Renewable, and Efficient Energy Act directed the Michigan Public Service Commission to create a Wind Energy Resource Zone Board to explore the potential for wind energy use in the state. The Board consulted with local governments in order to carry out its task and issued a report detailing its findings in order to identify a wind energy resource zone as the most productive portion of the state to begin large scale wind development. Finally, the Michigan legislature has created an expedited process for obtaining siting certificates for wind projects.

Overall, the states that have been most active in creating substantive legislation on wind energy systems, as opposed to creating financial or tax incentives for wind energy, tend to fall into two main camps. The first camp consists of those states that have focused their legislation on creating or defining property rights in wind resources — wind easements — in order to facilitate private transactions and investment in wind energy systems. Those states include Montana, Nebraska, North Dakota, and South Dakota. The second camp consists of those states that have supported increased wind development by creating statewide siting and permitting systems for wind energy systems above a certain size, some of which also preempt local zoning regulation for those systems. These states include Connecticut, Minnesota, New Hampshire, Ohio, Rhode Island, and Vermont. In states like Iowa, Texas, New York, Utah, and Illinois, the state legislatures have not officially recognized wind easements and any siting and permitting of wind energy systems takes place at the local level.

For those states with no statewide siting and permitting process, there is a wide range of local regulation of wind energy systems of various sizes.
    . . . .

_____

NOTES AND QUESTIONS

1. What public policy goals other than greenhouse gas emissions reductions are likely to be served by state policies structured to promote renewable energy and energy efficiency? In particular, to what extent could such policies be connected to economic development and job creation?

2. To what extent would a national RPS standard provide an even more effective approach to supporting a transition to renewable energy forming a greater share of the energy market? Gold and Thakar argue for such a standard elsewhere in the article excerpted above. *See* Gold & Thakar, *supra*, at 238-39. *See also* Lincoln L. Davies, *Power Forward: The Argument for a National RPS*, 42 Conn. L. Rev. 1339, 1343–44 (2010); Joshua P. Fershee, *Changing Resources, Changing Market: The Impact of a National Renewable Energy Portfolio Standard on the U.S. Energy Industry*, 29 Energy L.J. 49, 55–56 (2008). However, others, like Professor Jim Rossi, have cautioned that such a law would pose distributional, economic, and operational concerns that would need to be addressed. *See* Jim Rossi, *The Limits of a National Renewable Portfolio Standard*, 42 Conn. L. Rev. 1425 (2010).

3. As discussed in more depth in Chapter Three, significant property rights issues also arise with respect to siting both renewable energy projects and the transmission lines associated with them. Professor Ashira Ostrow has argued that Congress should enact what she terms a process preemption approach to address facility siting problems modeled on the U.S. approach to telecommunications siting, in which local regulators serve as the primary regulators but operate under federal constraints. In particular, she suggests that such process constraints on renewable energy include requirements that siting decisions be made within a reasonable period of time, supported by substantial evidence contained in a written record, and subject to expedited federal judicial review. *See* Ashira Pelman Ostrow, *Process Preemption in Federal Siting Regimes*, 48 Harv. J. on Legis. 289, 326–35 (2011). Professors Alexandra Klass and Elizabeth Wilson have explored the possibility of applying Ostrow's process preemption approach to the siting of transmission lines. Alexandra B. Klass & Elizabeth Wilson, *Renewable Energy and Transmission Challenges*, Vand. L. Rev. (forthcoming 2012) (draft manuscript on file with authors). What would be the benefits and limitations of such an approach?

4. STATE-LED LITIGATION

States also have had a major effect on climate change law through multi-state litigation. A key example of such litigation is the case of *Massachusetts v. EPA*, filed by 12 state attorneys general along with several environmental groups and local governmental entities. In this lawsuit, described at length in Chapter Three, the Supreme Court made the significant determination that greenhouse gases could be pollutants for the purpose of regulation under the Clean Air Act and that EPA had not properly carried out its statutory mandate with respect to determining whether to regulate greenhouse gases from motor vehicles.

State attorneys general also joined forces in filing a common law tort lawsuit alleging that the five largest emitters of carbon dioxide in the country are contributing to a public nuisance. In the case of *American Electric Power Co. v. Connecticut*, also discussed in depth in Chapter Three, eight states and other plaintiffs sued five major electric power generators that operate coal-fired power plants in the Midwest. Plaintiffs sought a court order to reduce their carbon dioxide emissions by "a specified percentage each year for at least a decade." 406 F. Supp. 2d 265, 270 (S.D.N.Y. 2005). The federal district court dismissed the case with the argument that the case presented a non-justiciable political question. *Id.* The Second Circuit reversed, 582 F.3d 309 (2d Cir. 2009), holding that the political question doctrine did not bar the suit; that plaintiffs had constitutional standing to bring the case; and that plaintiffs had successfully alleged a public nuisance claim under federal common law. The Supreme Court granted *certiorari* and ultimately decided that plaintiffs' federal common law claim was displaced by the Clean Air Act, 131 S. Ct. 2527, 2537 (2011).

Such state-led litigation is controversial. For some state representatives and other commentators, it is an appropriate mechanism through which states can influence federal policy and seek compensation or injunctive relief for alleged harms. For others, it represents activism and overreaching on the part of state attorneys general. The two statements below were made by the state attorneys general of Connecticut and Colorado at academic conferences. Both address the justifications for and propriety of state-led litigation to address climate change.

STATEMENT OF RICHARD BLUMENTHAL, ATTORNEY GENERAL OF CONNECTICUT IN SYMPOSIUM, THE ROLE OF STATE ATTORNEYS GENERAL IN NATIONAL ENVIRONMENTAL POLICY: WELCOME & GLOBAL WARMING PANEL, PART I

30 Colum. J. Envtl. L. 335, 340–41 (2005)

. . . .

Our reason for going to court is supported now more than ever before by indisputable scientific evidence. Clearly, from the standpoint of my constituents, Connecticut citizens, much of the Northeast, the rest of the country, there is evidence that climate change is resulting from CO_2, greenhouse gas emissions, that there are clear effects of that in estuaries disappearing, changes in forests, eroding shorelines, and all kinds of effects that we believe are directly attributable to changes that result in carbon dioxide. Our lawsuit spells out in detail why we think that is so. But it's a problem of immediate concern and immediate economic costs to the people we represent.

We had a theory in this lawsuit, which we have researched extensively: CO_2 emissions from power plants around the country are a direct cause of those climate changes, and we have sued the 5 major emitters of CO_2. These companies annually produce 650 tons of CO_2 at plants in 20 states. Together they account for 10% of all the CO_2 emissions in the country, about ¼ of the emissions from the US power sector, which accounts for 10% of the world's carbon dioxide emission. We have not sued all of the sources of CO_2, but they are major sources. This is based on federal and state nuisance law. We can sue any tortfeasor or joint tortfeasor for the kind of relief that we're seeking here. The principles on which we're suing are well established, I don't need to go through all the cases on public nuisance common law, beginning with *State of Georgia v. Tennessee Copper,* from 1907. Sulfur dioxide pollution from those smelters was polluting Georgia, and it sued a plant in a neighboring state and won. Other states since then have reaffirmed those principles, which are generally strict liability; we are prepared to establish negligence or intent, but we can prevail on a [strict liability] theory.

One of the key points is that we are seeking relief that includes no money damages. If you contemplate this lawsuit, you need to think tobacco without the money — we're trying to change the way the industry does business. We're not seeking millions of dollars. The relief we're seeking is about as different as could be in the sense that we want not a penny from these defendants. We want them to do the things necessary to reduce their emissions by about 3% a year, whether it's by new equipment or by operating more efficiently. We believe that goal is doable, realistic, affordable, and required by the law.

So your question may be that even if the federal government isn't acting, shouldn't federal law preempt the states? What right do you have as AG to deal with a national, and maybe global problem. States often fill a gap where the federal government refuses to act. The federal government has said it has no authority to act and that Congress has rejected efforts to cover this, given that CO_2 is not an ambient air problem and thus not covered by the Clean Air Act. For a variety of reasons, the federal government has taken a position that there's no federal law to deal with the problem. The preemption issue is far less troubling here than it was in tobacco. Many of the other defenses that were raised in the tobacco suit will be raised here, but I think they will be overcome — I think that we're on very solid ground, no[t] just in federal law but also in our state nuisance theory. Even if there were preemption, our state nuisance claims would be upheld, and for a variety of other reasons, I think the legal issues will be fairly straightforward for the court and the factual issues eventually will be resolved in our favor. There will undoubtedly be a battle of the experts on some issues, but many of the most important factual issues are no longer subject to legitimate scientific dispute. I think that we will be prepared to show the causal links between the plants, CO_2 emissions, global warming, and the harm done to our states. Let me just close by saying that this problem is not going to go away — the litigation is not going to go away. We're committed for the long term — we know we're in for a fight. We knew we were in for a fight against the tobacco companies, and they had vowed never to lose and they had never lost. When we began the suit against the tobacco companies, nobody gave us a prayer. The reason why the tobacco companies finally came to the table is because we went to trial.

JOHN W. SUTHERS, THE STATE ATTORNEY GENERAL'S ROLE IN GLOBAL
CLIMATE CHANGE

---

85 Denv. U. L. Rev. 757, 757–63 (2007–2008)

What should be the proper role of *state* attorneys general in regard to global climate change? I will first give you my answer to that question, and then elaborate on my response. I believe the proper role of state attorneys general in combating global warming is to enforce the civil and criminal laws passed by their respective state legislatures to protect environmental quality, to cooperate in the enforcement of federal laws designed to combat the problem, to contest federal positions that are contrary to states' rights and principles of federalism, and to properly represent the state health and environment agencies that are clients of the state attorney general.

Now as self-evident as that may sound, I would suggest to you that my view of the proper role of state AGs in this effort would be regarded with some disdain by a few of my AG colleagues, and certainly so among many environmental groups in this country who believe that state AGs have the very broad authority and responsibility to act in whatever the AGs believe is the broader public interest, whether or not they are statutorily vested with the authority to do so. You see, as to the state attorneys general, the global warming debate is a microcosm of a much larger debate about the proper role of state attorneys general. Let me frame the debate for you by alluding to my own experience.

When I was sworn in as attorney general of Colorado in January of 2005, I understood my role would be significantly different than my work as a district attorney or as United States Attorney. Those public offices did virtually nothing but litigation. The district attorney's office prosecuted criminal cases and had limited civil jurisdiction in consumer protection and public health areas. As U.S. Attorney, my office did all the criminal and civil litigation for the United States in the District of Colorado. As attorney general, I understood I would be legal advisor to all departments, agencies, boards, and commissions in Colorado State government. My office would issue legal opinions, both formal and informal, on a wide variety of subjects pertinent to the operation of the State. I also understood I would be involved in a broad range of civil litigation on behalf of the State of Colorado, both as plaintiff and defendant, in addition to the criminal prosecution responsibilities I had had.

But as to my role as the protector of the broad public interest, primarily in regard to Colorado's civil and criminal statutes relating to consumer protection and environmental protection, I still saw myself as assuming the familiar role of a law enforcer. In fact, I would be the chief law enforcement officer in Colorado. It would be my job to enforce criminal and civil laws passed by the state legislature to protect consumers from fraud and deception and to enforce a variety of statutes enacted to protect the public from air and water pollution and other health hazards.

And I do not believe I was naive. I was well aware that state attorneys general had been involved in some controversial litigation, including the massive civil suit against tobacco companies that had culminated in a settlement agreement in 1999 involving *as* much as $240 billion, and that many free market conservatives questioned whether that was a proper exercise of the State police power. I knew that several attorneys general, like Eliot Spitzer of New York, had made quite a name for themselves taking on corporate America, and that many on Wall Street and elsewhere thought they were overreaching . . .

Now what exactly is attorney general activism? Is it capable of definition or is it simply a case of "you know it when you see it"? Let me give you a few "I knew it when I saw it" examples and then try to define it.

In the aftermath of Hurricane Katrina in 2005, gas prices rose sharply. The public was angry, perceiving that the rise in price was more the result of corporate opportunism than market forces. The state AGs, all wanting to be perceived as diligent problem solvers, weighed in with their concerns. The Federal Trade Commission (FTC) and several AGs initiated investigations. Colorado had initiated gas pricing investigations in approximately eight out of the previous dozen years. I distinctly recall a nationwide phone conference in which the FTC gave the AGs a preview of the report they were issuing the next day. Essentially, the FTC found no systematic wrongdoing. It concluded that the rise in prices was attributable to market forces, including the highly volatile spot and futures markets. Various AG investigations reported similar conclusions. I thought that would be the end of the matter and expected the phone call to wrap up quickly. But a veteran attorney general from the Midwest interjected and made what I considered an amazing assertion, In fact, I had to write it down. "Just because we haven't found anything illegal, doesn't make it right and doesn't mean we shouldn't do anything about it," he said. "We need to do something about these obscene profits."

Folks, that is the mindset of an activist AG. Luckily, market forces shifted a short time later and attorney general interest in the issue declined at the same rate as gas prices.

As to AG activism on the issue of global warming, let me cite you to two cases. In 2006, shortly before he left office, California Attorney General Bill Lockyer filed suit against the world's six largest car makers. In this suit California sought to recover damages for all environmental damage caused by automobiles since their invention. In *California v. General Motors Corp.*, it was California's contention that cars are a "public nuisance" the manufacturers inflicted upon it. The suit ignored the fact that the California legislature long ago passed the nation's strictest auto emission standards and that the companies had specially equipped a significant portion of their fleet in order to comply with those standards. The suit also did not deal with the reality that California constructed an enormous highway system to accommodate this alleged public nuisance. The suit was eventually dismissed by the federal district court in the fall of 2007 on the grounds it raised political questions outside the jurisdiction of the courts. Folks, I believe this was a case of AG activism.

Several Eastern attorneys general, including Eliot Spitzer and his successor Andrew Cuomo, do not like coal fired power plants. So Spitzer, Richard Blumenthal in Connecticut, and several fellow state AGs sued the nation's five largest coal burning utilities, even though none of the utilities were located in their states. In *Connecticut v. American Electric Power Co., Inc.* the AGs sought a reduction in carbon dioxide emissions. The AGs viewed these emissions as a public nuisance and claimed they needed to bring the case because the federal government and coal burning utility companies had failed to implement any meaningful measures to address this matter of national and worldwide significance. The U.S. District Court in the Southern District of New York dismissed the action as raising non-justiciable political questions.

Ladies and gentlemen, therein lies the rub. Unlike some of my colleagues, I do not believe that state AGs have the authority to act in whatever they believe is the broader national or international interest and to usurp the jurisdictional authority of Congress and federal regulatory agencies in the process.

I believe many of these are in fact political or policy questions to be resolved by legislative bodies.

I also believe basic principles of federalism are being undermined. Over the last year, Andrew Cuomo, Eliot Spitzer's successor as Attorney General of New York, has taken creative legal steps in an attempt to deter new coal fired utility plants in Kansas and Colorado. To me, the notion that the attorney general of New York has the jurisdictional authority to attempt to block utility plants in Kansas and Colorado is an affront to the most basic tenets of federalism. If the attorneys general of a few Eastern states want to control carbon emissions in Colorado and Kansas, they need to lobby the legislators and regulators in those states and/or fight and win battles in Congress that will result in national air quality standards applicable to every state. Otherwise, they should leave it to the people of Colorado to regulate their own utilities. And incidentally, the new coal fired utility unit in Colorado had been approved as part of an agreement between industry and environmentalists because two older coal units would also be retrofitted as part of the deal and the three of them together would have less total emissions than the two currently operational units.

My definition of AG activism is this: It is when a state attorney general attempts to remedy a real or perceived problem through means other than that intended by those elected to make public policy. My test in determining whether to exercise state power to sue someone is simply this: Has a law been violated and is there sufficient evidence to prove it in court? I will not bring a legal action to stop conduct if a legislature has not provided me a means to do so either by express statutory authority or by statutory recognition that I retain certain common law powers. . . .

The aggressive litigation posture taken by some of my fellow state attorneys general has led critics to question whether they are engaged in a violation of the separation of powers. By using perceived common law powers to achieve public policy objectives they deem desirable, they are, in essence, legislating and regulating by litigation. They are shaping public policy, traditionally the legislative function. . . .

NOTES AND QUESTIONS

1. What do you think is the proper role of a state attorney general with respect to controversial issues like climate change? Do you agree more with the attorney general from Connecticut or the one from Colorado?
2. A public nuisance is defined as an unreasonable interference with rights held by the public in general. RESTATEMENT (SECOND) OF TORTS §821B(1) (1979). Typical public nuisance suits in the environmental arena are filed by state or local governments and seek to enjoin widely spread harms such as those from noise, dust, odors, or water pollution. How are the harms that climate change causes similar to and different from these more typically

litigated harms? For discussion, see generally Thomas Merrill, *Global Warming as a Public Nuisance*, 30 COLUM. J. ENVTL. L. 293 (2005); Ken Alex, *A Period of Consequences: Global Warming as Public Nuisance*, 26A STAN. ENVTL. L.J. 77 (2007); David A. Dana, *The Mismatch Between Public Nuisance Law and Global Warming*, 18 SUP. CT. ECON. REV. 9 (2010).

3. In California, the state attorney general has also focused within the state in pursuing climate change litigation. In 2007, the attorney general filed suit under the California Environmental Quality Act (CEQA) against the County of San Bernardino. The suit alleged that the county had failed to comply with CEQA by not adequately considering climate change in an update to its General Plan. As adopted, the update to the General Plan prescribed the goals and policies that would direct the future of land use, growth, and transportation through 2030 without estimating the increases in greenhouse gas emissions that the execution of the plan would cause. *See In re* People v. Cnty. of San Bernardino, No. CIVSS 0700329 (Cal. App. Dep't Super. Ct. 2007), *available at* http://ag.ca.gov/globalwarming/pdf/SanBernardino_complaint.pdf; *see also* Hari M. Osofsky, *Is Climate Change "International"? Litigation's Diagonal Regulatory Role*, 49 VA. J. INT'L L. 585, 610–13 (2009). In the settlement that was negotiated, the county agreed to amend its General Plan to include the goal of "reducing those greenhouse gas emissions reasonably attributable to the County's discretionary land use decisions and the County's internal government operations" and to adopt a Greenhouse Gas Emissions Reduction Plan that would inventory present and projected greenhouse gas emissions in the county. *See* Order Regarding Settlement, People v. Cnty. of San Bernardino, No. CIVSS 0700329 (Cal. App. Dep't Super. Ct. 2007), *available at* http://ag.ca.gov/cms_pdfs/press/2007-08-21_San_Bernardino_settlement_agreement.pdf. What effects do you expect that this litigation and settlement agreement would have on other localities in California?

5. ADAPTATION PLANNING

In addition to the activities that states have undertaken to mitigate greenhouse gas emissions, many states have become active in adaptation planning. According to the Center for Climate and Energy Solutions, about one-quarter of states have completed or are in the process of completing a state adaptation plan. *See U.S. Climate Policy Maps*, CTR. FOR CLIMATE AND ENERGY SOLUTIONS, http://www.pewcenter.org/what_s_being_done/in_the_states/state_action_maps.cfm (last visited Apr. 20, 2012).

California was the first state to a complete a state adaptation plan. Its 2009 Climate Adaptation Strategy was a response to a 2008 Executive Order requiring the California Resources Agency to "summarize the best known science on climate change impacts to California, assess California's vulnerability to the identified impacts and then outline solutions that can be implemented within and across state agencies to promote resiliency." Cal. Exec. Order No. S-13-08, *available at* http://gov.ca.gov/news.php?id=11036. An excerpt of the strategy follows.

CAL. NATURAL RES. AGENCY, 2009 CALIFORNIA CLIMATE ADAPTATION
STRATEGY 3–9 (2009)

http://resources.ca.gov/climate_adaptation/docs/Statewide_Adaptation_Strategy.pdf

The Golden State at Risk

Climate change is already affecting California. Sea levels have risen by as much as seven inches along the California coast over the last century, increasing erosion and pressure on the state's infrastructure, water supplies, and natural resources. The state has also seen increased average temperatures, more extreme hot days, fewer cold nights, a lengthening of the growing season, shifts in the water cycle with less winter precipitation falling as snow, and both snowmelt and rainwater running off sooner in the year.

These climate driven changes affect resources critical to the health and prosperity of California. For example, forest wildland fires are becoming more frequent and intense due to dry seasons that start earlier and end later. The state's water supply, already stressed under current demands and expected population growth, will shrink under even the most conservative climate change scenario. Almost half a million Californians, many without the means to adjust to expected impacts, will be at risk from sea level rise along bay and coastal areas. California's infrastructure is already stressed and will face additional burdens from climate risks. And as the Central Valley becomes more urbanized, more people will be at risk from intense heat waves.

If the state were to take no action to reduce or minimize expected impacts from future climate change, the costs could be severe. A 2008 report by the University of California, Berkeley and the non-profit organization Next 10 estimates that if no such action is taken in California, damages across sectors would result in "tens of billions of dollars per year in direct costs" and "expose *trillions* of dollars of assets to collateral risk." More specifically, the report suggests that of the state's $4 trillion in real estate assets "$2.5 trillion is at risk from extreme weather events, sea level rise, and wildfires" with a projected annual price tag of up to $3.9 billion over this century depending on climate scenarios. . . .

California understands the importance of addressing climate impacts today. The state strengthened its commitment to managing the impacts from sea level rise, increased temperatures, shifting precipitation and extreme weather events when Governor Arnold Schwarzenegger signed Executive Order (EO) S-13-08 on November 14, 2008. The order called on state agencies to develop California's first strategy to identify and prepare for these expected climate impacts.

The *2009 California Climate Adaptation Strategy* (CAS) report summarizes the best known science on climate change impacts in the state to assess vulnerability and outlines possible solutions that can be implemented within and across state agencies to promote resiliency. This is the first step in an ongoing, evolving process to reduce California's vulnerability to climate impacts.

The California Natural Resources Agency (CNRA) has taken the lead in developing this adaptation strategy, working through the Climate Action Team (CAT). Seven sector-specific working groups led by 12 state agencies, boards and commissions, and numerous stakeholders were convened for this effort. The strategy proposes a comprehensive set of recommendations designed to inform and guide California decision makers as they begin to develop policies that will protect the state, its residents and its resources from a range of climate change impacts.

. . . .

California's Climate Adaptation Strategy

As the climate changes, so must California. To effectively address the challenges that a changing climate will bring, climate adaptation and mitigation (i.e., reducing state greenhouse gas (GHG) emissions) policies must complement each other, and efforts within and across sectors must be coordinated. For years, the two approaches have been viewed as alternatives, rather than as complementary and equally necessary approaches.

Adaptation is a relatively new concept in California policy. The term generally refers to efforts that respond to the *impacts* of climate change — adjustments in natural or human systems to actual or expected climate changes to minimize harm or take advantage of beneficial opportunities.

California's ability to manage its climate risks through adaptation depends on a number of critical factors including its baseline and projected economic resources, technologies, infrastructure, institutional support and effective governance, public awareness, access to the best available scientific information, sustainably-managed natural resources, and equity in access to these resources.

As the *2009 California Climate Adaptation Strategy* illustrates, the state has the ability to strengthen its capacity in all of these areas. In December 2008, the California Air Resources Board released the state's *Climate Change Scoping Plan*, which outlines a range of strategies necessary for the state to reduce its GHG emissions to 1990 levels by 2020. Many climate mitigation strategies, like promoting water and energy efficiency, are also climate adaptation strategies. By building an adaptation strategy on existing climate science and frameworks like the Scoping Plan, California has begun to effectively anticipate future challenges and change actions that will ultimately reduce the vulnerability of residents, resources and industries to the consequences of a variable and changing climate. Now that the state has produced plans for climate mitigation and adaptation, closer coordination is needed to implement both approaches.

The strategies included in this report were approved by the CAT Team, which represents all of state government. Now, the CAT will lead in the coordination of measures and push to develop the necessary tools to effect adaptation protocols. California's mitigation (CAT) and adaptation (CAS) processes will be further integrated through extensive information exchange and consolidation of working groups from both efforts.

To ensure a coordinated effort in adapting to the unavoidable impacts of climate change, the *2009 California Climate Adaptation Strategy* was developed using a set of guiding principles:

- Use the best available science in identifying climate change risks and adaptation strategies.
- Understand that data continues to be collected and that knowledge about climate change is still evolving. As such, an effective adaptation strategy is "living" and will itself be adapted to account for new science.

- Involve all relevant stakeholders in identifying, reviewing, and refining the state's adaptation strategy.
- Establish and retain strong partnerships with federal, state, and local governments, tribes, private business and landowners, and non-governmental organizations to develop and implement adaptation strategy recommendations over time.
- Give priority to adaptation strategies that initiate, foster, and enhance existing efforts that improve economic and social well-being, public safety and security, public health, environmental justice, species and habitat protection, and ecological function.
- When possible, give priority to adaptation strategies that modify and enhance existing policies rather than solutions that require new funding and new staffing.
- Understand the need for adaptation policies that are effective and flexible enough for circumstances that may not yet be fully predictable.
- Ensure that climate change adaptation strategies are coordinated with the California Air Resources Board's AB 32 Scoping Plan process when appropriate, as well as with other local, state, national and international efforts to reduce GHG emissions.

The *2009 California Climate Adaptation Strategy* takes into account the long-term, complex, and uncertain nature of climate change and establishes a pro-active foundation for an ongoing adaptation process. Rather than address the detailed impacts, vulnerabilities, and adaptation needs of every sector, those determined to be at greatest risk are prioritized.

. . . .

Preliminary Recommendations

. . . .

It is recognized that implementation of the following strategies will require significant collaboration among multiple stakeholders to ensure they are carried out in a rational, yet progressive manner over the long term. These strategies distinguish between near-term actions that will be completed by the end of 2010 and long-term actions to be developed over time, and are covered in more detail in the sector chapters in Part II of this report as well as in initial efforts.

Key recommendations include:

1. A Climate Adaptation Advisory Panel (CAAP) will be appointed to assess the greatest risks to California from climate change and recommend strategies to reduce those risks building on California's Climate Adaptation Strategy. This panel will be convened by the California Natural Resources Agency, in coordination with the Governor's Climate Action Team, to complete a report by December 2010. The state will partner with the Pacific Council on International Policy to assemble this panel. A list of panel members can be found on the California adaptation Web site.

2. California must change its water management and uses because climate change will likely create greater competition for limited water supplies needed by the environment, agriculture, and cities. As directed by the recently signed water legislation (Senate Bill X71), state agencies must implement strategies to achieve a statewide 20 percent reduction in per capita water use by 2020, expand surface and groundwater storage, implement efforts to fix Delta water supply, quality, and ecosystem conditions, support agricultural water use efficiency, improve state-wide water quality, and improve Delta ecosystem conditions and stabilize water supplies as developed in the Bay Delta Conservation Plan.

3. Consider project alternatives that avoid significant new development in areas that cannot be adequately protected (planning, permitting, development, and building) from flooding, wildfire and erosion due to climate change. The most risk-averse approach for minimizing the adverse effects of sea level rise and storm activities is to carefully consider new development within areas vulnerable to inundation and erosion. State agencies should generally not plan, develop, or build any new significant structure in a place where that structure will require significant protection from sea level rise, storm surges, or coastal erosion during the expected life of the structure. However, vulnerable shoreline areas containing existing development that have regionally significant economic, cultural, or social value may have to be protected, and in-fill development in these areas may be accommodated. State agencies should incorporate this policy into their decisions and other levels of government are also encouraged to do so.

4. All state agencies responsible for the management and regulation of public health, infrastructure or habitat subject to significant climate change should prepare as appropriate agency-specific adaptation plans, guidance, or criteria by September 2010.

5. To the extent required by CEQA [California Environmental Quality Act] Guidelines Section 15126.2, all significant state projects, including infrastructure projects, must consider the potential impacts of locating such projects in areas susceptible to hazards resulting from climate change. Section 15126.2 is currently being proposed for revision by CNRA to direct lead agencies to evaluate the impacts of locating development in areas susceptible to hazardous conditions, including hazards potentially exacerbated by climate change. Locating state projects in such areas may require additional guidance that in part depends on planning tools that the CAS recommendations call for.

6. The California Emergency Management Agency (Cal EMA) will collaborate with CNRA, the CAT, the Energy Commission, and the CAAP to assess California's vulnerability to climate change, identify impacts to state assets, and promote climate adaptation/mitigation awareness through the Hazard Mitigation Web Portal and My Hazards Website as well as other appropriate sites. The transportation sector, led by Caltrans, will specifically assess how transportation nodes are vulnerable and the type of information that will be necessary to assist response to district emergencies. Special attention will be paid to the most vulnerable communities impacted by climate change in all studies.

7. Using existing research the state should identify key California land and aquatic habitats that could change significantly during this century due to climate change. Based on this identification, the state should develop a plan for expanding existing protected areas or altering land and water management practices to minimize adverse effects from climate change induced phenomena.

8. The best long-term strategy to avoid increased health impacts associated with climate change is to ensure communities are healthy to build resilience to increased spread of disease and temperature increases. The California Department of Public Health will develop guidance by September 2010 for use by local health departments and other agencies to assess mitigation and adaptation strategies, which include impacts on vulnerable populations and communities and assessment of cumulative health impacts. This includes assessments of land use, housing and transportation proposals that could impact health, GHG emissions, and community resilience for climate change, such as in the 2008 Senate Bill 375 regarding Sustainable Communities.

9. The most effective adaptation strategies relate to short and long-term decisions. Most of these decisions are the responsibility of local community planning entities. As a result, communities with General Plans and Local Coastal Plans should begin, when possible, to amend their plans to assess climate change impacts, identify areas most vulnerable to these impacts, and develop reasonable and rational risk reduction strategies using the CAS as guidance. Every effort will be made to provide tools, such as interactive climate impact maps, to assist in these efforts.

10. State fire fighting agencies should begin immediately to include climate change impact information into fire program planning to inform future planning efforts. Enhanced wildfire risk from climate change will likely increase public health and safety risks, property damage, fire suppression and emergency response costs to government, watershed and water quality impacts, and vegetation conversions and habitat fragmentation.

11. State agencies should meet projected population growth and increased energy demand with greater energy conservation and an increased use of renewable energy. Renewable energy supplies should be enhanced through the Desert Renewable Energy Conservation Plan that will protect sensitive habitat that will while helping to reach the state goal of having 33 percent of California's energy supply from renewable sources by 2020.

12. Existing and planned climate change research can and should be used for state planning and public outreach purposes; new climate change impact research should be broadened and funded. By September 2010, the California Energy Commission will develop the CalAdapt Web site that will synthesize existing California climate change scenarios and climate impact research and to encourage its use in a way that is beneficial for local decision-makers. Every effort will be made to increase funding for climate change research, focusing on three areas: linkages with federal funding resources, developing Energy Commission -led vulnerability studies, and synthesizing the latest climate information into useable information for local needs through the CalAdapt tool.

NOTES AND QUESTIONS

1. Given that climate change impacts will vary among the country's regions and localities, states seem a natural site for adaptation planning. As stated by Professor J.B. Ruhl, "It seems unlikely that the federal government could effectively devise a national adaptation strategy that fulfills the need of every state and local community." J.B. Ruhl, *Climate Change Adaptation and the Structural Transformation of Environmental Law*, 40 ENVTL. L. 363, 427 (2010). What do you think are the most important considerations in adaptation planning in Florida? Iowa? Texas? Do you think it would be useful for states to participate in regional bodies to jointly consider adaptation issues? If you were charged with dividing the country into regions for this purpose, what divisions would you propose? How would this approach fit into the federalism schemes described by Professor Glicksman in Chapter Three?

2. States and localities are also the "first responders" to the types of natural disasters that are expected to increase in prevalence with climate change such as hurricanes, floods, fires, and heat waves. States that are overwhelmed by a major disaster can request federal aid under the Stafford Act of 1988. Will the legal structure that governs disasters need to change because of climate change? To what extent should state and local governments be allowed to continue making potentially hazardous areas such as floodplains and the wildland-urban interface safe for development, and then seek federal assistance when disaster strikes? For a discussion of these issues, see Raymond J. Burby, *Hurricane Katrina and the Paradoxes of Government Disaster Policy: Bringing About Wise Governmental Decisions for Hazardous Areas*, 604 ANNALS AM. ACAD. POL. & SOC. SCI. 171 (2006).

3. How should the costs of adapting to climate change be distributed? Should the states or the federal government be responsible for the costs of adaptation measures such as constructing sea walls to fend off sea level rise and developing new water supplies? Professor Daniel Farber explains there is an argument for placing responsibility "at the lowest possible government level so that both costs and benefits would be concentrated on the same group." Daniel A. Farber, *Climate Adaptation and Federalism: Mapping the Issues*, 1 SAN DIEGO J. CLIMATE & ENERGY L. 259, 270 (2009). Under this view, federal tax dollars wouldn't be spent on protecting residences in coastal cities. Rather, states or localities would be responsible for assessing the taxes necessary to do so if they chose to. Yet there is also an argument for having society as a whole — through federal tax dollars — protect individuals from climate change: "This system achieves the maximum amount of loss-spreading, in essence providing social insurance against the risk of climate change." *Id.* at 272.

6. FEDERALISM: THE FEDERAL-STATE RELATIONSHIP

The present array of climate law developments in U.S. states points to a critical federalism question for the future: What should the respective roles of the federal and state governments be and how should they be coordinated? Chapter Three considered this question from the perspective of the federal government, whereas this section focuses on the role of the state.

A common approach in U.S. environmental law has been "cooperative federalism," wherein federal and state levels of government share authority in a cooperative manner. In the Clean Air Act, for example, Congress gave the federal agency broad authority to identify pollutants and establish regulatory standards for them. States, in turn, were authorized to take the primary role in implementing these standards by writing permits with facility-specific emissions limits and enforcing permit requirements.

Assuming the future — even if not short-term — passage of a federal climate law, some degree of cooperative federalism seems inevitable. However, its dimensions and characteristics are very much up for debate. Consider the following discussion, written by Professor Kirsten Engel when the passage of comprehensive climate change legislation looked more likely, regarding how state climate initiatives might fare with further development of federal climate law.

Kirsten H. Engel, Whither Subnational Climate Change Initiatives in the Wake of Federal Climate Legislation?

39 Publius: J. Federalism 432, 445-49 (2009)

[The] prospect of a federal climate regulatory regime poses two critical questions for state climate initiatives: (1) will the states nevertheless continue to push forward with climate-related initiatives — might any be dropped? — and (2) if they do, what ought to be the scope of federal preemption, if any, of such initiatives?

Will States and Localities Continue to Pursue Climate Mitigation Measures?

Whether states and localities continue to pursue any particular climate change policy is a function of two factors: the degree to which the motivations underlying the state or local government's pursuit of that policy is independent of and unrelated to the current lack of federal climate legislation and the degree to which future legislation preempts state and local action on that policy. With respect to the first factor, this article suggests an assortment of different motivations underlying state and local action on climate change: the prospect of achieving tangible emission reduction benefits through legal action to compel the federal government to regulate emissions nationally or obtain reductions from major emitters through court-ordered relief; the potential for credit-claiming and publicity-seeking, the prospects of developing new or expanded markets in renewable energy and energy efficiency technologies, the quest for energy cost savings and other co-benefits of climate mitigation, the chance to reap network-related benefits proffered by translocal organizations of government actors devoted to the climate change issue, the rewards of policy entrepreneurship, and a desire to counter the anticompetitive effects of subnational regulation.

Of this list, only a few seem to rely upon the current lack of federal climate legislation and hence to indicate a change in state and local climate action following the enactment of federal climate legislation. Most obviously, there will be little reason to sue EPA to compel it to regulate greenhouse gases should

Congress mandate such regulatory action in federal legislation. And certainly the existence of such legislation will weaken the cache associated with the smallest governing jurisdictions tackling the largest of environmental problems. Hence to the degree any of these initiatives are being driven by a local politician's quest for credit and publicity, federal legislation will definitely take the wind [out] of his or her sails.

A second area in which we should expect to see a downturn in state action is state-initiated common law public nuisance actions against large emitters of greenhouse gases, such as electric utilities. Nationally applicable emissions standards for the industries that have been targeted in these lawsuits should eliminate the regulatory disparity that drives emissions leakage. Again, this will of course not be the case if the federal legislation fails to enact standards applicable to the industries targeted in this litigation. Nationally applicable federal emissions standards that impose only a minimum standard, leaving states the discretion to impose more stringent standards (the framework employed in most federal environmental laws) will not eliminate the regulatory disparity where states decide to impose more stringent standards upon in-state facilities but the out-of-state facilities remain subject only to the minimum federal standards. But the fact that the out-of-state facilities are subject to a regime of emissions controls means that it will be difficult for states to argue that they constitute a public nuisance.

Federal climate legislation could also deal a blow to state's motivation to engage in at least some policy entrepreneurship. Again, however, the degree to which federal legislation will have this effect will depend upon the design of the legislation, most importantly, the extent to which the federal legislation makes room for states to continue to innovate in the climate policy realm, keeping robust the market for policy innovation. Similarly the extent to which the federal government adopts, in federal legislation, any of the policy innovations generated thus far by state and local governments may influence the degree to which states continue to be motivated to be climate policy entrepreneurs. The federal government's adoption of state innovations in federal legislation would appear to underscore the value of state and local policy innovation and thereby encourage its continuation.

However, because the remaining motivations — most importantly those driven by the prospect of reaping economic, networking and policy entrepreneurship benefits — appear unrelated to the current lack of federal climate legislation, there is every reason to believe that states will continue to push forward with these policies. Furthermore, federal climate legislation may prove to be a boon to states and local climate initiatives. Clean energy is now a federal priority. The $787 billion federal stimulus package, for example, contains large sums for energy efficiency, renewables, and technological development. Such federal investment should boost state efforts in these areas and encourage states to invest in clean energy research and development.

Will Congress Preempt State-Local Initiatives?

Assuming that state and local governments will continue to be motivated to pursue climate change policies, the extent to which they will, in fact, continue to exist will depend upon the degree to which Congress expressly or impliedly preempts state policies in the context of federal climate legislation. This in turn may depend upon the design of the federal regulatory program.

It seems likely that Congress will enact some sort of cap and trade program, administered by EPA, and applicable to the largest stationary industrial emitters of greenhouse gases such as electric utilities and other industries that burn large quantities of fossil fuels. The program may resemble, at least superficially, the cap and trade program put in place to control sulfur dioxide emissions from utilities under the acid rain trading program of the 1990 Amendments to the Clean Air Act. To date, nearly all of the major federal proposals for climate legislation employ a cap and trade program. . . .

Should Congress enact a cap and trade regime as predicted, the scope of federal preemption of state climate initiatives is likely to be sweeping with respect to those aspects of the program subject to federal regulation. Thus, should Congress follow the model of the Acid Rain Trading program for carbon dioxide emissions, states will be barred from, for example, restricting trades in greenhouse gas allowances distributed under the program. Similarly, should Congress follow, for greenhouse gas emissions from motor vehicles, the regulatory model employed generally for vehicle emission standards under the Clean Air Act §209(a), with the exception of California, states will be barred from promulgating their own vehicle emission standards (but can adopt standards identical to that of California).

The narrowness of a cap and trade regime focused on one or more high carbon dioxide-emitting sectors of the economy may actually be fairly favorable for the continuation of a robust field of state and local climate initiatives. Provided the courts do not interpret Congress's action in the area to preempt the entire field of greenhouse gas regulation most of the initiatives discussed in this article should be unaffected by such a program. Thus states should continue to retain authority to impose renewable portfolio standards to develop and implement green building energy efficiency standards, to provide tax credits and subsidies for energy efficiency and renewables, and to pursue all manner of land use and transportation planning. Under this scenario, probably the most uncertain area will be the preemptive effect of a federal cap and trade program upon the regional cap and trade programs, such as RGGI and, in the future, the WCI. . . .

Of course, there is no guarantee that a federal climate regulatory program will be limited to a cap and trade regime for only certain sectors of the economy. Congress may decide to regulate with a broader brush with the result that the risk of federal preemption is that much greater. With respect to such broader regulatory proposals, it is worthwhile noting that federal preemption has greater sway with respect to certain issues than with others. The economies of scale achieved by uniform product manufacturing standards supports strong preemption in the case of vehicle emissions standards. So too the efficiency benefits achieved by an unencumbered emissions trading market argue for strong preemption to the extent states might be regulating in a manner that undermines the fungibility of emissions allowances in the federal market.

Outside these concerns, however, it is important that Congress and the courts adopt a narrow approach to federal preemption. If anything, the quite remarkable history of state and local action on climate change underscores the benefits of overlapping regulatory jurisdiction of the states and federal government. For years, while the federal government largely ignored climate change, states and local governments stepped into the breach and began grappling with the problem with a vast array of initiatives. Some of these initiatives, such as building codes, lie in areas traditionally subject to state and local control, but others deal with topics, such as interstate emissions trading, that have traditionally been the domain of federal regulation. Some of the latter may serve as models for federal regulators but, in any case, they jumpstarted the regulatory developments that many regard as necessary to a less fossil-fuel dependent economy. State and local regulation thus serves as a backstop when the federal government fails to regulate. It also serves as an important source of regulatory innovations. Broad federal preemption should be disfavored because it will undermine important benefits that accrue from preserving broadly overlapping regulatory authority between the states and the federal government.

NOTES AND QUESTIONS

1. Like Professor Engel, Professor Alice Kaswan also argues against broad federal preemption. Alice Kaswan, *A Cooperative Federalism Proposal for Climate Change Legislation: The Value of State Autonomy in a Federal System*, 85 Denv. U. L. Rev. 791, 794–803 (2008). As she explains, "the states have a vital interest in establishing their own climate change goals and in asserting at least limited control over key implementation decisions." *Id.* at 797. In her view, the federal government should set minimum goals or standards for greenhouse gas reductions but allow states to exceed them. In this way, states could mandate additional emissions restrictions that, for example, encourage the development of a local renewable energy industry or reduce the emission of greenhouse gas co-pollutants that cause smog. The ability of states to go beyond federal minimum goals could also help protect against lapses or inadequacies in the federal government's implementation and enforcement of the law. Imagine that you represent the cement industry, a major emitter of greenhouse gases throughout the United States. What arguments would you make against such state autonomy and in favor of broad federal preemption?
2. States have often been considered in U.S. law as "laboratories" of policy innovation. The term comes from a 1932 Supreme Court decision in which Justice Brandeis observed that "[i]t is one of the happy incidents of the federal system that a single courageous State may, if its citizens choose, serve as a laboratory; and try novel social and economic experiments without risk to the rest of the country." *New State Ice Co. v. Liebmann*, 285 U.S. 262, 311 (1932). Do you think states have fulfilled this vision in the arena of climate law? Do you think they should continue to be able to do so even if Congress passes a new comprehensive federal climate law?

3. The Waxman-Markey Bill that the U.S. House of Representatives passed in 2009 adopted an interesting approach to the preemption of state cap-and-trade programs. With its proposed creation of a national cap-and-trade program, the bill provided that "no State or political subdivision thereof shall implement or enforce a cap that covers any capped emissions emitted during the years 2012 through 2017." The provision would have thus temporarily preempted the programs developed under California's AB 32, the WCI, and RGGI. Why do you think the House opted for this approach? If the bill had passed into law, what would have likely happened?

C. LOCALITIES: CITIES AND COUNTIES

Localities are the level of government closest to both the sources of greenhouse gases and the on-the-ground impacts of climate change. They are also most arguably connected to the will of the people, and they may be more responsive and nimble than higher levels of government. This section examines the innovative roles that localities are playing in climate change law and policy.

1. EMISSIONS REDUCTIONS

As primary decision makers in policy areas spanning from land use to waste management, local governments will arguably be essential to fashioning successful climate change policies. Professor Katherine Trisolini highlights four areas of "well-accepted local power" in which local governments can act to reduce greenhouse gas emissions.

KATHERINE A. TRISOLINI, ALL HANDS ON DECK: LOCAL GOVERNMENTS AND THE POTENTIAL FOR BIDIRECTIONAL CLIMATE CHANGE REGULATION

62 Stan. L. Rev. 669, 697-98, 707, 718, 723-24 (2010)

1. Buildings and Energy Efficiency

Building energy efficiency provides perhaps the most straightforward and dramatic opportunity to reduce greenhouse gas emissions downstream by shrinking demand. Improving buildings' environmental performance — through green building programs, efficiency standards, and/or building code changes — provides a particularly attractive means for reducing greenhouse gases. Mature, available, and well-studied technologies render building energy efficiency a technologically easy, proven, and often cost-effective emissions reduction strategy.

Because reduction in demand continues throughout a building's lifespan, employing these technologies reduces both immediate and long-term greenhouse gas emissions. Moreover, because these reductions are built in to the physical environment, construction or rehabilitation of existing building stock creates lasting emissions savings regardless of subsequent political changes. Forecasts of future construction underscore the potential to reduce emissions through improved building efficiency: between now and 2050, U.S. residents will build or replace an estimated 89 million residential units and construct 190 billion square feet of commercial, office, institutional, and other non-residential space.

Why is this a local issue? In the United States, local governments have significant power to regulate building construction and renovation through their traditional authority to adopt and enforce building codes . . . .

2. Zoning and Land Use Power: Reducing Vehicle Use

Local governments also substantially shape the built environment through their well-accepted power over zoning and land use. This power places local governments in a potentially critical position for reducing transportation emissions because land use and urban form shape vehicle usage. . . .

3. Waste and Garbage

Waste management, another typical and well-accepted area of local power, has the potential to decrease energy demand while simultaneously eliminating new sources of greenhouse gas emissions. Because landfills and sewage treatment plants generate methane from discrete sites, they can also generate power to displace demand for energy from greenhouse gas-intensive sources. . . .

4. Proprietary Functions of Local Governments . . .

Local governments' most direct (and likely least politically challenging) route to reducing downstream energy consumption is through targeting their own resources and operations. Potential reductions from proprietary activities alone may be substantial given the sheer number of local governments, the size of their operations, and the types of things that they own and operate. In 2002, the United States had nearly 40,000 general-purpose local governments. When combined with school districts and special use districts, the number is nearly 88,000.

The collective number of local employees as compared with the federal and state governments provides a rough sense of the size of local government operations. As of the 2006 census, local governments in the United States employed nearly twelve million full-time equivalent workers as compared to the federal government's 2.5 million and the collective 4.25 million of all fifty states combined. (Even discounting the employees from independent school districts and special purpose districts, general-purpose local governments still employed more people than the governments of all fifty states combined.) In addition to buildings, vehicles, lighting structures, and schools, local governments own utilities, airports, landfills, and ports, among many other things.

Large cities provide a particularly useful lens through which to grasp the potential impact of proprietary activities and operations. Los Angeles estimates that municipal operations accounted for nearly seventeen million metric tons of CO_2, comprising one-third of the carbon dioxide output from the area. Part of the reason this figure is so high is that, like a number of large local governments, the city owns its utility company. It also directly controls large sources of emissions, including several airports and the Port of Los Angeles.

Many mayors across the country have taken collaborative action on climate change policy. The U.S. Mayors Climate Protection Agreement below was endorsed at the 73rd Annual Meeting of the U.S. Conference of Mayors in 2005. As of 2011, 1,054 mayors from the 50 states, the District of Columbia and Puerto Rico, representing a total population of over 88,499,854 citizens, had signed onto it.

U.S. Conference of Mayors, The U.S. Mayors Climate Protection Agreement (As Endorsed by the 73rd Annual U.S. Conference of Mayors Meeting, Chicago, 2005)

http://www.usmayors.org/climateprotection/documents/mcpAgreement.pdf

A. We urge the federal government and state governments to enact policies and programs to meet or beat the target of reducing global warming pollution levels to 7 percent below 1990 levels by 2012, including efforts to: reduce the United States' dependence on fossil fuels and accelerate the development of clean, economical energy resources and fuel-efficient technologies such as conservation, methane recovery for energy generation, waste to energy, wind and solar energy, fuel cells, efficient motor vehicles, and biofuels;

B. We urge the U.S. Congress to pass bipartisan greenhouse gas reduction legislation that 1) includes clear timetables and emissions limits and 2) a flexible, market-based system of tradable allowances among emitting industries; and

C. We will strive to meet or exceed Kyoto Protocol targets for reducing global warming pollution by taking actions in our own operations and communities such as:

1. Inventory global warming emissions in City operations and in the community, set reduction targets and create an action plan;
2. Adopt and enforce land-use policies that reduce sprawl, preserve open space, and create compact, walkable urban communities;
3. Promote transportation options such as bicycle trails, commute trip reduction programs, incentives for car pooling and public transit;
4. Increase the use of clean, alternative energy by, for example, investing in "green tags," advocating for the development of renewable energy resources, recovering landfill methane for energy production, and supporting the use of waste to energy technology;
5. Make energy efficiency a priority through building code improvements, retrofitting city facilities with energy efficient lighting and urging employees to conserve energy and save money;
6. Purchase only Energy Star equipment and appliances for City use;

7. Practice and promote sustainable building practices using the U.S. Green Building Council's LEED [Leadership in Energy and Environmental Design] program or a similar system;
8. Increase the average fuel efficiency of municipal fleet vehicles; reduce the number of vehicles; launch an employee education program including anti-idling messages; convert diesel vehicles to bio-diesel;
9. Evaluate opportunities to increase pump efficiency in water and wastewater systems; recover wastewater treatment methane for energy production;
10. Increase recycling rates in City operations and in the community;
11. Maintain healthy urban forests; promote tree planting to increase shading and to absorb CO_2; and
12. Help educate the public, schools, other jurisdictions, professional associations, business and industry about reducing global warming pollution.

NOTES AND QUESTIONS

1. What benefits do you think mayors gain by joining the agreement? What drawbacks or risks exist? Does signing the statement commit a mayor to taking any particular actions?
2. An important organization in motivating local governments to act on climate change has been "ICLEI—Local Governments for Sustainability," established in 1990 by more than 200 local governments from 43 countries at the United Nations–sponsored World Congress of Local Governments for a Sustainable Future. *See Fast Facts*, ICLEI, http://incheon2010.iclei.org/incheon-iclei/iclei-fast-facts.html (last visited Apr. 20, 2012). ICLEI's Cities for Climate Protection Campaign assists cities in adopting and implementing emissions reductions policies. Local governments join the campaign by passing a resolution pledging to reduce their greenhouse gas emissions, and then ICLEI assists them through a five-step process that includes measuring their emissions; committing to an emissions reduction target; planning their actions; implementing their plan; and monitoring their emissions reductions. Which of these tasks do you think would be most difficult for local governments?
3. Green building is an active area of legal development at the local level. However, rather than developing their own green building rules, many municipalities are relying on the Leadership in Energy and Environmental Design (LEED) standards set by the U.S. Green Building Council (USGBC), a private organization. As described by Professor Sarah Schindler, cities have begun to incorporate LEED standards into their municipal codes, requiring for example that a local developer register with the USGBC and achieve a specific number of LEED checklist points prior to the issuance of a building permit. Sarah Schindler, *Following Industry's LEED®: Municipal Adoption of*

Private Green Building Standard, 62 FLA. L. REV. 285 (2010). Why would municipalities choose to accept LEED standards this rather than develop and enforce local standards? What tensions or conflicts could arise when a local government relies on a private building industry organization's standards in this way? What benefits could result?

2. ADAPTATION PLANNING

As suggested above, localities have a great deal of authority in the realms of law implicated by mitigation. In addition, localities will be on the front line for climate change adaptation. Many cities and counties have begun to study how climate change is likely to affect them and plan for these changes. The county of Miami-Dade, Florida provides an example.

ICLEI, INSTITUTIONALIZING CLIMATE PREPAREDNESS IN MIAMI-DADE COUNTY, FL 4, 7–9, 11–12 (2010)

http://www.icleiusa.org/action-center/learn-from-others/
ICLEI_Miami_DadeCase_Study_lowres.pdf

A Need for Climate Change Adaptation

As a coastal community located at sea level and surrounded by water on three sides, with typical land elevation only three to ten feet above mean high water, Miami–Dade County is acutely aware of the dangers posed by climate change. Climate changes, including sea level rise, increases in temperature, changes in precipitation patterns, and changes in the intensity and/or frequency of extreme events all threaten the health and safety of residents, the integrity of infrastructure, and the vitality of regional ecosystems. In 2007, the Organization for Economic Cooperation and Development (OECD) quantified the vulnerability of various municipalities across the world towards climate change and identified Miami–Dade County as having the highest amount of vulnerable assets exposed to coastal flooding (for the 2070's) with a projected potential cost of approximately $3.5 trillion. . . .

Moreover, the County's geographical location at the tip of a peninsula, its large, dense population, and the reality that many key economic drivers for the county are weather dependent (e.g. tourism and agriculture), have created a clear impetus to plan for climate change. . . .

. . . .

Preparing for Climate Change While Advancing Local Sustainability

Recognizing the increased urgency for dealing with climate change, the County created a formal Climate Change Advisory Task Force (Task Force) that has been instrumental in providing guidance and recommendations on both adaptation and mitigation issues to the Miami–Dade Board of County Commissioners. Created in June of 2006 through the adoption of Ordinance 06–113 sponsored by Commissioner Natacha Seijas, the Task Force includes 25 appointed members and over 150 additional individuals who represent key sectors of the community, such as non-profit organizations, universities, building and architecture firms, national parks representatives, regional and state planning agencies, private sector business, federal partners and community residents.

Seven sub-committees were formed to focus on key areas of concern with the County; each chaired by a member of the Task Force and comprised of participants from the Task Force and the public. The seven committees include:

- Built Environment Adaptation
- Economic, Social, and Health
- Alternative Fuels and Transportation
- Energy and Buildings
- Science Committee
- Intergovernmental Affairs
- Natural Systems Adaptation

Meeting monthly, the Task Force has been a vehicle for community engagement in the County's climate change efforts, ensuring that voices from important community sectors are integrated into long-term adaptation and mitigations strategies. While the Task Force does not have the authority to make decisions, it does provide critical input and feedback, and helps to facilitate support from the community. To date, fifty-seven recommendations have been forwarded to the Board of County Commissioners and several are already being implemented. Sample activities already underway in the County that have been recommended by the Task Force include:

- The County Manager met with key department directors in the fall of 2008 and began the discussion of how to start incorporating climate change planning into department strategic plans. The County partnered with the National Oceanic and Atmospheric Association (NOAA) in March 2010 to provide an initial introduction and training for climate adaptation to department heads and operational staff to expedite this process.
- Through the Southeast Florida Regional Climate Compact's Regional Vulnerability Assessment Technical Work Group and NOAA, the County and Compact partners have been working with the U.S. Geological Survey (USGS) and the U.S. Army Corps. of Engineers (USACE) to build consensus on climate vulnerability and sea level rise mapping and planning parameters, utilizing regional digital elevation data and models. This information will be used in conjunction with Miami–Dade County's Stormwater Master Plan to identify flood hazard prone areas and create planning maps and tools for use in the comprehensive planning and zoning process.
- County staff has contacted the National Park Service (NPS), U.S. Geological Survey (USGS), Everglades National Park (ENP) and the South Florida Water Management District (SFWMD) to establish a team to work on a Pilot Program to assess the feasibility of using existing monitoring efforts and the information collected during this monitoring as indicators or "vital signs" of climate change.

- The Evaluation and Appraisal Report that will be going to the Board of County Commissioners in January 2011 includes a recommendation for the County to initiate an analysis on climate change and its impacts on the built environment with an eye towards addressing development standards and regulations related to investments in infrastructure, development/redevelopment and public facilities in hazard prone areas.
- The Evaluation and Appraisal Report that will be going to the Board of County Commissioners in January 2011 also includes a recommendation for the County to establish Climate Change evaluation criteria, to be used to evaluate proposed new development and redevelopment or assess the suitability or proposed use(s), density and/or intensity of use(s), and the level or risk of exposure to climate change impacts, among others.
- County staff has begun working with the Epidemiology, Disease Control and Immunization Services program of the Miami–Dade Health Department to create a working group to track and analyze potential climate change-related health impacts.

. . . .

Challenges to Adaptation

Throughout Miami–Dade County's adaptation and sustainability process, the County has faced numerous challenges and overcome many obstacles which have resulted in a series of potential stumbling blocks that other communities should be cognizant of during their climate preparedness efforts:

- **Complexity of Issue:** Climate change is a complex issue with multiple impacts that span all agencies/departments, and all sectors of society. This can be an enormous hurdle to overcome and poses difficulty in conveying the need for action. Communities need to acknowledge this complexity but not let it be a barrier to action.
- **Scientific Uncertainty and Timeframe:** One significant obstacle to overcome is determining which climate change projections to utilize for planning from the numerous and varied impact projections that currently exist. The extended timeframe of projected impacts (e.g., 2050, 2100), in conjunction with shorter-term decision-making, create a challenging political dichotomy. This is further exacerbated by the reality that some impacts may not be felt until far into the future but require tough decisions to be made today.
- **Scale and Complexity of Data:** Vast amounts of data need to be gathered and analyzed in order to guide decision making. In addition, systems, programs, and security mechanisms need to be created to store and manage this data to ensure data accuracy and integrity. Creation of these systems can be a lengthy and resource-intensive process, but is important for tracking changes and success.
- **Competing and Immediate Needs:** Miami–Dade County provides all basic services to residents in the County. Climate change impacts will affect most of these services but can also be seen as a separate priority which creates competition between existing, more immediate needs and

the need to take action now to prepare for future challenges. Finding ways to integrate climate concerns into existing community concerns can lessen this competition.

- **Current Economic and Budget Constraints:** Communities across the U.S. are currently grappling with how to deliver basic services while facing a severe budget shortfall. Miami–Dade County is no different and is struggling with integrating climate adaptation and preparedness activities into operations, while also dealing with the reality that this is likely to create added burdens on already strained budgets.
- **Land Use Realities:** Can coastal development really be thwarted? In regards to climate change, it's clear that it should, but how can this become a reality? Making tough land-use decisions will require support from federal, state, regional, and local counterparts, which can be challenging to foster, but will be critical for success.
- **Turning Science in to Action:** How does a community translate complicated and often 'difficult-to-understand' issues into action? This, along with effective communication, is the key to moving forward and aggressively addressing and acting on climate change.
- **Effective Communication:** The most important stepping stone to climate change policy can often be the most challenging obstacle to overcome. Effective communication is pivotal in dealing with any community-wide issue.

NOTES AND QUESTIONS

1. With sea level rise, a critical question for coastal cities like Miami, Florida, will be whether to defend or retreat. As Niki L. Pace, Research Counsel with the Mississippi-Alabama Sea Grant Legal Program, explains:

> As shorelines encroach upon the built environment over the next century, coastal communities face a difficult decision—retreat inland or defend against rising seas. Further complicating this decision is the need to balance the public's interest in the water's edge with waterfront property owners' interest in safeguarding their investment. In response, some governments are increasingly limiting waterfront property owners' right to armor their waterfront property in favor of preserving the natural shoreline.
>
> Niki L. Pace, *Wetlands or Seawalls? Adapting Shoreline Regulation to Address Sea Level Rise and Wetland Preservation in the Gulf of Mexico*, 26 J. LAND USE & ENVTL. L. 327, 329 (2011).

The decision is made more difficult by scientific uncertainty regarding the magnitude of sea level rise. While the IPCC's 2007 Fourth Assessment projected a quarter- to half-meter sea level rise by 2100, more recent projection are in the one to two meter range. J.T. Overpeck & J.L. Weiss, *Projections of Future Sea Level Becoming More Dire*, 106 PROC. NAT'L ACAD. SCI. U.S. AM. 21461 (2009). What factors should cities consider in determining when to defend and when to retreat? Should urban and suburban coastlines be equally defended? Should wealthy and poor residential neighborhoods be equally defended? Should the United States and other wealthy countries help pay for the defense of large cities in poor countries? How, if at all, should the law attempt to address the unfairness that results from people having unequal capacity to defend or adapt?

2. Non-coastal cities will have many concerns other than sea level rise. The adaptation section of the Chicago Climate Action Plan focuses on reducing the urban heat island effect, protecting air quality, managing stormwater, and preserving urban vegetation. *See* CHICAGO CLIMATE ACTION PLAN 39–43 (2008), *available at* http://www.chicagoclimateaction.org/filebin/pdf/finalreport/CCAPREPORTFINALv2.pdf/. What do you think would be the main adaptation concerns for the city of Phoenix, Arizona?

3. Building on its work helping localities reduce emissions, ICLEI established a Climate Resilient Communities program to help localities plan for adaptation. After localities join this program, they follow a five-step process: conduct a climate resiliency study, set preparedness goals, develop a climate preparedness plan, implement the preparedness plan, and monitor resiliency. Even with the kind of assistance that ICLEI offers, why do you think that many localities are reluctant to plan for climate change? If counties and cities have limited resources to spend on climate change policy, how should they allocate these resources between mitigation and adaptation? How could localities reframe adaptation efforts under other policy goals to make adaptation more politically and economically viable?

4. How might local mitigation and adaptation efforts fit together? If a city begins to make plans to address significant impacts that it faces, could that help incentivize it to act to mitigate emissions as well? When could steps to mitigate and adapt be brought together and when might they conflict?

D. TRANSNATIONAL COLLABORATIONS

One of the most fascinating aspects of subnational action on climate change has been the extent to which subnational jurisdictions in different national jurisdictions have communicated and cooperated with each other. These collaborations have ranged from agreements like the Western Climate Initiative, which involves a confined geographic region, to those among cities, states, and provinces around the world made in conjunction with COP negotiations. Such collaborations not only raise national law questions regarding when subnational entities can interact transnationally, but also create challenging issues for state-centric models of international law. This section explores these agreements and their implications for multilevel climate change regulation.

1. REGIONALLY BASED TRANSNATIONAL COLLABORATIONS: THE CALIFORNIA EXAMPLE

California has been a leader in creating regionally based collaborations with other states and provinces, and its efforts therefore provide a useful model for exploring such collaborations. One important example of cross-national collaboration at the state level is the Western Climate Initiative, discussed above. In addition to including both U.S. states and Canadian provinces as partners, several Mexican states have signed on as "observers." Observer jurisdictions do not commit to the program's emissions reduction goals, but they are able to participate in the program's proceedings to facilitate the possibility of joining the program later. RGGI does not have any foreign jurisdictions as partners, but three Canadian provinces participate as observers.

Apart from the WCI, California has forged other state-level collaborations outside of the United States. Most significantly, it has sought to establish relationships with foreign jurisdictions that could serve as a reliable source of carbon offset credits generated from the reduction of deforestation and forest degradation (REDD). Emitters in California would be able to buy the REDD credits in lieu of reducing their in-state emissions, which would help lower the price of allowances in California's cap-and-trade program. Toward this end, California negotiated the following memorandum of understanding (MOU) with the states of Chiapas, Mexico, and Acre, Brazil.

GOVERNOR'S CLIMATE AND FORESTS (GCF) TASK FORCE,
MEMORANDUM OF UNDERSTANDING ON ENVIRONMENTAL COOPERATION
BETWEEN THE STATE OF ACRE OF THE FEDERATIVE REPUBLIC OF BRAZIL,
THE STATE OF CHIAPAS OF THE UNITED MEXICAN STATES, AND
THE STATE OF CALIFORNIA OF THE UNITED STATES OF AMERICA (NOV. 16, 2010)

http://www.gcftaskforce.org/documents/MOU_Acre_California_and_Chiapas.pdf

The State of Acre of the Federative Republic of Brazil, the State of Chiapas of the United Mexican States, and the State of California of the United States of America, hereinafter referred to as "the Parties":

ACKNOWLEDGING the friendship and excellent cooperation among the governments of the Federative Republic of Brazil, the United Mexican States, and the United States of America;

TAKING INTO ACCOUNT the global nature of environmental problems and the ability of joint efforts to enhance joint policies for environmental protection and sustainable natural resources, especially reducing emissions from deforestation;

RATIFYING the willingness to promote new mechanisms of dialogue and agreement that lead to the strengthening of relationships and productive mutual action;

CONSIDERING the opportunities for collaboration between the State of Acre, the State of Chiapas, and the State of California in combating climate change;

RECOGNIZING the importance and value of implementing climate mitigation and adaptation actions at sub-national levels, both in their own right and as a means to furthering national and international efforts;

Recognizing further the importance of focusing on issues of common interest between the Parties, such as reducing greenhouse gas emissions in the forest sector by preserving standing forests and sequestering additional carbon through the restoration and reforestation of degraded lands and forest, and through improved forest management practices;

Recognizing further that the Governors' Climate and Forests (GCF) Task Force is a unique subnational collaboration between 14 states and provinces from the United States, Brazil, Indonesia, Nigeria, and Mexico that seeks to integrate Reducing Emissions from Deforestation and Forest Degradation (REDD) and other forest carbon activities into emerging greenhouse gas (GHG) compliance regimes in the United States and elsewhere. As such, the GCF represents an important foundation for identifying enhanced partnerships.

EXPRESS their willingness to cooperate, in the search of joint actions that improve environmental quality and optimize the quality of life in the State of Acre, the State of Chiapas, and the State of California.

Article 1

This Memorandum of Understanding is intended to promote broader cooperation regarding environmental issues among the Parties within their respective purview and based on principles of reciprocity, information exchange and mutual benefit.

Article 2

The Parties will coordinate efforts and promote collaboration for environmental management, scientific and technical investigation, and capacity building, through cooperative efforts focused particularly on:

a. Reducing greenhouse gas emissions from deforestation and land degradation — otherwise known as "REDD" — and sequestration of additional carbon through the restoration and reforestation of degraded lands and forests, and through improved forest management practices.

b. Developing recommendations together to ensure that forest-sector emissions reductions and sequestrations, from activities undertaken at the sub-national level, will be real, additional, quantifiable, permanent, verifiable and enforceable, and capable of being recognized in compliance mechanisms of each party's state.

Article 3

In furtherance of the priorities referenced in Article 2, the Parties will develop the following method of cooperation, among others:

a. The states will develop a Sub-national REDD Working Group that will convene monthly between December 2010 through October 2011 to begin the process for developing a state to state sectoral REDD linkage recommendation that will provide the foundation for an eventual submittal to the California Air Resources Board, as defined in California's cap and trade program (CCR, Title 17, Sections 95991-95997) and to other necessary state entities to approve such a recommendation amongst the Parties. This group will weigh the legal, technical and economic considerations in developing sector-based credits generated by the Parties. This group should include no more than 15 representatives with experience developing sector-based REDD programs or directly involved with the states supplying the credits, or from the California state government.

The process should be led by a facilitator to ensure the group focuses on meeting the needs of ARB in their existing cap and trade regulations. Membership should be limited to a small number of representatives of each Party, a national representative from the selected states;, a limited number of NGO representatives and expert advisors including one on the social dimension of greenhouse gas mitigation, but no more than 2 project based standard organization representatives, and a facilitator.

b. Other methods developed between the Parties.

Article 4

The Parties will cooperate in the development of a workplan for the REDD Partnership Working Group containing cooperative actions.

The workplan will include all necessary provisions for implementing the cooperation activity agreed upon, including its scope, coordination and administration, resource allocation, expert and professional exchanges, administrative issues, and any other information deemed necessary for achieving the objective of this Memorandum of Understanding.

Independent of the formalization of work plans the Parties agree that collaboration proposals can be presented that allow the parties to optimize outcomes for achieving the objective of this Memorandum of Understanding.

Article 5

In activities of cooperation and information exchanges, if Parties deem it convenient, private and public sectors may be invited to participate, as well as public, academic and research institutions, or any other organization, as long as they can directly contribute to the achievement of the objective of this Memorandum of Understanding. Other states are also encouraged to participate as Observers to working group discussions.

Article 6

The Parties will finance activities referred to in this Memorandum of Understanding with resources allocated in their respective budgets, as these resources become available and as stipulated by their own legislation processes. Each Party will pay for expenses related to its own participation, unless alternative financial mechanisms can be used for specific activities, as appropriate and as approved by their respective appointing authority.

. . . .

Article 10

This Memorandum of Understanding can be modified by mutual consent of the Parties in writing, specifying the date of the entry into force of any such modifications.

Article 11

Termination of this Memorandum of Understanding can be made by any of the Parties, through written communication directed to the other Parties with thirty (30) days advance notice.

Article 12

The Parties acknowledge that this Memorandum of Understanding is only intended to provide for cooperation between the Parties, and does not create any legally binding rights or obligations. To the extent any other provision of this Memorandum of Understanding is inconsistent with this paragraph, this paragraph shall control.

NOTES AND QUESTIONS

1. This agreement was signed at the Third Governors' Global Climate Summit in 2010, and it built on agreements forged at the previous two such summits in 2008 and 2009. In 2008, nine governors from Brazil, Indonesia, and the United States signed an agreement to cooperate on forestry and climate change action and established a Governors' Climate and Forest (GCF) Task Force. *Governor Schwarzenegger Convenes Governors' Global Climate Summit*, Envtl. News Serv. (Nov. 18, 2008), http://www.ens-newswire.com/ens/nov2008/2008-11-18-02.html.

   At the 2009 summit, the GCF Task Force signed a letter addressed to the leaders of the United States, Indonesia, and Brazil calling for international leadership to reduce forestry-related greenhouse gas emissions. Also at the 2009 summit, the governor of California signed an agreement with the governor of China's Jiangsu Province to partner on climate and energy policy, representing China's first-ever subnational agreement to reduce greenhouse gas emissions. Newsroom, United Nations Development Programme, 30 Global Leaders Sign Declaration Before Next Climate Agreement (Oct. 2, 2009), *available at* http://content.undp.org/go/newsroom/2009/october/30-global-leaders-sign-declaration-in-advance-of-next-climate-agreement.en.

   What purposes do subnational events and agreements such as these serve? How important are they to the implementation of initiatives such as California's cap-and-trade program? In what ways might such agreements affect climate change law at larger scales?

2. In Article 12, the MOU states that it does not create any legally binding rights or obligations. Are legally binding rights and obligations necessary for a future agreement that would authorize the creation and transfer of carbon offset credits? Does the state of California have the constitutional authority to enter into an agreement with a foreign subnational jurisdiction that creates legal rights? See the discussion above on foreign affairs preemption. Consider also that the Constitution states that "no State shall enter into any Treaty, Alliance, or Confederation. U.S. Const. art. I, §10, cl. 1."

3. To what extent should California be viewed as a model, or as an anomaly, that few other U.S. states are likely to follow? Other U.S. states, in addition to California, have formed cross-border regional arrangements regarding energy. For example, the Midwestern Regional Transmission Organization

(MISO) provides regional grid management and open access to transmission facilities across all or part of 12 U.S. states and the Canadian province of Manitoba. *See About Us*, MISO, https://www.midwestiso.org/AboutUs/ Pages/AboutUs.aspx.

2. INTERNATIONALLY BASED TRANSNATIONAL COLLABORATIONS

Cities, states, and provinces have forged transnational collaborations on climate change in parallel with the UNFCCC meetings and independently of them. These agreements have no formal international legal status and have very limited integration with the official COP negotiations; these subnational entities are making voluntary pledges, which are not legally enforceable. However, the voluntary quality of these pledges does not diminish their potential impact on mitigation. In many instances, cities, states, and provinces are making more ambitious pledges than some of the UNFCCC nation-state parties and their emissions reductions are substantial in the aggregate.

States and provinces also have been collaborating transnationally on climate change under the auspices of the Governors' Global Climate Summits and the R20—Regions of Climate Action. The Governor's Global Climate Summit 3, held at University of California, Davis, in November 2010, was cohosted by then-California Governor Arnold Schwarzenegger, other subnational leaders, the United Nations Development Programme, and the United Nations Environment Programme. It aimed to create opportunities for mutual learning and partnership development, as well as officially launch R20, a subnational collaboration announced at the 2009 Copenhagen COP. The R20's mission is "To help states, provinces, regions and other subnational governments around the world develop, implement and communicate low-carbon and climate-resilient economic development projects, policies and best practices." *Mission*, R20 REGIONS OF CLIMATE ACTION, http://regions20.org/about-r20/ mission.

With respect to the cities, Local Governments for Sustainability (ICLEI), in partnership with the broader United Cities for Local Government (UCLG), has played a leading role in supporting local action around the world and organizing local efforts at the COP negotiations. Cities have collaborated over a series of COPs in the Local Government Climate Roadmap, initiated as a parallel agreement to the official Bali Roadmap at the 13th Conference of the Parties (COP 13) in Bali. The roadmap process highlights the role that local action plays in mitigation and adaptation actions worldwide while advocating for a strong and comprehensive post-2012 global climate agreement. *See Local Government Climate Roadmap*, ICLEI, http://www.iclei.org/index .php?id=7694.

The roadmap process gained momentum during the 14th Conference of the Parties (COP 14) in Poznan in 2008, and the 15th Conference of the Parties (COP 15) in Copenhagen in 2009 saw the participation of the largest local government delegation ever at a UNFCCC event. In the lead-up to the 16th Conference of the Parties in Cancun, local governments gathered at the World Mayors Summit on Climate (WMSC) 2010. They launched the "Global Cities

Covenant on Climate — the Mexico City Pact," which is excerpted below. As of its first progress report at the Durban COP, the Mexico City Pact had been signed by more than 207 cities and other local governments, including Bogotá, Johannesburg, Los Angeles, Buenos Aires, Rio de Janeiro, Istanbul, and Barcelona.

WORLD MAYORS SUMMIT OF CLIMATE, MEXICO CITY, MEXICO NOV. 21, 2010, GLOBAL CITIES COVENANT ON CLIMATE: "THE MEXICO CITY PACT" (2010)

http://www.wmsc2010.org/the-mexico-city-pact/

Acknowledging that cities play a strategic role in the fight against climate change, because they are centres of economic, political and cultural innovation, host to half of the world population, and manage vast public resources, infrastructure, investments and expertise;

Recalling that between 1992 and 2007, whilst the UNFCCC and its Kyoto Protocol were designed, numerous local governments demonstrated leadership and implemented innovative actions to combat climate change at the local level;

Reminding that as today half of the world's population lives in cities; that the International Energy Agency estimates that cities accounted for 67% of the world's primary energy demand and more than 70% of global CO_2 emissions in 2006. With continued urbanisation and urban growth, energy use in cities is projected to increase to 73% of the global total, and CO_2 emissions to 76%, by 2030;

Noting that since our cities are at increased risk of the devastating consequences of global climate change, particularly affecting the urban poor, many cities around the world, despite limited budgets and capacities, are already developing and implementing local adaptation strategies to address problems caused by climate change, even in the absence of a binding global commitment on adaptation;

Recognizing that since 2007, when national governments embarked on the UN Climate Roadmap, local governments signed the World Mayors and Local Governments Climate Protection Agreement and developed a parallel *Local Government Climate Roadmap* to mirror and influence the on-going work of the Conference of the Parties (COP), with the purpose of seeking recognition for local climate action within global climate governance;

Emphasizing that during COP15 in 2009, when the Copenhagen Accord was announced with national commitments and actions of governments, local governments published the *Copenhagen World Catalogue of Local Climate Commitments*, which identified more than 3,500 voluntary greenhouse gas reduction commitments of local governments in countries of Annex 1 and Non-Annex 1 countries;

Welcoming and seeking synergies with regional initiatives such as the Covenant of Mayors in Europe and the U.S. Conference of Mayors Climate Protection Agreement in the U.S.A;

Inviting more cities, local and regional governments to initiate action or accelerate their climate efforts, both in developed as well as in developing countries;

Acknowledging that our local commitments and actions must be measurable, reportable and verifiable in order to attract recognition and support from existing or new multilateral institutions and funding mechanisms;

Considering that the Intergovernmental Panel on Climate Change (IPCC) has determined that reductions in greenhouse gases emissions must limit the increase of global temperatures to less than 2 degrees Celsius by the end of this century;

Gathering on the eve of COP16, at the World Mayors Summit on Climate, in Mexico City on 21 November 2010, we state the following:

WE, THE MAYORS AND LOCAL AUTHORITY REPRESENTATIVES BY SIGNING THE GLOBAL CITIES COVENANT ON CLIMATE "THE MEXICO CITY PACT", WE COMMIT TO:

1. Reduce our local greenhouse gas emissions voluntarily

We shall promote measures, public policies, laws, plans and campaigns to reduce emissions of greenhouse gases in our cities, taking into account our individual resources and capacities to do so.

2. Adopt and implement local climate mitigation measures designed to achieve our voluntary reduction targets

If we have set targets for reducing GHG emissions, we will adopt and implement measures to achieve them, in areas such as sustainable transportation, proper waste management, energy efficiency, as well as implement low carbon options that help to green our local economies and lifestyles.

3. Develop local adaptation strategies to address the local impact of climate change

We shall design appropriate local adaptation plans and implement climate change adaptation and preparedness measures with operational mechanisms that improve the quality of life of our inhabitants, in particular the urban poor, who are most vulnerable to the harmful impacts of climate change.

4. Register our emission inventories, commitments, climate mitigation and adaptation measures and actions in a measurable, reportable and verifiable (MRV) manner

With a view to launch and follow-up on our commitments, we will enter our climate actions in the **carbonn Cities Climate Registry**. Acknowledging our common but differentiated responsibilities in responding to climate change, we agree to make our actions transparent and provide regular information and data so that our efforts can be measured, reported and verified.

5. Seek the creation of mechanisms that allow direct access to international funding for local climate actions

We will seek the development of mechanisms to directly access financing for our registered mitigation and adaptation actions and in doing so, we will seek the support of various national governments and multilateral funding institutions.

6. Establish a *Global Cities Covenant on Climate* Secretariat

We agree that a Global Cities Covenant on Climate Secretariat will be established to follow-up on actions arising from this instrument and to promote the Global Cities Covenant on Climate with other local and regional authorities. We request the Secretariat to undertake all efforts to facilitate cooperation, exchange and expertise on climate mitigation and adaptation among all signatories of the Global Cities Covenant on Climate.

7. Promote the involvement of civil society in the fight against climate change

We will engage our citizens in our actions to address climate change, and will support proposals from civil society that encourage changes in lifestyles that contribute to our local climate actions.

8. Advocate and seek partnerships with multilateral institutions and national governments on our local climate actions

We agree to cooperate actively with each other to advocate support before multilateral institutions and national governments — within the scope of the UNFCCC process and beyond —, to seek recognition and support for our measurable, reportable and verifiable local climate actions, and to implement subnational, national, regional and multilateral frameworks that are complementary to our climate actions and which may result from multilateral climate negotiations.

9. Promote partnerships and city-to-city cooperation

We agree to seek active partnerships and promote city-to-city cooperation among all signatories of the Global Cities Covenant on Climate, including sharing information and knowledge, capacity building and technology transfer in all areas relevant to climate mitigation and adaptation.

10. Spread the message of the Global Cities Covenant on Climate and, in particular, encourage and invite other leaders of local and sub-national governments to join our climate actions.

NOTES AND QUESTIONS

1. The cities that have signed the Mexico City Pact include rich and poor cities, large and small cities. What do cities share in common that enable them to band together in this way? How might differences among cities in wealth, size, or other characteristics make it difficult to agree on some issues or approaches?
2. Are subnational governments more able to reach agreement than nation-states because their agreements do not bind them in the same way? How do the consequences of noncompliance vary between these transnational

agreements among subnational governments and agreements among nation-states under international law?

3. The carbonn Climate Cities Registry (cCCR) referred to in the Mexico City Pact was established at the same 2010 World Mayors Summit. Registered cities are considered either "Signatory Cities," meaning that they have signed the Mexico City Pact and thereby expressed their willingness to report their commitments, emissions, and mitigation/adaptation actions as soon as possible; or "Pioneer Cities," meaning they have actually commenced reporting their commitments, emissions inventories, and actions through the registry. The goal is to "ensure that local climate action is measurable, reportable and verifiable, and that data are consistent with the standards of the global climate regime." *See* Carbonn Cities Climate Registry, http://citiesclimateregistry.org/ (last visited Apr. 19, 2012). The cCCR 2011 Annual Report released at the Durban COP detailed 107 energy and climate commitments, 90 greenhouse gas inventories, and 555 actions by 51 cities in 19 countries. *See id.* Why are cities interested in building the credibility of local climate actions? Might they hope that the reductions they make will be able to generate carbon offsets that could be purchased by companies or individuals? Also, what difficulties do you expect that cities will encounter in measuring and verifying their emissions reductions? How could being registered with the cCCR assist them?

4. At the 2011 COP 17 meeting in Durban, 114 mayors from 28 countries adopted the Durban Climate Change Adaptation Charter. They pledged to consider adaptation in key local government decisions, undertake local level impact and vulnerability assessments, and prepare long-term local adaptation strategies. Does the collaborative work of cities on climate change indicate the need for a rethinking of the nation-state centered model of international law, or does this action by subnational governments complement international negotiations among nation-states? Should the UNFCCC process be more inclusive of these governments and, if so, how would that work in practical terms? For further exploration of these questions, see Hari M. Osofsky, *Multiscalar Governance and Climate Change: Reflections on the Role of States and Cities at Copenhagen*, 25 Md. J. Int'l L. 64 (2010).

CHAPTER 6

NON-STATE ACTORS AND INITIATIVES: NGOS, CORPORATIONS, AND INDIVIDUALS

Although only governments have the authority to make climate change law, non-state actors play a critical role in its creation, implementation, and ultimate success. The term non-state actor generally refers to entities that are not part of the state or any subunit thereof, such as a province or municipality. Non-governmental organizations (NGOs), corporations, and individuals are key categories of non-state actors that contribute in a variety of ways to the development of climate change law and policy.

A. NON-GOVERNMENTAL ORGANIZATIONS

NGOs are generally private, non-profit, voluntary interest groups. The purposes of NGOs cover the entire range of human interests and may be domestic or international in scope. In this section, the NGOs of most interest are those that seek to influence domestic and international policymakers toward enacting new climate change law. It is worth noting, however, that many business NGOs also have been formed to influence climate change law, often with the aim of preventing or limiting regulation. Business NGOs are primarily discussed along with corporations in Section B, below.

1. INFLUENCE ON UNITED STATES LAW

In the United States, environmental NGOs, including those advocating for climate change policy, serve in a variety of roles. They shape legislation and regulation at federal, state, and local levels; bring litigation in order to enforce and/or develop environmental standards; and raise public awareness. Well-established NGOs in the United States have developed extensive expertise on climate change law and policy, and new single-issue NGOs have also emerged to work on this issue. The following excerpt from a speech by the Executive Director of the Natural Resources Defense Council (NRDC), a leading environmental NGO, describes the history of environmental NGOs' impact in the United States.

Peter Lehner, Environment, Law, and Nonprofits: How NGOs Shape Our Laws, Health, and Communities

26 Pace Envtl. L. Rev. 19, 19–26 (2009)

Now let me turn to the theme for tonight — the role of non-profits, or as they are more commonly known in the rest of the world, non-governmental organizations (NGOs), in shaping environmental law and in shaping our environment. Let me start with a timely observation that the role of NGOs in the environmental sphere, while not unique, is rare and is missing in other areas of U.S. law, perhaps most notably today securities and finance. We do not have organizations representing the public who have been watch-dogging our government's oversight of the financial markets. We don't have organizations that enforce against violators the mandates of insurance law to advance the public good, rather than just their private interests. We don't have people who know the banking system every bit as well as the bankers and the purported regulators, but who are there to speak for the public.

And imagine how different things would be right now if, over the last 25 years, we'd had such voices. Voices who pushed back at what has become an almost religious faith in unregulated markets; voices who asked loudly and persuasively whether some of the claims being made were not factually baseless; voices who were part of the negotiations when rules were being established to ensure there was transparency, fairness, and accountability.

That comparison with the financial world may be the best way I can describe the role environmental NGOs have had. For in the environmental arena, while we have not made all the progress we need to have made and while we have new and daunting challenges, we have not faced a full meltdown yet. We've done an okay job of cleaning up sewage and industrial pollution; we've created parks and other protected areas; cars are cleaner and air quality has improved in many areas; we've developed recycling programs and energy efficiency standards. As I'll mention, we now face the challenge of climate change, and we have far more to do to achieve clean air and water and preserve open space and wild species. But we face these challenges knowing what to do — if we can garner the political will — and with a track record of successes and failures on which to build.

Looking backwards, as we'll do together in a minute, we'll see that NGOs have had a critical role in shaping U.S. environmental laws, both in drafting them, and in transforming the sterile legislative words into meaningful protections, binding judicial precedent, and effective practices. And NGOs fundamentally altered what had been a bilateral, often isolated dialogue between polluter and regulator into a trilateral and often multilateral debate that included those affected in ways other than solely their pocket book. And looking forward, we'll see that NGOs, and the rest of the environmental law community cannot rest on their laurels or rely on only the tried-and-true. We have new challenges that will affect the very foundations of our country, our economy, and indeed our planet. I'll offer a few thoughts on what to do.

[A] critical step in the birth of environmental law occurred only [w]hen the Scenic Hudson Preservation Conference challenged a pump-storage facility on Storm King Mountain[. Before this case], only economic interests could get into court. Yet Scenic Hudson's members had other interests — "aesthetic, conservational, and recreational." In a seminal decision written in 1965 by Judge Oakes, the Second Circuit Court of Appeals held that such interests were sufficient for standing. Environmental litigation was born.

That case had another long-term ramification as well. Many of the lawyers in that case — Wall Street lawyers working largely pro bono — realized that environmental interests could not be protected by the occasional efforts of corporate lawyers; the environment needed full time environmental lawyers, experts in the field, but always representing the public. The lawyers who fought the Scenic Hudson battle — Stephan Duggan, Whitney North Seymour Jr, and David Sive — were some of the founders of NRDC, and at about the same time other environmental NGOs were also formed. So, not just environmental litigation, but environmental litigators were born.

It was in this setting that a group of about fifty people gathered, in 1969, at the Airlie House in Virginia's Shenandoah Mountains. Many of the lawyers who went on to work for NRDC, as well as for the Environmental Defense Fund and the Sierra Club Legal Defense Fund (now EarthJustice), hammered out legal approaches to defend the environment — whether to rely on the public trust, to build from common law, or to bring cases on the Fourteenth Amendment. Notables of the group, like former Vermont Governor Phillip Hoff and California Congressman Pete McCloskey, felt that in the then current political climate, new legislation was necessary and possible.

This was about 1970 and the time of the first Earth Day. Rachel Carson's 1962 Silent Spring had opened the nation's eyes to the impact of toxins. The image of the Cuyahoga River fire burned across Time Magazine. The public demanded action. And Congress, guided in large part by these new public interest environmental lawyers, responded by writing the National Environmental Policy Act, the Clean Air Act, the Clean Water Act, and other anti-pollution laws. Environmental laws, not just wilderness conservation laws. Thus, not just environmental litigation and environmental litigators, but modern environmental legislation was born.

Each of these new pieces of legislation, and the debates that preceded them, were heavily influenced by NGOs pressing for fast action, clear and aggressive targets, health-based mandatory standards rather than cost-based aspirational goals, frequent monitoring and public availability of environmental permits and records. NRDC, for example had a huge role in drafting the 1972 Clean Water Act. NGOs largely shaped the 1990 Clean Air Act. There is a lot to be said about the role of NGOs in the legislative process, but, as others have covered that, let me focus instead on the role of NGOs in bringing the words on paper to life. Let me give just a couple of examples.

In 1971, the Calvert Cliffs Coordinating Committee brought suit under NEPA [National Environmental Policy Act] against the Atomic Energy

Commission. That case converted what was thought of by the agency as a "paper tiger" into a major tool to get better decisions that strengthened the ability of NGOs to influence regulation. The requirement of environmental consideration "to the fullest extent possible" was no longer an escape hatch, but a mandate to set the highest standard for agencies. Tony Roisman, then a staff attorney at NRDC recalls of this era, "Government couldn't write a passable EIS. You could stop almost anything. Injunctions flowed like water from the courts." NEPA thus went from a vague hope to a major negotiating tool, shifting the balance of power between future polluters and the public. (This by the way continues to today — next week NRDC will be arguing a NEPA case in the U.S. Supreme Court.)

In the same year the Citizens to Protect Overton Park challenged the decision of the Federal Department of Transportation to build a freeway through a public park in Memphis. The citizens sued, arguing that the law prohibited DOT from putting the road through the park unless all other options were truly infeasible. The DOT brushed off this feasibility analysis. The Supreme Court reversed the decision of the DOT and said that Congress meant what it said. The Court transformed Section 4(f) of the federal transportation law from mere aspiration to a law with teeth and, as you all know, also established a framework of review to be used in future decisions. This case would only have been brought by an NGO.

The following year, 1972, in the Sierra Club v. Morton challenge to a ski resort in the Sierras, the Supreme Court ruled against the Sierra Club, but in so doing clearly laid out exactly what NGOs needed to do to get into court in the future: prove themselves or their members to be among those who would be injured by the challenged action. In his dissent to the majority opinion, Justice William O. Douglas noted the importance of this voice for the public, "[B]efore these priceless bits of Americana are forever lost . . . , the voice of the existing beneficiaries of these environmental wonders should be heard."

Similarly, when utilities figured out how to get around the regulations of the original Clean Air Act — by building their smokestacks higher, thereby pushing the pollutants higher into the atmosphere and dispersing them but also creating acid rain — NGOs, not EPA, pushed back. In 1974, NRDC sued the Tennessee Valley Authority, the largest violator, and ensured that the goal of the statute — cleaner air — was actually achieved. That win eliminated over one million tons of pollutants, and led to one of the largest sulfur dioxide cleanup programs in United States history.

And when, despite the Clean Air Act's mandate about ambient air quality standards for pollutants contributing to endangerment of public health, and despite ample evidence of the impact of lead on children's health and IQ, EPA did nothing, it was NGOs who gave life to the Act. In 1978 NRDC sued EPA to promulgate a National Ambient Air Quality Standard (NAAQS) for lead and also rules for controlling lead emissions in car exhaust. Thus, it was litigation and relentless pressure by NGOs that finally resulted in the phase-out of lead from gasoline. The result: in 1976 the average level of lead in the typical American was 12.8 micrograms/liter. By 1988 that level dramatically dropped to 2.8. And as NGOs continue to keep lead from other household substances, that level continues to drop.

And consider the Clean Water Act. It requires dischargers to have permits and to monitor their discharges. By comparing the reports to the permits, it is fairly easy to find violations. But polluters weren't used to the law and many did not take it seriously. The governments did not take it seriously either. So NGOs used the citizen suit provision to enforce the law against violators. River-keeper, often represented by the Pace Environmental Litigation Clinic, brought hundreds of cases to clean up this region. At one point, NRDC alone had more Clean Water Act enforcement cases than all of the Department of Justice. And look at the case law — it's almost all in cases brought by NGOs.

All these efforts required attributes that only the environmental NGOs possessed. They required a level of expertise in the science, the law — both the legislation and its regulations, and the reality of what was happening on the ground. This level of expertise is very hard for individuals, usually with other jobs or occupations, to obtain. These cases also require a dedication to the public interest, not to short-term political expedience, administrative turf, or corporate profits. And they required constant vigilance.

These NGOs were critical not just at the first decade of environmental law, but throughout our recent history. Take a story from the last forty-eight hours in Congress before passing the 1990 Clean Air Act amendments. Three NRDC lawyers knew the statute inside and out, and were keeping a close eye on the negotiated drafts. It was ten o'clock on a Friday night when the other side dropped what they called "technical amendments." At first glance it seemed to be highly-detailed, inconsequential editorial corrections. But David Hawkins, our Director of Air and Energy read it again. He caught a semi-colon inserted into a paragraph of 45 words. That semi-colon changed the entire meaning of the paragraph, expanding the eligibility for power plants to delay compliance. He called Congressional allies and they put that semi-colon in its grave. Imagine the level of expertise it takes to remove a semi-colon at 10pm on a Friday night.

Here's another example. In the 2007 Energy Act, there is a provision that will require lighting to be 25% more efficient by 2012 and 75% more efficient by 2020, effectively banning inefficient incandescent bulbs. This will save consumers billions of dollars and eliminate millions of tons of carbon dioxide pollution. It was also negotiated by NRDC and industry, and then was adopted almost verbatim by Congress. This followed a long-line of similar energy efficiency laws dating back to the 1970s negotiated by NGOs and industry and adopted by Congress.

And the work of environmental NGOs continues to the present. In the last eight years, for example, the Bush Administration has waged an unprecedented war on the environment. This is a non-partisan statement; this is simple fact. Environmental NGOs, very often NRDC and EarthJustice, but others as well, sometimes accompanied by other entities such as states, have had repeatedly to sue EPA and other federal agencies to overturn efforts to promulgate new regulations weakening the Clean Air Act, the Clean Water Act, the Endangered Species Act, and a host of other statutes. I've been personally involved on many of these challenges so it's tempting to go into them in more detail, but I'll spare you. Suffice it to say that, despite the deference usually paid to EPA in such cases (more on that later), we usually won. And as a direct result, millions of people will breathe cleaner air, enjoy healthier water, and have opportunities to be refreshed by real wild places.

This role of environmental NGOs is crucial and must continue in the future. The 2008 Climate Security Act that would cap CO_2 pollution and require emitters to purchase allowances for their CO_2 emissions, for example, was heavily influenced by NRDC as well as other NGOs. Without the NGOs, the bill would have looked very, very different, if existed at all. The cap would be higher, there would be fewer interim caps, there would be more allowances given away for free to polluters, fewer incentives for energy efficiency or clean energy. It's not just that NGOs represented the public interest, but that they had the scientific, technical, legal and political expertise to make their voice persuasive. The bill did not pass Congress, but it will soon — a carbon cap must become law very soon or we are all in deep trouble — and when it does, it will show the role and importance of environmental NGOs.

The same is true at the state level. The RGGI, the Regional Greenhouse Gas Initiative, recently created the first CO_2 auction in the U.S. It just announced that it brought in $38.6 million in revenue. Not bad for the first week. The RGGI also was heavily influenced by NGOs. And on the other side of the country, Governor Schwarz[e]negger just signed a law actually sponsored by NRDC and another NGO — that sort of thing can happen in California — establishing incentives for alternative transportation, green buildings and Smart Growth.

And the same important role of environmental NGOs can be seen at this local level as well. Hundreds of smaller local NGOs, often using legal tools created and refined by the larger national NGOs, have worked to clean up thousands of local streams or protects parks and forests. These local NGOs, while independent of the larger national ones I'm discussing, often followed the model and cultural trend set by larger groups. (And the larger NGOs, of course, benefit from the local knowledge and enthusiasm of the smaller groups.)

Climate change has been a harder issue to rally the public around than other important environmental issues, perhaps in part because climate change and human health are linked in a complex chain of causation over a substantial period of time. People easily understand that breathing polluted air can harm the lungs or that swimming in polluted water can cause skin rashes. In contrast, they often do not appreciate how many aspects of human health and well-being depend on a predictable climate. Also, people may not clearly see the link between climate change and environmental degradation. It is easier to understand the harms of deforestation or overfishing.

Moreover, climate-concerned NGOs have sometimes been divided on how to respond to the climate threat. Many environmental NGOs have traditionally opposed nuclear energy, an energy source viewed by others as climate-friendly. NGOs concerned with landscape aesthetics or wildlife may contest the siting of solar or wind energy facilities. With respect to regulatory policy, NGOs vary in the extent to which they are supportive of market-based regulations such as cap-and-trade programs or emissions taxes.

In the 2000s, litigation has been the advocacy approach through which U.S. environmental NGOs have had the most success thus far in advancing climate change law. U.S. environmental law has a history dating to the 1970s of allowing citizens to sue governmental agencies and/or private interests believed to be violating the law. Also, the Administrative Procedure Act (APA) of 1946 authorizes citizens to challenge judicial review of agency actions as being "arbitrary, capricious, an abuse of discretion, or otherwise not in accordance with law."

In the face of inadequate federal action on climate change in the 2000s, American environmentalists took the climate issue to court. The next reading contains the profiles of the 17 NGOs that petitioned the EPA in 1999 to regulate greenhouse gas emission from new motor vehicles. This petition ultimately led to the Supreme Court's landmark climate change decision in 2007, *Massachusetts v. EPA*, which is discussed in depth in Chapter Three.

INTERNATIONAL CENTER FOR TECHNICAL ASSESSMENT, PETITION FOR RULEMAKING AND COLLATERAL RELIEF SEEKING THE REGULATION OF GREENHOUSE GAS EMISSIONS FROM NEW MOTOR VEHICLES UNDER §202 OF THE CLEAN AIR ACT (1999)

http://209.200.74.155/doc/ghgpet2.pdf

Pursuant to the Right to Petition Government Clause contained in the First Amendment of the United States Constitution, the Administrative Procedure Act, the Clean Air Act, and the Environmental Protection Agency (EPA) implementing regulations, petitioners file this Petition for Rulemaking and Collateral Relief with the Administrator [of the Environmental Protection Agency] and respectfully requests her to undertake the following mandatory duties:

(1) Regulate the emissions of carbon dioxide (CO2) from new motor vehicles and new motor vehicle engines under §202(a)(1) of the Clean Air Act;

(2) Regulate the emissions of methane (CH4) from new motor vehicles and new motor vehicle engines under §202(a)(1) of the Clean Air Act;

(3) Regulate the emissions of nitrous oxide (N20) from new motor vehicles and new motor vehicle engines under §202(a)(1) of the Clean Air Act;

(4) Regulate the emissions of hydrofluorocarbons (HFCs) from new motor vehicles and new motor vehicle engines under §202(a)(1) of the Clean Air Act;

Petitioners

Petitioner *International Center for Technology Assessment* (CTA) . . . Formed in 1994, CTA seeks to assist the public and policy makers in better understanding how technology affects society. CTA is a non-profit organization devoted to analyzing the economic, environmental, ethical, political and social impacts that can result from the application of technology or technological systems.

Petitioner *Alliance for Sustainable Communities* . . . The Alliance was formed five years ago in order to bring together representatives of government at all levels, citizens and innovators to develop projects which express the primary relationship between people and the earth.

Petitioner *Applied Power Technologies, Inc.* (APT) . . . APT is a research & development concern bringing new energy conversion systems to the air-conditioning industry on behalf of the natural gas industry. APT will advent the deregulation and decentralization of power production by producing nearly pollution-free air-conditioning, refrigeration and related appliances which will convert clean natural gas into electric offsetting heat energy on-site of actual end usage.

Petitioner *Bio Fuels America* . . . Bio Fuels America is a not for profit, self funded, advocacy group that promotes renewable energies such as wind, sun and biomass.

Petitioner *The California Solar Energy Industries Association* (CAL SEIA) . . . CAL SEIA is a solar industry trade association with 70 member companies who do business in California. CAL SEIA's members include manufacturers of both solar thermal and photovoltaic technologies, as well as distributors, contractors, architects, engineers and utilities.

Petitioner *Clements Environmental Corporation* . . . Clements Environmental Corp. is a small environmental engineering firm specializing in the conversion of Municipal Solid Waste and other waste organics to biofuels and biochemicals.

Petitioner *The Earth Day Network* . . . The Earth Day Network [EDN] is a global alliance of environmental organizations. Under the banner "Clean Energy Now!", EDN is promoting a dramatic increase in energy efficiency and a rapid transition to renewable energy and away from reliance on coal and oil. The organization intends to use Earth Day 2000 to marshal 500 million people around the world to support policies that improve the environment and reverse global warming.

Petitioner *Environmental Advocates* . . . Environmental Advocates serves the people of New York as an effective and aggressive watchdog and advocate on virtually every important state environmental issue. Through advocacy, coalition building, citizen education and policy development, we work to safeguard public health and preserve our unique natural heritage. With thousands of individual supporters and over 130 organizational members, Environmental Advocates is truly the voice of New York's environmental community.

Petitioner *Environmental and Energy Study Institute* (EESI) . . . EESI is a non-profit organization founded in 1982 by a bipartisan group of Members of Congress. EESI promotes public policy that sustains people, the environment and our natural resources. EESI's wide-ranging audience includes Congress and other national policymakers, as well as state and local officials, industry leaders, the public interest community, the media, and the general public. EESI draws together timely information, innovative public policy proposals, policymakers, and stakeholders to seek solutions to environmental and energy problems.

Petitioner *Friends of the Earth* . . . Friends of the Earth is a national environmental organization dedicated to preserving the health and diversity of the planet for future generations. As the largest international environmental network in the world with affiliates in 63 countries, Friends of the Earth empowers citizens to have an influential voice in decisions affecting their environment.

Petitioner *Full Circle Energy Project, Inc.* . . . Full Circle Energy Project, Inc. is a non-profit organization founded to enable environmentally sensible and sustainable energy resources to supply at least 50% of the total energy used in the United States. Its primary focus is on reducing the amount of fossil fuels used by the transportation sector.

Petitioner *The Green Party of Rhode Island* . . . The Green Party of RI is a part of the international Green Party movement. In Rhode Island it has run candidates for a variety of offices, always focusing on environmental issues as well as justice, non violence, and democracy issues.

Petitioner *Greenpeace USA* . . . Greenpeace is one of the world's major environmental organizations with offices in 33 countries, including the United States of America, and over 3 million donating supporters worldwide. Greenpeace is a non-profit organization devoted to the protection of the environment with an emphasis on global environmental problems such as climate change and protection of the stratospheric ozone layer, prevention of nuclear, chemical and biological pollution, and defense of biodiversity.

Petitioner *National Environmental Trust* (NET) . . . NET was established in 1994 to help move specific environmental issues, ripe for action, into the public spotlight. Through use of opinion research, media relations, a grassroots network and government relations, NET has helped to advance policies which protect the environment in each of its campaign areas: global warming, clean air, forests protection and children's environmental health.

Petitioner *Network for Environmental and Economic Responsibility of the United Church of Christ [UCC]* . . . The Network for Environmental and Economic Responsibility (NEER) is a grassroots, volunteer movement committed to mobilizing UCC persons, networks and resources for a holistic ministry of learning, reflection, and action cognizant of the earth and its creatures. Network members believe that all living things on our planet are interdependent in a vast web of life.

Petitioner *New Jersey Environmental Watch* . . . New Jersey Environmental Watch is a church based organization in New Jersey that seeks better air in their area and elsewhere. Recently, it recorded 40 percent of our Sunday School children had been hospitalized for asthma. It is also in cancer alley and have greatly elevated cancer rates. The 14-lane New Jersey Turnpike passes through Elizabeth, NJ the bottom 40 percent of the Newark Airport is located there as well, and Elizabeth is immediately downwind of the huge Bayway Tosco refinery in Linden.

Petitioner *New Mexico Solar Energy Association* (NMSEA) . . . NMSEA is an all volunteer organization working to further solar and related arts, sciences, and technologies with concern for the ecologic, social and economic fabric of the region. It serves to inform public, institutional and government bodies and seeks to raise the level of public awareness of these purposes.

Petitioner *Public Citizen* . . . Public Citizen, founded by Ralph Nader in 1971, is a non-profit research, lobbying, and litigation organization based in Washington, DC. Public Citizen advocates for consumer protection and for government and corporate accountability, and is supported by over 150,000 members throughout the United States.

Petitioner *Solar Energy Industries Association* (SEIA) . . . The Solar Energy industries Association (SEIA), founded in 1974, is the U.S. industry organization composed of over 150 solar-electric and solar thermal manufacturers, component suppliers, national distibutors [*sic*] and project developers, and an additional 400 companies in the SEIA—affiliated state and regional chapters covering 35 states.

Petitioner *The SUN DAY Campaign* . . . The SUN DAY Campaign is a nonprofit network of 850+ businesses and organizations founded in 1991 to promote increased use of renewable energy and energy efficient technologies. Areas of work include research on sustainable energy technologies, electric utility restructuring, climate change, and the federal energy budget. Projects include publication of a weekly newsletter, an annual series of directories of sustainable energy organizations, and other studies.

NOTES AND QUESTIONS

1. Do you agree with Lehner's positive assessment of the contribution of NGOs to environmental law? Not all commentators celebrate the environmental litigation filed by NGOs. For example, at the other end of the spectrum, American Enterprise Institute scholar Michael Greve characterizes environmental NGOs as "bounty hunters" that are motivated to litigate by private economic reward rather than public benefit. Michael S. Greve, *The Private Enforcement of Environmental Law*, 65 TUL. L. REV. 339 (1990). What role do you think NGOs should play in the development of climate change law?

2. Another criticism of U.S. environmental NGOs is that they are not sufficiently diverse or focused on concerns of low-income communities of color. The environmental justice movement, which emerged in the United States in the 1990s to address the disproportionate distribution of environmental harms and benefits, lagged behind both the environmental and civil rights movements in this country. For an exploration of ongoing diversity concerns, see Faith R. Rivers, *Bridging the Black-Green-White Divide: The Impact of Diversity in Environmental Nonprofit Organizations*, 33 WM. & MARY ENVTL. L. & POL'Y REV. 449 (2009). Given the environmental justice concerns that arise both domestically and internationally in the context of climate change, how should U.S. NGOs work to address diversity concerns in their composition and agendas?

3. Note the many differences among the NGOs that jointly filed the U.S. EPA petition. A few are very large national NGOs; others appear to be small and operate in only one state. A few are traditionally environmentally focused and many are business NGOs advocating on behalf of alternative

energy companies. The list of petitioners also includes a public policy think tank, a political party, and a religious group. How do you think these petitioners came together to collaborate on this petition?

As discussed in depth in Chapter Three, NGOs have initiated many other legal cases relating to climate change with a wide variety of legal theories. The Center for Climate Law at Columbia University has assembled an exhaustive U.S. Climate Change Litigation Chart, *available at* http://www.climatecasechart.com. In addition to cases under the Clean Air Act, U.S. environmental groups have filed lawsuits to force the federal government to take action on climate change under the Endangered Species Act, Marine Mammal Protection Act, Clean Water Act, Global Change Research Act, Freedom of Information Act, Alternative Motor Fuels Act, and Energy Policy Act. *See, e.g.,* Natural Res. Def. Council v. Kempthorne, 2009 U.S. Dist. LEXIS 78424 (E.D. Cal. 2009); Ctr. for Biological Diversity v. Brennan, 571 F. Supp. 2d 1105 (N.D. Cal. 2007); Ctr. for Biological Diversity v. Office of Mgmt. & Budget, 546 F. Supp. 2d 722 (N.D. Cal. 2008).

NGOs also have initiated many lawsuits to ensure compliance with the National Environmental Policy Act, *see, e.g.,* Center for Biological Diversity v. National Highway Safety Administration, 538 F.3d 1172 (9th Cir. 2008), Friends of the Earth v. Mosbacher, 488 F.Supp.2d 889 (N.D. Cal. 2007), and to prevent the government from authorizing new coal-fired power plants, *see, e.g.,* Sierra Club v. Johnson, 541 F.3d 1257 (11th Cir. 2008); Appalachian Voices v. Chu, 262 F.R.D. 24 (D.D.C. 2009). Finally, in key public nuisance cases filed by state attorney generals such as *California v. GM* and *AEP v. Connecticut*, NGOs have worked behind the scenes to help do research and develop legal theories. *See* Kal Raustiala & Natalie Bridgeman, Nonstate Actors in the Global Climate Regime (2007) (Unpublished research paper, UCLA School of Law) (on file with authors). Aside from litigation, NGOs have played very important roles in policy research, public education, and information dissemination. Professor Daniel Esty finds that NGOs act as "intellectual competitors in the policymaking domain" by offering "alternative data or information, competing analyses, and new policy options." *See* Daniel C. Esty, *Toward Optimal Environmental Governance*, 74 N.Y.U. L. Rev. 1495, 1561 (1999). Esty also observes that NGOs are often more adept at disseminating important information about environmental problems and policy decisions than government. *See id.*

4. Environmental NGOs have played an important role in countries around the world. While a full analysis of their role is beyond the scope of this book, this note suggests a couple examples of the scholarly literature on environmental NGOs operating in other countries. For discussion of access to courts by environmental NGOs in the EU context, see Bilun Müller, *Access to the Courts of the Member States for NGOs in Environmental Matters under European Union Law: Judgment of the Court of 12 May 2011 — Case C-115/09 Trianel and Judgment of 8 March 2011 — Case C-240/09 Lesoochranarske Zoskupenie*, 23 J. Envtl. L. 505 (2011). For an article about the role of environmental NGOs in the Botswanan context, see Zein Kebonang & Kabelo Kenneth Lebotse, *Reflections on the Legislative Environment for Nongovernmental Organizations in Botswana*, 12 Int'l J. Not-for-Profit L. 54 (2010).

2. INFLUENCE ON INTERNATIONAL LAW

NGOs emerged as a force at the Earth Summit in 1992 in Rio de Janeiro, where the United Nations Framework Convention on Climate Change was signed. Nearly 1,500 NGOs were accredited to attend meetings, lobby governmental representatives, present documents, and meet among themselves. *See* Chiara Giorgetti, *Organizational Summary: The Role of Nongovernmental Organizations in the Climate Change Negotiations*, 9 Colo. J. Int'l Envtl. L. & Pol'y 115, 125 (1998). Professor Kal Raustiala observes: "As has long been the case in domestic [U.S.] environmental law, NGOs are now major actors in the formulation, implementation, and enforcement of international environmental law." Kal Raustiala, *The Participatory Revolution in International Environmental Law*, 21 Harv. Envtl. L. Rev. 537, 538 (1997).

In the excerpt below, which predates the Kyoto Protocol coming into force, Professor Raustiala categorizes NGO contributions to global climate change policy. He describes five roles that they play.

Kal Raustiala, Nonstate Actors in the Global Climate Regime, in International Relations and Global Climate Change 95, 95–117 (Urs Luterbacher & Detlef F. Sprinz eds., 2001)

---

http://graduateinstitute.ch/webdav/site/admininst/shared/iheid/800/luterbacher/
luterbacher%20chapter%205%20105.pdf

NGOs [Non-Governmental Organizations] activities directly relating to global climate policy and the FCCC [Framework Convention on Climate Change] process can be divided into five basic categories:

- Helping to set the international agenda and raise awareness of environmental challenges
- Providing policy advice and information
- Influencing the process of international negotiation through political pressure
- Monitoring governmental actions
- Assisting in the process of implementation

Setting the Agenda

[Environmental] NGOs have been great popularizers of environmental problems, and as such have focused—in conjunction with the news media and with scientific epistemic communities—significant public and government attention on climate change. They have often been the conduit between climatologists and the public, providing (at times oversimplified) distillations of the latest research and stimulating political action. In doing so they have kept the issue of climate change alive as one of the important problems governments must address, or at least appear to address. In the words of one former U.S. official, describing the NGO-organized Villach and Bellagio meetings that helped initiate the international climate change policy process that led to the FCCC: "The two workshops, the meetings of the Advisory Group on Greenhouse Gases and other activities . . . indeed played a significant catalytic role in establishing the IPCC [Intergovernmental Panel on Climate Change] . . . . Governments could no longer permit . . . NGOs to drive the agenda on the emerging climate issue." While NGOs vary widely in their approach to agenda setting, their public activities help frame issues politically and motivate political action. Greenpeace is often the most flamboyant. The day before COP-1 [the first conference of the parties to the FCCC] began, for example, three Greenpeace activists occupied a coal plant chimney near Cologne to focus attention on the source of a chief greenhouse gas, CO_2. At the opposite end of the spectrum are relatively dry and technical conferences and presentations held, often at the negotiations themselves, on various alternative energy sources and policy issues. The more private lobbying efforts of NGOs, which also vary substantially, can influence governmental assessments of the "climate change problem" and hence negotiating calendars and topics.

Providing Policy Recommendations

Climate change is a complex multidimensional problem that challenges governments to develop flexible, effective, and efficient policy responses. The nature of the problem, its depth and severity, the potential costs, and the potential impact of various solutions are all subject to great uncertainty. NGOs, to varying degrees, have devoted attention to these and other issues and often seek to develop and promote particular substantive assessments and practical policy measures. For governments that lack resources and expertise in this area, especially of the smaller, less developed states, NGOs in the aggregate may provide useful information that is relatively "costless." NGOs engage in and fund scientific research; NGOs in the United States have been particularly active in this regard. NGOs may serve as a "voice for the voiceless," or for those with limited political power, and thereby seek, in their own view, to provide both a human face and a concern for justice to the often technocratic and abstract process of regulation. Just as frequently, however, they are voices for the powerful.

In practice, as noted above, NGOs have made use of the access they have received to provide government delegations with policy analyses and recommendations, as well as critiques of proposed policies. These have come from both environmental and business NGOs. Since the FCCC has come into force meetings have proliferated, and NGO participation, both formal and informal, has become fairly regularized. For example, meetings of the Ad Hoc Group on the Berlin Mandate (AGBM), which negotiated the Kyoto Protocol, nearly always included at least one formal NGO intervention. These interventions typically addressed specific issues under negotiation and offered suggestions as well as critiques. . . .

     . . . .

Members of NGOs have also appeared on several government delegations and have acted as consultants for governments. One of the most prominent examples is the relation between the London-based Foundation of International Environmental Law and Development (FIELD) and the Alliance of Small Island States (AOSIS). Members of FIELD, mostly international lawyers, consulted extensively with members of AOSIS, appeared on their delegations, and at times acted as the delegation of certain AOSIS members. The tiny member governments of AOSIS, often lacking much indigenous expertise about climate change and the policy possibilities, became a more powerful negotiating force in conjunction with FIELD. Business NGOs have also played this role — for example, members of the U.S.-based Global Climate Coalition have been present on U.S. delegations to FCCC meetings.

Political Pressure

NGOs can apply political pressure both directly and internationally — at negotiations themselves — as well as indirectly and domestically through national-level lobbying and media action. The ultimate impact of direct pressure at negotiations is debatable. While many participants in international environmental negotiations emphasize the social pressures and atmosphere of negotiations, and NGOs can influence that atmosphere, ardor often cools. In the end, the efficacy of international accords rests on their ratification, implementation, and subsequent interpretation — actions relatively immune to the specific social climate of the negotiation process. National-level pressure has a firmer base in domestic politics. Particularly in the developed democracies, NGOs can be powerful organizations with a large and politically active membership. While climate change is currently low on the political radar in many states, in some industrialized democracies issues retain political salience. If the underlying problem is itself not politically salient, possible solutions including: gasoline taxes, mass transit subsidies, and the like, are controversial issues in nearly every industrial economy. These proposed solutions become domestic political issues on which NGOs often weigh in. Since international responses are the collective result of many national decisions, this indirect pathway of influence can be significant.

Indeed, the political power of environmental NGOs and the access they have gained in the climate negotiations has stimulated the activities of business NGOs to the point that the majority of observers at recent meetings are those representing business interests. In short, the international response to climate change has taken place in a politicized atmosphere, with many divergent interests represented. NGOs are important domestic actors that governments listen to in addition to, and regardless of, the "useful" roles enumerated above and below.

Monitoring Government Actions

Like most international environmental agreements, the FCCC uses a reporting process in which governments self-report on their actions with limited collective oversight. Other governments, therefore, have few means by which they can assess their counterparts' actions in a formal and transparent way. NGOs have helped "multilateralize" information about national actions by preparing analyses of what governments have claimed to do, what they have actually done, and what is likely in the future. For example, the Climate Action Network, a consortium of many environmental NGOs, has prepared comprehensive reports of climate pledges and actions, and has made them readily available to governments, private interests, and the media. While "enforcement" is too strong a word for this role, and often too much is made of NGO monitoring activity, through these and similar efforts NGOs have the potential to aid in achieving compliance with and implementation of the FCCC.

Implementation Activities

International agreements generally must be put into practice if they are to be effective. The implementation of accords and the resulting policy feedback is a central part of the politics of environmental cooperation. NGOs have, in other issue areas, played important roles in the implementation of environmental commitments. For the Convention on International Trade in Endangered Species (CITES), for example, NGOs have both been granted "bureau duties" (essentially running the CITES secretariat) and have played critical roles in CITES' monitoring and enforcement apparatus. Often, however, NGOs fail to sustain the same level of interest in regime implementation that they do in regime negotiation.

The FCCC did not contain clear programmatic or emissions commitments, beyond national reporting requirements and a vague emissions reduction pledge for industrialized states, until the negotiation of the Kyoto Protocol in 1997. The Kyoto Protocol, should it enter into force, will greatly expand the range of implementable obligations. The implementation of the Kyoto Protocol will depend heavily on the evolution of emissions trading, joint implementation programs, and the Clean Development Mechanism. As these mechanisms develop, NGOs may have greater opportunities to influence the implementation of the FCCC.

NOTES AND QUESTIONS

1. Non-state actors lack legal personality in classic approaches to international law. However, they have been able to participate in the development of the international climate treaties through their status as "observers." The admission of observers is governed by Article 7.6 of the UNFCCC:

   Any body or agency, whether national or international, governmental or non governmental, which is qualified in matters covered by the Convention, and which has informed the secretariat of its wish to be represented at a session of the Conference of the Parties as an observer, may be so admitted unless at least one third of the Parties present object.

   UNFCCC accreditation is a continuous process, and to date about 1,300 NGOs have been admitted as observers. The NGOs include representatives from business and industry, environmental groups, farming and agriculture, indigenous populations, local governments and municipal authorities, research and academic institutes, labor unions, women's groups, and youth groups.

   See Parties & Observers, United Nations Framework Convention on Climate Change, http://unfccc.int/parties_and_observers/items/2704.php (last visited Apr. 20, 2012).

The UNFCCC's procedural rules set forth how observers may participate. Rule 7(2) provides that "observers may, upon invitation of the President [of the Conference of the Parties], participate without the right to vote in the proceedings of any session in matters of direct concern to the body or agency they represent, unless at least one third of the Parties present at the session object." Draft Rules of Procedure of the COP and Its Subsidiary Bodies, rule 7(2), U.N.F.C.C.C. Conference of the Parties, 2d Sess., U.N. Doc. FCCC/CP/1996/2 (May 22, 1996), *available at* http://unfccc.int/resource/docs/cop2/02.pdf. Under Rule 30, COP meetings are ordinarily open to observers. *Id.* at Rule 30. How do you think the UNFCCC Parties—the sovereign states that are trying to negotiate the international agreement—perceive and deal with the participation of NGOs? How does NGO participation in treaty negotiations raise issues of accountability and legitimacy?

2. For a historical discussion of NGO access to international environmental treaty meetings, see Kal Raustiala, *The Participatory Revolution: in International Environmental Law*, 21 HARV. ENVTL. L. REV. 537, 543–52 (1997). Other important works focusing on NGO participation in international climate change law include Chiara Giorgetti, *The Role of Nongovernmental Organizations in the Climate Change Negotiations*, 9 COLO. J. INT'L ENVTL. L. & POL'Y 115 (1998); Chiara Giorgetti, *From Rio to Kyoto: A Study of the Involvement of Non-Governmental Organizations in the Negotiations on Climate Change*, 7 N.Y.U. ENVTL. L.J. 201 (1999); THOMAS PRINCEN & MATTHIAS FINGER, ENVIRONMENTAL NGOS IN WORLD POLITICS: LINKING THE LOCAL AND THE GLOBAL (1994); and MICHELE M. BETSILL & ELISABETH CORELL, NGO DIPLOMACY: THE INFLUENCE OF NONGOVERNMENTAL ORGANIZATIONS IN INTERNATIONAL ENVIRONMENTAL NEGOTIATIONS (2008). For a broader discussion of NGOs and international law, see Steve Charnovitz, *Nongovernmental Organizations and International Law*, 100 AM. J. INT'L L. 348 (2006).

3. NGOS AND THE DEVELOPMENT OF THE KYOTO PROTOCOL

The role of environmental NGOs has been particularly apparent in recent international climate change negotiations under the UNFCCC. In perhaps the most important example, NGOs significantly influenced the development of the Kyoto Protocol, which, as discussed in depth in Chapter Two, is the only climate change agreement with binding targets and timetables. In the reading that follows, Professor Michele Betsill analyzes how NGOs participated in the negotiation of the Kyoto Protocol and the influence they had on treaty outcomes.

MICHELE BETSILL, ENVIRONMENTAL NGOS AND THE KYOTO PROTOCOL
NEGOTIATIONS: 1995 TO 1997, IN NGO DIPLOMACY:
THE INFLUENCE OF NONGOVERNMENTAL ORGANIZATIONS
IN INTERNATIONAL ENVIRONMENTAL NEGOTIATIONS

46–64, Michele M. Betsill & Elisabeth Corell eds., 2008

ENGOs [Environmental NGOs] were extremely active participants in the Kyoto Protocol negotiations. More than forty organizations sent representatives to at least two of the negotiating sessions, with the largest delegations coming from Greenpeace, Friends of the Earth, and the World Wide Fund for Nature. The environmental community was dominated by northern NGOs. Only one-fourth of the ENGOs came from the South, and these organizations typically sent only one or two representatives to the negotiations. The climate change secretariat provided some funds (raised from individual countries) for NGO participation; however, the funds were often insufficient.

ENGOs coordinated their participation in the Kyoto Protocol negotiations under the umbrella of the Climate Action Network (CAN). CAN was formed in 1989 for environmental organizations interested in the problem of climate change and today has more than 280 members [note from editors: CAN had more than 700 members by 2011]. CAN is a loose organization divided into eight regions, each with its own coordinator: Africa, Australia, Central and Eastern Europe, Europe/United Kingdom, Latin America, South Asia, Southeast Asia, and the United States/Canada. CAN served as the voice of the environmental community during the Kyoto Protocol negotiations. Members met daily during each negotiating session, and these meetings were an important forum for sharing information, debating issues, and coordinating lobbying efforts. In between negotiating sessions, some CAN members met regularly with other members in their respective regions (e.g., Europe) to devise strategies for lobbying particular governments.

During the period 1995 to 1997 CAN had four objectives. First, CAN argued that the Protocol should include commitments for industrialized countries to reduce their GHG emissions 20 percent below 1990 levels by 2005. Second, they argued for strong review and compliance mechanisms to enhance the implementation of the commitments contained in the Protocol. Third, ENGOs objected to proposals to allow industrialized Parties to meet their commitments through emissions trading. Finally, CAN also opposed the idea of permitting Parties to get credit for emissions absorbed by sinks. The latter two objectives reflected CAN's position that industrialized states should achieve the majority of their emissions reductions through domestic policy changes. Throughout the negotiations CAN members framed the problem of climate change as an environmental crisis requiring immediate action.

CAN members employed a variety of strategies for promoting their position during the negotiations. Perhaps their most visible activity was the publication of a daily newsletter, *ECO*, at each of the negotiating sessions. *ECO*, which was widely read by all participants to the negotiations, served two purposes. First, it was a useful way for delegates to keep up with the day-to-day progress of the talks. Second, and most important in terms of exerting influence, CAN used *ECO* as a political forum for promoting their positions on a variety of issues, to discredit arguments put forth by opponents of emissions reductions (e.g., the oil producing states and the fossil-fuel industry and to put pressure on delegations to take aggressive measures to mitigate global climate change). Each issue contained a "fossil of the day" award given to the country that had most obstructed the negotiations the previous day. In addition CAN members used the pages of *ECO* to highlight their framing of climate change as an environmental crisis, regularly pointing to potential impacts such as more intense heat waves in Shanghai, stress to the Rocky Mountain ecosystem in the United States, damage to the Polish economy from more frequent floods, and significant declines in agricultural productivity in Africa and Asia.

CAN members also provided technical information to delegates. They publicized the potentially devastating impacts of climate change and conducted research on other scientific issues, such as the capacity of forests to serve as sinks. In addition several ENGOs produced their own cost-benefit analyses of various mitigation strategies and critiqued analyses produced by other organizations, highlighting how different assumptions lead to different predictions. During formal negotiating sessions, ENGOs held a variety of "side events" on technical issues related to the negotiations, although it should be noted that these events primarily attracted other NGOs and journalists rather than state delegates. CAN members devoted considerable time to evaluating proposals and identifying potential loopholes in the draft negotiating texts. As the negotiations progressed, such specialized knowledge was in demand by delegates who had to choose among policy options. It is important to note, however, that ENGOs did not have a monopoly on this type of knowledge and information during this period. Members of the scientific and business communities were also providing information on the physical impacts of climate change and the potential economic effects of various mitigation and adaptation options. These actors often provided contradictory information making it difficult for policy makers to uncover the "truth."

ENGOs had limited access to delegates during the negotiations, much more so than had been the case during the UNFCCC negotiations. This reportedly stemmed from an incident at a negotiating session prior to COP-1 where UN officials accused a prominent fossil-fuel lobbyist of orchestrating the floor debate by sending notes to OPEC delegates. As a result NGOs were denied access to the floor during plenary sessions, and by the sixth negotiating session, delegates met primarily in closed-door, "nongroup" sessions from which NGOs were excluded altogether. Formally, NGOs were kept up-to-date through daily briefings with the Chair of the negotiations, as well as their respective state delegations. Informally, CAN members relied on the relationships they had developed with members of state delegations over the years, gathering information through corridor meetings and cell phone conversations. The use of cell phones was one particularly notable innovation during the Kyoto Protocol negotiations. On several occasions government delegates reportedly called environmental representatives to get their opinion on proposals being discussed in closed-door sessions, which enabled ENGOs to contribute to debates while not physically in the room.

In addition CAN members resorted to more "subversive" measures; they lurked in corridors, hotel lobbies, and restrooms hoping to overhear conversations and/or corner key delegates; they even searched for draft documents and memos in trashcans and copiers. Overall, the problem of access was not insurmountable for the environmental community; as one representative noted, it just "wastes our time." CAN members had to devote considerable time and resources to following the negotiations. Nevertheless, they continued to keep up to date on the status of the talks and were often able to prepare strategies to counter proposals before they were formally introduced.

CAN members did have a few opportunities to participate directly in the Kyoto Protocol negotiations through informal roundtables and workshops organized to debate specific issues and proposals as well as formal statements delivered during plenary sessions. For example, during COP-2, Kiliparti Ramakrishna of the Woods Hole Research Center chaired a roundtable on possible impacts of industrialized emissions reductions on developing countries. Noting the involvement of the NGO community in this roundtable, Ramakrishna stated, "I hope delegates will agree with me that the inclusion of panelists from the nongovernmental community helped to enrich and enliven the discussion". CAN representatives (like all NGOs) were permitted to deliver a formal statement to the plenary during each of the negotiating sessions, usually one statement by a representative of a northern ENGO and one from a representative of a southern ENGO. CAN used this platform to highlight the latest scientific information on climate change impacts, as well as the potentially negative economic impacts on developing countries if industrialized states failed to limit their GHG emissions.

While specialized knowledge was the primary source of leverage employed by CAN during the negotiations, there is some evidence that ENGOs also capitalized on their perceived role as shapers of public views about climate change and the appropriateness of governments' responses. Several governments complained about how they were portrayed by CAN. For example, at the second negotiating session, both the Philippines and the Netherlands objected that their positions on targets had been misrepresented in ECO. Some environmental groups also organized demonstrations and protest activities to draw public and media attention to the negotiations and the issue of climate change, although these were largely done on an individual basis rather than through CAN.

Assessing ENGO Influence

In the Kyoto Protocol negotiations ENGOs were active participants in that at each of the negotiating sessions they provided a great deal of written and verbal information to the negotiators. Although their ability to interact directly with the delegates was somewhat compromised, the problem of access was not insurmountable. These factors are only part of the story in assessing NGO influence in international environmental negotiations. This section examines whether these activities had any effect on the negotiation process and/or outcome. . . .

The core issue in climate change negotiations between 1995 and 1997 was the establishment of binding targets and timetables for reducing GHG emissions. The central questions concerned who should be required to reduce their emissions and by *how much*?. . . .

The Protocol text requires that industrialized countries reduce their aggregate GHG emissions 5.2 percent below 1990 levels by the period 2008-2012, with each country committing to an individual target between an 8 percent decrease and a 10 percent increase (Article 3). This was largely a Japanese-brokered compromise between the American and EU positions, and by most accounts, a case of political horsetrading during the tough bargaining in closed-door sessions involving the EU leadership, the United States, and Japan over the final days (and ultimately hours) of COP-3 [in Kyoto]. The targets are not based on scientific or economic analysis and are far below what the international scientific community says is necessary to stabilize atmospheric concentrations of GHGs.

The CAN proposal for 20 percent reductions was never seriously considered during the Kyoto Protocol negotiations because many delegates questioned its political feasibility. While CAN members framed the threat of global warming as an imminent environmental crisis requiring immediate action, this same sense of urgency was not reflected in the statements made by state delegates. Most states appeared to accept global warming as a legitimate environmental threat, though they did not sense that climate change was an impending crisis, noting uncertainty about the timing, magnitude, and distribution of climate change impacts. They were more concerned instead about how to mitigate the economic costs of controlling GHG emissions.

In the absence of CAN, the Kyoto Protocol targets might have been even weaker. Specifically, ENGOs appear to have played an important role in shaping the positions of the United States and the European Union, two key actors in the negotiations. An important turning point in the negotiations came with the decision of then-US Vice President Al Gore to attend the Kyoto meeting and to instruct the American delegation to be more flexible in its negotiating position. Several observers suggested that ENGOs were instrumental by generating media attention to the negotiations, which in turn may have increased the pressure for Vice-President Gore to attend the meeting. One insider argued that the environmental community had nothing to do with Gore's decision to attend the meeting. According to this version of the story, Gore had always planned to attend but did not want to raise expectations in case something came up and he was unable to make the trip.

Even if ENGOs did not influence Gore's decision to attend COP-3, they do appear to have influenced what he said once he arrived. The Vice President's speech included a last-minute addition (i.e., it was not included in the prepared text that was distributed before the speech) stating, "I am instructing our delegation right now to show increased negotiating flexibility if a comprehensive plan can be put in place. . . ." Evidence suggests that American ENGOs convinced Gore to make this addition. Prior to his speech, the pages of ECO had been filled with calls for the United States to be more flexible in the negotiations, particularly in its opposition to a reduction target. High-level representatives of two American organizations reportedly conveyed this message to the Vice President (with whom they had established a close relationship during his tenure in the Senate) in a phone conversation during Gore's trip from the Osaka airport to the Kyoto convention hall. Indeed, when Gore uttered the word "flexibility," two executives from one of these organizations smiled, shook hands and gave each other congratulatory pats on the back. Following Gore's visit, the US delegation announced for the first time that it would agree to include targets for emissions reductions (rather than stabilization) in the Protocol.

In addition ENGO pressure seems to have been important in getting the European Union and developing countries to hold out for reduction targets before giving in on sinks and trading. By promoting an even higher reduction target, ENGOs made the EU proposal for 15 percent reductions look moderate. Moreover, Europeans are particularly concerned about how they are portrayed by the environmental community and thus were more willing to maintain a strong position than might otherwise have been the case. Commenting on the negotiations, EU Environment Commissioner Ritt Bjerregaard noted, "We are fortunate to have a lot of activist NGOs to push nations along." Interestingly, many environmentalists expressed satisfaction (and sometimes shock) that the Protocol contained any reduction commitments at all.

This analysis highlights the interaction between domestic and international channels of NGOs influence. At the domestic level, the environmental community failed to shape the US position, losing out to an aggressive campaign by members of the American fossil-fuel industry. Groups like the GCC [Global Climate Coalition] succeeded in framing the issue of climate change as a significant economic threat and mobilized opposition in Congress and the public, which in turn limited the ability of the Clinton administration to put forward a progressive position on targets and timetables. However, at the international level, the GCC did not have sufficient resources and organizational capabilities to ensure that the United States stuck to its position of opposing any reduction targets. Through CAN, American ENGOs joined their European counterparts in regular meetings with EU delegates, promoting their position that the Protocol must contain reduction targets and reminding European decision-makers that their constituents supported a commitment (thanks in large part to the domestic work of European ENGOs). In turn, the EU states (along with the G-77) maintained pressure on the United States to accept reduction targets. . . .

NOTES AND QUESTIONS

1. Professor Betsill concludes that CAN and other ENGOs had an important impact on the Kyoto negotiation process. Why do you think ENGOs have had more success influencing the development of climate change policy at the international level than at the domestic level in the United States?

2. At the COP 15 meeting in Copenhagen in 2009, NGO participation in negotiations was unexpectedly curtailed. *See* Dana R. Fisher, *Cop-15 in Copenhagen: How the Merging of Movements Left Civil Society Out in the Cold*, 10 GLOBAL ENVTL. POL. 11 (2010). A record number of NGO observers registered for the meeting: 20,000 individuals, about four times the number that registered for the COP-13 meeting in Bali in 2007. Unfortunately, conference organizers were not prepared to accommodate the high number of registrants, and they had to sharply limit attendance at negotiating sessions. Partly because of this shutout, and partly because of prior mobilization, the Copenhagen meeting featured large public protests outside the negotiation venue. Professor Dana Fischer suggests that these events at Copenhagen will continue to affect UNFCCC policies regarding observer access: "To ensure the safety of the Parties negotiating *inside*, the regime has little choice but to limit access to members of civil society. Ironically, the more civil society actors

try to participate . . . the less access they are likely to have." *Id.* at 16. How important do you think it is to have civil society access to treaty negotiations? What are the benefits and costs of such access?

3. As apparent from the fact that so many NGOs that are not strictly environmental NGOs have been admitted by the UNFCCC as observers (see above), climate change is no longer viewed as just (or even primarily) an environmental issue. Rather it is a human issue—a problem of human and social development. Framed in this way, civil society interest in climate change is poised to grow significantly. Most notably, the growing "climate justice" movement is built around the powerful idea that those who are least responsible for causing climate change are also those most likely to suffer directly from its early impacts. *See* J. Timmons Roberts, *The International Dimension of Climate Justice and the Need for International Adaptation Funding*, 2 ENVTL. JUST. 185 (2009).

B. CORPORATIONS

Businesses with a wide variety of stakes in the law and policy outcomes have mobilized to monitor and influence climate law and policy proceedings. The major interested industries include, among others, fossil fuel producers (coal, oil, natural gas), automobile manufacturers, insurers, power generators, and renewable energy suppliers (hydroelectric, solar, wind). Many businesses are also mobilizing internally. Even when not required to do so by law, a number of businesses are developing plans and taking actions to participate in carbon markets and reduce greenhouse gas emissions. This section explores the drivers of corporate climate-related activities and their implications.

1. THE OIL COMPANIES AND OTHER CARBON-INTENSIVE INDUSTRIES

Perhaps the businesses most naturally opposed to new climate change policies that would restrict emissions are those that constitute the fossil fuel industry. Climate change policy represents a direct effort to limit the sale and use of their products. For example, the oil industry, especially several giant companies such as BP, ExxonMobil, and Chevron, has played a significant role in influencing the debates about climate change policy in the United States and throughout the world. The following excerpt by Professor Simone Pulver, however, shows that the policy positions of oil companies have evolved over time and varied across the industry.

SIMONE PULVER, AN ENVIRONMENTAL CONTESTATION APPROACH TO ANALYZING THE CAUSES AND CONSEQUENCES OF THE CLIMATE CHANGE POLICY SPLIT IN THE OIL INDUSTRY

20 Org. & Env't 52, 52–55 (2007)

When climate change first emerged as an international policy concern in the late 1980s, the oil industry interpreted climate change as a threat to its primary product, gasoline. . . . In the face of the business threat embodied by climate change, oil companies from around the globe played an expected, obstructive role. They stood united in their opposition to any international effort to regulate carbon dioxide and other greenhouse gases. Led by the American oil majors Exxon, Mobil, Chevron, and Texaco, the oil industry argued against international action on climate change and questioned the findings of climate scientists. However, in the summer of 1997, the picture shifted. That May, John Browne, the Chief Executive Officer of British Petroleum (BP), made international head-lines by announcing that his company was splitting from the rest of the oil indus-try and would support international greenhouse gas regulation. After BP's announcement, Royal Dutch/Shell (Shell) and a few other oil companies also broke ranks and spoke out in support of international action on climate change. To date, there are two factions in the oil industry; those companies that support international and domestic climate regulation and those that oppose it. . . .

Implications of Greenhouse Gas Regulation for the Oil Industry

Understanding the implications of global climate change and greenhouse gas regulation for the oil industry requires an assessment in three timeframes: short term (5 to 10 years), medium term (50 years), and long term (70 to 100 years). Least controversial are the short-term implications of greenhouse gas regulation for the oil industry. In the immediate future, the production and consumption of fossil fuels will continue as usual. The structural dependence of national economies and transportation systems on coal, oil, and natural gas makes unlikely any dramatic changes in supply, demand, and price for fossil fuels during the next 5 to 10 years. Slightly more open to debate are the long-term implications of greenhouse gas regulation. The most plausible long-term scenario is that industrial and industrializing societies will shift away from fossil fuels to an economy based on alternative energy resources, such as renewable or nuclear energy. Under this scenario, global demand for coal, oil, and natural gas will decline. Concurrently, on the supply side, many regional oil reserves will have been exhausted. Other, less plausible, visions of the long-term future assume minor changes in the business-as-usual role of fossil fuels in the economy. They predict that as conventional oil supplies decline, synthetic fuel and unconventional sources of liquid fuels, such as tar sands, oil shale, and other hydrocarbons, will augment conventional oil supplies . . .

Most controversial are the medium-term effects of greenhouse gas regulation on the oil industry. Of greatest concern to oil companies are medium-term demand and price effects. The standard wisdom predicts that Kyoto-type greenhouse gas regulation will cause shifts in fuel demand from coal to oil to natural gas. However, modeling and analysis by the International Energy Agency suggest otherwise. Pershing argues that "a number of issues may affect whether there will be an impact on any individual fuel, what that impact will be, how that impact will vary across countries." Factors that will influence future fossil fuel demand include changes in regional distribu-tion of reserves in the next 20 years, growth in demand because of economic growth, allocation of demand depending on the marginal cost of production and transport, price sensitivity of demand, and fuel-specific concerns not related to climate change (for example, coal demand may decline because of local air quality concerns rather than global climate regulation). . . .

Beyond demand and price effects, oil companies are also concerned about medium-term effects on both shareholder value and facility regulations. Environmental costs related to spills, fines, and pollution abatement have long been a component of the profitability of the oil industry in terms of bottom-line operating costs. More recently, overall environmental performance has also been incorporated into assessments of shareholder value. In addition, the fate of the tobacco industry has inspired a set of arguments focusing on oil companies and climate change liability. Environmental advocates contend that oil companies, especially those that deny climate science and oppose climate regulation, are the potential targets of climate change–related litigation. Although the idea of liability for damages caused by changes in climate is purely speculative at this point, the financial burden of those damages could potentially exceed $100 billion. . . .

The Split in the Oil Industry

Overall then, in the early and mid-1990s, the prospects for and implications of greenhouse gas regulation were uncertain. First, although binding greenhouse gas emissions reductions were under discussion, the prospects for a successful negotiation of a binding international climate treaty remained uncertain up until the final days of the December 1997 Kyoto negotiations. Second, the concrete effects on the oil sector of Kyoto-type greenhouse gas reductions remain uncertain to date. In the face of this uncertainty, oil companies pioneered very different policy responses to the climate issue, which I categorize as either adversarial or cooperative (see Table 2).

ExxonMobil best exemplifies an adversarial climate policy. Since the first U.N. meeting on climate change in 1991, representatives from ExxonMobil have consistently questioned global assessments of climate science, describing them as uncertain and of doubtful validity and have argued that a policy approach of mandated reductions in greenhouse gas emissions is premature and likely to cause significant economic upheaval. ExxonMobil has communicated this message in a variety of ways, including direct interventions at meeting of the IPCC, through business lobbying groups like the Global Climate Coalition and International Petroleum Industry Environmental Conservation Association, through advertisements in leading newspapers, and through influence on national politics. In terms of its long-range strategy, ExxonMobil expects to continue as an oil company and is investing in technologies that complement a fossil fuel economy. They are investing capital in unconventional fossil fuel projects, including oil shale and tar sands, in fuels cells as an alternative to internal combustion engines, and in carbon capture and storage projects. However, the company is not diversifying into solar, wind, and other alternative energy technologies. Within the wider group of major oil companies, support for ExxonMobil's adversarial stance comes from the national oil companies of Saudi Arabia (Saudi Aramco), Venezuela (Petroleos de Venezuela), Iran (National Iranian Oil Corporation), and Indonesia (Pertamina), all members of the Organization of Petroleum Exporting Countries. In addition, PetroChina holds an adversarial position based on the claim that developing countries should not bear the burden of international climate regulation.

In contrast to the adversarial oil companies, BP, Shell, Norway's national oil company Statoil, and Mexico's national oil company Pemex are pursuing cooperative climate policies. They actively support the Kyoto Protocol, the international climate treaty that requires its industrialized country signatories to meet binding greenhouse gases emissions reduction targets and accept the findings of the IPCC, a collaborative effort among several thousand scientists who advise the U.N. climate change negotiations. In addition, both BP and Shell have committed to precautionary action on climate change, including investment in renewable energy technologies as alternatives to fossil fuels. In May 1997, Shell announced its commitment to invest $500 million in renewable energy during the next 5 years, establishing Shell International Renewables as a new core business area. Six months later, BP publicly committed to investing $160 million in solar energy. BP, Shell, and Pemex have also adopted emissions reduction targets. BP pledged to reduce company-wide greenhouse gas emissions by 10% from 1990 levels by 2010. Shell made a similar pledge but set itself a target date of 2002. Mimicking the international policy process, both companies piloted internal emissions trading systems as the policy tool to meet their targets. In addition, the cooperative companies have enlisted the collaboration of environmental NGOs in developing their emissions trading systems and their climate policies more broadly. In terms of long-range plans, both BP and Shell have referred to their future transformations from oil companies into energy service providers.

**Table 2: Elements of Adversarial vs.
Cooperative Oil Company Climate Policies**

Adversarial Climate Policy	Cooperative Climate Policy
Critical of climate science, particularly of assessment reports issued by the Intergovernmental Panel on Climate Change (IPCC)	Accept findings of IPCC and argue that current state of climate science merits precautionary action
Oppose regulation of greenhouse gas emissions, in particular the 1997 Kyoto Protocol formulated in the U.N.-sponsored international climate change negotiations	Support mandated reductions in greenhouse gas emissions and have taken on company-wide emissions reductions targets; support the Kyoto Protocol
Reject renewable energy technologies as viable alternatives to fossil fuels energy	Invest significant new funds into renewable technologies
Work independently, relying on in-house expertise	Partner with leading environmental NGOs such as Environmental Defense and World Wide Fund for Nature

NOTES AND QUESTIONS

1. In this article, Professor Pulver analyzes why the oil companies' approaches differed. Economic theory suggests that the answer would lie in market forces or firm-specific operational characteristics. Pulver, however, finds that economic factors do not explain the divergence between BP and Exxon-Mobil. Rather, she concludes that each company's decision-makers were embedded in different climate science and policy networks that led them to make different assessments of what course of action would be profitable. Why do you think BP and several other oil companies viewed a cooperative stance as the better approach? What are the various ways in which these companies might have benefitted from this approach?

2. Oil companies, particularly ExxonMobil, have been accused of mounting a misinformation campaign about climate change science. In January 2007, the Union of Concerned Scientists released a report claiming that Exxon-Mobil used the tobacco industry's disinformation tactics and "funneled about $16 million between 1998 and 2005 to a network of ideological and advocacy organizations that manufacture uncertainty on [climate change]." UNION OF CONCERNED SCIENTISTS, SMOKE, MIRRORS & HOT AIR: HOW EXXONMOBIL USES BIG TOBACCO'S TACTICS TO 'MANUFACTURE UNCERTAINTY' ON CLIMATE CHANGE 1 (2007).

   In February 2008, the city of Kivalina, Alaska, and a federally recognized tribe, the Alaska Native Village of Kivalina, sued ExxonMobil Corp. and 8 other oil companies, 14 power companies, and 1 coal company. In addition to alleging a public nuisance, the lawsuit also accused several of the defendants, including ExxonMobil and BP America, of a conspiracy to mislead the public regarding the causes and consequences of global warming. The lawsuit was dismissed by the district court in September 2009. *See* Kivalina v. ExxonMobil, 663 F. Supp. 2d 863 (N.D. Cal. 2009). Plaintiffs appealed to the Ninth Circuit in March 2010.

   To what degree do you think that businesses with very strong corporate interests in the outcome of climate policy should try to influence the public's perception of the science of climate change? Do you think companies should be legally liable if the information that they disseminate is inaccurate? For more on potential legal liability, see Angela Lipovich, *Smoke Before Oil: Modeling a Suit Against the Auto and Oil Industry on the Tobacco Tort Litigation Is Feasible*, 35 GOLDEN GATE U. L. REV. 429 (2005); J. Kevin Healy & Jeffrey M. Tapick, *Climate Change: It's Not Just a Policy Issue for Corporate Legal Counsel—It's a Legal Problem*, 29 COLO. J. ENVTL. L. 89 (2004).

3. Among energy sector companies, oil and coal suppliers have been most strongly opposed to mandatory emissions reduction; however, the coal companies have been more monolithic in their opposition than oil companies, likely in part because the coal industry is less diversified and has a smaller profit margin. Natural gas suppliers have been more likely to support emissions reductions because they would gain a competitive advantage based on the lower carbon content of their product. Nuclear and renewable energy companies have tended to be advocates of emissions reductions requirements, as they stand to profit from the transition away

from fossil fuels. In a similar way, some automobile companies have been more amenable to binding emissions reductions because they are further along in developing low-emissions vehicles. Power utilities may vary in their support for mandatory emissions reductions depending on their potential access to renewable energy sources. On how companies identify their comparative advantages and devise corporate strategy in the face of climate change and other environmental problems, see DANIEL C. ESTY & ANDREW S. WINSTON, GREEN TO GOLD: HOW SMART COMPANIES USE ENVIRONMENTAL STRATEGY TO INNOVATE, CREATE VALUE, AND BUILD COMPETITIVE ADVANTAGE (2006); EPA, A BUSINESS GUIDE TO U.S. EPA CLIMATE PARTNERSHIP PROGRAMS, EPA-100-B-08-001 (2008), *available at* http://www.epa.gov/partners/Biz_guide_to_epa_climate_partnerships.pdf.

2. BUSINESS-ENVIRONMENT COALITIONS

Part of the corporate strategy of some companies has been to work closely with climate-concerned NGOs on developing climate change law and policy. The most important such collaboration in the United States has been the U.S. Climate Action Partnership (USCAP). In 2007, 6 major environmental NGOs joined forces with 27 major oil companies, chemical companies, utilities, automobile manufacturers, and consumer product firms to issue "A Call for Action," urging "prompt enactment of national legislation in the United States to slow, stop and reverse the growth of greenhouse gas (GHG) emissions over the shortest time reasonably achievable." USCAP, A CALL FOR ACTION: CONSENSUS PRINCIPLES AND RECOMMENDATIONS FROM THE U.S. CLIMATE ACTION PARTNERSHIP: A BUSINESS AND NGO PARTNERSHIP (2007), *available at* http://docs.nrdc.org/global-warming/files/glo_07012201A.pdf.

In 2009, USCAP released a detailed framework for U.S. legislation to address climate change.

U.S. CLIMATE ACTION PARTNERSHIP, SUMMARY OVERVIEW: USCAP BLUEPRINT FOR LEGISLATIVE ACTION (2009)

http://www.us-cap.org/pdf/USCAP_Blueprint_Overview.pdf

The Blueprint is a direct response to requests by federal policymakers for a detailed consensus that could help inform legislation. While USCAP is a diverse organization, it does not include all stakeholders and we acknowledge that the Blueprint is not the only possible path forward. However, we believe the integrated package of policies we are recommending provides a pragmatic pathway to achieve aggressive environmental goals in a responsible and economically sustainable manner.

The United States faces an urgent need to reinvigorate our nation's economy, enhance energy security and take meaningful action to slow, stop and reverse GHG emissions to address climate change.

USCAP agrees that the science is sufficiently clear to justify prompt action to protect our environment. Each year of delayed action to control emissions increases the risk of unavoidable consequences that could necessitate even steeper reductions in the future, with potentially greater economic cost and social disruption.

To address these challenges successfully will require a fundamental shift in the way energy is produced, delivered and consumed in the US and around the globe. Thoughtful, comprehensive and tightly linked national energy and climate policy will help secure our economic prosperity and provide American businesses and the nation's workforce with the opportunity to innovate and succeed.

While we recognize that achieving the needed emission reductions is not free of costs, we also believe well-crafted legislation can spur innovation in new technologies, help to create jobs, and increase investment and provide a foundation for a vibrant, low-carbon economy.

International Principles

Climate change presents a global problem that requires global solutions. USCAP believes that international action is essential to meeting the climate challenge. U.S. leadership is essential for establishing an equitable and effective international policy framework for robust action by all major emitting countries. For this reason, action by the U.S. should not be contingent on simultaneous action by other countries. In our Blueprint we offer a set of principles to guide Congress and the Administration to address the global dimension of this problem.

Cap and Trade System Design

We believe the strongest way to achieve our emission reduction goals is a federal cap-and-trade program coupled with cost containment measures and complementary policies for technology research, development and deployment, clean coal technology deployment, lower-carbon transportation technologies and systems, and improved energy efficiency in buildings, industry and appliances. In a cap-and-trade system, one allowance would be created for each ton of GHG emissions allowed under the declining economy-wide emission reduction targets (the "cap"). Emitters would be required to turn in one allowance for each ton of GHG they emit. Those emitters who can reduce their emissions at the lowest cost would have to buy fewer allowances and may have extra allowances to sell to remaining emitters for whom purchasing allowances is their most cost-effective way of meeting their compliance obligation. This allows the economy-wide emission reduction target to be achieved at the lowest possible cost.

Targets and a Timetable for Action

USCAP believes the legislation should establish a mandatory, national economy-wide climate protection program that includes aggressive emission reduction targets for total U.S. emissions and for capped sectors. Equally important, it is imperative that the costs of the program be manageable. USCAP believes the recommended targets are achievable at manageable costs to the economy provided that a robust offsets program and other cost containment measures, along with other critically important policies as recommended in the Blueprint are enacted. In addition, Congress should require periodic assessment of emerging climate science and U.S. progress towards achieving emission reduction targets, and social, environmental and economic impacts in order to determine if legislative revisions are necessary to improve the nation's climate protection program.

Scope of Coverage and Point of Regulation

USCAP recommends the cap-and-trade program cover as much of the economy's GHG emissions as politically and administratively possible. This includes large stationary sources and the fossil-based CO_2 emitted by fuels used by remaining sources. The point of regulation for large stationary sources should be the point of emission. The point of regulation for transportation fuels should be at the refinery gate or with importers. Congress should establish policies to ensure carbon-based price signals are transparent to transportation fuel consumers and other end users, thereby encouraging them to make informed GHG-reduction choices. Emissions from the use of natural gas by residential and small commercial end users can be covered, for example, by regulating the utilities that distribute natural gas, often referred to as local distribution companies (LDCs).

Offsets and Other Cost Containment Measures

Adequate amounts of offsets are a critical component of the USCAP Blueprint. Emissions offsets are activities that reduce GHG emissions that are not otherwise included in the cap. USCAP recommends all offsets meet strong environmental quality standards (i.e., they must be environmentally additional, verifiable, permanent, measurable, and enforceable). We recommend that Congress should establish a Carbon Market Board (CMB) to set an overall annual upper limit for offsets starting at 2 billion metric tons with authority to increase offsets up to 3 billion metric tons, with domestic and international offsets each limited to no more than 1.5 billion metric tons in a given year. . . .

Allocation of Allowance Value

Emission allowances in an economy-wide cap-and-trade system will represent trillions of dollars in value over the life of the program. USCAP believes the distribution of allowance value should facilitate the transition to a low-carbon economy for consumers and businesses; provide capital to support new low- and zero-GHG-emitting technologies; and address the need for humans and the environment to adapt to climate change.

USCAP recommends that a significant portion of allowances should be initially distributed free to capped entities and economic sectors particularly disadvantaged by the secondary price effects of a cap and that free distribution of allowances be phased out over time. . . .

Complementary Measures

USCAP believes that policies and measures that are complementary to a cap-and-trade program are needed to create incentives for rapid technology transformation and to ensure that actual reductions in emissions occur in capped sectors where market barriers and imperfections exist that prevent the price signal from achieving significant reductions. . . .

Our Commitment

We, the members of the U.S. Climate Action Partnership, pledge to work with the President, the Congress, and all other stakeholders to enact an environmentally effective, economically sustainable, and fair climate change program consistent with our principles at the earliest practicable date.

NOTES AND QUESTIONS

1. One of the founding members of USCAP was the Pew Center for Global Climate Change (now called the Center for Climate and Energy Solutions). The Pew Center was established in 1998 as a non-profit, non-partisan, and independent organization with the mission of providing "credible information, straight answers, and innovative solutions in the effort to address global climate change." *See* Center for Climate and Energy Solutions, History and Mission, http://www.pewclimate.org/about/history_and_mission. The Pew Center has published over 100 reports and policy briefs relating to climate change and has served as host to the Business Environmental Leadership Council (BELC), which is the largest U.S.-based association of corporations focused on addressing climate change. In 2010, the Pew Center on Global Climate Change was named the world's top environmental think tank in a global survey of hundreds of scholars and experts conducted by researchers at the University of Pennsylvania. *See Pew Center Named Top Environmental Think Tank*, THOMASNET NEWS, Mar. 23, 2010, http://news.thomasnet.com/companystory/Pew-Center-named-top-environmental-think-tank-574532.

2. USCAP's *Blueprint* provided an important impetus to the political process. H.R. 2454, the legislation proposed by Representatives Waxman and Markey and passed by the House in 2009 (as discussed in Chapter Three) followed many of the recommendations set forth by USCAP. In 2010, as prospects dimmed for a new federal climate change law, three companies dropped out of USCAP. *See* Steven Mufson, *ConocoPhillips, BP and Caterpillar Quit USCAP*, WASH. POST, Feb. 17, 2010, http://www.washingtonpost.com/wp-dyn/content/article/2010/02/16/AR2010021605543.html.

3. The U.S. Chamber of Commerce opposed the Waxman-Markey Bill. As it stated,

> We opposed this specific legislation because it would not reduce the global level of greenhouse gases in the atmosphere. It is neither comprehensive nor international, and it falls short on moving renewable and alternative technologies into the marketplace and enabling our transition to a lower carbon future. It would also impose carbon tariffs on goods imported into the U.S., a move that would almost certainly spur retaliation from global trading partners.
>
> *Five Positions on Energy and the Environment*, USCHAMBER.COM, http://www.uschamber.com/issues/environment/five-positions-energy-and-environment (last visited Apr. 20, 2012).

The Chamber also stated that it supports a "comprehensive legislative solution that does not harm the economy, recognizes that the problem is international in scope, and aggressively promotes new technologies and efficiency." *See id.* In the fall of 2009, several high-profile companies dropped their membership with the U.S. Chamber of Commerce to voice their disagreement with the Chamber's position on climate legislation.

The Chamber's opposition to climate law extends to the possibility of regulating greenhouse gases under the existing Clean Air Act. In 2010, the Chamber filed a petition with the EPA asking the agency to reconsider its 2009 "endangerment finding" that greenhouse gas emissions endanger public health and welfare. After EPA rejected the Chamber's petition in 2010, the Chamber sued.

Is the Chamber of Commerce taking an unduly short-term view of its members' economic interests? In the medium- to long-term, does a governmental failure to control greenhouse gas emissions serve the interests of U.S. business? What responsibility does the Chamber of Commerce have to represent the interests of existing and future companies that stand to gain from new climate change policies or lose from climate change impacts?

3. VOLUNTARY CORPORATE COMMITMENTS

Some companies have committed to reducing their emissions even in the absence of governmental emissions reductions requirements. The Chicago Climate Exchange (CCX), founded in 2003, provided companies that set voluntary emissions reductions target with a trading mechanism through which to meet it. CCX members that reduced below their targets had surplus emissions allowances to sell or bank. CCX members that emitted above their targets could comply with their target by purchasing allowances. In the excerpt below, Professor Tseming Yang examines how CCX operated.

TSEMING YANG, THE PROBLEM OF MAINTAINING EMISSION "CAPS"
IN CARBON TRADING PROGRAMS WITHOUT FEDERAL GOVERNMENT INVOLVEMENT:
A BRIEF EXAMINATION OF THE CHICAGO CLIMATE EXCHANGE
AND THE NORTHEAST REGIONAL GREENHOUSE GAS INITIATIVE

17 Fordham Envtl. L. Rev. 271, 274–79 (2006)

As one alternative to a federally created carbon market, the Chicago Climate Exchange (CCX) is an example of a market created primarily by private entities. Commonly referred to as the "brainchild" of Richard Sandor, a former economist with the Chicago Board of Trade, it has received much publicity since it was created. The CCX describes itself as a "voluntary pilot Greenhouse Gas emission reduction and trading program for North America" that is "legally binding." It seeks to:

a) demonstrate unambiguously that a cross-section of North American private and public sector entities can reach agreement on a voluntary commitment to reduce Greenhouse Gas emissions and implement a market-based emission reduction program;

b) establish proof of concept by demonstrating the viability of a multi-sector and multi-national Greenhouse Gas emission cap-and-trade program supplemented by Project-based emission offsets.

The CCX began operating in 2003. Its members include not only large Fortune 500 companies such as Ford, DuPont, International Paper, American Electric Power, and BP America, but also smaller entities like Green Mountain Power and Central Vermont Public Services, both Vermont electric utility companies. Governmental entities participate as well, including the cities of Chicago, Berkeley, Oakland, and Aspen. In addition to full-fledged members, the CCX accepts participant members, which provide liquidity to the market and offset credits, and associate members, which have no or negligible emissions but trade for reasons other than compliance with emissions reduction commitments. The CCX allows non-business entities, primarily environmental organizations, to join as associate members. Some of them have purchased emissions allowances as a way of retiring them in much the same way some organizations have done in the acid rain trading program.

. . . .

Like other cap and trade emissions programs, the CCX seeks to achieve environmental gains by gradually reducing program-wide and individual members' emissions limits. The baseline used to measure reductions is the annual emissions average from 1998 to 2001. In 2003, the CCX capped emissions at 1% below the emissions baseline. Each subsequent year, emissions caps have been reduced by an additional 1% from the 2003 baseline. The 2006 cap is 4% below the 2003 baseline.

The original pilot period of the CCX was 2003-2006, after which the CCX was set to expire. However, CCX members have recently extended the operation of the pilot market period to 2010. For 2006-2010, emissions reductions are scheduled to progress at varying annual levels, resulting in an overall 6% reduction from 2003 baseline levels by 2010.

There is an annual "true-up" period, the time of reckoning when CCX members must account for whether emissions in the previous year match the number of carbon allowances each member holds. If a member's emissions exceed its individual emissions limit, it is given an opportunity to purchase additional allowances. However, the rules of the CCX impose limits on the purchase of offset and early action credits.

How does the CCX ensure that members do not exceed their overall emissions cap? Since the federal government does not currently limit greenhouse gas emissions, participants voluntarily accept the emissions limits. There is no formal governmental role in the policing of compliance. Rather, as an exempt commercial market under the Commodities Exchange Act, compliance with CCX rules, contained in the Rule Book, is monitored by the CCX itself and by the National Association of Securities Dealers (NASD).

This has given the widespread impression that the commitments undertaken by CCX members are unenforceable. In a recent description, it was said that "unlike Kyoto, CCX has no teeth." As a legal matter, that is incorrect.

Emissions control commitments are voluntarily undertaken by joining the CCX. However, subsequent compliance is arguably not voluntary at all. Because the CCX is a self-regulated, private entity, unsupervised by the CFTC [Commodity Futures Trading Commission] or other regulatory body, it is, in essence, a private contractual arrangement. When entities become CCX members, they agree "to abide by the rules of the Exchange as provided in the CCX Rulebook." Violations of CCX commitments would thus be enforceable as breaches of contractual obligations and lead to corresponding forms of liability. In other words, the CCX is as "voluntary" as any contract commitment is. CCX commitments may be made voluntarily, but they become legally binding once assumed.

What happens when a CCX member fails to limit its carbon emissions as required and then refuses to purchase the requisite carbon allowances? The rules of the CCX do not explicitly address the consequences of non-compliance with emissions limits. Presumably, the procedures governing Exchange rule violations more generally would be triggered. These provisions provide for punitive sanctions, including fines and suspension of trading privileges, when any CCX rules are violated. The ultimate sanction is termination of CCX membership. Since compliance with emissions limits and true-up are a Rulebook requirement, these provisions provide a mechanism for deterring or responding to non-compliance.

Because the CCX is a privately held company, much information about its operations is not publicly available. Thus, it is not clear whether the sanctions mechanism has ever been triggered. But given the small size and voluntary membership, consisting of companies that have a commitment to reducing their own greenhouse gas emissions, it is probably safe to assume that the mechanism has not been used. Even if an emissions limit is missed, the true-up period would provide ample opportunity to purchase the necessary carbon credits. At prices fluctuating between $1-4 per ton of carbon equivalent, that would seem to be a minor inconvenience for any company committed to enhancing or maintaining its green reputation. For 2003 and 2004, the CCX has reported the successful reduction of program-wide carbon emissions by over 8% and over 13%, respectively, below the relevant emissions reduction objectives.

NOTES AND QUESTIONS

1. The CCX facilitated corporate environmental self-regulation. Self-regulation differs from governmental regulation in that companies choose their environmental objectives and the methods to achieve them independently of the government, generally to gain some market advantage. *See* Jonathon Hanks, *Promoting Corporate Environmental Responsibility: What Role for 'Self-Regulatory' and 'Co-Regulatory' Instruments in South Africa?*, *in* THE GREENING OF BUSINESS IN DEVELOPING COUNTRIES: RHETORIC, REALITY AND PROSPECTS 187 (Peter Utting ed., 2002). A variety of market-based benefits may motivate self-regulation. For example, companies may be able to market themselves or

their products more favorably to customers and investors, and companies may experience cost-savings or productivity improvements, or both, that derive from their environmental improvements. Another possible benefit of self-regulation is that it may serve to preempt mandatory legislative or regulatory requirements, thus reducing future compliance costs. *See* Anna Alberini & Kathleen Segerson, *Assessing Voluntary Programs to Improve Environmental Quality*, 22 Envtl. & Resource Econ. 157, 157–84 (2002).

Which of these reasons do you think motivated the companies that joined CCX? For a critique of self-regulation in the context of industrial pollution control, see Sanford E. Gaines & Clíona Kimber, *Redirecting Self-Regulation,* 13 J. Envtl. L. 157, 157–84 (2001). The authors emphasize that industrial firms face significant information and other barriers to self-regulation and that self-regulation impairs public participation in setting environmental goals and assessing their achievement.

2. How does a consumer or citizen distinguish between real corporate commitment to environmental improvement and greenwashing? Greenwashing is defined as "disinformation disseminated by an organization so as to present an environmentally responsible public image." Concise Oxford English Dictionary (Judy Pearsall ed., 10th ed., 2003). Oft-used techniques of greenwashing include making green claims without proof and highlighting an environmentally positive aspect of a product or service while failing to mention other, often larger, negative aspects. Consider a company that advertises itself as a climate-conscious member of the CCX. If it buys allowances instead of reducing its emissions to comply with its target, would you consider the company an environmental leader or would you view this as a case of greenwashing?

3. In 2010, the CCX announced that it would terminate its emission allowance trading program after seven years of operation. *See Chicago Climate Exchange Closes Nation's First Cap-And-Trade System but Keeps Eye to the Future,* N.Y. Times, Jan. 3, 2011, http://www.nytimes.com/cwire/2011/01/03/03climatewire-chicago-climate-exchange-closes-but-keeps-ey-78598.html?pagewanted=all. Trading volumes and allowance prices had declined precipitously as it became apparent in 2009 that the U.S. Congress would not enact legislation that would support the creation of valuable carbon allowances. While CCX was a voluntary program, it depended in many ways on the expectation that a mandatory cap-and-trade program would be enacted in the future. Imagine yourself as the leader of a company that participated in the CCX. What would have been your reasons to join CCX, and would these reasons hold up after Congress failed to enact a climate change law instituting a federal cap-and-trade program?

C. INDIVIDUALS

We, as individuals and households, make decisions on a daily basis that have implications for climate change. These choices vary dramatically around the world and even within the developed world. Some people have the resources to make a wide range of consumption choices, while others face limitations based on their economic circumstances, the locally available options, or both.

Individuals with a wide range of choices decide, for example, which cars to buy and how much to drive them. They decide how much to light, heat, and cool their homes or apartments and how much to invest in efficient appliances. They decide how much stuff to buy. Yet these individual decisions are made in a larger social context. This context helps determine what cars and other consumer products are made; what forms of transportation and housing exist; and even how much consumption people feel is necessary to be happy.

This section confronts the difficult questions of how individual behavior affects climate change and how social norms and the law can influence climate-relevant individual behavior. Because people in developed countries produce many more greenhouse gas emissions than those in developing countries, this section focuses largely on the developed country context. It examines how to measure individual impact, how to transition to carbon neutrality, and how to use law as a tool of achieving these goals. However, the discussion also could apply to wealthier individuals in transitional and developing countries who produce more greenhouse gas emissions than the per capita norm.

1. MEASURING INDIVIDUAL IMPACT

For many years, much of U.S. environmental law, particularly air pollution law, has focused on regulating corporate emitters. To reduce the sulfur dioxide and nitrogen oxide emissions that cause acid rain and smog, for example, power plants and major industrial facilities have been heavily regulated. To some extent, greenhouse gas emissions also are an industrial pollution problem. Electricity generation by the electric power sector accounted for about one-third of U.S. greenhouse gas emissions and the industrial sector accounts for about one-fifth. U.S. EPA, Inventory of U.S. Greenhouse Gas Emissions and Sinks: 1990-2009, ES-14–ES-15 (2011), *available at* http://epa.gov/climatechange/emissions/downloads11/US-GHG-Inventory-2011-Complete_Report.pdf.

But individual choices—particularly by those who have the economic resources to consume heavily—also produce a great deal of emissions. The following excerpt from an article by Professors Michael Vandenbergh and Anne Steinemann explores the role of individual emissions in the overall U.S. emissions profile.

MICHAEL P. VANDENBERGH & ANNE C. STEINEMANN,
THE CARBON-NEUTRAL INDIVIDUAL

82 N.Y.U. L. Rev. 1673, 1687–95 (2007)

A recent New York Times editorial on climate change referred to the sources of carbon emissions as "industrial emissions," as if industrial emissions are synonymous with all emissions. This Part demonstrates that individual behavior is a discrete, overlooked source of enormous quantities of carbon dioxide emissions. It then presents a model that estimates the releases of carbon dioxide attributable to the average individual in the United States and to all individuals in the aggregate. The Part concludes by evaluating the significance of these emissions.

A. Individual Behavior as a Source Category

The framing of pollution sources exerts a powerful influence on the regulatory and social forces brought to bear on them. Identifying a source begins the process of attributing a quantity of emissions to that source, assigning blame for the harms caused by those emissions, and directing regulatory resources toward emissions reductions. Sources that are perceived as the largest emitters naturally attract the most public and regulatory attention.

Since the explosion of environmental regulation in the early 1970s, policymakers have focused most regulatory prescriptions on large industrial sources. In contrast, they have focused little regulatory attention on individuals and households. Framing pollution as an industrial problem generates remedies that involve industrial regulation. Thus, controlling emissions from automobiles becomes a matter of adopting technology-based standards on motor vehicle emissions, with little emphasis on the number and use of the vehicles. Controlling emissions from residential electricity use becomes a matter of adopting technology-based or market-allowance-based controls on electrical utilities, with far less emphasis on the amount of energy consumed in the home.

Assessments of the sources of carbon dioxide emissions have followed this traditional pattern. The presentation of 2004 carbon dioxide emissions data by the Energy Information Administration (EIA) of the Department of Energy demonstrates the point. Although the EIA identified industrial, commercial, transportation, and residential categories of emitters, it failed to identify individual behavior as a discrete source. Rather, it distributed the emissions attributable to individual behavior among at least two sectors: (1) residential (e.g., household electricity and direct energy use), and (2) transportation (personal driving, flying, and mass transportation). By dividing the emissions from individual behavior into two categories, one of which (transportation) includes emissions from many types of sources other than individuals, this framing obscures the size of the total emissions from individuals as a discrete source category. Other organizations that report emissions data also follow this approach. For example, a 2006 UN report divided greenhouse gas sources into several categories, none of which includes individual behavior as a discrete category.

A viable alternative is to begin by framing the sources of carbon emissions based on the types of policies or regulatory measures that might be effective in controlling them, and to work backward to determine the emissions that may be generated by these types of sources. If regulators begin by assuming that changing individual behavior is a viable means of achieving desired environmental outcomes, the analysis shifts. Then the question becomes, What behaviors are under the individual's control? With this framing in mind, the magnitude of the total contribution from individual behavior will come into focus as emissions from household activities and personal transportation are aggregated. The model presented below estimates the contribution of individual behavior using this approach.

B. A Model of Individual Carbon Dioxide Emissions

Not surprisingly, given the lack of attention to individuals' contributions to global warming, policymakers and scholars have developed few tools to assess the aggregate contribution of individual behavior to greenhouse gas emissions. To evaluate whether the carbon emissions from individual behavior are worthy of regulatory attention, we present the results of a model that estimates the carbon dioxide emissions in 2000 from the average individual in the United States and the aggregate emissions from all individuals. We provide an overview of the model here . . . .

1. Individual Behavior Defined

We define individual behavior to include only those behaviors that are under the direct, substantial control of the individual and that are not undertaken in the scope of the individual's employment. As a result, we include emissions from personal motor vehicle use, personal air travel, and mass transport. We exclude emissions from motor vehicle use and air travel undertaken in the course of employment (e.g., driving for a delivery service or flying on a business trip). Similarly, we include emissions attributable to household electricity use, but we exclude emissions attributable to the industrial production of household goods (e.g., the emissions resulting from the production, shipping, and retailing of appliances and food).

Although this conservative approach excludes many activities that contribute to climate change (e.g., the releases attributable to household appliance production), the emissions from these activities often vary widely depending on where and how the goods are produced, and the degree of individual control over them is often very limited. Furthermore, making individuals responsible for all emissions derived from consumer choices would make it possible to attribute virtually all emissions to individuals, yet it would not satisfy the initial objective of including only emissions that can be changed through laws and policies directed at individual behavior. For ease of analysis, we divide the emissions from individual behavior into household and transportation emissions.

a. Household Emissions

We estimate household emissions by using both top-down and bottom-up approaches. For the top-down approach, we calculate household energy consumption using EIA data for residential fuel consumption. We then convert household energy use into individual energy use. We use U.S. Census data indicating that the U.S. population in 2000 was roughly 281 million, and our calculation that the United States had just under 109 million households.

We divide household energy use into two categories: primary use and electricity use. The primary use category includes household energy consumption that does not require an external power generation source. Examples include space and water heaters, washing machines, and stoves that utilize coal, natural gas, petroleum, or wood. The EIA provides data on primary use. Using EIA conversion coefficients, we convert these forms of energy use into the amount of carbon dioxide emitted per household and per person.

We next obtain the total residential electricity use for 2000 using EIA data. We convert this electricity use into carbon emissions using the EIA coefficients, accounting for the fuel type used in the electricity generation. For example, electricity generated from fossil fuels generates carbon dioxide emissions, but sources such as nuclear energy and hydropower do not. We then calculate the total amount of carbon dioxide emissions from electricity consumption in pounds per household and pounds per individual.

To validate the top-down approach, we also calculate household carbon dioxide emissions using a bottom-up approach. We use EIA data on end-use electricity consumption for households in 2001 (2000 data were unavailable). For large numbers of household appliances, EIA data include the average use per household in kilowatt hours and the number of households utilizing these appliances. Thus, we can determine the amount of carbon dioxide emission-producing electricity used by each appliance and convert these values into total carbon dioxide emissions, emissions per household, and emissions per individual using the EIA conversion coefficients.

Our individual figure is a blended individual average that allocates to every person a share of carbon dioxide emissions regardless of behavior. The totals for the top-down and bottom-up approaches are remarkably similar, suggesting that the household estimate is reliable. We use the top-down approach in calculating the overall individual total.

b. Transportation Emissions

We divide individual transportation into three categories: automotive, air, and other. We include in the automotive category all personal vehicle use. We include in the air transportation category all air travel except business travel and freight. We assign rail and mass transit to the "other" category.

We translate EIA data on motor fuel consumed by personal vehicle use into pounds of carbon dioxide using the same conversion factors used in the household calculations, and we then convert the totals into pounds per person. We calculate emissions for domestic passenger air travel by multiplying energy intensity per passenger mile by the total number of domestic passenger miles, after reducing the total number of miles to exclude business travel. We convert the resulting figure into total pounds of carbon dioxide for all passenger air travel using the EIA coefficients. We then divide the total by the U.S. population to yield pounds of carbon dioxide per person. We calculate the rail and mass transit totals using a similar approach, although we do not reduce these totals for business travel.

2. Results

Table 1 presents the results of the individual behavior model. As it indicates, by merely including the behaviors over which individuals have direct, substantial control, the total emissions for the average American in 2000 equaled over 14,000 pounds (seven tons) of carbon dioxide.

Table 1: Individual Carbon Dioxide Emissions

Household	Pounds of CO_2 per Person
Primary	3494
Electricity	1922
Subtotal	5416
Transportation	
Automotive	7869
Air	857
Other	381
Subtotal	9107
Total (Mean Individual)	14,523
Total (All Individuals)	4.1 trillion

The total emissions for all 281 million Americans in 2000 was 4.1 trillion pounds. If calculated using 2006 data, the figure would likely be higher. The U.S. population reached roughly 300 million in 2006, while per-capita emissions have decreased only slightly since 2000.

C. Implications

Although the 4.1 trillion pound total is a tremendous amount, its importance is even more apparent in context. The 4.1 trillion pounds emitted by individuals constitute 32% of the roughly 12.7 trillion pounds emitted annually in the United States. By comparison, the entire industrial sector released 3.9 trillion pounds in 2000. The individual behavior figures also dwarf the subsectors that constitute the industrial sector. For example, the chemical-manufacturing and petroleum-refining industries, which were the top emitters among the manufacturing industries, emitted 686 billion pounds and 672 billion pounds of carbon, respectively, in 2002. Other industrial sectors had even lower totals, including iron and steel production (143.9 billion pounds), cement manufacture (90.8 billion), and aluminum production (13.7 billion).

Even more striking is the comparison of emissions from individual behavior in the United States with other sources worldwide. The United States released 24.4% of the world's carbon dioxide in 2000, suggesting that individual behavior in the United States accounted for roughly 8% of the world's carbon dioxide emissions. The significance of the 8% is clear when compared to the emissions of other continents and countries. The 4.1 trillion pounds attributable to U.S. individual behavior is larger than the total for sub-Saharan Africa (1.1 trillion pounds), South America (1.6 trillion), and Central America (1.0 trillion, including the Caribbean) combined, and it is roughly a third of all carbon dioxide emissions in Asia (15.6 trillion) and Europe (12.1 trillion).

NOTES AND QUESTIONS

1. You can become more aware of your individual impact by calculating your "carbon footprint." Try out a carbon footprint calculator at:

   - *Carbon Footprint Calculator: What's My Carbon Footprint?*, NATURE CONSERVANCY, http://www.nature.org/initiatives/climatechange/calculator/ (last visited Apr. 22, 2012);
   - *CoolClimate Carbon Footprint Calculator*, COOLCLIMATE NETWORK, http://coolclimate.berkeley.edu/uscalc (last visited Apr. 22, 2012); and
   - *Household Emissions Calculator*, U.S. EPA, http://www.epa.gov/climate change/emissions/ind_calculator.html (last visited Apr. 22, 2012).

   Once you input information relating, for example, to your motor vehicle and household energy use, these calculators estimate the total annual carbon emissions associated with your activities.

   How do these calculators vary in what they include and in their level of detail? How does your footprint vary when you use different calculators? What are the biggest contributors to your footprint and to what extent do you control those choices?

2. From calculating your carbon footprint, it becomes clear that its size will depend to some extent on characteristics of the built environment, which in many ways are not freely chosen by individuals. The average U.S. resident produces three times the amount of CO_2 emissions as a person in France or Denmark, in large part because people in the United States tend to live in bigger houses and drive bigger cars longer distances. *See What Makes Europe Greener than the US?*, GUARDIAN ENV. NETWORK, Sept. 29, 2009, *available at* http://www.guardian.co.uk/environment/2009/sep/29/europe-greener-us. What can individuals do to change the built environment to make it more climate-friendly?

3. A component of the carbon footprint that individuals have more control over is their consumption choices. Should consumer products be labeled in a way that communicates their "embedded carbon," the amount of carbon dioxide emitted in their manufacture and distribution? While labeling schemes may be imposed by government, in many instances NGOs initiate them and businesses voluntarily agree to participate. In 2007, the United Kingdom's Carbon Trust developed the "Carbon Reduction Label" (see Figure 6.1). The label indicates the total greenhouse gas emissions from every stage of the product's life cycle, including production, transportation, preparation, use, and disposal. Companies that display the label also commit to reducing the carbon footprint of the labeled product. A wide range of products has been labeled, including paving products, clothing, and foods. What are the benefits and limitations of a consumer-led approach of this sort?

Figure 6.1:   Carbon Trust's Carbon Reduction Label

Source: Label reprinted with permissions of Carbon Trust Footprinting Company Ltd.

4. How does the fact that individual behavior is a significant factor make it difficult to develop climate change policy in the United States? Do Americans fear that the government will try to control their lifestyle choices? Professor John Dernbach argues that Congress should write a climate change law that consciously engages individuals:

> [T]he legislation should contain findings and statements of purpose that pertain not just to the problem and proposed reductions, but also to the available opportunities and the important role that individuals can play. Climate change legislation, at a minimum, should also contain the same provisions for citizen participation as other environmental laws. In addition, Congress should consider supplementing national targets and timetables for emissions reductions with supplemental targets for per capita energy consumption and GHG emissions.
>
> The legislation should also require (1) the development and publication of a variety of public information; (2) public information about overall GHG emissions, including per capita GHG emissions and trends in those emissions; (3) more and better information about energy use and GHG emissions from goods and services, as well as information about individual GHG or carbon impacts; (4) more and better information about the choices that consumers have; and (5) information about the impacts of climate change in particular regions and economic sectors.
>
> Finally, the legislation should also provide individuals with as many incentives as possible to use those alternatives, including tax credits and other comparable incentives. Similarly, individuals should be able to generate and trade allowances for activities that are highly energy efficient or reduce GHG emissions in some other way. The government should also authorize the distribution of proceeds from allowances in ways that would, for example, reduce the cost of certain energy efficient products. Finally, the legislation should provide for rigorous analysis and monitoring of the effectiveness of various behavioral incentives, and for adjustments and modification of efforts in light of feedback and new information.
>
> John C. Dernbach, *Harnessing Individual Behavior to Address Climate Change: Options for Congress*, 26 Va. Envtl. L.J. 107, 109 (2008).

Do you agree with Dernbach's approach? What would be its benefits and limitations?

2. AN ETHIC OF CARBON NEUTRALITY?

A growing number of individuals and organizations are seeking to become carbon-neutral, which means that their net emissions (including offsets they purchase) would be zero. However, critics express skepticism about what carbon neutrality, and especially its heavy dependence on buying offsets, actually accomplishes. The following excerpt, also from the article by Professors Vandenbergh and Steinemann, explores the complexities of defining carbon neutrality, the prospects for carbon neutrality to become interwoven into society as a standard of appropriate behavior, and the limitations of this approach.

MICHAEL P. VANDENBERGH & ANNE C. STEINEMANN,
THE CARBON-NEUTRAL INDIVIDUAL

82 N.Y.U. L. Rev. 1687, 1717–25 (2007)

a. The Rising Popularity of Carbon Neutrality

The norm of carbon neutrality involves a perceived obligation to achieve zero net carbon emissions through a combination of reductions in carbon emissions and purchases of carbon offsets. The carbon-neutrality norm reflects the idiosyncrasies of the carbon emissions problem. Unlike many behaviors that contribute to environmental harms, individuals can achieve carbon neutrality not just by eliminating emissions but also by a combination of emissions reductions and offset purchases. Carbon neutrality has spread rapidly in the last several years, although largely among those who were already likely to adhere to environmental protection norms. Surveys on the adoption of the carbon-neutrality norm are not yet available, but a variety of sources provide anecdotal indications that the norm is becoming widespread. "Carbon neutrality" was Oxford Dictionary's "word of the year" for 2006. More than half a dozen companies, ranging from the predictable (Ben & Jerry's) to the surprising (Rupert Murdoch's News Corporation), have adopted carbon neutrality as an overall corporate goal. Many more firms have adopted programs that rely on customers to pay more at the time of purchase to help customers move in the direction of carbon neutrality by offsetting the carbon footprint of particular goods or services. Sports organizations, including the Australian Football League, FIFA (for the 2006 World Cup), and the National Football League have also begun adopting carbon neutrality for particular events or seasons.

Not-for-profit organizations and governments also are adopting carbon neutrality. California's most recent gubernatorial inauguration was carbon neutral. Several governments attempted to make a recent international summit meeting carbon neutral, although the effort faced political obstacles. New Zealand, the Vatican, the Canadian province of British Columbia, and at least one British town have announced their intention to become carbon neutral. The presidents of more than 150 colleges and universities in the

United States have signed a statement committing to take steps toward achieving carbon neutrality.

. . . .

b. The Characteristics of Carbon Neutrality

Several features of carbon neutrality may explain its rapid adoption. First, the concept is easy to understand and express. Studies suggest that simplicity is essential for many types of socially induced behavior changes because it enables individuals to notice, understand, and remember information. The simplicity comes at a cost, however: It may be possible to achieve the short- and long-term global emissions reduction targets through very large individual reductions rather than actual neutrality. A norm phrased as "no harmful carbon emissions" or "no more than your fair share" might accurately express this concept. Alternatively, some might argue that individuals in developed countries must become carbon negative to account for the needs of the developing world. Communicating the precise permissible levels of emissions to hundreds of millions of people in a way that generates desired levels of behavior change, however, would be impossible. Moreover, even if precise optimal emissions levels could be calculated, they would change from year to year.

Carbon neutrality also squares well with the abstract personal-responsibility norm: it enables individuals to be confident that regardless of others' behavior, they are not contributing to the harm. In short, carbon neutrality enables individuals to take personal responsibility for their contributions to climate change without reliance on uncertain or shifting estimates of the necessary reductions or of others' behavior.

Carbon neutrality may have achieved its current level of popularity because compliance is achievable without significant sacrifice for many individuals. Because carbon neutrality can be achieved through a mix of emissions reductions and offsets, it does not require massive behavior changes or financial costs. Many behavior changes can generate substantial emissions reductions at low cost. Furthermore, although the retail price of carbon offsets is likely to rise, it recently has been as low as $4 per ton of carbon. For example, some individuals may not be able to reduce motor vehicle use, but at least one retailer is selling offsets for the annual carbon emissions from a standard car for roughly $50.

Not surprisingly, psychological studies demonstrate that eliminating the barriers and availability of excuses for inaction are critically important steps for behavior change. Studies also demonstrate that once individuals have committed to a particular viewpoint or action, they tend to continue engaging in the behavior long after the original period of commitment has ended. Compliance with the carbon-neutrality norm does not require that individuals adopt other environmental beliefs, norms, or lifestyles that are inconsistent with their own. Moreover, it allows individuals to maintain control over the mix of behavior changes that they will use to achieve compliance. These points are essential. By adopting the carbon-neutrality norm, Ed Begley's wife can reduce her carbon footprint without making fences out of plastic milk jugs. More important, she can no longer assume that those who are unwilling to take the milk-jug route do not have an obligation to reduce their carbon footprint.

Empirical and theoretical studies support this analysis. Concrete norms that require wholesale changes in worldviews or clusters of abstract norms have little prospect for success. Those who do not subscribe to a worldview compatible with environmentalism will be more likely to reject information about climate change if they are forced to change their worldview rather than simply adopt new norms. Similarly, individuals are likely to reject a new norm that appears to divest them of control over daily life activities, as might be required if carbon neutrality could only be achieved through eliminating all carbon emissions. In some cases, individuals not only reject these types of behavior changes but also engage in reactance, acting in opposition to the perceived directive.

c. Criticisms of Carbon Neutrality

Carbon neutrality is not without critics. One concern is that offsets may not always provide genuine emissions reductions. For example, offsets may purport to displace a carbon-emitting activity that would not have occurred without the offset in the first place. Alternatively, the offset-generating activity may have uncertain scientific validity. In a worst-case scenario, offsets may be generated from the destruction of greenhouse gases that were only produced in the first place because of the market value of the offsets. A recent study identified substantial variation in the quality of the offsets available on the retail market, and a private standard is under development for retail carbon offsets. Thus far, personal carbon calculators have received less attention, but a forthcoming study concludes that these calculators lack transparency and vary widely in methodology and outputs.

A second concern is that even if offsets do reduce climate forcing at the levels advertised, the availability of offsets may undermine public support for government regulatory efforts and for individual behavior change that reduces emissions instead of offsetting them. These points are worthy of further empirical study, but it is equally likely that individuals who commit to carbon neutrality through offset purchases will become more supportive of government regulation and more likely to reduce their own emissions. Studies demonstrate that when individuals take affirmative steps to reduce their contributions to social harms, they expect reciprocity from others — in this case, industry, government, agriculture, and others. In addition, as discussed above, when individuals make a personal or public commitment to take an action, they are more likely to follow through on the action. Offsets that involve public commitments by individuals to reduce their carbon footprint thus may induce direct emissions reductions and may build public support for traditional regulatory measures.

A third concern is that as carbon neutrality spreads and more carbon offsets are purchased, the price of offsets is likely to rise. The price increase has at least two implications. First, compliance with the norm may decline if it requires higher costs to purchase offsets or more onerous behavior changes to achieve increased emissions reductions. Although an increase in offset prices is likely to occur, the widespread adoption of carbon neutrality will create incentives for private markets and government to provide alternatives for individuals to achieve emissions reductions. In addition, individuals who have adopted the carbon-neutrality norm may resist acting inconsistently with the norm even after it becomes more expensive to comply.

A second implication of the price increase is that it raises distributive justice concerns. If carbon neutrality can be achieved by offsets, and if offsets increase in price, the wealthy will be able to comply with the norm without facing substantial lifestyle disruptions, but the poor will not. Although this is a genuine concern, the remedy is not to abandon carbon neutrality or carbon offsets but rather to provide public or private subsidies to those who cannot afford offsets.

NOTES AND QUESTIONS

1. Although Professors Vandenberg and Steinemann are hopeful about public adoption of the carbon neutrality norm, public complacency is common, and apparently growing. A 2010 study asked, "How worried are you about global warming?" Fifty-three percent were "very worried" or "somewhat worried," while the rest were "not very worried" or "not at all worried." *See* ANTHONY LEISEROWITZ, ET AL., CLIMATE CHANGE IN THE AMERICAN MIND: AMERICANS' GLOBAL WARMING BELIEFS AND ATTITUDES IN JUNE 2010 (2010), *available at* http://environment.yale.edu/climate/files/ClimateBeliefsJune2010.pdf. The same survey found that 42 percent of Americans "strongly agree" or "somewhat agree" that "[t]he actions of a single individual won't make any difference in global warming." Two years earlier, only 31 percent strongly or somewhat agreed with this statement. *Id.* What are your responses to these questions and how have they changed over time?

2. Social scientists have conducted research to understand the barriers that prevent people from developing attitudes and actions that respond adequately to the significant threat of climate change. *See* Kari Marie Norgaard, *Cognitive and Behavioral Challenges in Responding to Climate Change* (World Bank Policy Research Working Paper 4940, 2009). Some of these barriers are psychological or conceptual. For example, people may judge as serious only those problems to which they feel that they can efficaciously respond: they stop paying attention to climate change when they realize that there is no easy solution for it. Or individuals may block out or distance themselves from information about climate change in order to maintain desirable emotional states. Other barriers are social and cultural. For example, information on the high carbon footprint of the United States contradicts patriotic national pride, and U.S. citizens who fail to respond to the issue of climate change benefit from their denial in economic terms.

3. Individuals and organizations in the United States that do seek to be carbon-neutral generally must rely at least in part on the purchase of carbon offsets. For example, an individual that takes a flight can purchase an amount of carbon offsets equivalent to the carbon emitted by the flight. The money is then spent to reduce emissions by that amount somewhere else, often through landfill methane destruction or reforestation projects. *See*

Katherine Hamilton et al., *Building Bridges: State of the Voluntary Carbon Markets 2010*, Ecosystem Marketplace & Bloomberg New Energy Finance (June 14, 2010). However, some studies have suggested that consumers do not always get what they pay for. An investigation by *The Christian Science Monitor* and the New England Center for Investigative Reporting found that individuals and businesses that participate in global carbon offset market are often "buying into projects that are never completed, or paying for ones that would have been done anyhow." Doug Struck, *Buying Carbon Offsets May Ease Eco-guilt But Not Global Warming*, CHRISTIAN SCI. MONITOR, Apr. 20, 2010, http://www.csmonitor.com/Environment/2010/0420/Buying -carbon-offsets-may-ease-eco-guilt-but-not-global-warming. What can businesses and/or NGOs do to increase the legitimacy and credibility of carbon offsets?

3. THE ROLE OF LEGAL MANDATES

To restrict many types of undesirable behaviors, governments rely on legal mandates and prohibitions rather than on social norms that may be ignored without legal penalty. According to Professor Katrina Kuh, the obstacles to using legal mandates to proscribe harmful individual behavior can be minimized by entrusting their design and enforcement to local, rather than state or federal, governments.

KATRINA FISCHER KUH, CAPTURING INDIVIDUAL HARMS

35 Harv. Envtl. L. Rev. 155, 195–203 (2011)

Traditional command and control regulation of industrial point sources relies heavily on the use of mandates, or direct proscriptions against environmentally harmful activities, and has achieved significant gains in reducing pollution from these sources. Scholars likewise recognize the potential utility of mandates in achieving changes in environmentally significant individual behavior, particularly when deployed in combination with other policy approaches. Most directly, mandates could, by imposing external sanctions for their violation, raise the costs of behaviors that harm the environment and change the calculation of a rational actor deciding whether to undertake the behavior. Coupling mandates with norms can have a synergistic effect because "when law aligns with social norms, the law can use state sanctions to supplement social sanctions" and thereby "increase . . . the total sanction from disobeying a norm" and encourage norm compliance.

For example, in a municipality with an anti-idling ordinance, a driver deciding whether to idle would balance the benefits (convenience, ease, etc.) against the costs (the possibility of a ticket). And, as described above, mandates could function in an expressive manner to influence behavior by triggering personal and/or social norms.

Direct proscriptions on environmentally harmful individual behaviors may in fact prove to be a necessary complement to other policy tools for regulating individual behavior, such as informational regulation, norm management, and price signals. Notably, there is uncertainty about the potential efficacy of norm management in changing individual behaviors and even champions of the use of norm management recognize that there are some behaviors that norm campaigns cannot succeed in changing and concede that a variety of policy approaches, beyond norm management, will likely be needed.

The application of mandates to individuals has, however, received little sustained attention in the literature focused on reducing individual environmental harms. This is likely so because of identified obstacles to the adoption and enforcement of mandates. In the words of one scholar:

> The use of command and control requirements to change individual environmentally significant behavior has been less successful and, at least in the near term, is unlikely to be effective, efficient, or politically feasible. The thousands or millions of potential regulatory targets for any given environmental problem, the widespread belief that individuals are not significant pollution sources, and the cognitive barriers to changing that belief all make individual behavior extremely difficult to regulate through command and control instruments, particularly at the federal level. . . . In particular, the cost of enforcement against large numbers of individuals makes behavior change based solely on the threat of formal legal sanctions unlikely. To the extent environmental harms caused by individuals are difficult to detect, enforcement is expensive and intrusive. Even if sufficient resources were devoted to the effort, the intrusiveness of enforcing these regulations may undermine compliance or produce a political backlash.

Numerous other scholars have likewise articulated the difficulties that arise in attempts to mandate changes in individual behaviors. Consistent with these gloomy prognostications, examples of failed or troubled mandates aimed at individual behavior abound, most notably, federal transportation control plans ("TCPs") under the Clean Air Act. In the mid-1970s, EPA imposed TCPs in areas where they found state-developed plans for meeting national air quality standards inadequate. The TCPs "contained a variety of measures, many of which required basic changes in the commuting practices of average citizens or imposed substantial new burdens on state or local governments." Specifically, TCPs included measures such as parking surcharges, elimination or reduction of employee parking, prohibitions on on-street parking by commuters, tolls, the retrofit of older cars with pollution control devices, and gas rationing. The TCPs occasioned immediate and vociferous public protest and were never implemented. Congress and the courts limited EPA's authority to implement transportation controls and EPA largely abandoned its attempts to implement the TCPs.

Mandates, then, receive little attention as a policy tool for addressing environmentally significant individual behaviors not because they would not be useful, but because of pessimism about feasibility. A few scholars have commented, without much analysis, that mandates on individual behavior may be more feasible if adopted and enforced at the local level. Michael P. Vandenbergh, for example, identifies examples of successful local efforts to influence individual behaviors (household waste and motor oil disposal programs) and observes that "some extension of local government controls over individual behavior, where combined with other regulatory instruments, thus may be effective." And in his detailed account of the failure of a federal trip reduction mandate included in the 1990 Clean Air Act Amendments, Craig N. Oren draws a distinction between federal and local mandates. He argues that federal mandates on mobile sources of air pollution (primarily individual drivers) in particular are "acceptable" only under certain conditions, in part because "such mandates impose a cost in loss of local autonomy, and deprive states and localities of their role as 'laboratories' for innovation." Although his critique of the federal trip reduction mandate is devastating, Oren's analysis leaves room for the possibility that locally tailored trip reduction measures could prove more successful.

A closer examination of the identified obstacles to the use of mandates to address individual behaviors supports the view that mandates may prove more feasible at the local level. Local development and enforcement of mandates addressed to individual behavior can minimize two chief obstacles to imposing mandates on individual environmental behavior, that such mandates are uncomfortably intrusive and difficult to enforce. These obstacles are explained in greater detail below, along with possibilities for minimizing these obstacles through local design and enforcement.

A. Intrusion Objections

Mandates are the most intrusive policy approach for changing behavior. By prohibiting or requiring conduct, mandates foreclose choice and, as applied to individual behaviors, can be "seen as an interference with individual liberty and an invasion of privacy." These objections may be particularly pronounced when the individual behavior subject to regulation "occurs at home or in the immediately surrounding area," as with many environmentally significant behaviors. Additionally, individuals may find government regulation more objectionable where the proscribed behavior is perceived to be in their self-interest, perhaps because it is convenient, is ingrained as a personal habit, or provides other value.

Local governments are, however, in a position to blunt some of the aforementioned intrusion objections. First, local governments already impose restrictions on day-to-day behaviors in myriad ways. Don't park on the south side of the street on Tuesdays between 10 a.m. and 1 p.m. Don't cross the street against the light. Shhhhh — you're being too loud. Get a license for your dog and keep it on a leash. Put your trash out no earlier than 5 p.m. the night before collection and retrieve it no later than 9 p.m. on the day of collection. Remove junk from your yard within forty-eight hours. Yard-sale signs must be smaller than six square feet in area, must be posted no earlier than 12 p.m. the day prior to the sale and taken down no later than 12 p.m. the day after the sale, and cannot be placed within ten feet from the street pavement. Indeed, localities already impose mandates on individual behaviors that harm the environment, including anti-idling, recycling, and air pollution ordinances. Many of these local mandates on behavior seem ripe for intrusion objections because the behavior being regulated occurs in or near the home and/or complying is inconvenient. However, these types of local rules are widely accepted. In a sense, then, individuals are already habituated or conditioned to accept local restrictions on behavior.

By way of specific example, imagine a hypothetical municipal ordinance setting an upper limit on water heater temperature. The ubiquity of municipal building, electrical, and fire codes that impose a variety of detailed requirements on property maintenance and operation makes the prospect of this type of regulation seem far less jarring and intrusive than, for example, a similar federal requirement. This may be especially true in particular areas (the Sagebrush Rebellion West) or moments in time (perhaps the present, as evidenced by the Tea Party movement) where opposition to an expanded role for the federal government characterizes the political mood.

Additionally, for many of the same reasons that local information can help identify barriers to behavior change, local information may also prove crucial when ascertaining whether a particular restriction will trigger insurmountable intrusion objections in a community and/or when designing mandates to avoid intrusion objections. For example, the Albion, New York Municipal Code cited above imposes a requirement that dogs be leashed, but includes an exception for hunting. It provides that a dog must be leashed "unless [it] is accompanied by its owner or a responsible person and under the full control of such owner or person. For the purpose of this chapter, a dog or dogs hunting in company of a hunter or hunters shall be considered as accompanied by its owner." Local knowledge about the use of hunting dogs is reflected in the design of the ordinance and helps to avoid resistance to the rule by avoiding interference with a locally-valued behavior. Knowledge about community attitudes and practices can thus help local governments select and structure mandates to be less intrusive.

Finally, while behavioral mandates can take the form of "straightforward coercion" such as bans or requirements, they can also impose less intrusive "time, place, and manner restrictions" that channel behavior while preserving some individual choice. As one scholar describes, with respect to how the law influences consumption, "lawmaking [can] frame[] individual choices in a way that directs them in a socially desirable way," or "benevolently guide[]" the decisions of its citizens. With respect to individual GHG emissions, for example, a municipality could reduce driving without altogether prohibiting it by closing roads to vehicle traffic during certain times, eliminating or reducing on-street parking, or barring single-occupancy vehicles from parking facilities at, for example, large sports arenas. The design and implementation of these types of restrictions is inextricably local.

B. Enforcement

Enforcement — in terms of both its practical and political feasibility — is frequently identified as the chief obstacle to mandates on environmentally significant individual behavior. A law aimed directly at individual behavior would need to be enforced against individuals. Individuals are, however, numerous, and may engage in environmentally significant behaviors in private spaces. Monitoring individual behavior can thus prove costly and pose serious logistical challenges. Significantly, however, local design and enforcement of mandates on individual behaviors can minimize the key enforcement challenges of expense, numerosity, and (in)visibility.

Local governments already possess an infrastructure that brings them into regular contact with their citizens and provides opportunities for both observation and enforcement. Local governments, for example, usually control household garbage collection, enforce local ordinances that address everything from noise to parking, issue permits for activities like sporting events, concerts, and parades, own and operate local parks and recreation facilities, and maintain local police, fire, and emergency response forces. Moreover, a variety of local special-use districts (school districts, water districts, local electric utilities, etc.) touch even more aspects of citizens' daily lives.

This existing infrastructure and contact could reduce both the expense associated with the enforcement of mandates on individual behavior and the challenges posed by numerosity. Enforcement of new mandates might be piggybacked on the enforcement of existing municipal rules and requirements, thereby potentially reducing expense. Local governments do not, for example, need to hire new "tire inspectors" to enforce a requirement that tires be kept inflated to appropriate levels. Tickets could be issued by the existing police force during traffic stops that would occur anyway. A requirement to lower water heater temperatures could be incorporated into the enforcement of the existing building code. And with respect to numerosity, local governments are accustomed to enforcing myriad laws on those individuals. Local governments are also in a better position to assess the visibility of behavior and make determinations about whether behavior can feasibly be subject to enforcement. As explained above, whether and how conduct is "visible" may depend on a variety of community-specific variables that local governments are in a better position to understand.

Local governments can also capitalize on knowledge of existing local norms to design laws so that they will be reinforced by existing norms. "Law might purposefully choose rules — that law would on its own have avoided — in order to gain this reinforcement . . . . There is, in other words, a cost to law's straying from norms, and law best does whatever it is that it is trying to do by [avoiding] these costs." Localities can deploy knowledge of local norms to craft mandates to piggyback on those norms, thereby increasing the likelihood of compliance apart from any independent enforcement efforts.

Finally, law may function to influence behavior even absent meaningful enforcement. Public involvement in state and federal policymaking is perhaps more limited and constrained than at the local level, where there may be more opportunities for democratic participation. Involvement at the local level may encourage compliance with local laws (regardless of opportunities for enforcement) because "people are more likely to comply with decisions and agreements they have played a role in formulating." Also, as described above, laws can influence behavior through their expressive function even in the absence of consistent enforcement. And, for a variety of reasons, the expressive value of local law may be particularly powerful. As one scholar argues, local laws may provide "a stronger signal of the local attitudes that matter most," and "an individual cares primarily about local attitudes because judgments of approval and disapproval are mostly local." Thus, we might expect "a larger expressive effect from local laws than state or federal laws, from local ordinances regulating smoking, recycling, and dogs more than state or federal statutes regulating speeding, motorcycle helmets or drunk driving." Accordingly, local governments may not only be in a better position to identify circumstances where enforcement is not feasible, they may also be best able to influence behavior through concededly unenforceable mandates by relying on their expressive function.

———

NOTES AND QUESTIONS

1. Many individuals may be willing to incur certain costs to reduce their individual and household carbon emissions, but they feel that unless many others do the same, their actions will not have a real impact in terms of reducing climate change. Legal mandates help solve this collective action problem, but they come up against the problems of intrusiveness and enforcement discussed by Professor Kuh. Do you agree with Professor Kuh that legal mandates relating to individual behavior will be acceptable to people if they are designed and enforced at the local level? Which of the following individual and household behaviors do you think local governments could regulate effectively using mandates? Which do you think would better addressed at the state or federal level using policies such as taxes and subsidies that affect the prices consumers pay?

   - Choosing a fuel-efficient car
   - Adopting efficient driving practices
   - Reducing driving by carpooling
   - Weatherizing your home
   - Replacing inefficient household appliances
   - Replacing inefficient heating and cooling units
   - Setting back thermostats
   - Washing laundry at lower temperatures
   - Line drying laundry
   - Installing low-flow showerheads and toilets
   - Eating less meat
   - Recycling all recyclables

2. Another way to directly use law to change individual and household behavior is through legal mandates that expand or reduce the consumer choices of individuals. California, for example, passed a zero-emissions vehicle (ZEV) mandate in 1990 that required major automobile makers to offer electric vehicles in order to continue sales of their gasoline-powered vehicles in the state. To learn about this mandate and its fate, see the film, *Who Killed the Electric Car?* (Sony Pictures 2006). Similarly, government could ban the sale of very low mileage per gallon passenger vehicles such as Hummers. The Energy Independence and Security Act (EISA) of 2007 set efficiency standards that will phase out traditional incandescent light bulbs between 2012 and 2014. Pub. L. No. 110-140, 121 Stat. 1492 (2007). Although the relevant

provisions of the Act are expected to save $13 billion in energy costs and prevent 100 million tons of carbon emissions, they have been held up as a symbol of big government that overreaches and intervenes in the private lives of Americans. Do you think that Congress should set efficiency standards for light bulbs, appliances, cars, and other products that effectively restrict consumer choices?

CHAPTER 7

THE FUTURE OF CLIMATE CHANGE LAW AND POLICY: RISKS AND POSSIBILITIES

This concluding chapter looks to the future of climate change law and policy. In so doing, it engages a question that has been lurking below the surface of the preceding chapters: What if we fail to mitigate adequately? The book up to this point has looked at international, national, subnational, and nongovernmental efforts to address climate change, but it is clear that none of these efforts are coming close to what scientists say are needed to minimize the risks of major climate change. Although the 2011 Durban climate change negotiations resulted in breakthroughs on a universal agreement and on a second Kyoto Protocol commitment period, these laudable steps forward will not significantly change the emissions scenarios over the next few years.

Given that troubling reality, this chapter explores the potential pathways that remain if we do not start to mitigate more aggressively soon. It considers two risky and potentially intertwined future scenarios, and the role that law might play in each of them. In the first scenario, which looks likely to be our path if mitigation efforts continue on their current course, major climate change transforms the globe, and leaders must contemplate significant relocation and reconstitution of law and society in response. In the second scenario, which also seems possible given our tendency to look for technological solutions to problems, the nations of the world decide to try to reverse climate change through geoengineering. These scenarios are not mutually exclusive; they could both happen to varying degrees, as well as in combination with current mitigation approaches. They might be proposed and decided upon in a deliberate way, or they might be undertaken as part of a hasty and desperate response to major climate change.

The primary way to avoid these two risky scenarios is through adequate mitigation that results in relatively limited climate change and accompanying adaptation. The book concludes by exploring how future lawyers and policymakers interested in this problem can work toward adequate mitigation and adaptation most effectively while preparing for this chapter's riskier scenarios.

A. SCENARIO ONE: INADEQUATE MITIGATION LEADS TO MAJOR IMPACTS AND ADAPTATION

Climate change already has begun to impact Arctic, low-lying coastal, and desert communities significantly. If we continue on our current emissions trajectory or even a slightly reduced one, climate change will likely affect an ever-greater swath of humanity. Moreover, the impacts of climate change are not distributed equally. Those who are most physically vulnerable are often in the places least able to adapt.

This reality raises not only profound justice questions, but also geopolitical, national security, and economic ones. As places become unlivable, climate change refugees will increase, as will the risk of armed conflict in some of the most impacted areas. This section engages those concerns, and considers the difficult human and legal issues that major climate change would raise.

1. MAINTAINING CARBON DIOXIDE LEVELS BELOW CRITICAL THRESHOLDS

Leading climate scientists claim that we must keep carbon dioxide below threshold levels in order to avoid the risk of major climate change. These scientists indicate that the safest approach is to keep carbon dioxide concentrations below 350 parts per million. However, we have already exceeded that threshold significantly—as monitored by the National Oceanic & Atmospheric Administration (NOAA) at the Mauna Loa Observatory, Hawaii, the atmospheric carbon dioxide concentration in 2011 exceeded 390 parts per million, *see Recent Mauna Loa CO₂*, NOAA, http://www.esrl.noaa.gov/gmd/ccgg/trends/ (last visited Apr. 22, 2012)—and is moving rapidly toward the riskier 450 parts per million.

The following excerpt from an article written by a number of climate scientists just before the Copenhagen negotiations explains why the 350 parts per million threshold is important. It describes the escalating risks as we exceed that concentration and have a greater risk of an over two degrees Celsius rise in temperature from pre-industrial levels.

JOHAN ROCKSTRÖM ET AL., A SAFE OPERATING SPACE FOR HUMANITY

461 Nature 472, 473 (2009)

Climate Change

Anthropogenic climate change is now beyond dispute, and . . . the international discussions on targets for climate mitigation have intensified. There is a growing convergence towards a '2 °C guardrail' approach, that is, containing the rise in global mean temperature to no more than 2 °C above the pre-industrial level.

Our proposed climate boundary is based on two critical thresholds that separate qualitatively different climate-system states. It has two parameters: atmospheric concentration of carbon dioxide and radiative forcing (the rate of energy change per unit area of the globe as measured at the top of the atmosphere). We propose that human changes to atmospheric CO_2 concentrations should not exceed 350 parts per million by volume [p.p.m.v.], and that radiative forcing should not exceed 1 watt per square metre above pre-industrial levels.

Transgressing these boundaries will increase the risk of irreversible climate change, such as the loss of major ice sheets, accelerated sealevel rise and abrupt shifts in forest and agricultural systems. Current CO_2 concentration stands at 387 p.p.m.v. and the change in radiative forcing is 1.5 W m^{-2} [watts per square meter].

There are at least three reasons for our proposed climate boundary. First, current climate models may significantly underestimate the severity of long-term climate change for a given concentration of greenhouse gases. Most models suggest that a doubling in atmospheric CO_2 concentration will lead to a global temperature rise of about 3 °C (with a probable uncertainty range of 2–4.5 °C) once the climate has regained equilibrium. But these models do not include long-term reinforcing feedback processes that further warm the climate, such as decreases in the surface area of ice cover or changes in the distribution of vegetation. If these slow feedbacks are included, doubling CO_2 levels gives an eventual temperature increase of 6 °C (with a probable uncertainty range of 4–8 °C). This would threaten the ecological life-support systems that have developed in the late Quaternary environment, and would severely challenge the viability of contemporary human societies.

The second consideration is the stability of the large polar ice sheets. Palaeo climate data from the past 100 million years show that CO_2 concentrations were a major factor in the long-term cooling of the past 50 million years. Moreover, the planet was largely ice-free until CO_2 concentrations fell below 450 p.p.m.v. (±100 p.p.m.v.), suggesting that there is a critical threshold between 350 and 550 p.p.m.v. Our boundary of 350 p.p.m.v. aims to ensure the continued existence of the large polar ice sheets.

Third, we are beginning to see evidence that some of Earth's subsystems are already moving outside their stable Holocene state. This includes the rapid retreat of the summer sea ice in the Arctic ocean, the retreat of mountain glaciers around the world, the loss of mass from the Greenland and West Antarctic ice sheets and the accelerating rates of sealevel rise during the past 10–15 years.

Adequate mitigation means staying below this destabilizing threshold, which we may be approaching as carbon dioxide concentrations continue to grow at levels beyond 350 parts per million. The more we exceed it, the greater the risks of major climate change impacts become. Organizations such as 350.org have formed around trying to keep concentrations below 350 parts per million and are exploring what measures are needed to do so.

The following excerpt from Professor Mary Wood explains, in human and biological terms, the importance of keeping carbon dioxide below destabilizing concentrations. It explores what the role of law could be in assisting needed transformation.

MARY CHRISTINA WOOD, "YOU CAN'T NEGOTIATE WITH A BEETLE":
ENVIRONMENTAL LAW FOR A NEW ECOLOGICAL AGE

50 Nat. Resources J. 167, 183–91 (2010)

IV. Climate Emergency and the Big Adaptation

. . . .

The crisis that eclipses all others today is climate change, a situation that creates enormous stakes for virtually every human being on Earth. In June 2007, a team of leading climate scientists warned that carbon dioxide and other greenhouse gas emissions have put Earth in "imminent peril"—literally on the verge of runaway climate heating that would impose catastrophic conditions on generations to come. Runaway heating threatens to melt the polar ice sheets and Greenland, kill the coral reefs, and turn the Amazon rainforest into savannah. It would bring floods, hurricanes, killer heat waves, fires, disease, crop losses, food shortages, and droughts of a caliber that is unimaginable to many. If unchecked, it will cause rising sea levels and inundation of coastal areas worldwide. Biologists warn that climate change could wipe out 40 percent to 70 percent of the world's species, triggering the kind of mass extinction that has not occurred on Earth for 55 million years. In the words of NASA Goddard Institute for Space Studies director, Jim Hansen, our continued carbon pollution will "transform the planet."

The implications for humanity, and the world's children, are unthinkable. If runaway heating comes to pass, it could mean death for millions or even billions of Earth's citizens. Even under the present heating scenarios, the United Nations estimates that the numbers of environmental refugees will climb to 50 million by 2010, and then to 1 billion by 2050. Desperate mass human migrations will pose unending threats to world security. Legal institutions that collapse under such stress will no longer provide stability, and many predict that a much hotter world would trigger the breakdown of civilization as we know it.

The global warming crisis has mind-blowing urgency, because of what scientists call the "tipping point." This is a climate tripwire, so to speak, a point at which humanity's carbon pollution kicks in dangerous natural feedback loops that could unravel the planet's climate system, despite any subsequent carbon reductions achieved by humanity. Due to carbon in the atmosphere from past releases, Earth is now precariously close to triggering these lethal feedbacks that would threaten civilization as we know it.

Some feedbacks are already underway. First, vast areas of permafrost are now melting, releasing carbon and methane. Scientists fear that such melting permafrost could release a billion tons of carbon dioxide a year to the atmosphere, creating what one science writer calls an "atmospheric tsunami." Second, as the polar ice caps melt, they, in turn, cause more planetary heating, because the ice, which reflects heat, turns to water, which absorbs heat—a phenomenon known as the "albedo flip." Third, the natural "sinks," such as oceans and forests, that have historically absorbed society's carbon pollution, have reached their limits and are now failing. Vast swaths of forest are dying and burning, both releasing carbon and eliminating carbon absorption capacity. Even the Amazon rainforest—the lungs of the planet—is now a significant source of carbon pollution. Finally, the oceans are so saturated with carbon that they are acidifying, creating conditions that are lethal to shellfish. These and other alarming feedbacks caused scientists to warn in 2007: "Recent greenhouse gas (GHG) emissions place the Earth perilously close to dramatic climate change that could run out of our control, with great dangers for humans and other creatures."

The world has only a narrow window of time to slash global emissions of carbon before the planet passes the tipping point. While just two years ago scientists believed the tipping point would be triggered at 450 parts per million of carbon in the atmosphere, some now believe the tipping point is below 350 parts per million. Present levels are at 387 parts per million. Analysts now repeatedly warn in the clearest terms possible that Earth is in a danger zone—a state of planetary emergency. Yet, following an aimless "business as usual" course, humanity continues to emit enormous amounts of carbon dioxide. Until the economic collapse of 2008, the yearly average increase in emissions was between 2 and 3 percent. As James Speth concludes, "[If we] keep doing exactly what we are doing today, [even] with no growth in the human population or the world economy . . . the world in the latter part of this century won't be fit to live in."

Even if humanity manages to prevent runaway heating, the natural world is already locked into extreme change. Due to the persistence of carbon already in the atmosphere, the world is projected to heat, at the very least, approximately 2.6 degrees Fahrenheit further. This is known as the heating "in the pipeline." In other words, this heating will occur despite cuts in GHG pollution. Projected effects from such irrevocable heating include increased storm intensity, a rise in sea levels, between 20 and 30 percent species loss, forest die-offs, drought, fire, crop loss, and a myriad of other harmful or deadly consequences.

The climate challenge boils down to two Herculean tasks, both of which put environmental law at the forefront of humanity's response. In climate circles, these tasks are tagged by the rather uninspiring terms "mitigation" and "adaptation." The first, "mitigation," means that humanity has to slash carbon emissions enough to prevent runaway heating. This is a huge challenge, since fossil fuels are the engine of modern industrial society and support virtually every aspect of human activity, including transportation, construction, food systems, and electricity use. The second term, "adaptation," means that humanity must figure out how to survive the heating that it can no longer avoid. No one really knows what the additional 2.6 degrees Fahrenheit will mean for daily living conditions, but it is certain to create radical change, given that the 1.6 degree Fahrenheit average temperature increase experienced so far is enough to prompt scientific predictions that the summer ice caps at the poles will vanish by 2012. The dual necessity of mitigation and adaptation is perhaps best captured by Thomas Friedman when he says: "Avoid the unmanageable and manage the unavoidable."

Mitigation and adaptation, together, create an imperative to protect natural resources immediately, across the board, for two basic reasons. First, doing so is the only means of avoiding the climate tipping point. Scientists make clear that we need to take urgent measures to draw down carbon pollution from currently dangerous levels. This not only means steep pollution reduction from obvious sources such as coal-fired power plants and cars, but also measures to preserve and enhance natural sinks such as forests and soils that can absorb carbon. In policy terms, this means a halt to much extractive old growth logging, wetland destruction, virgin land development, and industrial farming that damages soils.

Second, it is vital to protect the natural resources we still have in order to adapt to the irrevocable climate heating already underway and thereby maximize human survival. The Global Humanitarian Forum estimates that 300 million people — about 5 percent of the world's population — are already seriously impacted by climate change. Humanity now has to look at virtually all of its natural infrastructure in a different light, because many systems will fail, and as they do, natural resources will become ever more scarce. The reality is that humanity simply will not have all of the water, species, productive soils, and forests that it inherited from past generations. In the new world of climate heating, all remaining natural assets carry a premium for human survival and welfare.

For example, recent data show that the major rivers of the world are losing significant water due to climate change. Rivers across the United States are already over-appropriated, and 35 states in this country are engaged in water conflicts with their neighbors. In other parts of the world, such conflicts lead to war. As the glaciers melt due to global warming, the stable input into rivers disappears, and water sources collapse. Cities and farms in need of water will turn to other sources, including underground aquifers. But those sources may be contaminated due to pollution permitted under law by environmental agencies. Already in the United States, more than 700 chemicals have been detected in drinking water, and 129 of those are highly toxic. Any remaining uncontaminated water carries a premium of value to society.

Climate change also brings floods, pests, and temperature extremes, all of which are a blow to agricultural production. With global warming, food shortages are manifestly on the horizon. Already, 45 million people are chronically hungry due to climate change. According to the United Nations, by 2030 food prices will rise 20 percent and 75 percent of the world's population will be hungry. In just the past few years, Australia's extended drought has caused an 89 percent decline in rice production. The prospect of climate damage makes all of the remaining agricultural soils that much more valuable. But the valuable virgin soils are still gouged and paved over for strip malls, destination resorts, and subdivisions, all permitted under law by local land-use agencies.

Forests are part of the vital ecology of Earth. They provide vegetative cover for countless species and support the headwaters for major rivers and streams. The city of New York, for example, relies heavily on forests in the Catskills Mountains for its water supply. Portland, Oregon, and other cities in the Willamette Valley depend on the Bull Run watershed, which is encased by century-old trees. But due to climate heating, forests are dying at twice their normal rates, and mega-wild fires are devouring forestlands with unprecedented speed. Seemingly oblivious to the change, the U.S. Forest Service and state land agencies continue to allow harvests that shred the vegetative fabric supporting many crucial water sources.

One assumption seems solid: The more natural resources that are kept intact and functional, the more natural stock humans will be able to draw upon in the future, and the better odds humans will have to adapt to potentially devastating ecological change. Environmental management must incorporate a precautionary approach that places a premium on all remaining nature, for overlooked resources will undoubtedly host attributes that are crucial to future generations. The environmental law of the past was tailor-made for the transnational industrial age. Environmental law must be remade for what can be termed the "New Ecological Age." Agencies must significantly amplify the protection of vital resources, which means that they must strengthen their resistance to proposals for private profit that cause ecological damage.

Unfortunately, the dismal record of environmental law gives no basis for confidence that the approach of the past is suitable for the challenges ahead. Instead, a look at how environmental law operates reveals systemic dysfunction that permeates the entire structure. Operating with this dysfunction, agencies continue to authorize damage as if nature had unlimited abundance and capacity to heal—as if the end were not already in sight.

NOTES AND QUESTIONS

1. Professor Wood's article provides a pretty stark case for needed transformations in environmental law. If you were to design environmental law for the "New Ecological Age," what would that entail?
2. Climate scientists James Hansen, Makiko Sato, Pushker Kharecha, David Beerling, Robert Berner, Valerie Masson-Delmotte, Mark Pagan, Maureen Raymo, Dana L. Royer, and James C. Zachos have argued that the only way to avoid major climate change is to phase out coal until we have the technical capacity to effectively engage in carbon sequestration and storage. They explain: "Coal is the largest reservoir of conventional fossil fuels, exceeding combined reserves of oil and gas. The only realistic way to sharply curtail CO_2 emissions is to phase out coal use except where CO_2 is captured and sequestered." James Hansen et al., *Target Atmospheric CO_2: Where Should Humanity Aim?*, 2 OPEN ATMOSPHERE SCI. J. 217, 226 (2008). Is there any realistic way of achieving such a phase out? How would you go about doing so?

2. ENVIRONMENTAL JUSTICE DIMENSIONS OF MAJOR CLIMATE CHANGE

Although we have not yet hit a point where the climate has changed enough for most of the world's population to face serious consequences, a number of vulnerable populations already experience significant impacts.

This disproportionate distribution of harm, particularly given that the major emitters are generally not those facing the most severe harms in the near term, poses a serious environmental justice problem. While efforts exist under the UNFCCC to address some of these justice issues, such as through mechanisms to encourage technology transfer or provide adaptation funding, deep inequities remain.

The following excerpt by Professor Ruth Gordon details the unequal harm due to climate change faced by Africa, small island states, and indigenous peoples of the Arctic. It provides a window into both the current justice problem and the kinds of impacts that massive climate change potentially would cause more broadly in the future.

RUTH GORDON, CLIMATE CHANGE AND THE POOREST NATIONS:
FURTHER REFLECTIONS ON GLOBAL INEQUALITY

78 U. Colo. L. Rev. 1559, 1589-99 (2007)

III. The Asymmetrical Consequences of Global Warming: The View from the South

While the planet will undoubtedly survive the assault on its climate, regardless of how much damage humans cause, the impact upon its inhabitants, be they flora or fauna, is less certain. We do not know how many species will be lost as flora and fauna attempt to adapt to a rapidly changing climate, nor can we totally understand the potentially infinite effects upon ecosystems under severe stress. While we can readily observe the misfortunes of the polar bear, we cannot completely assess what is happening to rain forests that must quickly adapt, or the impact of losing coral reefs, which are sensitive to rising temperatures and greatly affect ocean ecosystems. We can only be humbled by what we do not know and by the scores of previously unanticipated effects that have already come to pass.

What we do know, however, is that southern-tier nations will be disproportionately affected by climate change, and many of these nations will be the least equipped to deal with these consequences. This Part will begin with a focus on African nations, which face a variety of harms and, because of their poverty, will have an especially difficult time dealing with them. It will then turn to small island nations, which face annihilation, and then briefly to the native peoples of the Arctic region, who are giving us a glimpse into one possible future. Both small island nations and Arctic peoples face the most catastrophic consequences: the total destruction of their habitat and thus of their culture, community, and way of life. For them, global warming means the unmitigated end of life as they have always known it.

A. Africa

Climate change is already a reality for poor African nations, with Kenya, Sudan, Ethiopia, Somalia, and Chad witnessing the consequences; indeed, the conflict in Darfur may be the first climate change conflict and an indication of similar future wars. Climate change is leading to "reduced rainfall and shrinking areas of arable land," and the number of food emergencies in sub-Saharan Africa each year has tripled since the 1980s. Desert lands are advancing into once-arable rain-fed areas, and wetter parts of Africa are getting wetter, often leading to devastating floods. Yet African nations have contributed very little to global warming, with emissions of less than 8% of the world's GHGs and most of this low sum coming from South Africa. The continent is particularly vulnerable to the effects of global warming, which will have a disproportionate impact on low-income unindustrialized nations, many of which also happen to be the nations that are, and will continue to be, least able to handle it. In other words, the world's poor will be shouldering yet another burden not of their making.

Africa is particularly at risk to climate change, in part because of its poverty and a lack of resources to deal with a problem that is beyond its control. Taken as a whole, it is the poorest continent in the world and probably the least industrialized. Technological and economic resources are minimal. Drought, floods, and food scarcity are already problems in some areas, and these problems are likely to multiply and intensify. In countries already vulnerable to drought, less rainfall is predicted, which will raise particular difficulties regarding water resources. Fourteen countries in Africa already suffer from water insufficiency, and it is estimated that another eleven nations will join this unenviable club within the next twenty-five years. Where water resources are shared, there is a potential for conflict as nations clash over an increasingly insufficient supply. Moreover, there are already discussions regarding the prospect of "climate change refugees," to portray the large scale and pervasive displacement of African peoples. Desertification is expected to intensify as there is less rainfall and land becomes increasingly scarce.

Global warming is expected to put an additional 80 to 120 million people at risk of hunger, and 70% to 80% of these people will be located in Africa. As weather patterns become more unpredictable, farmers are having a difficult time determining where and what to plant. Food insecurity is expected to increase as agricultural production declines due to lack of water and changing ecosystems. It is predicted that climate change could lead to a 5% drop in the production of food crops.

Rapidly changing ecosystems also raise the specter of risks to biodiversity and natural resource productivity. Many impoverished peoples depend on the diversity of surrounding ecosystems to support their way of life. Global warming, however, will have potentially devastating effects on habitats and the diversity found within already fragile ecosystems; between 25% and 40% of Africa's natural plant habitats could be lost by 2085. The Working Group on Climate Change and Development predicts that as plant species used in traditional medicines become extinct, local peoples' capacity to combat illnesses will become increasingly impaired. Vector- and water-borne diseases are expected to escalate, especially in areas with an inadequate health infrastructure. Heat stress, air pollution, water failures, water- and food-borne diseases, and food insecurity present other potential health hazards that are particularly problematic in the absence of sufficient medical services. Women may bear the brunt of these disasters, having limited access to land, education, and credit, while producing 80% of the crops. Their traditional knowledge may be crucial in addressing these issues, even if this knowledge alone is insufficient.

Finally, global warming is expected to intensify coastal erosion, flooding, and subsidence, problems that already plague Africa's coastal areas. Coastal zones are vulnerable to rising sea levels, with roads, bridges, buildings, and other infrastructure at risk of flooding, and populations that are vulnerable to the kind of disaster flooding brings. Rising sea levels could destroy an estimated 30% of Africa's coastal infrastructure.

B. Small Island States

Like their counterparts in impoverished nations, small island states did not contribute to climate change to any measurable extent; most are unindustrialized, relying mainly on tourism and light industry to support their economies. Yet, despite their lack of responsibility, these nations are likely to suffer especially abysmal consequences, including paying the ultimate price — their possible annihilation. This may be the definitive manifestation of unsustainability.

Small island states are "especially vulnerable to the effects of climate change, [such as] sea level rise and extreme events," and the prospect of rising oceans is especially dangerous and threatening. Climate change has been linked to deteriorating weather patterns that will include more severe storms, tornadoes, hurricanes, and cyclones, and islands are more likely to be in areas where many of these events take place. Predictions of how much the oceans will rise over the next one hundred years range from a best case scenario of .18 meters to a worst case of .59 meters, if melting glacial ice sheets are not taken into account. If this melting is included, in one hundred years, ocean levels could rise by four to six meters, and perhaps as high as seven meters. Many small island states are less than three to four meters above the present mean sea level, and thus the potential to be completely inundated is undeniable. Sea levels have already begun rising and pervasive and irreversible changes at the poles have commenced. The Kilinailau Islands have shrunk, and some have been cut in half by the sea. Salt water has encroached upon land, making it impossible to grow breadfruit and forcing the inhabitants to relocate. The island nations of Kiribati, Tuvalu, and Niue and the Marshall Islands are already beginning to contemplate relocating their inhabitants, looking toward Australia. Indeed, some inhabitants of islands in Kiribati have already been forced to relocate.

Rising sea levels will present other problems. They will exacerbate coastal and other low-lying area flooding, and intensify storm surges, erosion, and other coastal hazards. This in turn will threaten vital infrastructure, settlements, and facilities that support the livelihood of island peoples. Rising sea levels may also directly affect freshwater resources, agricultural production, and island biodiversity. By mid-century, water resources in many small islands are predicted to reach the point where they become inadequate to meet the needs of their inhabitants during low rain periods.

Increasing ocean temperatures may also stress ocean ecosystems, destroying habitats and altering migratory patterns of some ocean species. Coral reefs, which have been termed the rainforests of the ocean, are acutely sensitive to water temperature and thus are at particular risk. Coral reefs grow slowly and take many years to recover from damage. Their destruction has very serious implications because "fish depend on coral reefs for food and shelter, while coastal inhabitants depend on coral reefs for culture and food." Increasing ocean temperatures may also cause the migratory patterns of some ocean species to change, which could destroy habitats. In addition, higher temperatures may cause non-native species invasions to increase.

Finally, many island states heavily depend on tourism for income and foreign exchange, and there is little doubt that these negative effects have great potential to disrupt tourism. Beach erosion, soil salinization, increased stresses on coastal ecosystems, and damage to the infrastructure can only have a negative impact on tourism. Thus, at best, these nations face a tremendous assault upon their environment and, since their economies are intimately tied to the environment, their economies are likely to decline, perhaps drastically. At worst, they face the total destruction of their homes, cultures, and communities — that is the end of their existence as a community.

C. Native Communities of the North

Island nations might look to the societies of the Arctic as a window into their future. Arctic communities are already being displaced as their surroundings become uninhabitable. The Arctic is extremely vulnerable to the effects of current and projected climate change, and it is already experiencing some of "the most rapid and severe climate change on earth." Given this vulnerability, the region is already experiencing "deterioration in ice conditions, a decrease in the quantity and quality of snow, changes in the weather and weather patterns, and a transfigured landscape as permafrost melts at an alarming rate, causing slumping, landslides, and severe erosion in some coastal areas." One of the most important changes has been in the sea ice, which has diminished and become thinner, and is freezing later and thawing earlier. This has had a profound impact, as the Inuit depend on ice of a certain thickness to travel, hunt, harvest, and communicate between communities. "The quality, quantity and timing of snowfall have also changed," with implications for igloo building and travel. "Permafrost, which holds together unstable underground gravel and inhibits water drainage, is melting at an alarming rate, causing . . . landslides, severe erosion and loss of ground moisture, wetlands and lakes." This erosion has had a devastating effect on Inuit tribes, forcing relocations in some cases. There have been changes in water levels, more unpredictable weather, and changes in the location, characteristics, amount, and health of plant and animal species. "Increased temperatures and sun intensity have heightened the risk of previously rare health problems."

All of these changes have wrought profound changes upon the Inuit community, gravely affecting their way of life. The projected impact, however, may mean total destruction of their way of life. In the Arctic Climate Impact Assessment, it is predicted, inter alia, that:

- warming will increase four to seven degrees Celsius or twice the global average rate;
- precipitation will increase, winters will become shorter and warmer, and snow and ice cover will substantially decrease;

- reductions in sea ice will drastically shrink marine habitats for a number of species;
- land based creatures will likely be increasingly stressed as climate change alters breeding grounds, food sources, and migration routes;
- species ranges will shift northward;
- more diseases will shift from animals to humans;
- rising sea levels and a reduction in sea ice will result in higher waves and thus contribute to coastal erosion;
- thawing permafrost will weaken coastal lands; and
- flooding in coastal wetlands will increase.

The species upon which many indigenous peoples depend "not only for food and to support the local economy, but also as the basis for cultural and social identity," are at severe risk. Moreover, it will be increasingly difficult to safely travel to access these species, posing perhaps insurmountable challenges to human health and food security. Because of this intimate connection between Inuit culture and the health of their environment, the "widespread environmental upheaval resulting from climate change violates the Inuit's right to practice and enjoy the benefits of their culture."

NOTES AND QUESTIONS

1. What do you think are the most appropriate ways of addressing the injustices that Professor Gordon describes? Professor Maxine Burkett recommends setting up a reparations system at a global scale to address climate justice concerns. She argues that "any successful reparations effort must contain three critical elements: an apology, a monetary or other award that gives actual or symbolic weight to that apology, and, most importantly, a commitment by the perpetrator not to repeat the offending act, also known as the 'guarantee of nonrepetition.'" Maxine Burkett, *Climate Reparations*, 10 MELBOURNE J. INT'L L. 509, 527 (2009). How might such a system complement current efforts to engage in Clean Development Mechanism projects and establish an adaptation fund? What would be a reparations system's greatest benefits and limitations?

2. At a domestic level, Professor Alice Kaswan has argued for weaning our nation from fossil fuels and greening the energy grid as important mechanisms for addressing climate change justice. *See* Alice Kaswan, *Greening the Grid and Climate Justice*, 39 ENVTL. L. 1143 (2009). To achieve clean energy goals and also address justice concerns, Professor Burkett additionally argues that we need a domestic Clean Development Mechanism (CDM) that creates clean energy projects in low-income communities of color. As she explains:

   In the short term, adoption of the domestic CDM, though not the overarching remedy that environmental justice advocates would like to see most, is the remedy that is consistent with the current trajectory of policy-makers and, as such, is the most feasible approach. There are also significant advantages that attach to this solution. Besides meeting the theoretical and practical mandates of the environmental justice movement, it is an important engine for emergent economic development opportunities across the nation's rural and urban communities. This and the struggle for more fundamental systemic changes can, and should, be done concurrently.

The additional, though less obvious, benefit of this analysis is that it sets a framework for how the United States can meet its responsibilities and obligations to poor and of-color communities throughout the globe. Climate justice, in other words, can forcefully encourage the United States to consider the consequences of its political and economic character and incorporate the attendant moral obligations into its choice of solutions. If the environmental justice movement cannot curb the excesses of the United States' political economy, however, it will surely be ill-equipped to do so on a global scale. There is a growing sense that the continued relevance of the movement is hinged on its ability to have consequence in the fate of the global poor and of-color. The environmental justice movement, therefore, must be a critical and consequential crafter of domestic, and ultimately global, solutions.

Maxine Burkett, *Just Solutions to Climate Change: A Climate Justice Proposal for a Domestic Clean Development Mechanism*, 56 Buff. L. Rev. 169, 242–43 (2008).

What do you think about the possibility of developing a domestic CDM as part of our domestic efforts to address climate change injustice?

3. CLIMATE CHANGE REFUGEES

If major climate change takes place, many people will need to move from their communities and, in some cases, their countries. This relocation will not only pose issues for those forced to leave, but also for those receiving them. These concerns raise questions about the legal structures needed to manage these shifts.

The following excerpt from an article by Professors Bonnie Docherty and Tyler Giannini details the looming problem of migration induced by climate change. It describes the inadequacy of our existing refugee and climate change legal frameworks to address the needs of these migrants.

Bonnie Docherty & Tyler Giannini, Confronting a Rising Tide: A Proposal for a Convention on Climate Change Refugees

---

33 Harv. Envtl. L. Rev. 349, 349–61 (2009)

I. Introduction

Climate change will force millions of people to flee their homes over the coming century. Rising sea levels threaten to envelop small island states. Desertification will make swaths of currently occupied land uninhabitable. More intense storms will drive people, at least temporarily, to relocate to safer ground. Studies predict that by 2050 the number of climate change refugees may dwarf the number of traditional refugees — that is, those entitled to protection under the 1951 Refugee Convention and its 1967 Protocol. Climate change is an environmental phenomenon, yet most scientists agree that human activities around the world contribute to it. Because the nature of climate change is global and humans play a contributory role, the international community should accept responsibility for mitigating climate-induced displacement. States should develop an innovative, international, and interdisciplinary approach that can be implemented before the situation reaches a crisis stage. To date, no such satisfactory solution exists.

. . . .

II. Foundational Issues

Studies predict that, over the coming decades, environmental disruptions caused by climate change will lead tens, and perhaps hundreds, of millions of people to leave their homes and in some cases their countries. At the same time, both international legal frameworks and their associated institutions have gaps in their mandates that make it difficult for them to address the problem adequately. The existing refugee and climate change regimes in particular are ill-suited to handle this foreseeable migration. Any solution to the population flows resulting from climate change will require a new holistic and interdisciplinary approach because the problem does not fit solely within a human rights or an international environmental law framework.

A. The Emerging Problem of Climate Change Migration

Acknowledgment of the emerging problem of climate change migration has grown over the past two decades. As early as 1990, the Intergovernmental Panel on Climate Change ("IPCC"), a United Nations scientific body that won the 2007 Nobel Peace Prize for its comprehensive and objective reports on climate change, highlighted the effect of climate change on humans. It stated that "[t]he gravest effects of climate change may be those on human migration as millions are uprooted by shoreline erosion, coastal flooding and agricultural disruption." More recently, the United Nations Office of the High Commissioner for Human Rights ("OHCHR") has begun to pay specific attention to climate change, noting that it could affect hundreds of millions of people in numerous ways, including through "permanent displacement." In February 2008, the Deputy High Commissioner for Human Rights said:

> By 2050, hundreds of millions more people may become permanently displaced due to rising sea levels, floods, droughts, famine and hurricanes. The melting or collapse of ice sheets alone threatens the homes of 1 in every 20 people. Increased desertification and the alteration of ecosystems, by endangering communities' livelihoods, are also likely to trigger large population displacements.

Thus, experts in both the environmental and human rights communities have expressed concern about the seriousness of climate change migration.

Estimates of the number of people who will flee their homes because of climate change vary depending on the definition of the class of displacees and the source of the data. While some research urges caution in attempting to predict a number, other studies present figures ranging from 50 million to 200 million displaced persons before 2100. Norman Myers, for example, observed in 1995 that "global warming could put large numbers of people at risk of displacement by the middle of next century if not before." Myers continued:

> Preliminary estimates indicate the total [number] of people at risk of sea-level rise in Bangladesh could be 26 million, in Egypt 12 million, in China 73 million, in India 20 million, and elsewhere 31 million, making an aggregate total of 162 million. At the same time, at least 50 million people could be at risk through increased droughts and other climate dislocations.

The oft-cited 2006 Stern Review, a major British government study on climate change, notes that while Myers' estimate of 150 to 200 million persons has not been "rigorously tested," such numbers "remain in line with the evidence presented . . . that climate change will lead to hundreds of millions more people without sufficient water or food to survive." Estimates for displacement in Egypt and the Mekong Delta alone run as high as ten million for each area. By comparison, the Office of the United Nations High Commissioner for Refugees ("UNHCR"), the central United Nations organ that deals with traditional refugees, reported that globally in 2006 there were fewer than ten million refugees as defined by the 1951 Refugee Convention. Regardless of the exact figure of those displaced by climate change, experts have recognized this burgeoning problem.

The displaced will include both those who relocate within a country and those who leave their home state. In reviewing climate change's impact on security in 2008, the German Advisory Council on Global Change observed that "[i]t is likely that growing numbers of people will be affected by environmentally-induced migration and migration movements will more and more frequently take place across national borders." This transboundary displacement could have negative effects around the globe. According to the German Advisory Council, climate change has "implications not only for the affected societies but for the international system as a whole. . . . Migration, for example, could become unmanageable." While exact numbers of those who will cross borders in such situations is difficult to predict at present, the numbers will be substantial—likely in the millions given the consistent projections of much higher levels of overall displacement.

Observers predict that climate change migration will particularly affect certain hotspots, especially small island states, coastal zones, and regions of Africa and Asia. Floods and the frequency and intensity of storms will likely increase internal and international displacement, particularly in Asia. Sea-level rise will probably be most acute for small island states and areas of Asia. Glacial melts have been linked to environmental migration in South Asia. Drought and water scarcity will probably have the greatest impact on people who live in Africa and Asia.

Three categories of climate change effects—rising sea levels; an increasing quantity and intensity of storms; and drought, desertification, and water shortages—are expected to contribute most to migration flows. The number of people forced to migrate may dramatically increase as these effects become more pronounced. These impacts are among the most agreed-upon consequences of climate change and appear to be those most likely to result in forced transnational flight. Such migration may occur temporarily, as when people flee a severe storm, or on a more permanent basis, as either an entire state or a substantial part of a state becomes uninhabitable.

The prospect of entire nations disappearing is real for small island states. Their low elevation (sometimes only a few meters above sea level) and large coastal areas will exacerbate the effects of climate-induced disruptions. The Maldives, for example, could see portions of its capital flooded by 2025. Other states, including Kiribati, Tuvalu, the Marshall Islands, and several Caribbean islands, are also considered threatened. Although there has been much publicity about rising sea levels and potentially "sinking states," storms or water shortages also pose significant risks to small island states. Any of these effects of climate change could cause inhabitants to flee their country.

While some states may cease to exist, others may lose portions of territorial lands, which would in turn spur migration. Climate change will greatly affect coastal zones in certain regions, particularly in Asia. Major disruptions loom for certain low-lying, shoreline areas, such as those in Bangladesh, regions of which will be submerged. Eighty percent of Bangladesh is a delta, and the country is "specially susceptible to the impacts of global warming, including enhanced typhoons, storm surges and sea-level rise." In 1995, half of Bhola Island in Bangladesh became permanently flooded, leaving homeless 500,000 people, who have been described as some of the world's first climate change refugees. In all, scientists predict rising sea levels may ultimately swallow more than twenty percent of Bangladesh's land.

While the exact numbers of people who will be forced to cross borders because of climate change is not known, there are growing indications that the numbers are significant. This displacement may overwhelm not only receiving states but also the international legal system, which has yet to develop an adequate legal regime or institutionalized response to the problem.

B. The Legal Gap

Neither of the most relevant legal frameworks—namely refugee law and climate change law—precisely and definitively addresses the issue of climate change refugees, a term that in this Article refers to those who flee climate-induced disruptions across national boundaries and that will be defined in detail below. While broad principles of international law may have some normative value and provide arguments for assisting these refugees, there is a clear lacuna in the existing international legal system. No legal instrument specifically speaks to the issue of climate change refugees, and no international institution has the clear mandate to serve this population, which needs human rights protection and humanitarian aid. Discussing the relationship between climate change, migration, and human rights in February 2008, OHCHR's Deputy Commissioner of Human Rights emphasized the importance of "reflect[ing] upon gaps in protection." In short, displacement due to climate change is a de facto problem currently lacking a de jure solution.

1. Lack of Legal Frameworks

In principle, refugee and climate change law offer possibilities for addressing the problem of climate change migration. Despite proposals for them to do so, however, neither regime has embraced the notion of providing rights and aid to those who flee environmental disruption.

The refugee regime's narrow definition of refugee restricts its power to help with the climate change situation. The 1951 Refugee Convention defines a refugee as someone with a "well-founded fear of being persecuted for reasons of race, religion, nationality, membership of a particular social group or political opinion." Most commentators do not believe that environmental refugees, a concept that gained traction decades after the Refugee Convention's adoption, fall within its scope. They argue that climate change refugees have not been persecuted in the same way that traditional refugees have. Climate change refugees can, and still do, look to their home states for protection in ways that those fleeing traditional persecution, often at the hands of the state, do not. There has also been little political mobilization to amend the Refugee Convention's core definition, leaving the Convention too narrow an instrument to look to for protection for climate change refugees. The UNFCCC applies directly to climate change, but it too has legal limitations for dealing with climate change refugees. As an international environmental law treaty, the UNFCCC primarily concerns state-to-state relations; it does not discuss duties that states have to individuals or communities, such as those laid out in human rights or refugee law. It is also preventive in nature and less focused on the remedial actions that are needed in a refugee context. Finally, although the UNFCCC has an initiative to help states with adaptation to climate change, that program does not specifically deal with the situation of climate change refugees. Like the refugee regime, the UNFCCC was not designed for, and to date has not adequately dealt with, the problem of climate change refugees.

2. Lack of Institutions

Even if a legal framework for providing protection and aid to climate change refugees could be found in international law, the practical reality is that the international community and existing institutions are not addressing the problem. No comprehensive response, either internationally or nationally, has emerged, and small ad hoc initiatives are unlikely to provide the consistency and breadth needed for a long-term solution.

UNHCR has not instituted protections for environmental refugees and has not viewed its mandate as including such protections. Given the potential number of climate change refugees, UNHCR is likely concerned about expanding its mandate to include a population that would overwhelm its institutional capacity.

The UNFCCC's existing institutions are also ill-suited to take on the climate change refugee problem at present. Its adaptation efforts focus primarily on prevention and mitigation of climate change itself, rather than assistance for those who cross borders to flee climate change's effects. In sum, because neither the refugee nor the climate change regime was specifically created to solve such climate-induced dislocation, a major legal and policy void needs to be filled.

C. A Broad, Interdisciplinary Legal and Policy Framework

Climate change is expected to spark migration, and the lack of existing law and institutions will exacerbate the situation. A number of other factors, however, play a role in the emerging climate change refugee problem and should inform the solution. Conditions beyond environmental disruption, such as poverty, can contribute to displacement that is primarily caused by climate change. Climate-induced problems may lead to circumstances, such as armed conflict, that increase population flows. Various stresses, including population growth and poor governance, affect countries' abilities to prevent the need for relocation and to cope with any displacement that occurs. Climate change migration also involves a wide range of actors, including individuals, communities, home and host states, and the international community more broadly, which complicates efforts to deal with climate change migration fairly and effectively. A holistic approach to the climate change refugee problem should consider the needs and positions of parties and encompass a variety of relevant disciplines, including law, science, economics, technological innovation, development, and poverty alleviation.

The climate change refugee instrument that this Article proposes is only part of a larger framework for tackling foreseeable climate change migration. Because there are limits to what the law can achieve, other policy efforts are likely to be just as critical. Policies that help decrease the factors that compel people to leave are important. For example, the UNFCCC's 2007 Bali Action Plan promotes national initiatives to support sustainable development, economic diversification, conservation of forests, and technology transfers. In the context of considering climate change's impact on security, the German Advisory Council recommends the use of multiple disciplines, such as water management, poverty reduction, and agricultural programs, to help prevent security concerns from arising in their most severe form. The climate change refugee instrument should thus complement, rather than replace, other efforts that can reduce the need for individuals to flee their nations and generally mitigate the situation.

In addition, more inclusive approaches that apply to all those who flee climate change disruptions should supplement the binding climate change refugee instrument. Internally displaced persons ("IDPs"), who involuntarily leave their homes but not their countries because of climate change, should be part of the framework to deal with climate change displacement more broadly. Such displacement fits under the rubric of improving human security and well-being. In some situations, such as when a state fails in its responsibility to protect a community, IDPs may have as much need as refugees for international assistance. The issue of climate change IDPs is beyond the scope of this Article, but it deserves attention as the international community develops ways to deal with climate change migration.

D. Conclusion

The international community is now faced with the emergence of climate change-induced migration that will likely lead to millions of refugees crossing state borders during the next century. As evidenced by the inadequacies of the existing refugee and climate change frameworks, there is a clear need for a more specific and specialized legal instrument to fill the gap that presently exists within international law. While that instrument should be viewed as one piece of a larger solution to the problem of displacement, it would be a critical step toward mitigating the burgeoning crisis of climate change refugees.

. . . .

NOTES AND QUESTIONS

1. Lester Brown first used the term "environmental refugee" in 1976, and since then it and other variations have been used to describe people who are relocating in significant part due to environmental factors. The situations in which people migrate are often complex, with poverty and political instability interacting with the environmental factors involved. Professor Gaim Kibreab argues that this complexity makes a clear understanding of the precise role of climate change in migration difficult. He notes:

> Although the warming of the earth's climate system is not any longer controversial, its social impacts, for example, on precipitation, food insecurity, land use changes and overall agricultural production are still ambiguous. More equivocal are also the impact of climate change on human migration. This should not be construed to imply that climate change is an irrelevant factor in causing migration—be it forced or voluntary. What is emphasized is the fact that climate change operates in interaction with other multiple factors from which it is impossible to isolate. The claim that climate change causes population displacement is based on the wrong assumption that displacement is partly mono-causal and climate change can be isolated from other inextricably interwoven drivers of migration or displacement.
>
> The reason the available estimates of people displaced by climate change are unreliable is due to the fact that migration is the result of multiple causes and, therefore, it is difficult to isolate the role of the environment from the other drivers of migration. . . .
>
> Therefore there is need for concerted international action not only in terms of addressing the root causes of climate change and in mitigating its detrimental consequences, but also in meeting the protection and assistance needs of those who are affected. In the presence of political will, negotiated scheme of burden-sharing, international and regional solidarity, investment in poor and vulnerable countries' disaster preparedness and effective early warning systems, the protection and assistance needs of many of the persons whose displacement is induced by environmental change can be met within the framework of the existing international protection regime manifested in the 1951 U.N. Convention, the 1967 Protocol, the 1969 OAU Convention, the 1984 Cartagena Declaration and the 1998 Guidelines on the Principles of Internal Displacement.
>
> Gaim Kibreab, *Climate Change and Human Migration: A Tenuous Relationship?*, 20 FORDHAM ENVTL. L. REV. 357, 400–01 (2009).

How should strategies for relocation related to climate change deal with its multi-factor character?

2. How should we address the gaps in the law regarding climate change refugees? In the above article, Professors Docherty and Giannini argue for a new instrument on the issue. In an alternative approach, Professor Katrina Wyman explores justifications for and possible implementation of a right to resettle grounded in the right to a safe haven. *See* Katrina Miriam Wyman, *Sinking States, in* Property in Land and Other Resources 439 (Daniel H. Cole & Elinor Ostrom eds., 2012). In a third variation, Professor Elizabeth Burleson suggests that these issues be dealt with in the adaptation mechanisms under the UNFCCC. *See* Elizabeth Burleson, *Essay: Climate Change Displacement to Refugee*, 25 J. Envtl. L. & Litig. 19 (2010). What do you think would be the best approach?

4. NATIONAL SECURITY CONCERNS

The impacts of major climate change would be massively destabilizing at subnational, national, regional, and international levels. In some circumstances, resulting resource scarcity or shifting of particular ethnic groups might lead to armed conflict. Even when they do not, climate change will still cause significant shifts in the geopolitical map that will also raise national security concerns.

The United Nations Security Council debated these issues for the first time in April 2007. The following excerpt from that debate illuminates some of the complexities at the intersection of climate change with peace and security.

Press Release, Security Council, Security Council Holds
First-Ever Debate on the Impact of Climate Change on Peace and Security,
Hearing over 50 Speakers, U.N. Press Release SC/9000 (Apr. 17, 2007)

http://www.un.org/News/Press/docs/2007/sc9000.doc.htm

With scientists predicting that land and water resources will gradually become more scarce in the coming years, and that global warming may irreversibly alter the face of the planet, the United Nations Security Council today held its first-ever debate on the impact of climate change on security, as some delegates raised doubts over whether the Council was the proper forum to discuss the issue.

The day-long meeting, called by the United Kingdom, aimed to examine the relationship between energy, security and climate, and featured interventions from more than 50 delegations, representing imperiled island nations and industrialized greenhouse gas emitters alike. While some speakers praised the initiative, there were reservations from developing countries, which saw climate change as a socio-economic development issue to be dealt with by the more widely representative General Assembly. Many delegations also called for the United Nations to urgently consider convening a global summit on the issue.

The session was chaired by British Foreign Secretary, Margaret Beckett, whose country holds the presidency of the 15-nation Council for April. She said that recent scientific evidence reinforced, or even exceeded, the worst fears about climate change, as she warned of migration on an unprecedented scale because of flooding, disease and famine. She also said that drought and crop failure could cause intensified competition for food, water and energy.

She said that climate change was a security issue, but it was not a matter of narrow national security—it was about "our collective security in a fragile and increasingly interdependent world". By holding today's debate, the Council was not seeking to pre-empt the authority of other bodies, including the General Assembly and the Economic and Social Council. The decisions that they came to, and action taken, in all those bodies required the fullest possible understanding of the issues involved. "[So] climate change can bring us together, if we have the wisdom to prevent it from driving us apart," she declared.

Calling for a "long-term global response" to deal with climate change, along with unified efforts involving the Security Council, Member States and other international bodies, Secretary-General Ban Ki-moon said that projected climate changes could not only have serious environmental, social and economic implications, but implications for peace and security, as well.

"This is especially true in vulnerable regions that face multiple stresses at the same time—pre-existing conflict, poverty and unequal access to resources, weak institutions, food insecurity and incidence of diseases such as HIV/AIDS," he said. The Secretary-General outlined several "alarming, though not alarmist" scenarios, including limited or threatened access to energy increasing the risk of conflict, a scarcity of food and water transforming peaceful competition into violence and floods and droughts sparking massive human migrations, polarizing societies and weakening the ability of countries to resolve conflicts peacefully.

China's representative was among those who argued that the Council was not the proper forum for a debate on climate change. "The developing countries believe that the Security Council has neither the professional competence in handling climate change—nor is it the right decision-making place for extensive participation leading up to widely acceptable proposals," he said.

The issue could have certain security implications, but, generally speaking, it was, in essence, an issue of sustainable development. The United Nations Framework Convention on Climate Change had laid down the fundamental principles for the international community's response to climate change. The Kyoto Protocol had set up targets for developed countries—limited, but measurable—for reducing greenhouse gas emissions. To effectively respond to climate change, he said it was necessary to follow the principle of "common, but differentiated, responsibilities" set forth in the Convention, respect existing arrangements, strengthen cooperation and encourage more action.

The representative of Pakistan, speaking on behalf of the "Group of 77" developing countries and China, agreed, saying that the Council's primary duty was to maintain international peace and security. Other issues, including those related to economic and social development, were assigned to the Economic and Social Council and the General Assembly. The ever-increasing encroachment of the Security Council on the roles and responsibilities of the other main organs of the United Nations represented a "distortion" of the principles and purposes of the Charter, infringed on the authority of the other bodies and compromised the rights of the Organization's wider membership.

But Papua New Guinea's representative, who spoke on behalf of the Pacific Islands Forum, said that the impact of climate change on small islands was no less threatening than the dangers guns and bombs posed to large nations. Pacific island countries were likely to face massive dislocations of people, similar to population flows sparked by conflict. The impact on identity and social cohesion were likely to cause as much resentment, hatred and alienation as any refugee crisis.

"The Security Council, charged with protecting human rights and the integrity and security of States, is the paramount international forum available to us," he said. The Forum did not expect the Council to get involved in Climate Change Convention negotiations, but it did expect the 15-member body to keep the issue of climate change under continuous review, to ensure that all countries contributed to solving the problem and that those efforts were commensurate with their resources and capacities. It also expected the Council to review sensitive issues, such as implications for sovereignty and international legal rights from the loss of land, resources and people.

Singapore's speaker said that, while it was obvious that there was some discomfort about the venue and nature of today's debate, it was equally obvious that climate change was "the" global environmental challenge. Given their paucity of resources, developing countries would be the hardest hit, and some had their survival at stake. But it was not only the poor that would suffer. There was broad consensus that it was necessary to act to arrest what "we ourselves are responsible for". Many of the problems caused by climate change could only be tackled if nations worked together.

"Let us view our procedural disagreements against this backdrop," he said. While it might be difficult to quantify the relationship between climate change and international peace and security, there should be no doubt that climate change was an immediate global challenge, whose effects were transboundary and multifaceted. He was not advocating that the Security Council play a key role on climate change, but neither could he deny that body "some sort of a role, because it seems obvious to all but the wilfully blind that climate change must, if not now, then eventually have some impact on international peace and security.

Also participating in today's debate were the Minister for Foreign Affairs of Slovakia, the Under-Secretary of State for Foreign Affairs of Italy, the Federal Minister for Economic Cooperation and Development of Germany (on behalf of the European Union), the Minister for Development and Cooperation of the Netherlands and the Minister for State and Foreign Affairs of the Maldives.

Others taking part in the meeting were the representatives of Belgium, Ghana, Congo, Qatar, United States, France, Indonesia, Panama, South Africa, Russian Federation, Peru, Switzerland, Japan, Namibia, Barbados, Ukraine, Egypt, Australia, New Zealand, Tuvalu, Bangladesh, Venezuela, Sudan (on behalf of the African Group), Solomon Islands, Palau, Denmark, Iceland, Marshall Islands, Philippines, Mexico, Brazil, India, Republic of Korea, Norway, Federated States of Micronesia, Argentina, Cuba (on behalf of the Non-Aligned Movement), Liechtenstein, Bolivia, Cape Verde, Costa Rica, Israel, Canada, Mauritius and Comoros.

NOTES AND QUESTIONS

1. The countries participating in this interchange disagreed about whether the U.N. Security Council was an appropriate venue for addressing these issues. What do you think about the venue and about the substantive issues being discussed?
2. Professor David Caron is exploring the economic, geopolitical, and security consequences of Arctic melting. He argues that we are in a transitional state between a frozen Arctic Ocean and a fully melted one, with the sea now accessible for part of the year. Once the Arctic Ocean is fully melted, there will be difficult questions of national and international control and access. How do you think an open Arctic Ocean should be managed?
3. A dozen retired U.S. generals and admirals served as a Military Advisory Board to assess how climate change could affect this country's national security over a 30- to 40-year timeframe. The board's primary findings and recommendations were:

> Finding 1: Projected climate change poses a serious threat to America's national security. . . . Finding 2: Climate change acts as a threat multiplier for instability in some of the most volatile regions of the world. . . . Finding 3: Projected climate change will add to tensions even in stable regions of the world. . . . Finding 4: Climate change, national security, and energy dependence are a related set of global challenges. . . .
>
> . . . .
>
> Recommendation 1: The national security consequences of climate change should be fully integrated into national security and national defense strategies. . . . Recommendation 2: The U.S. should commit to a stronger national and international role to help stabilize climate change at levels that will avoid significant disruption to global security and stability. . . . Recommendation 3: The U.S. should commit to global partnerships that help less developed nations build the capacity and resiliency to better manage climate impacts. . . . Recommendation 4: The Department of Defense should enhance its operational capability by accelerating the adoption of improved business processes and innovative technologies that result in improved U.S. combat power through energy efficiency. . . . Recommendation 5: The Department of Defense should conduct an assessment of the impact on U.S. military installations worldwide of rising sea levels, extreme weather events, and other projected climate change impacts over the next 30 to 40 years.
>
> CNA CORP., NATIONAL SECURITY AND THE THREAT OF CLIMATE CHANGE 44–48 (2007), *available at* http://www.cna.org/reports/climate.

B. SCENARIO TWO: EFFORTS TO REVERSE CLIMATE CHANGE THROUGH GEOENGINEERING

As the prospects of bringing emissions down to the levels that scientists say are needed to avoid the most serious impacts of climate change seem increasingly poor, some scientists and policymakers have begun to consider whether a technological solution to climate change is possible. Specifically, they hope to reverse climate change by altering key components of the climate system in ways that reduce greenhouse gases already in the environment or limit their warming effects. These strategies are referred to as geoengineering.

This section explores the scenario in which we attempt to reverse climate change through these geoengineering approaches. It begins by considering the capacity of current science and technology to reverse climate change and the direction that this research is going. It then turns to the limited legal regime currently applicable to geoengineering. It concludes with an assessment of the risks and benefits of attempting to solve climate change in this fashion.

1. THE STATE OF THE SCIENCE AND TECHNOLOGY

The science and technology of geoengineering are developing rapidly, and numerous leading groups of scientists are considering different options. Geoengineering approaches, as a physical matter, largely fall into two categories. The first, known as solar radiation management (SRM), involves increasing the reflectivity of the earth to decrease the warming. SRM techniques do not address the root causes of climate change, but might work rapidly to stop the planetary heating and its associated harms (though not some of the other problems like ocean acidification). The second, known as carbon dioxide removal (CDR), involves physically removing carbon from the environment in a variety of ways. CDR addresses the root causes of climate change, but tends to be slower in its impacts.

The following excerpt from Professor Albert Lin describes the growing interest in finding technological fixes for climate change and some of the leading proposed methods for using geoengineering to address climate change. It focuses on two widely discussed approaches: putting aerosols into the atmosphere and fertilizing the ocean.

Albert C. Lin, Geoengineering Governance, Issues in Legal Scholarship, Apr. 2009, at 1, 1–7

http://www.degruyter.com/view/j/ils.2009.8.3/ils.2009.8.3.1112/ils.2009.8.3.1112.xml?format=INT

Mounting evidence of the seriousness of the climate change problem has prompted increased domestic and international efforts to slow or counter expected changes. The main focus of such efforts has been to curb greenhouse gas (GHG) emissions, whether through cap-and-trade schemes, vehicle emission standards, land use regulation, or other tools. Recent proposals in Congress have called for an 80% reduction in U.S. GHG emissions from 2005 levels by the year 2050, and according to widely accepted estimates, GHG emissions must decrease by at least 50% worldwide within the same period if the most serious climate change impacts are to be avoided.

Global and national-level efforts to reduce emissions, however, have been relatively unsuccessful thus far. Internationally, the Kyoto Protocol called for reductions of up to eight percent in GHG emissions from 1990 levels by industrialized countries during the period from 2008 to 2012, yet even this modest goal appears out of reach. Meanwhile, atmospheric GHG concentrations have continued rising steadily, as have mean global temperatures. Indeed, observations of actual changes in climate, such as the rate of glacial retreat and the extent of polar ice melt, have tended to exceed predictions regarding such changes.

The difficulties associated with achieving the drastic emissions reductions needed to avoid the more serious risks of climate change have led scientists, scholars, and policymakers to begin to consider potential technological approaches to the problem. One such approach, carbon capture and sequestration (CCS), would capture CO_2 from power plants and compress it for sequestration in stable geological formations underground or in the oceans. CCS is not a perfect solution: some of the sequestered CO_2 would likely return to the atmosphere over time; additional energy would be required to separate, compress, and inject CO_2; and surface releases of CO_2 at high concentrations could result in deaths or cause harm to flora and fauna. Nevertheless, policymakers consider CCS to be a low-risk abatement strategy, the design of potential regulatory regimes for CCS is underway, and implementation of CCS projects has begun.

Another, more controversial, technological approach to climate change is geoengineering. Geoengineering refers to various techniques, such as the release of aerosols into the stratosphere or the fertilization of the oceans, that focus on mitigating the consequences of higher GHG concentrations, rather than on reducing GHG emissions or capturing emissions before they are released into the environment. To date, the debate over geoengineering technologies among policymakers and scientists has tended to concern whether or not they should be deployed in response to the climate change problem. What has received less attention are the preliminary yet fundamental questions of geoengineering governance. These questions include: who should decide whether geoengineering research or deployment should go forward, how such decisions should be made, and what mechanisms should be in place to address the risk of deployment by rogue actors.

. . . .

I. The Basics of Geoengineering

In contrast to relatively uncontroversial technologies that reduce GHG emissions through increased energy efficiency or the use of renewable energy, geoengineering technologies involve projects that are intended specifically to mitigate the effects of GHG emissions once they are released. This intent, combined with the grand scale of these projects, are defining features of geoengineering proposals, scientist David Keith has suggested. This Part provides a brief overview of leading geoengineering proposals, including potential risks associated with each.

A. Albedo Modification

Some geoengineering proposals seek to reduce the amount of energy the Earth absorbs by modifying the Earth's albedo (i.e., reflectivity). Examples of such proposals include (1) the release of particles into the stratosphere, and (2) the use of space-based deflectors. Each of these technologies presents its own engineering challenges and environmental risks. Scientists have observed that the addition of sulfur to the stratosphere, either through natural activity such as volcanic eruptions or through human activity that generates SO_2 and other pollutants, produces a cooling effect by causing more sunlight to be reflected into space. Chemical and micro-physical processes convert the SO_2 into light-reflecting particles (or aerosols) that remain in the stratosphere for one to two years, counteracting the warming effect associated with higher GHG concentrations. While the deliberate release of SO_2 might stabilize global average temperatures to some degree, it would not necessarily prevent significant local climate changes from taking place. Nevertheless, the use of stratospheric aerosols is probably the most seriously discussed geoengineering proposal because of its relative technical and economic feasibility.

There could be substantial environmental and safety impacts associated with implementing such a scheme, however. One serious concern involves ozone depletion: scientists have found that the release of particles by large volcanic eruptions damages the stratospheric ozone layer that provides protection from the sun's ultraviolet rays. The addition of SO_2 particles to the stratosphere is likely to have a similar effect. Another shortcoming of the release of aerosols is that there would be little or no effect on atmospheric GHG concentrations. This means that such a scheme would only provide temporary relief from any warming effect; the release of aerosols would have to continue for several hundred years to allow the oceans to absorb gradually the CO_2 currently being released by humans. This form of geoengineering, in other words, would only buy time to reduce GHG emissions or to find other means of countering climate change.

Meanwhile, cessation of aerosol release after such a program had been in place for some time could cause far more rapid climate change than would have occurred in the absence of any initial geoengineering efforts. Furthermore, the release of aerosols would do nothing to counter the problem of ocean acidification. The acidity of the ocean is directly correlated to GHG levels, and increased acidity could lead to the loss of many of the Earth's coral reefs, which serve as important marine habitat. Elevated GHG levels would affect terrestrial ecosystems as well, as plant species that flourish under high concentrations of atmospheric CO_2 gain a competitive advantage over other species, leading to changes in habitat and biodiversity. In addition to these concerns, there may be other adverse effects that we cannot currently anticipate.

An alternative albedo modification approach that could sidestep some of these problems would deploy deflectors in outer space. Under one such proposal, a fleet of almost-transparent discs the size of dustbin lids would be launched into orbits that would keep them between the Earth and the sun, reducing sunlight by nearly two percent, an amount sufficient to counter the warming effect of a doubling of atmospheric GHG concentrations. The use of space-based deflectors would avoid the aforementioned risks (such as ozone depletion) associated with tinkering with the Earth's atmosphere via aerosol releases. The deflectors, however, would have to be replaced at the end of their useful lives, lest rapid climate change occur, and would generate debris that could interfere with Earth-orbiting spacecraft. And compared to the use of stratospheric aerosols, this approach would be far more costly and would face immensely more complicated barriers to implementation.

Finally, albedo modification proposals in general would reduce the amount of sunlight reaching the Earth, and thus likely would have other effects that are not yet fully understood. Sunlight plays a key role in global hydrology, for instance, and reduced solar forcing could disrupt the Asian and African monsoons that are vital to food supplies in those regions of the world.

B. Enhancing Oceanic Sinks

Another set of geoengineering proposals involves the addition of micronutrients to the oceans in order to increase the uptake of carbon by phytoplankton. The theory underlying ocean fertilization proposals is that unavailability of various micronutrients limits biological productivity in certain oceanic regions, such that adding a relatively small amount of the limiting micronutrients will drastically increase phytoplankton populations. While some of the carbon absorbed by phytoplankton will return to the surface ocean through natural decay processes, the sinking of dead phytoplankton will remove the rest of the carbon to the deep ocean and prevent it from reentering the atmosphere. The most common ocean fertilization proposal involves iron. Ice-core data reveals that relatively abundant iron supplies from atmospheric dust during glacial periods coincided with lower atmospheric CO_2 concentrations, leading some scientists to conclude that iron is the most important limiting micronutrient. Although an iron fertilization scheme would require significant quantities of iron, global supplies of this micronutrient are sufficient to support the execution of the proposal at a relatively moderate cost.

Experimental studies, however, have yielded unimpressive results regarding the amount of CO_2 that an iron fertilization scheme would ultimately remove from the atmosphere. Uncertainties surround the rate of vertical mixing in the oceans (which would be necessary to remove carbon from the atmosphere), the form of iron that would optimize phytoplankton growth, and the presence of other nutrients necessary for iron fertilization to be effective. Moreover, ocean fertilization schemes risk significant alteration of marine ecosystems. Phytoplankton form the foundation of marine food webs, and changes in their populations could lead to unpredictable changes in ecosystems, as well as heightened production of methane and other GHGs. Perhaps ameliorating these concerns somewhat, the iron fertilization process can be halted fairly readily if serious negative consequences arise.

As noted above, the growing number of high-level scientific meetings on geoengineering serves as an indicator that this approach is being taken more seriously. These meetings often involve disagreements among scientists as they grapple with the physical uncertainties and ethical implications of deliberate manipulation of the climate system.

The following article describes one such meeting in 2007. It provides the historical context for the meeting and the ethical complexities that arose.

Eli Kintisch, Scientists Say Continued Warming Warrants Closer Look at Drastic Fixes

318 Science 1054 (2007)

Should scientists study novel ways to alter Earth's climate to counteract global warming? Last week, a group of prominent researchers who gathered here gave a qualified "yes" — after agreeing that the road to understanding the science is fraught with booby traps and that deliberately tinkering with the climate could make the problem worse. Some even admitted to being surprised by their affirmative answer.

"My objective going [into the meeting] was to stop people from doing something stupid," says climate modeler David Battisti of the University of Washington, Seattle. But rising temperatures and carbon emissions, combined with little meaningful action by politicians, convinced him and his colleagues that it was time for mainstream climate science to look more closely at geoengineering. Even so, Battisti suspects that the participants share the hope of many of those who took part in the Manhattan Project to build the atom bomb: that society would never have to use the knowledge they provided. "It would be incomprehensible that we deploy this," Battisti says, emphasizing the greater need to cut carbon emissions.

Organized by the University of Calgary and Harvard University, the event allowed 50 elite climate, energy, and economics researchers to explore and debate geoengineering. For decades, the subject has been mostly confined to the pages of science fiction and unfunded by research agencies. But a 2006 paper in *Climatic Change* by Nobelist Paul Crutzen (*Science*, 20 October 2006, p. 401) served as an "enabler" to drive discussion among scientists of the once-taboo topic, says Harvard environmental chemist Scot Martin. Harvard geochemist Daniel Schrag and physicist David Keith of the University of Calgary in Canada then decided to organize the Cambridge event.

One reason most scientists have been leery of probing the topic was the fear that if such technical fixes were taken seriously, public support for cutting carbon emissions would be even more difficult to achieve. "The very best would be if emissions of the greenhouse gasses could be reduced so much that the [geoengineering] experiment would not have to take place," Crutzen wrote last year. "Currently, this looks like a pious wish."

Some scientists, however, have been thinking about geoengineering for quite some time. The field's roots lie in dueling Soviet and U.S. weather-modification programs of the 1960s. Since then, advocates have dreamed up schemes to fight warming by blocking sunlight with giant space shades or by creating sea clouds to increase the albedo of the ocean. In 1997, physicist and Star Wars stalwart Lowell Wood and colleagues affiliated with Livermore Berkeley National Laboratory suggested using aerosols to mimic the cooling effect of volcanoes, and a handful of modeling papers since have simulated that effect.

One of Wood's central points is that the aerosol method is cheap. In 1992, recalls Harvard physicist Robert Frosch, a National Academies' panel on climate resisted his suggestion to include the cost of geoengineering options in a figure on possible solutions to global warming. One relatively simple option: Inject sulfur dioxide into the stratosphere to reduce the amount of solar energy reaching Earth's surface. "Nobody wanted to put the geoengineering line on the figure because it looked too [economically] easy," Frosch told participants.

That cost was a major factor behind the discussions here, with a number of preliminary technical studies hinting that the SO_2 option could be deployed for a few billion dollars a year. That amount could make geoengineering attractive to politicians looking for radical fixes in a warming world. "The decision on whether to do this will not be made by this group," Schrag told his colleagues sitting in the wood-paneled premises of the American Academy of Arts and Sciences. But what scientists can do, he said, is offset the input of groups driven by profit or ideology with solid research on the possible side effects of various geoengineering techniques.

And to get started, the group certainly suggested plenty of side effects. Atmospheric dynamicists attacked the few modeling studies that have simulated geoengineering efforts for down-playing details such as ocean currents or complex feedbacks. (Modelers defended their studies, which use simplified models, as preliminary.) Ecologists pointed out that artificial cooling could lead to serious drying in the tropics and that any fix that lowers Earth's temperature wouldn't address the problem of the steadily acidifying ocean.

Modeler Raymond Pierrehumbert of the University of Chicago in Illinois warned that geoengineering could become a global addiction. "I don't actually work on geoengineering," he told the group. "But now that the genie's out of the bottle, I feel I have to." In one unpublished experiment, Pierrehumbert simulated a future scenario, presumably in the next century, in which the amount of atmospheric CO_2 had quadrupled but Earth was kept cool by a yearly dose of geoengineering. His model showed that a halt in the geoengineering effort—"by, say, a war or revolution"—would result in an 7°C temperature jump in the tropics in 30 years. That rise, he says, would trigger unimaginable ecological effects.

Sallie Chisholm, an MIT biological oceanographer, urged caution. She told *Science* that her colleagues are down-playing the difficulty of determining how "inherently unpredictable" biospheric feedbacks will react to "turning the temperature knob. . . . We cannot predict the biosphere's response to an intentional reduction in global temperature through geoengineering."

Other scientists were more willing to entertain the idea of studying climate manipulation but warned about a likely public backlash. Political scientist Thomas Homer-Dixon of the University of Toronto in Canada talked about street protests. "Some people may consider geoengineering to be an act of ultimate hubris," he says. "It's going to provoke fear, anger, guilt, and despair."

Others, however, viewed public alarm about geoengineering as a potentially positive effect. "If they see us talking about this as a last-ditch effort, it might increase their alarm" and drive them to cut emissions, explained Harvard climate dynamicist Peter Huybers during one of the sessions. By the end of the 2-day event, participants were stunned that they had come so far. "In this room, we've reached a remarkable consensus that there should be research on this," announced climate modeler Chris Bretherton of the University of Washington, Seattle. Nobody dissented.

Mixed in with his new sense of "responsibility," Battisti says, is dismay that the climate problem has grown so serious as to drive scientists to contemplate steps that, in theory, might lead to more serious problems than continued warming. After speaking on the phone with his wife from his hotel room, Battisti confessed, "I told her this meeting is terrifying me."

———————

In a further sign of the shift toward serious consideration of geoengineering, the Intergovernmental Panel on Climate Change (IPCC) will be including geoengineering for the first time in its upcoming Fifth Assessment Report. It is currently convening discussions among experts about how geoengineering fits into the science, impacts and adaptation, and mitigation aspects of its report.

The following excerpt describes the IPCC's efforts on these issues. It provides an overview of the motivations behind and core goals of a summer 2011 meeting to frame the IPCC's reporting on geoengineering.

IPCC, Busan, S. Kor., Oct. 11-14, 2010, The IPCC Fifth Assessment Report (AR5), Proposal for an IPCC Expert Meeting on Geoengineering, 32d Session, IPCC-XXXII/Document 5

http://ipcc.ch/meetings/session32/doc05_p32_proposal_EM_on_geoengineering.pdf

1. Background

Geoengineering, or the deliberate large-scale manipulation of the planetary environment, is increasingly being discussed as a potential strategy to counteract anthropogenic climate change. Prevailing uncertainty in the sensitivity of the climate system to anthropogenic forcing, inertia in both the coupled climate-carbon cycle and social systems, and the potential for irreversibilities and abrupt, nonlinear changes in the Earth system with possible significant impacts on human and natural systems call for research into possible geoengineering options to complement climate change mitigation efforts.

Geoengineering methods can be largely classified into two main groups: Solar Radiation Management (SRM) and Carbon Dioxide Removal (CDR). While both approaches aim to reduce global temperatures, they clearly differ in their modes of action, the timescales over which they are effective, their effects on temperature and other climate variables (e.g., precipitation), and other possible consequences.

SRM techniques attempt to offset the effects of increased greenhouse gas concentrations by reducing the amount of solar radiation absorbed by the Earth. This may be achieved by increasing the surface reflectivity of the planet, for example by brightening human structures, planting crops with a higher albedo, or covering deserts with reflective material. Other techniques aim to enhance marine cloud reflectivity by introducing sea salt aerosols in low clouds, mimic the effects of volcanic eruptions by injecting sulphate aerosols into the lower stratosphere, or place shields or deflectors in space to reduce the amount of incoming solar radiation.

CDR techniques aim to address the cause of climate change by removing greenhouse gases from the atmosphere. This would include advanced land use management strategies to protect or enhance land carbon sinks, and the use of biomass for both carbon sequestration (including biochar) and as a carbon neutral energy source. The removal of carbon dioxide from the atmosphere, either through the enhancement of natural weathering processes or direct capture from ambient air are further examples, as well as the enhancement of oceanic CO_2 uptake through ocean fertilisation with scarce nutrients or the enhancement of upwelling processes.

Major uncertainties exist regarding the effects of these techniques on the physical climate system and on biogeochemical cycles, their possible impacts on human and natural systems, and their effectiveness and costs. SRM, for example, could impact regional precipitation patterns while offering no solution for CO_2-induced ocean acidification. Unilateral action may have environmental side effects on other countries and regions, and may not appropriately address the global scale of the issue. Thus, geoengineering itself may constitute "dangerous anthropogenic interference with the climate system" (Article 2, UNFCCC), and consideration needs to be given to international governance frameworks.

2. Expert Meeting

Current discussions that suggest geoengineering as an option to support climate mitigation efforts remain rather abstract and lack comprehensive risk assessments that take into account possible adverse impacts over short and longer time frames. The understanding of the physical science basis of geoengineering is still limited and IPCC will, for the first time, assess this in several chapters of the WGI [Working Group I] contribution to AR5. Improved scientific understanding of the impacts of geoengineering proposals on human and natural systems will be assessed by WGII [Working Group II]. WGIII [Working Group III] needs to take into account the possible impacts and side effects and their implications for mitigation cost in order to define the role of geoengineering within the portfolio of response options to anthropogenic climate change. Furthermore, this includes an evaluation by WGIII of options for appropriate governance mechanisms.

2.1 Objectives

The aim of the proposed expert meeting is to discuss the latest scientific basis of geoengineering, its impacts and response options, and to identify key knowledge gaps. The expert meeting would be organised by Working Group III with a cross-Working-Group focus. The following issues will be discussed in more detail:

- different geoengineering options, their scientific basis and associated uncertainties;
- associated potential risks and related knowledge gaps;
- effect of impacts and side effects on mitigation cost and the role within the portfolio of mitigation options
- suitability of existing governance mechanisms for managing geoengineering, including social, legal and political factors
- key knowledge gaps that could be filled in the shorter and longer terms.

2.2 Expected Outcome

The expert meeting will provide a platform for exchange and discussion among experts from the different disciplines in order to better address the important cross-cutting issue of geoengineering. This should also encourage the consistent treatment of geoengineering options across the WGs' assessments that will build the basis for the AR5 Synthesis Report. The Expert Meeting will produce a report that could include summaries of keynote presentations, abstracts of expert contributions, reports from breakout group discussions, and a noncomprehensive bibliography of recent literature related to geoengineering.

3. Organization

A Scientific Steering Committee will be formed with relevant experts in geoengineering from the IPCC Working Groups.

Timing: first half of 2011

Duration: 2 to 3 days

Participants: About 40 invited experts, with broad international representation. It is proposed that 25 journeys for experts from developing countries and economies in transition including Co- and Vice-Chairs from all Working Groups are allocated as part of the line item "expert meetings related to the AR5" in the IPCC Trust Fund budget for 2011. Participants will be needed with expertise in:

- WGI: clouds/aerosols & climate, carbon cycle & climate, coupled climate–carbon cycle projections
- WGII: impacts on human and natural systems
- WGIII: bottom-up modelling experts, risk analysis, integrated assessment modelling groups, governance and international cooperation.

NOTES AND QUESTIONS

1. Geoengineering is a broad term that could be applied in its least invasive variation to carbon sequestration and storage efforts (though carbon storage and sequestration is often differentiated from geoengineering, as in the Lin article) and in its most intrusive variation to active changes in the ocean or atmosphere. Carbon storage and sequestration raises its own set of legal issues and risks. For example, Professors Alexandra Klass and Elizabeth Wilson have explored the complex property law questions raised by injecting carbon into the pore space of deep subsurface rock and potential solutions to these legal dilimmas. *See* Alexandra B. Klass & Elizabeth J. Wilson, *Climate Change, Carbon Sequestration, and Property Rights*, 2010 U. Ill. L. Rev. 363 (2010). Do you feel differently about efforts to capture greenhouse gases than you do about efforts to change the climate system? Why or why not?

2. Those advocating for more aggressive mitigation often have avoided focusing on either adaptation or geoengineering for fear of causing disincentives for greenhouse gas emissions reduction. Is there a way to explore those topics while minimizing such risks? As explored in the excerpt from the Intergovernmental Panel on Climate Change's latest report in Chapter One, adaptation will happen in any mitigation scenario because of the extent of our past greenhouse gas emissions, and a focus on adaptation may help people engage the consequences of mitigation failures more concretely. Is there an equivalent argument that could be made in the geoengineering context?

2. LEGAL DILEMMAS

The legal regime dealing directly with geoengineering is extremely limited. However, international and domestic law on several other topics may apply to geoengineering efforts to reverse climate change. This multiplicity of applicable law poses a significant governance challenge because these treaties and statutes function largely separately from one another. As scientists and policymakers consider the option of geoengineering more seriously, addressing this simultaneous overlap and fragmentation of applicable law is critical.

Moreover, geoengineering raises two phases of governance challenges. The first phase involves research about geoengineering techniques. Because research projects that move beyond modeling often involve some level of implementation, there have been numerous international efforts to create a governance model for the research. The second phase involves full-scale implementation. Although few are arguing for immediate, full-scale implementation, the international mechanisms for it need to be established before such calls become more mainstream.

Many efforts have been made to address the phase one concerns. In a recent example, as the Durban climate change negotiations commenced in December 2011, the Royal Society, Environmental Defense Fund, and TWAS (The Academy of Sciences for the Developing World, *formerly* the Third World Academy of Sciences) published a short report under the auspices of a collaborative project called the Solar Radiation Management Governance Initiative (SRMGI). Based on a March 2011 expert conference, the report presented nine emerging conclusions regarding the governance of SRM research.

ENVIRONMENTAL DEFENSE FUND, THE ROYAL SOCIETY & TWAS,
SOLAR RADIATION MANAGEMENT: THE GOVERNANCE OF RESEARCH 9–10 (2011)

---

http://www.srmgi.org/files/2012/01/DES2391_SRMGI-report_web_11112.pdf

Message 1

Nothing now known about SRM provides justification for reducing efforts to mitigate climate change through reduced GHG emissions, or efforts to adapt to its effects. The evidence to date indicates that it could be very risky to deploy SRM in the absence of strong mitigation or sustainable CDR methods.

Message 2

Research into SRM methods for responding to climate change presents some special potential risks. Governance arrangements for managing these risks are mostly lacking and will need to be developed if research continues.

Message 3

There are many uncertainties concerning the feasibility, advantages and disadvantages of SRM methods, and without research it will be very hard to assess these.

Message 4

Research may generate its own momentum and create a constituency in favour of large-scale research and even deployment. On the other hand, ignorance about SRM technology may not diminish the likelihood of its use, and in fact might increase it.

Message 5

A moratorium on all SRM-related research would be difficult if not impossible to enforce.

Message 6

Some medium and large-scale research may be risky, and is likely to need appropriate regulation.

Message 7

Considering deployment of SRM techniques would be inappropriate without, among other things, adequate resolution of uncertainties concerning the feasibility, advantages and disadvantages. Opinion varied on whether a moratorium on deployment of SRM methods would be appropriate at this stage.

Message 8

The development of effective governance arrangements for potentially risky research (including that on SRM) which are perceived as legitimate and equitable requires wide debate and deliberation. SRMGI has begun, and will continue to foster, such discussion.

Message 9

International conversations about the governance of SRM should be continued and progressively broadened to include representatives of more countries and more sectors of society. Appropriate international organisations should also be encouraged to consider the scientific, practical and governance issues raised by the research of SRM methods.

An examination of the details of particular geoengineering schemes high-lights the overwhelming legal complexity. The following excerpt by Professor Randall Abate and Mr. Andrew Greenlee provides an example of the difficulties of regulating the leading CDR technique of ocean iron fertilization under existing international law. The article describes ambiguity and, at times, conflict among the treaties that would likely apply to this type of geoengineering and their applicability to recent controversial efforts by private companies to attempt projects.

RANDALL S. ABATE & ANDREW B. GREENLEE, SOWING SEEDS UNCERTAIN: OCEAN IRON FERTILIZATION, CLIMATE CHANGE, AND THE INTERNATIONAL ENVIRONMENTAL LAW FRAMEWORK

27 Pace Envtl. L. Rev. 555, 555–61, 572–89 (2010)

Introduction

In a world plagued by the effects of climate change, ocean iron fertilization and other geoengineering techniques could help to respond and adapt to this global environmental crisis. Nevertheless, the international community, consistent with its reactions to other science-inspired responses to modern problems, has approached the promise of ocean iron fertilization with a half-hearted embrace and a surplus of healthy skepticism.

The controversy surrounding ocean iron fertilization reached a critical juncture in the past year. On January 7, 2009, a team of researchers from Germany's Alfred Wegener Institute for Polar and Marine Research and India's National Institute of Oceanography embarked on an expedition to the Antarctic Peninsula to assess the potential of ocean iron fertilization as a new approach to address climate change. The LOHAFEX team proposed to dump six tons of dissolved iron sulfate over 116 square miles of ocean surface between 200 and 500 nautical miles north or northwest of South Georgia Island to induce rapid growth of a phytoplankton bloom. In theory, such blooms can absorb massive amounts of carbon dioxide from the atmosphere and subsequently fall to the ocean floor, creating a "carbon sink" that effectively sequesters carbon, offsets global emissions of carbon dioxide, and mitigates some of the impacts of global warming.

Despite its laudable intentions, the LOHAFEX ocean iron fertilization proposal drew significant opposition. On January 13, 2009, the German Environment Ministry requested that the German Research Ministry immediately halt the expedition. The Environment Ministry raised concerns about the compatibility of the project with the decisions of the 9th Meeting of the Conference of the Parties to the Convention on Biological Diversity (CBD); the lack of an independent assessment into the potential environmental impacts of the experiment; and the adverse international response to the project by members of the media, who might view the project as a government-subsidized entrance into what could become a multi-billion dollar market. The German Research Ministry responded to these concerns by temporarily halting the project.

Several days later, however, the German Environment Ministry reversed its course and decided to allow the project to proceed. Research Minister Annette

Schavan declared that "[a]fter a study of expert reports, I am convinced there are no scientific or legal objections against the . . . ocean research experiment LOHAFEX." Shortly thereafter, the German Environment Ministry issued a press release reiterating its objections and voicing its regret over the decision to allow the experiment to proceed.

Private enterprises proposing ocean iron fertilization experiments have also stirred controversy. Planktos, a company based in the United States, announced plans to use similar technology to generate carbon credits that might be sold or traded. When warned by the United States Environmental Protection Agency (EPA) that such research activities might violate the Ocean Dumping Ban Act of 1988, Planktos responded that its activities would no longer be conducted with a U.S.-flagged vessel. Though Planktos later abandoned the project after failing to secure adequate funding, other commercial outfits such as Climos, which recently announced its plans to engage in iron fertilization of up to 40,000 square kilometers of ocean, are attempting to profit using a similar business model.

The dire threats posed by climate change have inspired innovative methods of carbon sequestration, including ocean iron fertilization as one of a variety of tools to mitigate the threat. However, there is little concrete data available about the environmental consequences of ocean iron fertilization or the efficacy of ocean iron fertilization as a method of carbon sequestration. Moreover, because ocean iron fertilization activities generally take place on the high seas, beyond the jurisdiction of domestic legal regimes, it is unclear which sources of international law should regulate the two categories of ocean iron fertilization projects: (1) the small-scale research activities that have taken place to date, and (2) the large-scale, and potentially more dangerous, ventures contemplated by private companies.

. . . .

I. The Science of Ocean Iron Fertilization

Ocean iron fertilization involves adding iron to the sea to artificially stimulate the rapid growth of phytoplankton, whose photosynthetic activity could potentially absorb enough heat-trapping carbon dioxide to help cool the atmosphere of the Earth. In practice, this strategy requires spreading iron particles in ocean areas where iron exists in such low concentrations that its absence limits phytoplankton growth. These waters include the Southern Ocean and the equatorial and northern regions of the Pacific Ocean.

Proponents emphasize the vast potential of ocean iron fertilization as a way to rapidly deploy "carbon sinks" that could draw large amounts of carbon dioxide from the atmosphere. The addition of relatively small amounts of iron offers the possibility of large increases in carbon sequestration and rapid mitigation of climate change at a relatively low financial cost. A pioneer of this method, the late John Martin, famously quipped, "[g]ive me half a tanker of iron, and I'll give you an ice age." Yet critics point to three major flaws with this strategy: (1) it may be less efficient than it seems; (2) it could raise a host of foreseeable and unforeseeable adverse environmental consequences; and (3) its effectiveness is difficult to measure.

. . . .

II. The Existing Legal Framework

A regulatory framework for ocean iron fertilization requires the use of international law because the vast majority of waters best suited for ocean iron fertilization are located in the high seas, beyond the 200-mile jurisdictional boundaries of any coastal nation's exclusive economic zone. Three international environmental law treaties govern ocean iron fertilization: (1) UNCLOS; (2) the CBD; and (3) the London Convention and Protocol. This part of the article addresses the legality of ocean iron fertilization under each of these treaties and considers the initial responses under these treaties to the legal challenges that ocean iron fertilization has presented.

A. The United Nations Convention on the Law of the Sea

UNCLOS provides the basic legal framework for both the protection of the world's oceans and the use of the resources contained therein. UNCLOS is widely regarded as "the constitution for ocean governance." Its provisions codify the customary international law obligation binding on all states, including non-party nations such as the United States, to prevent practices that damage the marine environment of other nations or areas beyond national jurisdiction.

UNCLOS Article 192 expresses the broad general obligation of all states "to protect and preserve the marine environment." Likewise, Article 145 provides in principle that "necessary measures shall be taken . . . with respect to activities in the Area to ensure effective protection for the marine environment from harmful effects which may arise from such activities." While these broad obligations are qualified somewhat by provisions that allow parties the sovereign right to exploit the natural resources in areas within their territorial control, states are nevertheless required to take all necessary measures to: (1) prevent, reduce and control pollution of the marine environment, (2) prohibit the transfer of damage or hazards from one area to another, and (3) protect rare and fragile ecosystems, as well as the habitat of depleted, threatened, or endangered species from pollution.

> Under Article 1(1)(4), UNCLOS defines pollution as:
> [T]he introduction by man, directly or indirectly, of substances or energy into the marine environment . . . which results or is likely to result in such deleterious effects as harm to living resources and marine life, hazards to human health, hindrance to marine activities, including fishing and other legitimate uses of the sea, impairment of quality for use of sea water and reduction of amenities.

Under this definition, it is not the nature of the substance introduced into the environment that brings an activity within its prohibitions, but the potential deleterious effects that its introduction may have. Proponents of ocean iron fertilization might argue that this definition of pollution would not cover their activities because such activity has not "resulted" nor is it "likely to result" in the deleterious effects proscribed because this same result occurs naturally and the dire results predicted by some are largely based on modeling that operates under the assumption of worst case scenarios. Alternatively, proponents may argue that ocean iron enrichment could have a net positive effect because the phytoplankton blooms stimulate the base of the food chain.

One way for critics to respond to this line of argument, which emphasizes the uncertainty surrounding ocean iron fertilization, is to invoke the precautionary principle. The precautionary principle provides that "where there are threats of serious or irreversible damage, lack of scientific certainty shall not be used as a reason for postponing cost-effective measures to prevent environmental degradation." A corollary to this principle is that the burden of proof falls on those who propose to engage in activity that may harm the environment.

Unlike the majority of modern environmental legal and regional seas agreements, however, UNCLOS does not contain an express endorsement of the precautionary principle. However, some scholars have read the pollution provisions of UNCLOS to contain an implicit endorsement of the precautionary principle because the definition of pollution refers to actions that "result or are likely to result" in the proscribed deleterious effects. Under this reading, the obligations to prevent pollution are triggered even when no direct causal link has been established, so long as environmental harm is likely. Even assuming that the probability of harm does not rise to the level of likelihood, the party advocating the action should nevertheless bear the burden of proof that the action is benign.

The problem with the precautionary principle in this context, however, is that the action proposed seeks to address the catastrophic environmental consequences of inaction in the face of climate change. In other words, when the threat of environmental degradation posed by mitigation measures such as ocean iron fertilization is considered in the context of the more significant threat of large-scale environmental degradation from global warming, concerns regarding the risks of ocean iron fertilization become less compelling. Advocates for ocean iron fertilization could argue that this climate change mitigation strategy is a cost-effective measure that could prevent the serious and irreversible environmental damage caused by climate change, and that lack of scientific certainty should not prevent its evaluation as a potentially critical mitigation tool. This inversion of the logic of the precautionary principle, along with the absence of the principle in the language of UNCLOS, diminishes the applicability of the precautionary principle in the ocean iron fertilization context.

There is, however, another way to bring ocean iron fertilization activities within the regulatory ambit of UNCLOS. Article 194 provides that states must act to prevent, reduce, and control pollution from all sources, which includes "dumping." Dumping is defined as "any deliberate disposal of wastes or other matter from vessels, aircraft, platforms or other man-made structures at sea." Article 210 of UNCLOS requires states to adopt laws and regulations to prevent and regulate dumping that must be no less effective than internationally agreed global rules and standards. UNCLOS delegates the promulgation of global rules and standards regarding "dumping" to other international treaties, and endorses the recently enacted rules and standards under the CBD and the London Protocol, which specifically address iron fertilization on the high seas. It is to these two treaty regimes that the analysis now turns.

B. The Convention on Biological Diversity

The 1992 Convention on Biological Diversity (CBD) seeks to conserve biodiversity and encourage the sustainable use of its components, including genetic resources. The protection of marine and coastal areas within the framework of the CBD emerged as an important agenda item in the mid-1990s following the conclusion of the Jakarta Mandate in 1995 and the adoption of a program of related works in 1998.

Parties to the CBD directly addressed ocean iron fertilization at the May 2008 Ninth Meeting of the Conference of the Parties in Bonn. Section C of Decision IX/16 urged States to use the utmost caution when considering proposals for large-scale ocean iron fertilization and declared that such large-scale operations were not justified. Decision IX/16 further recommended that parties and governments act in accordance with the precautionary principle to ensure that ocean iron fertilization activities do not take place until there is: (1) an adequate scientific basis on which to justify such activities, including assessing associated risks; and a (2) global, transparent, and effective regulatory mechanism for these activities.

Decision IX/16 established an exception for "small-scale" scientific research studies undertaken within "coastal waters." It qualified the exception by authorizing only those experiments justified by the need to gather specific scientific data, provided that the studies were subject to a thorough prior assessment of the potential impacts of the research studies on the marine environment. Finally, Decision IX/16 distinguished between research conducted for scientific purposes and research conducted for generating and selling carbon offsets or any other commercial purposes, and forbade ocean iron fertilization activities designed to promote research in the latter category.

Interpreting the effect of Decision IX/16 has raised some important questions. First, Decision IX/16 fails to define "small-scale" activities that would fit within the scientific research exception of the framework. When compared to the vast expanse of the oceans, one thousand square miles might be considered to be "small scale." Yet such an experiment would far exceed the scope of any experiments yet undertaken. Second, Decision IX/16 calls for the restriction of research activities to "coastal waters." Yet this limitation deprives scientists of the most useful regions for experimentation — the iron-deficient high seas of the Southern Ocean. This language was likely included in an attempt to internalize the externalities perceived to be present on the high seas. However, Decision IX/16 essentially imposes a moratorium on ocean iron fertilization experiments, particularly since the international system has not yet framed a global, transparent, and effective regulatory mechanism as required under this CBD decision.

C. The London Convention and Protocol

Both the 1972 London Convention on the Prevention of Marine Pollution by Dumping of Wastes and Other Matter and its more recent incarnation, the 1996 London Protocol, provide rules and standards that pertain generally to marine pollution and, more specifically, to ocean iron fertilization. Parties to the London Convention cannot dump any prohibited substances without first undergoing an environmental impact assessment, obtaining a permit, and complying with the monitoring requirements of Annex 2 of the London Protocol.

By contrast, under the stricter London Protocol, dumping of any waste or other matter is prohibited, except for five categories of substances listed in Annex 1. Parties to the London Protocol must additionally abide by the precautionary principle under Article 3 of the Protocol. Article 3 requires the adoption of "appropriate preventative measures" whenever an activity is "likely to cause harm" even when there is "no conclusive evidence to prove a causal relation between inputs and their effects." However, both the London Convention and the London Protocol provide an exception to these restrictions whereby the "placement of matter for a purpose other than the mere disposal thereof does not qualify as dumping," provided that such placement is not contrary to the aims of the Convention or Protocol.

On May 8, 2007, the Scientific Group of the London Convention and the Scientific Group of the London Protocol released a joint Statement of Concern about Ocean Fertilization. This document stated that the current knowledge about the practice was insufficient to justify large-scale projects and characterized iron fertilization as largely a speculative endeavor. It also noted the risk of negative impacts that large-scale projects posed to the marine environment. Ultimately, the joint statement recommended that any operations be carefully evaluated to ensure that activities were not contrary to the aims of the London Convention and the London Protocol.

The parties to the London Convention and Protocol revisited this topic in London in October 2008 and agreed to adopt Annex Six Resolution LC-LP.1 on the Regulation of Ocean Fertilization (Annex Six Resolution). This resolution stated that the scope of the London Convention and Protocol includes ocean iron fertilization activities, which it defined as any activity undertaken by humans with the principal intention of stimulating primary productivity in the oceans. The resolution further stated that "legitimate scientific research" should be regarded as "placement of matter for a purpose other than mere disposal" under both the London Convention and the London Protocol. As such, this resolution exempted from the prohibitions of both treaties ocean iron fertilization projects that qualify as "legitimate scientific research."

The Annex Six Resolution does not specify what activities constitute "legitimate scientific research." The resolution merely provides that proposals should be assessed on a case-by-case basis using an assessment framework to be developed by the Scientific Groups under the London Convention and Protocol, which should include tools for determining whether the proposed activity is contrary to the aims of the Convention and Protocol. Until such guidance is available, the resolution urges contracting parties to use utmost caution and the "best available guidance" to evaluate whether the proposal will ensure protection of the marine environment consistent with the Convention and Protocol. Finally, the resolution expressly forbids any ocean iron fertilization activities other than legitimate scientific research and states that such projects cannot qualify for any exemption from the definition of dumping.

The Intersessional Technical Working Group on Ocean Fertilization had its first meeting from February 9-13, 2009 under the Chairmanship of Dr. Chris

Vivian. Delegations from eighteen Contracting Parties to the London Convention attended, as did delegations from fifteen members of the Contracting Parties to the London Protocol. Several non-governmental organizations, including Greenpeace International, as well as an intergovernmental organization, the North Pacific Marine Science Organization, also attended the meeting. The group convened to develop an assessment framework on ocean fertilization and compile information for the contracting parties on ocean iron fertilization and its impacts on the marine environment.

The Group agreed to draft a Risk Assessment and Management Framework for Scientific Research involving Ocean Fertilization. The parties agreed this would be a "work in progress," and would serve as a preliminary model for a final framework that the governing bodies would adopt in October 2009. The South African delegation suggested that the project not monetize any carbon offsets generated nor use such offsets for meeting targets of the Kyoto Protocol. However, the Group decided that such a policy matter should be considered at a meeting of the governing bodies. Finally, the delegations of Brazil and Argentina expressed concern about the LOHAFEX experiment and requested a report from the German and Indian sponsors on how the experiment might impact their coastal areas and EEZs [Exclusive Economic Zones].

The draft framework proposed at the meeting was designed to serve as a tool to assess scientific research proposals on a case-by-case basis to determine if a proposed activity would comport with the London Convention or Protocol. This guidance would also help "determine whether a project is legitimate scientific research," characterize the risks to the marine environment on a "project-specific basis," and "collect the necessary information to develop a management strategy." The elements of the assessment, which the sponsor of the proposed project would present to a national regulator, would include: (1) problem formulation and initial assessment that would define the parameters of the experiment; (2) site selection and description; (3) exposure assessment that would describe the movement and fate of the added substances; (4) an effects assessment; (5) a risk characterization that would estimate the likelihood for adverse impacts and the magnitude of those impacts; and (6) a list of risk management procedures.

The framework further requires that the sponsor of a project provide evidentiary support for key assumptions and explain the potential impacts to countries that might be affected. The approval for projects would only be issued for defined periods of time and within defined areas, and sponsors would also have to report on the conduct of the experiment, as well as compliance with the conditions set forth by the Secretariat. Finally, the assessment and approval documentation would be made publicly available.

Interestingly, neither the language of the Annex Six Resolution nor the subsequent draft framework includes any reference to the language of the CBD Decision IX/16, which limits research to "small-scale" experiments in "coastal waters" in its criteria for permitted ocean fertilization research. Since the resolution and framework came after the CBD Decision and refer to the CBD Decision in their text, it is reasonable to conclude that the parties to the London Convention and Protocol considered and rejected these limitations.

The omission of this language perhaps reflects the findings of the UNESCO Intergovernmental Oceanographic Commission ad hoc Consultative Group on Ocean Fertilization (IOC ad hoc group), a group of five leading scientists on ocean iron fertilization that was formed at the request of the Scientific Groups of the IMO in advance of the Resolution of the London Convention and Protocol. In a statement released by the IOC ad hoc group in June 2008, the group sharply criticized the limitations imposed by the CBD decision. It railed against the "arbitrary" and "new" limitation of scientific research to "coastal waters" as "counterproductive" given that the most useful scientific experiments to date have taken place on the open ocean.

The IOC ad hoc group statement also stressed that the size of the activity should not be determinative, noting that ocean iron fertilization projects conducted only over one square kilometer might be damaging if undertaken over a coral reef, while ocean fertilization undertaken over thousands of square kilometers might be benign. The statement further maintained that "small-scale" was a relative term and it expressly approved of larger experiments as a means to diminish the dilution of iron near the center of smaller experiments and obtaining better data relating to vertical transport of carbon dioxide. It endorsed experiments as large as 200 kilometers by 200 kilometers as clearly justified.

The IOC ad hoc group conceded that it lacked expertise in international law or policy, but it nevertheless offered two alternatives to policy makers of the London Convention and Protocol. The first called for an independent committee composed of scientists and representatives from the policy, legal, and industry sectors that would assess each proposed fertilization activity on the basis of the risks posed to the environment. This committee would have veto power over those projects it considered to fall below a clearly defined threshold of damage to the environment. The second suggestion would allow "legitimate scientific experiments"—those with defensible scientific goals and public disclosure of methods and results—to proceed, while delaying those activities designed to generate carbon credits or other monetary gain until environmental safeguards can be developed and enacted.

The IMO London Convention and Protocol Working Group on Ocean Fertilization (Working Group), which met in Guayaquil, Ecuador in May 2008, reviewed the IOC ad hoc group input and information from other international organizations with special expertise in ocean iron fertilization issues. The Working Group issued three recommendations for the scientific and legal groups: (1) it requested advice from the Legal Intersessional Correspondence Group regarding the appropriateness of the phrase "contrary to the aims of the Convention/Protocol;" (2) it requested that the London Convention and Protocol consolidate new information on scientific research on ocean iron fertilization as it becomes available and make it available for use in assessing proposals; and (3) it recommended that Annex 3 be used as the list of considerations for evaluating ocean iron fertilization activities.

There are some indications that the CBD is retreating from its de facto moratorium on ocean iron fertilization. A draft CBD document entitled "Scientific Synthesis on the Impacts of Ocean Fertilization on Marine Biodiversity" noted the need for international oversight for all ocean iron fertilization activities. In addition, it called for the adoption of an assessment framework to validate side effects and, surprisingly, for legitimate scientific research to advance the collective understanding of biogeochemical processes within the global oceans.

The London Convention and Protocol Correspondence Group reviewed this document and stated that the CBD draft could serve as a background paper for the London Convention and Protocol. However, it noted that the document does not offer an assessment framework for scientific research proposals involving ocean iron fertilization, nor does it provide the level of technical guidance necessary to ensure precautionary protection of the marine environment. The Group further noted that the CBD document "contained gaps" and served a different purpose—to compile and synthesize available scientific information on potential impacts on marine biodiversity—than that of the Correspondence Group.

Based on the text of the Annex Six Resolution released by the London Convention and Protocol, the extent to which the statements of the IOC ad hoc group or the Scientific Working Group were considered is unclear. Nor does the resolution offer any indication as to the applicability of the limitations imposed by the CBD Decision IX/16. However, it is clear that the London Convention and Protocol do not authorize sanctions for violations. While voluntary compliance with the London Convention and Protocol is reported to be high, it is unclear whether the prohibition provides sufficient deterrence for commercial enterprises that might engage in large-scale ocean iron fertilization research to test their methods in advance of expected future carbon trading.

III. The LOHAFEX Project and the Need for a New Legal Framework

If one of the goals of international environmental law is to provide clear guidelines so that states may regulate entities subject to their jurisdiction, then the LOHAFEX project provides an ideal illustration of the shortcomings of the current legal framework governing ocean iron fertilization. This part of the article examines the legality of the LOHAFEX expedition under existing international environmental law and illustrates why a new legal framework is necessary.

The LOHAFEX project fails to comply with the mandate of CBD Decision IX/16, which restricts ocean iron fertilization projects to "small-scale" studies within "coastal waters." Neither the decision, nor Article 2, of CBD defines "small-scale" or "coastal waters," but the proposed site in the Southern Ocean does not appear to qualify as coastal waters.

The risk assessment prepared by the Alfred Wegener Institute, the German group that co-sponsored the experiment, does not claim that the site falls within coastal waters. Instead, the assessment states that its proposed approach complies with the requirements of the CBD. It first references the recent CBD decision, placing emphasis on the stated need for further research to assess the impact on the ecosystem and the efficacy of iron fertilization. It then asserts that the proposal is based on "intercomparisons . . . of previous iron fertilisation experiments all carried out in the Southern Ocean including coastal waters that provide the basis for the assessment of the impact of such experiments on the environment." It later describes the location as "downstream from an extensive land mass" (the Antarctic Peninsula), which "contains waters with coastal plankton species." With regard to the "small-scale" requirement, the assessment describes the spatial scale as "small in respect to the surrounding environment" and small "in comparison to natural iron enrichments by coastal waters or icebergs."

According to the assessment, the LOHAFEX experiment: (1) fulfills the need to assess its impact on the ecosystem; (2) fits within the scope of the term "coastal waters" because the subject matter has previously been studied in coastal water and coastal plankton live in the water; and (3) satisfies the "small-scale" requirement if compared to the size of the Southern Ocean and natural iron enrichments. This argument is hardly an ironclad legal defense. Therefore, it is reasonable to conclude, as did the German Environment Ministry, that the experiment would not comply with a strict interpretation of CBD Decision IX/16.

In response to a letter from a non-governmental organization (NGO) that alleged that a violation of the CBD had occurred, the Bureau of the Conference of the Parties to the CBD addressed the issue of the LOHAFEX expedition in Nairobi, Kenya on February 19, 2009. After the German representative left the room to let the Bureau discuss the course of action, the Executive Secretary noted that the issue of implementation of COP decisions was not addressed in the rules of procedure and that the responsibility to implement COP decisions lay with the parties at the national level. Nevertheless, the Bureau members felt compelled to issue a formal response to the NGO. The Bureau concluded that it was up to Germany to respond to the letter from the NGO. The Bureau also indicated that it would send a letter to Germany and India to convey the Bureau's concerns about the LOHAFEX expedition.

This interaction highlights the decentralized nature of international law. Instead of providing a centralized enforcement mechanism, the CBD (and the other treaties discussed above) relies on states to police the activities of nationals within their jurisdiction. While the results might have disappointed the expectations of observers in favor of more concrete action against Germany in response to the LOHAFEX expedition, the CBD Bureau's response demonstrates that its members shared the concerns that the NGO expressed regarding possible violations of the CBD's restrictions on ocean iron fertilization.

By contrast, the legal justification for the LOHAFEX expedition appears somewhat stronger under the London Convention and Protocol Resolution, whose terms do not include the restrictions of the CBD resolution. The project would very likely meet the threshold requirement that it be a scientific research project. However, the Scientific Groups under the London Convention and Protocol have not yet issued an assessment framework. Therefore, as a party to the Convention and Protocol, Germany must "use utmost caution and the best available guidance to evaluate the . . . proposal to ensure 'protection of the marine environment consistent with the Convention and Protocol.'" The risk assessment plausibly maintains that the naturally occurring iron enrichment in the region is much larger in scale than the level of iron to be deposited in the proposed experiment; therefore, it would cause no greater ecological damage than that presently occurring naturally. Accordingly, Germany could reasonably conclude that this experiment fits within the scientific research exception to the resolution.

As demonstrated by the foregoing analysis, these two overlapping treaties impose different levels of obligations for scientific research projects that seek to conduct ocean iron fertilization, with the CBD imposing several highly restrictive terms that are conspicuously absent in the London Convention and Protocol. Yet the German Ministry of Research still allowed the project to move forward, despite the uncertainty regarding its compliance with the CBD and over the objections of the Ministry of the Environment. The rationale for this decision is unclear, but press releases from both the Alfred Wegener Institute and the Indian National Institute of Oceanography used the ambiguity and incongruity in international legal instruments to justify the LOHAFEX expedition.

IV. Foundations for a New Legal Framework

The unclear and conflicting mandates in the existing legal framework governing the LOHAFEX project illustrate the need for a new legal framework to regulate scientific research on ocean iron fertilization. First, and most importantly, the new legal framework would harmonize the incongruous treaty obligations in the existing framework to ensure that states understand whether actors subject to their jurisdiction are in compliance with international law. Second, the framework would address ground rules for those parties seeking to capitalize on ocean iron fertilization through the trade of carbon credits, as well as for those parties that wish to engage in scientific research. In lieu of an artificial distinction based on the motivation of those looking to explore ocean iron fertilization, the new framework would treat all parties equally and distinguish proposed activities on the basis of the scope of the project. Third, the proposed legal framework would include differentiated standards for small-scale and large-scale ocean iron fertilization projects.

. . . .

NOTES AND QUESTIONS

1. One dominant concern for those considering geoengineering is whether it can be tested effectively in smaller scale ways. For example, Alan Robock, Martin Bunz, Ben Kravitz, and Georgiz Stenchikov argue that "geoengineering [referring to SRM] cannot be tested without full-scale implementation." Alan Robock et al., *A Test for Geoengineering?*, 327 SCIENCE 530 (2010). If the only real test for some approaches to geoengineering is actual implementation, how should that affect our assessment of the phase one and phase two governance options?

2. The Abate and Greenlee excerpt reinforces that a good deal of law already applies to particular geoengineering approaches to climate change. Can these complex issues be addressed adequately through applying existing conventions to these new issues? How should conflicts among them be resolved? What are the benefits and limitations of existing law?

3. Professor Albert Lin has argued for addressing geoengineering under the UNFCCC agreements, perhaps through a protocol focused on the issue. He argues that failing to engage these issues through that framework increases the risk of undesirable deployment of this technology. *See* Albert C. Lin, *Geoengineering Governance,* Issues in Legal Scholarship, Apr. 2009, at 1, 1–7, *available at* http://www.bepress.com/ils/vol8/iss3/art2. Based on what you have learned of the UNFCCC process, what would be the advantages and disadvantages of addressing geoengineering in that forum?
4. If a new agreement specifically on geoengineering were crafted, what would be the ideal process for doing so? What should it include? Who should be involved in crafting it? Should it be a treaty among nation-states, or a soft law instrument that includes more stakeholders?

3. THE POSSIBILITIES AND RISKS OF A TECHNOLOGICAL FIX

Geoengineering to reverse climate change not only poses technical, scientific, and legal complexities, but also raises difficult ethical and strategic policy issues. These concerns range from workability and cost-effectiveness to the appropriateness of intentional human interference in the climate system. For geoengineering to be taken seriously as a solution to climate change, policymakers must grapple with these issues.

The following excerpt from Jay Michaelson, which predates the latest wave of interest in geoengineering, aims to provide such a foundation. It lays out some of the objections to geoengineering and responds to them.

JAY MICHAELSON, GEOENGINEERING: A CLIMATE CHANGE MANHATTAN PROJECT

17 Stan. Envtl. L.J. 73, 122–30 (1998)

IV. In Defense of Geoengineering

A. "It Just Won't Work"/"It Will Do More Harm than Good"

Immodest proposals should elicit skepticism. When one faces a costly proposal involving unproven and potentially dangerous technology, particularly when it involves interfering with a system as complex as the Earth's climate, it is natural to expect Babel-like failure to follow Babel-like arrogance. Geoengineering has a checkered history, at best, from the Army Corps of Engineers' choking of the Everglades to the Soviet Union's attempts to reverse the flow of Siberian rivers to grow cotton and melt part of the Arctic ice cap. What if the Big Fix leaves us worse off than we were before?

The danger of altering the Earth's climatic systems, when we cannot even successfully maintain a tiny "Biosphere II," was well expressed by the National Academy of Sciences:

> Geoengineering options have the potential to affect greenhouse warming on a substantial scale. However, precisely because they might do so, and because the climate system and its chemistry are poorly understood, these options must be considered extremely carefully. . . . Some of these options are relatively inexpensive to implement, but all have large unknowns concerning possible

environmental side-effects. They should not be implemented without careful assessment of their direct and indirect consequences.

The response to such concerns, however, should be caution, not dismissal. Regarding primary efficacy, there is good evidence that some geoengineering proposals — iron seeding or particulate scattering, for example — show considerable promise. Though . . . it is far too early to be certain of success, it is also far too early to be dismissive. While the case for technological optimism is "uneasy," the case for technological pessimism — in the face of a century of technological progress that shows little sign of abating — is just plain weak.

Regarding secondary effects, caution should inspire more research, not less. A global "sunscreen" may also cause acid rain or affect the ozone layer, but it may not: what is needed by policymakers are answers from scientists. Of course, as any scientist knows, "answers" are more often estimates and prognostications than definite results. If this turns out to be the case at the end of Phase One of a Climate Change Manhattan Project, then Phase Two should proceed carefully. In the case of the "sunscreen" dust proposal, we could proceed gradually, releasing less dust than Mount Pinatubo did in 1991. In any event, we should not let panic at the scale of the problem or the danger for unintended effects replace calm investigation of the possibilities before us. What is important to remember, again, is (1) that we can progress slowly and cautiously, and (2) that we have not yet even begun to do so.

Clearly, it would be easy — and tragic — for confidence to turn to hubris, and for would-be climate engineers to repeat old mistakes. This consequentialist objection does not undermine the principle of a geoengineering project, however, or the efficacy of geoengineering as a policy tool. Nor does the objection recognize that some geoengineering techniques have already produced favorable and reliable experimental data. Finally, this complaint does not adequately consider the uncertain and grave context in which climate change policies are made. We are already in a mess; the question is how best to clean it up.

B. "It Costs Too Much"

Although the relative economy of geoengineering is treated above . . . , two objections remain based not on geoengineering's cost relative to that of preventive regulation, but on its cost alone. It may be that the up-front investment in geoengineering makes it either (1) impractical or (2) counterproductive.

1. The High Cost of Geoengineering Makes It Impractical

The first major cost-based objection to geoengineering is that it is simply impractical to expect the nations of the world to spend billions of dollars on ocean seeding in an era of shrinking budgets and (in the United States, at least) suspicion of cooperative international activity. The obvious rebuttal is that some geoengineering proposals may turn out to be quite affordable — particulate matter spreading, for example. Nevertheless, even if geoengineering techniques demand large up-front investments, the objection is answerable.

Assuming arguendo that geoengineering will be expensive up front, it still seems less different to throw money at a problem than to enforce a restrictive and costly regulatory regime. Even if the price tag is high, the geoengineering project remains affordable in terms of political economy because it minimizes costs that factor into the political calculus, such as social costs and efficiency costs borne by distributionally advantaged (politically powerful) parties. . . . So long as the cost of a geoengineering project is not so astronomical as to prevent consideration of the political economies, it is likely to be more "affordable" in political-economic terms than any other option currently on the table.

Two more general responses to the contention that geoengineering's potentially high cost makes it impractical are warranted. First, any serious debate on climate change must recognize that a geoengineering project is not a decorative boondoggle; it is a necessary measure taken to prevent serious degradation to the earth's environment that would have huge attendant costs for many human interests. If serious debate were to emerge, geoengineering's "sticker shock" might wane in the context of rational reflection of the costs of climate change itself. Second, and in a similar vein, the fairness of a "polluter pays" approach as embodied in geoengineering may itself help ameliorate the reluctance of the polluters to pay. Thus, the charge that the cost of a geoengineering project renders it impractical is rebuttable by reconsidering the political economy of geoengineering as compared with regulatory solutions and recalling that notions of propriety and fairness also have political value, however attenuated.

2. The High Cost of Geoengineering Makes It Inefficient at Best, Counterproductive at Worst

Even if we can afford geoengineering, the cost-objector may retort, perhaps there is a better investment. Instead of throwing billions of dollars at a dubious plan to cool the Earth, perhaps we would be better off allowing developing countries to progress technologically (and thus adapt better to a changed climate) and coaxing private enterprise to develop zero-emission vehicles, nano-technological carbon-eaters, or some other decentralized "Small" Fix. One might even argue, as Gregg Easterbrook has, that geoengineering is a misappropriation of funds, because, while climate change is a problem, it is not as severe as more prosaic challenges such as providing safe drinking water or curbing urban pollution in the developing world.

In response, the first objection is really just a variation on "wait and see," and as such is a high-risk proposal. Perhaps nanotechnology will save the world. But perhaps it will not. In the meantime, climate change policymakers must develop strategies to cope with today's (and tomorrow's) problems in the best possible way. A successful strategy may include grants to private enterprise to develop climate-friendly technologies. Just as we ought not put all our hopes in a Big Fix, however, we should not put all our hopes in the white knight of as-yet-unknown technology.

The second objection — that geoengineering is inefficient or perhaps even inhumane in the face of widespread malnutrition and disease — is basically an argument against any climate change strategy, and it is simply not borne out by the facts. The Easterbrook policy of "give me a fish today, and let the ocean burn tomorrow" is particularly inept in light of the probability that the most serious effects of climate change will be felt by the developing world. Moreover, many local problems (e.g., the lack of safe drinking water) are difficult for the "international community" to address, for reasons of high transaction costs, national sovereignty, and the myriad of difficulties associated with any long term, overseas commitment. The concept of a Climate Change Manhattan Project, on the other hand, allows and encourages the developing world to be a free rider on a project financed mostly (one would presume) by the industrialized nations of the world. Finally, since it restricts growth less in the developing world than would regulation, a Climate Change Manhattan Project allows developing nations to more quickly progress away from the serious environmental threats of unsafe water, unhealthy air, and topsoil loss, through proven means such as sewage treatment, newer (cleaner) automobiles and factories, and modern agriculture.

C. "It Is Unnatural"

One intuitive objection to intentionally manipulating the climate is that it is unnatural. Surely, "Nature knows best." And if it does, geoengineering is misguided, not only because of the practical risks just addressed, but because human interference with the Earth's climate is both unethical and profoundly unwise. Seen in this light, geoengineering is a question not of Nordhaus's risk proposals, but of Bill McKibben's "The End of Nature." Almost all aspects of the natural world, the argument runs, are somewhat less "Other" than they were, something closer to a manufactured event than they once had been. These may seem like "soft" concerns, of minimal consequence to a policymaker. However, supposedly soft concerns often translate into very "hard" political preferences. More importantly, soft concerns define who we are and why we live. Ultimately, the hardest and driest economic calculations reduce to the "soft" inner preferences of putatively rational actors, who reveal themselves in myriad expressions of utility. If geoengineering is seen as cutting the Earth's nose off to spite its face by a majority of people, then it is not a good policy since it fails to achieve the environmental objectives in which we are interested.

Several responses to the unnaturalness objection are possible. First, the need to mitigate climate change may simply outweigh the aesthetic valuation of the natural world. The costs of coping with dead forests and shifting agricultural zones are not scare tactics, but serious concerns that may outweigh eco-aesthetic (or even religious) reservations about a man-made sky. If the consequences of global warming track the more acute predictions of greenhouse "doomsayers," this is certainly the case: few may insist on the integrity of Gaia if millions of people (and animals) will starve.

Second, one may respond fatalistically by noting that geoengineering is no more a direct alteration of the environment than the everyday effects of millions of cars and factories. Any refusal to tinker with Nature is an illusion: we have already done so, and the only remaining question is whether to continue to do so negligently, or to begin to tinker benevolently. It would be better to "let the meadow be," and not move mounds of Earth around with bulldozers, but not once the meadow has already been plowed over.

Finally, one may counter wilderness-aesthetes on their own terms by replying that while geoengineering is an ugly interference with nature, it removes even uglier ones. Global warming is no mere abstract, aesthetic injury. While problematic, geoengineering is actually right in the context of global warming insofar as "a thing is right when it tends to preserve the integrity, stability, and beauty of the biotic community." We are not cutting off our nose to spite our face; we are performing corrective plastic surgery.

It is true that the ethical and aesthetic objections favor preventive regulation that would avoid the initial ecological insult. Yet climate change policies must be viewed in terms of their effects. What will work best? If geoengineering fulfills Leopold's above-quoted dictum best, it seems the most ethical choice. To be sure, the objections are strong: it was Henry David Thoreau who said that "[i]n wildness is the preservation of the world." And it is also true that, at first, geoengineering seems like the ultimate betrayal of this ideal. But if models of climate change are correct, New England will experience a warming of 1.5 to 4.5 degrees Celsius, which will render Walden woods unable to sustain its native flora. What then?

D. "It Subverts Other Efforts"

While there is a chance that geoengineering will work, there is also a chance that it will not. In the meantime, one might object, a focus on geoengineering subverts other efforts to attain sensible reductions in GHG emissions. Stephen Schneider voices this concern in his account of the 1992 National Research Council panel on climate change policy, where some worried that "even the very thought that we could offset some aspects of inadvertent climate modification by deliberate climate modification schemes could be used as an excuse by those who would be negatively affected by controls on the human appetite to continue polluting and using the atmosphere as a free sewer." This political concern is warranted. Insofar as the Big Fix lulls us into thinking that we have done all we need to do about global warming, it is, as one environmentalist put it, a classic "high risk-high gain" policy. Either it works, or we are in a lot of trouble.

By way of response, it must be conceded that geoengineering can be a high risk option. But it does not have to be. First, geoengineering should be developed in parallel with emissions reductions. Recall that economists believe a sizable amount of GHG emissions can be reduced quite cheaply. Surely, those inexpensive reductions should be pursued vigorously to produce a "safety cushion" while the potential of geoengineering is evaluated. Second, wise geoengineering is timely geoengineering. As stated above, we ought not wait until remediation is necessary before exploring the option: we must build the drill before the cavity develops. If Phase One of the Climate Change Manhattan Project begins now, a reasoned set of answers to many geoengineering questions may emerge well in advance of the "point of no return" for climate change regulation.

Geoengineering undoubtedly strengthens the hand of the procrastinator, but prompt and wise policy planning cuts against the complacent position. We must begin now. Advocates correctly fear putting their eggs into an untested basket, but we need not drop the emissions-reductions basket to grab hold of the geoengineering one. Proponents of geoengineering must take responsibility for ensuring that the policy does not degenerate into simple procrastination.

———————

NOTES AND QUESTIONS

1. Does Michaelson's list of potential objections seem like a complete one? Are you persuaded by his responses to those objections?

2. Geoengineering could be approached as an alternative to difficult mitigation choices or as a complement to them. For example, Professor Albert Lin has argued that pursuing geoengineering in lieu of mitigation would be a mistake. He proposes an adaptive approach that explores how geoengineering might complement mitigation over time.

   However, in doing so, he takes a different approach than Michaelson to the issue of how to decide when geoengineering strategies are appropriate. Lin explains:

   > A critical initial question would involve the baseline from which geoengineering governance decisions would be made. Given the widespread unease and uncertainty associated with geoengineering proposals, the international community should begin with a default presumption against the implementation of any geoengineering project. Such a presumption is also warranted by the difficulty of reversing course after a geoengineering project has already been operating for many years: suddenly stopping a long-running aerosol release program, for instance, would almost surely cause a rapid warming that both human and nonhuman populations would struggle to adjust to. Notwithstanding any presumption against geoengineering deployment, an adaptive governance approach counsels in favor of revisiting that presumption at regular intervals.
   >
   > Regularly revisiting the issue offers several advantages. First, this would allow the parties to take account of updated information regarding climate change and its impacts, the success (or lack thereof) of efforts to reduce emissions, and geoengineering risks and refinements. Review of the issue must be sufficiently frequent to allow the parties to respond to "climate surprises"—unexpectedly rapid or large climate changes that are not accounted for in most climate models, which tend to assume relatively smooth increases in GHG concentrations and temperature. Second, a schedule to periodically reconsider the issue reduces the stakes involved in each vote, thereby ameliorating the tendency for parties to assume entrenched positions that make agreement more difficult and increasing the likelihood that parties will be willing to agree to a nonconsensus decisionmaking process. Third, repeated consideration of geoengineering can foster a continuing international dialogue on the matter. Such a dialogue essentially would serve as ongoing negotiations that can lead to the building of coalitions or the formation of consensus on an issue. In addition, consistent views or decisions with regard to the conditions under which geoengineering may be deployed can also promote the formation of norms and even customary international law to govern the conduct of nations and institutions with respect to geoengineering.

Albert C. Lin, *Geoengineering Governance,* Issues in Legal Scholarship, Apr. 2009, at 1, 1–7, *available at* http://www.bepress.com/ils/vol8/iss3/art2.

What do you think our baseline presumptions should be?

3. Simone Tilmes, Rolf Müller, and Ross Salawitch have argued that proposed sulfur aerosol geoengineering schemes would accelerate ozone depletion. Simone Tilmes et al., *The Sensitivity of Polar Ozone Depletion to Proposed Geoengineering Schemes*, 320 Science 1201 (2008). Arguments such as these raise difficult questions about what precaution means in this context. Is it more dangerous to take measures to reverse climate change that may have other ecosystem consequences or to opt out of a potential solution to climate change? Or, in a more nuanced variation, how can we ensure that we minimize collateral ecosystem impacts in geoengineering schemes?

C. CHOOSING OUR FUTURE

This final section revisits the question of what would be required to mitigate adequately. It analyzes both the economics of mitigation and potential political and legal pathways forward. It concludes by providing an opportunity for reflection on where to go from here.

1. THE ECONOMIC, POLITICAL, AND GOVERNANCE CHALLENGES OF MITIGATING ADEQUATELY

In 2007, Sir Nicholas Stern published a lengthy assessment of the economics of climate change which argues that the costs of impacts and adaptation far exceed those of aggressive mitigation. *See* Nicholas Stern, The Economics of Climate Change: The Stern Review (Cambridge Univ. Press, 2007). While this assessment resulted in a firestorm of commentary, with some agreeing with and some disputing his claims, it remains the most significant analysis to date of our economic choices.

The following excerpt provides a Summary of Conclusions from the *Stern Review*. It provides an overview of the core components of Stern's assessment.

Nicholas Stern, Stern Review on the Economics of Climate Change: Summary of Conclusions

---

http://www.hm-treasury.gov.uk/d/Summary_of_Conclusions.pdf

There is still time to avoid the worst impacts of climate change, if we take strong action now.

The scientific evidence is now overwhelming: climate change is a serious global threat, and it demands an urgent global response. This Review has assessed a wide range of evidence on the impacts of climate change and on the economic costs, and has used a number of different techniques to assess costs and risks. From all of these perspectives, the evidence gathered by the Review leads to a simple conclusion: the benefits of strong and early action far outweigh the economic costs of not acting. Climate change will affect the basic elements of life for people around the world — access to water, food production, health, and the environment. Hundreds of millions of people could suffer hunger, water shortages and coastal flooding as the world warms. Using the results from formal economic models, the Review estimates that if we don't act, the overall costs and risks of climate change will be equivalent to losing at least 5% of global GDP each year, now and forever. If a wider range of risks and impacts is taken into account, the estimates of damage could rise to 20% of GDP or more. In contrast, the costs of action — reducing greenhouse gas emissions to avoid the worst impacts of climate change — can be limited to around 1% of global GDP each year.

The investment that takes place in the next 10-20 years will have a profound effect on the climate in the second half of this century and in the next. Our actions now and over the coming decades could create risks of major disruption to economic and social activity, on a scale similar to those associated with the great wars and the economic depression of the first half of the 20th century. And it will be difficult or impossible to reverse these changes. So prompt and strong action is clearly warranted. Because climate change is a global problem, the response to it must be international. It must be based on a shared vision of long-term goals and agreement on frameworks that will accelerate action over the next decade, and it must build on mutually reinforcing approaches at national, regional and international level.

Climate change could have very serious impacts on growth and development.

If no action is taken to reduce emissions, the concentration of greenhouse gases in the atmosphere could reach double its pre-industrial level as early as 2035, virtually committing us to a global average temperature rise of over 2°C. In the longer term, there would be more than a 50% chance that the temperature rise would exceed 5°C. This rise would be very dangerous indeed; it is equivalent to the change in average temperatures from the last ice age to today. Such a radical change in the physical geography of the world must lead to major changes in the human geography — where people live and how they live their lives.

Even at more moderate levels of warming, all the evidence — from detailed studies of regional and sectoral impacts of changing weather patterns through to economic models of the global effects — shows that climate change will have serious impacts on world output, on human life and on the environment. All countries will be affected. The most vulnerable — the poorest countries and populations — will suffer earliest and most, even though they have contributed least to the causes of climate change. The costs of extreme weather, including floods, droughts and storms, are already rising, including for rich countries. Adaptation to climate change — that is, taking steps to build resilience and minimize costs — is essential. It is no longer possible to prevent the climate change that will take place over the next two to three decades, but it is still possible to protect our societies and economies from its impacts to some extent — for example, by providing better information, improved planning and more climate-resilient crops and infrastructure. Adaptation will cost tens of billions of dollars a year in developing countries alone, and will put still further pressure on already scarce resources. Adaptation efforts, particularly in developing countries, should be accelerated.

The costs of stabilising the climate are significant but manageable; delay would be dangerous and much more costly.

The risks of the worst impacts of climate change can be substantially reduced if greenhouse gas levels in the atmosphere can be stabilised between 450 and 550ppm CO_2 equivalent (CO_2e). The current level is 430ppm CO_2e today, and it is rising at more than 2ppm each year. Stabilisation in this range would require emissions to be at least 25% below current levels by 2050, and perhaps much more. Ultimately, stabilisation — at whatever level — requires that annual emissions be brought down to more than 80% below current levels.

This is a major challenge, but sustained long-term action can achieve it at costs that are low in comparison to the risks of inaction. Central estimates of the annual costs of achieving stabilisation between 500 and 550ppm CO_2e are around 1% of global GDP, if we start to take strong action now.

Costs could be even lower than that if there are major gains in efficiency, or if the strong co-benefits, for example from reduced air pollution, are measured. Costs will be higher if innovation in low-carbon technologies is slower than expected, or if policy-makers fail to make the most of economic instruments that allow emissions to be reduced whenever, wherever and however it is cheapest to do so.

It would already be very difficult and costly to aim to stabilise at 450ppm CO_2e. If we delay, the opportunity to stabilise at 500-550ppm CO_2e may slip away.

Action on climate change is required across all countries, and it need not cap the aspirations for growth of rich or poor countries.

The costs of taking action are not evenly distributed across sectors or around the world. Even if the rich world takes on responsibility for absolute cuts in emissions of 60-80% by 2050, developing countries must take significant action too. But developing countries should not be required to bear the full costs of this action alone, and they will not have to. Carbon markets in rich countries are already beginning to deliver flows of finance to support low-carbon development, including through the Clean Development Mechanism. A transformation of these flows is now required to support action on the scale required.

Action on climate change will also create significant business opportunities, as new markets are created in low-carbon energy technologies and other low-carbon goods and services. These markets could grow to be worth hundreds of billions of dollars each year, and employment in these sectors will expand accordingly. The world does not need to choose between averting climate change and promoting growth and development. Changes in energy technologies and in the structure of economies have created opportunities to decouple growth from greenhouse gas emissions. Indeed, ignoring climate change will eventually damage economic growth.

Tackling climate change is the pro-growth strategy for the longer term, and it can be done in a way that does not cap the aspirations for growth of rich or poor countries.

A range of options exists to cut emissions; strong, deliberate policy action is required to motivate their take-up.

Emissions can be cut through increased energy efficiency, changes in demand, and through adoption of clean power, heat and transport technologies. The power sector around the world would need to be at least 60% decarbonised by 2050 for atmospheric concentrations to stabilise at or below 550ppm CO_2e, and deep emissions cuts will also be required in the transport sector.

Even with very strong expansion of the use of renewable energy and other low carbon energy sources, fossil fuels could still make up over half of global energy supply in 2050. Coal will continue to be important in the energy mix around the world, including in fast-growing economies. Extensive carbon capture and storage will be necessary to allow the continued use of fossil fuels without damage to the atmosphere. Cuts in non-energy emissions, such as those resulting from deforestation and from agricultural and industrial processes, are also essential.

With strong, deliberate policy choices, it is possible to reduce emissions in both developed and developing economies on the scale necessary for stabilisation in the required range while continuing to grow.

Climate change is the greatest market failure the world has ever seen, and it interacts with other market imperfections. Three elements of policy are required for an effective global response. The first is the pricing of carbon, implemented through tax, trading or regulation. The second is policy to support innovation and the deployment of low-carbon technologies. And the third is action to remove barriers to energy efficiency, and to inform, educate and persuade individuals about what they can do to respond to climate change.

Climate change demands an international response, based on a shared understanding of long-term goals and agreement on frameworks for action.

Many countries and regions are taking action already: the EU, California and China are among those with the most ambitious policies that will reduce greenhouse gas emissions. The UN Framework Convention on Climate Change and the Kyoto Protocol provide a basis for international co-operation, along with a range of partnerships and other approaches. But more ambitious action is now required around the world.

Countries facing diverse circumstances will use different approaches to make their contribution to tackling climate change. But action by individual countries is not enough. Each country, however large, is just a part of the problem. It is essential to create a shared international vision of long-term goals, and to build the international frameworks that will help each country to play its part in meeting these common goals.

Key elements of future international frameworks should include:

- *Emissions trading:* Expanding and linking the growing number of emissions trading schemes around the world is a powerful way to promote cost-effective reductions in emissions and to bring forward action in developing countries: strong targets in rich countries could drive flows amounting to tens of billions of dollars each year to support the transition to low-carbon development paths.

- *Technology cooperation:* Informal co-ordination as well as formal agreements can boost the effectiveness of investments in innovation around the world. Globally, support for energy R&D [Research & Development] should at least double, and support for the deployment of new low-carbon technologies should increase up to five-fold. International cooperation on product standards is a powerful way to boost energy efficiency.
- *Action to reduce deforestation:* The loss of natural forests around the world contributes more to global emissions each year than the transport sector. Curbing deforestation is a highly cost-effective way to reduce emissions; largescale international pilot programmes to explore the best ways to do this could get underway very quickly.
- *Adaptation:* The poorest countries are most vulnerable to climate change. It is essential that climate change be fully integrated into development policy, and that rich countries honour their pledges to increase support through overseas development assistance. International funding should also support improved regional information on climate change impacts, and research into new crop varieties that will be more resilient to drought and flood.

Addressing the economics of climate change raises important governance questions. Economic transformation will not take place automatically. The "business as usual" scenario in the various climate models reflects this difficulty. Without intervention, rapid increases in atmospheric concentrations of greenhouse gases will continue. But widespread disagreement exists over what would constitute a more appropriate and effective climate change governance structure.

The following excerpt by Professor David Held and Mr. Angus Fayne Hervey propose one version of such a structure. It outlines the core elements of a governance approach that incorporates democratic principles.

DAVID HELD & ANGUS FANE HERVEY, DEMOCRACY, CLIMATE CHANGE AND GLOBAL GOVERNANCE: DEMOCRATIC AGENCY AND THE POLICY MENU AHEAD 14–16 (2009)

www.policy-network.net/publications_download.aspx?ID=3426

4. The Political Elements of a Democratic Global Deal

Climate change is a problem with global causes and consequences. A coordinated international effort is therefore required to achieve cost effective and successful mitigation policies. However, the nature of the problem also means that international agreements will be difficult to reach. Countries and regions have very different interests in achieving a solution, implying a highly contested distribution of costs and benefits. In addition, developing countries, given their relatively small contribution to historical emissions, object to having their development impeded by restrictions. Finally, the challenges associated with enforcing a global solution may make some nations reluctant to participate, adding a source of uncertainty about how cost-effective the policies will be. However, despite the vigorous debate surrounding the type of policies required to combat climate change and how they should or should not be implemented, there is considerable overlap on what the political elements of a global deal might look like. At the most general level, most commentators agree that it should be broadly inclusive, multi-faceted, state-centric and sustainable.

Participation

The key requirement is participation from all countries, and most importantly, participation by the most powerful democracy in the world. The world has been waiting for the United States to join the collective effort against climate change; there is now reason to believe that it is ready to act. The integration of less developed states is also crucial, as already noted. Even if the developed states of the world were to cut their emissions to zero by 2050, without significant cuts in the rest of the world the overall goal of keeping a global rise in temperatures to under 2°C would be missed. Developing countries need to be convinced that they can simultaneously reduce their emissions and increase their growth rate by increasing their energy efficiency. They need, for instance, to eliminate distortions in their energy markets, such as large oil subsidies. But for most developing countries, the cheapest form of energy is coal (or other high-emission energy sources), and in those cases, there is a real trade-off. Money spent to reduce GHG emissions is money that could be spent to provide education, better health and clean water, or to grow faster. In such cases, developed countries, it can be argued, should pay for the incremental costs. However, as Victor et al. have pointed out, this is unlikely to happen — it is simply unrealistic to expect industrialised nations to contribute the tens or hundreds of billions of dollars needed for such a compensation scheme when official development assistance (including for wars in Iraq and Afghanistan) currently stands at around $100 billion for all purposes. Moreover, the countries that would get the most compensation, such as China, are now [the] west's most potent economic competitors.

Offset Schemes and Financial Incentives

The alternative is some form of offset scheme that allows industrialised nations to fund emissions reductions in developing nations, and counting those reductions towards their own legal commitments. The idea is that this would require industrialised nations to pay a majority of the costs while also laying a foundation for the creation of a global emissions trading market. This was the aim behind the creation of the Clean Development Mechanism (CDM). However, although the CDM has, after a difficult start, been successful in creating a global market for GHGs, its design is fundamentally flawed, and it has done very little to actually cut emissions or to assist host countries in achieving sustainable development.

Another important requirement will be the prevention of deforestation, which contributes 17% of current carbon emissions, almost twice as much as transport. Developing countries' tropical forests are an important source of carbon sequestration, yet they are not provided with any compensation for these environmental services. Providing them with financial incentives will help to reduce emissions from forested lands and invest in low-carbon paths to sustainable development. In this regard, encouraging steps have been made in the implementation of the United Nations Fund for Reducing Emissions from Deforestation and Forest Degradation (UN-REDD). However, the establishment of a final framework for the transfer of funds is still some years away, with a final agreement only likely to come into effect after 2012. Moreover, there are serious concerns about the appropriate geographical scale of accounting and incentive mechanisms, monitoring, land tenure, elite capture of funds and the potential for fraud.

Participation and deliberation on a global scale are necessary, yet in their current forms, existing instruments of global environmental governance are ill-equipped to achieve results. What is needed are representative institutions armed with the capacity and legitimacy required to translate policy commitments into real world outcomes. If a global deal is going to work it must have an answer to the problem of governance, and embody an institutional structure that shapes and determines decisions which reflect the whole world in an even-handed way. Recourse to inclusive and broadly representative global decision-making channels is the most appropriate and effective way of doing this, and strengthening mechanisms of global governance will be key to constructing a global democratic response to the issue.

5. Democracy and the Policy Menu Ahead

The challenge of tackling climate change will require the development of considerable additional institutional capacity and policy innovation. The goal of achieving this capacity, and the means to get there, will be undermined if countries of all stages of development are not directly involved in the shaping of solutions. Current policy development demonstrates this concern. The short term path to effective environmental governance is to integrate a broader set of interests into existing multilateral governance capacity. The existing mandate of the GEF [Global Environmental Fund] could be broadened in order to help coordinate and fund international environmental agreements and reflect developing country priorities. Complementary to this, the UNEP [United Nations Environmental Program] could increase its status and responsibilities by becoming a specialised UN agency, with all the compulsory UN funding that this entails. The central challenge in the years ahead of compliance monitoring and enforcement could be facilitated through a formal international mechanism for settling environmental disputes through mediation and arbitration, potentially similar to the World Bank's investment dispute body. Enhancing the capacities and responsibilities of the GEF and the UNEP in this way would be a step toward the more consolidated and formal institutional capacity of a World Environmental Organisation as a longer term goal, driven perhaps by the G2 + 1 (the USA, China and the EU), but accountable to the G195.

The Key Role of the State

In all of these challenges, states remain the key actors, as they hold the key to both domestic and international policymaking. The implementation of international agreements will be up to individual states, emissions trading and carbon pricing will require domestic legislation, and technological advance will need state support to get off the ground. However, state strategies at the domestic level should involve the creation of incentives, not overly tight regulation. Governments have an important role in "editing" choice, but not in a way that precludes it altogether. This approach is represented in the form of what Giddens calls "the ensuring state," whose primary role is help energise a diversity of groups to reach solutions to collective action problems. The state, so conceived, acts as a facilitator and an enabler, rather than as a top-down agency. An ensuring state is one that has the capacity to produce definite outcomes. The principle goes even further; it also means a state that is responsible for monitoring public goals and for trying to make sure they are realised in a visible and legitimate fashion.

This will require a return to planning—not in the old sense of top down hierarchies of control, but in a new sense of flexible regulation. This will require finding ways to introduce regulation without undermining the entrepreneurialism and innovation upon which successful responses will depend. It will not be a straightforward process, because planning must be reconciled with democratic freedoms. There will be push and pull between the political centre, regions and localities, which can only be resolved through deliberation and consultation. Most importantly, states will require a long term vision that transcends the normal push and pull of partisan politics. This will not be easy to achieve.

All this takes place in the context of a changing world order. The power structure on which the 1945 multilateral settlement was based is no longer intact, and the relative decline of the west and the rise of Asia raises fundamental questions about the premises of the 1945 multilateral order. Democracy and the international community now face a critical test. However, addressing the issue of climate change successfully holds out the prospect of reforging a rule-based politics, from the nation-state to the global level. . . . By contrast, failure to meet the challenge could have deep and profound consequences, both for what people make of modern democratic politics and for the idea of rule-governed international politics. Under these conditions, the structural flaws of democracy could be said to have tragically trumped democratic agency and deliberative capacity.

NOTES AND QUESTIONS

1. Professor Ilya Somin has disputed the need for such governance approaches regarding climate change:

> In my view, such global governance is neither necessary nor sufficient to prevent global warming. As co-blogger Eric Posner points out, an effective

climate change deal requires the agreement of only about 20 or so major emitting nations, such as the US, China, India, Russia, and several major European States. Obviously, most of these states would suffer serious harm if catastrophic global warming scenarios turn out to be true. They therefore have strong incentives to reach a deal. Collective action problems are not a serious danger when a solution only requires the cooperation of a few major actors, each of whom knows their participation is essential to the success of the overall project. There is little incentive to free-ride if the potential "free-rider" knows that the problem can't be solved without his participation.

Ilya Somin, *Do We Need Global Governance to Combat Global Warming?*, THE VOLOKH CONSPIRACY (Dec. 21, 2009, 8:11 PM), http://volokh.com/2009/12/21/do-we-need-global-governance-to-combat-global-warming/.

Do you agree with Professor Somin? What are the strongest arguments for and against this position?

2. The book began with a quote from United Nations Secretary General Ban Ki-moon arguing for the importance of the world facing its 50-50-50 challenge of reducing greenhouse gas emissions by at least 50 percent as population increases by at least 50 percent by 2050. Press Release, Secretary General, Better Global Governance Needed to Help Most Vulnerable, Stave Off Climate Change, Meet 'New Generation' Challenges, Says Secretary-General in Marrakesh, U.N. Press Release SG/SM/13188 (Oct. 18, 2010), *available at* http://www.un.org/News/Press/docs/2010/sgsm13188.doc.htm. Do you think that the options proposed in the above readings are promising ways of meeting this challenge or do you prefer other approaches, such as the one Professor Somin proposes? Which ones do you think are most promising?

2. A VISION FOR EFFECTIVE CLIMATE CHANGE LAW

Regardless of one's opinion on climate science, economics, or politics, a fundamental reality remains. If we do not take aggressive steps to mitigate climate change, there is a risk that we will face the devastation of the first scenario laid out in this chapter. Those who disagree with consensus climate science, or with Stern's analysis, might view that risk as very low or long-term, but even they are hard pressed to deny that any risk exists. Those who agree with IPCC assessments and the science emerging since the Fourth Assessment Report suggesting that climate change may be happening even faster than we expected likely will view this risk as very high.

This risk frames the core question of the book: What is the most appropriate role of law in addressing climate change moving forward? Answering it requires deciding how you view the risks and what you think the appropriate international or transnational governance strategies are. The latter task necessitates a further decision about how subnational and nongovernmental actors should fit into those governance strategies and how dominant the UNFCCC structure should be in them.

This question is not simply a hypothetical one. As students interested in thoughtfully engaging the hard questions posed by the problem of climate change, a problem that seems very unlikely to go away in the near term, you represent the best hope for the creative solutions that our future so desperately needs. We encourage you to use your understanding of current approaches to climate change law and policy to envision an alternative future and the steps that will get us there.

INDEX